Recovering Biblical Manhood and Womanhood

Recovering Biblical Manhood & Womanhood

A RESPONSE TO EVANGELICAL FEMINISM

EDITED BY
JOHN PIPER & WAYNE GRUDEM

CROSSWAY BOOKS
A PUBLISHING MINISTRY OF
GOOD NEWS PUBLISHERS
WHEATON, ILLINOIS

Recovering Biblical Manhood and Womanhood.

Published by Crossway Books, a publishing ministry of
Good News Publishers, Wheaton, Illinois 60187.

Cover design: Josh Dennis

Cover photo: Photos.com

First printing, 1991

Printed in the United States of America

Reprint ISBN 13: 978-1-58134-806-4
Reprint ISBN 10: 1-58134-806-1

This book is sponsored by the Council on Biblical Manhood and Womanhood, P.O. Box 317, Wheaton, IL 60189.

Readers may order booklets of chapters 1, 3, 4, 13, 22, and 23 by writing the Council on Biblical Manhood and Womanhood, P.O. Box 317, Wheaton, IL 60189. Other chapters may be available as booklets in the near future.

Library of Congress Cataloging-in-Publication Data

Recovering Biblical manhood and womanhood /John Piper and
Wayne Grudem, editors.
p. cm.
Includes bibliographical references and index.
1. Sex role—Religious aspects—Christianity—Miscellanea.
2. Sex role—Biblical teaching—Miscellanea. 3. Men (Christian theology)—Miscellanea. 4. Woman (Christian theology)—Miscellanea. 5. Men (Christian theology)—Biblical teaching—Miscellanea. 6. Woman (Christian theology)—Biblical teaching—Miscellanea. I. Piper, John, 1946- .
II. Grudem, Wayne, 1948
BT708.R415 1991 261.8'343—dc20 90-20258
ISBN 0-89107-586-0

BP 15 14 13 12 11 10 09 08 07
31 30 29 28 27 26 25 24 23 22 21

To Noël and Margaret

Table of Contents

Preface (2006)

A conservative backlash against radical feminism has reverberated through pop culture during the last twenty years; simultaneously, egalitarianism has been steadily encroaching to where it is now the cultural norm. Two decades ago few would have believed that American women today (some of them mothers and wives) would be fighting in the American armed forces in the deserts of Iraq. Although there are occasional protests against this newly regnant egalitarianism—even at the secular level—there is no question that the culture is predominantly egalitarian. Against this backdrop, the re-release of *Recovering Biblical Manhood and Womanhood: A Response to Evangelical Feminism* (*RBMW*) is most timely, and it will continue to serve a vital role in shaping current evangelical attitudes about gender roles in the church and home.

While evangelical complementarians have delivered an impressive body of exegetical and theological argument, from the Danvers Statement in 1987–1988, to the *RBMW* in 1991, and to Wayne Grudem's *Evangelical Feminism and Biblical Truth* in 2004, there has been a continuing erosion of commitment to the church's classic understanding of what the Bible teaches about male-female role relationships. An increasing number of evangelical publishers (once bastions of conservatism regarding gender roles) are publishing books from a feminist perspective, and some of them now refuse to print anything that assumes or advances complementarianism. Likewise, well-regarded campus ministries have adopted and implemented functionally egalitarian patterns of ministry, and many evangelical faculties, even in the most conservative of institutions, promote egalitarianism.

Sadly, perhaps the most significant factor in the weakening of biblically defined roles in marriage, family, and the church is the teaching and practice within a growing number of evangelical congregations. Ministers are embracing egalitarianism; they no longer believe or teach what the Bible says about male and female roles. Among those ministers who continue to believe, a large number assume that gender distinctions are not of vital importance; consequently, their congregations follow the culture rather than the Bible. Increasing numbers of men entering the ministry have little or no formal training, so they lack a thorough grasp of biblical teaching so as to equip their officers and congregations with the truth.

As a result, there are complementarians conceding their biblical stance on the issue, wittingly or unwittingly. Some conservative evangelicals are serving in denominational settings where the battle over women's ordination was fought years ago; they tend to see this as an issue of the past. These leaders believe our challenge is to empower women to serve more broadly and visibly, thereby unleashing the fetters in which the church has wrongfully bound them. They say that as long as women are not ordained to the pastorate, or maybe to eldership, Scripture is being obeyed. They claim that women can do anything in the church that non-ordained men can do, as if that secures a biblical view and answers all the practical matters relating to the ministry of women in the church. Still other evangelicals are looking for a middle ground between evangelical egalitarianism and complementarianism. Unfortunately, all of these proposals so far appear to be nothing more than a repackaging of egalitarianism.

It is clear that the upcoming generation has not been introduced to the church's time-honored understanding of the Scriptures on matters pertaining to gender roles. To this new generation we must stress that complementarianism is cause for celebration rather than apology because it provides the relational framework in which men and women experience covenantal privileges and responsibilities. Both men and women are image bearers of the living God and equals before the cross. When male and female live and work together as God intended, there is nothing more beautiful, satisfying, delightful, and God-glorifying—a truth to be lived and celebrated, shouted from the rooftops, and proclaimed in the streets.

By contrast, egalitarianism cannot come to grips with the unique creation of man as male and female, and its upholders assert that there is no legitimate difference between men and women in the home and church, at least not one that allows for male spiritual leadership. As a result, egalitarianism devalues God's creation design and redemptive calling of women. It fails to do justice to the distinctions that exist between the sexes and wrongly equates any acknowledgment of role distinctions with inequality and discrimination. Wise pastors, godly Christian women, and many others involved in ministry realize that preaching, teaching, and discipleship must promote a practical embrace of biblical womanhood in the local church.

We can make headway by emphasizing to our congregations the important distinction between masculinity and femininity. However, such distinction will further erode if the church continues to devalue it. Additionally, we must promote healthy, heterosexual, monogamous marriages. In order for this to happen, the church must make biblical application to contemporary marriage. Teaching and learning the biblical distinctions in our mutual marital responsibilities and ways of relating is essential. Contrarily, egalitarianism is part of the disintegration of marriage in our culture, whether explicit or implicit, witting or unwitting.

We must also lead Christian women toward a joyous embrace of godly, male leadership in the church as we simultaneously direct their men toward a self-denying, other-serving embrace of the leadership role. For this to happen, ministers and other church leaders must teach what the Bible says about qualified church leadership, even amidst the opposing claims of egalitarians, which are becoming more pronounced and histrionic. They often view the exercise of male leadership as domination or abuse, so bravery is required when addressing the Bible's teaching on male-female roles and functions in the home and church. Meanwhile, many evangelicals have been stung by accusations of chauvinism; as a result, they want to placate the culture's suspicion of male clergy. They desire to reach a hostile culture and are afraid of alienating it with unpopular views. Such evangelicals believe the biblical view but don't preach and teach it, instead doing their best to disguise it in church life. However, blurring distinctions by means of covert androgyny will only further weaken our churches.

The current controversy necessitates a strong restatement of the complementarian position, mainly because Scripture is utterly clear on gender distinctives in both home and church. It is never safe to act contrary to biblical teaching; therefore, a Bible-embracing church will work to ensure that men and women in the congregation embrace it in its totality. Gender distinctives will be boldly, clearly, and lovingly proclaimed from the pulpit, as well as discreetly and appropriately applied in the context of discipleship. When God-given distinctives are denied, altered, or ignored, disaster occurs in marriages, families, and churches. Blurring spousal roles can lead not only to marital failure but also to gender confusion in children.

Another reason why complementarianism is vitally important to the spiritual health of Christian congregations is the cultural transition confronting them. Male-female role relationships, the definition of the family, homosexual rights—all of these are bellwethers of our culture. These indicate a mega-shift from a Judeo-Christian framework to a pagan worldview. Until about 1970, our culture fed off the residue of traditional Christianity; since that time we have seen a dramatic and rapid shift to an essentially pagan ethos. Unfortunately, this ungodly framework is being imported into the church by self-avowed Christian leaders through their compromise on the subject of biblical manhood and womanhood. Bruce Ware, professor of theology at Southern Baptist Seminary, says:

> Today the primary areas in which Christianity is pressured by the culture to conform are on issues of gender and sexuality. Post-moderns and ethical relativists care little about doctrinal truth claims. These seem to them innocuous, archaic, and irrelevant to life. What they do care about, and care about with a vengeance, is whether their feminist agenda and sexual perversions are tolerated, endorsed, and expanded in an increasingly neo-pagan landscape. Because that is what they care most about. It is precisely here that Christianity is most vulnerable. To lose the battle here is to subject the church to increasing layers of departure and surely it will not be long until ethical departures (the church yielding to the pressures, for instance, of women's ordination to the pastoral ministry) will yield to even more central doctrinal departures, like questioning whether Scripture's inherent teaching about manhood and womanhood renders it fundamentally untrustworthy for the Christian life. I find it instructive that when Paul warns about departure from the faith in the latter days, he lists first "ethical compromises and the searing of the conscience" as a prelude to the doctrinal departures.[1]

Ware points out that ethical compromise is followed by doctrinal sellout. We evangelicals care about doctrine; however, if we capitulate to the current ethical reordering, doctrinal unfaithfulness is certain to follow. The church has been called to counter and bless the culture, not to copy and baptize it. All too often our churches reflect, rather than constructively engage, worldly culture. Perhaps worst of all, many evangelical leaders claim that if we want to reach the lost, we must become like them. This is a recipe for disaster. Dorothy Sayers refuted this notion: "It is not the business of the church to conform Christ to men, but men to Christ."[2] That is precisely the challenge we face in this area of biblical manhood and womanhood. Will the church shape her values to the prevailing cultural mores and norms, or will she positively impact and influence our culture?

At the core of this topic lies the fundamental issue of biblical authority. If we write off, ignore, or distort the Bible's teaching on gender roles, then we are bound to do so with everything the Bible teaches. Indeed, the Bible is so clear on male-female distinction that ministers find it challenging to uphold biblical truth from the pulpit, knowing what kind of reaction they may provoke in hearers who have been steeped in a feminist culture. This is where the manhood-womanhood issue becomes an issue of scriptural authority. Are we going to perform a hermeneutical twist when the Bible's teaching makes us culturally uncomfortable, or are we going to let the lion loose, let God be God, and let his Word speak and rule in our lives? If we deny biblical teaching about manhood and womanhood, the possibility of a definitive interpretation is lost. If we can wrest egalitarianism from the Bible, we can pervert it to say anything we wish.

Pagan ideas underlie evangelical egalitarianism, based, as it is, on ideas borrowed from cultural feminism. Egalitarianism must always lead to an eventual denial of the gospel. When the biblical distinctions of male and female are denied, Christian discipleship is irretrievably damaged because there can be no talk of cultivating distinctively masculine or feminine virtue. One can only speak of a vague androgynous discipleship. But that's not how God made us. We need masculine males and feminine females in order to generate the kind of discipleship that results in a commitment to complementarianism.

From the complementarian viewpoint, the gender controversy of the past twenty years has revolved around faithfulness to the Bible. Such was the emphasis when *RBMW* originated fifteen years ago, and it is the emphasis underlying this reissue of the book. We are reminded here of Paul's letters to Timothy and Titus and his exhortation to hold fast the Word and deal decisively with those who undermine it. All too often, however, we are enticed by worldly substitutes. When facing hardship, we are apt to seek a friend before turning to the Psalms. When tempted to doubt God's provision, we turn to human leaders before going to the words of Jesus. When angry, we seek someone who will justify us rather than the wisdom of Proverbs. Within us all is the tendency to turn to the uninspired books of men ahead of the inspired Book of God. This fleshly pull has impacted how the current gender discussion is progressing. Complementarians continue to articulate a compelling vision of God's beautiful design for men and women, yet much of this articulation amounts to no more than a defense against the onslaught of new interpretations, definitions, and approaches from an egalitarian subset within evangelicalism.

Egalitarians often claim that we cannot look to the Bible to settle these types of disputes; rather, we should look to church history or elsewhere. Most of the new egalitarian arguments are rooted outside of the Bible and instead seek credibility through history, archaeology, and manipulation of original Bible language. Each of these arguments is an attack on one of the perfections of Scripture: its authority, sufficiency, verbal plenary inspiration, and clarity. When these areas are undermined, the inerrancy of Scripture is ultimately at stake. In 1978 the *Chicago Statement on Biblical Inerrancy* issued this warning:

> We are conscious too that great and grave confusion results from ceasing to maintain the total truth of the Bible whose authority one professes to acknowledge. The result of taking this step is that the Bible that God gave loses its authority, and what has authority instead is a Bible reduced in content according to the demands of one's critical reasonings and in principle reducible still further once one has started. This means that at bottom independent reason now has authority, as opposed to Scriptural teaching. If this is not seen and if for the time being basic Evangelical doctrines are still held, persons denying the

> full truth of Scripture may claim an Evangelical identity while methodologically they have moved away from the Evangelical principle of knowledge to an unstable subjectivism, and will find it hard not to move further.[3]

Many of those leading the egalitarian movement continue to profess a high view of Scripture and a trust in the total truthfulness of the Bible, even while their practice contradicts their profession. Paul's charge to Timothy, "guard the good deposit" (1 Tim. 6:20), is what keeps complementarians in the battle and gives us the impetus to encourage one another to stand firm. So much is at risk in this debate: the health of the home and church; the way in which we understand the Christ-church paradigm; how we apply God's Word to the Christian life; and the way we raise masculine sons and feminine daughters.

In the middle of all of this, *Recovering Biblical Manhood and Womanhood* is still the bedrock text. The subtitle, *A Response to Evangelical Feminism,* continues to fit simply because the biblical arguments for complementarianism are the same. Unbiblical interpretations will come and go, but the Bible will maintain the same clear and consistent message of God's good design for men and women. That is why many of the evangelical feminist arguments have changed in the last decade whereas the complementarian defenses have not. This is why the book you hold in your hand will be a valuable resource for decades to come, and it is our prayer that many in the body of Christ will embrace God's design for men and women, and that homes and churches will be strengthened as we yield ourselves to the Word of God.

J. Ligon Duncan, Ph. D.
Senior Minister, First Presbyterian Church
Jackson, MS

Chairman of the Board,
Council on Biblical Manhood
and Womanhood

Adjunct Professor of Theology
Reformed Theological Seminary

Randy Stinson, Ph. D.
Executive Director
Council on Biblical Manhood
and Womanhood

Assistant Professor of Family
and Gender Studies
Southern Baptist Theological Seminary

Preface (1991)

A controversy of major proportions has spread through the church. It began over 20 years ago in society at large. Since then an avalanche of feminist literature has argued that there need be no difference between men's and women's roles—indeed, that to support gender-based role differences is unjust discrimination. Within evangelical Christianity, the counterpart to this movement has been the increasing tendency to oppose any unique leadership role for men in the family and in the church. "Manhood" and "womanhood" as such are now often seen as irrelevant factors in determining fitness for leadership.

Many evangelical Christians have defended this position in writing. They include Letha Scanzoni and Nancy Hardesty (1974), Paul Jewett of Fuller Seminary (1975), Richard and Joyce Boldrey of North Park College (1976), Patricia Gundry (1977), Berkeley and Alvera Mickelsen of Bethel College and Seminary (1979), Catherine Clark Kroeger (1979), E. Margaret Howe of Western Kentucky University (1982), Gilbert Bilezikian of Wheaton College (1985), Aida Spencer of Gordon-Conwell Seminary (1985), Gretchen Gaebelein Hull (1987), and many others, in articles, lectures, and classroom teaching. Although they have disagreed on details, their common theme has been the rejection of a unique leadership role for men in marriage and in the church.

Yet these authors differ from secular feminists because they do not reject the Bible's authority or truthfulness, but rather give *new interpretations* of the Bible to support their claims. We may call them "evangelical feminists" because by personal commitment to Jesus Christ and by profession of belief in the total truthfulness of Scripture they still identify themselves very clearly with evangelicalism. Their arguments have been detailed, earnest, and persuasive to many Christians.

What has been the result? Great uncertainty among evangelicals. Men and women simply are not sure what their roles should be. Traditional positions have not been totally satisfactory, because they have not fully answered the recent evangelical feminist arguments. Moreover, most Christians will admit that selfishness, irresponsibility, passivity, and abuse have often contaminated "traditional" patterns of how men and women relate to each other.

But the vast majority of evangelicals have not endorsed the evangelical feminist position, sensing that it does not really reflect the pattern of Biblical truth. Within our churches, we have had long discussions and debates, and still the controversy shows signs of intensifying, not subsiding. Before the struggle ends, probably no Christian family and no evangelical church will remain untouched.

We have edited this book in the hope that it might lead to a constructive solution to this controversy. Our *secondary* purpose is to respond to evangelical feminist writings like those mentioned above—hence the subtitle, *A Response to Evangelical Feminism*. We consider these authors to be brothers and sisters in Christ, and we have endeavored to respond to them in sincerity and love. Yet we also consider their essential position to be wrong in the light of Scripture, and ultimately harmful to the family and the church. Therefore we have tried to respond to them in detail and with clarity, and we have in many cases attempted to show that their interpretations of Scripture are simply not persuasive, and should not be accepted by Christians.

But our *primary* purpose is broader than that: We want to help Christians recover a noble vision of manhood and womanhood as God created them to be —hence the main title, *Recovering Biblical Manhood and Womanhood*. Our vision is not entirely the same as "a traditional view." We affirm that the evangelical feminist movement has pointed out many selfish and hurtful practices that have previously gone unquestioned. But we hope that this new vision—a vision of Biblical "complementarity"—will both correct the previous mistakes and avoid the opposite mistakes that come from the feminist blurring of God-given sexual distinctions.

We hope that thousands of Christian women who read this book will come away feeling affirmed and encouraged to participate much more actively in many ministries, and to contribute their wisdom and insight to the family and the church. We hope they will feel *fully equal* to men in status before God, and in importance to the family and the church. We pray that, at the same time, this vision of equality and complementarity will enable Christian women to give wholehearted affirmation to Biblically balanced male leadership in the home and in the church.

Similarly, we desire that every Christian man who reads this book will come away feeling in his heart that women are indeed *fully equal* to men in personhood, in importance, and in status before God, and, moreover, that he can eagerly endorse countless women's ministries and can freely encourage the contribution of wisdom and insight from women in the home and church, without feeling that this will jeopardize his own unique leadership role as given by God.

On an even deeper level, we hope that every woman reading this book will come away saying, "I understand much more fully what it means to be a woman, and I am *thankful* that God made me a woman, remarkably different from a man, yet immeasurably valuable in God's sight and in His plan for the world." And we hope that every man reading this book will come away saying, "I understand much more fully what it means to be a man, and I am *thankful* that God made me to be a man, remarkably different from a woman, yet immeasurably valuable in God's sight and in His plan for the world."

If that happens, then perhaps the path will be opened for clearing away much confusion, for diffusing much frustration over male-female relationships, and for healing many of the heartaches that smolder deep within millions of men and women who have been the victims of a society without direction on how to understand our wonderful gift of sexual complementarity.

A brief note about terms: If one word must be used to describe our position, we prefer the term *complementarian*, since it suggests both equality and beneficial differences between men and women. We are uncomfortable with the term "traditionalist" because it implies an unwillingness to let Scripture challenge traditional patterns of behavior, and we certainly reject the term "hierarchicalist" because it overemphasizes structured authority while giving no suggestion of equality or the beauty of mutual interdependence.

Twenty-two authors from many denominational backgrounds contributed to this book, and it is inevitable that not every author would agree with every detail in the chapters written by the other authors or by the editors. Where there are occasional differences in details, we have attempted to call attention to that fact in the notes, and we must say here that the positions advocated in the chapters are those of the individual authors. Yet the authors share a common commitment to the overall viewpoint represented in the book, and in every case the editors felt that the chapters were consistent with the position endorsed by the Danvers Statement published by the Council on Biblical Manhood and Womanhood in 1988 (see Appendix 2). It is commitment to that position that has guided the inclusion of articles in the book.

Many people have helped in correspondence, typing and editing, and compiling the indexes and we wish especially to thank Debbie Rumpel, Carol Steinbach, Mary Morris, Tammy Thomas, Noël Piper, John O. Stevenson, Eric Hoehn, Caren Hoehn, and E. Calvin Beisner for their accurate and tireless help. Lane Dennis of Crossway Books has been an eager supporter of this project from the start, and Fieldstead and Company provided an early and generous grant that enabled the project to get off the ground. We also acknowledge with appreciation the responsible, solidly Biblical work of several evangelical scholars whose earlier books defended a view compatible with the one represented here, especially George W. Knight III (1977, 1985), Susan T. Foh (1979), Stephen B. Clark (1980), and James Hurley (1982).

The Council on Biblical Manhood and Womanhood has sponsored and endorsed this as its first book project, and we are grateful for the support of the Council in this work. (A list of Council members appears in Appendix 2.)

Most of all, we want to thank our wives, Noël Piper and Margaret Grudem, who have faithfully supported us in this work and in their prayers, and who have for many years of marriage (22 and 21 years, respectively) been partners with us in the exciting task of discovering more and more the true nature of Biblical manhood and womanhood, in all its fullness and joy. For this we thank God, the giver of every perfect gift, to whom alone be glory.

John Piper and Wayne Grudem
January, 1991

NOTE ON HOW TO USE THIS BOOK:

We do not expect that many people will read a book of this length from cover to cover. The book is arranged so that people can read first the chapters that interest them most. Those who want an overview of the book may read chapters 1 and 2. Those interested in discussion of specific Biblical texts can turn to chapters 3–11, while theological questions are treated especially in chapters 12–14. Specialized studies (from history, biology, psychology, sociology, and law) are found in chapters 15–19, and questions of practical application are treated in more detail in chapters 20–25. Finally, in chapter 26 we give a careful response to the statement issued by Christians for Biblical Equality, and then try to put the whole controversy in perspective and express our hopes for the future.

Foreword
For Single Men and Women (and the Rest of Us)

John Piper

We know you are there—almost sixty million of you in America. And we are listening. One of the most important things we have learned is that we do not know what it is like to be single in America today—at least not the way you know it. Margaret Clarkson made this very plain to us:

> Because married people were all single once, they tend to think that they know all there is to know about singleness. I suggest that this is not so; that there is a vast difference between being single at 25 or 30, with marriage still a viable possibility, and being single at 45 or 50 or 60, with little or no prospect of ever being anything else. Singleness has a cumulative effect on the human spirit which is entirely different at 50 than at 30.[1]

What I would like to do in this foreword is try to let single people do as much of the talking as possible—people like Jesus and the Apostle Paul and some contemporary men and women who serve in the single life. This way we will be listening and speaking at the same time. I realize I am going to filter all of this through my happily married lens. It is futile in one sense for me to write this chapter, except that I do not put it forward as something definitive about the single experience today, but as a call to married folks to listen and a statement to single folks that this book and this issue have to do with you, even though many of its chapters deal with marriage. Enough singles have read this foreword already to let me know that some things I say hit the nail on the head and some things do not fit their experience at all. My hope is to listen closely enough and speak truly enough that married and single people will be helped along in the conversation.

We also pray that in the process there will be tremendous encouragement and challenge for your faith and ministry. We believe the vision of manhood and womanhood in this book is utterly relevant for single people. Why this is so will become clear before we come to the end of this foreword.

We hear at least eight important theses on singleness when we tune in to Jesus and His contemporary single followers.[2]

I. Marriage, as we know it in this age, is not the final destiny of any human.

My mother was killed in a bus collision near Bethlehem in Israel in 1974. She was fifty-six years old and had been married to my father for thirty-seven years. As the grief began to heal, God gave my father another wonderful wife. I rejoice in this. But it has caused me to take much more seriously the words of Jesus to the Sadducees concerning marriage in the resurrection. They told Jesus about a woman who was widowed seven times. "At the resurrection," they asked, "whose wife will she be?" Jesus answered, "When the dead rise, they will neither marry nor be given in marriage; they will be like the angels in heaven" (Mark 12:25).

This is important to me because it means my father will not be a bigamist in the age to come. Why? Because in the resurrection, marriage as we know it will not exist. This has profound significance for singleness in this life. It means that if two wives will not be one too many, then no wives will not be one too few. If love in the age to come is transposed into a key above and beyond the melody of marriage in this life, then singleness here will prove to be no disadvantage in eternity.

In fact, there is some warrant for thinking that the kinds of self-denial involved in singleness could make one a candidate for greater capacities for love in the age to come. No one has left anything for the sake of the kingdom, says the Lord Jesus, who will not receive back far more (Matthew 19:27-30). Many unmarried people have strengthened their hands with this truth. For example, Trevor Douglas, a single missionary with Regions Beyond Missionary Union, working in the Philippines among the Ifugao people, wrote in 1988:

> In the end, however, Christians know that Jesus will more than make up for every cost incurred by being a single male missionary. As I have applied his promises in Matthew 19:27-30 to myself, I see a tremendous exchange taking place in eternity. The social cost of not fitting in a couple's world will be exchanged for socializing with Jesus around his throne. I'll trade the emotional cost of loneliness and the family hurt for companionship with new fathers, mothers, and families. I'll exchange the physical cost for spiritual children. And when I'm snubbed, I love to think of eternity and the privilege of going from the last of the gospel preachers to the head of the line. The rewards are worth everything.[3]

II. Jesus Christ, the most fully human person who ever lived, was not married.

In 1987, I wrote an editorial for the Minneapolis *Star-Tribune* during a volatile controversy over advertising condoms on television.[4] The concern of the networks was to help curb the spread of AIDS. My basic point was: "In the act of endorsing protection from disease, the ads also endorse its cause, namely, sexual promiscuity." I said that the claim that condoms make for "safe" sex betrayed an incredible naiveté about human nature.

My argument went like this: "Personhood is deeper and more significant than what is physical. Only a superficial view of personhood says we will be 'safe' if we can avoid a disease while pursuing acts that Western civilization has overwhelmingly called immoral and that the Bible indicts as dishonoring to our creator. . . . Not only the Biblical teaching but also the testimony of human conscience in varied cultures around the world have said for centuries that extramarital sex and homosexual activity are destructive to personhood, to relationships and to the honor of God, who made our sexuality to deepen and gladden the union of man and woman in marriage."

You can imagine that this did not go unchallenged. I got a letter from one young man who spoke for a certain group of single people when he said, "My girlfriend and I have lots of good sex together. We think your ideas are repressive leftovers from the Victorian era that make people neurotic and miserable. We think our sexuality is part of our personhood, and not to enjoy it is to be incomplete people. We have no intention of getting married to meet the expectations of any puritans. And we think a life of slavery to virginity would mean being only half human."[5]

When I wrote back to this man, the centerpiece of my response was this: The most fully human person who has ever lived, or ever will live, is Jesus Christ, and He never once had sexual intercourse.

This can be powerfully liberating to single people who may think at times, "This one thing I will never have, sexual relations, and in not having it I will not be all I was meant to be." To this thought Jesus, the virgin, says, "A student is not above his teacher, but everyone who is fully trained will be like his teacher" (Luke 6:40). We will always have mountains of truly human Christ-likeness yet to climb, but sexual intercourse is not one of them. For He never knew it. And He is infinitely whole.

The paradox we may feel in this is captured in the title of Luci Swindoll's book on singleness: *Wide My World, Narrow My Bed*. Single by choice at forty-nine (when she wrote the book), she shows that the narrow path of the Son of Man, who had no place to lay his head (not even on a woman's shoulder), leads into a wide world of wonder and freedom and joy and love.[6]

Cheryl Forbes illustrates how she and other single women and men have been inspired by the "wideness" of Jesus' single life:

> Jesus is the example to follow. He was single. He was born to serve. . . . He had deep friendships among all sorts of people—men, women, single, married. That was his work, an intimate part of his ultimate mission of dying on the cross for our sins. . . . His relationships with Mary, Martha, Peter, and the other disciples helped prepare him for his death. No one can love in the abstract. He allowed himself to be interrupted by needy children, distraught fathers, hungry men and sick women. . . . Jesus sought to make himself vulnerable.[7]

III. The Bible celebrates celibacy because it gives extraordinary opportunity for single-minded investment in ministry for Christ.

Paul said that he wished everyone could know the freedom for ministry that he enjoyed as a single person (1 Corinthians 7:7). He went on to explain,

> I would like you to be free from concern. An unmarried man is concerned about the Lord's affairs—how he can please the Lord. But a married man is concerned about the affairs of this world—how he can please his wife—and his interests are divided. An unmarried woman or virgin is concerned about the Lord's affairs: Her aim is to be devoted to the Lord in both body and spirit. But a married woman is concerned about the affairs of this world—how she can please her husband. I am saying this for your own good, not to restrict you, but that you may live in a right way in undivided devotion to the Lord. (1 Corinthians 7:32-35).

Many single people give thanks for this truth in their own lives. It seems to come out most often in a cherished freedom for flexible scheduling and for risk-taking. As a single missionary in Kenya, Rhena Taylor wrote:

> Being single has meant that I am free to take risks that I might not take were I a mother of a family dependent on me. Being single has given me freedom to move around the world without having to pack up a household first. And this freedom has brought to me moments that I would not trade for anything else this side of eternity.[8]

Trevor Douglas similarly describes the freedom for risk that he has experienced:

> The first advantage [of being single] is that it's best adapted to perilous situations. . . . In rugged life among primitive tribes, in guerrilla-infested areas, or in disease and famine, the single man has only himself to worry about. . . . Paul claims that being single and male best fits the "shortness" of the time. Doing God's work is a momentary thing. Advantages and opportunities come and go very quickly. The single lifestyle enables one to get the most out of the time God gives for his work. . . . One of my chief delights is that I don't have to fit my ministry around a family schedule. I don't have to be home at a certain time each night. My time is the Filipinos' time.[9]

Douglas quotes one of his heroes, another single missionary with radical single-mindedness, David Brainerd:

> I cared not where or how I lived, or what hardships I went through, so that I could but gain souls for Christ. While I was asleep I dreamed of these things, and when I awoke the first thing I thought of was this great work. All my desire was for the conversion of the heathen, and all my hope was in God.[10]

A single friend at our church read this third point and responded like this to balance the scales:

> I believe that singles have flexibility in scheduling but are not totally free from anxiety. While I'm happy to be free from balancing husband and family needs and ministry, I must face other "practical" needs should Jesus tarry—retirement, housing, finances, etc. The reality is that single women have to plan for the future as singles. We must be good stewards with the resources we have,

but studies show that women don't earn the same salaries that men do for the same tasks. And in ministry everyone earns less than in the secular world, but it's a choice that has been made, but that doesn't mean I don't feel the tension.

How do singles balance a career that requires more than forty hours a week plus other outside commitments (continuing education, etc.) with the "extraordinary opportunity for single-minded investment in ministry"? I think there will be those singles who interpret this to mean that because they are not married they are "expected" to devote every non-working hour to ministry— something not expected from those who are married. I don't think that is what you are saying.

Unfortunately there are many in the church who reinforce this error in thinking. This thinking can turn into an abusive situation. Singles can be guilted and shamed into doing too much. I believe there must be a caution to singles not to become "over-invested." Singles must protect their spiritual, physical, and emotional health as well as those who are married. Singles need to be affirmed to take time to develop nurturing relationships ("family").

IV. The Apostle Paul and a lot of great missionaries after him have renounced marriage for the sake of the kingdom of God.

"Don't we have the right to take a believing wife along with us, as do the other apostles and the Lord's brothers and Cephas?" (1 Corinthians 9:5). With these words Paul shows that it was normal and permissible for him as an apostle to have a wife. But he chose not to use this legitimate right (cf. 1 Corinthians 9:15). He was the first of a long line of single men and women who have renounced marriage for the sake of the gospel, as Jesus said some would: "For some . . . have renounced marriage because of the kingdom of heaven" (Matthew 19:12).

This renunciation has, in most cases, required immense courage and devotion to Christ. Ada Lum, a single woman working with International Fellowship of Evangelical Students in Southeast Asia, told this moving story of devotion:

> Flying from Rome to Munich I had warm fellowship with an attractive and spirited nun. I learned this was her first visit home to Germany after thirty years as a missionary. No wonder she was excited! I could also tell that she loved Christ and had served him happily even through the war in the Philippines, where she had been imprisoned in an enemy camp. We talked about our faith in Jesus Christ and our walk with him. Then she showed me her plain gold ring on the inside of which was inscribed, "Wed to Christ." But there certainly was nothing neurotic about her. She was refreshingly human![11]

Mary Slessor was doing work in the interior of Calabar, West Africa, at the end of the nineteenth century and was deeply desirous of a companion. Her hope centered on Charles Morrison, a man who was working with the mission on the coast. They were engaged, but the mission would not allow him to transfer to the interior because of his poor health. She would have to move to Duke Town. She wrote:

> It is out of the question. I would never take the idea into consideration. I could not leave my work for such a reason. To leave a field like Okoyong without a worker and go to one of ten or a dozen where the people have an open Bible and plenty of privilege! It is absurd. If God does not send him up here then he must do his work and I must do mine where we have been placed. If he does not come I must ask the Committee to give me someone else for it is impossible for me to work the station alone.[12]

With similar single-minded devotion to her calling, Lottie Moon broke an engagement with a brilliant young scholar because he "adopted the Darwinian theory of evolution." Years later she said, "God had first claim on my life, and since the two conflicted, there could be no question about the result."[13]

Elisabeth Elliot tells of a conversation she had with Gladys Aylward, missionary to China:

> She had been a missionary in China for six or seven years before she ever thought of wanting a husband. When a British couple came to work near her, she began to watch the wonderful thing they had in marriage, and to desire it for herself. Being a woman of prayer she prayed—a straightforward request that God would call a man from England, send him straight out to China, and have him propose. She leaned toward me on the sofa on which we were sitting, her black eyes snapping, her bony little forefinger jabbing at my face. "Elisabeth," she said, "I *believe* God answers prayer! He *called* him." Then, in a whisper of keen intensity, "but he *never* came."[14]

One of the reasons the choice to be single can be courageous is that for some it is the choice of very painful loneliness. Trevor Douglas illustrates this with a story from one of his friends:

> Perhaps loneliness takes the heaviest toll. At creation, God knew that man needed companionship. The single male missionary forfeits that legitimate need and embraces loneliness. I well remember how a fellow single missionary brother poured out his heart to me. "Christmas is especially bad," he said. "That's the hardest. Once I was invited to spend Christmas with a family, but after I got there I wished I had never gone. I felt like they were just trying to do me a favor. I felt like an intruder. Next Christmas, I drove off in my car far away, rented a motel room, and sat there and cried."[15]

The courage to be single (and I realize that marriage requires its kind of courage too) is not just found among missionaries. Many young men and women in more ordinary circumstances have made incredibly hard decisions to avoid a marriage they at first thought was right. Elva McAllaster writes a whole chapter on such stories under the title "The Courage to Stay Single." For example:

> Mara had the courage. She was already wearing a diamond when she began to realize that Larry's moods were so unpredictable that, in spite of all the qualities for which she adored him, he was not good husband material. Nor was he ready to be a father. She thought of his moods—those black moods—and she shuddered, and stood by her courage.[16]

> Mervin had courage, too. He was already engaged, as a matter of fact, when he began to feel ominous intensities of penned-in and nailed-down limitation. He knew it would make him feel like sixteen varieties of a heel to break the engagement, but he knew increasingly that Erma was wrong for him. Wrong, wrong, wrong. When Erma nervously wanted the wedding to be sooner than they had first planned, her insecurity liberated Mervin's emotions, and his emotions liberated his whole future—as he would now describe it.[17]

The point is this: singleness has been a noble and courageous path for ministry ever since Jesus and the Apostle Paul chose it "because of the kingdom of heaven." It is no sign of weakness to want to be married. It is normal, and it is good. The courage comes when you sense God calling you to singleness (for this chapter of your life) and you accept the call with zeal and creative planning for His glory.

V. The Apostle Paul calls singleness a gift from God.

"I wish that all men were [single] as I am. But each man has his own gift from God; one has this gift, another has that" (1 Corinthians 7:7). In essence, Jesus pointed to the same thing in Matthew 19:12 when He said, "The one who can accept this should accept it."

With the gift comes the grace to be chaste. Margaret Clarkson is right: "His commands are his enablings." She reminds the single person, after dealing with her own single sexuality for more than forty years, that chastity is not only commanded but possible, year after year, as a gift from God. She quotes John White's *Eros Defiled* to make the point:

> Just as the fasting person finds he no longer wishes for food while the starving person is tortured by mental visions of it, so some are able to experience the peace of sexual abstinence when they need to. Others are tormented. Everything depends upon their mindset or attitude. The slightest degree of ambivalence or double-mindedness spells ruin.
>
> I cannot stress this principle enough. Neither hunger for food nor hunger for sex increases automatically until we explode into uncontrollable behavior. Rather, it is as though a spring is wound up, locked in place, ready to be released when the occasion arises. And should that occasion not arise (and here I refer especially to sex), *I need experience no discomfort.*"[18]

Single people do not always discover singleness as a gift at the beginning of their journey. Ada Lum admits that it was a process for her to come to this place:

> For a long time I did not consider that my single status was a gift from the Lord. I did not resent it—to be frank, in my earlier idealistic period I thought that because I had chosen singleness I was doing God a favor! But in later years I was severely tested again and again on that choice. Then, through Paul's words and life and my subsequent experiences, it gently dawned on me that God had given me a superb gift![19]

But single people are not generally treated as the bearers of a superb and special gift from God. They are sometimes treated as abnormal in the church. Perhaps the only text people can think of is Genesis 2:18, "It is *not good* for the man to be alone." Conclusion: singleness is not good. Trevor Douglas candidly describes the cost of being a single man in this kind of atmosphere:

> Jesus admitted that singleness is costly, so much so that not everyone can endure it. The obvious cost is the attitude that single men might be gay, or at least slightly strange, and perhaps anti-female. Our North American society is structured definitely for couples. Not so the tribe of Ayangan Ifugaos among whom I work. Although 99 percent of the men are married, they don't look at the one percent as weird. The social cost only hits me when I return home—in the churches, among Christians, who, of all people, should know better.[20]

Well, is it good or not good to be alone? If it is not good—not God's will—how can it be called a "gift from God"? How could Jesus, who never sinned, have chosen it for Himself? How could Paul say it was a great asset for ministry?

Two answers: First, Genesis 2:18 was a statement about man before the fall. Perhaps, if there had been no fall, there would have been no singleness.[21] Everyone would have had a perfectly compatible personality type for someone; people and situations would have matched up perfectly; no sin would have made us blind or gullible or hasty; and no great commission—no lostness, no famine, no sickness, no misery—would call for extraordinary measures of sacrifice in marriage and singleness. But that is not our world. So sometimes—many times—it *is* good for a person to be alone.

But second, almost no one has to be really alone. That's the point of the next thesis. But let me include here another insight from another single person who read this foreword:

> I believe that Genesis 2:18 extends beyond the principle of marriage. As a general rule, it is definitely not good for man (or woman) to be alone. God created us to function within relationships. Most of the time, it will not be necessary for the single person to be alone, even though the marriage relationship does not exist. Many married people are very much alone emotionally. Sometimes marriage keeps one from being alone, but not always.

VI. Jesus promises that forsaking family for the sake of the kingdom will be repaid with a new family, the church.

"I tell you the truth, no one who has left home or brothers or sisters or mother or father or children or fields for me and the gospel will fail to receive a hundred times as much in this present age (homes, brothers, sisters, mothers, children and fields—and with them, persecutions) and in the age to come, eternal life" (Mark 10:29-30). Many singles have discovered these hundreds of family members in the body of Christ. It is often not their fault when they haven't. But many have. Margaret Clarkson's large-hearted book, *So You're Single*, is even dedicated "TO MY MARRIED FRIENDS whose love and friendship have so enriched my life." She obviously found a "family" in many of the families in her life.

Dietrich Bonhoeffer, the German pastor who was hanged for conspiring to assassinate Hitler, was single. He knew the needs of single people for family, and was moved, in large measure for this reason, to write his little book, *Life Together*. He said simply, the single person "needs another Christian who speaks God's Word to him."[22] That is what the church is for.

Elisabeth Elliot comes at this need for family from another side, and asks, "How may a single woman enter into the meaning of motherhood if she can have no children?" She answers:

> She *can* have children! She may be a spiritual mother, as was Amy Carmichael, by the very offering of her singleness, transformed for the good of far more children than a natural mother may produce. All is received and made holy by the One to whom it is offered.[23]

This ideal is not a reality for many singles. But Jesus had a great vision of hundreds of wonderful relationships growing up in the lives of single people who choose the kingdom road of obedient singleness rather than accepting marriage from an unbeliever. We who are leaders in the churches should open our eyes to make the same discovery that Frank Schneider made:

> For the first time in years of Christian service, we were aware of an affluence of intelligent, capable, loyal, energetic, talented single adults who only wanted someone to care enough to recognize they exist. Some lonely, some deeply hurt, others very self-sufficient and quite in control, but all desiring fellowship in a Christian atmosphere where they can feel they belong.[24]

VII. God is sovereign over who gets married and who doesn't. And He can be trusted to do what is good for those who hope in Him.

Job speaks not just for those who had and lost, but also for those who never had, when he says, "Naked I came from my mother's womb, and naked I will depart. The LORD gave and the LORD has taken away; may the name of the LORD be praised" (Job 1:21). God rules in these affairs, and we will be the happier when we bow before His inscrutable ways and confess, ". . . no good thing does he withhold from those whose walk is blameless" (Psalm 84:11). "He who did not spare his own Son, but gave him up for us all—how will he not also, along with him, graciously give us all things?" (Romans 8:32).

Margaret Clarkson's personal statement of submission rings with the strength that comes from bowing before the sovereignty of God:

> Through no fault or choice of my own, I am unable to express my sexuality in the beauty and intimacy of Christian marriage, as God intended when he created me a sexual being in his own image. To seek to do this outside of marriage is, by the clear teaching of Scripture, to sin against God and against my own nature. As a committed Christian, then, I have no alternative but to live a life of voluntary celibacy. I must be chaste not only in body, but in mind and spirit as well. Since I am now in my 60's I think that my experience of what this means is valid. I want to go on record as having proved that for those who are committed to do God's will, his commands are his enablings. . . .

> My whole being cries out continually for something I may not have. My whole life must be lived in the context of this never-ceasing tension. My professional life, my social life, my personal life, my Christian life—all are subject to its constant and powerful pull. As a Christian I have no choice but to obey God, cost what it may. I must trust him to make it possible for me to honor him in my singleness.
>
> That this *is* possible, a mighty cloud of witnesses will join me to attest. Multitudes of single Christians in every age and circumstance have proved God's sufficiency in this matter. He has promised to meet our needs and he honors his word. If we seek fulfillment in him, we shall find it. It may not be easy, but whoever said that Christian life was easy? The badge of Christ's discipleship was a cross.
>
> Why must I live my life alone? I do not know. But Jesus Christ is Lord of my life. I believe in the sovereignty of God, and I accept my singleness from his hand. He could have ordered my life otherwise, but he has not chosen to do so. As his child, I must trust his love and wisdom."[25]

Ann Kiemel Anderson gave poetic expression to what thousands of Christian singles have discovered about the relationship of desire for marriage and devotion to a sovereign God:

> *Jesus, if this is Your will,*
> *then YES to being single.*
> *In my deepest heart, i want to marry,*
> *to belong to a great man;*
> *to know that i am linked to his life . . .*
> *and he to mine . . .*
> *following Christ and our dreams together . . .*
> *but You know what i need.*
> *if i never marry, it is YES to You.*[26]

VIII. Mature manhood and womanhood are not dependent on being married.

This is why the rest of this book is relevant for single people, even when it is dealing with marriage. The question every man and woman should ask earnestly is this: "What does it mean to be a woman and not a man?" Or: "What does it mean to be a man and not a woman? What is my masculine or feminine personhood (not just anatomy and physiology)?" We are persuaded from Scripture that masculinity and femininity are rooted in who we are by nature. They are not simply reflexes of a marriage relationship. Man does not become man by getting married. Woman does not become woman by getting married.

But it is clear that the form that a man's leadership, provision, and protection take varies with the kind of relationship a man has with a woman—from the most intimate relationship of marriage to the most casual relationship with a stranger on the street. And the form that a woman's affirmation of that leadership takes will also vary according to the relationship. Mature femininity does not express itself in the same way toward every man. A mature woman who is not married, for example, does not welcome the same kind of strength and leadership from other men that she would welcome from her husband. But she will affirm the strength and leadership of men in some form in all her relationships with worthy men. I know this will need a lot of explanation. That is what I try to do in Chapter 1.

The point here is simply to stress that for single people sexual personhood counts. It does not first emerge in marriage. No one is ready for marriage who has not discovered in practical ways how to live out his mature masculinity or her mature femininity. Paul Jewett is right:

> Sexuality permeates one's individual being to its very depth; it conditions every facet of one's life as a person. As the self is always aware of itself as an "I," so this "I" is always aware of itself as himself or herself. Our self-knowledge is indissolubly bound up not simply with our human being but with our sexual being. At the human level there is no "I and thou" per se, but only the "I" who is male or female confronting the "thou," the "other," who is also male or female.[27]

This is not dependent on marriage. Ada Lum illustrates this for single women:

> At any age the single woman needs to respect herself as a sexual being whom God created. She is not less sexual for not being married. *Sex* has to do with biological drive for union with one of the opposite sex. *Sexuality* has to do with our whole personhood as a woman or a man. It has to do with the ways we express ourselves in relation to others. It has to do with being warm, understanding, receptive sexual beings when we relate to another female or to a child or to a man who is the least prospect for a husband! . . . I try to treat him as I do my two brothers. I enjoy Leon and Dick. I respect them. I like to hear them talk about masculine things in masculine ways. I am pleased when they treat me thoughtfully. . . . With care and discretion a single woman can and should be a real woman to the men around her.[28]

Cheryl Forbes gives another illustration of one kind of feminine expression as a single person:

> To be single is not to forego the traditional "womanly" pursuits. Whether you live alone or with a husband and children, a house or apartment is still a home that requires "homemaking." And marital status has nothing to do with the desire for warm, comfortable, aesthetically pleasing surroundings. God gave each of us a desire for beauty; it is part of our desire for him, who is loveliness incarnate. Why should a single woman reject that part of her image as a creature of God? . . . I am a better and more imaginative cook now than I was five years ago. I am free to experiment on myself and my friends. I have the time and the money to entertain people around the dinner table, something I might not want or be able to do if I cooked for a family three times a day every day.[29]

The point is that, married or single, your manhood or your womanhood matters. You dishonor yourself and your Maker if you disregard this profound dimension of your personhood. Our culture is pressing us on almost every side to discount this reality and think of ourselves and each other merely in terms of a set of impersonal competencies and gender-blind personality traits. It has the appearance of promoting justice. But the failure to take into account the profound and complementary differences of masculine and feminine personhood is like assigning a truck driver the task of writing the choreography for two ballet artists.

Our prayer is that God will give to millions of single Christians in our day a deep understanding and appreciation for their own distinct sexual personhood, that Christ will be magnified more and more in you as you offer His gift of singleness back to Him in radical freedom from the way of the world, and that you will grow deeper and deeper in joyful devotion (on the Calvary road) to the triumphant cause of Jesus Christ.

I close this foreword with a final word of hope from a woman of deep insight and long singleness. Margaret Clarkson looks back over a lifetime of singleness and extends a hand to those just starting:

> When Christian was crossing the River at the close of *Pilgrim's Progress*, his heart failed him for fear. He began to sink in the cold, dark waters. But Hopeful, his companion, helped him to stand, calling out loudly, "Be of good cheer, my brother; I feel the bottom, and it is good." Then Christian recovered his faith, and passed safely through the waters to the Celestial City.
>
> If there are singles who find the waters of singleness dark and deep, who feel, "I sink in deep waters; the billows go over my head; all his waves go over me," this is my message to you concerning singleness: "Be of good cheer, my brother, my sister; I feel the bottom, and it is good."[30]

I

Vision and Overview

1

A Vision of Biblical Complementarity

Manhood and Womanhood Defined According to the Bible

John Piper

When I was a boy growing up in Greenville, South Carolina, my father was away from home about two-thirds of every year. And while he preached across the country, we prayed—my mother and my older sister and I. What I learned in those days was that my mother was omni-competent.

She handled the finances, paying all the bills and dealing with the bank and creditors. She once ran a little laundry business on the side. She was active on the park board, served as the superintendent of the Intermediate Department of our Southern Baptist church, and managed some real estate holdings.

She taught me how to cut the grass and splice electric cord and pull Bermuda grass by the roots and paint the eaves and shine the dining-room table with a shammy and drive a car and keep French fries from getting soggy in the cooking oil. She helped me with the maps in geography and showed me how to do a bibliography and work up a science project on static electricity and believe that Algebra II was possible. She dealt with the contractors when we added a basement and, more than once, put her hand to the shovel. It never occurred to me that there was anything she couldn't do.

I heard one time that women don't sweat, they glow. Not true. My mother sweated. It would drip off the end of her long, sharp nose. Sometimes she would blow it off when her hands were pushing the wheelbarrow full of peat moss. Or she would wipe it with her sleeve between the strokes of a swingblade. Mother was strong. I can remember her arms even today thirty years later. They were big, and in the summertime they were bronze.

But it never occurred to me to think of my mother and my father in the same category. Both were strong. Both were bright. Both were kind. Both would kiss me and both would spank me. Both were good with words. Both prayed with fervor and loved the Bible. But unmistakably my father was a man and my mother was a woman. They knew it and I knew it. And it was not mainly a biological fact. It was mainly a matter of personhood and relational dynamics.

When my father came home he was clearly the head of the house. He led in prayer at the table. He called the family together for devotions. He got us to Sunday School and worship. He drove the car. He guided the family to where we would sit. He made the decision to go to Howard Johnson's for lunch. He led us to the table. He called for the waitress. He paid the check. He was the one we knew we would reckon with if we broke a family rule or were disrespectful to Mother. These were the happiest times for Mother. Oh, how she rejoiced to have Daddy home! She loved his leadership. Later I learned that the Bible calls this "submission."

But since my father was gone most of the time, Mother used to do most of those leadership things too. So it never occurred to me that leadership and submission had anything to do with superiority and inferiority. And it didn't have to do with muscles and skills either. It was not a matter of capabilities and competencies. It had to do with something I could never have explained as a child. And I have been a long time in coming to understand it as part of God's great goodness in creating us male and female. It had to do with something very deep. I know that the specific rhythm of life that was in our home is not the only good one. But there were dimensions of reality and goodness in it that ought to be there in every home. Indeed they ought to be there in varying ways in all mature relationships between men and women.

I say "ought to be there" because I now see that they were rooted in God. Over the years I have come to see from Scripture and from life that manhood and womanhood are the beautiful handiwork of a good and loving God. He designed our differences and they are profound. They are not mere physiological prerequisites for sexual union. They go to the root of our personhood. This chapter is an attempt to define some of those differences as God wills them to be according to the Bible.

* * * * *

Let me say a word about that phrase, "according to the Bible." The subtitle of this chapter is "Manhood and Womanhood Defined *According to the Bible.*" What that means is that I have made every effort to bring the thinking of this chapter into *accord* with what the Bible teaches. At the same time, however, I have not tried to include a detailed exegetical argument for every assertion.

There are three main reasons that seem to justify this approach:

First, for the purposes of this chapter, it seemed best to present the Biblical vision of manhood and womanhood as clearly and concisely as possible, and to leave the comprehensive technical discussion for the following chapters. I have also tried in articles,[1] sermons,[2] and unpublished papers to give credible account of the Biblical foundations of what I say here.

Second, I have tried to include enough Biblical argumentation in this essay, especially in the footnotes, to show why I believe this vision of manhood and womanhood is in fact "*according to the Bible.*" I hope it will be obvious that my reflections are not the creation of an independent mind, but the fruit of a tree planted firmly in the soil of constant meditation on the Word of God.

Third, experience has taught me that there are two ways to commend a vision of manhood and womanhood. One way has to do with rational argumentation concerning factual evidences. For example, an evangelical Christian wants to know, Does the Bible really teach this vision of manhood and womanhood? So one way of commending the vision is by patient, detailed, careful exegetical argumentation.

But there is another way to commend the vision. A person also wants to know, Is the vision beautiful and satisfying and fulfilling? Can I live with it? This is not a bad question. Commending Biblical truth involves more than saying, "Do it because the Bible says so." That sort of commendation may result in a kind of obedience that is so begrudging and so empty of delight and hearty affirmation that the Lord is not pleased with it at all.

So there is a second task needed in winning people over to a vision of manhood and womanhood. Not only must there be thorough exegesis, there must also be a portrayal of the vision that satisfies the heart as well as the head. Or to put it another way: we must commend the beauty as well as the truth of the vision. We must show that something is not only right but also good. It is not only valid but also valuable, not only accurate but also admirable.

This chapter is meant to fit *mainly* into the second category. Not merely, but mainly. It is designed to show that our vision of manhood and womanhood is a deeply satisfying gift of grace from a loving God who has the best interests of his creatures at heart. The vision is not onerous or oppressive. It does not promote pride or self-exaltation. It conforms to who we are by God's good design. Therefore it is fulfilling in the deepest sense of that word.

* * * * *

The tendency today is to stress the equality of men and women by minimizing the unique significance of our maleness or femaleness. But this depreciation of male and female personhood is a great loss. It is taking a tremendous toll on generations of young men and women who do not know what it means to be a man or a woman. Confusion over the meaning of sexual personhood today is epidemic. The consequence of this confusion is not a free and happy harmony among gender-free persons relating on the basis of abstract competencies. The consequence rather is more divorce, more homosexuality, more sexual abuse, more promiscuity, more social awkwardness, and more emotional distress and suicide that come with the loss of God-given identity.

It is a remarkable and telling observation that contemporary Christian feminists devote little attention to the definition of femininity and masculinity. Little help is being given to a son's question, "Dad, what does it mean to be a man and not a woman?" Or a daughter's question, "Mom, what does it mean to be a woman and not a man?" A lot of energy is being expended today minimizing the distinctions of manhood and womanhood. But we do not hear very often what manhood and womanhood *should* incline us to do. We are adrift in a sea of confusion over sexual roles. And life is not the better for it.

Ironically the most perceptive thinkers recognize how essential manhood and womanhood are to our personhood. Yet the meaning of manhood and womanhood is seen as unattainable. For example, Paul Jewett, in his very insightful book, *Man as Male and Female*, argues persuasively that maleness and femaleness are essential, not peripheral, to our personhood:

> Sexuality permeates one's individual being to its very depth; it conditions every facet of one's life as a person. As the self is always aware of itself as an 'I,' so this 'I' is always aware of itself as *himself* or *herself*. Our self-knowledge is indissolubly bound up not simply with our *human* being but with our *sexual* being. At the human level there is no 'I and thou' *per se*, but only the 'I' who is male or female confronting the 'thou,' the 'other,' who is also male or female.[3]

He cites Emil Brunner to the same effect: "Our sexuality penetrates to the deepest metaphysical ground of our personality. As a result, the physical differences between the man and the woman are a parable of psychical and spiritual differences of a more ultimate nature."[4]

After reading these amazing statements concerning how essential manhood and womanhood are to our personhood and how sexuality "conditions every facet of one's life," it is stunning to read that Jewett does not know what manhood and womanhood are. He says,

> Some, at least, among contemporary theologians are not so sure that they know what it means to be a man in distinction to a woman or a woman in distinction to a man. It is because the writer shares this uncertainty that he has skirted the question of ontology in this study.[5]
>
> All human activity reflects a qualitative distinction which is sexual in nature. But in my opinion, such an observation offers no clue to the ultimate meaning of that distinction. It may be that we shall never know what that distinction ultimately means. But this much, at least, seems clear: we will understand the difference—what it means to be created as man or woman—only as we learn to live as man and woman in a true partnership of life.[6]

Surely this is a great sadness. We know that "sexuality permeates one's individual being to its very depth." We know that "it conditions every facet of one's life as a person." We know that every I-thou encounter is an encounter not of abstract persons but of male or female persons. We know that physical differences are but a parable of male and female personhood. But, alas, we do not know who we are as male and female. We are ignorant of this all-pervasive dimension of our identity.

But what about Jewett's prescription for hope in the face of this stunning ignorance of who we are? He suggests that we discover who we are "as man or woman" by experiencing a "true partnership" as man *and* woman. The problem with this is that we cannot know what a "true partnership" is until we know the nature of the partners. A true partnership must be true to who the partners are. A true partnership must take into account the sexual reality "that conditions every facet of their life." We simply cannot know what a "true" partnership is until we know what truly "permeates [our] personhood to the very depths." If we are really ignorant of what true manhood and womanhood are, we have no warrant to prescribe the nature of what *true* partnership will look like.

The sexual turmoil of our culture is not surprising when we discover that our best Christian thinkers claim not to know what masculinity and femininity are, and yet acknowledge that these are among the most profound aspects of personhood that "condition every facet of one's life"! How shall parents rear daughters to be women and sons to be men when even the leading teachers of the church do not know what manhood and womanhood are?

The conviction behind this chapter is that the Bible does not leave us in ignorance about the meaning of masculine and feminine personhood. God has not placed in us an all-pervasive and all-conditioning dimension of personhood and then hidden the meaning of our identity from us. He has shown us in Scripture the beauty of manhood and womanhood in complementary harmony. He has shown us the distortions and even horrors that sin has made of fallen manhood and womanhood. And he has shown us the way of redemption and healing through Christ.

To be sure, we see "through a glass dimly." Our knowledge is not perfect. We must be ever open to new light. But we are not so adrift as to have nothing to say to our generation about the meaning of manhood and womanhood and its implications for our relationships. Our understanding is that the Bible reveals the nature of masculinity and femininity by describing diverse responsibilities for man and woman while rooting these differing responsibilities in creation, not convention.

When the Bible teaches that men and women fulfil different roles in relation to each other, charging man with a unique leadership role, it bases this differentiation not on temporary cultural norms but on permanent facts of creation. This is seen in 1 Corinthians 11:3-16 (especially vv. 8-9, 14); Ephesians 5:21-33 (especially vv. 31-32); and 1 Timothy 2:11-14 (especially vv. 13-14).[7] In the Bible, differentiated roles for men and women are never traced back to the fall of man and woman into sin. Rather, the foundation of this differentiation is traced back to the way things were in Eden before sin warped our relationships. Differentiated roles were corrupted, not created, by the fall.[8] They were created by God.

* * * * *

This leads me then to attempt at least a partial definition of manhood and womanhood. This is risky business. Every word we choose could be misunderstood. Unsympathetic readers could jump to conclusions about practical implications that are not implied. I would simply plead for the application of that great principle of good criticism: Before assessing an author's position, express an understanding of it in a way the author would approve.

I would commend the following descriptions of masculinity and femininity for consideration. It will be very important to read them in the light of the subsequent comments. These are not exhaustive descriptions of all that masculinity or femininity mean. But they are intended to embrace both married people and single people. Even where I illustrate manhood and womanhood in the dynamics of a marriage relationship, I hope single people will see an application to other relationships as well. The definitions are not exhaustive, but they touch all of us. They are an attempt to get at the heart, or at least an indispensable aspect, of manhood and womanhood.[9]

> AT THE HEART OF MATURE MASCULINITY IS A SENSE OF BENEVOLENT RESPONSIBILITY TO LEAD, PROVIDE FOR AND PROTECT WOMEN IN WAYS APPROPRIATE TO A MAN'S DIFFERING RELATIONSHIPS.

> AT THE HEART OF MATURE FEMININITY IS A FREEING DISPOSITION TO AFFIRM, RECEIVE AND NURTURE STRENGTH AND LEADERSHIP FROM WORTHY MEN IN WAYS APPROPRIATE TO A WOMAN'S DIFFERING RELATIONSHIPS.

The Meaning of Masculinity

Here we take the definition of masculinity a phrase at a time and unfold its meaning and implications.

> AT THE HEART OF MATURE MASCULINITY IS A SENSE OF BENEVOLENT RESPONSIBILITY TO LEAD, PROVIDE FOR AND PROTECT WOMEN IN WAYS APPROPRIATE TO A MAN'S DIFFERING RELATIONSHIPS.

"AT THE HEART OF . . ."

This phrase signals that the definitions are not exhaustive. There is more to masculinity and femininity, but there is not less. We believe this is at the heart of what true manhood means, even if there is a mystery to our complementary existence that we will never exhaust.

". . . MATURE MASCULINITY . . ."

A man might say, "I am a man and I do not feel this sense of responsibility that you say makes me masculine." He may feel strong and sexually competent and forceful and rational. But we would say to him that if he does not feel this sense of benevolent responsibility toward women to lead, provide and protect, his masculinity is immature. It is incomplete and perhaps distorted.

"Mature" means that a man's sense of responsibility is in the process of growing out of its sinful distortions and limitations, and finding its true nature as a form of love, not a form of self-assertion.

". . . A SENSE OF . . ."

I use the word "sense" because to be masculine a man must not only be responsible, but sense or feel that he is. If he does not "sense" or "feel" and "affirm" his responsibility, he is not mature in his masculinity.

The word "sense" also implies the fact that a man can be mature in his masculinity when his circumstances do not put him in any relationship where he actually has the possibility to relate to any woman. He may be in combat or out to sea away from women. He may be in prison. He may have a job on an oil rig in the North Atlantic. He may be a monk. Or his style of life may simply make interaction with women very limited.

A man can be properly masculine in those circumstances if he has the sense of benevolent responsibility to lead, provide for and protect women. This sense need not be actualized directly in order to qualify for mature masculinity. For example, his "sense" of responsibility will affect how he talks about women and the way he relates to pornography and the kind of concern he shows for the marriages of the men around him.

The word "sense" also implies that a man may not be physically able to provide for or protect his family and yet be mature in his masculinity. He may be paralyzed. He may have a disabling disease. His wife may be the main breadwinner in such a circumstance. And she may be the one who must get up at night to investigate a frightening noise in the house. This is not easy for the man. But if he still has a sense of his own benevolent responsibility under God he will not lose his masculinity.

His sense of responsibility will find expression in the ways he conquers self-pity, and gives moral and spiritual *leadership* for his family, and takes the initiative to *provide* them with the bread of life, and *protect* them from the greatest enemies of all, Satan and sin.

Someone might ask: So is a woman masculine if she is a single parent and provides these same things for her children? Are these only for men to do? I would answer: A woman is not unduly masculine in performing these things for her children if she has the sense that this would be properly done by her husband if she had one, and if she performs them with a uniquely feminine demeanor.

However, if a woman undertakes to give this kind of leadership toward her husband she would not be acting in a properly feminine way, but would be taking up the masculine calling in that relationship. If the husband is there but neglects his responsibility and does not provide leadership for the children, then the mature, feminine mother will make every effort to do so, yet in a way that says to the husband, "I do not defy you, I love you and long with all my heart that you were with me in this spiritual and moral commitment, leading me and the family to God."

". . . BENEVOLENT . . ."

This word is intended to show that the responsibility of manhood is for the *good* of woman. Benevolent responsibility is meant to rule out all self-aggrandizing authoritarianism (cf. Luke 22:26). It is meant to rule out all disdaining condescension and any act that makes a mature woman feel patronized rather than honored and prized (cf. 1 Peter 3:7). The word "benevolent" is meant to signal that mature masculinity gives appropriate expression to the Golden Rule in male-female relationships (Matthew 7:12).

". . . RESPONSIBILITY . . ."

The burden of this word is to stress that masculinity is a God-given *trust* for the good of all his creatures, not a *right* for men to exercise for their own self-exaltation or ego-satisfaction. It is less a prerogative than a calling. It is a duty and obligation and charge. Like all God's requirements it is not meant to be onerous or burdensome (1 John 5:3). But it is nevertheless a burden to be borne, and which in Christ can be borne lightly (Matthew 11:30).

The word "responsibility" is chosen to imply that man will be uniquely called to account for his leadership, provision and protection in relation to women. This is illustrated in Genesis 3:9 when God says to Adam first, "Where are you?" Eve had sinned first, but God does not seek her out first. Adam must give the first account to God for the moral life of the family in the garden of Eden. This does not mean the woman has no responsibility, as we will see. It simply means that man bears a unique and primary one.

". . . TO LEAD . . ."

One problem with language is that words tend to carry very different connotations for different people. Hence the word "lead" will sound strong and domineering to some, but moderate and servant-like to others.

Another problem is that one word carries many different nuances and implications for different contexts and situations. For example, the word "lead" could refer to what people do when they direct an orchestra, or persuade a friend to go to the zoo, or inspire a group for a cause, or command a military platoon, or make the first suggestion about where to eat, or take the driver's seat when a group gets in the car, or take the initiative in a group to push the button in an elevator, or choose a door and open it for another to go through, or chair a committee, or sing loud enough to help others, or point a lost motorist to the freeway entrance, or call the plays on a football team, or call people together for prayer.

Therefore, I need to explain in some detail what I have in mind by the mature masculine responsibility to lead. Otherwise false ideas could easily come into people's minds that I do not intend. Following are nine clarifying statements about the meaning of mature masculine leadership.

1. Mature masculinity expresses itself not in the demand to be served, but in the strength to serve and to sacrifice for the good of woman.

Jesus said, "Let the greatest among you become as the youngest and the leader as one who serves" (Luke 22:26). Leadership is not a demanding demeanor. It is moving things forward to a goal. If the goal is holiness and Heaven, the leading will have the holy aroma of Heaven about it — the demeanor of Christ.

Thus after saying that "the husband is the head of the wife as Christ is the head of the church," Paul said, "Husbands, love your wives as Christ loved the church and *gave himself up for her*, that he might sanctify her" (Ephesians 5:23, 25). Jesus led his bride to holiness and heaven on the *Calvary* road. He looked weak, but he was infinitely strong in saying NO to the way of the world. So it will be again and again for mature men as they take up the responsibility to lead.

2. Mature masculinity does not assume the authority of Christ over woman, but advocates it.

The leadership implied in the statement, "The husband is the head of the wife *as Christ is the head of the church*" (Ephesians 5:23), is not a leadership that gives to the man all the rights and authority that Christ has. The analogy between Christ and the husband breaks down if pressed too far, first because, unlike Christ, all men sin. Christ never has to apologize to his church. But husbands must do this often.

Moreover, unlike Christ, a husband is not preparing a bride merely for himself but for another, namely Christ. He does not merely act as Christ, but also for Christ. At this point he must not be Christ to his wife lest he be a traitor to Christ. Standing in the place of Christ must include a renunciation of the temptation to be Christ. And that means leading his wife forward to depend not on him but on Christ. And practically, that rules out belittling supervision and fastidious oversight. She also stands or falls before her own master, Jesus Christ.

3. Mature masculinity does not presume superiority, but mobilizes the strengths of others.

No human leader is infallible. Nor is any man superior to those he leads in every respect. Therefore a good leader will always take into account the ideas of those he leads, and may often adopt those ideas as better than his own. This applies to husbands at home and elders in the church and all the other places where leadership is critical.[10] A man's leadership is not measured by his obliviousness to the ideas and desires of others. A leader of peers may be surrounded by much brighter people than himself. He will listen and respond. And if he is a good leader, they will appreciate his initiative and guidance through the ups and downs of decision-making. The aim of leadership is not to demonstrate the superiority of the leader, but to bring out all the strengths of people that will move them forward to the desired goal.

In Ephesians 5:28-29 the wife is pictured as part of the man's body as the church is part of Christ's body. So in loving his wife a man is loving himself. This is clearly an application to marriage of Jesus' command, "Love your neighbor as yourself." This rules out a leadership that treats a wife like a child. A husband does not want to be treated that way himself.

Moreover Christ does not lead the church as his daughter but as his wife. He is preparing her to be a "fellow-heir" (Romans 8:17), not a servant girl. Any kind of leadership that in the name of Christlike headship tends to produce in a wife personal immaturity or spiritual weakness or insecurity through excessive control or picky supervision or oppressive domination has missed the point of the analogy in Ephesians 5. Christ does not create that kind of wife.

4. *Mature masculinity does not have to initiate every action, but feels the responsibility to provide a general pattern of initiative.*

In a family the husband does not do all the thinking and planning. His leadership is to take responsibility *in general* to initiate and carry through the spiritual and moral planning for family life. I say "in general" because "in specifics" there will be many times and many areas of daily life where the wife will do all kinds of planning and initiating. But there is a general tone and pattern of initiative that should develop which is sustained by the husband.

For example, the leadership pattern would be less than Biblical if the wife in general was having to take the initiative in prayer at mealtime, and get the family out of bed for worship on Sunday morning, and gather the family for devotions, and discuss what moral standards will be required of the children, and confer about financial priorities, and talk over some neighborhood ministry possibilities, etc. A wife may initiate the discussion and planning of any one of these, but if she becomes the one who senses the general responsibility for this pattern of initiative while her husband is passive, something contrary to Biblical masculinity and femininity is in the offing.[11]

Psychologist James Dobson is so concerned about the recovery of the leadership of husbands at home that he calls it "America's greatest need."

> A Christian man is obligated to lead his family to the best of his ability. . . . If his family has purchased too many items on credit, then the financial crunch is ultimately his fault. If the family never reads the Bible or seldom goes to church on Sunday, God holds the man to blame. If the children are disrespectful and disobedient, the primary responsibility lies with the father . . . not his wife. . . . In my view, America's greatest need is for husbands to begin guiding their families, rather than pouring every physical and emotional resource into the mere acquisition of money.[12]

5. Mature masculinity accepts the burden of the final say in disagreements between husband and wife, but does not presume to use it in every instance.
In a good marriage decision-making is focussed on the husband, but is not unilateral. He seeks input from his wife and often adopts her ideas. This is implied in the love that governs the relationship (Ephesians 5:25), in the equality of personhood implied in being created in the image of God (Genesis 1:27), and in the status of being fellow-heirs of the grace of life (1 Peter 3:7). Unilateral decision-making is not usually a mark of good leadership. It generally comes from laziness or insecurity or inconsiderate disregard.

On the other hand dependence on team input should not go to the point where the family perceives a weakness of indecision in the husband. And both husband and wife should agree on the principle that the husband's decision should rightly hold sway if it does not involve sin. However, this conviction does not mean that a husband will often use the prerogative of "veto" over the wishes of his wife or family. He may, in fact, very often surrender his own preference for his wife's where no moral issue is at stake. His awareness of his sin and imperfection will guard him from thinking that following Christ gives him the ability of Christ to know what's best in every detail. Nevertheless, in a well-ordered Biblical marriage both husband and wife acknowledge in principle that, if necessary in some disagreement, the husband will accept the burden of making the final choice.

6. Mature masculinity expresses its leadership in romantic sexual relations by communicating an aura of strong and tender pursuit.
This is very difficult to put into words. But sexual relations are so basic to human life we would be delinquent not to at least try to say how masculinity expresses itself here.

It is the mingling of tenderness with strength that makes the unique masculine quality of leadership in sexual relations. There is an aura of masculine leadership which rises from the mingling of power and tenderness, forcefulness and affection, potency and sensitivity, virility and delicateness. It finds expression in the firmness of his grasp, the strength of taking her in his arms, the sustaining of verbal adoration, etc. And there are a hundred nuances of masculine pursuit that distinguish it from feminine pursuit.

It is important to say that there is, of course, a feminine pursuit in sexual relations. This is why the word "initiate" is not an exact way of describing masculine leadership in sexual relations. The wife may initiate an interest in romance and may keep on initiating different steps along the way. But there is a difference. A feminine initiation is in effect an invitation for the man to do his kind of initiating. In one sense then you could say that in those times the man is *responding*. But in fact the wife is inviting him to lead in a way as only a man can, so that she can respond to him.

It will not do to say that, since the woman can rightly initiate, therefore there is no special leadership that the man should fulfil. When a wife wants sexual relations with her husband she wants him to seek her and take her and bring her into his arms and up to the pleasures that his initiatives give her.

Consider what is lost when women attempt to assume a more masculine role by appearing physically muscular and aggressive. It is true that there is something sexually stimulating about a muscular, scantily clad young woman pumping iron in a health club. But no woman should be encouraged by this fact. For it probably means the sexual encounter that such an image would lead to is something very hasty and volatile, and in the long run unsatisfying. The image of a masculine musculature may beget arousal in a man, but it does not beget several hours of moonlight walking with significant, caring conversation. The more women can arouse men by doing typically masculine things, the less they can count on receiving from men a sensitivity to typically feminine needs. Mature masculinity will not be reduced to raw desire in sexual relations. It remains alert to the deeper personal needs of a woman and mingles strength and tenderness to make her joy complete.

7. Mature masculinity expresses itself in a family by taking the initiative in disciplining the children when both parents are present and a family standard has been broken.
Mothers and fathers are both to be obeyed by their children (Ephesians 6:1). Mothers as well as fathers are esteemed teachers in the home (Proverbs 1:8; 6:20; 31:1). They carry rights of authority and leadership toward their children, as do their husbands. They do not need to wait till Dad gets home from work to spank a disobedient child.

But children need to see a dynamic between Mom and Dad that says, Dad takes charge to discipline me when Mom and Dad are both present.[13] No woman should have to take the initiative to set a disobedient child right while her husband sits obliviously by, as though nothing were at stake. Few things will help children understand the meaning of responsible, loving masculinity better than watching who takes the responsibility to set them right when Mom and Dad are both present.

8. Mature masculinity is sensitive to cultural expressions of masculinity and adapts to them (where no sin is involved) in order to communicate to a woman that a man would like to relate not in any aggressive or perverted way, but with maturity and dignity as a man.
This would mean dressing in ways that are neither effeminate nor harsh and aggressive. It would mean learning manners and customs. Who speaks for the couple at the restaurant? Who seats the other? Who drives the car? Who opens the door? Who walks in front down the concert hall aisle? Who stands and who sits, and when? Who extends the hand at a greeting? Who walks on the street side? How do you handle a woman's purse? Etc. Etc. These things change from culture to culture and from era to era. The point is that masculine leadership will not scorn them or ignore them, but seek to use them to cultivate and communicate a healthy pattern of complementarity in the relationships between men and women.[14] Mature masculinity will not try to communicate that such things don't matter. Mature masculinity recognizes the pervasive implications of manhood and womanhood, and seeks to preserve the patterns of interaction that give free and natural expression to that reality. A dance is all the more beautiful when the assigned steps are natural and unself-conscious.

9. Mature masculinity recognizes that the call to leadership is a call to repentance and humility and risk-taking.
We are all sinners. Masculinity and femininity have been distorted by our sin. Taking up the responsibility to lead must therefore be a careful and humble task.

We must admit as men that historically there have been grave abuses. In each of our lives we have ample cause for contrition at our passivity or our domination. Some have neglected their wives and squandered their time in front of the television or putzing around in the garage or going away too often with the guys to hunt or fish or bowl. Others have been too possessive, harsh, domineering, and belittling, giving the impression through act and innuendo that wives are irresponsible or foolish.

We should humble ourselves before God for our failures and for the remaining tendency to shirk or overstep our responsibilities. The call to leadership is not a call to exalt ourselves over any woman. It is not a call to domineer, or belittle or put woman in her place. She is, after all, a fellow-heir of God and destined for a glory that will one day blind the natural eyes of every man (Matthew 13:43). The call to leadership is a call to humble oneself and take the responsibility to be a servant-leader in ways that are appropriate to every differing relationship to women.

It is a call to risk getting egg on our faces; to pray as we have never prayed before; to be constantly in the Word; to be more given to planning, more intentional, more thoughtful, less carried along by the mood of the moment; to be disciplined and ordered in our lives; to be tenderhearted and sensitive; to take the initiative to make sure there is a time and a place to talk to her about what needs to be talked about; and to be ready to lay down our lives the way Christ did if that is necessary.

". . . PROVIDE FOR . . ."

"At the heart of mature masculinity is a sense of benevolent responsibility to lead, *provide for . . .*"

The point of saying that man should feel a responsibility to provide for woman is not that the woman should not assist in maintaining support for the family or for society in general. She always has done this historically because so much of the domestic life required extraordinary labors on her part just to maintain the life of the family. Today in many cultures women carry a tremendous breadwinning role in the field, often while the men do far less strenuous tasks. It is possible to be excessively demanding or excessively restrictive on a woman's role in sustaining the life of the family. Proverbs 31 pictures a wife with great ability in the business affairs of the family.

What I mean when I say that a man should feel a benevolent responsibility to *provide* is this: when there is no bread on the table it is the man who should feel the main pressure to do something to get it there. It does not mean his wife can't help — side by side in a family enterprise or working in a different job. In fact, it is possible to imagine cases where she may have to do it all — say, if he is sick or injured. But a man will feel his personhood compromised if he, through sloth or folly or lack of discipline, becomes dependent over the long haul (not just during graduate school!) on his wife's income.

This is implied in Genesis 3 where the curse touches man and woman in their natural places of life. It is not a curse that man must work in the field to get bread for the family or that woman bears children. The curse is that these spheres of life are made difficult and frustrating. In appointing the curse for his rebellious creatures God aims at the natural sphere of life peculiar to each. Evidently God had in mind from the beginning that the man would take special responsibility for sustaining the family through bread-winning labor, while the wife would take special responsibility for sustaining the family through childbearing and nurturing labor. Both are life-sustaining and essential.

The point of this Genesis text is not to define limits for what else the man and the woman might do. But it does suggest that any role reversal at these basic levels of childcare and breadwinning labor will be contrary to the original intention of God, and contrary to the way he made us as male and female for our ordained roles.[15] Supporting the family is primarily the responsibility of the husband. Caring for the children is primarily the responsibility of the wife.

Again I stress that the point here is not to dictate the details of any particular pattern of labor in the home. The point is that mature manhood senses a benevolent responsibility before God to be the primary provider for his family. He senses that if God were to come and call someone to account for not meeting the family's needs God would come to the husband first (Genesis 3:9).

The same is true for a social grouping of men and women who are not married. Mature men sense that it is primarily (not solely) their responsibility to see to it that there is provision and protection. The covenant of marriage does not create a man's sense of benevolent responsibility to provide the basic necessities of food and shelter. In marriage the sense of responsibility is more intense and personal. But this dimension of mature manhood is there in a man apart from marriage.

". . . PROTECTION . . ."

"At the heart of mature masculinity is a sense of benevolent responsibility to lead, provide for and *protect* . . ."

Suppose a man and a woman (it may be his wife or sister or friend or a total stranger) are walking along the street when an assailant threatens the two of them with a lead pipe. Mature masculinity senses a natural, God-given responsibility to step forward and put himself between the assailant and the woman. In doing this he becomes her servant. He is willing to suffer for her safety. He bestows honor on her. His inner sense is one of responsibility to protect her because he is a man and she is a woman.

There is a distorted and sinful masculinity that might claim an authority and leadership that has the right to tell the woman to step in front of him and shield him from the blows and let him escape. But every man knows this is a perversion of what it means to be a man and a leader. And every wife knows that something is amiss in a man's manhood if he suggests that she get out of bed 50% of the time to see what the strange noise is downstairs.

She is not condemned as a coward because she feels a natural fitness in receiving this manly service. And she may well be more courageous than he at the moment. She may be ready to do some fearless deed of her own. A man's first thought is not that the woman at his side is weak, but simply that he is a man and she is a woman. Women and children are put into the lifeboats first, not because the men are necessarily better swimmers, but because of a deep sense of honorable fitness. It belongs to masculinity to accept danger to protect women.

It may be that in any given instance of danger the woman will have the strength to strike the saving blow. It may be too that she will have the presence of mind to think of the best way of escape. It may be that she will fight with tooth and claw to save a crippled man and lay down her life for him if necessary. But this does not at all diminish the unique call of manhood when he and his female companion are confronted by a danger together. The dynamics of mature masculinity and femininity begin the drama with him in front and her at his back protected — however they may together overcome the foe or suffer courageously together in persecution. A mature man senses instinctively that as a man he is called to take the lead in guarding the woman he is with.[16]

". . . WOMEN . . ."

"At the heart of mature masculinity is a sense of benevolent responsibility to lead, provide for and protect *women* . . ."

I do not say "wives" because there is a sense in which masculinity inclines a man to feel a responsibility for leadership and provision and protection toward women in general, not just toward wives or relatives. Masculinity and femininity are rooted in who we are by nature. They are not simply reflexes of a marriage relationship. Man does not become man by getting married. But it is clear that the *form* which leadership, provision and protection take will vary with the kind of relationship a man has with a woman — from the most intimate relationship of marriage to the most casual relationship with a stranger on the street. This is why the description of masculinity must conclude with the following phrase.

" . . . IN WAYS APPROPRIATE TO A MAN'S DIFFERING RELATIONSHIPS"

Ephesians 5:22, Titus 2:5 and 1 Peter 3:1, 5 exhort wives to be subject to "your own" (*idiois*) husbands. This term "your own" shows that the relationship of leadership and submission between a woman and her husband should be different from the relationship of leadership and submission which she may have with men in general. Husbands and wives have responsibilities to each other in marriage that they do not have to other men and women.

But this does not mean that there is no way that maleness and femaleness affect the relationship of men and women in general. That a man has a unique responsibility for leadership in his own home does not mean that his manhood is negligible in other settings. It is not negligible. But it is very diverse. The responsibility of men toward women will vary according to the kind of relationship they have. Husband and wife will have different responsibilities than a pastor and female parishioner will have. And those responsibilities will in turn be different from the differing responsibilities of men and women in business, recreation, government, neighborhood, courtship, engagement, etc. The possibilities of women and men meeting each other and having dealings with each other are extremely diverse and beyond counting. And my persuasion is that mature masculinity will seek appropriate expressions of manhood in each of these relationships.

These expressions of manhood will include acts of defense and protection, a readiness to serve with strength, and a pattern of initiative. I have touched on all three of these. But it may be helpful to focus once more on this idea of a pattern of initiative that is appropriate for differing relationships. The point here is that even though a man will not take initiating steps of leadership with a stranger or with a colleague the same way he will with his wife, his mature manhood will seek a pattern of initiative appropriate for the relationship.

For example, if a man works as a lawyer in a law firm with other lawyers, some of whom are women, he will of course not initiate many of the kinds of discussion that he might with his wife. In fact one of the special initiatives mature masculinity will take is to build protections against the development of any kind of inappropriate intimacy with his female colleagues. It is not *primarily* the responsibility of women to build procedural and relational guidelines to protect themselves from the advances of ill-behaved men. Primarily it is the responsibility of mature manhood to establish a pattern of behaviors and attitudes—a kind of collegial choreography—that enable men and women to move with freedom and ease and moral security among each other.

If, in the course of the day, a woman in the law firm calls a meeting of the attorneys, and thus takes that kind of initiative, there are still ways that a man, coming to that meeting, can express his manhood through culturally appropriate courtesies shown to the women in the firm. He may open the door; he may offer his chair; he may speak in a voice that is gentler.[17]

It is true that this becomes increasingly difficult where a unisex mentality converts such gentlemanly courtesies into offenses and thus attempts to shut out every means of expressing the realities of manhood and womanhood. It will be a strain for mature Christian men and women to work in that atmosphere. But it may be that through intelligent discussion and courteous, caring behaviors they may have a redeeming effect even on what their colleagues think and feel about manhood and womanhood.

We must reckon with the possibility that in the various spheres of life it is possible that role relationships emerge for men and women that so deeply compromise what a man or woman senses is appropriate for their masculine or feminine personhood that they have to seek a different position. This is what J. I. Packer implies when he makes the following perceptive observation:

> While I am not keen on *hierarchy* and *patriarchy* as terms describing the man-woman relationship in Scripture, Genesis 2:18-23 . . . and Ephesians 5:21-33 . . . continue to convince me that the man-woman relationship is intrinsically nonreversible. By this I mean that, other things being equal, a situation in which a female boss has a male secretary, or a marriage in which the woman (as we say) wears the trousers, will put more strain on the humanity of both parties than if it were the other way around. This is part of the reality of the creation, a given fact that nothing will change.[18]

This brings us back to the basic insight of Paul Jewett, namely, that

> Our self-knowledge is indissolubly bound up not simply with our *human* being but with our *sexual* being. At the human level there is no 'I and thou' *per se*, but only the 'I' who is male or female confronting the 'thou,' the 'other,' who is also male or female.

I believe this is true and that God has not left us without a witness to the meaning of our masculine and feminine personhood. I have tried to unfold at least some of what that masculine personhood involves. Now we turn to the meaning of mature femininity.

The Meaning of Femininity

A significant aspect of femininity is how a woman responds to the pattern of initiatives established by mature masculinity. This is why I have discussed masculinity first. Much of the meaning of womanhood is clearly implied in what I have said already about manhood—in the same way that the moves of one ballet dancer would be implied if you described the moves of the other. Nevertheless it is important now to focus on the description of womanhood given earlier and unfold its meaning for the sake of a balanced and attractive portrait of manhood and womanhood.

> AT THE HEART OF MATURE FEMININITY IS A FREEING DISPOSITION TO AFFIRM, RECEIVE AND NURTURE STRENGTH AND LEADERSHIP FROM WORTHY MEN IN WAYS APPROPRIATE TO A WOMAN'S DIFFERING RELATIONSHIPS.[19]

"AT THE HEART OF . . ."

Again, this phrase signals that the definition of femininity is not exhaustive. There is more to femininity, but not less. I believe this is at the heart of what true womanhood means, even if there is a mystery to our complementary existence that we will never exhaust.

". . . MATURE FEMININITY . . ."

The word "mature" implies that there are distortions of femininity. False or immature stereotypes are sometimes identified as the essence of femininity. Ronda Chervin, in her book *Feminine, Free and Faithful*, gives a list of what people commonly consider "positive feminine traits" and "negative feminine traits." The participants in her workshops say positively that women are

> responsive, compassionate, empathetic, enduring, gentle, warm, tender, hospitable, receptive, diplomatic, considerate, polite, supportive, intuitive, wise, perceptive, sensitive, spiritual, sincere, vulnerable (in the sense of emotionally open), obedient, trusting, graceful, sweet, expressive, charming, delicate, quiet, sensually receptive (vs. prudish), faithful, pure.

Chervin lists the following women who exhibit many of these traits: Ruth, Naomi, Sarah, Mary (Jesus' mother), Cordelia of *King Lear*, Melanie in *Gone with the Wind*, Grace Kelly, and Mother Teresa of Calcutta. On the other hand people often stereotype women with negative traits:

> weak, passive, slavish, weepy, wishy-washy, seductive, flirtatious, vain, chatterbox, silly, sentimental, naive, moody, petty, catty, prudish, manipulative, complaining, nagging, pouty, smothering, spiteful.[20]

It is plain then that when we talk of femininity we must make careful distinctions between distortions and God's original design. "Mature femininity" refers not to what sin has made of womanhood or what popular opinion makes of it, but what God willed for it to be at its best.

". . . IS A FREEING DISPOSITION . . ."

I focus on mature femininity as a *disposition* rather than a set of behaviors or roles because mature femininity will express itself in so many different ways depending on the situation. Hundreds of behaviors may be feminine in one situation and not in another. And the specific acts that grow out of the disposition of womanhood vary considerably from relationship to relationship, not to mention from culture to culture.

For example, the Biblical reality of a wife's submission would take different forms depending on the quality of a husband's leadership. This can be seen best if we define submission not in terms of specific behaviors, but as a *disposition* to yield to the husband's authority and an *inclination* to follow his leadership.[21] This is important to do because no submission of one human being to another is absolute. The husband does not replace Christ as the woman's supreme authority. She must never follow her husband's leadership into sin. She will not steal with him or get drunk with him or savor pornography with him or develop deceptive schemes with him.

But even where a Christian wife may have to stand with Christ against the sinful will of her husband, she can still have a spirit of submission—a disposition to yield. She can show by her attitude and behavior that she does not like resisting his will and that she longs for him to forsake sin and lead in righteousness so that her disposition to honor him as head can again produce harmony.[22]

The disposition of mature femininity is experienced as freeing. This is because it accords with the truth of God's purpose in creation. It is the truth that frees (John 8:32). There are sensations of unbounded independence that are not true freedom because they deny truth and are destined for calamity. For example, two women may jump from an airplane and experience the thrilling freedom of free-falling. But there is a difference: one is encumbered by a parachute on her back and the other is free from this burden. Which person is most free? The one without the parachute feels free—even freer, since she does not feel the constraints of the parachute straps. But she is not truly free. She is in bondage to the force of gravity and to the deception that all is well because she feels unencumbered. This false sense of freedom is in fact bondage to calamity which is sure to happen after a fleeting moment of pleasure.

That is the way many women (and men) today think of freedom. They judge it on the basis of immediate sensations of unrestrained license or independence. But true freedom takes God's reality and God's purpose for creation into account and seeks to fit smoothly into God's good design. Freedom does include doing what we want to do. But the mature and wise woman does not seek this freedom by bending reality to fit her desires. She seeks it by being transformed in the renewal of her desires to fit in with God's perfect will (Romans 12:2). The greatest freedom is found in being so changed by God's Spirit that you can do what you love to do and know that it conforms to the design of God and leads to life and glory.

God does not intend for women to be squelched or cramped or frustrated. But neither does he intend for women to do whatever seems to remove these feelings without regard to the appropriateness of the action. Sometimes freedom comes from outward changes in circumstances. Sometimes it comes from inward changes of the heart and mind. Many today say, for example, that true freedom for a lesbian would be the liberty to act according to her sexual preference.[23] But I would say that true freedom cannot ignore God's judgment on homosexual activity and God's will for men and women to be heterosexual in their sexual relations. Therefore true freedom is not giving in to our every impulse. It is the sometimes painful and exhilarating discovery of God's power to fight free from the bondage of our sinful selves.[24]

I believe that the femininity to which God calls women is the path of freedom for every woman. It will not look the same in every woman. But it will lay responsibilities on all women in the same way that mature masculinity lays responsibilities on all men. Some of these we express very naturally. Others of them we must grow into by prayer and faith and practice. But this process of growth is no more confining than the growth of a young woman toward patterns of mature behavior that enable her to act with natural freedom in the company of adults.

"... TO AFFIRM, RECEIVE AND NURTURE STRENGTH AND LEADERSHIP FROM WORTHY MEN ..."

"At the heart of mature femininity is a freeing disposition *to affirm, receive and nurture strength and leadership from worthy men* in ways appropriate to a woman's differing relationships."

The "strength and leadership" referred to here is what was described above concerning the responsibility of mature masculinity to lead, provide and protect. The quality of that strength and leadership is captured in the phrase, "from worthy men." I recognize that there is strength and leadership that is unworthy of a woman's affirmation. I do not mean to define femininity merely as a response to whatever sinful men may happen to offer up. Mature femininity is rooted in a commitment to Christ as Lord and is discerning in what it approves. Mature femininity has a clear, Biblical vision of mature masculinity. Woman delights in it as man delights in mature femininity. Each gives the other the greatest scope for natural, pure, mature expression. But when a man does not possess mature masculinity the response of a mature woman is not to abandon her femininity. Rather, her femininity remains intact as a desire for things to be as God intended them to be. But she also recognizes that the natural expression of her womanhood will be hindered by the immaturity of the man in her presence.

My definition of the heart of femininity includes three words to describe the response of a woman to the strength and leadership of worthy men: affirm, receive and nurture.

"Affirm" means that mature women advocate the kind of masculine-feminine complementarity that we are describing here. This is important to stress because there may be occasions when women have no interaction with men and yet are still mature in their femininity. This is because femininity is a disposition to *affirm* the strength and leadership of worthy men, not just to *experience* it firsthand. It is also true, as we will see below, because there are unique feminine strengths and insights that women embody even before they can be given to any man.

"Receive" means that mature femininity feels natural and glad to accept the strength and leadership of worthy men.[25] A mature woman is glad when a respectful, caring, upright man offers sensitive strength and provides a pattern of appropriate initiatives in their relationship. She does not want to reverse these roles. She is glad when he is not passive. She feels herself enhanced and honored and freed by his caring strength and servant-leadership.

"Nurture" means that a mature woman senses a responsibility not merely to receive, but to nurture and strengthen the resources of masculinity. She is to be his partner and assistant. She joins in the act of strength and shares in the process of leadership. She is, as Genesis 2:18 says, "a helper suitable for him."

This may sound paradoxical—that she strengthens the strength she receives, and that she refines and extends the leadership she looks for. But it is not contradictory or unintelligible. There are strengths and insights that women bring to a relationship that are not brought by men. I do not mean to imply by my definition of femininity that women are merely recipients in relation to men. Mature women bring nurturing strengths and insights that make men stronger and wiser and that make the relationship richer.[26]

Note: We need to heed a caution here about the differing strengths of men and women. Whenever anyone asks if we think women are, say, weaker than men, or smarter than men, or more easily frightened than men or something like that, a good answer would go like this: women are weaker in some ways and men are weaker in some ways; women are smarter in some ways and men are smarter in some ways; women are more easily frightened in some kinds of circumstances and men are more easily frightened in other kinds of circumstances.

It is very misleading to put negative values on the so-called weaknesses that each of us has by virtue of our sexuality. God intends for all the "weaknesses" that are characteristically masculine to call forth and highlight woman's strengths. And God intends for all the "weaknesses" that are characteristically feminine to call forth and highlight man's strengths.

A person who naively assumes that men are superior because of their kind of strength might consider these statistics from 1983: six times more men than women are arrested for drug abuse. Ten times more men than women are arrested for drunkenness. Eighty-three percent of serious crimes in America are committed by men. Twenty-five times more men than women are in jail. Virtually all rape is committed by men.[27]

I point that out to show that boasting in either sex as superior to the other is a folly. Men and women as God created them are different in hundreds of ways. One helpful way to describe our equality and differences is this: Picture the so-called weaknesses and strengths of man and woman listed in two columns. If you could give a numerical value to each one the sum at the bottom of both columns is going to be the same. Whatever different minuses and pluses are on each side of masculinity and femininity are going to balance out. And when you take those two columns from each side and lay them, as it were, on top of each other, God intends them to be the perfect complement to each other, so that when life together is considered (and I don't just mean married life) the weaknesses of manhood are not weaknesses and the weaknesses of woman are not weaknesses. They are the complements that call forth different strengths in each other.[28]

If it is true that manhood and womanhood are to complement rather than duplicate each other, and if it is true that the way God made us is good, then we should be very slow to gather a list of typical male weaknesses or a list of typical female weaknesses and draw a conclusion that either is of less value than the other. Men and women are of equal value and dignity in the eyes of God—both created in the image of God and utterly unique in the universe.[29]

". . . IN WAYS APPROPRIATE TO A WOMAN'S DIFFERING RELATIONSHIPS . . ."

"At the heart of mature femininity is a freeing disposition to affirm, receive and nurture strength and leadership from worthy men *in ways appropriate to a woman's differing relationships.*"

Mature femininity does not express itself in the same way toward every man. A mature woman who is married, for example, does not welcome the same kind of strength and leadership from other men that she welcomes from her husband. But she will affirm and receive and nurture the strength and leadership of men *in some form* in all her relationships with men. This is true even though she may find herself in roles that put some men in a subordinate role to her. Without passing any judgment on the appropriateness of any of these roles one thinks of the following possible instances:

Prime Minister and her counsellors and advisors.
Principal and the teachers in her school.
College teacher and her students.
Bus driver and her passengers.
Bookstore manager and her clerks and stock help.
Staff doctor and her interns.
Lawyer and her aides.
Judge and the court personnel.
Police officer and citizens in her precinct.
Legislator and her assistants.
T.V. newscaster and her editors.
Counsellor and her clients.

One or more of these roles might stretch appropriate expressions of femininity beyond the breaking point. But in any case, regardless of the relationships in which a woman finds herself, mature femininity will seek to express itself in appropriate ways. There are ways for a woman to interact even with a male subordinate that signal to him and others her endorsement of his mature manhood in relationship to her as a woman. I do not have in mind anything like sexual suggestiveness or innuendo. Rather, I have in mind culturally appropriate expressions of respect for his kind of strength, and glad acceptance of his gentlemanly courtesies. Her demeanor—the tone and style and disposition and discourse of her ranking position—can signal clearly her affirmation of the unique role that men should play in relationship to women owing to their sense of responsibility to protect and lead.

It is obvious at this point that we are on the brink of contradiction—suggesting that a woman may hold a position of leadership and fulfill it in a way that signals to men her endorsement of their sense of responsibility to lead. But the complexities of life require of us this risk. To illustrate: it is simply impossible that from time to time a woman not be put in a position of influencing or guiding men. For example, a housewife in her backyard may be asked by a man how to get to the freeway. At that point she is giving a kind of leadership. She has superior knowledge that the man needs and he submits himself to her guidance. But we all know that there is a way for that housewife to direct the man that neither of them feels their mature femininity or masculinity compromised. It is not a contradiction to speak of *certain kinds* of influence coming from women to men in ways that affirm the responsibility of men to provide a pattern of strength and initiative.

But as I said earlier, there are roles that strain the personhood of man and woman too far to be appropriate, productive and healthy for the overall structure of home and society. Some roles would involve kinds of leadership and expectations of authority and forms of strength as to make it unfitting for a woman to fill the role. However, instead of trying to list what jobs might be fitting expressions for mature femininity or mature masculinity, it will probably be wiser to provide several guidelines.

It is obvious that we cannot and should not prohibit women from influencing men. For example, *prayer* is certainly a God-appointed means women should use to get men to where God wants them to be. Praying women exert far more power in this world than all political leaders put together. This kind of powerful influence is compounded immensely when one considers the degree to which the world is shaped and guided by the effects of how men and women are formed by their mothers. This influence is perhaps more effective than all the leadership of men put together.

So the question should be put: what kind of influence would be inappropriate for mature women to exercise toward men? It would be hopeless to try to define this on a case-by-case basis. There are thousands of different jobs in the church and in the world with an innumerable variety of relationships between men and women. More appropriate than a black-and-white list of "man's work" and "woman's work" is a set of criteria to help a woman think through whether the responsibilities of any given job allow her to uphold God's created order of mature masculinity and femininity.

Here is one possible set of criteria. All acts of influence and guidance can be described along these two continuums:

Personal ____________ Non-personal
Directive____________ Non-directive

To the degree that a woman's influence over man is personal and directive it will generally offend a man's good, God-given sense of responsibility and leadership, and thus controvert God's created order.

A woman may design the traffic pattern of a city's streets and thus exert a kind of influence over all male drivers. But this influence will be non-personal and therefore not necessarily an offense against God's order. Similarly, the drawings and specifications of a woman architect may guide the behavior of contractors and laborers, but it may be so non-personal that the feminine-masculine dynamic of the relationship is negligible.

On the other hand, the relationship between husband and wife is very personal. All acts of influence lie on the continuum between personal and non-personal. The closer they get to the personal side, the more inappropriate it becomes for women to exert directive influence.

But the second continuum may qualify the first. Some influence is very directive, some is non-directive. For example, a drill sergeant would epitomize directive influence. It would be hard to see how a woman could be a drill sergeant over men without violating their sense of masculinity and her sense of femininity.

Non-directive influence proceeds with petition and persuasion instead of directives. A beautiful example of non-directive leadership is when Abigail talked

David out of killing Nabal (1 Samuel 25:23-35). She exerted great influence over David and changed the course of his life; but she did it with amazing restraint and submissiveness and discretion.

When you combine these two continuums, what emerges is this: If a woman's job involves a good deal of directives toward men, they will, in general, need it to be non-personal.

The God-given sense of responsibility for leadership in a mature man will not generally allow him to flourish long under personal, directive leadership of a female superior. J. I. Packer suggested that "a situation in which a female boss has a male secretary" puts strain on the humanity of both (see note 18). I think this would be true in other situations as well. Some of the more obvious ones would be in military combat settings if women were positioned so as to deploy and command men; or in professional baseball if a woman is made the umpire to call balls and strikes and frequently to settle heated disputes among men. And I would stress that this is not necessarily owing to male egotism, but to a natural and good penchant given by God.

Conversely, if a woman's relation to man is very personal, then the way she offers guidance will need to be non-directive. The clearest example here is the marriage relationship. The Apostle Peter speaks of a good wife's meek and tranquil spirit that can be very winsome to her husband (1 Peter 3:4). A wife who "comes on strong" with her advice will probably drive a husband into passive silence, or into active anger.

It is not nonsense to say that a woman who believes she should guide a man into new behavior should do that in a way that signals her support of his leadership. This is precisely what the Apostle Peter commends in 1 Peter 3:1ff. Similarly in the workplace it may not be nonsense in any given circumstance for a woman to provide a certain kind of direction for a man, but to do it in such a way that she signals her endorsement of his unique duty as a man to feel a responsibility of strength and protection and leadership toward her as a woman and toward women in general.

The Biblical Vision of Complementarity

In the following chapters we hope to show, with more detailed exegetical argumentation, that the vision of masculine and feminine complementarity sketched in this essay is a Biblical vision — not a perfect portrayal of it, no doubt, but a faithful one. This is the way God meant it to be before there was any sin in the world: sinless man, full of love, in his tender, strong leadership in relation to woman; and sinless woman, full of love, in her joyful, responsive support for man's leadership. No belittling from the man, no groveling from the woman. Two intelligent, humble, God-entranced beings living out, in beautiful harmony, their unique and different responsibilities. Sin has distorted this purpose at every level. We are not sinless any more. But we believe that recovery of mature manhood and womanhood is possible by the power of God's Spirit through faith in his promises and in obedience to his Word.

In the home when a husband leads like Christ and a wife responds like the bride of Christ, there is a harmony and mutuality that is more beautiful and more satisfying than any pattern of marriage created by man. *Biblical headship* for the husband is the divine calling to take primary responsibility for Christlike, servant-leadership, protection and provision in the home. *Biblical submission* for the wife is the divine calling to honor and affirm her husband's leadership and help carry it through according to her gifts.[30] This is the way of joy. For God loves his people and he loves his glory. And therefore when we follow his idea of marriage (sketched in texts like Genesis 2:18-24; Proverbs 5:15-19; 31:10-31; Mark 10:2-12; Ephesians 5:21-33; Colossians 3:18-19; and 1 Peter 3:1-7) we are most satisfied and he is most glorified.

The same is true of God's design for the leadership of the church.[31] The realities of headship and submission in marriage have their counterparts in the church. Thus Paul speaks of authority and submission in 1 Timothy 2:11-12. We will try to show that "*authority*" refers to the divine calling of spiritual, gifted men to take primary responsibility as elders for Christlike, servant-leadership and teaching in the church. And "*submission*" refers to the divine calling of the rest of the church, both men and women, to honor and affirm the leadership and teaching of the elders and to be equipped by them for the hundreds and hundreds of various ministries available to men and women in the service of Christ.

That last point is very important. For men and women who have a heart to minister—to save souls and heal broken lives and resist evil and meet needs—there are fields of opportunity that are simply endless. God intends for the entire church to be mobilized in ministry, male and female. Nobody is to be at home watching soaps and ballgames while the world burns. And God intends to equip and mobilize the saints through a company of spiritual men who take primary responsibility for leadership and teaching in the church.

The word "primary" is very important. It signals that there are different kinds and levels of teaching and leading that will not be the sole responsibility of men (Titus 2:3; Proverbs 1:8; 31:26; Acts 18:26). Mature masculinity will seek by prayer and study and humble obedience to discover the pattern of ministry involvement for men and women that taps the gifts of every Christian and honors the God-given order of leadership by spiritual men.

There are many voices today who claim to know a better way to equip and mobilize men and women for the mission of the church. But we believe that manhood and womanhood mesh better in ministry when men take primary responsibility for leadership and teaching in the church; and that mature manhood and womanhood are better preserved, better nurtured, more fulfilled and more fruitful in this church order than in any other.

If I were to put my finger on one devastating sin today, it would not be the so-called women's movement, but the lack of spiritual leadership by men at home and in the church. Satan has achieved an amazing tactical victory by disseminating the notion that the summons for male leadership is born of pride and fallenness, when in fact pride is precisely what prevents spiritual leadership. The spiritual aimlessness and weakness and lethargy and loss of nerve among men is the major issue, not the upsurge of interest in women's ministries.

Pride and self-pity and fear and laziness and confusion are luring many men into self-protecting, self-exalting cocoons of silence. And to the degree that this makes room for women to take more leadership it is sometimes even endorsed as a virtue. But I believe that deep down the men—and the women—know better.

Where are the men with a moral vision for their families, a zeal for the house of the Lord, a magnificent commitment to the advancement of the kingdom, an articulate dream for the mission of the church and a tenderhearted tenacity to make it real?

When the Lord visits us from on high and creates a mighty army of deeply spiritual men committed to the Word of God and global mission, the vast majority of women will rejoice over the leadership of these men and enter into a joyful partnership that upholds and honors the beautiful Biblical pattern of mature manhood and mature womanhood.

A Closing Challenge to Men and Women

Several years ago the women of our church asked for a morning seminar in which I would lay out my vision of manhood and womanhood and discuss it with them. I was eager for this opportunity. We spent all of Saturday morning together. It was very encouraging for me. They had many hard questions, but as a whole were wonderfully supportive of the vision I shared. Not all the women of our church see things exactly the same way; but those who came out that Saturday morning were enthusiastic about the kind of manhood and womanhood portrayed in this book.

I closed the seminar with a personal (fifteen-point) challenge to the women of our church. It has some parts that show the special emphases of our fellowship, but I thought it would be a helpful and practical way to conclude this essay. To balance the ledger I have written a corresponding challenge to men. Ten of the points are virtually identical for men and women (1-8, 12-13). I realize that these challenges are weighted heavily toward the relational dynamics of married men and women. But I want to emphasize that I regard singleness as an excellent calling, followed by no less than Jesus and the Apostle Paul. The definitions of masculinity and feminity spelled out in this book and the challenges that follow do not assume the necessity to be married in order to be fully man or fully woman.

My earnest challenge and prayer for you is . . .

Women	*Men*
1. That all of your life—in whatever calling—be devoted to the glory of God.	1. That all of your life—in whatever calling—be devoted to the glory of God.
2. That the promises of Christ be trusted so fully that peace and joy and strength fill your soul to overflowing.	2. That the promises of Christ be trusted so fully that peace and joy and strength fill your soul to overflowing.
3. That this fullness of God overflow in daily acts of love so that people might see your good deeds and give glory to your Father in Heaven.	3. That this fullness of God overflow in daily acts of love so that people might see your good deeds and give glory to your Father in Heaven.
4. That you be women of the Book, who love and study and obey the Bible in every area of its teaching; that meditation on Biblical truth be the source of	4. That you be men of the Book, who love and study and obey the Bible in every area of its teaching; that meditation on Biblical truth be the source of

hope and faith; that you continue to grow in understanding through all the chapters of your life, never thinking that study and growth are only for others.

5. That you be women of prayer, so that the Word of God will be opened to you, and so the power of faith and holiness will descend upon you; that your spiritual influence may increase at home and at church and in the world.

6. That you be women who have a deep grasp of the sovereign grace of God which undergirds all these spiritual processes; and that you be deep thinkers about the doctrines of grace, and even deeper lovers of these things.

7. That you be totally committed to ministry, whatever your specific calling; that you not fritter away your time on soaps or women's magazines or unimportant hobbies or shopping; that you redeem the time for Christ and his Kingdom.

8. That, if you are single, you exploit your singleness to the full in devotion to God (the way Jesus and Paul and Mary Slessor and Amy Carmichael did) and not be paralyzed by the desire to be married.

9. That, if you are married, you creatively and intelligently and sincerely support the leadership of your husband as deeply as obedience to Christ will allow; that you encourage him in his God-appointed role as head; that you influence him spiritually primarily through your fearless tranquillity and holiness and prayer.

10. That, if you have children, you accept responsibility with your hus-

hope and faith; that you continue to grow in understanding through all the chapters of your life, never thinking that study and growth are only for others.

5. That you be men of prayer, so that the Word of God will be opened to you, so the power of faith and holiness will descend upon you; that your spiritual influence may increase at home and at church and in the world.

6. That you be men who have a deep grasp of the sovereign grace of God which undergirds all these spiritual processes; and that you be deep thinkers about the doctrines of grace, and even deeper lovers of these things.

7. That you be totally committed to ministry, whatever your specific calling; that you not fritter away your time on excessive sports and recreation or unimportant hobbies or aimless diddling in the garage; but that you redeem the time for Christ and his Kingdom.

8. That, if you are single, you exploit your singleness to the full in devotion to God (the way Jesus and Paul and Mary Slessor and Amy Carmichael did) and not be paralyzed by the desire to be married.

9. That, if you are married, you love your wife the way Christ loved the church and gave himself for her; that you be a humble, self-denying, upbuilding, happy spiritual leader; that you consistently grow in grace and knowledge so as never to quench the aspirations of your wife for spiritual advancement; that you cultivate tenderness and strength, a pattern of initiative and a listening ear; and that you accept the *responsibility* of provision and protection in the family, however you and your wife share the labor.

10. That, if you have children, you accept primary responsibility, in part-

band (or alone if necessary) to raise up children in the discipline and instruction of the Lord—children who hope in the triumph of God—sharing with your husband the teaching and discipline they need, and giving them the special attachment they crave from you, as well as that special nurturing touch and care that you alone are fitted to give.

11. That you not assume that secular employment is a greater challenge or a better use of your life than the countless opportunities of service and witness in the home, the neighborhood, the community, the church, and the world; that you not only pose the question: career or full-time homemaker?, but that you ask just as seriously: full-time career or freedom for ministry? That you ask: Which would be greater for the Kingdom—to work for someone who tells you what to do to make his or her business prosper, or to be God's free agent dreaming your own dream about how your time and your home and your creativity could make God's business prosper? And that in all this you make your choices not on the basis of secular trends or upward lifestyle expectations, but on the basis of what will strengthen the faith of the family and advance the cause of Christ.

12. That you step back and (with your husband, if you are married) plan the various forms of your life's ministry in chapters. Chapters are divided by various things—age, strength, singleness, marriage, employment, children at home, children in college, grandchildren, retirement, etc. No chapter has all the joys. Finite life is a series of tradeoffs. Finding God's will, and living for the glory of Christ to the full in every chapter is what makes it a suc-

nership with your wife (or as a single parent), to raise up children in the discipline and instruction of the Lord—children who hope in the triumph of God; that you establish a pattern of teaching and discipline that is not solely dependent on the church or school to impart Bible knowledge and spiritual values to the children; and that you give your children the time and attention and affection that communicates the true nature of our Father in Heaven.

11. That you not assume advancement and peer approval in your gainful employment are the highest values in life; but that you ponder the eternal significance of faithful fatherhood and time spent with your wife; that you repeatedly consider the new possibilities at each stage of your life for maximizing your energies for the glory of God in ministry; that you pose the question often: Is our family molded by the culture, or do we embody the values of the Kingdom of God? That you lead the family in making choices not on the basis of secular trends or upward lifestyle expectations, but on the basis of what will strengthen the faith of the family and advance the cause of Christ.

12. That you step back and (with your wife, if you are married) plan the various forms of your life's ministry in chapters. Chapters are divided by various things—age, strength, singleness, marriage, employment, children at home, children in college, grandchildren, retirement, etc. No chapter has all the joys. Finite life is a series of tradeoffs. Finding God's will and living for the glory of Christ to the full in every chapter is what makes it a suc-

cess, not whether it reads like somebody else's chapter or whether it has in it what only another chapter will bring.

13. That you develop a wartime mentality and lifestyle; that you never forget that life is short, that billions of people hang in the balance of heaven and hell every day, that the love of money is spiritual suicide, that the goals of upward mobility (nicer clothes, cars, houses, vacations, food, hobbies) are a poor and dangerous substitute for the goals of living for Christ with all your might and maximizing your joy in ministry to people's needs.

14. That in all your relationships with men (not just in marriage) you seek the guidance of the Holy Spirit in applying the Biblical vision of manhood and womanhood; that you develop a style and demeanor that does justice to the unique role God has given to man to feel responsible for gracious leadership in relation to women—a leadership which involves elements of protection and provision and a pattern of initiative; that you think creatively and with cultural sensitivity (just as he must do) in shaping the style and setting the tone of your interaction with men.

15. That you see the Biblical guidelines for what is appropriate and inappropriate for men and women not as arbitrary constraints on freedom, but as wise and gracious prescriptions for how to discover the true freedom of God's ideal of complementarity; that you not measure your potential by the few roles withheld, but by the countless roles offered; that you look to the loving God of Scripture and dream about the possibilities of your service to him, with the following list as possibilities for starters:

cess, not whether it reads like somebody else's chapter or whether it has in it what only another chapter will bring.

13. That you develop a wartime mentality and lifestyle; that you never forget that life is short, that billions of people hang in the balance of heaven and hell every day, that the love of money is spiritual suicide, that the goals of upward mobility (nicer clothes, cars, houses, vacations, food, hobbies) are a poor and dangerous substitute for the goals of living for Christ with all your might and maximizing your joy in ministry to people's needs.

14. That in all your relationships with women (not just in marriage) you seek the guidance of the Holy Spirit in applying the Biblical vision of manhood and womanhood; that you develop a style and demeanor that expresses your God-given responsibility for humble strength and leadership, and for self-sacrificing provision and protection; that you think creatively and with cultural sensitivity (just as she must do) in shaping the style and setting the tone of your interaction with women.

15. That you see the Biblical guidelines for what is appropriate and inappropriate for men and women not as license for domination or bossy passivity, but as a call to servant leadership that thinks in terms of responsibilities not rights; that you see these principles as wise and gracious prescriptions for how to discover the true freedom of God's ideal of complementarity; that you encourage the fruitful engagement of women in the countless ministry roles that are Biblically appropriate and deeply needed. For example:

OPPORTUNITIES FOR MINISTRY

Ministries to the handicapped
- Hearing impaired
- Blind
- Lame
- Retarded

Ministries to the sick
- Nursing
- Physician
- Hospice care—cancer, AIDS, etc.
- Community health

Ministries to the socially estranged
- Emotionally impaired
- Recovering alcoholics
- Recovering drug-users
- Escaping prostitutes
- Abused children, women
- Runaways, problem children
- Orphans

Prison ministries
- Women's prisons
- Families of prisoners
- Rehabilitation to society

Ministries to youth
- Teaching
- Sponsoring
- Open houses and recreation
- Outings and trips
- Counseling
- Academic assistance

Sports ministries
- Neighborhood teams
- Church teams

Therapeutic counseling
- Independent
- Church-based
- Institutional

Audiovisual ministries
- Composition
- Design
- Production
- Distribution

Writing ministries
- Free-lance
- Curriculum development
- Fiction
- Non-fiction
- Editing
- Institutional communications
- Journalistic skills for publications

Teaching ministries
- Sunday school: children, youth, students, women
- Grade school
- High school
- College

Music ministries
- Composition
- Training
- Performance
- Voice
- Choir
- Instrumentalist

Evangelistic ministries
- Personal witnessing
- Parachurch groups
- Home Bible studies
- Outreach to children
- Visitation teams
- Counseling at meetings
- Telephone counseling

Radio and television ministries
- Technical assistance
- Writing
- Announcing
- Producing

Theater and drama ministries
- Acting
- Directing
- Writing
- Scheduling

Social ministries
- Literacy
- Pro-life
- Pro-decency
- Housing
- Safety
- Beautification
- Drug rehabilitation

Pastoral care assistance
- Visitation
- Newcomer welcoming and assistance
- Hospitality
- Food and clothing and transportation

Prayer ministries
- Praying
- Mobilizing for prayer events
- Helping with small groups of prayer
- Coordinating prayer chains
- Promoting prayer days and weeks and vigils

Missions
- All of the above across cultures

Support ministries
- Countless "secular" jobs that undergird other ministries

The awesome significance of motherhood

Making a home as a full-time wife

I realize this list is incomplete and reflects my own culture and limitations. But it is worth the risk, I think, to make clear that that the vision of manhood and womanhood presented in this book is not meant to hinder ministry but to purify and empower it in a pattern of Biblical obedience.

The ninth affirmation of the Danvers Statement[32] is perhaps the crucial final thing to say so that the aim of this book is not misunderstood.

> With half the world's population outside the reach of indigenous evangelism; with countless other lost people in those societies that have heard the gospel; with the stresses and miseries of sickness, malnutrition, homelessness, illiteracy, ignorance, aging, addiction, crime, incarceration, neuroses, and loneliness, no man or woman who feels a passion from God to make His grace known in word and deed need ever live without a fulfilling ministry for the glory of Christ and the good of this fallen world.

2

An Overview of Central Concerns:

Questions and Answers

John Piper and Wayne Grudem

This chapter offers an overview of the vision of manhood and womanhood presented in this book with cogent summary responses to the most common objections. Because every effort to answer one question (on this or any important issue) begets new questions, the list of questions here is not exhaustive. Nonetheless, we hope to give enough trajectories that readers can track the flight of our intention to its appointed target: the good of the church, global mission, and the glory of God.

1. Why do you regard the issue of male and female roles as so important?

We are concerned not merely with the behavioral roles of men and women but also with the underlying nature of manhood and womanhood themselves. Biblical truth and clarity in this matter are important because error and confusion over sexual identity leads to: (1) marriage patterns that do not portray the relationship between Christ and the church[1] (Ephesians 5:31-32); (2) parenting practices that do not train boys to be masculine or girls to be feminine; (3) homosexual tendencies and increasing attempts to justify homosexual alliances (see question 41); (4) patterns of unbiblical female leadership in the church that reflect and promote the confusion over the true meaning of manhood and womanhood.

God's gift of complementary manhood and womanhood was exhilarating from the beginning (Genesis 2:23). It is precious beyond estimation. But today it is esteemed lightly and is vanishing like the rain forests we need but don't love. We believe that what is at stake in human sexuality is the very fabric of life as God wills it to be for the holiness of His people and for their saving mission to the world. (See the "Rationale" of the *Danvers Statement* in Appendix Two.)

2. What do you mean (in question 1) by "unbiblical female leadership in the church"?

We are persuaded that the Bible teaches that only men should be pastors and elders. That is, men should bear *primary* responsibility for Christlike leadership and teaching in the church. So it is unbiblical, we believe, and therefore detrimental, for women to assume this role. (See question 13.)

3. Where in the Bible do you get the idea that only men should be the pastors and elders of the church?

The most explicit texts relating directly to the leadership of men in the church are 1 Timothy 2:11-15; 1 Corinthians 14:34-36; 11:2-16. The chapters in this book on these texts will give the detailed exegetical support for why we believe these texts give abiding sanction to an eldership of spiritual men. Moreover, the Biblical connection between family and church strongly suggests that the headship of the husband at home leads naturally to the primary leadership of spiritual men in the church. (See Chapter 13.)

4. What about marriage? What did you mean (in question 1) by "marriage patterns that do not portray the relationship between Christ and the church"?

We believe the Bible teaches that God means the relationship between husband and wife to portray the relationship between Christ and His church. The husband is to model the loving, sacrificial leadership of Christ, and the wife is to model the glad submission offered freely by the church.

5. What do you mean by submission (in question 4)?

Submission refers to a wife's divine calling to honor and affirm her husband's leadership and help carry it through according to her gifts. It is not an absolute surrender of her will. Rather, we speak of her *disposition to yield* to her husband's guidance and her *inclination* to follow his leadership. (See pages 46-49) Christ is her absolute authority, not the husband. She submits "out of reverence for Christ" (Ephesians 5:21). The supreme authority of Christ qualifies the authority of her husband. She should never follow her husband into sin. Nevertheless, even when she may have to stand with Christ against the sinful will of her husband (e.g., 1 Peter 3:1, where she does not yield to her husband's unbelief), she can still have a *spirit* of submission—a *disposition* to yield. She can show by her attitude and behavior that she does not like resisting his will and that she longs for him to forsake sin and lead in righteousness so that her disposition to honor him as head can again produce harmony.

6. What do you mean when you call the husband "head" (in question 5)?

In the home, Biblical headship is the husband's divine calling to take primary responsibility for Christlike leadership, protection, and provision. (See pages 36-45 on the meaning of mature manhood, and question 13 on the meaning of "primary.")

7. Where in the Bible do you get the idea that husbands should be the leaders in their homes?

The most explicit texts relating directly to headship and submission in marriage are Ephesians 5:21-33; Colossians 3:18-19; 1 Peter 3:1-7; Titus 2:5; 1 Timothy 3:4, 12; Genesis 1-3. The chapters of this book relating to these texts give the detailed exegetical support for why we believe they teach that headship includes primary leadership and that this is the responsibility of the man. Moreover, in view of these teaching passages, the pattern of male leadership that pervades the Biblical portrait of family life is probably not a mere cultural phenomenon over thousands of years but reflects God's original design, even though corrupted by sin.

8. When you say a wife should not follow her husband into sin (question 5), what's left of headship? Who is to say what act of his leadership is sinful enough to justify her refusal to follow?

We are not claiming to live without ambiguities. Neither are we saying that headship consists in a series of directives to the wife. Leadership is not synonymous with unilateral decision making. In fact, in a good marriage, leadership consists mainly in taking responsibility to establish a pattern of interaction that honors both husband and wife (and children) as a store of varied wisdom for family life. Headship bears the primary responsibility for the moral design and planning in the home, but the development of that design and plan will include the wife (who may be wiser and more intelligent). None of this is nullified by some ambiguities in the borderline cases of conflict.

The leadership structures of state, church, and home do not become meaningless even though Christ alone is the absolute authority over each one. The New Testament command for us to submit to church leaders (Hebrews 13:17) is not meaningless even though we are told that elders will arise speaking perverse things (Acts 20:30) and should be rebuked (1 Timothy 5:20) rather than followed when they do so. The command to submit to civil authorities (Romans 13:1) is not meaningless, even though there is such a thing as conscientious objection (Acts 5:29). Nor is the reality of a man's gentle, strong leadership at home nullified just because his authority is not above Christ's in the heart of his wife. In the cases where his leadership fails to win her glad response, we will entrust ourselves to the grace of God and seek the path of Biblical wisdom through prayer and counsel. None of us escapes the (sometimes agonizing) ambiguities of real life.

9. Don't you think that stressing headship and submission gives impetus to the epidemic of wife abuse?

No. First, because we stress Christlike, sacrificial headship that keeps the good of the wife in view and regards her as a joint heir of the grace of life (1 Peter 3:7); and we stress thoughtful submission that does not make the husband an absolute lord (see question 5). Second, we believe that wife abuse (and husband abuse) have some deep roots in the failure of parents to impart to their sons and daughters the meaning of true masculinity and true femininity. The confusions and frustrations of sexual identity often explode in harmful behaviors. The solution to this is not to minimize gender differences (which will then break out in menacing ways), but to teach in the home and the church how true manhood and womanhood express themselves in the loving and complementary roles of marriage.

10. But don't you believe in "mutual submission" the way Paul teaches in Ephesians 5:21, "Submit to one another"?

Yes, we do. But "the way Paul teaches" mutual submission is not the way everyone today teaches it. Everything depends on what you mean by "mutual submission." Some of us put more stress on reciprocity here than others (see note 6 on page 493 in Chapter 8, and the discussion in Chapter 10, pages 198-201). But even if Paul means complete reciprocity (wives submit to husbands and husbands submit to wives), this does not mean that husbands and wives should submit to each other *in the same way*. The key is to remember that the relationship between Christ and the church is the pattern for the relationship between husband and wife. Are Christ and the church mutually submitted? They aren't if submission means Christ yields to the authority of the church. But they are if submission means that Christ submitted Himself to suffering and death for the good of the church. That, however, is not how the church submits to Christ. The church submits to Christ by affirming His authority and following His lead. So mutual submission does not mean submitting to each other *in the same ways*. Therefore, mutual submission does not compromise Christ's headship over the church and it should not compromise the headship of a godly husband.

11. If head *means "source" in Ephesians 5:23 ("the husband is the head of the wife"), as some scholars say it does, wouldn't that change your whole way of seeing this passage and eliminate the idea of the husband's leadership in the home?*

No. But before we deal with this hypothetical possibility we should say that the meaning "source" in Ephesians 5:23 is very unlikely. Scholars will want to read the extensive treatment of this word in Appendix One. But realistically, lay people will make their choice on the basis of what makes sense here in Ephesians. Verse 23 is the ground, or argument, for verse 22; thus it begins with the word *for*. "Wives, submit to your husbands as to the Lord. *For* the husband is the head of the wife. . . ." When the headship of the husband is given as the *ground* for the submission of the wife, the most natural understanding is that headship signifies some kind of leadership.

Moreover, Paul has a picture in his mind when he says that the husband is the head of the wife. The word *head* does not dangle in space waiting for any meaning to be assigned to it. Paul says, "For the husband is the head of the wife as Christ is the head of the church, *His body*" (Ephesians 5:23). The picture in Paul's mind is of a body with a head. This is very important because it leads to the "one flesh" unity of husband and wife in the following verses. A head and its body are "one flesh." Thus Paul goes on to say in verses 28-30, "In this same way, husbands ought to love their wives as their own bodies. He who loves his wife loves himself. After all, no one ever hated his own body, but he feeds and cares for it, just as Christ does the church—for we are members of his body." Paul carries through the image of Christ the Head and the church His body. Christ nourishes and cherishes the church because we are limbs of His body. So the husband is like a head to his wife, so that when he nourishes and cherishes her, he is really nourishing and cherishing himself, as the head who is "one flesh" with this body.

Now, if *head* means "source," what is the husband the source of? What does the body get from the head? It gets nourishment (that's mentioned in verse 29). And we can understand that, because the mouth is in the head, and nourishment comes through the mouth to the body. But that's not all the body gets from the head. It gets guidance, because the eyes are in the head. And it gets alertness and protection, because the ears are in the head.

In other words if the husband as head is one flesh with his wife, his body, and if he is therefore a source of guidance, food, and alertness, then the natural conclusion is that the head, the husband, has a primary responsibility for leadership, provision, and protection. So even if you give *head* the meaning "source," the most natural interpretation of these verses is that husbands are called by God to take primary responsibility for Christlike servant-leadership, protection, and provision in the home, and wives are called to honor and affirm their husbands' leadership and help carry it through according to their gifts.[2]

12. Isn't your stress on leadership in the church and headship in the home contrary to the emphasis of Christ in Luke 22:26, ". . . the greatest among you should be like the youngest, and the one who rules like the one who serves"?

No. We are trying to hold precisely these two things in Biblical balance, namely, leadership and servanthood. It would be contrary to Christ if we said that servanthood cancels out leadership. Jesus is not dismantling leadership, He is defining it. The very word He uses for "leader" in Luke 22:26 is used in Hebrews 13:17, which says, "Obey your *leaders* and submit to them, for they are keeping watch over your souls, as ones who will have to give an account." Leaders are to be servants in sacrificially caring for the souls of the people. But this does not make them less than leaders, as we see in the words *obey* and *submit.* Jesus was no less leader of the disciples when He was on His knees washing their feet than when He was giving them the Great Commission.

13. In questions 2 and 6, you said that the calling of the man is to bear "primary responsibility" for leadership in the church and the home. What do you mean by "primary"?

We mean that there are levels and kinds of leadership for which women may and often should take responsibility. There are kinds of teaching, administration, organization, ministry, influence, and initiative that wives should undertake at home and women should undertake at church. Male headship at home and eldership at church mean that men bear the responsibility for the overall pattern of life. Headship does not prescribe the details of who does precisely what activity. After the fall, God called Adam to account first (Genesis 3:9). This was not because the woman bore no responsibility for sin, but because the man bore *primary* responsibility for life in the garden—including sin.

14. If the husband is to treat his wife as Christ does the church, does that mean he should govern all the details of her life and that she should clear all her actions with him?

No. We may not press the analogy between Christ and the husband that far. Unlike Christ, all husbands sin. They are finite and fallible in their wisdom. Not only that, but also, unlike Christ, a husband is not preparing a bride merely for himself, but also for another, namely, Christ. He does not merely act *as* Christ, he also acts *for* Christ. At this point he must not be Christ to his wife, lest he be a traitor to Christ. He must lead in such a way that his wife is encouraged to depend on Christ and not on himself. Practically, that rules out belittling supervision and fastidious oversight.

Even when acting as Christ, the husband must remember that Christ does not lead the church as His daughter, but as His wife. He is preparing her to be a "fellow-heir," not a servant girl (Romans 8:17). Any kind of leadership that, in the name of Christlike headship, tends to foster in a wife personal immaturity or spiritual weakness or insecurity through excessive control, picky supervision, or oppressive domination has missed the point of the analogy in Ephesians 5. Christ does not create that kind of wife.

15. Don't you think that these texts are examples of temporary compromise with the patriarchal status quo, while the main thrust of Scripture is toward the leveling of gender-based role differences?

We recognize that Scripture sometimes *regulates* undesirable relationships without *condoning* them as permanent ideals. For example, Jesus said to the Pharisees, "Moses permitted you to divorce your wives because your hearts were hard. But it was not this way from the beginning" (Matthew 19:8). Another example is Paul's regulation of how Christians sue each other, even though "[t]he very fact that you have lawsuits among you means you have been completely defeated already" (1 Corinthians 6:1-8). Another example is the regulation of how Christian slaves were to relate to their masters, even though Paul longed for every slave to be received by his master "no longer as a slave, but better than a slave, as a dear brother" (Philemon 16).

But we do not put the loving headship of husbands or the godly eldership of men in the same category with divorce, lawsuits, or slavery. The reason we don't is threefold:

(1) Male and female personhood, with some corresponding role distinctions, is rooted in God's act of creation before the sinful distortions of the status quo were established. (See Chapters 3 and 10.) This argument is the same one, we believe, that evangelical feminists would use to defend heterosexual marriage against the (increasingly prevalent) argument that the "leveling thrust" of the Bible leads *properly* to homosexual alliances. They would say No, because the leveling thrust of the Bible is not meant to dismantle the created order of nature. That is our fundamental argument as well. (2) The redemptive thrust of the Bible does not aim at abolishing headship and submission but at transforming them for their original purposes in the created order. (3) The Bible contains no indictments of loving headship and gives no encouragements to forsake it. Therefore it is wrong to portray the Bible as overwhelmingly egalitarian with a few contextually relativized patriarchal texts. The contra-headship thrust of Scripture simply does not exist. It seems to exist only when Scripture's aim to redeem headship and submission is portrayed as undermining them. (See Question 50, for an example of this hermeneutical flaw.)

16. Aren't the arguments made to defend the exclusion of women from the pastorate today parallel to the arguments Christians made to defend slavery in the nineteenth century?

See the beginning of our answer to this problem in question 15. The preservation of marriage is not parallel with the preservation of slavery. The existence of slavery is not rooted in any creation ordinance, but the existence of marriage is. Paul's regulations for how slaves and masters related to each other do not assume the goodness of the institution of slavery. Rather, seeds for slavery's dissolution were sown in Philemon 16 ("no longer as a slave, but better than a slave, as a dear brother"), Ephesians 6:9 ("Masters . . . do not threaten [your slaves]"), Colossians 4:1 ("Masters, provide your slaves what is right and fair"), and 1 Timothy 6:1-2 (masters are "brothers"). Where these seeds of equality came to full flower, the very institution of slavery would no longer be slavery.

But Paul's regulations for how husbands and wives relate to each other in marriage *do* assume the goodness of the institution of marriage—and not only its goodness but also its foundation in the will of the Creator from the beginning of time (Ephesians 5:31-32). Moreover, in locating the foundation of marriage in the will of God at creation, Paul does so in a way that shows that his regulations for marriage also flow from this order of creation. He quotes Genesis 2:24, "they will become one flesh," and says, "I am talking about Christ and the church." From this "mystery" he draws out the pattern of the relationship between the husband as head (on the analogy of Christ) and the wife as his body or flesh (on the analogy of the church) and derives the appropriateness of the husband's leadership and the wife's submission. Thus Paul's regulations concerning marriage are just as rooted in the created order as is the institution itself. This is not true of slavery. Therefore, while it is true that some slave owners in the nineteenth century argued in ways parallel with our defense of distinct roles in marriage, the parallel was superficial and misguided.

Mary Stewart Van Leeuwen points out, from 1 Timothy 6:1-6, that, according to the nineteenth-century Christian supporters of slavery, "even though the institution of slavery did not go back to creation . . . the fact that Paul based its maintenance on a revelation from Jesus himself meant that anyone wishing to abolish slavery (or even improve the slaves' working conditions) was defying timeless Biblical norms for society."[3] The problem with this argument is that Paul does not use the teachings of Jesus to "maintain" the institution of slavery, but to regulate the behavior of Christian slaves and masters in an institution that already existed in part because of sin. What Jesus endorses is the kind of inner freedom and love that is willing to go the extra mile in service, even when the demand is unjust (Matthew 5:41). Therefore, it is wrong to say that the words of Jesus give a foundation for slavery in the same way that creation gives a foundation for marriage. Jesus does not give any foundation for slavery, but creation gives an unshakeable foundation for marriage and its complementary roles for husband and wife.

Finally, if those who ask this question are concerned to avoid the mistakes of Christians who defended slavery, we must remember the real possibility that it is not we but evangelical feminists today who resemble nineteenth century defenders of slavery in the most significant way: using arguments from the Bible to justify conformity to some very strong pressures in contemporary society (in favor of slavery then, and feminism now).

17. Since the New Testament teaching on the submission of wives in marriage is found in the part of Scripture known as the "household codes" (Haustafeln), *which were taken over in part from first-century culture, shouldn't we recognize that what Scripture is teaching us is not to offend against current culture but to fit in with it up to a point and thus be willing to change our practices of how men and women relate, rather than hold fast to a temporary first-century pattern?*

This is a more sophisticated form of the kind of questions already asked in questions 15 and 16. A few additional comments may be helpful. First of all, by way of explanation, the "household codes" refer to Ephesians 5:22-6:9, Colossians 3:18-4:1, and less exactly 1 Peter 2:13-3:7, which include instructions for pairs of household members: wives/husbands, children/parents, and slaves/masters.

Our first problem with this argument is that the parallels to these "household codes" in the surrounding world are not very close to what we have in the New

Testament. It is not at all as though Paul simply took over either content or form from his culture. Both are very different from the nonbiblical "parallels" that we know of.[4]

Our second problem with this argument is that it maximizes what is incidental (the little that Paul's teaching has in common with the surrounding world) and minimizes what is utterly crucial (the radically Christian nature and foundation of what Paul teaches concerning marriage in the "household codes"). We have shown in questions 15 and 16 that Paul is hardly unreflective in saying some things that are superficially similar to the surrounding culture. He bases his teaching of headship on the nature of Christ's relation to the church, which he sees "mysteriously" revealed in Genesis 2:24 and, thus, in creation itself.

We do not think that it honors the integrity of Paul or the inspiration of Scripture to claim that Paul resorted to arguing that his exhortations were rooted in the very order of creation and in the work of Christ in order to justify his sanctioning temporary accommodations to his culture. It is far more likely that the theological depth and divine inspiration of the apostle led him not only to be very discriminating in what he took over from the world but also to sanction his ethical commands with creation only where they had abiding validity. Thus we believe that there is good reason to affirm the enduring validity of Paul's pattern for marriage: Let the husband, as head of the home, love and lead as Christ does the church, and let the wife affirm that loving leadership as the church honors Christ.

18. But what about the liberating way Jesus treated women? Doesn't He explode our hierarchical traditions and open the way for women to be given access to all ministry roles?

We believe the ministry of Jesus has revolutionary implications for the way sinful men and women treat each other. "[S]hould not this woman, a daughter of Abraham, whom Satan has kept bound for eighteen long years, be set free . . .?" (Luke 13:16). Everything Jesus taught and did was an attack on the pride that makes men and women belittle each other. Everything He taught and did was a summons to the humility and love that purge self-exaltation out of leadership and servility out of submission. He put man's lustful look in the category of adultery and threatened it with hell (Matthew 5:28-29). He condemned the whimsical disposing of women in divorce (Matthew 19:8). He called us to account for every careless word we utter (Matthew 12:36). He commanded that we treat each other the way we would like to be treated (Matthew 7:12). He said to the callous chief priests, ". . . prostitutes are entering the kingdom of God ahead of you" (Matthew 21:31). He was accompanied by women, He taught women, and women bore witness to His resurrection life. Against every social custom that demeans or abuses men and women the words of Jesus can be applied: "And why do you break the command of God for the sake of your tradition?" (Matthew 15:3).

But where does Jesus say or do anything that criticizes the order of creation in which men bear a primary responsibility to lead, protect, and sustain? Nothing He did calls this good order into question. It simply does not follow to say that since women ministered to Jesus and learned from Jesus and ran to tell the disciples that Jesus was risen, this must mean that Jesus opposed the loving headship of husbands or the limitation of eldership to spiritual men. We would not argue that merely because Jesus chose twelve men to be His authoritative apostles, Jesus must have favored an eldership of only men in the church. But this argument would be at least as valid as arguing that anything else Jesus did means He would oppose an eldership of all men or the headship of husbands. The effort to show that the ministry of Jesus is part of a major Biblical thrust against gender-based roles can only be sustained by *assuming* (rather than demonstrating) that He meant to nullify headship and submission rather than rectify them. What is clear is that Jesus radically purged leadership of pride and fear and self-exaltation and that He also radically honored women as persons worthy of the highest respect under God.

19. Doesn't the significant role women had with Paul in ministry show that his teachings do not mean that women should be excluded from ministry?

Yes. But the issue is not whether women should be excluded from ministry. They shouldn't be. There are hundreds of ministries open to men and women. We must be more careful in how we pose our questions. Otherwise the truth is obscured from the start.

The issue here is whether any of the women serving with Paul in ministry fulfilled roles that would be inconsistent with a limitation of the eldership to men. We believe the answer to that is No. Tom Schreiner has dealt with this matter more fully in Chapter 11. But we can perhaps illustrate with two significant women in Paul's ministry.

Paul said that Euodia and Syntyche "contended at my side in the cause of the gospel, along with Clement and the rest of my fellow workers" (Philippians 4:2-3). There is wonderful honor given to Euodia and Syntyche here for their ministry with Paul. But there are no compelling grounds for affirming that the nature of the ministry was contrary to the limitations that we argue are set forth in 1 Timothy 2:12. One must *assume* this in order to make a case against these limitations. Paul would surely say that the "deacons" mentioned in Philippians 1:1 along with the "overseers" were fellow workers with him when he was there. But if so, then one can be a "fellow worker" with Paul without being in a position of authority over men. (We are assuming from 1 Timothy 3:2 and 5:17 that what distinguishes an elder from a deacon is that the responsibility for teaching and governance was the elder's and not the deacon's.)

Phoebe is praised as a "servant" or "deacon" of the church at Cenchreea who "has been a great help [or "patroness"] to many people, including me" (Romans 16:1-2). Some have tried to argue that the Greek word behind "help" really means "leader." This is doubtful, since it is hard to imagine, on any count, what Paul would mean by saying that Phoebe became his leader.[5] He could of course mean that she was an influential patroness who gave sanctuary to him and his band or that she used her community influence for the cause of the gospel and for Paul in particular. She was a very significant person and played a crucial role in the ministry. But to derive anything from this that is contrary to our understanding of 1 Timothy 2:12, one would have to *assume* authority over men here since it cannot be shown.

20. But Priscilla taught Apollos didn't she (Acts 18:26)? And she is even mentioned before her husband Aquila. Doesn't that show that the practice of the early church did not exclude women from the teaching office of the church?

We are eager to affirm Priscilla as a fellow worker with Paul in Christ

(Romans 16:3)! She and her husband were very influential in the church in Corinth (1 Corinthians 16:19) as well as Ephesus. We can think of many women in our churches today who are like Priscilla. Nothing in our understanding of Scripture says that when a husband and wife visit an unbeliever (or a confused believer—or anyone else) the wife must be silent. It is easy for us to imagine the dynamics of such a discussion in which Priscilla contributes to the explanation and illustration of baptism in Jesus' name and the work of the Holy Spirit.

Our understanding of what is fitting for men and women in that kind of setting is not an oversimplified or artificial list of rules for what the woman and man can say and do. It is rather a call for the delicate and sensitive preservation of personal dynamics that honor the headship of Aquila without squelching the wisdom and insight of Priscilla. There is nothing in this text that cannot be explained on this understanding of what happened. We do not claim to know the spirit and balance of how Priscilla and Aquila and Apollos related to each other. We only claim that a feminist reconstruction of the relationship has no more warrant than ours. The right of Priscilla to hold an authoritative teaching office cannot be built on an event about which we know so little. It is only a guess to suggest that the order of their names signifies Priscilla's leadership. Luke may simply have wanted to give greater honor to the woman by putting her name first (1 Peter 3:7), or may have had another reason unknown to us. Saying that Priscilla illustrates the authoritative teaching of women in the New Testament is the kind of precarious and unwarranted inference that is made again and again by evangelical feminists and then called a major Biblical thrust against gender-based role distinctions. But many invalid inferences do not make a major thrust.

21. Are you saying that it is all right for women to teach men under some circumstances?

When Paul says in 1 Timothy 2:12, "I do not permit a woman to teach or to have authority over a man; she must be silent," we do not understand him to mean an absolute prohibition of all teaching by women. Paul instructs the older women to "teach what is good. Then they can train the younger women" (Titus 2:3-4), and he commends the teaching that Eunice and Lois gave to their son and grandson Timothy (2 Timothy 1:5; 3:14). Proverbs praises the ideal wife because "She speaks with wisdom, and faithful instruction is on her tongue" (Proverbs 31:26). Paul endorses women prophesying in church (1 Corinthians 11:5) and says that men "learn" by such prophesying (1 Corinthians 14:31) and that the members (presumably men and women) should "teach and admonish one another with all wisdom, as you sing psalms, hymns and spiritual songs" (Colossians 3:16). Then, of course, there is Priscilla at Aquila's side correcting Apollos (Acts 18:26).

It is arbitrary to think that Paul had every form of teaching in mind in 1 Timothy 2:12. Teaching and learning are such broad terms that it is *impossible* that women not teach men and men not learn from women *in some sense*. There is a way that nature teaches (1 Corinthians 11:14) and a fig tree teaches (Matthew 24:32) and suffering teaches (Hebrews 5:8) and human behavior teaches (1 Corinthians 4:6; 1 Peter 3:1).

If Paul did not have every conceivable form of teaching and learning in mind, what did he mean? Along with the fact that the setting here is the church assembled for prayer and teaching (1 Timothy 2:8-10; 3:15), the best clue is the coupling of "teaching" with "having authority over men." We would say that the teaching inappropriate for a woman is the teaching of men in settings or ways that dishonor the calling of men to bear the primary responsibility for teaching and leadership. This primary repsonsibility is to be carried by the pastors or elders. Therefore we think it is God's will that only men bear the responsibility for this office.

22. *Can't a pastor give authorization for a woman to teach Scripture to the congregation, and then continue to exercise oversight while she teaches?*

It is right for all the teaching ministries of the church to meet with the approval of the guardians and overseers (=elders) of the church. However, it would be wrong for the leadership of the church to use its authority to sanction the de facto functioning of a woman as a teaching elder in the church, only without the name. In other words, there are two kinds of criteria that should be met in order for the teaching of a woman to be biblically affirmed. One is to have the endorsement of the spiritual overseers of the church (=elders). The other is to avoid contexts and kinds of teaching that put a woman in the position of functioning as the de facto spiritual shepherd of a group of men or to avoid the kind of teaching that by its very nature calls for strong, forceful pressing of men's consciences on the basis of divine authority.

23. *How can you be in favor of women prophesying in church but not in favor of women being pastors and elders? Isn't prophecy at the very heart of those roles?*

No. The role of pastor/elder is primarily governance and teaching (1 Timothy 5:17). In the list of qualifications for elders the prophetic gift is not mentioned, but the ability to teach is (1 Timothy 3:2). In Ephesians 4:11, prophets are distinguished from pastor-teachers. And even though men learn from prophecies that women give, Paul distinguishes the gift of prophecy from the gift of teaching (Romans 12:6-7; 1 Corinthians 12:28). Women are nowhere forbidden to prophesy. Paul simply regulates the demeanor in which they prophesy so as not to compromise the principle of the spiritual leadership of men (1 Corinthians 11:5-10).

Prophecy in the worship of the early church was not the kind of authoritative, infallible revelation we associate with the written prophecies of the Old Testament.[6] It was a report in human words based on a spontaneous, personal revelation from the Holy Spirit (1 Corinthians 14:30) for the purpose of edification, encouragement, consolation, conviction, and guidance (1 Corinthians 14:3, 24-25; Acts 21:4; 16:6-10). It was not necessarily free from a mixture of human error, and thus needed assessment (1 Thessalonians 5:19-20; 1 Corinthians 14:29) on the basis of the apostolic (Biblical) teaching (1 Corinthians 14:36-38; 2 Thessalonians 2:1-3). Prophecy in the early church did not correspond to the sermon today or to a formal exposition of Scripture. Both women and men could stand and share what they believed God had brought to mind for the good of the church. The testing of this word and the regular teaching ministry was the responsibility of the elder-teachers. This latter role is the one Paul assigns uniquely to men.[7]

24. *Are you saying then that you accept the freedom of women to publicly prophesy as described in Acts 2:17, 1 Corinthians 11:5, and Acts 21:9?*

Yes.[8]

25. *Since it says in 1 Corinthians 14:34 that "women should remain silent in the churches," it doesn't seem like your position is really Biblical because of how much speaking you really do allow to women. How do you account for this straightforward prohibition of women speaking?*

The reason we believe Paul does not mean for women to be *totally* silent in the church is that in 1 Corinthians 11:5 he permits women to pray and prophesy in church: "[E]very woman who *prays* or *prophesies* with her head uncovered dishonors her head." But someone may ask, "Why do you choose to let 1 Corinthians 11:5 limit the meaning of 1 Corinthians 14:34 rather than the other way around?"

To begin our answer, we notice in both 1 Corinthians 14:35 and 1 Corinthians 11:6 that Paul's concern is for what is "shameful" or "disgraceful" for women (*aischron* in both verses and only here in 1 Corinthians). The issue is not whether women are competent or intelligent or wise or well-taught. The issue is how they relate to the men of the church. In 1 Corinthians 14:34 Paul speaks of *submission*, and in 1 Corinthians 11:3 he speaks of man as *head*. So the issue of shamefulness is at root an issue of doing something that would dishonor the role of the men as leaders of the congregation. If *all* speaking were shameful in this way, then Paul could not have condoned a woman's praying and prophesying, as he does in 1 Corinthians 11:5 precisely when the issue of shamefulness is what is at stake. But Paul shows in 1 Corinthians 11:5-16 that what is at stake is not *that* women are praying and prophesying in public but *how* they are doing it. That is, are they doing it with the dress and demeanor that signify their affirmation of the headship of the men who are called to lead the church?

In a similar way we look into the context of 1 Corinthians 14:33-36 to find similar clues for the *kind* of speaking Paul may have in mind when he says it is "shameful" for a woman to speak. We notice again that the issue is not the ability or the wisdom of women to speak intelligently but how women are relating to men (*hypotassesthōson*—"let them be in submission"). Some kind of interaction is taking place that Paul thinks compromises the calling of the men to be the primary leaders of the church. Chapter 6 of this book argues in detail that the inappropriate interaction relates to the testing of prophecies referred to in 1 Corinthians 14:29. Women are taking a role here that Paul thinks is inappropriate. This is the activity in which they are to be silent.[9] In other words, what Paul is calling for is not the total silence of women but a kind of involvement that signifies, in various ways, their glad affirmation of the leadership of the men God has called to be the guardians and overseers of the flock.

26. *Doesn't Paul's statement that "There is . . . neither male nor female . . . for you are all one in Christ Jesus" (Galatians 3:28) take away gender as a basis for distinction of roles in the church?*

No. Most evangelicals still agree that this text is not a warrant for homosexuality. In other words, most of us do not force Paul's "neither male nor female" beyond what we know from other passages he would approve. For example, we know from Romans 1:24-32 that Paul does not mean for the created order of different male and female roles to be overthrown by Galatians 3:28.

The context of Galatians 3:28 makes abundantly clear the sense in which men and women are equal in Christ: they are equally justified by faith (v. 24), equally free from the bondage of legalism (v. 25), equally children of God (v. 26), equally clothed with Christ (v. 27), equally possessed by Christ (v. 29), and equally heirs of the promises to Abraham (v. 29).

This last blessing is especially significant, namely, the equality of being a fellow-heir with men of the promises. In 1 Peter 3:1-7, the blessing of being joint heirs "of the gracious gift of life" is connected with the exhortation for women to submit to their husbands (v. 1) and for their husbands to treat their wives "with respect as the weaker partner." In other words, Peter saw no conflict between the "neither-male-nor-female" principle regarding our inheritance and the headship-submission principle regarding our roles. Galatians 3:28 does not abolish gender-based roles established by God and redeemed by Christ.

27. How do you explain God's apparent endorsement of women in the Old Testament who had prophetic or leadership roles?

First, we keep in mind that God has no antipathy toward revealing His will to women. Nor does He pronounce them unreliable messengers. The differentiation of roles for men and women in ministry is rooted not in women's incompetence to receive or transmit truth, but in the primary responsibility of men in God's order to lead and teach. The instances of women who prophesied and led do not call this order into question. Rather, there are pointers in each case that the women followed their unusual paths in a way that endorsed and honored the usual leadership of men, or indicted their failures to lead.

For example, Miriam, the prophetess, focused her ministry, as far as we can tell, on the women of Israel (Exodus 15:20). Deborah, a prophetess, judge, and mother in Israel (Judges 4:4; 5:7), along with Jael (Judges 5:24-27), was a living indictment of the weakness of Barak and other men in Israel who should have been more courageous leaders (Judges 4:9). (The period of the judges is an especially precarious foundation for building a vision of God's ideal for leadership. In those days God was not averse to bringing about states of affairs that did not conform to His revealed will in order to achieve some wise purpose [cf. Judges 14:4].) Huldah evidently exercised her prophetic gift not in a public preaching ministry but by means of private consultation (2 Kings 22:14-20). And Anna the prophetess filled her days with fasting and prayer in the temple (Luke 2:36-37).

We must also keep in mind that God's granting power or revelation to a person is no sure sign that this person is an ideal model for us to follow in every respect. This is evident, for example, from the fact that some of those God blessed in the Old Testament were polygamists (e.g. Abraham and David). Not even the gift of prophecy is proof of a person's obedience and endorsement by God. As strange as this sounds, Matthew 7:22, 1 Corinthians 13:2, and 1 Samuel 19:23-24 show that this is so. Moreover, in the case of each woman referred to above we have an instance of a charismatic emergence on the scene, not an installation to the ordinary Old Testament office of priest, which was the responsibility of men.

28. Do you think women are more gullible than men?

First Timothy 2:14 says, "Adam was not the one deceived; it was the woman who was deceived and became a sinner." Paul gives this as one of the reasons why he does not permit women "to teach or have authority over a man." Historically this has usually been taken to mean that women are more gullible or deceivable than men and therefore less fit for the doctrinal oversight of the church. This may be true (see question 29). However, we are attracted to another understanding of Paul's argument.

We think that Satan's main target was not Eve's peculiar gullibility (if she had one), but rather Adam's headship as the one ordained by God to be responsible for the life of the garden. Satan's subtlety is that he knew the created order God had ordained for the good of the family, and he deliberately defied it by ignoring the man and taking up his dealings with the woman. Satan put her in the position of spokesman, leader, and defender. At that moment both the man and the woman slipped from their innocence and let themselves be drawn into a pattern of relating that to this day has proved destructive.

If this is the proper understanding, then what Paul meant in 1 Timothy 2:14 was this: "Adam was not deceived (that is, Adam was not approached by the deceiver and did not carry on direct dealings with the deceiver), but the woman was deceived and became a transgressor (that is, she was the one who took up dealings with the deceiver and was led through her direct interaction with him into deception and transgression)."

In this case, the main point is not that the man is undeceivable or that the woman is more deceivable; the point is that when God's order of leadership is repudiated it brings damage and ruin. Men and women are both more vulnerable to error and sin when they forsake the order that God has intended.

29. But it does look as if Paul really thought Eve was somehow more vulnerable to deception than Adam. Wouldn't this make Paul a culpable chauvinist?

No. When someone asks if women are weaker than men, or smarter than men, or more easily frightened than men, or something like that, perhaps the best way to answer is this: women are weaker in some ways and men are weaker in some ways; women are smarter in some ways and men are smarter in some ways; women are more easily frightened in some circumstances and men are more easily frightened in others. It is dangerous to put negative values on the so-called weaknesses that each of us has. God intends for all the "weaknesses" that characteristically belong to man to call forth and highlight woman's strengths. And God intends for all the "weaknesses" that characteristically belong to woman to call forth and highlight man's strengths.

Even if 1 Timothy 2:14 meant that in some circumstances women are characteristically more vulnerable to deception, that would not settle anything about the equality or worth of manhood and womanhood. Boasting in either sex as superior to the other is folly. Men and women, as God created us, are different in hundreds of ways. Being created equally in the image of God means at least this: that when the so-called weakness and strength columns for manhood and for womanhood are added up, the value at the bottom is going to be the same for each. And when you take those two columns and put them on top of each other, God intends them to be the perfect complement to each other.

30. If a woman is not allowed to teach men in a regular, official way, why is it permissible for her to teach children, who are far more impressionable and defenseless?

This question assumes something that we do not believe. As we said in question 21, we do not build our vision on the assumption that the Bible assigns women their role because of doctrinal or moral incompetence. The differentiation of roles for men and women in ministry is rooted not in any supposed incompetence, but in God's created order for manhood and womanhood. Since little boys do not relate to their women teachers as man to woman, the leadership dynamic ordained by God is not injured. (However, that dynamic would be injured if the pattern of our staffing and teaching communicated that Bible teaching is *only* women's work and not the *primary* responsibility of the fathers and spiritual men of the church.)

31. *Aren't you guilty of a selective literalism when you say some commands in a text are permanently valid and others, like, "Don't wear braided hair" or "Do wear a head covering," are culturally conditioned and not absolute?*

All of life and language is culturally conditioned. We share with all interpreters the challenge of discerning how Biblical teaching should be applied today in a very different culture. In demonstrating the permanent validity of a command, we would try to show from its context that it has roots in the nature of God, the gospel, or creation as God ordered it. We would study these things as they are unfolded throughout Scripture. In contrast, to show that the specific forms of some commands are limited to one kind of situation or culture, 1) we seek for clues in the context that this is so; 2) we compare other Scriptures relating to the same subject to see if we are dealing with limited application or with an abiding requirement; and 3) we try to show that the cultural specificity of the command is *not* rooted in the nature of God, the gospel, or the created order.

In the context of Paul's and Peter's teaching about how men and women relate in the church and the home, there are instructions not only about submission and leadership, but also about forms of feminine adornment. Here are the relevant verses with our literal translation:

1 Timothy 2:9-10, "Likewise the women are to adorn themselves in respectable apparel with modesty and sensibleness, not in braids and gold or pearls or expensive clothing, but, as is fitting for women who profess godliness, through good works."

1 Peter 3:3-5, "Let not yours be the external adorning of braiding hair and putting on gold or wearing clothes, but the hidden person of the heart by the imperishable (jewel) of a meek and quiet spirit, which is precious before God."

It would be wrong to say these commands are not relevant today. One clear, abiding teaching in them is that *the focus* of effort at adornment should be on "good works" and on "the hidden person" rather than on the externals of clothing and hair and jewelry. Neither is there any reason to nullify the general command to be modest and sensible, or the warning against ostentation. The only question is whether wearing braids, gold, and pearls is intrinsically sinful then and now.

There is one clear indication from the context that this was not the point. Peter says, "Let not yours be the external adorning of . . . wearing clothes." The Greek does not say "fine" clothes (*NIV* and *RSV*), but just "wearing clothes" or, as the *NASB* says, "putting on dresses." Now we know Peter is not condemning the use of clothes. He is condemning the misuse of clothes. This suggests, then, that the same thing could be said about gold and braids. The point is not to warn against something intrinsically evil, but to warn against its misuse as an expression of self-exaltation or worldly-mindedness. Add to this that the commands concerning headship and submission are rooted in the created order (in 1 Timothy

2:13-14) while the specific forms of modesty are not. This is why we plead innocent of the charge of selective literalism.

32. *But doesn't Paul argue for a head covering for women in worship by appealing to the created order in 1 Corinthians 11:13-15? Why is the head covering not binding today while the teaching concerning submission and headship is?*

The key question here is whether Paul is saying that creation dictates a head covering or that creation dictates that we use culturally appropriate expressions of masculinity and femininity, which just happened to be a head covering for women in that setting. We think the latter is the case. The key verses are: "Judge for yourselves: Is it proper for a woman to pray to God with her head uncovered? Does not nature itself teach you that if a man has long hair, it is a disgrace to him, but that if a woman has long hair, it is her glory? For long hair is given to her as a covering" (1 Corinthians 11:13-15).

How did nature teach that long hair dishonored a man and gave women a covering? Nature has not endowed women with more hair than men. In fact, if nature takes its course, men will have more hair than women because it will cover their face as well as their head. There must be another way that nature teaches on this subject! We believe custom and nature conspire in this pedagogy. On the one hand, *custom* dictates what hair arrangements are generally masculine or feminine. On the other hand, *nature* dictates that men feel ashamed when they wear symbols of femininity. We could feel the force of this by asking the men of our churches, "Does not nature teach you not to wear a dress to church?" The teaching of nature is the *natural* inclination of men and women to feel shame when they abandon the culturally established symbols of masculinity or femininity. Nature does not teach what the symbols should be.

When Paul says that a woman's hair "is given to her for a covering" (v. 15), he means that nature has given woman the hair and the inclination to follow prevailing customs of displaying her femininity, which in this case included letting her hair grow long and drawing it up into a covering for her head. So Paul's point in this passage is that the relationships of manhood and womanhood, which are rooted in the created order (1 Corinthians 11:7-9), should find appropriate cultural expression in the worship service. Nature teaches this by giving men and women deep and differing inclinations about the use of masculine and feminine symbols.

33. *How is it consistent to forbid the eldership to women in our churches and then send them out as missionaries to do things forbidden at home?*

We stand in awe of the faith, love, courage, and dedication that have moved thousands of single and married women into missions. The story told by Ruth Tucker in *Guardians of the Great Commission: The Story of Women in Modern Missions*[10] is great. Our prayer is that it will inspire thousands more women—and men!—to give themselves to the great work of world evangelization.

Is this inconsistent of us? Is it true that we are sending women as missionaries to do "things forbidden" at home? If so, it is a remarkable fact that the vast majority of the women who over the centuries have become missionaries also endorsed the responsibility of men in leadership the way we do (Tucker, p. 38). And the men who have most vigorously recruited and defended women for missions have done so, not because they disagreed with our vision of manhood and womanhood, but because they saw boundless work available in evangelism—some that women could do better than men.

For example, Hudson Taylor saw that when a Chinese catechist worked with a "missionary-sister" instead of a European male missionary, "the whole work of teaching and preaching and representing the mission to outsiders devolves upon him; he counts as the head of the mission, and must act independently."[11] The paradoxical missionary strength of being "weak" was recognized again and again. Mary Slessor, in an incredible display of strength, argued that she should be allowed to go alone to unexplored territory in Africa because "as a woman she would be less of a threat to native tribesmen than a male missionary would be, and therefore safer."[12]

Another example is A. J. Gordon, the Boston pastor, missionary, statesman, and founder (in 1889) of Gordon-Conwell Theological Seminary. He strongly promoted women in missions, appealing especially to the prophesying daughters of Acts 2:17. But for all his exuberance for the widest ministry of women in mission he took a view of 1 Timothy 2:12 similar to ours:

> Admit, however, that the prohibition is against public teaching; what may it mean? To teach and to govern are the special functions of the presbyter. The teacher and the pastor, named in the gifts to the Church (Eph. 4:11), Alford considers to be the same; and the pastor is generally regarded as identical with the bishop. Now there is no instance in the New Testament of a woman being set over a church as bishop and teacher. The lack of such example would lead us to refrain from ordaining a woman as pastor of a Christian congregation. But if the Lord has fixed this limitation, we believe it to be grounded, not on her less favored position in the privileges of grace, but in the impediments to such service existing in nature itself.[13]

We admit that there are ambiguities in applying Paul's instructions about an established church to an emerging church. We admit that there are ambiguities in separating the Priscilla-type counsel from the official teaching role of 1 Timothy 2:12. We could imagine ourselves struggling for Biblical and cultural faithfulness the way Hudson Taylor did in a letter to Miss Faulding in 1868:

> I do not know when I may be able to return, and it will not do for Church affairs to wait for me. You cannot take a Pastor's place in name, but you must help (Wang) Lae-djun to act in matters of receiving and excluding as far as you can. You can speak privately to candidates, and can be present at Church meetings, and might even, through others, suggest questions to be asked of those desiring baptism. Then after the meeting you can talk privately with Lae-djun about them, and suggest who you think he might receive next time they meet. Thus he may have the help he needs, and there will be nothing that any one could regard as unseemly.[14]

We do not wish to impede the great cause of world evangelization by quibbling over which of the hundreds of roles might correspond so closely to pastor/elder as to be inappropriate for a woman to fill. It is manifest to us that women are fellow workers in the gospel and should strive side by side with men (Philippians 4:3; Romans 16:3,12). For the sake of finishing the Great

Commission in our day, we are willing to risk some less-than-ideal role assignments.

We hope that we are not sending men or women to do things that are forbidden at home. We are not sending women to become the pastors or elders of churches. Neither has the vast majority of women evangelists and church planters sought this for themselves. We do not think it is forbidden for women to tell the gospel story and win men and women to Christ. We do not think God forbids women to work among the millions of lost women in the world, which according to Ruth Tucker "was the major justification of the Women's Missionary Movement."[15] Even if a woman held a more restrictive view than ours, the fact that over two-thirds of the world's precious lost people are women and children means that there are more opportunities in evangelism and teaching than could ever be exhausted. Our passion is not to become the watchdogs of where women serve. Our passion is to join hands with all God's people, *in God's way*, to "declare his glory among the nations" (Psalm 96:3).

34. Do you deny to women the right to use the gifts God has given them? Does not God's giving a spiritual gift imply that He endorses its use for the edification of the church.

Having a spiritual gift is not a warrant to use it however we please. John White is right when he writes, "Some people believe it to be impossible that the power of the Holy Spirit could have unholy consequences in an individual's life. But it can."[16] Spiritual gifts are not only given by the Holy Spirit, they are also regulated by the Holy Scriptures. This is clear from 1 Corinthians, where people with the gift of tongues were told not to use it in public when there was no gift of interpretation, and prophets were told to stop prophesying when someone else had a revelation (14:28-30). We do not deny to women the right to use the gifts God has given them. If they have gifts of teaching or administration or evangelism, God does want those gifts used, and He will honor the commitment to use them within the guidelines given in Scripture.

35. If God has genuinely called a woman to be a pastor, then how can you say she should not be one?

We do not believe God genuinely calls women to be pastors. We say this not because we can read the private experience of anyone, but because we believe private experience must always be assessed by the public criterion of God's Word, the Bible. If the Bible teaches that God wills for men alone to bear the primary teaching and governing responsibilities of the pastorate, then by implication the Bible also teaches that God does not call women to be pastors. The church has known from its earliest days that a person's personal *sense* of divine leading is not *by itself* an adequate criterion for discerning God's call. Surely there is a divine sending of chosen ministers (Romans 10:15); but there is also the divine warning concerning those who thought they were called and were not: "I did not send or appoint them" (Jeremiah 23:32).

Probably what is discerned as a divine call to the pastorate in some earnest Christian women is indeed a call to ministry, but not to the pastorate. Very often the divine compulsion to serve comes upon Christians without the precise avenue of service being specified by the Holy Spirit. At this point we should look not only at our gifts but also at the teaching of Scripture regarding what is appropriate for us as men and women.

36. What is the meaning of authority when you talk about it in relation to the home and the church?

This question is crucial because the New Testament shows that the basic relationships of life fit together in terms of authority and compliance. For example, the relationship between parents and children works on the basis of the right of the parents to require obedience (Ephesians 6:1-2). The civil government has authority to make laws that regulate the behavior of citizens (Romans 13:1-7; Titus 3:1; 1 Peter 2:13-17). Most social institutions have structures that give to some members the right to direct the actions of others. The military and business come most readily to mind (Matthew 8:9; 1 Peter 3:18-20). The church, while made up of a priesthood of believers, is governed in the New Testament by servant-leaders whom the people are called to follow (1 Thessalonians 5:12; Hebrews 13:7, 17; 1 Timothy 3:5; 5:17). And in marriage the wife is called to submit to the sacrificial headship of her husband (Ephesians 5:22-33; Colossians 3:18-19; 1 Peter 3:1-7). Finally, the source of all this authority is God's authority, which is absolute.

What becomes clear as soon as we try to give a definition to this authority is that its form changes from one relationship to another. We would define authority in general as the *right* (Matthew 8:9) and *power* (Mark 1:27; 1 Corinthians 7:37) and *responsibility* (2 Corinthians 10:8; 13:10) *to give direction to another*. This applies perfectly to God in all His relationships. But it applies in very different ways to the different human relationships.

For example, with regard to the *power* to direct others, the state is invested with the sword (Romans 13:4); parents are given the rod (Proverbs 13:24); businesses can terminate an employee (Luke 16:2); and elders can, with the church, excommunicate (Matthew 18:17; 1 Corinthians 5:1-8). Similarly, the extent of the *right* to direct others varies with each relationship. For example, parents have the right to be directly involved in the minutest details of their children, teaching them to hold their forks correctly and sit up straight. But the government and the church would not have such extensive rights.

For Christians, *right* and *power* recede and *responsibility* predominates. "Jesus called them together and said, 'You know that the rulers of the Gentiles lord it over them, and their high officials exercise authority over them. Not so with you. Instead, whoever wants to become great among you must be your servant'" (Matthew 20:25-26). Authority becomes a burden to bear, not a right to assert. It is a sacred duty to discharge for the good of others. Excommunicating a church member is a painful last resort. A spanked child is enfolded in affection. Employers show mercy. But none of this is the abolition of authority structures, only their transformation as loving responsibility seeks to outrun rights and power.

The transformation of authority is most thorough in marriage. This is why we prefer to speak of leadership and headship rather than authority. The Bible does not give warrant to husbands to use physical power to bring wives into submission. When Ephesians 5:25-27 shows Christ bringing His bride toward holiness, it shows Him suffering for her, not making her suffer for Him. The husband's authority is a God-given burden to be carried in humility, not a natural right to flaunt with pride. At least three things hinder a husband from using his authority (leadership!) to justify force: 1) the unique intimacy and union implied in the phrase "one flesh"—". . . no one ever hated his own body, but he feeds and cares for it . . ." (Ephesians 5:29-31); 2) the special honor commanded in 1 Peter 3:7 as to a joint heir of the grace of life; 3) the aim to cultivate shared maturity in Christ, not childish dependence.

Thus authority in general is the right, power, and responsibility to direct others. But the form and balance of these elements will vary in the different relationships of life according to the teachings of Scripture.

37. If a church embraces a congregational form of governance in which the congregation, and not the elders, is the highest authority under Christ and Scripture, should the women be allowed to vote?

Yes. Acts 15:22 says, "Then it seemed good to the apostles and the elders, with the whole church, to choose men from among them and send them to Antioch." This seems to be a Biblical expression of the priesthood of all believers (1 Peter 2:9; Revelation 1:6; 5:10; cf. Matthew 18:17). The reason we do not think this is inconsistent with 1 Timothy 2:12 is that the authority of the church is not the same as the authority of the individuals who make up the church. When we say the congregation has authority, we do not mean that each man and each woman has that authority. Therefore, gender, as a part of individual personhood, is not significantly in view in corporate congregational decisions.

38. In Romans 16:7, Paul wrote, "Greet Andronicus and Junias, my relatives who have been in prison with me. They are outstanding among the apostles, and they were in Christ before I was." Isn't Junias a woman? And wasn't she an apostle? And doesn't that mean that Paul was willing to acknowledge that a woman held a very authoritative position over men in the early church?

Let's take these three questions one at a time.

1. Was Junias a woman? We cannot know. The evidence is indecisive. We did a complete search of all the Greek writings from Homer (B.C. ninth century?) into the fifth century A.D. available now on computer through the *Thesaurus Linguae Graecae* (Pilot CD ROM #C, University of California at Irvine, 1987), which contains 2,889 authors and 8,203 works. We asked the computer for all forms of *Iounia-* so that we would pick up all the possible cases. (We did not search for the possible first declension masculine genitive *Iouniou*, which morphologically *could* come from a masculine *Iounias*, because there is no way to tell if *Iouniou* might come from the man's name *Iounios*; so that all these genitive forms would be useless in establishing a masculine *Iounias*.)

The result of our computer search is this: Besides the one instance in Romans 16:7 there were three others.

> 1. Plutarch (ca. A.D. 50-ca. 120), in his *Life of Marcus Brutus*, wrote about the tension between Brutus and Cassius, ". . . though they were connected in their families, Cassius having married Junia, the sister of Brutus (*Iounia gar adelphē Broutou sunoikei Kassios*)."[17]
>
> 2. Epiphanius (A.D. 315-403), the bishop of Salamis in Cyprus, wrote an *Index of Disciples*, in which he includes this line: "Iounias, of whom Paul makes mention, became bishop of Apameia of Syria" (*Index disciplulorum*, 125.19-20). In Greek, the phrase "of whom" is a masculine relative pronoun (*hou*) and shows that Epiphanius thought Iounias was a man.
>
> 3. John Chrysostom (A.D. 347-407), in preaching on Romans 16:7, said in

reference to Junias, "Oh! how great is the devotion of this woman, that she should be even counted worthy of the appellation of apostle!"[18]

What we may learn from these three uses is that Junias was used as a woman's name in the time around the New Testament (Plutarch). The Church Fathers were evidently divided as to whether Paul was using Junias that way, Epiphanius assuming it is masculine, Chrysostom assuming it is feminine. Perhaps somewhat more weight may be given to the statement by Epiphanius, since he appears to know more specific information about Junias (that he became bishop of Apameia), while Chrysostom gives no more information than what he could deduce from Romans 16:7).[19]

Perhaps more significant than either of these, however, is a Latin quotation from Origen (died 252 A.D.), in the earliest extant commentary on Romans: He says that Paul refers to "Andronicus and Junias and Herodian, all of whom he calls relatives and fellow captives (*Andronicus, et Junias, et Herodion, quos omnes et cognatos suos, et concaptivos appellat*)" (Origen's commentary on Romas, preserved in a Latin translation by Rufinus, c. 345-c.410 A.D., in J. P. Migne, *Patrologia Graeca*, vol. 14, col. 1289). The name Junias here is a Latin masculine singular nominative, implying—if this ancient translation is reliable—that Origin (who was one of the ancient world's most proficient scholars) thought Junias was a man. Coupled with the quotation from Epiphanias, this quotation makes the weight of ancient evidence support this view.

Masculine names ending in *-as* are not unusual even in the New Testament: Andrew (*Andreas*, Matthew 10:2), Elijah (*Elias*, Matthew 11:14), Isaiah (*Esaias*, John 1:23), Zacharias (Luke 1:5). A. T. Robertson (*Grammar of the Greek New Testament* [New York: Hodder and Stoughton, 1914], pp. 171-173) shows that numerous names ending in *-as* are shortened forms for clearly masculine forms. The clearest example in the New Testament is Silas (Acts 15:22) from Silvanus (1 Thessalonians 1:1; 1 Peter 5:12).

So there is no way to be dogmatic about what the form of the name signifies. It could be feminine or it could be masculine. Certainly no one should claim that Junia was a common woman's name in the Greek speaking world, since there are only these three known examples in all of ancient Greek literature. Moreover the fact that Andronicus and Junias, like Prisca and Aquila (16:3), are given as a pair does not demand that they be husband and wife, because in 16:12 two women are greeted as a pair: "Greet Tryphena and Tryphosa, those women who work hard in the Lord." Andronicus and Junias could be addressed as two men, since Tryphena and Tryphosa are addressed as two women.

2. Was Junias an apostle? Possibly so, but this is not certain. Grammatically "of note among the apostles" could mean that the apostles held Andronicus and Junias in high regard. Thus they would not be themselves apostles. But this is unlikely because Paul himself is an apostle and would probably not refer to them in the third person. On the other hand, since Andronicus and Junias were Christians before Paul was, it may be that their longstanding ministry (reaching back before Paul's) is precisely what Paul might have in mind when he says "of note among the apostles." They may well have been known among the apostles before Paul was even converted. Here again we cannot be certain.

3. Did Junias have a very authoritative position in the early church? Probably not. The word *apostle* is used for servants of Christ at different levels of author-

ity in the New Testament. Revelation 21:14 refers to "the twelve apostles of the Lamb" (cf. Matthew 19:28; Acts 1:15-26). The twelve had a unique role in bearing witness to the resurrection of Jesus. Paul counted himself among the privileged group by insisting on having seen and been called by the risen Christ (Galatians 1:1, 12; 1 Corinthians 9:1-2). Very closely related with this unique inner ring were the missionary partners of Paul, Barnabas (Acts 14:14) and Silvanus and Timothy (1 Thessalonians 2:6), as well as James, the Lord's brother (Galatians 1:19) and perhaps others (1 Corinthians 15:7).

Finally, the word *apostle* is used in a broad sense as "messenger," for example, of Epaphroditus in Philippians 2:25, and of several "messengers of the churches" in 2 Corinthians 8:23. Therefore, if Andronicus and Junias were apostles, they were probably among the third group serving in some kind of itinerant ministry. If Junias is a woman, this would seem to put her in the same category with Priscilla, who with her husband seemed to do at least a little travelling with the Apostle Paul (Acts 18:18). The ministry would be significant but not necessarily in the category of an authoritative governor of the churches like Paul (2 Corinthians 10:8; 13:10).

39. Paul seems to base the primary responsibility of man to lead and teach on the fact that he was created first, before woman (1 Timothy 2:13). How is this a valid argument when the animals were created before man, but don't have primary responsibility for leading him?

The contextual basis for this argument in the book of Genesis is the assumption throughout the book that the "firstborn" in a human family has the special right and responsibility of leadership in the family. When the Hebrews gave a special responsibility to the "firstborn," it never entered their minds that this responsibility would be nullified if the father happened to own cattle before he had sons. In other words, when Moses wrote this, he knew that the first readers would not lump animals and humans together as equal candidates for the responsibilities of the "firstborn." We shouldn't either.

Once this concern with the priority of animals is out of the way, the question that evangelical feminists must come to terms with is why God should choose to create man and woman sequentially. It won't do just to say, "Sequence doesn't *have* to mean leadership priority." The question is: "What *does* this sequence mean?" Why didn't God create them simultaneously out of the same dust? In the context of all the textual pointers assembled by Ray Ortlund Jr. in his chapter on Genesis 1-3, we think the most natural implication of God's decision to bring Adam onto the scene ahead of Eve is that he is called to bear the responsibility of headship. That fact is validated by the New Testament when Paul uses the fact that "Adam was formed first, then Eve" (1 Timothy 2:13) to draw a conclusion about male leadership in the church.

40. Isn't it true that the reason Paul did not permit women to teach was that women were not well-educated in the first century? But that reason does not apply today. In fact, since women are as well-educated as men today, shouldn't we allow both women and men to be pastors?

This objection does not match the data in the Biblical text, for at least three reasons: (1) Paul does not give lack of education as a reason for saying that women cannot "teach or have authority over a man" (1 Timothy 2:12), but rather points back to creation (1 Timothy 2:13-14). It is precarious to build an argument on a reason Paul did *not* give, instead of the reason he did give.

(2) Formal training in Scripture was not required for church leadership in the New Testament church—even several of the apostles did not have formal Biblical training (Acts 4:13), while the skills of basic literacy and therefore the ability to read and study Scripture were available to men and women alike (note Acts 18:26; Romans 16:1; 1 Timothy 2:11; Titus 2:3-4). The papyri show "widespread literacy" among Greak-speaking women in Egypt, and, in Roman society, "many women were educated and witty" (*Oxford Classical Dictionary*, ed. N. Hammond and H. Scullard [second edition; Oxford: Clarendon Press, 1970], p. 1139).

(3) If any woman in the New Testament church was well-educated, it would have been Priscilla, yet Paul was writing 1 Timothy 2:12 to Ephesus (1Timothy 1:3), the home church of Priscilla and Aquila. Beginnning in 50 A.D., Paul had stayed at the home of Priscilla and Aquila in Corinth for eighteen months (Acts 18:2, 11), then they had gone with Paul to Ephesus in 51 A.D. (Acts 18:18-19, 21). Even by that time Priscilla knew Scripture well enough to help instruct Apollos (Acts 18:26). Then she had probably learned from Paul himself for another three years, while he stayed at Ephesus teaching "the whole counsel of God" (Acts 20:27, RSV; cf. v. 31; also 1 Corinthians 16:19), and no doubt many other women in Ephesus followed her example and also learned from Paul. Aquila and Priscilla had gone to Rome sometime later (Romans 16:3), about 58 A.D., but apparently had returned, for they were in Ephesus again at the end of Paul's life (2 Timothy 4:19), about 67 A.D. Therefore it is likely that they were back in Ephesus in 65 A.D., about the time Paul wrote 1 Timothy (persecution of Christians began in Rome in 64 A.D.). Yet not even well-educated Priscilla, nor any other well-educated women in Ephesus, were allowed to teach men in the public assembly of the church: writing to Ephesus, Paul said, "I do not permit a woman to teach or to have authority over a man" (1 Timothy 2:12). The reason was not lack of education, but creation order.

41. Why do you bring up homosexuality when discussing male and female role distinctions in the home and the church (as in question 1)? Most evangelical feminists are just as opposed as you are to the practice of homosexuality.

We bring up homosexuality because we believe that the feminist minimization of sexual role differentiation contributes to the confusion of sexual identity that, especially in second and third generations, gives rise to more homosexuality in society.

Some evangelicals who once disapproved of homosexuality have been carried by their feminist arguments into approving of faithful homosexual alliances. For example, Gerald Sheppard, a professor of Old Testament Literature at Emmanuel College in the University of Toronto, was nurtured in a conservative evangelical tradition and attended an evangelical seminary. In recent years he has argued for the ordination of women to the pastorate. He has also moved on to say, "On a much more controversial matter, the presence of gay and lesbian Christians and ministers in our churches is for me a similar issue. . . . I believe that the Gospel—as Evangelicals Concerned recognizes—should lead us at least to an affirmation of gay and lesbian partnerships ruled by a Biblical ethic analogous to that offered for heterosexual relationships."[20]

Another example is Karen J. Torjesen, who argues that removing hierarchy in sexual relations will probably mean that the primacy of heterosexual marriage will have to go:

> It would appear that, in Paul, issues of sexuality are theologically related to hierarchy, and therefore the issues of Biblical feminism and lesbianism are irrefutably intertwined. We need to grapple with the possibility that our conflicts over the appropriate use of human sexuality may rather be conflicts rooted in a need to legitimate the traditional social structure which assigns men and women specific and unequal positions. Could it be that the continued affirmation of the primacy of heterosexual marriage is possibly also the affirmation of the necessity for the sexes to remain in a hierarchically structured relationship? Is the threat to the "sanctity of marriage" really a threat to hierarchy? Is that what makes same-sex relations so threatening, so frightening?[21]

The Evangelical Women's Caucus was split in 1986 over whether there should be "recognition of the presence of the lesbian minority in EWCI."[22] We are glad that many evangelical women distanced themselves from the endorsement of lesbianism. But what is significant is how many evangelical feminists considered the endorsement "a step of maturity within the organization" (e.g., Nancy Hardesty and Virginia Mollenkott). In other words, they view the movement away from role distinctions grounded in the natural created order as leading inevitably to the overthrow of normative heterosexuality. It seems to us that the evangelical feminists who do not embrace homosexuality will be increasingly hard put to escape this logic.

Paul Jewett, too, seems to illustrate a move from Biblical feminism toward endorsing certain expressions of homosexuality. In his defense of equal roles for men and women in *Man as Male and Female* in 1975, he said that he was uncertain "what it means to be a man in distinction to a woman or a woman in distinction to a man."[23] That seemed to us to bode ill for preserving the primacy of heterosexuality. In 1983, he reviewed the historical defense of homosexuality by John Boswell, who argued that Paul's meaning in Romans 1:26-27 was that the only thing condemned was homosexual behavior by heterosexuals, not by homosexuals who acted according to their "nature." Jewett rejected this interpretation with the words, "For [Paul] the 'nature' against which a homosexual acts is not simply his individual nature, but the generic human nature in which he shares as an individual."[24]

This was gratifying, but it seemed strange again to us that he would say homosexual behavior is a sin against "generic *human* nature" rather than *masculine* or *feminine* nature. Then, in 1985, Jewett seemed to give away the Biblical case for heterosexuality in a review of Robin Scroggs' book, *The New Testament and Homosexuality*. Scroggs argues that the passages that relate to homosexual behavior in the New Testament "are irrelevant and provide no help in the heated debate today" because they do not refer to homosexual "inversion," which is a natural orientation, but to homosexual "perversion."[25] Jewett says, "If this is the meaning of the original sources—and the scholarship is competent, the argument is careful and, therefore, the conclusion is rather convincing—then what the New Testament is against is something significantly different from a homosexual orientation which some people have from their earliest days."[26]

Not only have we seen evangelical feminists carried by the logic of their position toward endorsing homosexuality, but we also see the clinical evidence that there is no such thing as a "homosexual child." George Rekers, Professor in the Department of Neuropsychiatry and Behavioral Sciences at the Medical School of the University of South Carolina, has argued this in many technical journals and some popular works. (For example, *Shaping Your Child's Sexual Identity* [Grand Rapids: Baker Book House, 1982]; *The Christian in an Age of Sexual Eclipse* [Wheaton: Tyndale House, 1981]. See also Chapter 17.) What Rekers means is that there are dynamics in the home that direct the sexual preferences of the child. Especially crucial is a father's firm and loving affirmation of a son's masculinity or a daughter's femininity.[27] But, we ask, how can this kind of affirmation be cultivated in an atmosphere where role differences between masculinity and femininity are constantly denied or minimized? If the only significant role differentiation is based on competency and has no root in nature, what will parents do to shape the sexual identity of their tiny children? If they say that they will do nothing, common sense and many psychological studies tell us that the children will be confused about who they are and will therefore be far more likely to develop a homosexual orientation.

To us it is increasingly and painfully clear that Biblical feminism is an unwitting partner in unravelling the fabric of complementary manhood and womanhood that provides the foundation not only for Biblical marriage and Biblical church order, but also for heterosexuality itself.

42. *How do you know that your interpretation of Scripture is not more influenced by your background and culture than by what the authors of Scripture actually intended?*

We are keenly aware of our fallibility. We feel the forces of culture, tradition, and personal inclination, as well as the deceitful darts of the devil. We have our personal predispositions, and have no doubt been influenced by all the genetic and environmental constraints of our past and present. The history of exegesis does not encourage us that we will have the final word on this issue, and we hope we are not above correction. But we take heart that some measure of freedom from falsehood is possible, because the Bible encourages us not to be conformed to this age but to be transformed by the renewing of our minds (Romans 12:1-2).

Whether feminists are more influenced by the immense cultural pressure of contemporary egalitarian assumptions, or we are more influenced by centuries of patriarchalism and by our own masculine drives is hard to say. It does little good for us to impugn each other on the basis of these partially subconscious influences. It is clear from the literature that we all have our suspicions.

Nonetheless, our confidence in the convictions we hold is based on five facts: 1) We regularly search our motives and seek to empty ourselves of all that would tarnish true perception of reality. 2) We pray that God would give us humility, teachability, wisdom, insight, fairness, and honesty. 3) We make every effort to submit our minds to the unbending and unchanging grammatical and historical reality of the Biblical texts in Greek and Hebrew, using the best methods of study available to get as close as possible to the intentions of the Biblical writers. 4) We test our conclusions by the history of exegesis to reveal any chronological snobbery or cultural myopia. 5) We test our conclusions in the real world of contemporary ministry and look for resonance from mature and godly people. In humble confidence that we are handling the Scriptures with care, we lay our vision now before the public for all to see and debate in public forum.

43. *Why is it acceptable to sing hymns written by women and recommend books written by women but not to permit them to say the same things audibly?*

We do *not* say that a woman cannot say the same things audibly. When Paul says, ". . . be filled with the Spirit. Speak to one another with psalms, hymns and spiritual songs," (Ephesians 5:18-19), we imagine women in the congregation reciting or singing for the church what God had given them (perhaps, in some cases, as a kind of "prophecy" mentioned in 1 Corinthians 11:5). Moreover, we rejoice in the inevitable fact that the men as well as the women will learn and be built up and encouraged by this poetic ministry.

Nor would we say that what a woman writes in books and articles cannot be spoken audibly. The issue for us is whether she should function as part of the primary teaching leadership (=eldership) in a fellowship of women and men. We have not, of course, ruled out either small or worldwide ministries of teaching other women. Neither have we ruled out occasional lectureships and periodic addresses (as distinct from recognized Bible teaching in the church) in which women address men as well as women, for example, at the Urbana Missions Conference or any number of local and national conferences and convocations.

We use the qualifiers *occasional* and *periodic* because the regularity of teaching one group of people is part of what constitutes the difference between *official* teaching leadership, which is withheld from women in 1 Timothy 2:12, and the *unofficial* guidance given by Priscilla and Aquila in Acts 18:26. We recognize that these lectures and addresses *could* be delivered in a spirit and demeanor that would assault the principle of male leadership. But it is not necessary that they do so. This is most obvious when the woman publicly affirms that principle with intelligence and gladness. We also recognize the ambiguities involved in making these distinctions between the kinds of public speaking that are appropriate and inappropriate. Our expectation is not that we will all arrive at exactly the same sense of where to draw these lines, but that we might come to affirm together the underlying principles. Obedient, contemporary application of ethical teachings (e.g., the teachings of Jesus on poverty and wealth, anger and forgiveness, justice and non-retaliation) has always been laden with difficult choices.

44. *Isn't giving women access to all offices and roles a simple matter of justice that even our society recognizes?*

We are aware that increasingly the question is being posed in terms of justice. For example, Nicholas Wolterstorff says, "The question that women in the church are raising is a question of justice. . . . Women are not asking for handouts of charity from us men. They are asking that in the church—in the church of all places—they receive their due. They are asking why gender is relevant for assigning tasks and roles and offices and responsibilities and opportunities in the church."[28]

Clearly, we think gender *is* relevant for determining the justice of roles and responsibilities. Perhaps the best way to show *why* is to cite an article from the *Minneapolis Star-Tribune* from March 7, 1989 (p. 11A), entitled, "Gay Adults Should Not be Denied the Benefits of Marriage." The author, Thomas B. Stoddard, told the story of two lesbians, Karen Thompson and Sharon Kowalski, of Minnesota. "Thompson and Kowalski are spouses in every respect," he writes, "except the legal." (Every jurisdiction in the United States refuses to permit two individuals of the same sex to marry.) "They exchanged vows and rings; they lived together until Nov. 13, 1983—when Kowalski was severely injured when her car was struck by a drunk driver. She lost the capacity to walk or to speak more than several words at a time, and needs constant care. Thompson sought a court ruling granting her guardianship over her partner, but Kowalski's parents opposed the petition and obtained sole guardianship. They moved Kowalski to a nursing home 300 miles away from Thompson and forbade all visits."

Stoddard uses this story to illustrate the painful effects of the "monstrous *injustice*" of "depriving millions of gay American adults the marriages of their choice." His argument is that gay marriages "create families and promote social stability. In an increasingly loveless world, those who wish to commit themselves to a relationship founded upon devotion should be encouraged, not scorned. Government has no legitimate interest in how that love is expressed."

This raises a very fundamental question: How does natural existence relate to moral duty? Or: What moral constraints does our birth as male or female put upon us? Does God intend that our maleness confront us with any moral demands that are different from the moral demands with which God confronts a woman by virtue of her femaleness?

The answer is not simple. On the one hand we would cry, No! The Ten Commandments apply equally to man and woman with no distinctions. But on the other hand, most of us would also cry, Yes! It is a sin for a man to marry a man. But it is not a sin for a woman to marry a man (Romans 1:26-27). If this is so, we *cannot* say that what we are by *nature* (gender) is unimportant in determining our moral duty in relation to other people.

When a man stands before a woman, the moral duty that confronts him is not identical with his duty when he stands before a man. God has ordained that the natural and moral world intersect, among other places, at the point of our sexuality.

Until the recent emergence of gay pride, scarcely anyone would have accused God of discriminating against woman by giving only to men the right to marry women. Historically, it did not seem unjust that *solely* on the basis of gender God would exclude half the human race as lawful spouses for women. It seemed "fitting" and "natural" and "right" ("just") that a large array of marital feelings and actions should be denied to women and men in their relations to half the human race.

The reason there was no worldwide revolt against this enormous limitation of our freedom was probably that it squared with what most of us felt was appropriate and desirable anyway. In His mercy God has not allowed the inner voice of nature to be so distorted as to leave the world with no sense of moral fitness in this affair.

It may be that evangelical feminists would say that gender *is* relevant in defining justice in regard to *marriage* because nature teaches by the *anatomy* and *physiology* of man and woman what is just and right. But we ask, Is that really the only basis in nature for marriage? Are we left only with anatomical differences as the ground of heterosexual marriage? One of the theses of this book is that the natural fitness of man and woman for each other in marriage is rooted in something more than anatomy. There is a profound female or male personhood portrayed in our differing bodies. As Emil Brunner put it:

> Our sexuality penetrates to the deepest metaphysical ground of our personality. As a result, the physical differences between the man and the woman are a parable of psychical and spiritual differences of a more ultimate nature.[29]

Or as Otto Piper said, "Though [the difference between the sexes] has a sexual basis, its actuality covers all aspects of personal life."[30]

Perhaps, if evangelical feminists, who do not endorse the justice of homosexual marriages, would agree that the basis of their position is not mere anatomy but also the deeper differences of manhood and womanhood, then they could at least understand why we are hesitant to jettison such deeper differences when thinking through the nature of justice in other relational issues besides who may marry whom. The point of our book is that Scripture and nature teach that personal manhood and womanhood are indeed relevant in deciding not only whom to marry but also who gives primary leadership in the relationship.

45. Isn't it true that God is called our "helper" numerous times in the Bible with the same word used to describe Eve when she was called a "helper" suitable for man? Doesn't that rule out any notion of a uniquely submissive role for her, or even make her more authoritative than the man?

It is true that God is often called our "helper," but the word itself does not imply anything about rank or authority. The context must decide whether Eve is to "help" as a strong person who aids a weaker one, or as one who assists a loving leader. The context makes it very unlikely that *helper* should be read on the analogy of God's help, because in Genesis 2:19-20 Adam is caused to seek his "helper" first among the animals. But the animals will not do, because they are not "fit for him." So God makes woman "from man." Now there is a being who is "fit for him," sharing his human nature, equal to him in Godlike personhood. She is infinitely different from an animal, and God highlights her value to man by showing how no animal can fill her role. Yet in passing through "helpful" animals to woman, God teaches us that the woman is a man's "helper" in the sense of a loyal and suitable assistant in the life of the garden. The question seems to assume that because a word (like *helper*) has certain connotations ("Godlikeness")in some places it must have them in every place. This would be like saying that because God is described as one who "works" for us, therefore no human who "works" is responsible to his boss, since the word couldn't have that meaning when used of God.

46. Literally, 1 Corinthians 7:3-4 says, "Let the husband render to the wife the debt, likewise also the wife to the husband. The wife does not have authority over her own body, but the husband (does); and likewise also the husband does not have authority over his own body but the wife (does). Do not deprive each other except perhaps by agreement for a season that you might give time to prayer. . . ." Doesn't this show that unilateral authority from the husband is wrong?

Yes. But let's broaden our answer to get the most from this text and guard it from misuse.

This text could be terribly misused by unloving men who take it as a license for thoughtless sexual demands, or even lewd and humiliating erotic activity. One can imagine a man's sarcastic jab: "The Bible says that you do not have authority over your body, but I do. And it says, you *owe* me what I want." The reason we say this would be a *misuse* is because the text also gives to the wife the authority to say, "The Bible says that you do not have authority over your body, but I do, and I tell you that I do not want you to use your body to do that to me" (v. 4b). Another reason we know this would be a misuse is that Paul says decisions in this sensitive area should be made "by agreement" (v. 5).

This text is not a license for sexual exploitation. It is an application to the sexual life of the command, "Honor one another above yourselves" (Romans 12:10). Or: "In humility consider others better than yourselves" (Philippians 2:3). Or: "[D]o not use your freedom to indulge the sinful nature; rather, serve one another in love" (Galatians 5:13). The focus is not on what we have a right to take, but on the debt we have to pay. Paul does not say, "Take what you want." He says, "Do not deprive each other." In other words, when it lies within your power to meet your spouse's needs, do it.

There is a wonderful mutuality and reciprocity running through this text from verse 2 to verse 5. Neither husband nor wife is given more rights over the body of the other. And when some suspension of sexual activity is contemplated, Paul repudiates unilateral decision making by the wife or the husband. "Do not deprive each other except *by mutual consent* and for a time" (v. 5).

What are the implications of this text for the leadership of the husband? Do the call for mutual yielding to sexual need and the renunciation of unilateral planning nullify the husband's responsibility for general leadership in the marriage? We don't think so. But this text definitely shapes that leadership and gives added Biblical guidance for how to work it out. It makes clear that his leadership will not involve selfish, unilateral choices. He will always strive for the ideal of agreement. He will take into account the truth that her sexual needs and desires carry the same weight as his own in developing the pattern of their intimacy.

This text makes it crystal clear that leadership is not synonymous with having to get one's way. This text is one of the main reasons we prefer to use the term *leadership* for the man's special responsibility rather than *authority*. (See question 36.) Texts like this transform the concept of authority so deeply as to make the word, with its authoritarian connotations, easily misunderstood. The difference between us and the evangelical feminists is that they think the concept disappears into mutuality, while we think the concept is shaped by mutuality.

47. *If you believe that role distinctions for men and women in the home and the church are rooted in God's created order, why are you not as insistent about applying the rules everywhere in secular life as you are in the home and the church?*

As we move out from the church and the home we move further from what is fairly clear and explicit to what is more ambiguous and inferential. Therefore our emphasis moves more and more away from specific role recommendations (like the ones made in Scripture), and instead focuses on the realization of male and female personhood through the more subjective dimensions of relationship like demeanor, bearing, attitudes, courtesies, initiatives, and numerous spoken and unspoken expectations.

We believe the Bible makes clear that men should take primary responsibility for leadership in the home and that, in the church, the primary teaching and governing leadership should be given by spiritual men. We take this to be a Biblical expression of the goodness and the wisdom of God concerning the nature of leadership in these roles and the nature of manhood and womanhood. That is, rather than leaving to us to judge for ourselves whether mature manhood and womanhood would be preserved and enhanced through the primary leadership of men or women in these spheres, God was explicit about what would be good for us. However, when it comes to all the thousands of occupations and professions, with their endlessly varied structures of management, God has chosen not to be specific about which roles men and women should fill. Therefore we are not as sure in this wider sphere which roles can be carried out by men or women in ways that honor the unique worth of male and female personhood. For this reason we focus (within some limits) on how these roles are carried out rather than which ones are appropriate. (See Chapter 1, pp. 44-45, 50-52.)

48. How can a Christian single woman enter into the mystery of Christ and the church if she never experiences marriage?

Elisabeth Elliot has given an answer to this that we prefer to quote rather than try (in vain) to improve:

> The gift of virginity, given to every one to offer back to God for His use, is a priceless and irreplaceable gift. It can be offered in the pure sacrifice of marriage, or it can be offered in the sacrifice of a life's celibacy. Does this sound just too, too high and holy? But think for a moment—because the virgin has never known a man, she is free to concern herself wholly with the Lord's affairs, as Paul said in 1 Corinthians 7, "and her aim in life is to make herself holy, in body and spirit." She keeps her heart as the Bride of Christ in a very special sense, and offers to the Heavenly Bridegroom alone all that she is and has. When she gives herself willingly to Him in love she has no need to justify herself to the world or to Christians who plague her with questions and suggestions. In a way not open to the married woman her daily "living sacrifice" is a powerful and humble witness, radiating love. I believe she may enter into the "mystery" more deeply than the rest of us.[31]

49. Since many leading evangelical scholars disagree on the questions of manhood and womanhood, how can any lay person even hope to come to a clear conviction on these questions?

Two of the concerns that prompted us to form the Council on Biblical Manhood and Womanhood were: 1) "the increasing prevalence and acceptance of hermeneutical oddities devised to reinterpret apparently plain meanings of Biblical texts;" and 2) "the consequent threat to Biblical authority as the clarity of Scripture is jeopardized and the accessibility of its meaning to ordinary people is withdrawn into the restricted realm of technical ingenuity."[32]

Serious students of the Bible must walk a fine line between two dangers. On the one side there is the oversimplification of the process of interpretation that neglects the disciplines of historical and grammatical study. On the other side there is the temptation to pull rank on lay people and emphasize inaccessible data and complicated contextual problems so much that they despair of confident understanding. We realize that there are "some things that are hard to understand [in Paul's letters], which ignorant and unstable people distort, as they do the other Scriptures, to their own destruction" (2 Peter 3:16). This will guard us from overstating the simplicity of Scripture.

But we believe the emphasis should fall on the usefulness of all Scripture. "*All Scripture* is God-breathed and *useful* for teaching, rebuking, correcting and training in righteousness, so that the man of God may be thoroughly equipped for every good work" (2 Timothy 3:16). We do not want to discourage any serious lay person that the usefulness of Scripture is out of his or her reach. We also want to stress that under divine inspiration the Apostle Paul was committed to clarity and forthrightness in his writing: ". . . we have renounced secret and shameful ways; we do not use deception, nor do we distort the word of God. On the contrary, by setting forth the truth plainly we commend ourselves to every man's conscience in the sight of God" (2 Corinthians 4:2).

We would also encourage lay people to view controversies over important issues not only as evidence of our sin and ignorance but also as evidence that truth matters, that it is worth striving for, and that harmful error is not carrying the day unopposed. Paul said to the Corinthians, "I hear that when you come together as a church, there are divisions among you, and to some extent I believe it. No doubt there have to be differences among you to show which of you have God's approval" (1 Corinthians 11:18-19). We are far from doubting the genuine Christian standing of evangelical feminists. This will be made very clear in Chapter 26. The point here is that controversy is necessary where truth matters and serious error is spreading. Lay people should therefore take heart that the battle for truth is being fought. They should realize that many of the plain things they virtually take for granted in their faith today were once hotly disputed and were preserved for them through controversy.

On this issue of manhood and womanhood we encourage lay people to consider the arguments available to them, think for themselves, saturate themselves in Scripture, and pray earnestly for what Paul promised in Philippians 3:15: "[I]f on some point you think differently, that too *God will make clear to you.*" For more guidance in this process we refer you to what is said above in question 42 and to Chapter 26, pp. 418-420, where we discuss the guidance of the Spirit in this matter.

50. If a group of texts is hotly disputed, wouldn't it be a good principle of interpretation not to allow them any significant influence over our view of manhood and womanhood?

No, this would not be a good principle of interpretation. First, because almost every text about precious and important things is disputed in some way and by some Christians. Never in history has there been so much pluralism under the banner of the Bible as there is today. Second, imagine what it would mean if we took no stand on things because they were disputed. It would mean that Satan's aim to mislead us would be made much easier. He would not have to overthrow the truth of Biblical texts; he would only have to create enough confusion that we would put the important ones aside. Third, leaving Satan out for a moment, we are all biased and would very likely use this principle of interpretation to justify neglecting the texts that do not suit our bias while insisting that the ones that suit our bias are crystal clear.

This, it seems to us, is the Achilles heel of the hermeneutical approach adopted by Gretchen Gaebelein Hull in her book *Equal to Serve*. She takes one set of texts to be clear and undisputed, then takes another set to be obscure and disputed, and then says that the obscure ones should not have a crucial say in shaping our understanding of the issue. Specifically, she takes Genesis 1-2, the examples of Deborah, Huldah, Miriam, Abigail, etc., the ministry of Jesus to women, the examples of ministering women in the New Testament, plus texts on the redemptive equality of women (like 2 Corinthians 5:14-21), and infers that they *clearly* teach that male headship, in any distinctive form, is wrong. But all the texts in the New Testament that seem to teach an abiding role distinction for women and men she says are obscure and cannot make their contribution to the shape of our vision of manhood and womanhood. In the following lines she illustrates her method *vis à vis* the love of God and then applies it to the issue at hand:

> Everything I know about God indicates that He is indeed love, so loving that He came Himself to die for me. Therefore I put to one side passages like the Imprecatory Psalms or the Canaanite Wars that I do not understand. But I do *not* throw out the known truth "God is love," simply because some passages about the nature of God puzzle me.
>
> So we should also treat the three "hard passages" about women [1 Corinthians 11:2-16; 14:33b-36; 1 Timothy 2:8-15], which we find in the New Testament and which appear to place specific restrictions on women only. To these we could add Colossians 3:18; Ephesians 5:22-24; and 1 Peter 3:1-6. . . . Therefore we may legitimately put these Scripture portions aside for the very reason that they *remain* "hard passages"—hard exegetically, hard hermeneutically, and hard theologically.[33]

In this way, very crucial texts are silenced by the governing theme of "sex-blind" egalitarianism which is itself built on texts the meanings of which are also disputed. This illustrates the danger of a principle that says, if a text is disputed, don't use it. Our procedure should be rather to continue to read Scripture carefully and prayerfully, seeking a position that dismisses no texts but interprets all the relevant texts of Scripture in a coherent way. And then we are to obey that consistent teaching.

51. Since there is significant disagreement in the church over the issues of men's and women's roles, should we not view this issue as having a very low level of importance in defining denominational, institutional and congregational standards of belief and practice?

We need to realize first that significant disagreement in the church does not mean that the issue at stake is unimportant. The history of doctrinal controversy teaches us that very important matters (as well as less important ones) have been the subject of serious controversy. In fact the length and intensity of a controversy may be evidence of the importance of the issue, not of its unimportance.

If we examine the lists of expected standards for most denominations, institutions, and congregations, we discover that some articles (perhaps most) were included because a controversy swirled around that truth and a stand needed to be taken for the health of the church and the cause of the kingdom of Christ. This means that many precious truths may not be included in our doctrinal and ethical standards at any given point in history because they were simply taken for granted in the absence of controversy. For example, until recently, standards have not generally included explicit statements on homosexual practice or certain kinds of drug abuse.

Today most Christian denominations, institutions, and congregations have long taken for granted the primary responsiblity of a husband to lead his family and the primary responsibility of spiritual men to lead the church. Therefore, these Biblical truths have not received explicit statement in the formal standards. Their absense is *not* a sign of their relative unimportance but (almost the exact opposite) of their deep, pervasive, and long-standing worth in the Christian community.

Thus we have the anomalous situation today that institutional affirmations of faith and practice include things far less important, we believe, than what is at stake in the heart of this issue. For example, we would say that the health and mission of the church are less at stake in the issues of infant and believer's baptism, premillenialism, and the divisions over presbyterian, congregational, or episcopal polity.

Moreover, not to take a stand on this issue in our culture is to take a very decisive stand because of the relentless pressure for change being applied on many sides by feminists. Public advocacy on this issue results in so much criticism that many Christian leaders strive to avoid it. But there is no avoiding it. It is a massive issue that goes to the depths of who we are as persons and therefore touches all of life. Our counsel here is not to set out a specific strategy to preserve God's gift of sexual complementarity. Rather, we simply plead for Christian leaders to awaken to the importance of what is at stake and seek the wisdom from above for how to act for the good of the church and the glory of God.

II

Exegetical and Theological Studies

3

Male-Female Equality and Male Headship

Genesis 1–3

Raymond C. Ortlund, Jr.

Why go all the way back to the first three chapters of the Bible, if our concern is with manhood and womanhood today? Because as Genesis 1-3 go, so goes the whole Biblical debate. One way or the other, all the additional Biblical texts on manhood and womanhood must be interpreted consistently with these chapters. They lay the very foundation of Biblical manhood and womanhood.

My purpose in this essay is to demonstrate from Genesis 1-3 that both *male-female equality* and *male headship*, properly defined, were instituted by God at creation and remain permanent, beneficent aspects of human existence.

Let me define *male-female equality*:

> *Man and woman are equal in the sense that they bear God's image equally.*

Let me also define *male headship*:

> *In the partnership of two spiritually equal human beings, man and woman, the man bears the primary responsibility to lead the partnership in a God-glorifying direction.*

The model of headship is our Lord, the Head of the church, who gave Himself for us.[1] The antithesis to male headship is male domination. By male domination I mean the assertion of the man's will over the woman's will, heedless of her spiritual equality, her rights, and her value. *My essay will be completely misunderstood if the distinction between male headship and male domination is not kept in mind throughout.*

Evangelical feminism argues that God created man and woman as equals in a sense that excludes male headship. Male headship/domination (feminism acknowledges no distinction) was imposed upon Eve as a penalty for her part in the fall. It follows, in this view, that a woman's redemption in Christ releases her from the punishment of male headship.[2]

What, then, did God intend for our manhood and womanhood at the creation? And what did God decree as our punishment at the fall? The first two chapters of Genesis answer the first question and the third chapter answers the second.

What God Intended at Creation

Genesis 1:26-28

> [26]Then God said, "Let us make man in our image, after our likeness; and let them have dominion over the fish of the sea, and over the birds of the air, and over the cattle, and over all the earth, and over every creeping thing that creeps upon the earth."
>
> [27]So God created man in his own image,
> in the image of God he created him;
> male and female he created them.
>
> [28]And God blessed them, and God said to them, "Be fruitful and multiply, and fill the earth and subdue it; and have dominion over the fish of the sea and over the birds of the air and over every living thing that moves upon the earth." [*RSV*][3]

In verse 26, God announces His intention to make man. This divine fanfare, unparalleled in the creation account, sets the making of man apart as a special event. God seems almost to jeopardize His unique glory by sharing His image and rule with a mere creature. Nevertheless, such a one God now intends to create. Verse 26, then, has the force of riveting our attention on God's next creative work, the zenith of His genius and benevolence.

Verse 26 teaches the glory of man in three ways. First, God says, "Let us make man. . . ." In verse 24 God had said, "Let the earth bring forth living creatures. . . ." By the sheer power of His spoken will, God had caused the living creatures to emerge from the earth "by remote control as it were."[4] In the creation of man, however, God Himself acted directly and personally.

Second, man was created to bear the image or likeness of God. Taking in the whole of Scripture, I think it probable that the image of God in man is the soul's personal reflection of God's righteous character. To image God is to mirror His holiness.[5] Other interpreters construe the image of God in a more general sense, including human rationality, conscience, creativity, relationships, and everything we are *as man*.[6] But however one interprets the *imago Dei*, God shared it with man alone. Man is unique, finding his identity upward in God and not downward in the animals.

The third indication of man's greatness in verse 26 is his special calling under God: ". . . and let them have dominion. . . ." Man stands between God above and the animals below as God's ruling representative. Man is the crown of creation.

In verse 27, God fulfills His purpose as declared in verse 26. In describing God's supreme creative act, Moses shifts from prose to poetry:

So God created man in his own image,
in the image of God he created him;
male and female he created them.[7]

Each of these three lines makes a point. Line one asserts the divine creation of man. *We came from God.* Line two overlaps with line one, except that it highlights the divine image in man. *We bear a resemblance to God.* Line three boldly affirms the dual sexuality of man. *We are male and female.* Nowhere else in Genesis 1 is sexuality referred to;[8] but human sexuality, superior to animal sexuality, merits the simple dignity given it here. Further, Moses doubtless intends to imply the equality of the sexes, for both male and female display the glory of God's image with equal brilliance: ". . . in *the image of God* he created him; *male and female* he created them." This is consistent with God's intention, stated in verse 26, that both sexes should rule: ". . . and let *them* rule. . . ."

Finally, in verse 28, God pronounces His benediction on man. In verse 22, God spoke His blessing out over the mass of the lower creatures. But here in verse 28 we read, "God blessed them and said *to them*. . . ." With man alone, male and female alike without distinction, God shares an I-thou relationship. In His benediction the Creator also authorizes male and female together to carry out their mission to rule the lower creation.

To sum up: Man was created as royalty in God's world, male and female alike bearing the divine glory equally.

Most evangelical feminists would heartily agree with this interpretation of the text. Genesis 2 and 3 are more controversial. But I must challenge two points of feminist interpretation before moving on to chapter two.

First, in commenting on verse 26, Gilbert Bilezikian notes that God refers to "them," both male and female, as "man." He writes:

> . . . the designation "man" is a generic term for "human beings" and . . . encompasses both male and female. This fact is made especially clear in Genesis 5:2 where the word *man* designates both male and female: "He created them male and female; at the time they were created, he blessed them and called them 'man.'" (NIV)[9]

This is a striking fact, indeed. It demands explanation. After all, if any of us modern people were to create a world, placing at its apex our highest creature in the dual modality of man and woman, would we use the name of only one sex as a generic term for both? I expect not. Our modern prejudices would detect a whiff of "discrimination" a mile away. But God cuts right across the grain of our peculiar sensitivities when He names the human race, both man and woman, "man."[10]

Why would God do such a thing? Why would Moses carefully record the fact? Surely God was wise and purposeful in this decision, as He is in every other. Surely His referring to the race as "man" tells us something about ourselves. What aspect of reality, then, might God have been pointing to by this means? Bilezikian continues:

> Thus, when God declares, "Let us make man in our image . . " the term *man* refers to both male and female. Both man and woman are God's image-bear-

ers. There is no basis in Genesis 1 for confining the image of God to males alone.[11]

Who, I wonder, is teaching that men only bear God's image? No contributor to this volume will be found saying that. But not only is Bilezikian's argument diverted by a non-issue, it also fails to explain what the text of verse 26 does say.

How may we understand the logic of God's decision to describe the human race as "man"? Let me suggest that it makes sense against the backdrop of male headship. Moses does not explicitly teach male headship in chapter 1; but, for that matter, neither does he explicitly teach male-female equality. We see neither the words "male-female equality" nor "male headship" here or anywhere in Genesis 1-3. What Moses does provide is a series of more or less obvious hints as to his doctrine of manhood and womanhood. The burden of Genesis 1:26-28 is male-female equality. That seems obvious—wonderfully obvious! But God's naming of the race "man" whispers male headship, which Moses will bring forward boldly in chapter two.

God did *not* name the human race "woman." If "woman" had been the more appropriate and illuminating designation, no doubt God would have used it. He does not even devise a neutral term like "persons." He called us "man," which anticipates the male headship brought out clearly in chapter two, just as "male and female" in verse 27 foreshadows marriage in chapter two. Male headship may be personally repugnant to feminists, but it does have the virtue of explaining the sacred text.

Some contend that, in principle, one ought not to refer to the human race as "man." Such terminology is unfair to half the population, they insist. I am not arguing that one must always use "man" in social and theological discourse to avoid misrepresenting the truth. I am arguing, however, that, in light of Genesis 1:26-27 and 5:1-2, one may not call this linguistic practice unjust or insensitive without impugning the wisdom and goodness of God.

My second challenge is directed at the concept of the image of God found in feminist interpretation. Aida Bensançon Spencer writes, "Male and female are together needed to reflect God's image."[12] That is, man and woman together as collective man, rather than the man and the woman separately as individuals, reflect the image of God. Leaving us in no doubt about her meaning, Spencer makes this claim:

> There is no possibility, according to [Genesis 1:26-27], that Adam, the male, could by himself reflect the nature of God. Neither is it possible for Adam, the female, by herself to reflect God's nature. Male and female are needed to reflect God's nature.[13]

There is *no possibility*, in light of Genesis 1:26-27, that either the man or the woman alone could display the image of God? What, then, of Genesis 5:1 and 3?

> When God created man, he made him in the likeness of God. . . . When Adam had lived 130 years, he had a son in his own likeness, in his own image; and he named him Seth.[14]

God created man in His image. Later, Adam had a son in *his* image.

Implication? Adam, who was in God's image, passed the divine image (albeit flawed by sin) on to his son Seth. The divine image resided in the *individuals* Adam and Seth. So Spencer's insistence on a collective divine image in man-plus-woman is unwarranted. Genesis 1:26-27 can and should be construed to say that each individual created by God bore His image, male and female alike.

For this reason, Spencer's practical application of the *imago Dei* to church leadership lacks force. She writes:

> Females as well as males are needed in positions of authority in the church to help people better to comprehend God's nature. God's image needs male and female to reflect God more fully.[15]

Even if it were true that the *imago Dei* would necessarily be incomplete in a single individual, it would still not follow that both men and women are needed *in positions of church authority* "to help people better to comprehend God's nature."

Genesis 2:18-25

There is a paradox[16] in the creation account. While Genesis 1 teaches the equality of the sexes as God's image-bearers and vice-rulers on the earth, Genesis 2 adds another, complex dimension to Biblical manhood and womanhood. The paradox is this: God created male and female in His image equally, but He also made the male the head and the female the helper.

For clarity's sake, let me restate my definition of male headship (not male domination):

> *In the partnership of two spiritually equal human beings, man and woman, the man bears the primary responsibility to lead the partnership in a God-glorifying direction.*

That is, God calls the man, with the counsel and help of the woman, to see that the male-female partnership serves the purposes of God, not the sinful urges of either member of the partnership.

What will now emerge clearly from Genesis 2 is that male-female equality does not constitute an undifferentiated sameness. Male and female are equal as God's image-bearers. They are spiritually equal, which is quite sufficient a basis for mutual respect between the sexes. But the very fact that God created human beings in the dual modality of male and female cautions us against an unqualified equation of the two sexes. This profound and beautiful distinction, which some belittle as "a matter of mere anatomy," is not a biological triviality or accident. It is God who wants men to be men and women to be women; and He can teach us the meaning of each, if we want to be taught. We ourselves can feel intuitively the importance of distinct sexual identity when we see, for example, a transvestite. A man trying to be a woman repulses us, and rightly so. We know that this is perverse. Sexual confusion is a significant, not a slight, personal problem, because our distinct sexual identity defines who we are and why we are here and how God calls us to serve Him.

God has no intention of blurring sexual distinctness in the interests of equality *in an unqualified sense*. In fact, there are many areas of life in which God has no intention of levelling out the distinctions between us. Consider the obvious: God does not value intellectual or aesthetic equality among people. He does not value equality in finances, talents, and opportunity. It is God who deliberately ordains inequalities in many aspects of our lives. When I came from the womb, I had only so much potential for physical, intellectual, and aesthetic development. Some are born with less than I was, others with more. Because God is ultimately the One who shapes our lives, I have to conclude that God is not interested in unlimited equality among us. And because God is also wise, I further conclude that unlimited equality must be a false ideal. But the Bible does teach the equal personhood and value and dignity of all the human race—men, women, and children—and that must be the only equality that matters to God. One measure of our wisdom as God's image-bearers is whether we share this perspective with God. One measure of our reconciliation with God is whether His sovereign decrees draw from us a response of worship or resentment.

How, then, does Genesis 2 teach the paradoxical truths of male-female equality and male headship? The crucial verses are 18-25, but we should first establish the context.

God created the man first (2:7) and stationed him in the Garden of Eden to develop it and to guard it (2:15). God laid a dual command on the man. First, the man was commanded to partake freely and joyfully of the trees God had provided (2:16). Second, the man was commanded not to eat of one tree, lest he die (2:17). Here we see both God's abundant generosity and man's moral responsibility to live within the large, but not unrestricted, circle of his God-ordained existence. For the man to step outside that circle, to attempt an autonomous existence, freed from God, would be his ruin.

That is the scene as we come to verse 18, which hits us from the blind side:

> The LORD God said, "It is not good for the man to be alone. I will make him a helper suitable for him."

Amid all this stunning perfection in the Garden of Eden, God said, "There is something wrong here. The man ought not to be alone." God put His finger on the one deficiency in Paradise. The man needed "a helper suitable for him."

Surprisingly, however, God did not immediately create this helper. Instead, God paraded the animals before the man for him to name them (2:19-20). Why? Because the man did not yet see the problem of his aloneness. And so God translated the man's objective aloneness into a feeling of personal loneliness by setting him to this task. In serving God, the man encountered his own need.

This is so, because the task of naming the animals entailed more than slapping an arbitrary label on each beast. The task required the man to consider each animal thoughtfully, so that its name was appropriate to its particular nature. Out of this exercise, it began to dawn on the man that there was no creature in the garden that shared *his* nature. He discovered not only his own unique superiority over the beasts, which the privilege of naming them in itself implied; he also discovered his own solitude in the world.[17] We may surmise that an aching longing welled up within the man for the companionship of another creature on his level.

And so God performs the first surgical operation (2:21-22). Imagine the scene: As the last of the beasts plods off with its new name, the man turns away with a trace of perplexity and sorrow in his eyes. God says, "Son, I want you to lie down. Now close your eyes and sleep." The man falls into a deep slumber. The Creator goes to work, opening the man's side, removing a rib, closing the wound, and building the woman. There she stands, perfectly gorgeous and uniquely suited to the man's need. The Lord says to her, "Daughter, I want you to go stand over there. I'll come for you in a moment." She obeys. Then God touches the man and says, "Wake up now, son. I have one last creature for you to name. I'd like to know what you think of this one." And God leads Eve out to Adam, who greets her with rhapsodic relief:

> This is now bone of my bones
> and flesh of my flesh;
> she shall be called woman,
> because she was taken out of man. (2:23)

These are the first recorded human words, and they are poetry. What do they express? The joy of the first man in receiving the gift of the first woman: "This creature alone, Father, out of all the others—this one at last meets my need for a companion. She alone is my equal, my very flesh. I identify with her. I love her. I will call her Woman, for she came out of Man." The man perceives the woman not as his rival but as his partner, not as a threat because of her equality with himself but as the only one capable of fulfilling his longing within.

This primal event explains why we see men and women pairing off today, as Moses teaches in verse 24: "For this reason a man will leave his father and mother and be united to his wife, and they will become one flesh." The Garden of Eden is where it all started—not in the social evolution of mankind but in the original, pre-fall creation by God. At its very heart, marriage is not a human custom, variable according to changing times; it is a divinely created institution, defined for all ages and all cultures in our shared, primeval, perfect existence.

And what does marriage mean? What distinguishes this particular social institution? Moses reasons that marriage is the re-union of what was originally and literally one flesh—only now in a much more satisfying form, we would all agree. This is why "He who loves his wife loves himself. For no man ever hates his own flesh."[18] Becoming "one flesh" as husband and wife is symbolized and sealed by sexual union, it is true. But the "one flesh" relationship entails more than sex. It is the profound fusion of two lives into one, shared life together, by the mutual consent and covenant of marriage. It is the complete and permanent giving over of oneself into a new circle of shared existence with one's partner.

Lastly, verse 25 seals the creation account with a reminder of the perfection in which Adam and Eve[19] first came together: "The man and his wife were both naked, and they felt no shame." They felt no shame because they had nothing to hide. They lived in perfect integrity together.

In the conspicuous phrase, "a helper suitable for him" (2:18, 20),[20] we encounter the paradox of manhood and womanhood. On the one hand, the woman alone, out of all the creatures, was "suitable for him." She alone was Adam's equal. A man may enjoy a form of companionship with a dog, but only on the dog's level. With a wife, a man finds companionship on his own level, for she is his equal.

On the other side of the paradox, the woman is the man's helper. The man was not created to help the woman, but the reverse. Doesn't this striking fact suggest that manhood and womanhood are distinct and non-reversible? Doesn't this make sense if we allow that, while the man and the woman are to love each other as equals, they are not to love each other *in the same way*?[21] The man is to love his wife by accepting the primary responsibility for making their partnership a platform displaying God's glory, and the woman is to love her husband by supporting him in that godly undertaking.

So, was Eve Adam's equal? Yes and no. She was his spiritual equal and, unlike the animals, "suitable for him." But she was not his equal in that she was his "helper." God did not create man and woman in an undifferentiated way, and their mere maleness and femaleness identify their respective roles. A man, just by virtue of his manhood, is called to lead for God. A woman, just by virtue of her womanhood, is called to help for God.

Must the male headship side of the paradox be construed as an insult or threat to women? Not at all, because *Eve was Adam's equal in the only sense in which equality is significant for personal worth*. Woman is just as gifted as man "with all the attributes requisite to attaining wisdom, righteousness and life."[22] In a parallel sense, a church member has as much freedom and opportunity to achieve real significance as does a church elder; but the elder is to lead, and the member is to support. There is no cause for offense.

Why then do some godly people resist this teaching so energetically? One reason is a smothering male domination asserted in the name of male headship. When truth is abused, a rival position (in this case, feminism) that lacks *logically* compelling power can take on *psychologically* compelling power. But male domination is a personal moral failure, not a Biblical doctrine.

If we define ourselves out of a reaction to bad experiences, we will be forever translating our pain in the past into new pain for ourselves and others in the present. We must define ourselves not by personal injury, not by fashionable hysteria, not even by personal variation and diversity, but by the suprapersonal pattern of sexual understanding taught here in Holy Scripture.

The paradox of Genesis 2 is also seen in the fact that the woman was made *from* the man (her equality) and *for* the man (her inequality). God did not make Adam and Eve from the ground at the same time and for one another without distinction. Neither did God make the woman first, and then the man *from* the woman *for* the woman. He could have created them in either of these ways so easily, but He didn't. Why? Because, presumably, that would have obscured the very nature of manhood and womanhood that He intended to make clear.[23]

Another indication of the paradox is that Adam welcomes Eve as his equal ("bone of my bones and flesh of my flesh"), yet he also names her ("she shall be called Woman").[24] God charged the man with naming the creatures and gave him the freedom to exercise his own judgment in each case. In doing so, Adam brought the earthly creation under his dominion. This royal prerogative extended to Adam's naming of his helper.[25] Nevertheless, the name he gives her, "Woman," springs from his instantaneous recognition of her as the counterpart to "Man."[26]

Let us note this carefully. In designating her "Woman" the man interprets her identity in relation to himself. Out of his own intuitive comprehension of who she is, he interprets her as feminine, unlike himself, and yet as his counterpart and equal. Indeed, he sees in her his very own flesh. And he interprets the woman not only for his own understanding of her, but also for her self-understanding. God did not explain to the woman who she was in relation to the man, although He could have done so. He allowed Adam to define the woman, in keeping with Adam's headship. Adam's sovereign act not only arose out of his own sense of headship, it also made his headship clear to Eve. She found her own identity in relation to the man as his equal and helper *by the man's definition*. Both Adam and Eve understood the paradox of their relationship from the start.

Still another signal of the paradox is detected in verse 24. Because the woman alone is the man's very flesh, their re-union in marriage is a "one flesh" relationship. Adam could not have joined himself to a lesser creature without degrading himself. But it is the man who leaves his parents to found a new household with his new wife at his side. His wife does not leave her family to initiate the new household; this is the responsibility of the head.

Genesis 2 supplements Genesis 1 by showing that God's commission that we "have dominion over the earth" (1:26, 28) as male and female works out practically through marriage. And in marriage the man heads the home for God and the wife helps him to fulfill the divine calling.

We ought to be sufficiently agile intellectually and emotionally to accept this paradoxical truth. Christians, of all people, have a reason to live with paradox. After all, God exists as one Godhead in three Persons, equal in glory but unequal in role. Within the Holy Trinity the Father leads, the Son submits to Him, and the Spirit submits to both (the Economic Trinity). But it is also true that the three Persons are fully equal in divinity, power, and glory (the Ontological Trinity). The Son submits, but not because He is God, Jr., an inferior deity. The ranking within the Godhead is a part of the sublime beauty and logic of true deity. And if our Creator exists in this manner, should we be surprised and offended if His creaturely analog on earth exists in paradoxical form?

But what does evangelical feminism have to say about Genesis 2? Spencer adopts a most eccentric view of "a helper suitable for him."[27] She dissects the Hebrew word translated "suitable for him" (*k^{e}negdô*) into its three constituent parts: *k^{e}* + *neged* + *ô*, that is (very roughly), "*as* + *before* + *him*." Spencer then paraphrases the sense as "a helper 'as if in front of him.'" This is not strictly incorrect, but it would be more effectively paraphrased, "a helper corresponding to him." That is, the woman is a helper suitable for the man, on his level, in contrast to the animals. But Spencer goes further in interpreting the *neged* element in the construction: "'Front' or 'visible' seems to suggest superiority or equality."[28] A helper *superior* to Adam? Spencer cites as evidence favoring her view the fact that the noun *nagîd* means "leader," which it does. She reasons as follows:

> The same preposition [*neged*] *when converted into a noun* (*nagîd*) signifies "a leader, ruler, prince or king," an "overseer." Literally it signifies the "one in front."[29]

There is no evidence, however, that *neged* is "converted into a noun" to become *nagîd*.[30] By Spencer's line of reasoning we could argue that the English adjective "front" converts into the noun "frontier," suggesting that the word "front" connotes sparse habitation and primitive living conditions. This is simply invalid reasoning. Moreover, if *neged* means "superior to," then what are we to make of, say, Psalm 119:168? "All my ways are before (*neged*) you." Is the psalmist saying, "All my ways are superior to you, O Lord"? Not only is that an unbiblical notion, the whole burden of Psalm 119 is the excellency and authority of the law over the psalmist. The *neged* element in *k^enegdô* merely conveys the idea of direct proximity or anteposition.[31] The woman, therefore, is a helper corresponding to the man, as his counterpart and equal.

It is the word "helper" that suggests the woman's supportive role. Spencer argues, however, that this description of Eve "does not at all imply inherent subordination."[32] She adduces the fact that God Himself is portrayed in Scripture as our "Helper," which He is. She then interprets this fact: "If being 'one who helps' inherently implies subordination, then, in that case, God would be subordinate to humans!"[33] This reasoning is not really fallacious. The fallacy lies in the implication of what she says, namely, that God cannot be subordinate to human beings. It is entirely possible for God to subordinate Himself, in a certain sense, to human beings. He does so whenever He undertakes to help us. He does not "un-God" Himself in helping us; but He does stoop to our needs, according to His gracious and sovereign will.

Similarly, I subordinate myself to my children when I help them with their homework. I do not empty my mind of my own knowledge; but I do come down to their level to see their questions from their perspective and to point them toward solutions they can understand. Their needs set my agenda. In this sense I subordinate myself to my children whenever I help them with their homework.

So it is with God. When He helps His people, He retains His glorious deity but (amazingly!) steps into the servant role, under us, to lift us up. He is the God who emptied Himself and came down to our level—below us, to the level of slavery—to help us supremely at the Cross. Therefore, the fact that the Old Testament portrays God as our Helper proves only that the helper role is a glorious one, worthy even of the Almighty. This Biblical fact does not prove that the concept of helper excludes subordination. Subordination is entailed in the very nature of a helping role.

I see this fallacy again and again in feminist argumentation. "Subordination = denigration" and "equality = indistinguishability." Whence this insight into reality? Is the Son of God slighted because He came to do the will of the Father? Is the church denigrated by her subordination to her Lord? Are church members less than "fully redeemed" on account of their submission to their pastors and elders? Are children less than "fully human" by virtue of their submission to their parents?[34]

"But," someone will say, "doesn't hierarchy in marriage reduce a woman to the status of a slave?" Not at all. The fact that a line of authority exists from one person to another in both slavery and marriage, and, for that matter, in the Holy Trinity, in the Body of Christ, in the local church, in the parent-child relationship—the fact that a line of authority exists from one person to another in all of these relationships does not reduce them all to the logic of slavery. Feminists seem to be reasoning that, because *some* subordination is degrading, *all* subordination must necessarily be degrading. On the contrary, what Biblical headship requires and what slave-holding forbids is that the head respect the helper as an equally significant person in the image of God.

Why then this arbitrary equation of submission with dehumanization in manhood and womanhood? For what logical reason *must* equality be defined in terms of position and role? This thinking did not spring up out of evangelical soil. It grew up out of worldly soil, and it has been transplanted into evangelical soil and is sustained there artificially by the potent fertilizers of the worldliness and doctrinal confusion widespread in the evangelical movement.

Bilezikian concludes his discussion of Genesis 2 with the following statement:

> Whenever the principle of equal rights is denied and one sex is subjected to another, a natural outcome is the denial of the right of privacy for the subordinated party. Violation and exploitation ensue. The obscenities of rape, prostitution and pornography are the sinful results of male dominance. To strip a woman naked and hold her down under the power of a knife, a fistful of money, or the glare of a camera is the supreme expression of man's rule over woman. Such rulership was not a part of God's creation ideal.[35]

I challenge this intemperate statement at several levels. First, the issue is framed in terms of "equal rights." That sounds noble, but does God really grant husbands and wives equal rights *in an unqualified sense*? Surely God confers upon them equal worth as His image-bearers. But does a wife possess under God all the rights that her husband has *in an unqualified sense*? As the head, the husband bears the primary responsibility to lead their partnership in a God-glorifying direction. Under God, a wife may not compete for that primary responsibility. It is her husband's just because he is the husband, by the wise decree of God. The ideal of "equal rights" in an unqualified sense is not Biblical.

Second, the "natural outcome" of godly male headship is female fulfillment, not a denial of female rights. And anyway, in a one-flesh relationship, who has a "right of privacy"? I am an open book to my wife—not that I always enjoy that, but it is true. After nineteen years of marital intimacy with her in every sense, privacy is more than a moot point; the very idea is inane. If you wish to preserve your right to privacy, don't get married![36]

Third, how is it that in the last twenty years or so, as we have increasingly lost our understanding of male headship and as feminist ideals have been aggressively pursued throughout our society—how is it that, under these conditions, sexual exploitation and confusion and perversity have exploded in incidence? Male headship is not to blame. Male domination and feminism are the two viruses attacking our sexuality today. They vandalize God's creation and multiply human misery. How can anyone who loves God's glory, who feels for people, and who cherishes the gift of our sexuality not be inflamed at the enormities being committed by these two monsters, male domination and feminism?

Finally, Bilezikian asserts that such perversities as rape, prostitution and pornography are "the supreme expression of man's rule over woman." But if we define "man's rule" from Holy Scripture as godly male headship, then the supreme expression of it is the woman's nobility, fulfillment, and joy.

Bilezikian's incautious paragraph simply asserts the feminist perspective without evidence or argumentation. Neither does he show any awareness of the nuances of the position he earlier claimed to be answering—a position, like ours, which advocates male headship without male domination.[37]

What God Decreed at the Fall

How did our fall into sin affect God's original, perfect, and paradoxical ordering of the sexes? What did He decree as our punishment at the fall?

Those who deny the creation of male headship in Genesis 1-2 often argue that, in Genesis 3, God imposed male headship/domination (no distinction is allowed) upon the woman after the fall. As the corollary to this interpretation, they go on to argue that redemption in Christ reverses this decree and reinstates the woman to "full equality" with the man. We have seen, however, that God built male headship (not male domination) into the glorious, pre-fall order of creation. Our purpose here is to summarize the doctrine of manhood and womanhood taught in Genesis 3, especially in verses 16-19, and then to challenge feminist interpretation of this passage.

Genesis 3 is one of *the* crucial chapters of Holy Scripture. If it were suddenly removed from the Bible, the Bible would no longer make sense. Life would no longer make sense. If we all started out in Edenic bliss, why is life so painful now? Genesis 3 explains why. And if something has gone terribly wrong, do we have any hope of restoration? Genesis 3 gives us hope.

Because Paul in 1 Timothy 2:14 cites the woman's deception as warrant for male headship to be translated from the home into the church,[38] we will survey the narrative of that deception on our way to verses 16-19.

In verses 1-5, Satan, masquerading in the guise of the serpent, draws Eve into a reconsideration of her whole life. To paraphrase and amplify his reasoning,

> "Queen Eve," the serpent inquires in astonishment and disbelief, "something is bothering me. Is it really true that God forbade you two to eat of any of these trees? That perplexes me. After all, didn't He pronounce everything 'very good'? And hasn't He put both you and King Adam in charge of it all? Our loving Creator wouldn't impose so severe a limitation on you, would He? I don't understand, Eve. Would you please explain this problem to me?"

Eve hadn't even known there was a "problem." But the Serpent's prejudiced question unsettles her. It knocks her back on her heels. And so the Serpent engages Eve in a reevaluation of her life *on his terms*. She begins to feel that God's command, which Adam had shared with her,[39] has to be defended: "We *are* allowed to eat of these trees, serpent. But there is this one tree here in the center of the Garden—God said, 'Don't eat of it; don't even touch it, lest you die'." God had actually said, "You shall *freely* eat from *any* tree, with only one exception." But Eve's misquote reduces the lavish generosity of God's word to the level of mere, perhaps grudging, permission: "We *may* eat from the trees." Already the Garden doesn't look quite the same to Eve. No longer is the Tree of Life at the center of things (cf. 2:9). She doesn't even mention it. Now, in her perception of reality, the forbidden tree is at the center. Life is taking on a new, ominous feel. Eve also enlarges God's prohibition with her own addition, "you may not touch it." In her mind, the limitation is growing in significance. At the same time, she tones down God's threat of punishment: "you shall *surely* die" becomes the weaker "lest you die."

With Eve's view of the consequences of sin weakened, the Serpent springs on that point: "You will not surely die." Now we see that he hasn't been seeking information at all. He knows exactly what God had said. And then the Serpent pretends to let Eve in on an important secret:

> "Eve, I'm going to do you a favor. I hate to be the one to break this to you, but you deserve to know. God has a motive other than love for this restriction. The truth is that God wants to hold you back, to frustrate your potential. Don't you realize that God Himself has this knowledge of good and evil? He knows what will enrich life and what will ruin life. And He knows that this fruit will give you two that same knowledge, so that you will rise to His level of understanding and control. Eve, it may come as a shock to you, but God is holding out on you. He is not your friend; He is your rival.
>
> "Now, Eve, you have to outwit Him. I know this Garden seems pleasant enough; but, really, it is a gigantic ploy, to keep you in your place, because God feels threatened by what the two of you could become. This tree, Eve, is your only chance to reach your potential. In fact, Eve, if you *don't* eat of this tree, you will surely die!"

It was a lie big enough to reinterpret all of life and attractive enough to redirect Eve's loyalty from God to Self. The lie told her that obedience is a suicidal plunge, that humility is demeaning, and that service is servility. *And so Eve begins to feel the aggravation of an injustice which, in reality, does not exist.*

Having planted the lie in her mind, the serpent now falls silent and allows Eve's new perception of reality to take its own course (3:6). With Moses' enablement, we can imagine what her thoughts might have been:

> "It doesn't *look* deadly, does it? In fact, it makes my mouth water! How could a good God prohibit such a good thing? How could a just God put it right here in front of us and then expect us to deny ourselves its pleasures? It's intriguingly beautiful, too. And with the insight it affords, I can liberate us from dependence upon our Creator. And who knows? If He finds out we've caught on to Him, He'll take this tree away and we'll be stuck in this prison forever! Let's eat it now while we have the chance!"

After his careful, detailed description of Eve's deception, Moses describes the actual act of Adam and Eve's sin very simply, as a matter of fact, without a hint of shock: ". . . she took some and ate it. She also gave some to her husband, who was with her, and he ate it" (3:6b).[40]

Mark well what the text says and what it does not say. The text does not say, ". . . she took some and ate it. Her husband, who was with her, also took some and ate it." What actually happened is full of meaning. Eve usurped Adam's headship and led the way into sin. And Adam, who (it seems) had stood by passively, allowing the deception to progress without decisive intervention—Adam, for his part, abandoned his post as head. Eve was deceived; Adam forsook his responsibility. Both were wrong and together they pulled the human race down into sin and death.

Isn't it striking that we fell upon an occasion of sex role reversal? Are we to repeat this confusion forever? Are we to institutionalize it in evangelicalism in the name of the God who condemned it in the beginning?

But if Adam and Eve fell into sin together, why does Paul blame Adam for our fall in Romans 5:12-21? Why doesn't Paul blame both Adam and Eve? Why does Genesis 3:7 say that it was only after *Adam* joined in the rebellion that the eyes of *both* of them were opened to their condition? Why does God call out to

Adam, "Where are you?" (Genesis 3:9)?[41] Why doesn't God summon both Adam and Eve to account together? Because, as the God-appointed head, Adam bore the primary responsibility to lead their partnership in a God-glorifying direction.

This may explain why Satan addressed Eve, rather than Adam, to begin with. Her calling was to help Adam as second-in-command in world rulership. If the roles had been reversed, if Eve had been created first and then Adam as her helper, the Serpent would doubtless have approached Adam. So Eve was not morally weaker than Adam. But Satan struck at Adam's headship. His words had the effect of inviting Eve to assume primary responsibility at the moment of temptation: "*You* decide, Eve. *You* lead the way. Wouldn't *you* rather be exercising headship?" Just as Satan himself fell through this very kind of reasoning, so he used it to great effect with Eve. Presumably, she really believed she could manage the partnership to both Adam's and her own advantage, if she would only assert herself. Adam, by contrast, defied God with eyes wide open.[42]

When confronted by God, Adam does not actually lie. He just shifts the blame to Eve: "The man said, 'The woman you put here with me—she gave me some fruit from the tree, and I ate it'" (3:12). Why is it that we all feel Adam's face-saving, despicable hypocrisy in his factual, but evasive, reply to God? Because we recognize, if only intuitively, that Adam bears the final responsibility for what happened. Eve, when challenged, can only hang her head and admit, "The serpent deceived me" (3:13).

In 3:14-15, God curses the Serpent, condemning him to humiliation and to ultimate defeat under the victorious offspring of the woman.[43] Our only hope as a fallen race is God's merciful promise to defeat our enemy, which He will accomplish through human instrumentality.

In verse 16 God decrees a just settlement with the woman:

> I will greatly increase your pains in childbearing;
> with pain you will give birth to children.
> Your desire will be for your husband,
> and he will rule over you.

God's decree is two-fold. First, as a mother, the woman will suffer in relation to her children. She will still be able to bear children. This is God's mercy providing the means by which He will carry out His death sentence on the Serpent. But now the woman will suffer in childbirth. This is God's severity for her sin. The new element in her experience, then, is not childbirth but the pain of childbirth.

Second, as a wife, the woman will suffer in relation to her husband. The exact content of her marital suffering could be defined in either of two ways. Either she will suffer conflict with her husband, or she will suffer domination by him.[44] The form and logic of Genesis 4:7b bear a most striking resemblance to our passage:[45]

3:16b: *w*^{e}*'el-'îšēḵ t*^{e}*šûqāṯēḵ' w*^{e}*hû' yimšol-bāḵ*
4:7b: *w*^{e}*'ēlêḵā t*^{e}*šûqāṯô w*^{e}*'attāh timšol-bô*

And 4:7b reads, "[Sin's] desire is for you, but you must master it." To paraphrase and amplify the sense: "Sin has a desire, Cain. It wants to control you. But you must not allow sin to have its way with you. You must rule over it."

How does this parallel statement illuminate the interpretation of 3:16? Most importantly, it clarifies the meaning of the woman's "desire." Just as sin's desire is to have its way with Cain, God gives the woman up to a desire to have her way with her husband. Because she usurped his headship in the temptation, God hands her over to the misery of competition with her rightful head. This is justice, a measure-for-measure response to her sin.[46]

The ambiguous element in the equation is the interpretation of the words translated in the NIV, "and he will rule over you." We could draw one of two conclusions. First, God may be saying, "You will have a desire, Eve. You will want to control your husband. But he must not allow you to have your way with him. He must rule over you."

If this is the sense, then God is requiring the man to act as the head God made him to be, rather than knuckle under to ungodly pressure from his wife. Accordingly, 3:16b should be rendered: "Your desire will be for your husband, but he must rule over you."[47] In this case, we would take "rule" as the exercise of godly headship. This interpretation matches the reasoning in 4:7 more nearly, but another view is possible.

Second, God may be saying, "You will have a desire, Eve. You will want to control your husband. But he will not allow you to have your way with him. He will rule over you." If this is the true sense, then, in giving the woman up to her insubordinate desire, God is penalizing her with domination by her husband. Accordingly, 3:16b should be rendered: "Your desire will be for your husband, and he will rule over you."[48] The word "rule" would now be construed as the exercise of ungodly domination. As the woman competes with the man, the man, for his part, always holds the trump card of male domination to "put her in her place."

But however 3:16 should be interpreted, nothing can change the fact that God created male *headship* as one aspect of our pre-fall perfection. Therefore, while many women today need release from male domination, the liberating alternative is not female rivalry or autonomy but male headship wedded to female help.[49] Christian redemption does not redefine creation; it restores creation, so that wives learn godly submission and husbands learn godly headship.

In 3:17-19, God decrees His judgment upon Adam:

> "Because you listened to your wife and ate from the tree about which I commanded you, 'You must not eat of it,'
>
> "Cursed is the ground because of you;
> through painful toil you will eat of it all the days of your life.
> "It will produce thorns and thistles for you,
> and you will eat the plants of the field.
> "By the sweat of your brow you will eat your food
> until you return to the ground,
> since from it you were taken;
> for dust you are and to dust you will return."

God gives Adam up to the painful and ultimately futile attempt to eke out a living from the cursed ground. Notice four things in the text. First, work is not Adam's punishment, just as childbearing was not Eve's punishment. The new punitive element is his pain in working the ground and his ultimate defeat in it. After a lifetime of survival by the sweat of his brow, the ground from which he was first taken will swallow him up in death.

The second important point here is God's rationale for this punishment. God does not say, "Because you have eaten of the tree which I commanded you, 'You shall not eat of it'. . . ." God does say, "*Because you listened to your wife* and ate from the tree. . . ." Adam sinned at two levels. At one level, he defied the plain and simple command of 2:17. That is obvious. But God goes deeper. At another level, Adam sinned by "listening to his wife."[50] He abandoned his headship. According to God's assessment, this moral failure in Adam led to his ruination.[51]

The third interesting point is the very fact that God addresses Adam with this introductory statement, "Because you have listened. . . ." God does not address Eve in this way, but God does issue a formal indictment to Adam before his sentencing. Why? Because Adam was the head, the finally responsible member of the partnership. His disobedience, not Eve's, was the pivotal factor in the fall. Notice this. God says, "It is because of *you*, Adam, that the ground is cursed" (verse 17). God does not say, "It is because of you both, Adam and Eve," as if they shared equal responsibility in an unqualified sense.

The fourth point here is that God told Adam alone that he would die. But Eve died, too. Why then did God pronounce the death sentence on Adam alone? Because, as the head goes, so goes the member.

By these dreadful, and yet hopeful, oracles of destiny, God shapes for us the existence we all share today. Under these conditions, our pain alerts us to a great truth: This life is not our fulfillment. This life is not meant to be a final experience. Our pain and limitations point us to God, to the eternal, to the transcendent, where our true fulfillment lies.

Adam understood this truth, I think. Instead of turning away from the bar of God's justice in bitterness and despair, Adam turns to his wife and says, "I believe God's promise. He has not cast us adrift completely. He will give us the final victory over our enemy and we will again enjoy the richness and fullness of life in God. And because you are the mother of all those who will truly live, I give you a new name—Eve, Living One. I believe God, and I honor you."[52] In contrast to the cruel, cutting words of verse 12, Adam reaches out in love to Eve and they are reunited in faith and hope.

I personally find that, after studying this profound and moving passage on its own terms, it is depressing to read feminist commentary. A work of truth and beauty is being defaced. For example, Bilezikian writes:

> The fall had spawned the twin evils of woman's suffering in labor and of man's laboring in suffering. As a result of Satan's work, man was now master over woman, just as the mother-ground was now master over man. For these reasons, it is proper to regard both male dominance and death as being antithetical to God's original intent in creation. Both are the result of sin, itself instigated by Satan. Their origin is satanic.[53]

I respond in two ways. First, Bilezikian misrepresents the opposing view. Responsible interpreters do not advocate demeaning, oppressive "male dominance." They advocate selfless male headship, in which the man undertakes to serve his wife and family by providing the leadership that will glorify God and benefit them without regard for the price the man must pay to fulfill that responsibility. Headship calls us men to lay down our lives for our families.

Second, if Bilezikian would still argue that the exercise of male *headship* is satanic, then I must conclude that he is profoundly misguided. In his Conclusion he refers to "the repulsive pagan practice whereby one spouse exercises power over the other."[54] If the mere exercise of headship power is repulsive and pagan (and, presumably, satanic as well), then is it repulsive when a parent exercises power over his child? It can be. But *must* it be?[55] Is it pagan when a church elder exercises power over a church member? It can be. But *must* it be?[56] Is it satanic when Christ exercises power over His church? That *cannot* be! His headship over us is our salvation. It follows, therefore, that the ugliness and paganism evident in other relationships must be blamed not on the exercise of power itself but on sinful abuses of the exercise of rightful power. The origin of marital misery lies not in male headship, which God created for our blessing, but in a multitude of other, personal factors.

Bilezikian also labors to mitigate the moral repugnance of Eve's role in the conspiracy of Genesis 3. He seems to wish for Eve a sort of victim status in the affair. One must read his entire presentation to appreciate this unusual moral perspective, but let me quote him at one point:

> The only ray of hope in the statement of the curse appears in relation to the woman. In Adam all die, but Eve, as the mother of the living, shall bring forth life—and from her seed will issue redemption.[57]

But does the Bible set Adam and Eve off as death over against life? Paul, in Romans 5, sets Adam and *Christ* off as death over against life. Bilezikian's feminism seems to have swept him away into an anti-male prejudice that completely misses the point of Genesis 3.

Concluding Appeal

Male-female equality and male headship, properly defined, are woven into the very fabric of Genesis 1-3. Non-evangelical feminists recognize this. To quote one such writer, "Feminist theology must create a new textual base, a new canon. . . . Feminist theology cannot be done from the existing base of the Christian Bible."[58] Evangelical feminists, however, cannot create a new feminist canon without losing their evangelical credentials. So they reinterpret the sacred canon that exists to suit their purposes. I do not charge that they do so consciously. God alone knows our secret thoughts. But all of us know the stripping experience of discovering, to our dismay, that we have been making the Bible say things it does not really say. To make such a discovery and then to change is simply to grow in grace.

What might be the principial source of evangelical feminist blindness to the Biblical text? Consider the following. *There is no necessary relation between personal role and personal worth*. Feminism denies this principle. Feminism insists that personal role and personal worth must go together, so that a limitation in role reduces or threatens personal worth. But why? What logic is there in such a claim? Why must my position dictate my significance? The world may reason that way. But doesn't the gospel teach us that our glory, our worth, is measured by our personal conformity to Christ?[59] Or have we lost confidence in the gospel's perspective on reality? The absurdity of feminism lies in its irrational demand that a woman cannot be "a serious person" unless she occupies a position of headship.

Fortunately, this type of reasoning has already been put to the test in real life, so we can see its practical consequences. Look at the world. Is it any wonder that we see all around us a mass stampede for power, recognition, status, prestige, and so on? But the world's reasoning is invalid. Authority does not authenticate my person. Authority is not a privilege to be exploited to build up my ego. Authority is a responsibility to be borne for the benefit of others without regard for oneself. This alone is the Christian view.

Ironically, feminism shares the very premise upon which male domination is founded, namely, that my personal significance is measured according to my rung on the ladder, and my opportunity for personal fulfillment enlarges or contracts according to my role. By this line of reasoning, the goal of life degenerates into competition for power, and no one hungers and thirsts for true fulfillment in righteousness. No wonder both male domination and feminism are tearing people apart!

I appeal to my readers in the name of God, I appeal to you on the ground of Genesis 1-3, to reconsider rationally the basis of your personal significance. Your glory is found only in the image of God within you, as you resemble His holy character, whatever niche you may occupy in His larger scheme of things.

4

Women in the Life and Teachings of Jesus

James A. Borland

This chapter has two goals: (1) to show that Jesus placed a high value on women, and (2) to show that Jesus recognized role distinctions for men and women. Jesus' high regard for women is seen in how He recognized their intrinsic equality with men, in how He ministered to women, and in the dignity He accorded to women during his ministry. Jesus' recognition of role distinctions for men and women is demonstrated by His choosing only men to serve as His apostles with their primary tasks of preaching, teaching, and governing. Women, however, served in other important capacities, such as praying, providing financial assistance, ministering to physical needs, voicing their theological understanding, and witnessing to the resurrection.

Some may question whether Jesus' teaching and practice regarding the status of women harmonize with the rest of Biblical truth. Was His teaching radically different from Old Testament revelation? Are Jesus and Paul contradictory? Is a wife's submission to her husband a one-way street, or are there mutual aspects involved in the teaching about submission?[1]

Different positions have been taken relative to these questions, ranging from that of radical feminists[2] to more traditional evangelical views. The evangelical community seeks to interpret the text as inspired and authoritative. Such is the case with a number of evangelical feminists who are discarding the more traditional viewpoints.[3] For Hull, Bilezikian, and others, sex roles are essentially unimportant. They see no "subordination of women to men" in home, church, or society, but rather a "mutual submission and therefore equal opportunity for men and women to serve in both church and society."[4] Equal opportunity to serve as an ordained elder, bishop, pastor, or teacher is one of their primary concerns.

One starting place for the evidence in the New Testament is to examine the position of women in the life and teachings of our Lord Jesus Christ. The evidence in the four Gospels demonstrates that our Lord placed a high value on women, while He continued to recognize role distinctions for men and women.

I. Christ Placed a High Value on Women.

The place of women in the first-century Roman world and in Judaism has been well-documented and set forth in several recent books.[5] Most frequently, women were regarded as second-class citizens. Even the Old Testament presents situations where women were depersonalized. But such indications do not equal endorsement. God never authorized or approved behavior that depersonalized women. There are other things recorded in Scripture such as child sacrifice, polygamy, ritualistic sex in religion, and wife abuse that have never been sanctioned by God.

The cultural mores and the historical setting into which God spoke His revelation must be distinguished from that revelation itself. Only God's Word is inspired, not human folkways and customs.[6] Moreover, later cultural developments and deviations from God's truth must not be confused with revelation from God.

Jesus' regard for women was much different from that of His contemporaries. Evans terms Jesus' approach to women as "revolutionary" for His era.[7] But was His treatment of women out of character with Old Testament revelation, or with later New Testament practice? Other chapters in this volume will show that it was not.

A. Jesus Demonstrated the High Value He Placed on Women by Recognizing Their Intrinsic Value as Persons.

For Christ, women have an intrinsic value equal to that of men. Jesus said, ". . . at the beginning the Creator 'made them male and female'" (Matthew 19:4; cf. Genesis 1:27). Women are created in the image of God just as men are. Like men, they have self-awareness, personal freedom, a measure of self-determination, and personal responsibility for their actions.

Scanzoni and Hardesty point out that "Jesus came to earth not primarily as a male but as a person. He treated women not primarily as females but as human beings."[8] Jesus recognized women as fellow human beings. Disciples come in two sexes, male and female. Females are seen by Jesus as genuine persons, not simply as the objects of male desire.[9] Hurley believes "the foundation-stone of Jesus' attitude toward women was his vision of them as *persons* to whom and for whom he had come. He did not perceive them primarily in terms of their sex, age or marital status; he seems to have considered them in terms of their relation (or lack of one) to God."[10]

Examples of this even-handed treatment of women by Jesus are found in the four Gospels. First, Jesus regularly addressed women directly while in public. This was unusual for a man to do (John 4:27). The disciples were amazed to see Jesus talking with the Samaritan woman at the well of Sychar (John 4:7-26). He also spoke freely with the woman taken in adultery (John 8:10-11).[11] Luke, who gives ample attention to women in his Gospel, notes that Jesus spoke publicly with the widow of Nain (Luke 7:12-13), the woman with the bleeding disorder (Luke 8:48; cf. Matthew 9:22; Mark 5:34), and a woman who called to Him from a crowd (Luke 11:27-28). Similarly, Jesus addressed a woman bent over for eighteen years (Luke 13:12) and a group of women on the route to the cross (Luke 23:27-31).

A second aspect of Jesus' regard for the full intrinsic value of women is seen in *how* He spoke to the women He addressed. He spoke in a thoughtful, caring manner. Each synoptic writer records Jesus addressing the woman with the bleeding disorder tenderly as "daughter" (references above) and referring to the bent woman as a "daughter of Abraham" (Luke 13:16). Bloesch infers that "Jesus called the Jewish women 'daughters of Abraham' (Luke 13:16), thereby according them a spiritual status equal to that of men."[12]

Third, Jesus did not gloss over sin in the lives of the women He met. He held women personally responsible for their own sin as seen in His dealings with the woman at the well (John 4:16-18), the woman taken in adultery (John 8:10-11), and the sinful woman who anointed His feet (Luke 7:44-50). Their sin was not condoned, but confronted. Each had the personal freedom and a measure of self-determination to deal with the issues of sin, repentance, and forgiveness.

Jesus' regard for the intrinsic equality of women and men is also exhibited in his view of divorce and lust. In His treatment of divorce (Matthew 5:32; 19:9; Mark 10:11-12; Luke 16:18), Jesus clearly regards women not as property but as persons. They have legitimate rights and should be respected. Evans succinctly notes, "Women are not objects to be dismissed at will."[13]

Jesus' condemnation of the sin of lust was crucial in allowing Him and His followers to enjoy social contact as male and female, something nearly foreign to the Jewish mores of His age. Jesus said that "anyone who look sat a woman lustfully has already committed adultery with her in his heart" (Matthew 5:28). Why not separate men and women to avoid temptation as the rabbis practiced? Because Jesus came to seek and to save, to teach and to reach (Luke 19:10). That included women as well as men. Jesus' disciples were to have a righteousness that "surpasses that of the Pharisees" (Matthew 5:20).

Jesus "called upon his disciples to discipline their thoughts rather than to avoid women."[14] Lust does not have to be fed but can be controlled. Jesus demanded such control from His disciples, allowing males and females to associate together and to work in harmony with one another. Although such social contact between the sexes would be unthinkable to first-century rabbis, Jesus' teaching about the sinfulness of lust helps to explain the relationship men and women sustain both in His earthly ministry and in the apostolic church.[15] In the early church, women frequently labored together with men (Acts 16:14-15; Romans 16:3, 12; Philippians 4:3).

B. Jesus Demonstrated the High Value He Placed on Women by Ministering to Women.

Another way in which Jesus showed the high value He placed on women was in ministering to them in a vital and practical manner—both physically and spiritually. Numerous healings and the casting out of demons from women display Jesus' care and concern for women. Several such incidents are only briefly recorded. Jesus healed Peter's mother-in-law and allowed her in return to minister to Him (Mark 1:30-31; Matthew 8:14-15; Luke 4:38-39). Jesus also was concerned for a widow in Nain (Luke 7:11-15). He met her as she was weeping just before burying her only son. With compassion, He spoke to her and raised her son to life. Later, Christ healed a woman who was hopelessly bent over for eighteen years (Luke 13:10-17). Courageously, on the sabbath and inside the synagogue before hostile religious leaders, Jesus helped and defended this poor woman. He spoke to her, tenderly placed His hands on her, and caused her to stand erect, for which she glorified God. He then acknowledged her equal standing with men in Israel's religious heritage by referring to her as a daughter of Abraham (cf. John 8:33, 39).

Mentioned in all three Synoptic Gospels are two additional interwoven stories. Illustrating great faith while breaking religious and social customs, a poor woman, rendered ceremonially unclean for twelve years by a bleeding disorder, touched Jesus in a large crowd (Matthew 9:20-22; Mark 5:25-34; Luke 8:43-48). Instead of rebuking her, Jesus addressed her tenderly as "daughter," publicly strengthened her faith, and bid her go in God's peace.[16] Jesus then proceeded to the house of Jairus, who, with his wife, had just lost a twelve-year-old daughter. In addition to being rendered ceremonially unclean by the woman's touch in the crowd (Leviticus 15:19-22), Jesus also touched the dead girl and restored her to her parents (Matthew 9:23-25; Mark 5:35-43; Luke 8:49-56). Jesus' ministry to needy and hurting women is clearly seen in these events. From the bottom of the social order to the top (the girl's father was a ruler of the synagogue), Jesus aided women just as He did men.

Another woman, a foreigner, a Canaanite of Syrophoenicia, whose daughter was demon-possessed, asked Jesus' help (Matthew 15:21-28; Mark 7:24-30). She was persistent, intelligent, and witty, and exemplified *great faith*, a phrase elsewhere applied only to a centurion (Matthew 8:10; Luke 7:9). In rabbinic writings women are seldom presented positively and rarely illustrate faith or theological acumen.[17] But Jesus used her as an illustration of His previous teaching about defilement (Matthew 15:10-20; Mark 7:14-23). Jesus' disciples considered this Gentile woman unclean (cf. Acts 10:28). Jesus tested her spiritual tenacity, enlarged her understanding of spiritual truth, then granted her request, complimenting her for her faith.

The fourth Gospel records Jesus' concern for His mother's welfare as voiced in His dying words to John (19:26-27). Jesus wanted His mother to be cared for properly after His death.

Besides ministering to physical needs, Jesus dealt with women spiritually. The foremost example of this is found in John 4. Jesus spoke with the Samaritan woman as an individual and met her specific needs. Jesus apparently showed her the same attention, care and interest He showed to men. In fact, an interesting contrast is evident between Nicodemus (chapter 3) and the Samaritan woman (chapter 4). He was secretive; she was open. He doubted; she accepted. Jesus also taught her specific religious truths about God, worship, and the Messiah. As great as these particulars are, some feminists have exaggerated the details and surmised additional concepts to enhance the role of women.[18] However, three aspects of this occasion do stand out. (1) Jesus spoke to *a woman* (v. 27), which amazed the disciples. (2) She was a Samaritan (v. 9). (3) He taught her religious truth in contrast to the current rabbinic practices. This point is more fully developed in a later section of this chapter. Two other passages (John 7:53-8:11 and Luke 7:37-50), commented on above, show Christ meeting similar spiritual needs in other women.

Two additional incidents deserve mention. On one occasion a woman spoke up from the crowd saying how blessed Jesus' mother was to bear and nurse Him (Luke 11:27-28). Jesus did two important things. He gave her His undivided attention by listening to her comment, and He mildly corrected her and pointed her toward further spiritual understanding. He said that hearing and keeping the Word of God are the primary spiritual tasks. Jesus does not deny His mother's place of importance, but goes beyond it to a wider spiritual truth.

An additional story concerns Salome, Zebedee's wife (cf. Matthew 27:56; Mark 15:40; 16:1), ambitiously seeking positions of utmost power and honor for her two sons, James and John. She seems to have "worshiped" with a selfish motive (Matthew 20:20-22). This incident comes only shortly after Jesus' promise of thrones to the twelve (Matthew 19:28). In fact, the disciples "thought that the kingdom of God was going to appear at once" (Luke 19:11). They were anxious to secure their positions of authority. James and John may have asked through their mother, not desiring a further rebuke from Christ for seeking preeminence (Mark 9:34-37; Luke 9:46-48). Again, Jesus' mild rebuff is turned into a spiritual lesson on humility and self-sacrifice. Jesus was consistently willing to dialogue and interact with women.

Thus, Jesus showed how highly He valued women by ministering to them and meeting their needs—even the need to be heard. He healed women, dialogued with them, and showed women the same care and concern He showed to men.

C. Jesus Demonstrated the High Value He Placed on Women by According Them Dignity in His Ministry.

Jesus accorded dignity to women in His ministry in three ways: (1) by employing women as illustrations in His teaching, (2) by teaching women theological truths, and (3) by having women participate in His life and ministry. As indicated above in Section A (and also note 5), women were not always held in high repute by many of Jesus' contemporaries. Jesus' ministry gave a renewed respect to the place of women in His society.

First, women were employed by Jesus quite freely as illustrations in His teaching. Mention of the queen of the south (Matthew 12:42; cf. Luke 11:31) reminded His audience how a foreign queen travelled far to find the truth, but it was also used to warn of coming judgment for those who reject Christ. Jesus likened the kingdom of heaven to the leaven worked into bread dough by a woman (Matthew 13:33). Some debate whether the leaven represents the rapid expansion of God's kingdom or rather the spread of evil (cf. Matthew 16:6, 12). In either case, Jesus chose to use an illustration that would no doubt awaken the interest of His female listeners.

Jesus also taught (Matthew 24:41; cf. Luke 17:34-37) that at the time of His second coming (in power and glory) women would be about their daily tasks, in this case grinding grain on a hand-mill. These women as well as men will be divided and judged over their relationship to Christ. One goes to judgment (Luke 17:37), while the other enters into the kingdom. Another parable Jesus taught mentioning women almost exclusively is that of the ten virgins (Matthew 25:1-10). Jesus used them as examples of readiness (or lack of the same) for Christ's kingdom.

Jesus mentioned the widow of Zarephath (Luke 4:26) as an example of those outside Israel who receive God's blessings. The healing of the leper Naaman (Luke 4:27; cf. 2 Kings 5:2-4) illustrated the same point one verse later, but brought thoughts to mind of the faithful witness of the Israelite maid.

Jesus' parable of lost things (sheep, shekel, and son) in Luke 15 presents some interesting parallels between the shepherd and the woman. Jesus uses male and female, each with different roles, with neither elevated or depreciated.[19] Both serve to illustrate God's seeking the lost and rejoicing over their salvation.

The need for steadfast prayer was illustrated by a widow's persistence before a corrupt judge (Luke 18:1-5). Female hearers must have taken heart to hear Jesus praise a woman's persistence in their male-dominated culture. Jesus also commented on a poor widow who gave all she had to God in the women's court of the temple (Luke 21:1-4; cf. 20:1; Mark 12:41-44). Her heart attitude allowed her to give a much larger percentage (she gave 100 percent) than all the others because she must have trusted God to fully meet her needs.

Jesus not only chose women to illustrate His teaching, but also was concerned that women should be allowed to sit under His teaching as well. This may not seem surprising to those ready to enter the twenty-first century, but it was unusual in Jesus' day.

Feminists see Luke 10:38-42 as crucial in showing women being taught by Christ. Hull calls it "the most significant encounter . . . because it taught that women should prefer studying theology over a preoccupation with domestic chores."[20] Unfortunately, Hull misrepresents "traditionalists" when she reports them as saying women should not study theology.[21] Certainly, women *are* to learn and apply the Word of God. This is vitally important. But actually, the application is much broader than Hull implies. *Every* believer must make countless decisions throughout life, constantly choosing to act as a pupil with Jesus as the teacher. It does not mean that other duties or Christian graces are to be ignored, but it does imply that some things ("what is better," v. 42) are more important than other things. There are no role distinctions for learning from Christ.

On a later visit of Jesus to Bethany, it was Martha who was taught by Jesus while Mary sat in the house (John 11:20). For Martha, "Her growth is his goal, even in the midst of her tears of mourning for her brother" (Lazarus).[22] Jesus instructed her about the resurrection, and even that He was the resurrection and the life (John 11:25-26). Thereupon, Martha gave a superb confession about Christ, saying, "Yes, Lord, I believe that You are the Christ, the Son of God, who is to come into the world" (John 11:27, NKJV). On two other occasions Christ personally taught female disciples, even if in non-traditional teaching settings. On His way to the crucifixion, Jesus gave an extended proverb to a group of wailing women (Luke 23:27-31). He said, "Daughters of Jerusalem, do not weep for me; weep for yourselves and for your children. For the time will come when you will say, 'Blessed are the barren women, the wombs that never bore and the breasts that never nursed!'" He was saying that the future would see a worse judgment, probably using an *a fortiori* argument. If Christ, whom Pilate declared to be an innocent man, could be crucified, what will happen to those whom Rome judges to be guilty? Christ's final teaching to a woman is contained in His post-resurrection words to Mary Magdalene concerning His ascension (John 20:17). Jesus asks Mary to convey His words to the others, which she does (20:18).

An additional way that Jesus accorded dignity to women during His ministry was in having women participate in His life and ministry. Luke 2 mentions both the briefest and the most extensive of female associations in the life of Jesus. Anna of Asher was a godly, aged prophetess who resided in the temple area (Luke 2:36-38). She gave thanks for Jesus, whom she recognized as Messiah, when His parents presented him to God at six weeks of age (Luke 2:22; cf. Exodus 13:12, 15; Leviticus 12:2-6). Luke purposely pairs her actions with those of Simeon, just as he balances Zachariah's story with that of Mary's. Care is taken to show female participation.

The woman whom God chose to have the most extensive association with Jesus was His mother, Mary. But apart from the annunciation and birth narratives of Matthew and Luke, she is mentioned only five times in the Gospels—the trip to Jerusalem (Luke 2:41-51); the Cana wedding (John 2:1-11); accompanying Jesus to Capernaum (John 2:12); asking for Jesus (Matthew 12:46-50; Mark 3:31-35; Luke 8:19-21); and at the cross (Matthew 27:56; Mark 15:40; John 19:25-27). Mary's life was significant for at least three reasons. (1) She was a first-hand witness of Jesus' divine origin *and* true humanity. (2) She was a tremendous model of godliness, faith, dedication, and patience, among other good qualities. (3) She, along with other women, was incorporated into the new life of the church at Pentecost.[23]

Other women who participated in Christ's life fit into one of two groups—(1) those who served Him in some way, and (2) those who witnessed to His resurrection.

In the first category were two one-time participants as well as a group of women who served more frequently. Two women served Christ by anointing Him. Luke records an anointing of His feet by a notoriously sinful woman (7:36-50). The other Gospels tell of Mary's anointing of His head and feet with a pound of precious spikenard (Matthew 26:6-13; Mark 14:3-9; John 12:2-8). These women served Christ out of love and appreciation, but Mary's anointing was even more significant because she did it with a view to His approaching death (Matthew 26:12; Mark 14:8; John 12:7). Mary had true spiritual insight, no doubt gained from Jesus' teaching. They both were truly thankful, and Christ accepted their thanks while healing, forgiving, and liberating as the different cases called for.

Those who ministered to Christ more frequently included Martha in Judea and a group of women in Galilee. Luke 10:40 records Martha attempting to get a meal ready for about fifteen persons. Jesus did not order her to stop serving but gently corrected her attitude about Mary. Martha served at another supper just a week before Christ's death (John 12:2), suggesting that her service was more than just occasional.

Luke 8:2-3 recounts another group of women who ministered to Jesus and His disciples financially.[24] They may have served Jesus in other general ways as well, since the term is used of these women twice elsewhere without any reference to money (Matthew 27:56; Mark 15:41).[25] Their labor was important and some of their names are recorded—Mary Magdalene, Joanna, Susanna, Mary the mother of James and Joses, and Salome. There were also many others (Luke 8:3). We are not told how often these women travelled with Christ and the apostles. Hurley has suggested that they were more active while Jesus was in the Galilee region near their homes,[26] but Matthew 27:56 mentions their travel with Christ all the way to Jerusalem. Apparently when Jesus travelled in Judea (most of John's Gospel) and Samaria, He may sometimes have had the apostles make other arrangements for food and other provisions (Luke 9:52).

A final indication of the dignity accorded women in the ministry of Jesus is seen in the importance given to women in the resurrection accounts. In Christ's day, women were not considered reliable witnesses. Josephus warns, for example, "But let not the testimony of women be admitted, on account of the levity and boldness of their sex."[27] Still, God chose to use women as His initial witnesses to His disciples.

It may be an overstatement to say that the women sent from the tomb were "certainly . . . given a 'quasi-apostolic role.'"[28] To invent the role of a quasi-apostle seems foreign to the intent of these passages. The uniqueness of the role of an apostle will be discussed in the next major section of this chapter.

The question remains, why were the women chosen as witnesses of the resurrection? Was God bestowing a special honor on these women? Was God trying to indicate larger roles for women in His new community of believers? I believe both were intended.

All four Gospel writers bestow a great honor on the women who lovingly and with servant hearts came early to the tomb to anoint Jesus' body, thus paying their last respects. What if they were frightened and surprised by what they saw and heard (Matthew 28:5-8; Mark 16:5-8; Luke 24:2-9; John 20:1-2)? They still faithfully bore witness of Jesus' resurrection to His disciples and, no doubt, to countless others in the months and years that followed.

Some have contrasted the faith of the women witnesses with the unbelief of the apostles, but as Hurley notes, "Neither the women nor the disciples were really ready for the resurrection. The women had to be convinced by the angel."[29] The important point is that God did use women along with men at this strategic juncture in human history.

These women not only were the first witnesses to Jesus' resurrection, but also stand perpetually as examples for all believers. These women led the way in proclaiming the gospel—that Christ died for our sins, was buried, but rose again for our justification the third day. The duty and high privilege of witnessing for Christ is still open to every believer, without distinction as to gender.

II. Christ Recognized Role Distinctions for Men and Women.

Christ not only valued women very highly, but also demonstrated a clear role distinction between men and women. Nowhere is this issue seen more clearly than in Jesus' selection of only men for the role of apostle. Many Biblical feminists question the significance of this obvious role distinction, or explain it as cultural or as temporary. Siddons's brief comment is that dangers in travel and the "male-dominated" social structure of the time were reasons for the apostles' being only men.[30]

But Jesus was not averse to breaking social customs when He felt it necessary. He criticized Pharisees to their face in public (Matthew 23:13-36), healed on the sabbath (Mark 1:21-27; Luke 13:14; John 5:8-10), and cleansed the temple (John 2:14-17; Matthew 21:12-13). Against custom, Jesus spoke to the Samaritan woman (John 4:7-9), ate with tax collectors and sinners (Matthew 9:11), and even ate with unwashed hands (Mark 7:1-23)! The point is that when moral issues were at stake, Jesus did not bend to cultural pressure. No, it was not social custom or cultural pressure that caused Jesus to appoint an all-male group of apostles. Had He so desired, He could easily have appointed six men and their wives as apostles, since the wives of the apostles frequently accompanied them (1 Corinthians 9:5). But no such arrangement was initiated.

In fact, Jewish culture did accept women into positions of leadership. Just three decades before Herod the Great took over as king, Israel was ruled for years by Queen Alexandra. The fact that an occasional judge (Deborah, Judges 4-5), or ruler (Athaliah, 2 Kings 11:3) was a woman also demonstrates that female leadership was possible. Even though many women have excellent leadership qualities, God still has clear role distinctions in mind when apostleship and eldership are considered.

After spending all night in prayer (Luke 6:12), Jesus chose His twelve apostles (Matthew 10:2-4; Mark 3:13-19). Apostleship was to involve leadership, rulership, and the reception of special revelation. Several functions of the apostles were immediately discernible: (1) The apostles were to be with Christ, undoubtedly to learn extensively and to be trained firsthand (Mark 3:14-15). (2) The apostles were the obvious official leaders in the early church. See Acts 2:14; 5:12, 18, 40, 42; 6:2-4; 9:29; 15:2, and Galatians 1:17. (3) Special rulership was committed to the apostles. Christ promised that the apostles would sit on twelve thrones ruling over the twelve tribes of Israel (Matthew 19:28; Luke 22:30). (4) Christ promised the apostles reception of special revelation (John 16:13-15) and a special teaching ministry of the Holy Spirit (John 14:26). (5) As a testimony of the fact that male leadership in the church has been permanently established by Christ, the names of the twelve apostles are forever inscribed on the very foundations of heaven itself. "Now the wall of the city had twelve foundations, and on them were the names of the twelve apostles of the Lamb" (Revelation 21:14, *NKJV*).

None of the above roles was performed by the women who followed Christ or ministered to Him. Though highly valued and given a new dignity by Christ, their roles were different from those of the men Christ selected for His top leadership positions. Women gave to Christ, served Him, fellowshipped with Him, accompanied Him, learned from Him, prayed, and testified of their salvation[31] or of Christ's resurrection. But no woman in Christ's ministry was called, commissioned, or named as an apostle, or even performed in the role of an apostle. These roles and functions Christ reserved for men.[32]

Spencer discounts these distinctions implied in Christ's choice of men as His apostles. She reasons, "If Jesus' choice of twelve male disciples signifies that females should not be leaders in the church, then, consistently his choice also signifies that Gentiles should not be leaders in the church."[33] In another setting Spencer voiced the same argument. "If the twelve included only Jews, why should we not say that only Jews can be pastors/elders?"[34]

Her logic can be seen in the following syllogism:

A. Jesus chose only male apostles.
B. Jesus chose only Jewish apostles.
C. Therefore, church elders must be male and Jewish.

Of course, the argument is invalid, so the conclusion is unproven. Historically, we know it to be false. Spencer wants us to see that Gentiles *did* occupy eldership positions in scores of "Gentile" churches founded by Paul. She would like us to conclude that if Jewishness is not required for eldership, neither should maleness be required.

But even a superficial analysis of the New Testament reveals that the Jews occupied a *unique* position during Christ's earthly ministry. Jesus was born to be a "ruler who will be the shepherd of my people Israel" (Matthew 2:6). Jesus was termed "the consolation of Israel" (Luke 2:25), and He proclaimed, "I was not sent except to the lost sheep of the house of Israel" (Matthew 15:24). He announced a soon-coming kingdom (Mark 1:15) and sent His apostles at first only to the Jews (Matthew 10:6), promising them eventual rulership over the twelve tribes of Israel (Matthew 19:28; Luke 22:30; cf. Acts 1:6). Considering the Jewishness of Christ's mission to redeem Israel (Luke 24:21), it is not surprising to find all Jews on the initial list of apostles. It was not cultural pressure but God's plan to bring salvation through the Jews that led to twelve Jewish apostles.

With the resurrection, Christ's mission expanded to include Gentiles (Matthew 28:19) "in this one body" (Ephesians 2:16), the church. Gentiles were not only saved, but became elders in the new organizational units of local churches. A Gentile (Luke) wrote two books of the New Testament (Luke and Acts), and several Gentiles such as Titus and Epaphroditus were Paul's apostolic assistants and coworkers. Thus, Jewish apostles were unique and foundational, but Gentiles rapidly came to assume leadership in the church.

But was maleness, like Jewishness, to be discarded as a requirement for apostle or elder? Was maleness only foundational as well? There is clearly a difference in this case. First, the church did not start as all male and then later become both male and female. Christ's followers were male and female from the beginning, and both men and women were present at the beginning of the church at Pentecost (Acts 1:14). Second, from all we can tell, male leadership was perpetuated by those whom Christ initially taught, trained, and to whom He committed the future leadership of His church. Since Acts continually reminds us of the leading of Christ and of the Holy Spirit in the work of the church and its leaders, the assumption is that leadership choices were also made in that manner.

That male leadership is to continue as the norm is borne out almost immediately once the church begins. In Acts 1:15-26, the first and only replacement apostle was selected. Evans asserts that women no doubt met the requirements to be an apostle "as set out in Acts 1:21-22."[35] She overlooks, however, that one of the very conditions listed is to be a male—". . . it is necessary to choose one of the *men* [Greek *andron*] who have been with us . . ." (Acts 1:21, emphasis added).[36]

A further example is not the direct teaching of Jesus, but additionally strongly suggests that male leadership in the church was Jesus' intention. This comes out of the selection instructions and results in Acts 6, where the first leaders besides the apostles were appointed. Plenty of women were numbered among the believers according to Acts 1:14; 5:1 and 5:14. A problem arose regarding the neglect of certain women (Acts 6:1). The church was told to select seven qualified *men* (*andras*, Acts 6:3). If the instruction had been to look for seven "human beings" (*anthropous*), and then only men had been selected, we might say their choice was cultural or perhaps happenstance. Instead, the choice of men was deliberate.

Therefore, we can conclude that in the choice of the twelve apostles, in the choice of only men to write the New Testament Scriptures, in the other leadership tasks given uniquely to the apostles, in the pattern of male leadership followed by those whom Jesus taught most closely, and even in the twelve names inscribed on the foundations of the heavenly city, Jesus clearly affirmed an abiding role distinction between men and women and an abiding leadership role for men.

But even though clear role distinction is seen in Christ's choice of the apostles and in the exclusive type of work they were given to perform, no barriers need exist between a believer and the Lord Jesus Christ, regardless of gender. Jesus demonstrated only the highest regard for women, in both His life and teaching.

He recognized the intrinsic equality of men and women, and continually showed the worth and dignity of women as persons. Jesus valued their fellowship, prayers, service, financial support, testimony and witness. He honored women, taught women, and ministered to women in thoughtful ways.

As a result, women responded warmly to Jesus' ministry. Have things changed too drastically today for us to see this same Jesus? Not at all. Modern women can find the same rich fulfillment in serving Christ as did the Marys and Marthas of Judea, or the Joannas and Susannas of Galilee.

5

Head Coverings, Prophecies, and the Trinity

1 Corinthians 11:2-16

Thomas R. Schreiner

Introduction

> [2]I praise you for remembering me in everything and for holding to the teachings, just as I passed them on to you. [3]Now I want you to realize that the head of every man is Christ, and the head of the woman is man, and the head of Christ is God. [4] Every man who prays or prophesies with his head covered dishonors his head. [5]And every woman who prays or prophesies with her head uncovered dishonors her head—it is just as though her head were shaved. [6]If a woman does not cover her head, she should have her hair cut off; and if it is a disgrace for a woman to have her hair cut or shaved off, she should cover her head. [7]A man ought not to cover his head, since he is the image and glory of God; but the woman is the glory of man. [8]For man did not come from woman, but woman from man; [9]neither was man created for woman, but woman for man. [10]For this reason, and because of the angels, the woman ought to have a sign of authority on her head. [11]In the Lord, however, woman is not independent of man, nor is man independent of woman. [12]For as woman came from man, so also man is born of woman. But everything comes from God. [13]Judge for yourselves: Is it proper for a woman to pray to God with her head uncovered? [14]Does not the very nature of things teach you that if a man has long hair, it is a disgrace to him, [15]but that if a woman has long hair, it is her glory? For long hair is given to her as a covering. [16]If anyone wants to be contentious about this, we have no other practice—nor do the churches of God.

First Corinthians 11:2-16 has some features that make it one of the most difficult and controversial passages in the Bible.[1] For instance: How does verse 2 relate to verses 3-16? What does Paul mean by the word *head* in verse 3? Can we identify the custom regarding the adornment of women in the passage? In what sense is woman *the glory* of man (verse 7)? What does Paul mean when he says that the woman is to have authority on her head (verse 10)? Can we comprehend the reason why a woman is to have authority on her head, namely, *because of the angels* (verse 10)? And finally, what does the word *nature* mean in verse 14?

The difficulties with this text could lead one to say that it should not be used to establish any doctrine or teaching on the role relationship of men and women. Indeed, one might claim that only clear passages should be used to form a doctrine, and this passage is too obscure. No one, or at least few people, would argue that women should be adorned with veils today, leading some to say that this passage is culturally bound and no longer viable in the twentieth century.

In contrast to this position, I will argue that the central thrust of the passage is clear. There are difficulties, but some of the key issues are not as difficult as it has been claimed, and the issues that remain obscure do not affect the central teaching of the passage. Also, while wearing head coverings no longer speaks to our culture, there is an abiding principle in this text that is applicable to the twentieth century.

The Relation of 11:2 to 11:3-16

How does verse 2 relate to the following verses? Verse 2 says, "Now I praise you because you remember me in everything, and hold firmly to the traditions, just as I delivered them to you." The following verses (11:3-16), however, do not seem to be an example of the Corinthians holding fast to the Pauline traditions. The behavior of the Corinthian women is contrary to the custom of Paul and the other churches, according to verse 16. Presumably, Paul would not instruct the Corinthians regarding proper adornment for women if they were already following his instructions in this matter. It is probably the case, then, that 11:2 functions as a complimentary introduction before Paul begins to criticize the Corinthians on certain practices. Indeed, 11:2 is most likely the introductory statement for all of chapters eleven through fourteen. Even though the Corinthians are not following the traditions regarding women (11:3-16), the Lord's Supper (11:17-34), and spiritual gifts (12:1-14:40), the situation of the church is not bleak in every respect.

What is the Adornment for Women in this Passage?

One of the perplexing questions in this passage is this: What custom regarding adornment is referred to here? We cannot treat this complex question in detail, but the two most probable suggestions can be set forth: (1) The custom Paul recommends is for women to wear shawls. (2) Paul objects to long, loose hair that falls down the back; he wants women to follow the usual custom of piling their hair up on top of their heads.

In favor of the view that Paul is speaking against women wearing their hair loose and falling down the back are the following arguments:[2] (1) There is no extant evidence that full veiling, familiar in Islam, was current in Paul's time. Therefore, the custom described cannot be veiling. (2) The same Greek word that describes the practice of the Corinthian women in 11:5 (*akatakalyptos*) ["unveiled," according to RSV] is used in Leviticus 13:45 (LXX)[3] about a leper's hair, which is to hang *unloosed*. The problem with the Corinthian women, then, is that they were wearing their hair loose and flowing down their backs. (3) The word *apokalyptō* , which is somewhat related to *akatakalyptos*, is used in

Numbers 5:18, where a woman suspected of adultery had to unbind her hair and wear it loosely. The wearing of long, loose hair by an adulteress would support the idea that wearing one's hair loose was considered shameful. (4) Respectable women in Paul's time did not appear in public with their hair long and flowing down their backs. They wore their hair piled up on their heads in a bun. Paul wants the Corinthian women to adhere to this custom.

Despite these arguments in favor of the view that Paul is commanding the wearing of hair on top of the head by women, it is probable that Paul is speaking of wearing a head covering of some kind, such as a shawl.[4] That a shawl rather than a full veil is in Paul's mind is indicated by the word *covering* (*peribolaios*) in 11:15, which is not the usual word for veil but probably refers to a wraparound. The evidence in favor of this position is as follows: (1) The verb translated as "cover" in the NIV (*katakalyptō*) occurs three times in verses 6-7, and related cognate words occur in verses 5 and 13. These words most often refer to a covering of some kind. For example, the angels who saw the glory of Yahweh in the temple *covered* their faces (Isaiah 6:2). Judah thought Tamar, his daughter-in-law, was a harlot because she *covered* her face (Genesis 38:15). Since the word almost universally means "to cover" or "to hide," the text is probably referring to a hair covering of some kind.[5]

(2) Philo (30 B.C. - A.D. 45) uses the same words Paul does in 1 Corinthians 11:5, "head uncovered" (*akatakalyptō tē kephalē*), and it is clear that Philo is speaking of a head covering being removed because the priest had just removed her kerchief (*Special Laws*, 3:60). *Akatakalyptos* also means "uncovered" in Philo, *Allegorical Interpretation* II,29, and in Polybius 15,27.2 (second century B.C.). Moreover, it is simply a negative adjective based on the verb *katakalyptō* , which commonly means "cover, veil." (3) Esther 6:12 (LXX) employs the same expression found in verse four, *kata kephalēs*, of Haman, who hurried home mourning, covering his head in shame. He probably used part of his garment to do this. (4) A similar expression occurs in Plutarch (46-120 A.D.), where it is specifically stated that the head is covered with part of the toga (*himation*).[6]

Verse 15 seems to create a difficulty if Paul is speaking of a head covering. Verse 15 says that her "long hair is given to her for a covering." But if her hair is given to her for a covering, then a woman would not need to wear another covering over her hair. However, it is improbable that the only covering that Paul requires is a woman's hair, for we have already seen that the words for covering that Paul uses in verses 4-6 and verse 13 point to a veil or a shawl. Indeed, if all Paul has been requiring is long hair, then his explanation of the situation in verses 4-6 is awkward and even misleading. Verse 15 can be explained in such a way that Paul is not rejecting his earlier call for a shawl. The word *for* (*anti*) in verse 15 probably indicates not substitution but equivalence.[7] In other words, Paul is not saying that a woman has been given long hair *instead of* a covering. Rather, he is saying that a woman has been given long hair *as* a covering. His point seems to be that a woman's long hair is an indication that she needs to wear a covering.[8]

To sum up: the custom recommended here is a head covering of some kind, probably a shawl. The importance of identifying this custom can be exaggerated, unless one believes that the custom of the day should be applied to our culture. The major point of the text is clear: women are to adorn themselves in a certain way. The precise kind of head covering Paul had in mind is no longer clear. What is more important, and we turn to this next, is: Why does Paul want the women to adorn themselves in a certain way?

The Function of 11:3 in the Argument and the Meaning of *Head*

Probably the most crucial question in this passage is what Paul means by the word *head* (*kephalē*) in verse 3: "Now I want you to realize that the head of every man is Christ, and the head of the woman is man, and the head of Christ is God." Two answers are being suggested today: *source* and *authority*.[9] The meaning of this word has been extensively debated in the literature, and we will not cover all the ground again. Instead, three reasons will be given to defend *authority* as the best understanding of the word *head*.

(1) Even if we were to grant that the word *head* can mean "source" in a few instances, Wayne Grudem has shown that the meaning "authority" is indisputable in a number of passages, while the meaning "source" is never certainly attested. Grudem is correct in saying that those who oppose the meaning "authority" demand more examples of this meaning than they would with almost any other word. Usually, three or four clear examples are of great value, and Grudem provides a number that are decisive.

(2) Even if it were demonstrated that *head* does mean "source" in a few passages, it never bears that meaning in the Septuagint, and that is the relevant piece of literature with which Paul would have been most familiar. The use of *head* in the Septuagint is minimized by the Mickelsens because Paul was writing to Greeks who did not know the Old Testament well.[10] But this is an unconvincing argument. Paul appeals to the Old Testament either allusively or by quotation often when writing to Gentile converts. Most evangelicals agree that the Greek Old Testament is the most important source for Paul's theology, and of course this would apply to his use of words as well.

(3) A crucial usage, of course, is in Paul's own writings. It is precisely here that the evidence for "source" is weakest. Compare, for example, a passage on the same basic topic, men and women, in Ephesians 5:22ff. Paul says that "the husband is the head of the wife as Christ is the head of the church" (verse 23). In what meaningful sense can one say that a husband is the source of his wife? Wives do not exist by virtue of their husband's existence. Wives do not derive their life from their husbands. The meaning "source" here makes Paul's statement hard to comprehend since it is difficult to see how husbands are the source of their wives. Some have said that Paul is speaking of Adam as the source of Eve. But what is the evidence for this? Paul clearly speaks of husbands and wives in general in verses 22 and 24, and it would be strained and unusual to see a sudden reference to Adam and Eve in 5:23. Further support for *head* meaning "authority" is found in 5:22 and 5:24, for there Paul calls on women *to submit* to their husbands, which accords nicely with the notion that *head* denotes authority.

Paul uses the word *head* with the meaning "authority" in Ephesians 1:22 as well. Beginning with 1:20ff, he says that God raised Christ from the dead, seated Him at His right hand far above all other authorities and powers, subjected all things under His feet, and gave Him as head over all things to the church. The entire context focuses on the enthronement of Christ and His exaltation. The focus on the exaltation of Christ in the context suggests that the meaning of *head* is "authority."

Such an interpretation is confirmed by a parallel passage in Colossians 2:10. There Christ is said to be "the head over every power and authority." Here *head* must mean "authority," not "source," because the same rulers and authorities are also spoken of in Colossians 2:15, and there they clearly refer to the demonic powers that were publicly humiliated and led in a triumphal procession through Jesus' death and resurrection. Paul is not saying to the Colossians in 2:10 that Jesus is "the source" of these demonic powers; his point is that Jesus is sovereign over them, that He rules over them.

The texts that are sometimes used to argue that Paul could use the word *head* to mean "source" are Colossians 1:18; 2:19; Ephesians 4:15. In each case, the asserted meaning is possible but doubtful, since the meaning "source" for this word is not clearly found in the Septuagint, elsewhere in Paul, or in the rest of the New Testament. In Colossians 1:18, Christ is said to be the head over the church, and the concept of authority accords well with the context (Colossians 1:15-20). Colossians 2:19 and Ephesians 4:15 could be translated as "source," but Paul is probably saying in these two passages that the Sovereign of the church is also the One who sustains and strengthens the church.

Now we return to 1 Corinthians 11:3. If our interpretation is correct, then Paul is saying that Christ is the authority over every man, man is the authority over woman, and God is the authority over Christ. Since Paul appeals to the relation between members of the Trinity, it is clear that he does not view the relations described here as merely cultural, or the result of the fall.

C. Kroeger objects that to make God the head over Christ is to fall into the christological heresy of making Christ subordinate to God.[11] But this would only be a heresy if one asserted that there was an ontological difference (a difference in nature or being) between Father and Son. The point is not that the Son is essentially inferior to the Father. Rather, the Son willingly submits Himself to the Father's authority. The difference between the members of the Trinity is a functional one, not an essential one.

Such an interpretation is confirmed by 1 Corinthians 15:28: "When [Christ has subjected all things to Himself], then the Son himself will be made subject to him who put everything under him, so that God may be all in all." Paul did not see such subjection of the Son to the Father as heretical because the Son was not essentially inferior to the Father. Instead, He will subject Himself voluntarily to the Father's authority. The Son has a different function or role from the Father, not an inferior being or essence.

This point is often missed by evangelical feminists. They conclude that a difference in function necessarily involves a difference in essence; i.e., if men are in authority over women, then women must be inferior. The relationship between Christ and the Father shows us that this reasoning is flawed. One can possess a different function and still be equal in essence and worth. Women are equal to men in essence and in being; there is no ontological distinction, and yet they have a different function or role in church and home. Such differences do not logically imply inequality or inferiority, just as Christ's subjection to the Father does not imply His inferiority.

In fact, some evangelical feminists recently have made misleading statements regarding the issue of subordinationism in the doctrine of the Trinity. R. C. and C. Kroeger define subordinationism as "A doctrine that assigns an inferiority of being, status, *or role* to the Son or Holy

Spirit within the Trinity" (italics mine).[12] They also say, "Some apply a doctrine of subordination of woman to man on the basis of a similar relationship within the Trinity (1 Corinthians 11:3)."[13] G. Bilezikian says, "Nowhere in the Bible is there a reference to a chain of command within the Trinity. Such 'subordinationist' theories were propounded during the fourth century and were rejected as heretical."[14]

Such statements reflect a serious misunderstanding of both the doctrine of the Trinity and the nature of subordinationism. The Kroegers' definition of subordinationism fails to make the historic and crucial distinction between essence and role. What the church condemned was a subordinationism that predicated a difference of essence or being among Father, Son, and Spirit. The distinct role of the Son does not imply that He is essentially inferior to the Father. The addition of the word *inferiority* before the word *role* in the Kroegers' definition is especially distorting because a distinct role does not logically imply inferiority. That the Kroegers are inconsistent regarding the definition of subordinationism is evident in that elsewhere in their article they define it correctly: "The Nicene fathers ascribed to the Son and Spirit an equality of being or essence, but a subordination of order."[15] What the Nicene fathers called a subordination of order is another way of saying that they saw a subordination in role, or a subordination in the economic Trinity. The Nicene fathers rightly saw that this did not imply that the Son and the Spirit were inferior in nature to the Father. The Kroegers' earlier definition of subordinationism, then, makes sense only if they conclude that the Nicene fathers were heretical.

Bilezikian is even less careful. He says that there is not the slightest evidence in the Bible for "a chain of command within the Trinity." I would not use the phrase "chain of command," but that the Son submits to the Father is clear from 1 Corinthians 15:28. It is clear that this subjection of the Son to the Father is *after* His earthly ministry, so how anyone can say that there is no hint of a difference of order or role within the Trinity is difficult to see. Whenever Scripture says that God sent the Son into the world (e.g., John 3:17), we see subordination in role: the Father commands and sends; the Son obeys and comes into the world to die for our sins.

The notion that there is a subordination in function or in the economic Trinity but an equality of essence is also part of the historic heritage of evangelical theology. John Calvin says of Tertullian's understanding of the Trinity, "Nor am I displeased with Tertullian's definition, provided it be taken in the right sense, that there is a kind of distribution or economy in God which has no effect on the unity of essence."[16] What Calvin means by "distribution or economy" is a difference of role, and thus he concludes that a different role does not rule out equality of being or essence.

Charles Hodge says about the Nicene Creed:

> The creeds are nothing more than a well-ordered arrangement of the facts of Scripture which concern the doctrine of the Trinity. They assert the distinct personality of the Father, Son and Spirit; their mutual relation as expressed by those terms; their absolute unity as to substance or essence, and their consequent perfect equality; *and the subordination of the Son to the Father*, and of the Spirit to the Father and the Son, *as the mode of subsistence and operation.*

> These are Scriptural facts, to which the creeds in question add nothing; and it is in this sense they have been accepted by the Church universal.[17]

The distinction between being and role is also reflected in Louis Berkhof. He says, "There can be no subordination as to essential being of the one person of the Godhead to the other, and therefore no difference in personal dignity. . . . The only subordination of which we can speak, *is a subordination in respect to order and relationship*."[18]

To sum up, both Bilezikian and the Kroegers have wrongly defined subordinationism, thereby misleading readers with regard to the historic and evangelical doctrine of the Trinity.

Another argument used for the translation "source" in 1 Corinthians 11:3 is that Paul says woman came from man in verse 11:8, and this obviously suggests the idea of source. Surely this understanding of verse 8 is correct, but verse 8 does not explicate the meaning of *head* in verse 3. Instead, Paul uses this argument from source to prove that woman is the glory of man.

The order of Paul's statement in 1 Corinthians 11:3 has caused some question. If Paul is teaching hierarchy here, why does he not write (1) "the head of Christ is God," (2) "the head of every man is Christ," and (3) "the head of the woman is man"? Instead, Paul places "the head of Christ is God" as the last statement in the verse. Some suggest that this rules out any hierarchical understanding. But we have already seen that the clear meaning of *head* is "authority," and thus a hierarchy is definitely established. Why, then, does Paul place "the head of Christ is God" last? I think Paul added the headship of God over Christ right after asserting the headship of man over woman in order to teach that the authority of man over woman does not imply the inferiority of women or the superiority of men. Some Corinthians may have concluded that the headship of man over woman diminished woman's worth. Paul anticipates this objection and adds that God is the head over Christ. And even though God (i.e., the Father) is the head over Christ, He is not essentially greater than Christ. So too, even though women are under men's authority, they are not essentially inferior. Paul follows this same pattern in 11:7-12. In 11:7-10, he says women were created for man's glory and sake. But in 11:11-12, he shows that this does not involve the inferiority of women.

The Relation of 11:4-6 to 11:3

We have spent considerable time on 11:3 because it is fundamental to the whole passage. Verses 4-6 flow from the theological principle enunciated in 11:3. Since Christ is the authority over men, and since men are the authority over women, it follows that no man should wear a head covering when he prays and prophesies, while a woman should.

Paul objects to men wearing head coverings in verse 4 because such adornment would be disgraceful. Why? Because that is what women wore (11:5-6), and thus a man who wore such a head covering would be shamefully depicting himself as a woman. Conversely, if women do not wear head coverings, their failure to be adorned properly would be shameful (11:5) because they would be dressing like men. That the shame involved is due to appearing like a man is confirmed by Paul's explanation in 11:5b-6. A woman's failure to wear a head covering is analogous to her having her hair cut short or shaved. Every woman in the culture of that day would have been ashamed of appearing in public with her head shaved or her hair cut short, because then she would have looked like a man.

Paul explicitly says in 11:15 that a woman's "long hair" is her "glory." And if a man has long hair, it is a dishonor to him (11:14). If we compare verse 14 with verse 15, it is clear that for a man to wear long hair is a dishonor to him because such long hair is the particular glory of a woman, i.e., because if a man wears long hair, he looks like a woman. If we examine verses 5 and 6 in light of verses 14-15, we see that for a woman to wear her hair short or to shave her hair is contrary to what brings her glory, namely, long hair. Indeed, to keep her hair short is to wear it the way a man does (cf. 11:14). Thus, we can conclude that Paul wants women to wear head coverings while praying and prophesying because to do otherwise would be to confuse the sexes and give the shameful impression that women are behaving like men.

On whom or what is the man or woman bringing shame if he or she is not adorned properly? In verse 4, Paul says that the man who has a head covering "dishonors his head." In verse 5 he says that the woman without a head covering "dishonors her head." What does he mean by the word *head* in these verses? The word clearly refers to authority in 11:3, as we have seen above. It refers to one's physical head in verses 4 (first use), 5 (first use), 7, and 10. Two interpretations are possible in our context, and they are not necessarily incompatible.

On the one hand, to disgrace one's head may mean that one disgraces oneself. Three arguments can be used to defend this interpretation. (1) The word *head* can simply refer to one's self. In Acts 18:6, Paul says to the resistant Jews in Corinth, "Your blood be on your own heads!" He clearly means that the responsibility for rejecting the gospel message lies only with themselves. (2) The parallel with verses 14 and 15 suggests that *head* means "oneself." In verse 14, Paul says "if a man has long hair, it is a disgrace to *him*" (my italics). Now this thought in verse 14 is remarkably close to the idea that a man who wears a head covering "dishonors his head" (11:4). In the same way, if a woman's wearing long hair "is *her* glory" (verse 15, my italics), then the disgrace and shame described in verses 5 and 6 must refer to the disgrace she brings on herself. (3) Verses 4-6 forge a close relationship between one's physical head and disgracing the head. It is legitimate to infer that those who do not adorn their physical heads in a proper way bring shame on their heads, i.e., their own selves.

On the other hand, dishonoring the head in verses 4 and 5 may refer to the head described above in verse 3. Thus, a man who wears a head covering brings dishonor on his head, Christ. The woman who fails to wear a head covering brings dishonor on her head, man. Three arguments support this interpretation. (1) Verses 4-6 are an inference or conclusion drawn from the fundamental proposition in verse 3. Why does Paul want women to wear head coverings? Because such head coverings reflect the role relationship intended between man and woman. Since man is the head of woman, woman ought to adorn herself with a head covering. Failure to do so is to bring shame on one's head, namely, man. Such an understanding of *head* accords well with the intended connection between verse 3 and verses 4-6. (2) If Paul only wanted to say that one was disgracing oneself, he could have used a reflexive pronoun in verses 4 and 5. By using the word *head* in an obviously metaphorical way, Paul suggests a connection with the metaphorical use of that word in verse 3. (3) Paul says in verse 7 that "woman is the glory of man." He probably means by *glory* that the woman is intended to bring honor to the man. She should honor him because he is the head, i.e., the authority (11:3). This suggests that a woman disgraces her head, i.e., man, by not wearing a head covering (11:5), and man disgraces his head, Christ, by wearing a head covering (11:4).

Paul might have intended both senses here. They are not mutually exclusive. A woman who does not wear a head covering both disgraces herself and brings dishonor on her authority, who is man. A man who wears a head covering dishonors himself and his authority, Jesus Christ. If one does not conform to the role God intended, one brings dishonor on oneself and on one's authority. A child who rebels against a parent brings grief on himself and his parents (Proverbs 10:1; 17:25). We can conclude, then, that if a woman failed to wear a head covering and so dressed like a man, she brought shame both on herself and—because her behavior was a symbol of her rebellion against the created order, i.e., the intended relation between man and woman—on the man. Her failure to wear a head covering communicated rebellion and independence to everyone present in worship.[19]

We should pause to note here that Paul allows women to pray and prophesy in public assembly, according to 11:5. Some scholars have thought that women's prayer and prophecy were permitted only in private, since Paul says women should keep silent in church (1 Corinthians 14:34). But the praying and prophesying were probably in the public assembly for the following reasons: (1) The context favors the idea these chapters describe public worship. The subsequent topics focus on the Lord's Supper (11:17-34) and spiritual gifts (12:1-14:40), and these relate to public worship. (2) Prophecy was given to edify the community when gathered (1 Corinthians 14:1-5, 29-33a); it was not a private gift to be exercised alone. (3) Even if the meetings were in a home, such meetings would have been considered public assemblies, since many churches met in houses (cf. Romans 16:5; Philemon 2). (4) First Corinthians 14:33b-36 is best understood not to forbid *all* speaking by women in public, but only their speaking in the course of the congregation's judging prophesies (cf. 14:29-33a). Understood in this way, it does not contradict 11:5. It simply prohibits an abuse (women speaking up and judging prophecies in church) that Paul wanted to prevent in the church at Corinth.

So, Paul thinks women should pray and prophesy in public. Yet he wants them to do so with a head covering. I understand the major burden of 11:3-6, then, to be as follows: Women can pray and prophesy in public, but they must do so with a demeanor and attitude that supports male headship because in that culture wearing a head covering communicated a submissive demeanor and feminine adornment.[20] Thus, Paul does not forbid women to participate in public worship, yet he does insist that in their participation they should evidence a demeanor that is humble and submissive to male leadership.

The Function of 11:7-10 in the Argument

In verses 7-10, Paul explains further why he wants the women to wear head coverings and why the men should not wear them. A man (verse 7a) should not wear a covering "since he is the image and glory of God." But a woman should wear a covering because she "is the glory of man" (verse 7b). Paul is not denying that women are created in God's image, for he is referring to the creation accounts here and was well aware that Genesis teaches that both men and women are created in God's image (Genesis 1:26-27). The focus here is on the word *glory*, which is used in both parts of the sentence. What does Paul mean when he says that man is the glory of God, while woman is the glory of man? Both the subsequent and preceding verses give us some clue. We will investigate the succeeding verses first.

In verses 8-9, two reasons are given why women are the glory of men. First, in verse 8, Paul writes that women are the glory of men because "man did not come from woman, but woman from man." Paul is obviously thinking of Genesis 2:21-23, where woman is made out of man's rib. What is Paul's point here? Since woman came from man, she was meant to be his glory, i.e., she should honor him. That "honor" is the meaning of the *glory* is suggested also by verses 14-15. Paul says that long hair is a woman's "glory" in verse 15. Conversely, he says that "if a man has long hair, it is a *dishonor* to him." It is clear that these two verses function as a contrast. It is glorious for a woman to have long hair, but dishonorable for a man. From the contrast between the words *dishonor* and *glory*, we can conclude that another way of translating *glory* in verse 15 would be with the word *honor*. Paul's point is that one should always honor and respect the source from which one came. And woman honors man by wearing a head covering, thereby showing that man is the head, i.e., the authority.

Second, verse 9 explains that woman is man's glory since man was not created because of woman, but woman because of man. Paul once again alludes to Genesis 2. Woman was created to accompany man (Genesis 2:18) and in order to be a helper for him (2:20). If woman was created for man's sake, i.e., to help him in the tasks God gave him, then it follows that woman should *honor* man.

The thrust of 11:7b-9 is that women should wear a head covering because she is man's glory, i.e., she was created to honor him. Now we have already seen that if she does not wear a head covering (11:5-6), she dishonors her head, i.e., she does not honor him and she brings dishonor on herself. Thus, the use of the word *dishonor* in 11:4-6 supports the notion that *glory* in verse 7 has the meaning *honor*. But how do we know that woman was created to bring honor to man? Paul proves this in 11:8-9. Woman was created to bring honor to man because (1) the source of woman is man (this should not be confused with saying that the source of a wife is her husband, a wrong view of Ephesians 5:23 with which we have already dealt), and such an origin indicates a different role in the created order, and (2) woman was created because of man, i.e., in order help him in his tasks.

We ought to note in particular the significance of 11:8-9 in the argument. Evangelical feminists often claim that any role distinctions between males and females are due only to the fall. But their argument fails for two reasons.

First, Paul argues from creation, not from the fall. The distinctions between male and female are part of the created order, and Paul apparently did not think redemption in Christ negated creation. Feminists also often contend that the creation accounts in Genesis 1-2 do not support any role distinctions between the sexes. They think the creation accounts prove egalitarianism.[21] Nevertheless, Paul obviously interpreted Genesis 2 as revealing a distinction in roles between men and women. This is clear not only in 1 Corinthians 11, but also in 1 Timothy 2:8-15. The burden of proof lies squarely on the evangelical feminists, for they need to demonstrate clearly that Paul was not appealing to creation in order to justify role distinctions between men and women. Thus far they have not argued their case satisfactorily.

Second, Paul explicitly uses the argument from source in 11:8 to argue for the wearing of coverings by women. Thus, contrary to evangelical feminists, Paul uses an argument from source, which is rooted in the order of creation, to support the idea of a difference in roles between men and women. We have already argued that Paul means "authority" by the word *head* in verse 3, and here Paul even employs an argument from source to defend a distinction between the roles of men and women.

How does verse 10 fit into the structure of the argument? Paul says, "Therefore the woman ought to have *a symbol of* authority on her head, because of the angels" (NASB). The verse is controversial, but it seems to be another argument in favor of women wearing head coverings. The word *therefore* (NASB) (*dia touto*) points back to verses 8-9. We should note the structure of verses 7-10. Paul begins (11:7) by saying that man should not wear a head covering "since he is the image and glory of God." Woman, though, "is the glory of man." Then, in verses 8-9, Paul explains why men should not wear head coverings and why women are the glory of men. We have already seen that he grounds the distinction between men and women in creation. Finally, in verse 10 he draws an inference from verses 8-9: that women should wear head coverings. It would be easy to miss the structure of these verses because verses 8-9 function as a parenthesis and support the commands in both verse 7 and verse 10. It might help to show the structure of the verses as follows: (1) Men ought not to wear head coverings (11:7). (2) Support for this command (11:8-9). (3) Therefore, women ought to wear head coverings (11:10). Verses 7 and 10 are substantially parallel. Paul begins the passage by saying that men "ought not" (*ouk opheilei*) to wear head coverings (11:7), and he concludes it by saying that women "ought" (*opheilei*) to wear head coverings (verse 10). The reasons given in verses 8-9 support both commands.

But what does Paul mean when he speaks of a woman having authority on her head? English versions often have added a word to the Greek text in order to make the meaning plainer. Thus, the NASB translates verse 10 to say that "the woman ought to have *a symbol of* authority on her head." The RSV says that a woman should "have a veil on her head," and the NIV says a woman should have "a sign of authority on her head." But the Greek text literally says "the woman ought to have authority on her head." The words *symbol* (NASB), *veil* (RSV), and *sign* (NIV) are not in the Greek text. All the text says is that a woman should have authority (*exousia*) on her head. The word *authority* has been translated by the English versions in a passive sense so that Paul seems to be saying that a woman should have a sign or symbol of a man's authority on her head, namely, a head covering or veil.

But M. Hooker has contended that such translations are misguided. She says that the word *authority* nowhere else has a passive meaning; it is always active.[22] What she means is that the word must refer to a woman's own authority over her head: she has the right and authority to prophesy. Thus, according to Hooker, the verse is not saying that a woman must wear a head covering to show her submission to a man's authority. Instead, wearing a head covering indicates that a woman has the right to prophecy. If Hooker is correct, Paul here is trumpeting the authority of women, not requiring their submission to men.

Hooker's view, however, should be rejected for seven reasons. (1) As we pointed out above, the structure of the text is such that verses 7 and 10 are parallel. A man should not wear a head covering (11:7), but a woman should (11:10). The *therefore* in verse 10 refers back to verses 8-9, which explain *why* a woman should have a sign of authority: because woman came from man and was created for man. The reasons given in verses 8-9 for wearing a head covering, which is required in verse 10, clearly show that the issue is a woman's proper role relationship to a man. (2) Hooker's view focuses on the authority or right, i.e., the *freedom* of a woman to prophesy, but the focus of the verse is not on freedom. Instead, the text says "the woman ought (*opheilei*) to have authority on her head." The word *ought* shows that a command is being given here to women as to how they ought to adorn themselves when they prophesy (cf. 11:5); it communicates an obligation, not a freedom.

(3) Understanding Paul as commanding women to wear a head covering as a sign of submitting to male authority fits best with the preceding verses in the passage. Nothing is clearer in verses 3-9 than that Paul wants the woman to wear a head covering because such adornment appropriately distinguishes women from men. Indeed, the focus on male headship over women in verse 3 shows that Paul wants women to wear a head covering in order to show that they are submissive to male headship. If Paul were suddenly focusing on the "right" and "authority" of women, as Hooker thinks, he would be contradicting what he has said in the preceding verses.[23] (4) The qualification given in verse 11 (see explanation below) fits best with a command for women to have a head covering as a symbol of submission to men. Paul begins verse 11 with *However*. In verses 11-12, he guards against the misunderstanding that women are somehow inferior to men. But he would not need to say this if he had just affirmed women's authority and right to prophesy in such strong terms in verse 10. But since, in verse 10, Paul really concludes his argument as to why women should wear head coverings as a sign of submission to male headship, he senses a need to qualify his point in verses 11-12.

(5) Furthermore, it is not at all strained to see *exousia* in verse 10 as "sign of authority" or "symbol of authority." The standard lexicon for New Testament literature sees such a symbolic understanding of *exousia* as a viable possibility.[24] One can easily see why something worn on the head can become a sign or symbol of something. The dragon, in Revelation 12:3, has seven heads on which are seven crowns. Clearly, these crowns symbolize the dragon's authority and power. When Jesus returns on a white horse (Revelation 19:11-12) "on his head are many crowns," symbolizing His kingly authority. In an example very similar to 1 Corinthians 11:10, Diodorus of Sicily (1.47.5, written ca. B.C. 60-30) refers to a stone statue that has "three *kingdoms* on its head (*echontōn treis basileias epi tēs kephalēs*)," but it clearly means in the context that the statue has three crowns, which are symbols of governing kingdoms. We can conclude, then, that it is not at all unusual for something on the head to be a symbol of something else.

(6) Hooker, however, says that the word *authority* always refers to a person's own authority, not the authority of someone else. The problem with Hooker's analysis is that *exousia* in most other contexts does not refer to a physical symbol of some authority. It is the particular context of this paragraph, as verses 4-9 show, that makes it clear that Paul is speaking of a symbol of authority.[25] To say there are no other examples of *exousia* being used this way is not decisive,

since there are not many other parallel examples of *authority* even being used symbolically. Moreover, the example from Diodorus is also helpful here. The text describes a statue of the mother of King Osymandias, and reads as follows:

> There is also another statue of his mother standing alone, a monolith twenty cubits high, and it has three kingdoms on its head, signifying that she was both daughter and wife and mother of a king (1.47.5).

Here the three crowns (which Diodorus calls kingdoms) all represent someone else's authority—the authority of the woman's father (who was a king), husband (who was a king), and son (who was a king). In no case is the woman's own authority symbolized by the crowns she wears. Similarly, the head covering of the woman in 1 Corinthians 11 may well represent the authority of the man to whom she is subject in authority.

(7) Even if *authority* has an active meaning here, it refers to the man's authority, not the woman's, in this context. Paul explicitly says the woman "ought" to have "authority" on her head, and the most sensible explanation is that she ought to wear a head covering as a symbol of man's authority over her.

In verse 10, Paul also gives a new reason for wearing the coverings: "because of the angels." What does he mean? We don't know for sure. The best solution is probably that the angels are good angels who assist in worship and desire to see the order of creation maintained.[26]

The Qualification in 11:11-12

First Corinthians 11:3-10 is a sustained argument in favor of male headship and female submission, yet with full participation in worship for women (something Christians today need to remember more often). Verses 11-12 function as a qualification so that the Corinthians will not misunderstand Paul's argument. Woman and man stand in interdependence in the Lord (11:11). Paul proves this statement in verse 12. Man is the source of woman, but all men ever since Adam have come into the world through women. Paul anticipates the problem that could arise if one stressed his argument in verses 3-10 too rigidly. Male and female could almost be construed as different species, and men as more valuable than women. That is not Paul's point at all. There is a profound interdependence and mutuality present in the male-female relationship, and neither sex can boast over the other because the sexes are interdependent. Ultimately "everything comes from God."

Verses 11-12 demonstrate that Paul would utterly reject the notion that women are inferior or lesser human beings. Sad to say, some traditionalists have treated women in this way. Mutuality is also an element of the relationship between men and women. Women are created in the image of God, and men have no greater worth because of their God-given responsibility to lead.

At the opposite extreme, some evangelical feminists have drawn a wrong deduction from verses 11-12. For example, Bilezikian asserts that if Paul sees men and women as equal and both created in God's image, then any role distinctions must be eliminated because they would contradict the affirmation of equality.[27] Such a distinctively modern way of thinking has little to do with how Paul thought. The text before us makes it plain that Paul thought role distinctions and equality were not contradictory. People can be equal in essence and yet have different functions. The fairest way to read Paul is to let his own writings strike the balance. Verses 3-10 make it clear that he believed in role distinctions; verses 11-12 show that he did not thereby believe women were inferior or less important. Those who focus only on verses 11-12 effectively shut out verses 3-10. It is a mistake to exclude either teaching; we must hold them together as Paul did.

The Concluding Argument for Head Coverings in 11:13-16

Paul returns in the final paragraph (verses 13-16) to the main burden of the text: women's wearing head coverings. This is another indication that verses 11-12 do not cancel out the commands given in verses 4-9. Here Paul appeals to the Corinthians' own judgment (11:13), confident that "the very nature of things" will instruct them with respect to what is fitting or proper. What is the content of the instruction given by nature? Nature teaches that "if a man has long hair, it is a disgrace to him," while "if a woman has long hair, it is her glory."

What is the meaning of the word *nature* (*physis*) here? Is Paul simply saying that *human tradition and customs* have made a distinction between the hair length of men and women? The use of the word *practice* (*sunētheia*) in 11:16 could support this interpretation. But Paul's use of *nature* elsewhere and the use of *teach* suggest that he is referring to the natural and instinctive sense of right and wrong that God has planted in us, especially with respect to sexuality. This sense of what is appropriate or fitting has been implanted in human beings from creation.[28] Romans 1:26-27 is an illuminating parallel because the same word is used. Women and men involved in a homosexual relationship have exchanged the natural function of sexuality for what is contrary to nature, i.e., they have violated the God-given created order and natural instinct, and therefore are engaging in sexual relations with others of the same sex.

Nature teaches, then, in the sense that the natural instincts and psychological perceptions of masculinity and femininity are manifested in particular cultural situations. Thus, a male instinctively and naturally shrinks away from doing anything that his culture labels as feminine. So, too, females have a natural inclination to dress like women rather than men. Paul's point, then, is that how men and women wear their hair is a significant indication of whether they are abiding by the created order. Of course, what constitutes long hair is often debated—what is appropriately masculine or feminine in hairstyle may vary widely from culture to culture.[29]

The function of verses 13-15 in the argument is to show that the wearing of a head covering by a woman is in accord with the God-given sense that women and men are different. For a woman to dress like a man is inappropriate because it violates the distinction God has ordained between the sexes. And, according to Paul, if a woman prophesies in church without wearing the symbol of being under male authority—i.e., if she prophesies while dressed like a man—she is in effect negating the distinction between men and women that God has ordained from creation.

In verse 16, Paul concludes his argument by saying, "But if one is inclined to be contentious, we have no other practice, nor have the churches of God." Now, some have said that Paul actually rejects the wearing of head coverings by women with these words because the Greek literally says "we have no *such practice*" (*toiautēn sunētheian*), and thus they conclude that the practice of wearing head coverings is renounced here by Paul. But such an understanding is surely wrong. Paul in this verse is addressing the contentious, who, the previous context makes clear, *do not want to wear a head covering*. The practice of certain Corinthian women who *refuse to wear a head covering* is what Paul refers to when he says "we have no such practice." Thus, he says to the contentious that both the apostolic circle ("we") and the rest of the churches adhere to the custom of head coverings. The instructions Paul has given reflect his own view of the matter and the practice of the other churches. Those who see this advice as limited only to the Corinthian situation have failed to take this verse seriously enough. Paul perceives his instructions here as binding for *all churches* in the Greco-Roman world. Indeed, the other churches already adhere to the practice Paul recommends here. Such a universal word at the conclusion of the text is a strong indication that the principle that underlies this passage cannot simply be dismissed as cultural.

Significance of This Text for Today's World

The significance of this text for the twentieth century must be examined briefly. Am I suggesting that women return to wearing coverings or veils? No.[30] We must distinguish between the fundamental principle that underlies a text and the application of that principle in a specific culture. The fundamental principle is that the sexes, although equal, are also different. God has ordained that men have the responsibility to lead, while women have a complementary and supportive role. More specifically, if women pray and prophesy in church, they should do so under the authority of male headship. Now, in the first century, failure to wear a covering sent a signal to the congregation that a woman was rejecting the authority of male leadership. Paul was concerned about head coverings only because of the message they sent to people in that culture.

Today, except in certain religious groups, if a woman fails to wear a head covering while praying or prophesying, no one thinks she is in rebellion. Lack of head coverings sends no message at all in our culture. Nevertheless, that does not mean that this text does not apply to our culture. The principle still stands that women should pray and prophesy in a manner that makes it clear that they submit to male leadership. Clearly the attitude and the demeanor with which a woman prays and prophesies will be one indication of whether she is humble and submissive. The principle enunciated here should be applied in a variety of ways given the diversity of the human situation.

Moreover, both men and women today should dress so that they do not look like the opposite sex. Confusion of the sexes is contrary to the God-given sense that the sexes are distinct. For example, it would be wrong for a twentieth-century American male to wear a dress in public. It would violate his masculinity. Everything within a man would cry out against doing this because it would violate his appropriate sense of what it means to be a man. The point is not that women should not wear jeans or pants, but that in every culture there are certain kinds of adornment which become culturally acceptable norms of dress for men and women.

Finally, we should note that there is a connection forged in this passage between femininity and the proper submission of women to men. The women in Corinth, by prophesying without a head covering, were sending a signal that they were no longer submitting to male authority. Paul sees this problem as severe because the arrogation of male leadership roles by women ultimately dissolves the distinction between men and women. Thus, this text speaks volumes to our culture today, because one of the problems with women taking full leadership is that it inevitably involves a collapsing of the distinctions between the sexes. It is hardly surprising, as the example of the Evangelical Woman's Caucus demonstrates, that one of the next steps is to accept lesbianism.[31] Paul rightly saw, as he shows in this text, that there is a direct link between women appropriating leadership and the loss of femininity. It is no accident that Paul addresses the issues of feminine adornment and submission to male leadership in the same passage.

In conclusion, we should affirm the participation of women in prayer and prophecy in the church. Their contribution should not be slighted or ignored. Nevertheless, women should participate in these activities with hearts that are submissive to male leadership, and they should dress so that they retain their femininity.

6

"Silent in the Churches": On the Role of Women in 1 Corinthians 14:33b-36[1]

D. A. Carson

> [33b]As in all the congregations of the saints, [34]women should remain silent in the churches. They are not allowed to speak, but must be in submission, as the Law says. [35]If they want to inquire about something, they should ask their own husbands at home; for it is disgraceful for a woman to speak in the church.

I. Introduction

The interpretation of 1 Corinthians 14:33b-36 is by no means easy. The nub of the difficulty is that in 1 Corinthians 11:2-16, Paul is quite prepared for women to pray and prophesy, albeit with certain restrictions; but here, a first reading of the text seems to make the silence he enjoins absolute. The solutions that have been advanced are, like devils in certain instances of demon possession, legion. I can do no more than list a few and mention one or two of my hesitations about them before turning to the interpretation I find most contextually and exegetically secure.

The demarcation of the passage to be studied deserves some comment, since the precise link between verse 33a and verse 33b, and therefore between verses 33b and verse 34, is disputed. Do we read, "For God is not a God of disorder but of peace, as in all the congregation of the saints"; or "As in all the congregations of the saints, women should remain silent in the churches"? The latter is stylistically inelegant, for in Greek the words rendered "congregations" and "churches" by the NIV are the same word: i.e., "As in all the churches of the saints, women should remain silent in the churches." But what some see as stylistic inelegance, others see as powerful emphasis achieved by repetition. Moreover, if verse 33b is linked with what precedes, it is uncertain just what the line of thought is. In the sentence, "For God is not a God of disorder but of peace, as in all the congregations of the saints," what is being compared? God and the congregations of the saints? God's peaceful order with what is in all the congregations of the saints? The sentence can be salvaged only by understanding an additional phrase, such as: "*and this principle must be operative in your church*, as in all the congregations of the saints."

On the whole, it seems best to take verse 33b with what follows. But even if someone prefers the other option, little is changed in the interpretation of verses 34-36, since the phrase "in the churches" (in the plural) is found *in verse 34*.

II. The Text-Critical Question

A number of scholars have noted the complexities of the textual evidence supporting the authenticity of these verses and have dismissed verses 34-36, or some part of them, as a late gloss of no relevance in establishing Pauline theology.[2] Not a few of these writers exercise a similar source-critical skill with all the other passages in the Pauline corpus that seem to restrict women in any way. The authentic Paul, they argue, is the Paul of passages like 1 Corinthians 11:2-16 and Galatians 3:27ff. I confess I am always surprised by the amount of energy and ingenuity expended to rescue Paul from himself and conform him to our image. In any case, the view that verses 34-36 contain a major gloss is so much a minority report, especially since all manuscripts include the passage, that until recently most discussions and refutations could afford to be cursory. In short, most were satisfied that, whatever the textual complexities, the evidence that these verses are original and in their original location (and not, as in some manuscripts, with verses 34-35 placed after 14:40), is substantial.[3]

With the publication of the recent and generally excellent commentary by Fee,[4] however, the view that verses 34-35 constitute a non-Pauline interpolation has gained wider credence. Before turning to interpretations of the text as it stands, it has become important to think through the reasoning of those who omit it.

The relevant textual evidence is quickly stated. Verses 34-35 appear in all known manuscripts, either in their present location, or, in the case of all Western witnesses, after verse 40 (D F G 88* a b d f g Ambrosiaster Sedulius-Scotus). In addition, Codex Fuldensis (a Latin manuscript written between A.D. 541 and A.D. 546 by order of Bishop Victor of Capua) places the verses after verse 40, but also inserts them in the margin after verse 33. It appears that, despite the uniformity of the Western tradition, Victor, or those who worked at his bidding, became aware of the placement of the verses outside their own tradition and signalled their hesitation in this way.

Thus, although the overwhelming majority of manuscripts support the placing of verses 34-35 after verse 33, one must offer an explanation of the Western textual tradition. Fee's solution is that when the epistle came from Paul's hand the verses were not there, but were added later. His argument is essentially twofold. *First*, he appeals to transcriptional probability. In particular, he refers to Bengel's first principle, perhaps the most important single text-critical principle: the form of the text that best explains the origin of all other forms is most likely the original. As a matter of mere logical possibility, one must opt, Fee says, for one of the following: (1) Paul wrote the words after verse 33 and someone later deliberately transposed them to a position after verse 40; (2) Paul wrote the words after verse 40 and someone deliberately transposed them to a position after verse 33; (3) Paul did not write the words at all; rather, they were an early marginal gloss (that is, a later editor's addition written in the margin) subsequently inserted into the text at two different places.[5] Fee judges that good historical reasons are available to support the third option, but none for either of the first two. The gloss itself, quite apart from the location of its insertion, may well have been created toward the end of the first century to achieve a reconciliation between 1 Timothy 2 and 1 Corinthians 14 or to thwart a rising feminist movement (the existence of which some find attested in 1 Timothy 2). This means, of course, that verse 33b must be read with verse 33a (cf. discussion above) and that verse 36 follows immediately (as the letter came from Paul).

If Fee's reconstruction of events is correct, the gloss must have been extraordinarily early to have managed to find its way into *every* manuscript. This becomes rather unlikely under the assumption that the gloss was inserted at the *end* of the first century, by which time this epistle had been circulating for four decades. It is hard to believe that none of the earliest copies had any influence on the second- and third-century textual traditions to which we have access. Most commentators are rightly reluctant, therefore, to postulate an original omission where no manuscript that has come down to us attests the omission. Moreover, most glosses of substantial size, like this one, seek to explain the text, or clarify the text, or elucidate the text (e.g. John 5:4; Acts 8:37; 1 John 5:7b-8); they do not introduce major problems of flow into the text. The difficulty is so great in this case that we are asked to believe in a glossator who is Biblically informed enough to worry about harmonization with 1 Timothy 2 but who is so thick he cannot see that he is introducing a clash between 1 Corinthians 14 and 1 Corinthians 11. In short, unless there are overwhelming reasons for rejecting both of the other two options, this third choice should be dismissed as both weak and speculative. Bengel's first principle is convincing; Fee's application of it is not.

It is not widely argued that Paul originally wrote the disputed words after verse 40. That leaves us with the first option, namely, that Paul wrote verses 34-35 after verse 33, but that someone later deliberately transposed them to follow verse 40. This is the majority view. Fee rejects it on the ground that no historical reason has been advanced to justify such transposition. In particular, he says, "(a) displacements of this kind do not occur elsewhere in the New Testament; and (b) no *adequate* [emphasis his] reason can be found for such a displacement were these words originally in the text after verse 33."[6]

Neither objection is weighty. On the first point, Fee himself concedes, in a footnote,[7] that the adulterous woman pericope (John 7:53-8:11 in English Bibles) is a remarkable exception: it found its way into no fewer than five locations in our manuscripts. As for his argument that "no *adequate* reason can be found for such a transposition," I am doubtful that Fee will find the reason I shall advance "adequate," but adequacy is in part in the eye of the beholder. Customarily it is suggested that some scribe transposed it to a position after verse 40 because that produces less strain in the flow of the passage than its location after verse 33. Fee does not find this suggestion "adequate" because (1) the position after verse 40 is scarcely an improvement, and if there is no improvement there is no motive for transposition; and (2) judging by the stability of the textual tradition in the Eastern church, it was not common for copyists to mess around with the order of Paul's epistles. Again, however, a different reading of the evidence is possible. (i) Although a location for verses 34-35 after verse 40 is not without difficulties, it does have, on a superficial reading, one marked advantage over that attested by the majority of the manuscript evidence. The position after verse 33 (again, on a superficial reading) breaks up the flow of the argument. Verses 37-40 are still demonstrably talking about tongues, prophecy, spiritual gifts, authority in the church—the very topics that have dominated chapter 14. True, to put verses 34-35 after verse 40 is still to leave some awkwardness, but at least the awkwardness of breaking up what appears to be a cohesive unit of thought is alleviated. Thus, when verse 40 ends up by insisting that everything be done "in a fitting and orderly way," it is easy to imagine some copyist thinking that what appear to be regulations governing the conduct of women in the assembly could be subsumed fairly easily under that principle. The role of women is then nicely tucked in between two major topics: spiritual gifts (chapters 12-14) and the resurrection (chapter 15). (ii) As for the stability of the textual tradition in the Eastern church, most textual critics acknowledge that the majority of the most "creative" glosses and emendations occurred early in the transmission of the text. Certainly in the West, by the time of Jerome there were protests about the sloppy quality of many copies and translations (as witness the well-known protest of "Pope" Damasus). All it would take to introduce the transposition was one copyist, presumably early enough to capture the Western tradition, making what he felt was an improvement. That the history of the Eastern textual tradition is remarkably stable is scarcely relevant, since most of that "history" is much later.

If we set aside Fee's view of the transcriptional probabilities, we must still evaluate his *second* text-critical appeal, namely, intrinsic probability. Fee makes three points:

(1) He strongly argues that one can make the best sense of the structure of Paul's argument "without these intruding sentences,"[8] i.e., by omitting these two verses. Of course, appeals to "intrinsic probability" are amongst the weakest, against the principle of *lectio difficilior potior* ("the more difficult reading is preferable," a principle that, strangely, Fee does not mention): all things being equal, the most difficult reading has the greatest claim to authenticity, since it can be demonstrated that scribes tended to smooth out perceived rough spots, not invent difficulties. Clearly, on intrinsic grounds inclusion of verses 34-35 after verse 33 is the *lectio difficilior*, the "harder reading." Methodologically, the only time the *lectio difficilior* should be overthrown by appealing to "intrinsic probability" occurs when the external evidence is strongly against the *lectio difficilior*. Despite Fee's treatment of the transcriptional probabilities, this is simply not the case.

But what Fee unwittingly accomplishes is to set out one important criterion for an acceptable interpretation of the passage: it must make sense of the *flow* of the passage, or it should be dismissed as unlikely. In other words, while it may be freely admitted that the passage makes sense if verses 34-35 are excised, both the transcriptional probabilities and the principle of *lectio difficilior* argue that these two verses are original; and if so, then the most credible interpretation is the one that shows how a thoughtful reading of the last half of the chapter makes ample sense of the flow of Paul's thought, *with verses 34-35 included after verse 33*.

(2) Fee sees "even greater difficulty" in "the fact that these verses stand in obvious contradiction to 11:2-16, where it is assumed without reproof that women pray and prophesy in the assembly."[9] All sides in the debate understand that this is the nub of the problem. Even so, it may be doubted whether this makes the shorter text "intrinsically" more "probable." It may instead be further fod-

der for the *lectio difficilior*. And again, Fee's concern points the way to another criterion of an adequate interpretation: it must explain how the two passages, 11:2-16 and 14:33b-36, can stand consistently in the same letter, *each within its own context.*

Fee forcefully rejects this approach, because he insists on taking "They are not allowed to speak" as an absolute statement that *cannot* be reconciled with 11:2-16. At the merely formal level, of course, he is right: the statement is absolute. But qualifications to a statement can be present even when they are not part of the syntactical unit in question. The qualifications *may* be part of the larger context or the flow of the argument: in other words, there may be discourse considerations. Consider, for example, 1 John 3:9: "No one who is born of God will continue to sin, because God's seed remains in him; he cannot go on sinning, because he has been born of God." We may agree that the meaning of "God's seed" could be taken a couple of different ways, and that the NIV rendering, just cited, exaggerates the force of the present tense verbs, but after all our caveats are in, this is an extraordinarily strong statement. Even so, responsible exegesis must not only fit it into the flow of 1 John 3 but also take note of 1 John 1:6, 8, 10, where all pretensions to sinless perfection are specifically denied.

So also here: the prohibition in 1 Corinthians 14:34 is strong, but, as we shall see, the context argues it is not as strong as Fee thinks. Moreover the sanction granted to women to pray and prophesy (in 1 Corinthians 11:2-16) has one or two more curbs on it than Fee thinks. In the last analysis, Fee's judgments based on "intrinsic probability" are in part the result of his insistence on an absolute disjunction between two texts where more sympathetic exegesis sees a way forward. The disjunction he draws is not demanded by the text; it is self-generated.

(3) Finally, Fee joins other scholars who have noted that there are some usages in these two verses that are not typically Pauline— though it must be said that he prejudges this issue by saying, rather more strongly, that they "seem quite foreign to Paul."[10] Of course, many passages that all concede are Pauline contain one or more *hapax legomena* (expressions that occur only once, whether once in the Pauline corpus, or once in the New Testament). In light of this, we ought to be very careful about relegating any passage to the level of redactional addition where part of the argument turns on odd usage. This is not to say that such arguments are never valid: I myself have argued against the authenticity of John 7:53-8:11, in part by appealing to usage. But even there, where the usage arguments are considerably stronger than here (in part because the text is much longer), the usage arguments would not be judged very powerful were it not for the very strong manuscript evidence favoring omission—evidence entirely lacking in this instance.

In any case, the atypical usages in this passage are not all of a piece. Several of the ones commonly listed (but not, thankfully, by Fee) occur in Ephesians, Colossians, or the Pastorals, but so convinced are some scholars that these epistles are deutero-Pauline that they conclude 1 Corinthians 14:34-35 must be deutero-Pauline as well. I refer to such items as the verbs *to permit* (*epitrepō*), which occurs in 1 Timothy 2:12, also dealing with women, and *to subordinate [oneself]* (*hypotassō*), which is found in Ephesians and Colossians. Although "churches [NIV 'congregations'] of the saints" is not found elsewhere in Paul, neither is it part of the disputed text: it occurs at the end of verse 33—which of course does not bother Conzelmann, since he, without any text-critical warrant, assigns all of verses 33b-36 to a later redactor.[11] Fee carefully distances himself from this kind of speculation and suggests that 1:2 offers adequate reason for this form of expression.[12] This rather goes to show that reasons can usually be found to explain unique usages. But when it comes to verses 34-35, Fee magnifies several alleged peculiarities. In particular, he thinks that the use of "the Law" in verse 34 is un-Pauline.[13] I shall comment on that expression below.

In brief, neither Fee's appeal to transcriptional probability nor his appeal to intrinsic probability is very convincing. With all respect to a brother whose text-critical prowess is far greater than my own, his arguments in this case sound a bit like the application of a first-class mind to the defense of a remarkably weak position.

III. Unsatisfying Interpretations

If we grant that verses 34-35 are authentic and were included after verse 33 when the epistle left Paul's hand, it is all the more important to weigh the various interpretations that have been offered. The following list is not exhaustive. It is broadly comprehensive, and not in any particular order.

(1) Some continue to see the demand for silence as an absolute rule. This is done in one of two ways. *First*, several seek to escape the tension between 11:2-16 and 14:33b-36 by arguing that only the latter passage has reference to the public assembly; the former deals only with the home or with small group gatherings.[14] In that case, nothing in 1 Corinthians prevents the interpreter's taking the prohibition of chapter 14 absolutely, so far as the church assembly is concerned.

This interpretation does not seem very likely, for: (a) Paul thinks of prophecy primarily as revelation from God delivered through believers *in the context of the church*, where the prophecy may be evaluated (14:23-29). (b) Distinctions between "smaller house groups" and "church" may not have been all that intelligible to the first Christians, who commonly met in private homes. When the "church" in a city was large enough (as certainly in Jerusalem, Antioch, Ephesus, and possibly Corinth) to overflow the largest private accommodation, it must have been rather difficult, once opposition was established, to find a public venue large enough to accommodate *all* the believers of that city; i.e., the house groups in such instances *constituted* the assembly of the church. (c) The language of 11:16 ("If anyone wants to be contentious about this, we have no other practice—nor do the churches of God.") seems to suggest a *church* concern, not merely the concern of private or small-group piety. The "we"/"church of God" parallel either means that Paul has never allowed the practice, and the churches have followed his lead; or that Paul and the church in Ephesus (from which he is writing) constitute the "we" that have not followed the practice, and again the other churches have adopted the same stance. Either way, when Paul adopts the same tone elsewhere (see especially 14:33b, 36), he is talking about conduct *in an assembly*. (d) The immediately succeeding verses (11:17-34) are certainly devoted to an ordinance designed for the assembly. (e) If someone points out that 11:2-16, unlike 14:33b-36, does not include the phrase "in the church," it must also be observed that 11:2-16 does not *restrict* the venue to the private home or small group. (f) Whether the restriction in 11:2-16 requires some kind of hat or a distinctive coiffure, it becomes faintly ridiculous in proportion to the degree of privateness envisaged. If the restriction pertains to every venue *except* the church assembly, does this mean the Christian wife must postpone her private prayer until she has hurried to her chambers and donned her headpiece? The restriction is coherent only in a public setting. (g) Above all, the universality of the promise of Joel, cited at Pentecost, that the Holy Spirit would be poured out on men and women such that both would prophesy as constituent members of the community of the new covenant, seems somehow less than transparent if the women may display their inheritance only outside the gathered messianic community.

The *second* way in which some understand the prohibition in 14:33b-36 as an absolute rule, thereby requiring creative measures in the exegesis of 11:2-16, is by taking the permission granted in the latter passage to be mere concession: women may indeed pray and prophesy (under the restriction of the head covering, whatever that is); but this is conceded with extreme reluctance to those who cannot manage to submit to the rule of chapter 14.[15] But the praying and prophesying exercised by women in chapter 11 is not cast as a concession. Moreover, the church enjoyed the heritage of Pentecost and the fulfillment of the Joel prophecy, as we have seen, which promised that both men *and women* would have the Spirit poured out on them and that in consequence they would prophesy (Acts 2:16).

(2) Some are willing to leave a contradiction, and say no more.[16] But apart from any bearing this might have on the doctrine of Scripture, it is hard to believe that Paul could contradict himself as boldly as some think he has within the space of a few pages.

(3) Equally unlikely is the view of Kähler, to the effect that the subordination Paul had in mind is not of women to men, but of women to the order of worship he is establishing.[17] But we must ponder why women are singled out. Do not men also have to submit to the ecclesiastical structures Paul is setting forth? Moreover, the verb for "submit" or "subordinate" normally involves subordination of a person or persons to a person or persons, not to an order, procedure, or institution.

(4) To her credit, Fiorenza suggests[18] that the reasoning behind many such judgments is based on theological bias; so she is prepared to let Paul be Paul. Whatever the restriction, she thinks it is placed on wives only. After all, 1 Corinthians 7 displays Paul's "ascetic preference for the unmarried state";[19] thus it is "apparent that Paul here is 'taking over bourgeois moral concepts which denote not absolute but conventional values.'"[20] Fiorenza finds Paul's attitude surprising since we know of missionary *couples* in the New Testament. Paul derives his stance from "the Jewish Hellenistic propaganda tradition" that "places the demand for subordination of wives in the context of the Law."[21] Verse 36 betrays the fact that Paul expects strong response from the church against these restrictions; for indeed, Paul himself recognizes that his argument "sounds preposterous" and "goes against the accepted practice of the missionary churches in the Hellenistic urban centers. He therefore claims for his regulations the authority of the Lord (verse 37)."[22]

Here we have Paul not only strapped into a bourgeois mentality but also guilty of the worst sort of religious jingoism: knowing what he says is preposterous and preparing for the backlash by appealing to the Lord's authority! I confess I cannot help entertaining the suspicion that Fiorenza's exegesis tells us more of her than it does of Paul.

(5) Another cluster of interpretations argues that the problems behind Paul's demand for silence are local, probably doctrinal or cultural.[23] These positions are defended with varying degrees of sophistication. The argument that some of the women were too noisy[24] cannot be taken very seriously, for we must ask why Paul then bans *all* women from talking. And were there *no* noisy men? Nor is it plausible that the women are silenced because they were uneducated; for again, we must ask why Paul doesn't silence uneducated *people*, not just women. And since Paul's rule operates in *all* the churches (verses 33b-34), it would be necessary to hold that *all* first-century Christian women were uneducated—which is palpable nonsense.[25]

A more sophisticated version of this approach argues that women were exploiting their emancipation, refusing the ruling of verse 29, and falling into various heresies. The "Law" to which Paul appeals in verse 34 is his own prior ruling, alluded to again in verse 37. Moreover, verse 36 makes it clear that the crucial issue at stake was the Word of God: "The Corinthians were claiming to have originated the divine message, with their women giving the lead."[26] The doctrinal error may have been related to 15:12—a claim to have already been raised; and this claim "may well have carried with it—on the part of the women—a tacit denial of their married state on the ground that as 'risen ones' they no longer owed marital allegiance."[27]

But none of this is convincing, and some of it is misleading. There is *no* evidence that Paul ever uses the word *law* to refer to his own ruling. There is, as we shall see, a much more natural interpretation of that word. Surely the thrust of verse 36 is the charge that the Corinthians were trying to stand apart from the other churches (cf. 14:33b). In other words, verse 36 does not *define* the problem but *describes* the attitude that supports it. And what evidence is there here that the women "gave the lead"? Moreover, the attempt to link this situation with a similar one in 1 Timothy arouses all the same kinds of objections about the exegesis of 1 Timothy.

There is a more foundational objection: These approaches are unbearably sexist. They presuppose that there was a major heresy in which one of the following was true: (a) *only* women were duped, yet Paul arbitrarily silences *all* the women, regardless of whether they were heretics or not; (b) both some men and some women were duped, but Paul silences only the latter, thus proving to be a chauvinist; or (c) Paul was entirely right in his ruling, because *all* the women and *only* women in *all* of the Pauline churches were duped—which perhaps I may be excused for finding hard to believe. Has that ever happened in the history of the church? The truth of the matter is that this passage raises no question of heresy, but if it did, some explanation would still have to be given for the fact that Paul's response silences women, not heretics.

(6) Yet another cluster of interpretations attempts to resolve the difficulty by ascribing verses 34-35, or some parts of them, to the position of the Corinthians, perhaps even to a quote from their letter.[28] There are many variations to this cluster, but the central purpose of these approaches is to assign the parts that do not seem to cohere with Paul's thought as enunciated elsewhere to the Corinthian position Paul is setting out to refute. If the law (verse 34) means the Old Testament, one must find some place where women are told to be silent, and (we are told) there isn't one. Therefore *law* must refer to something else. One common view is that it represents *Torah*, which in the first instance means "teach-

ing," but was commonly used to cover both Scripture and associated Jewish traditions. So the law, here, refers to Jewish tradition that the Corinthians have unwisely adopted. Verses 34-35 summarize that position. Paul's horrified response is given in verse 36, and the fact that the word "only" (*monous*) is masculine may suggest that Paul is saying, in effect, "Did the word of God originate with *you men only*?" Moreover, it has been argued that the first word of verse 36 must not be taken here as a comparative particle ("Or") but as a disjunctive particle, expressing shock and overturning what immediately precedes ("*What*! Did the word of God originate with you men only?").[29]

Again, however, the arguments are not as convincing as they first seem. We may conveniently divide a response into four parts:

(a) That the word for "only" is masculine is irrelevant: people considered generically are regularly found in the masculine gender in Greek.[30] It is more natural to read verse 36 as addressed to the church, not just to the men in the church.

(b) It is very doubtful that verses 34-35 constitute a quotation, perhaps from the Corinthians' letter. During the last decade and a half, one notable trend in Corinthian studies has been to postulate that Paul is quoting the Corinthians in more and more places—usually in places where the commentator does not like what Paul is saying! That Paul does quote from the Corinthians' letter no one disputes. But the instances that are almost universally recognized as quotations (e.g., 6:12; 7:1b; 8:1b) enjoy certain common characteristics: (i) they are short (e.g., "Everything is permissible for me," 6:12); (ii) they are usually followed by sustained qualification (e.g., in 6:12 Paul goes on to add "but not everything is beneficial . . . but I will not be mastered by anything"—and then, following one more brief quotation from their letter, he devotes several verses to the principle he is expounding); (iii) Paul's response is unambiguous, even sharp. The first two criteria utterly fail if we assume verses 34-35 are a quotation from the letter sent by the Corinthians.[31]

(c) Moreover, although Paul uses the word *law* in several ways, he *never* uses it to refer to Jewish tradition, and the full expression found here, "the law says," occurs only twice elsewhere in Paul (Romans 3:19; 1 Corinthians 9:8), both with reference to the Mosaic law, and the former, judging by the wealth of quotations that immediately precede it, to the Scriptures, to what we would refer to as the Old Testament (cf. verse 21). Fee argues that the usage of "the law" here is probably not Pauline, since no passage is explicitly cited, and it is Paul's practice to provide a text.[32] But the number of passages where this thesis can be tested is small. More importantly, I shall argue below that the reason Paul does not cite a text is that he has already refereed to the text he has in mind, specifically when he was earlier dealing with the roles of women. When Fee adds, "Nowhere else does he appeal to the Law in this absolute way as binding on Christian behavior,"[33] he seems to be confusing two issues. It is true that Paul does not make simple appeals *to the Mosaic covenant*, "the law" in that sense, as a basis for Christian conduct. When he appears to do so, there are usually mitigating factors: e.g., in Romans 13:8-10, Christian love is the *fulfillment* of the law, where "fulfillment" must be understood in a salvation-historical sense. But Paul can appeal to *Scripture*, "the law" in that sense, as a basis for Christian conduct, and where he does so, the appeal, as here, is usually correlative (as in 1 Corinthians 9:8 and 14:21). In short, neither the suggestion that "the law says" here refers to extra-biblical oral tradition, nor the view that it is here used in an un-Pauline way, can be reasonably substantiated.

(d) Although it is true that the first word in verse 36 is probably a disjunctive particle, nevertheless the proffered explanation does not follow. Odell-Scott and Manus understand verses 33b-35 as the proposition against which the disjunctive "What!" responds. In other words, Paul allegedly cites the Corinthian view that women must be silent, and then replies with some exasperation, "What! Did the word of God originate with you?" He thereby *dismisses* the content of verses 34-35. Bilezikian wants to render the word by "Nonsense!"[34] Kaiser specifically appeals to Thayer's *Lexicon*, which lists 1 Corinthians 14:36 as an instance of the principle that this disjunctive particle may appear (in Kaiser's citation of Thayer) "before a sentence contrary to the one preceding [it]. . . . "[35] However, Kaiser has not quoted enough of Thayer's context to convey his meaning accurately. To quote in full, Thayer says that the disjunctive may appear "before a sentence contrary to the one just preceding, to indicate that if one be denied or refuted the other must stand: Mt. xx.15 (i.e., *or*, if thou wilt not grant this, *is thine eye* etc.)." In other words, Thayer does not say that the disjunctive particle in question is here used to *contradict* the preceding clause, and thus *dismiss* it, but that it is used to introduce a "sentence contrary to the one just preceding," *not* in order to dismiss the preceding, but in order "to indicate that if one be denied or refuted the other must stand." To put the matter another way, he is saying that the construction is a form of logical argument that is used to *reinforce* the preceding clause, as Thayer's example from Matthew 20:15 shows. There, the first part finds the landowner saying to the grumbling workers, "Don't I have the right to do what I want with my own money?" As Jesus proceeds, He certainly does *not* want to overturn the principle articulated by this rhetorical question; *of course* the landowner has that right. But since the workers have not accepted this principle, Jesus introduces a "sentence contrary to [this one]" to force the workers to see the preposterous nature of their criticism. To use the language of Thayer (who is quoting the King James Version in italics and inserting ordinary lettering to show the true force of the disjunctive particle), and filling in the words hidden behind his "etc.": "*or*, if thou wilt not grant this, *is thine eye evil, because I am good?*" In the NIV, using the same change of typefaces to make the point, we obtain "*Or*, if you are not willing to admit the truth I am affirming, *are you envious because I am generous?*" In other words, if the workers "deny or refute" the first clause (which both the landowner and Jesus affirm), then at least they had better face up to the second (to use Thayer's expression, "to indicate that if [the first] one be denied or refuted the other must stand").

Thayer then goes on to list several other exemplary passages: Romans 3:29; 1 Corinthians 9:6; 10:22; 11:14 (he points out that there is a textual variant there); 14:36 (the passage at hand). Consider Romans 3:29. In the preceding verse, Paul insists, "For we maintain that a man is justified by faith apart from observing the law." The next word, at the beginning of verse 29, is the disjunctive particle in question: "*Or* [is] God the God of Jews only? Is he not the God of Gentiles too? Yes, of Gentiles too, since there is only one God. . . . " Certainly neither Paul nor Thayer (and presumably not Kaiser) wants to overturn what Paul wrote in verse 28. Rather, using a rhetorical device, Paul goes on to say, in effect, "If you want to deny or refute this truth, then at least face up to this: monotheism itself demands that God is not the God of Jews only, but of all."

Exactly the same sort of reasoning occurs in the other passages Thayer quotes. He then adds, *as part of the same article in his lexicon*, two extrapolations of this usage of the disjunctive particle : (a) *ē agnoiete*, "or don't you know," citing Romans 6:3; 7:1 [cf. 6:14]; (b) *ē ouk oidate*, "or don't you know," citing Romans 11:2; 1 Corinthians 6:9, 16, 19. In each case the flow of the argument demands that the words that succeed the expression *are used to enforce, rather emphatically, what some among the readers are in danger of trying to deny or refute: the clause that precedes it*. In short, Kaiser has not understood Thayer's point.

Worse yet is Bilezikian's discussion of some of the relevant passages in Paul. For example, he writes: "In [1 Corinthians] 6:1-2, Paul challenges the Corinthians for their propensity to go into litigations against each other before pagan courts, rather than to submit their contentions to fellow believers. He counters this situation with '(nonsense!) do you not know that the saints will judge the world?'"[36] Again, however, it is important to listen to the text itself. In verse 1, Paul writes, "If any of you has a dispute with another, dare he take it before the ungodly for judgment instead of before the saints?" The verb *dare* in this rhetorical question proves beyond contradiction that in this context the assumed answer is "No!" In other words, *the question itself* is a rhetorical device for forbidding such litigation. Verse 2 then begins with the disjunctive particle: "*Or* [do] you not know that the saints will judge the world?" Thus, using exactly the same reasoning that Thayer employs, we conclude that verse 2 *reinforces* the truth of verse 1, the truth that Christians should *not* enter into the litigation in question. Bilezikian has simply not understood what is being affirmed under the force of the rhetorical question.

There is even less excuse for this failure in understanding when he turns to 1 Corinthians 6:15-16, for Paul himself inserts, after the rhetorical question but before the disjunctive particle, the words *mē genoito*: "Never" (NIV), "God forbid" (KJV). Once again, verse 16 emphatically reinforces the truth of verse 15, if the rhetorical question is read in any sort of responsible way.

Bilezikian does not even have a rhetorical question to fall back on when he treats 1 Corinthians 6:8-9. To quote him again: "In 6:9, having exposed the misbehavior of brethren who wrong and defraud each other, [Paul] counters with '(nonsense!) do you not know that the unrighteous will not inherit the kingdom of God?'"[37] Again, let Paul speak. In verses 7-8, as part of his denunciation of the same Corinthian practices, he writes: "Why not rather be wronged? Why not rather be cheated? Instead, you yourselves cheat and do wrong, and you do this to your brothers." Paul does not now want to turn around and say that they have *not* been acting this way: clearly, they have been, and the burden of his remark is that they should not be. Equally clearly, however, some Corinthians are slow to accept his denunciation. They would prefer to "deny or refute" (Thayer's terms) Paul's contention. So Paul goes on: "*Or* [do] you not know that the wicked will not inherit the kingdom of God?" In other words, if you want to buck at what I am writing in verses 7-8, at least you had better swallow what I say now in verse 9—and of course the effect is to reinforce, emphatically so, the burden of verses 7-8.

In every passage he treats on this matter, Bilezikian demonstrates, quite remarkably, that he does not understand what he has cited. In one instance (1

Corinthians 11:13), he refers to the particle *ē* even though no Greek edition known to me includes that particle.[38]

All scholars make mistakes, I no less than others. But the sheer vehemence that has surrounded the treatment of this particle in recent years attests that we are facing more than an occasional lapse of exegetical judgment. We are facing an ideology that is so certain of itself that in the hands of some, at least, the text is not allowed to speak for itself.[39] The brute fact is this: *in every instance in the New Testament where the disjunctive particle in question is used in a construction analogous to the passage at hand, its effect is to reinforce the truth of the clause or verse that precedes it.* Paul's point in 14:36 is that some Corinthians want to "deny or refute" what Paul has been saying in verses 34-35. So he continues, "*Or* [if you find it so hard to grant this, then consider:] did the word of God originate with you? Or are you the only people it has reached?" This is part and parcel of Paul's frequent insistence in this letter that the Corinthian church return to the common practice and perspective of the other churches (1:2; 4:17; 7:17; 11:16; 14:33) and to wholehearted submission to apostolic authority (14:37-38).[40]

(7) There is in addition a variety of interpretations that cut more or less independent swathes. For instance, Ellis[41] sees the restriction applied to wives only, in the light of the distinctions in roles he thinks Paul does expect to be maintained in the Christian home. Perhaps these women were even questioning their own husbands' prophecies, provoking some very embarrassing situations. But in much of the ancient world, marriage meant an *improvement* to women in freedom and social status. Even if these verses deal primarily with the *married* woman, I suspect both Paul and his readers would assume the *a fortiori* argument: if married women are enjoined to be silent, then how much more the single ones? Besides, does Ellis really think that Christian women enjoyed full freedom and perfect egalitarianism in function in the church as long as they were single, and then from the day of their marriage onward became silent for fear of offending the husbands to whom they were to submit? These considerations effectively dismiss those interpretations that admit that Paul insists on certain role distinctions between the sexes but limit such distinctions to the home, denying that they have any bearing on the church.

All of these interpretations share another quite decisive weakness. They do not adequately explain why these words should be found here, in this context, dealing with prophecy and tongues. After all, Paul has not yet abandoned the subject (as is clear from verses 37-40). If we accept the text as it stands, we must ask why Paul seems to interrupt the flow of his thought to add this little unrelated section into his chapter.

IV. An Interpretation Constrained by the Context

Another interpretation has been set out by various writers and meets the objections put to it. The view has been ably defended elsewhere;[42] I can merely sketch it here. Paul has just been requiring that the church in Corinth carefully weigh the prophecies presented to it. Women, of course, may participate in such prophesying; that was established in chapter 11. Paul's point here, however, is that they may *not* participate in the oral weighing of such prophecies. That is not permitted in any of the churches. In that connection, they are not allowed to speak—

"as the law says." Apparently in sympathy with the view that makes this appeal to "law" a feature of the *Corinthian* position, Evans suggests that to take this as *Paul's* appeal to law sounds "strangely unlike" him.[43] That is a rather strange assessment, since Paul in this chapter has already appealed once to "the law" (cf. 14:28), by which he means the Old Testament Scriptures. By this clause, Paul is probably not referring to Genesis 3:16, as many suggest,[44] but to the creation order in Genesis 2:20b-24,[45] for it is to that Scripture that Paul explicitly turns on two other occasions when he discusses female roles (1 Corinthians 11:8, 9; 2 Timothy 2:13). The passage from Genesis 2 does not enjoin silence, of course, but it does suggest that because man was made first and woman was made for man, some kind of pattern has been laid down regarding the roles the two play. Paul understands from this creation order that woman is to be subject to man—or at least that wife is to be subject to husband. In the context of the Corinthian weighing of prophecies, such submission could not be preserved if the wives participated: the first husband who uttered a prophecy would precipitate the problem.

More broadly, a strong case can be made for the view that Paul refused to permit any woman to enjoy a church-recognized teaching authority over men (1 Timothy 2:11ff.),[46] and the careful weighing of prophecies falls under that magisterial function. This does not mean that women should not learn: let them ask their husbands about various aspects of these prophecies, once they return home. Why should the Corinthians buck not only the practice of all the churches (verse 33b) but also the Scriptures themselves (verse 36)? Are they so enamored with the revelations that they have received that they dare to pit them against the authentic deposit found in Scripture and in the apostolic tradition? And if they feel they are merely interpreting that tradition under the promptings of the Spirit, are they not troubled to see that all the churches have translated the same texts, and the same Gospel, into quite different ecclesiastical practices? Are you the only people the word of God has reached (cf. verse 36b)?[47]

Several final observations on this interpretation may prove helpful. *First*, this interpretation fits the flow of chapter 14. Although the focus in the second part of the chapter is still on tongues and prophecy, it is still more closely related to the order the church must maintain in the enjoyment of those grace gifts. Verses 33b-36 fall happily under the description. The immediately preceding verses deal with the evaluation of prophets; these verses (verses 33b-36) further refine that discussion. The general topic of 1 Corinthians 12-14 has not been abandoned, as the closing verses of chapter 14 demonstrate. There is no other interpretation of these disputed verses that so neatly fits the flow of the argument.

Second, this interpretation makes sense not only of the flow but also of the structure of the passage. Chapter 14 is dominated by a discussion of the relative places of tongues and prophecy. Most of the chapter does not here concern us. Verses 26 and following, however, clearly deal with practical guidelines for the ordering of these two gifts in the assembly. Verse 26 is fairly general. Verses 27-28 deal with practical constraints on tongues speakers. In verse 29, Paul turns to prophecy and writes, "Two or three prophets should speak, and the others should weigh carefully what is said." The two parts of this verse are then separately expanded upon: the first part ("Two or three prophets should speak") is treated in verses 30-33a, where constraints are imposed on the *uttering* of prophecies; the second part ("and the others should weigh carefully what is said") is treated in verses 33b-36, where constraints are imposed on the *evaluation* of prophecies.[48]

Third, the major objection that has been set against it is that it seems inconsistent for Paul to permit women to prophesy and then to forbid them to weigh prophecies. But the objection carries little weight *provided* that such prophecy does not have the same authority status that the great writing prophets of the Old Testament enjoyed (whether or not such authority was immediately recognized). Elsewhere I have argued at length that "prophecy" in the New Testament is an extraordinarily broad category, extending all the way from the product of the pagan Muse (Titus 1:12) to Old Testament canonical prophecy. In common church life, it was recognized to be Spirit-prompted utterance, but with no guarantee of divine authority in every detail, and therefore not only in need of evaluation (1 Corinthians 14:29) but necessarily inferior in authority to the deposit of truth represented by the Apostle Paul (14:37-38).[49] In certain respects, then, it is perfectly proper for Paul to elevate teaching above prophecy, especially if the teaching is considered part of the non-negotiable apostolic deposit that serves in part as one of the touchstones enabling the congregation to weigh the prophecies that are granted to the church, and especially if the prophecies themselves, unlike the apostolic deposit, are subject to ecclesiastical appraisal. It does not mean, of course, that the utterances of any particular teacher need not be verified; I am not saying that prophecy must be evaluated, but teaching need not be. The New Testament includes too many passages that encourage the church to take responsibility for evaluating teachers and teaching (1 Timothy 1:3; 6:3-5; Titus 1:9-14; Hebrews 13:9; 2 Peter 2:1, etc.). But it *does* mean that prophecy cannot escape such evaluation, and it presupposes that there is a deposit of apostolic teaching, a given content, that is non-negotiable and that can serve as the criterion both of further teaching and of prophecy.

Fourth, this is not all that the Bible has to say about relationships between men and women in Christ. I have said nothing, for instance, about the command for men to love their wives even as Christ loved the church—an exquisitely high standard characterized by unqualified self-giving. Nor have I listed the many things Paul expects Christian women to do. Above all, I have not devoted space to the fact that in a Greek *ekklēsia*, i.e., a public meeting, women were not allowed to speak at all.[50] By contrast, women in the Christian *ekklēsia*, borne along by the Spirit, were *encouraged* to do so. In that sense, Paul was not trapped by the social customs of Corinth: the gospel, in his view, truly freed women from certain cultural restrictions. But that does not mean that *all* distinctions in roles are thereby abolished. I would be prepared to argue, on broader New Testament grounds, that the distinctive roles that remain are in Paul's view part and parcel of living in this created order, in the tension between the "already" and the "not yet"—in the period between the bestowal of the eschatological Spirit and the consummation of all things, when there is neither marriage nor giving in marriage.

And *fifth*, if this interpretation is correct, and there are some role distinctions between men and women to be observed, it is essential to recognize that this teaching is for our good, not for our enslavement. That is a theme I would dearly love to enlarge upon; but I shall pass it by.

7

Role Distinctions in the Church
Galatians 3:28

S. Lewis Johnson, Jr.

> [26]You are all sons of God through faith in Christ Jesus, [27]for all of you who were baptized into Christ have clothed yourselves with Christ. [28]There is neither Jew nor Greek, slave nor free, male nor female, for you are all one in Christ Jesus. [29]If you belong to Christ, then you are Abraham's seed, and heirs according to the promise. (Galatians 3:26-29)

Introduction

Never could the Apostle Paul have envisioned the place of Galatians 3:28 in contemporary evangelical literature. The issues of sexual equality and societal roles in modern society, however, have done what Paul could not have imagined.

In fact, the text has taken on a large and, for some, a crucial place in the discussion of the roles of the sexes in the Church of Jesus Christ. While traditionally commentators have discussed Paul's words in the context of the Biblical doctrine of justification by faith, that has become a secondary matter. One can understand this to some extent, since the vigorous debate over sex roles has, in effect, lifted it from its exegetical underpinnings and set it as a lonely text, a kind of proof text, in the midst of swirling theological debate. This is not without justification, but it also is not without peril. I am referring to the human tendency to forget sound hermeneutics and find things that are not really in the text. Listen to some of the comments about the text from both sides of the debate. Ronald and Beverly Allen call Galatians 3:28 "the feminist *Credo* of equality."[1] In a recent book, Mary Hayter refers to the text as "a crux" and "the locus classicus" for those who believe Scripture does not discriminate between male and female.[2] George Knight, a long-time defender of the historic orthodox interpretation of the text, nevertheless refers to Paul's statement as containing "momentous words."[3]

Paul King Jewett, professor of systematic theology at Fuller Theological Seminary, in a well-written, careful, and scholarly book, begins his discussion of the text by entitling it, "The Magna Carta of Humanity."[4] Jewett does not believe that Paul fully implemented his "magnificent affirmation," but at least he made a beginning in carrying it out by advancing beyond the rabbis and associating with women in his work.[5] In this Paul Jewett is not as bold as Robert Jewett, who speaks of the text as providing grounds for a Pauline breakthrough. He entitles a paper regarding the text, "The Sexual Liberation of the Apostle Paul."[6]

Both sides of the debate have admitted that Galatians 3:28 has not always been handled well. Klyne R. Snodgrass, in his significant article, has said, "This text, like some others, has become a hermeneutical skeleton key by which we may go through any door we choose. More often than not, Galatians 3:28 has become a piece of plastic that people have molded to their preconceived ideas."[7] James B. Hurley, holding a different view of the text, agrees, contending that much of the debate has arisen over "an abuse of Galatians 3:28."[8]

A fresh attempt to resolve some of the questions may arise from an overly ambitious expectation, but I believe it is a worthy aim. My method will be simple. After a brief survey of ancient interpretations, the apostle's argument in Galatians 3:26-29 will be summarized. The remainder of the paper will be devoted to the more important interpretations of the phrase "male nor female" (NIV).

I. Some Ancient Interpretations of Galatians 3:28

The following comments represent no claim to completeness or profundity, being merely a survey of some of the ways in which Galatians 3:28 was interpreted or handled in the ancient Christian world. As a matter of fact, the text did not loom large in that world and, while acknowledging my limited knowledge of that time, I have not yet found one extensive treatment of the text. I can only conclude that the early church regarded Galatians 3:28 as a text that was pellucidly clear.

Ignatius (d. 98-117), the Bishop of Antioch, wrote from Troas a letter to the Philadelphians on his way to martyrdom in Rome during Trajan's reign. There is no allusion to Galatians 3:28 in the shorter version of the letter, generally regarded as genuine. In the longer recension, however, there is an allusion to it. After exhorting wives to be "subject to your husbands in the fear of God" (cf. Ephesians 5:22), there occur the words, "Masters, be gentle towards your servants, as holy Job has taught you; for there is one nature, and one family of mankind. For 'in Christ there is neither bond nor free.'"[9] The new relation to Christ has its application to everyday life.

Justin Martyr (c. 100-165), Christian apologist, in his *Dialogue with Trypho*, likens his conversion to the symbolic picture of the high priest Joshua in Zechariah 3:1-10. He writes, in a text thought by some to be an allusion to Galatians 3:28, "Even so we, who through the name of Jesus have believed as one man in God the Maker of all," but Justin offers no expansion of the words, "as one man."[10]

Clement of Alexandria (c. 155-c. 220), the first known Christian scholar, in his *Protrepticos*, or *Exhortation to the Heathen*, xi, speaking of the great benefits conferred on man by Christ's coming, refers to Galatians 3:28 as support for the unity of those who have received wisdom in Christ. There is a new man, in whom there is neither barbarian, nor Jew, nor Greek, nor male, nor female. The status of believers in Christ is the leading idea.[11]

Hippolytus (d. 236), an elder and teacher of the Church in Rome, in *The Refutation of All Heresies*, refers to the text in discussion of the claims of the

Naassenes, who had used it in support of their claims of an everlasting substance above, which is hermaphrodite, possessing both male and female natures.[12]

Gregory of Nyssa (330-c. 395), the Cappadocian father and bishop of Nyssa, in "On Virginity," alludes to the text to show that both male and female are candidates for marriage to the true wisdom, Christ, in spiritual virginity, or disengagedness of heart from the worldly to the spiritual.[13]

John Chrysostom (c. 344/354-407), bishop of Constantinople, in his commentary on Galatians, discusses the text in some detail, asserting that the apostle ardently desires to convey the depth of our union with Christ. We "have all one form and one mold, even Christ's," he says. "He that was a Greek, or Jew, or bond-man yesterday, carries about with him the form, not of an Angel or Archangel, but of the Lord of all, yea displays in his own person the Christ."[14] He makes no reference to the clause "male nor female," evidently not finding that as pertinent as the two other antitheses.

Surprisingly, Augustine (354-430), the Bishop of Hippo, the greatest of the Latin fathers, rarely alluded to Galatians 3:28 in his writings. In his Second Discourse on Psalm Twenty-six there is one allusion. Speaking of waiting on the Lord, he writes, "He who has lost endurance has become weak and womanish. Let both men and women take heed of this, for man and woman are one in the one Man. He is no longer man or woman who lives in Christ."[15] The allusion is clear, and it is plain that he has in mind a oneness, a unity, of status in Christ. He says nothing of how this status relates to function in the church.

Martin Luther (1483-1546), the great German Reformer, in his important commentary on Galatians, devotes three pages to Galatians 3:28. He reminds the woman to "obey her husband," and warns that, "if the woman would be the man," that would be nothing but "confusion." All the faithful have "the same Christ" that all the saints had. Clearly, Luther sees the text as meaning that all believers have the same status in Christ, but in other spheres, such as the family, a submission within the equality all have in Christ is Biblical.[16]

John Calvin (1509-1564), Biblical theologian and commentator that he was, alludes or refers to Galatians 3:28 many times. In his commentary on Galatians he stresses the unity of believers in the one Christ. In his *Institutes* he, while again acknowledging the liberty believers have in Christ, nevertheless points out that the liberty of all in Christ has its limits, for "the same apostle who bids us stand and not submit to the 'yoke of bondage' [Galatians 5:1] elsewhere forbids slaves to be anxious about their state [1 Corinthians 7:21], unless it be that spiritual freedom can perfectly well exist along with civil bondage."[17] In other words, the master teacher from Geneva taught that freedom truly exists within limits and restrictions of a different order.

From this brief survey it appears that none of the major teachers in the history of the church thought Galatians 3:28 abolished the male-female role distinction in marriage or the church.

II. The Pauline Argument in Galatians 3:26-29

The General Context

The Epistle to the Galatians, most likely the first of Paul's letters, centers the attention of the reader on two dominant themes: (1) the justification of the believer in the Lord Jesus Christ apart from legal works, and (2) the ministry of the Holy Spirit as the indwelling energizer of the spiritual life in Christ.

The close affinity of Galatians with Romans is universally acknowledged. "The Epistle to the Galatians," Bishop Lightfoot said many years ago, "stands in relation to the Roman letter as the rough model to the finished statue; or rather, if I may press the metaphor without misapprehension, it is the first study of a single figure, which is worked into a group in the later writing."[18] One is written out of first indignant reaction to heresy, while the other is written calmly and at leisure.[19] That is probably ultimately the source of the remark of my old New Testament teacher, Professor Everett Harrison, "Romans tells us what the gospel is; Galatians tells us what it is *not*."[20]

Commentators on the letter have generally agreed that it falls into three sections. The opening two chapters are largely personal, containing a defense of his gospel and apostleship. The following section, also of two chapters, contains the exposition, in strongly argumentative form, of the heart of his gospel, the doctrine of justification by faith alone apart from legal works. The letter's final two chapters conclude with a hortatory appeal to practice the principles and responsibilities of the Christian life through the energy of the indwelling Spirit of God.

The Immediate Context

Galatians 3:28 falls within Paul's exposition of the purpose of the law, that is, to be a slave-guardian on the path toward maturity and unrestricted enjoyment of sonship (cf. 3:24; 4:1-7).[21] With the sonship has come a glorious freedom before God releasing all the faithful, whether Gentiles, slaves, or women, from life under the Old Covenant's bondage. The saints, enriched by the enjoyment of Abrahamic promises, are clothed with Christ in garments of freedom, family membership with heirship. This Paul now develops, negating any claim by the Judaizers that the Old Covenant life is a better life.

The Exegetical Analysis

Verse twenty-six, beginning with its explanatory "for" (see NASB; NIV leaves this out) justifies the new status. The apostle writes, "For you are all sons of God through faith in Christ Jesus" (NASB). The children have attained their majority and are sons, freemen of God, through a faith that has brought them into union with Christ.[22] The second person plural of the subject, "you are," with the modifying adjective, "all," underlines the participation of the Galatians in the new status. The universal privilege of sonship in the present age through union with Christ is Paul's point, and it sets the tone of the context for interpreting verse twenty-eight. Paul's emphasis is on spiritual status in Christ, "the spiritual privilege of being the sons of God."[23]

In verse twenty-seven Paul continues his exposition, explaining how the relation of sonship came into being. He writes, "For all of you who were baptized into Christ have clothed yourselves with Christ" (NASB). "For" declares that through baptism, a unifying incorporation into Him, the Galatians have put on Christ (cf. Romans 6:3-5; 1 Corinthians 12:13).

The discussion of the relation of faith and baptism, raised here because of the juxtaposition of faith with baptism, as well as the fact that union with Christ is traced to both, cannot be handled here due to the limitations of space. The discussions of Calvin,[24] Ridderbos,[25] Fung,[26] Betz,[27] Bruce,[28] and Dunn[29] provide a wide range of views. I would only echo Bruce's point that the apostle, who had learned so clearly and pointedly in his conversion experience the insufficiency of trust in the Old Covenant rite of circumcision, could never have ascribed a saving efficacy, a conveyance of grace by the performance of the rite, to water baptism, the New Covenant ordinance.[30] "It is absurd to say," Calvin comments, in harmony with Bruce, "that the grace of the Holy Spirit should be so bound to the external sign."[31]

If the apostle were thinking of the reality lying behind water baptism, that is, the baptism of the Holy Spirit by which believers are through faith united to Christ (cf. 1 Corinthians 12:13), then the text makes good sense. In Calvin's terms, he would be using the sign to signify the sense connected with the truth that the sign signifies, that is, the spiritual reality behind the sign. That, he contends, is the sense he uses when speaking of believers.

The final words, "have put on Christ," represent a metaphor probably derived from Hebrew tradition (cf. Isaiah 61:10; 64:6; Zechariah 3:3-4) and may have come to be associated with the taking off of one's clothes before baptism and the putting of them on again afterwards.[32] If the apostle were thinking of a Roman metaphor, he may have had in mind the Roman custom by which a youth, on attaining manhood, removed the crimson-bordered toga *praetexta*, the garment of childhood, and put on the toga *virilis*, the garment of manhood. At that time the young man would take his place in the family councils, taking on the responsibilities of maturity and enjoying the freedom that went with his new position. Since the apostle has just said that the Galatians have attained the position of adult sonship and will add heirship in a moment (v. 29), that "pagan" custom (Bruce's word) should not be dismissed lightly.

Verse twenty-eight points to a second issue of the universal sonship of believers: "There is neither Jew nor Greek, there is neither slave nor free man, there is neither male nor female; for you are all one in Christ Jesus" (NASB). The human distinctions of race, social rank, and sex are in some sense nullified in Christ. The crucial question is: In what sense? Betz contends, "There can be no doubt that Paul's statements have social and political implications of even a revolutionary dimension."[33] When a New Testament exegete uses the expression, "There can be no doubt," it often is a flag to the exegetical community that there is very good reason to doubt the statement. Let us see if that is true here.

The three antitheses are chosen with a view to fundamental distinctions in ancient society. In fact, as often noted, the apostle seems to have in mind the morning prayer of Jewish men, which can be traced back as far as about A.D. 150, in which the men thanked God that they were not born a Gentile, a slave, or a woman. Apparently the Jewish men intended no belittling of Gentiles, slaves, or women, so both Bruce and Snodgrass explain. Those classes were simply limited in certain spiritual privileges open to Jewish males.[34] In fact, similar formulas existed among the Gentiles.[35]

The three distinctions, important for Jewish life, are declared by Paul to be invalid in Christ. The first distinction, that between Jew and Greek, should be understood in a religious sense primarily, centering in the Abrahamic Covenant's rite of circumcision. Without circumcision a Gentile could not inherit the promises, being spiritually depraved and lost, without God in the world (cf. Ephesians 2:11-13), but now by the blood of the Messiah the Gentiles have been brought nigh by sovereign pardoning grace and have become heirs of the

Abrahamic promises. It is, of course, quite clear from the apostle's literature that the national distinction between Israel and the Gentiles still exists both in the world (cf. 1 Corinthians 10:32) and in the believing community (cf. Romans 9:1-11:36; Galatians 6:16). In Christ, however, both are heirs of the promised blessings, as Paul has indicated already (cf. 3:14) and will underline shortly (verse 29).

The second antithesis touches the inferiority of slaves, so marked in the ancient world and in Israelitish society. For Paul a Christian slave, too, inherits the promises equally, being "the Lord's freedman" (1 Corinthians 7:22). The Epistle to Philemon provides a vivid illustration of this (Philemon 8-20; cf. Colossians 4:9), and also in principle provides just grounds for the abolition of slavery itself. Yet here again, the distinction of slave and freedman still existed within the church (cf. 1 Corinthians 7:17-24). In fact, the vast majority of the New Testament commentators have taken the position that the apostle, while affirming the irrelevancy of the institution of slavery for status and relationship within the church, nevertheless did not feel it necessary to raise the issue of its retention in the society of the time (cf. 1 Corinthians 7:21-24; Colossians 3:22-25). It is difficult to see the "revolutionary dimension" of Paul's statement here.

The third antithesis, "there is not male and female" (Greek text; see *NASB* margin) contains a slight change of construction, probably due to influence from Genesis 1:27.[36] The distinction in sex also has no relevance to the status of believers in Christ Jesus. The reason Paul gives, introduced by the "for" of the last clause, is that Jew and Greek, slave and freedman, male and female are "one person in Christ Jesus" (*NEB*; cf. verse 29).

Concerning this last antithesis, Bruce comments, "It is not their distinctiveness, but their inequality of religious role, that is abolished 'in Christ Jesus.'"[37] Professor Bruce complains that Paul's other bans of discrimination on racial and social grounds have been accepted "*au pied de la lettre*" (literally), or *litteratim ac verbatim*, to use a Latin phrase, while this one has met with restrictions, since people have related it only to "the common access of men and women to baptism, with its introduction to their new existence 'in Christ.'"[38] He insists that the denial of discrimination holds good for the new existence "'in Christ' in its entirety," although he admits that circumcision involved a form of discrimination against women that was removed in its demotion from the position of religious law. Other inequities among Jewish and particularly among Gentile women existed.

Bruce argues that, if leadership may be given to Gentiles and to slaves in the church fellowship, then why not to women? Can superiority and inferiority of status have place in the society of which our Lord said, "whoever wants to be first must be slave of all" (cf. Mark 10:44)?[39] Certainly Paul welcomed the service of women in the Gentile mission (cf. Philippians 4:3, etc.) and permitted, many believe, their exercise of prayer and prophecy in church gatherings. Does this mean that the apostle affirmed women in the church offices and permitted their teaching in the church meetings? Professor Bruce does appear to admit that other Pauline passages may provide restrictions on female activities, but he contends that such passages "are to be understood in relation to Gal. 3:28, and not *vice-versa*."[40] We are reserving a fuller discussion of the questions surrounding the third antithesis for the third division of this paper, but perhaps three points ought to be noted here. First, the antitheses are not parallel, for the distinction between male and female is a distinction arising out of creation, a distinction still maintained in family and church life in the New Testament. Second, it must also be remembered that in this context Paul is not speaking of relationships in the family and church, but of standing before God in righteousness by faith. And, third, the apostle in his later letters, such as 1 Corinthians and 1 Timothy, does set forth just such restrictions as Bruce mentions.

Verse 29, "If you belong to Christ, then you are Abraham's seed, and heirs according to the promise," forms a triumphant conclusion to the apostle's argument. Christ's people are God's sons, baptized by the Spirit into spiritual union with Him, the Son, Abraham's Seed. And if believers belong to Abraham's Seed, then they are heirs to the unconditional covenantal promises in their Representative. Thus, heirship is grounded in faith apart from the works of the Law. Those who would seek to be justified by the works of the Law are rejected. What a telling refutation of the Judaizers and their doctrine of justification and heirship by legal works! The full and complete equality that all possess in Christ is a magnificent thing to behold, and the reference to the discussion over male/female relationships must not be missed. The richness of the oneness, without any denial at all of role distinctions, is the preeminent thrust of the section we have been considering. Justified by faith in Christ, both male and female are "sons of God" (verse 26), both are "in Christ Jesus" (verse 26), united to Him in eternal union through the baptism of the Holy Spirit (verse 27), both have clothed themselves with Christ and are one in Him (verse 28). We belong to Christ and, as if that were not enough, the apostle adds that we all, both male and female, are the patriarch's believing offspring and heirs of the stunning promises made to him (verse 29). The context contains no denial at all of role distinctions and, in fact, to inject the feminist agenda at this point dims the splendor of these grand truths.

III. Modern Interpretations of Galatians 3:28

A. The Feminist Argument

To interact with modern interpretations of Galatians 3:28 has been made a daunting task by the plethora of written materials, books, and articles, both popular and scholarly, that has emerged in recent years. To limit my comments, I will concentrate attention on the position of Paul King Jewett and Klyne R. Snodgrass, scholars who have given two extensive and widely accepted statements of the meaning of Galatians 3:28 from the perspective that would see no limitation on women's roles in the church.

Jewett's basic position in his well-written, thoughtful, and scholarly work, *Man as Male and Female: A Study in Sexual Relationships from a Theological Point of View*, is that the Bible is basically contradictory on the question of the relation of men and women in Christ and the church. The Biblical narratives and Jesus' attitude to women are incompatible with female subordination, but Paul, following rabbinic exegesis, teaches subordination in certain New Testament passages, such as 1 Corinthians 11 and 1 Timothy 2.[41] The apostle manifests a bit of an "uneasy conscience" in his exegesis of the Old Testament, but he still affirms female subordination.[42]

To some extent the apostle redeems himself, for he is the author of a brilliant piece of Biblical insight in his remarkable statement of Galatians 3:28. That is really the last word on the subject of female equality, and Jesus Himself neither said nor did anything beyond Paul's word here.[43] Paul, however, did not implement his Christian insight thoroughly, which has left us with the problem of the man/woman question. The church must press on to the full implementation of his Galatians 3:28 insight, abandoning, of course, his shortcomings in his other epistles.

Critique: What can we say in response to Jewett? First, Jewett acknowledges that Paul, in the three pairs of antitheses—Jew/Greek, bond/free, male/female—"thinks preeminently *coram Deo*," that is, of men before God.[44] Further, he later admits that this should be, "beyond all doubt," the principal concern of the church. Historic orthodoxy would certainly agree with this, and I am grateful for his clear enunciation of the point.

On the first antithesis, that of Jew/Greek, Jewett states that Paul saw the "social implications" of the text clearly enough. He illustrates this from Paul's withstanding of Peter in Antioch over Peter's actions when the men came from James in Jerusalem, and Peter returned to the teaching of Judaism about eating with the Gentiles (cf. Galatians 2:11-14). Jewett's point is that Paul did not say, as the men from Jerusalem must have said, "Jews and Greeks are one in Christ, but in other respects, such as in the table fellowship traditions, they are different and must follow the discriminatory traditions. We may enjoy spiritual fellowship with the Gentiles, but the social traditions still obtain."

This is not quite the point of the apostle. As he goes on to say, he does not rebuke Peter because he has failed to see the "social implications" of the oneness in Christ, but because he had seen them and was now returning to "the weak and worthless elemental things" (cf. 4:9). As Paul saw it, Peter's actions were a clear attack on the doctrine of justification by faith alone. To observe the Jewish food laws was simply a step along the way to circumcision as necessary to salvation, a step along the way to the view that, if Gentile believers were not able to have table fellowship with Jewish believers *as Gentile believers*, then their Christianity was second class.[45]

We may grant Jewett's claim that the essence of the gospel's proclamation of oneness or equality in Christ demanded a walk in harmony with that position. We may legitimately ask, however, if distinction of roles of believers within that equality necessarily violates that equality, especially since the apostle later in some detail sets out the distinctions of roles, offices, and gifts within the family (cf. Ephesians 5:22-6:9; Colossians 3:18-4:1) and the church (cf. 1 Corinthians 11:2-16; 12:1-31; 1 Timothy 2:9-15) with no suggestion of a loss of equality in Christ.

Jewett finds Paul's vision not so clear in the second antithesis, slave/free. While Philemon contains a hint that he would have had Onesimus freed by his master, the apostle does not confront Philemon with a demand for freedom. Paul is relegated by Jewett to the ignominious attitude of the churchmen in the time of the Civil War who played the wimp and did not fight for abolition.

In the antithesis of male/female, the apostle was still more cautious. Jewett contends that Paul spoke of women as being subordinate and unequal. However, for a former rabbi he did in a remarkable way act out the truth of no male and female. He greeted women by name (cf. Romans 16:6, 12, 15), and he named Priscilla before her husband (cf. Romans 16:3), after having commended Phoebe as a servant of the church at Cenchraea (16:1-2).[46]

Jewett's contention that these things constitute a remarkable acting out of the truth of male/female oneness is overdrawn. Sufficiently explanatory of all of this is the fact that all believers have become one in Christ Jesus, sharing equally the redemption that Christ has won by His atoning sacrifice. In other words, the implications of redemption, the joint blessings of covenantal union with our Lord, account for Paul's actions. As Jewett says, "How many rabbis had ever said that a man should love his wife *as Yahweh loved Israel*?"[47] The response of prominent women to Paul's preaching in Thessalonica and Berea may have included appreciation of "the profound worth which they perceived they had, as *persons*, to the Savior he preached,"[48] but it is more likely that they responded first and foremost because they sensed their sin and rejoiced in redemption by sovereign grace.

One final question interests me. Professor Jewett lays great stress on the fact that males and females must learn to live in partnership rather than in any form of hierarchy. He does not, however, spell out in detail what this means specifically and how sexual egalitarianism will work. Does this mean that he is willing to leave this to each body of Christians to decide for themselves? Does Scripture then leave us with no clear, normative guidance beyond the principle of Galatians 3:28?[49]

The position of Klyne Snodgrass, professor of Biblical literature at North Park Theological Seminary, is not dissimilar to Jewett's, although his approach to the questions is different.

Snodgrass affirms "the unity and equality that all persons experience in Christ," and surprisingly he admits that equality and hierarchy are "not necessarily antithetical ideas."[50] But this concession turns out to rest on an unusual definition of hierarchy.[51]

Snodgrass also appeals, like Jewett, to Galatians 2:11-14 and contends that Galatians 3:28 has "social implications." To Snodgrass, the social implications of Galatians lead to the ministry of women as they did in the New Testament. This, as he indicates later, means "ecclesiastical equality," a term, however, which he does not carefully define.[52]

With refreshing candor, Snodgrass admits that Galatians 3:28 does not answer all our questions about the role of women in society. He sees 1 Corinthians 14:33b-36 and 1 Timothy 2:11-15 as strong challenges to his views on *ecclesiastical* equality, as statements "necessitated by specific problems in Corinth and Ephesus." They are texts "less direct in their application."[53]

Snodgrass contends that the prophesying of women in 1 Corinthians 11:5 cannot be separated from "authoritative teaching and preaching."[54] This view explains aspects of his stand for "ecclesiastical equality," but unfortunately it cannot stand the test of Biblical exegesis.[55]

Critique: We might mention incidentally that Snodgrass deplores the "ironhanded"[56] view of traditionalists regarding Scripture, namely, that Scripture cannot contradict Scripture, but surely commitment to the non-contradictory unity of Scripture cannot legitimately be called "ironhandedness." It is the view of our Lord and His apostles. It would seem to be more perilous to me to pick and choose subjectively among competing texts by less reliable norms.

First, Snodgrass considers five passages parallel to Galatians 3:26-28 in the Pauline corpus: 1 Corinthians 7:17-27; 11:11-12; 12:13; Colossians 3:9-11; and Romans 10:12-13, to be "of major significance" for his position.[57] Only one of the five, however, mentions explicitly the male/female antithesis. Perhaps Paul did not give it the "explosive" force that Snodgrass sees in it. The other two antitheses seem of more importance for him, and Snodgrass calls the Jew/Gentile issue *the* (italics his) issue dominating Paul's concerns throughout his ministry.

Second, Snodgrass thinks that hierarchy arises only from the time of Genesis 3, but a more thoughtful exegesis locates the principle earlier, just as 1 Corinthians 11 and 14, Ephesians 5, and 1 Timothy 2 indicate.[58] What Genesis 3 sets forth is the effect of the fall on an already determined relationship (see Genesis 2:7, 18-25 and the apostle's use of the passage in his letters).

Third, Snodgrass stresses the conflict between Paul and Peter in Antioch as indicating how far-reaching the social implications of his statement in Galatians are (cf. Galatians 2:11-14). We have dealt with this in the critique of Jewett's claims.

Fourth, Snodgrass tends to think that, because women performed certain legitimate forms of ministry in the New Testament, such as ministering to our Lord and to Paul in personal ways and ministering to the church in Christian service, as every reader of the Bible acknowledges, the church must grant women, who have full equality in Christ, the office of elder, the oversight of the body, and the freedom to teach the gathered church. That does not follow. Christian service is the responsibility of all believers, but that does not prove that the office of elder is open to all. Christian teaching is a sovereign gift of the Spirit that not all have (cf. Romans 12:6-8; 1 Corinthians 12:6, 11, 29; 1 Peter 4:10-11).[59]

In other words, and to conclude this section, one must not try to answer all questions of Christian office and ministry from Galatians 3:28, as Snodgrass acknowledges in one place.[60]

"It seems precarious," Fung wisely declares, "to appeal to this verse in support of any view of the role of women in the Church, for two reasons: (a) Paul's statement is not concerned with the role relationships of men and women within the Body of Christ but rather with their common initiation into it through (faith and) baptism; (b) the male/female distinction, unlike the other two, has its roots in creation, so that the parallelism between the male/female pair and the other pairs may not be unduly pressed."[61] I find that eminently Biblical and reasonable.

B. The Historic Orthodox Argument

Historic orthodoxy, as noted in the brief survey of the Fathers' views, has contended that Galatians 3:28 affirms the full equality of males and females "*in Christ*," as Paul says. All are equal in Christ, the church, and family, but the phrase, "in Christ," refers to the mystical and universal, the representative and covenantal union of all believers in the Lord. In the context of Galatians, the apostle simply affirms that every believer in Christ inherits fully the Abrahamic promises by grace apart from legal works.

The phrase, "in the church," when the subject of office and function is in view, refers to the visible body of believers. In the visible body, equality coexists with divinely mandated leadership and submission, just as it does in the family (cf. Ephesians 5:22-6:9). This is not to lead to abuse, offense, or exploitation, for all of us are essential and equally important in our positions and functions within the body, as Paul points out (cf. 1 Corinthians 12:12-30). The existence of elders in the church, appointed by the Holy Spirit to rule in the body, does not destroy our equality in Christ (cf. Acts 20:28; 1 Thessalonians 5:12-13; 1 Timothy 5:17; Hebrews 13:7, 17, 24).

The ultimate and telling proof that equality and submission may coexist in glorious harmony is found in the mediatorial mission of the Son of God, "God from God, Light from Light, true God from true God" (Nicaea), who completed it in the true liberation of submission to His Father (cf. John 8:21-47; 1 Corinthians 15:24-28; cf. 11:3).

There is little need to multiply footnotes to document that this has been the view of historic orthodoxy to the present and, in fact, is still the majority view, although presently under vigorous attack. The very fact that its opponents call the view of historic orthodoxy "the traditional view" acknowledges its historical primacy.

There arises at this point, however, a matter worthy of serious consideration: If the Christian church has held this view for centuries with Bible in hand, then we may presume that there exists some good reason for that fact. The Lord Jesus Christ promised the church the gift of the permanently indwelling Spirit to provide understanding of the Scriptures (cf. John 16:12-15; Psalm 36:9). We have reason to believe that His promise has been kept, and that the church has received that light in understanding the Word of God. Widespread agreement in such understanding by orthodox believers should not be abandoned without the most careful consideration of objections, both exegetical and theological.

To treat the church's historical understanding of Scripture lightly is to forget that it is the believing body that, through the centuries, carries on the theological enterprise with the Word in hand and accompanied by the enlightening Spirit. Thus, the largest part of any theologian's work comes from reverent consideration and response to the Christian theological tradition. The creeds of the church, the results of serious spiritual and theological strife, are more important than the views of individuals. We should begin our discussions with the assumption that *the church is probably right*, unless exegetical and theological study compel us otherwise. "The proclamation of new discoveries," Abraham Kuyper, the famed founder of the Free University of Amsterdam, wrote, "is not always a proof of devotion to the truth, it is sometimes a tribute to self-esteem."[62]

Conclusion

There is no reason to claim that Galatians 3:28 supports an egalitarianism of function in the church. It does plainly teach an egalitarianism of privilege in the covenantal union of believers in Christ. The Abrahamic promises, in their flowering by the Redeemer's saving work, belong universally to the family of God. Questions of roles and functions in that body can only be answered by a consideration of other and later New Testament teaching.

8

Husbands and Wives as Analogues of Christ and the Church: Ephesians 5:21-33 and Colossians 3:18-19

George W. Knight III

The longest statement in the New Testament on the relationship of husbands and wives is Ephesians 5:21-33. The parallel account, Colossians 3:18-19, succinctly states the main points of Paul's teaching. We shall use the Ephesians account as the basis for this chapter and relate the Colossians material to it.

Before we inquire into the particular truths the apostle articulates in Ephesians 5:22-33, we should determine the flow of his presentation. Paul ties his previous discussion to his treatment of husbands and wives with a summary preview: "submit to one another out of reverence for Christ" (verse 21).[1] Then he addresses the respective parties: wives (verses 22-24) and husbands (verses 25-31). He asks wives to submit to their husbands as their heads as the church submits to Christ as her head. He asks husbands to love their wives as Christ loved the church. Paul compares the relationship of husband and wife to that between Christ and the church (notice the comparatives "as" and "just as" in verses 22, 23, 24, 25).

Paul not only compares marriage to the relationship between Christ and His church but also expands on the latter. Thus, some verses focus almost exclusively on Christ and the church (e.g., verses 26, 27). After these instructions and comparisons, Paul cites Genesis 2:24 in verse 31 and makes a final reference to the relationship of Christ and His church in verse 32. He concludes by summarizing his instructions in verse 33 with two key concepts: a husband is to love his wife and a wife is to respect her husband.

This passage abounds with instructions for marriage. The key ideas appear in the flow of the argument: submission to one another in the fear of the Lord (verse 21); submission by the wife to her husband as her head, as the church submits to Christ its head (verses 22-24); love by the husband for his wife, as Christ loves the church (verses 25-30); the appeal to Genesis 2:24 (verse 31); and the concluding summary (verse 33) with its emphasis on the husband's love and the wife's respect.

We will examine each of these in turn to ascertain its particular importance both in isolation and in its contribution to the whole passage. Limitations of space and the focus of our study demand that details about Christ and the church outside the comparison with marriage be omitted from consideration here.

Submit to One Another in the Fear of Christ

Verse 21 provides a transition from the verses that precede to those that follow. Even though the verb "submit to" is appropriately rendered as an imperative, as are others that precede it ("speak," verse 19; "sing and make music," verse 19), it (like them) is a participle that concludes the string of exhortations begun by Paul in verse 18 with the true imperative "be filled with the Spirit." "Submit to one another" thus concludes the list of things that should characterize Spirit-filled living by the redeemed. Furthermore, in a couple of important manuscripts, no verb appears in verse 22, so that "submit to" from verse 21 has to be understood as functioning in verse 22 as well. In other important manuscripts, the verb appears in verse 22 as well.[2] Both readings tie the two verses together, since the same verb is either understood or repeated. Hence verse 21 needs to be considered in its transitional role.

Three ideas are so inherent to the thought of this verse that we must consider them in order properly understand this verse and its relevance for the passage as a whole. They are (1) the meaning of "submit to one another," (2) the significance of the qualifier "out of reverence for Christ," and (3) how this call for submission to one another relates to the specific instructions to wives and husbands.

What is Meant by "Submit to One Another"?

In the admonition "submit to one another,"[3] the verb (*hupotassō*) has as its basic meaning "to subject or subordinate." Here Paul's use of the middle voice focuses on what one does to oneself: one submits oneself to others. The Bauer-Arndt-Gingrich-Danker *Greek-English Lexicon* rightly describes this as "submission in the sense of voluntary yielding in love" (p. 848, section 1bb). This voluntary yielding to others is a characteristic of the Christian community and is urged elsewhere in the New Testament. Compare, e.g., "In humility consider others [*allēlous*, the same word as in Ephesians] better than yourselves" (Philippians 2:3).[4] This admonition is based on the example of Jesus (Philippians 2:5), who insisted on a servant mentality in imitation of Him: ". . . whoever wants to become great among you must be your servant, and whoever wants to be first must be your slave—just as the Son of Man did not come to be served, but to serve" (Matthew 20:26-28; cf. Mark 10:43-45; cf. also Luke 22:26, 27).

Furthermore, the Apostle Peter, like the Apostle Paul, both urges particular people (younger men) to submit to particular people (elders) and all to submit to one another: "Young men . . . be submissive to (*hupotagēte*) those who are older. All of you, clothe yourselves with humility toward one another (*allēlōn* again) . . . " (1 Peter 5:4-5). Similarly, Paul urges masters to "Treat your slaves *in the same way*" (*ta auta* , Ephesians 6:9) as their slaves were to treat them, i.e., "with respect and fear, and with sincerity of heart" (verse 5). This implies reciprocity between masters and slaves. The exhortation to Christians in Ephesians 5:21 is thus, like these other passages, a general exhortation to mutual submission to "one another."

Submission in Reverence for Christ

The motivation for submission to one another is to be "reverence (*phobō*) for Christ" (5:21). Reverence, or fear (*phobos*), here is not dread, because Scripture elsewhere teaches that God's love in us casts out such fear (1 John 4:18; cf. also Romans 8:15). Rather, it is respectful reverence for Christ that recognizes who has asked this of us and that He will hold us accountable for our actions (cf., for this sense in Paul, 2 Corinthians 5:11; 7:1). This statement reminds us that—because in our sinful rebellion we would not obey our Lord—we will only submit to others when Christ has made us subject to Himself, and then we *will* submit to one another because He insists that we do so. Paul makes this point elsewhere when, in writing about interpersonal relationships—including those of men and women—he says forcefully, "What I am writing to you is the Lord's command" (1 Corinthians 14:37). Thus verse 21, explicitly insisting that believers submit to one another, sets the tone for the entire section.

How Verse 21 Is a Transition

But then the question naturally arises, how is the content of verse 21 related to verses 22-33? At least two answers have been given. First, one might answer that this verse is a general statement of the specifics spelled out for wives, children, and servants. That is, certain ways in which Christians are to submit to others are then specified.[5] It is argued that the key word *submit* is picked up with reference to wives in verses 22 and 24 and for children and servants by the concept of obedience (6:1, 5). Furthermore, this would seem to parallel Peter's approach when he urges Christians, "Submit yourselves for the Lord's sake to every authority instituted among men . . ." (1 Peter 2:13) and spells this out in terms of the submission servants (2:18ff.) and wives are to give (3:1ff.). Even if the following answer is more adequate, this suggestion need not be rejected so long as it does not exclude the more comprehensive understanding.

Second, one might answer that the relationship of verse 21 to verses 22-23 is that verse 21 states a general and comprehensive principle before Paul moves to the specific roles of husbands and wives, parents and children, and masters and slaves, so that the specific is considered in the light of the general. On this view, Paul reminds all in the congregation of their need for mutual submission in the Body of Christ before writing of the specific duties each has in his particular situation. This seems to do more justice to the explicit reciprocal pronoun used, "one another" (*allēlōn*). Furthermore, it is in line with the contextual understanding found elsewhere in Paul and Peter where a similar exhortation is given (Philippians 2:3, "let each of you regard one another . . ." [NASB]; 1 Peter 5:5, "all of you clothe yourselves with humility toward one another" [NASB).[6]

First Peter 5:5 is particularly instructive, because there Peter urges "all of you" to be humble toward one another immediately after urging the younger ones to be subject to their elders. Thus Peter calls on the elders among "all of you" to be humble toward younger men at the same time as he calls on younger men to submit to those same elders. Just as Peter expresses both ideas in one verse (1 Peter 5:5), so also Paul expresses the general note of mutual submission in verse 21, followed by the specific submission of wives to husbands, for example, in verses 22ff. So Paul wants to remind all Christians, men and women, of their duty to be submissive to one another before reminding wives of their particular responsibility to their husbands in marriage. This puts particular, unidirectional submission in the context of general, mutual submission and relates specific duties, roles, and responsibilities to the general Christian concept of mutual submission.

It is sometimes urged that mutual submission alone is in view in the section on wives and husbands, and that therefore wives are not being called to a unique or distinct submission to their husbands.[7] Since, however, verse 21 is a transition verse to the entirety of the section on household responsibilities, consistency would demand that the sections on children and parents and on servants and masters also speak only of mutual submissiveness and not of different roles. Since this is self-evidently not so for the section on children and parents, on the one hand, and masters and servants, on the other, the implication is that distinguishable roles and specific submission are also taught in the section on husbands and wives. Of course, it could be argued that the command given husbands to love their wives is but another way of calling them to mutual submission. But even if that were so, Paul still calls the husband "the head" of the wife and therefore the one to whom she should submit in everything (verses 22-24). Thus this section cannot be teaching only mutual submission rather than the specific submission of wives to husbands in the overall context of mutual submission. The mutual submission to which all are called and that defines the larger context and sets the tone does not, therefore, rule out the specific and different roles and relationships to which husbands and wives are called in the verses addressed to them.

Submission and Headship

In the main portion of the section addressed to wives and husbands (verses 22-30) and the concluding summary (verse 33), Paul delineates his teaching along three lines: (1) the role each has (submission, headship), (2) the attitude with which each fulfills his or her role (love, respect), and (3) the analogy of marriage to the relationship of Christ and His church.

The Roles of Wives and Husbands

Paul commands wives to "be subject to your own husbands, as to the Lord" (verse 22, NASB). The operative verb "be subject to" or "submit to" (*hupotassō*) reappears in verse 24, where Paul writes that wives should submit "to their husbands in everything" "as the church submits to Christ." This is the essence of the apostle's teaching to wives, since in Colossians 3:18 it is the entirety of his charge: "Wives, submit (*hupotassō*) to your husbands, as is fitting in the Lord."[8] Furthermore, this particular exhortation to the wife to submit to her husband is the universal teaching of the New Testament. Every passage that deals with the relationship of the wife to her husband tells her to "submit to" him, using this same verb (*hupotassō*): Ephesians 5:22; Colossians 3:18; 1 Peter 3:1; Titus 2:4f.[9] Sampley summarizes the matter when he says concerning the household instructions for wives that the form "reduced to its barest details would include: Wives, be submissive to (possibly 'your own') husbands."[10]

The meaning of *hupotassō*, used consistently in the charge to wives, is the same as its meaning in verse 21, that is, "submission in the sense of voluntary yielding in love."[11] This is no abandonment of the great New Testament truth also taught by the Apostle Paul that "there is neither . . . male nor female, for you are all one in Christ Jesus" (Galatians 3:28). Rather, it is an appeal to one who is equal by creation and redemption to submit to the authority God has ordained.

Her equality is evident in the verb form always used in this admonition and in the fact that it is wives who are addressed, not husbands. (The New Testament never commands husbands to subordinate their wives, i.e., to force them to submit.) The voice of the verb is not active but middle/passive, with the meaning either of subjecting oneself (middle) or of allowing oneself to be in subjection (passive), with the middle voice most likely here. Thus the admonition is similar to the request in Hebrews that Christians (who are equal in creation and redemption to one another and therefore also equal to elders) are to "Obey your leaders and submit to their authority" (Hebrews 13:17) and Peter's instruction that young men "be submissive (*hupotagēte*) to those who are older" (1 Peter 5:5). Just as certain men can be given authority in the church, implying no superiority for them or inferiority for those subject to them, so also wives may be asked to subject themselves to their husbands without any suggestion of inferiority/superiority. The Apostle Peter makes this clear when he insists that husbands, to whom he has asked wives to submit (1 Peter 3:1ff.), "treat them with respect as the weaker partner and as heirs with you of the gracious gift of life" (1 Peter 3:7).

The Nature of Wives' Submission

The submission wives are to render is delineated by four key concepts: (1) "to your own husbands" (in the Greek text, left out of the NIV; see NASB), (2) "as to the Lord" (both of these first two concepts appear in verse 22; for the second cf. also Colossians 3:18, "as is fitting in the Lord"), (3) "for the husband is the head of the wife" (verse 23), and (4) "as the church submits to Christ" (verse 24).[12] Paul does not ask every woman to submit to every man, but rather asks wives to submit to their own (*idiois*) husbands. Paul is not insisting that every relationship between a woman and a man is one of submission and headship, but that where leadership is an ingredient of the situation, as in marriage, the woman should submit to that leadership (headship) of the man. Similarly, for example, in the family of God, the church, where leadership is involved, Paul insists that women not take on that role but submit to the leadership of men (cf. 1 Timothy 2:11, 12; 1 Corinthians 14:34ff. and the chapters in this volume dealing with these passages). Here specifically he commands each wife to submit to the headship of her own husband.

The Nature of Husbands' Headship

Paul gives the basis for his charge to wives in verse 23: "For ("because," *hoti*) the husband is the head (*kephalē*) of the wife." It has been assumed already that this word *head* (*kephalē*) implies authority. Not all agree. Some say that it means "source." I refer the reader to the chapter by Wayne Grudem on this subject as well as the standard Greek lexicons for the data. Suffice it to say here that Paul indicates the significance of "head" (*kephalē*) by saying that "the husband is the head of the wife *as* Christ is head of the church" (verse 23). It is evident that Christ is the head of the church as the authority over it because the following verse speaks of the church as submitting to Christ. The two concepts mutually explain one another: the church submits to Christ's authority because He is the head or authority over it.

This reference to Christ as head follows two previous references to Him as head where the note of authority is equally present. In the first, Ephesians 1:22, Paul writes that Christ is head over "everything" and that God has "*placed all things under* (*hupotassō*) his feet." In the second, Ephesians 4:15, Christ is designated the head of the church, His body, and it is His authority and power that cause the growth of the body for the building up of itself in love. It is virtually certain that in comparing the headship of the husband over the wife to the headship of Christ over the church, the apostle is using the term *kephalē* for the husband as he does for Christ, namely, as one who has authority and is the leader.

When we ask how that headship was established, we are aided by Paul's treatment of this question in 1 Corinthians 11:1ff., where he explicitly relates the headship of a man over a woman to that of Christ over every man and of God over Christ. In this context, Paul refers to Genesis 2:21-24 and states that the order of creation of man and woman and the fact that woman was created to help the man (and not vice versa) demonstrate that God had established man as the head over the woman by this divine action and its inherent intent (1 Corinthians 11:8-9). Paul thus affirms that male headship is a divine appointment. This understanding certainly informs his use of the same term *kephalē* in Ephesians and is therefore the basis on which he commands the wife to submit to the husband as her head. It is evident in Ephesians 5 itself that Paul has Genesis 2 and its principles in mind, because he quotes Genesis 2:24 at Ephesians 5:31. What he has explicitly said in 1 Corinthians 11:8, 9 informs his statement in Ephesians 5:23, and his quotation of Genesis 2:24 in Ephesians 5:31 demonstrates that the principles of Genesis 2 inform his statements in Ephesians.

The Extent of Wives' Submission

Paul concludes this section to wives, verses 22-24, by indicating that wives should submit to their husbands "in everything" (*en panti*). The phrase is all-encompassing: submission must encompass all aspects of life. This removes the misunderstanding that some may have had, or others may still have, that Paul is speaking simply about submission in sex or some other narrow realm. Since by God's decree marriage partners are "one flesh," God wants them to function together under one head, not as two autonomous individuals living together. Since Paul is concerned about that unity, we should be concerned about it too.

Paul does not feel it necessary to add to the phrase *in everything* that all disobedience to God is excepted (cf. Acts 5:29, "We must obey God rather than men!"; cf. also Acts 4:19, 20).[13] This goes without saying. Nor does he mean by this to stifle the wife's thinking and acting. Rather, he wants that thinking and acting to be shared with her husband (as his is to be shared with her) and for her to be willing to submit to his leadership "in everything." The wife should not act unilaterally. Just as the church should willingly submit to Christ in all things and, if it does so, will not find that stifling, demeaning, or stultifying of growth and freedom, so also wives should willingly submit to their husbands in all things and, if they do so, will not find that stifling, demeaning, or stultifying.

But does this mean husbands can rule their wives insensitively? Of course not! Paul rules out elsewhere the idea that anyone in authority should "lord it over" those he leads (2 Corinthians 1:24), just as Peter insists that the elders to whom young men submit must not lord it over those under them (1 Peter 5:3). Paul takes this for granted here. He handles the question of the use (or misuse) of the husband's authority shortly in his words to the husband. To that we will turn momentarily. The important thing for the wife to know is that she should submit to her husband "in everything," that is, that her submission is coextensive with all aspects of their relationship.

With the words *submit to* and *head*, the apostle states the basic roles of wives and husbands, respectively. God established those roles at creation, and they have as their analogue the roles of Christ and His church. Thus Paul can urge this special relationship of wife and husband because God in creation established it and Christ in His redeeming love to the church models and substantiates it for the redeemed community. W. J. Larkin puts this consideration adeptly when he says that "the instruction for conduct in marriage in Ephesians 5:22-33 becomes unquestionably binding when seen as a reflection of Christ's relation to the church."[14]

Instructions to husbands and wives in the New Testament always focus first on wives and their responsibility to submit to their husbands (Ephesians 5:22-24; Colossians 3:18; 1 Peter 3:1ff.). Both Peter and Paul reaffirm the role relationship God established by creation before they deal with how men and women should conduct themselves in that relationship. *The divinely instituted form must come first, before one talks about how to live within it.* This is a permanently significant lesson.

Furthermore, Paul always addresses those under authority before those in authority: wives before husbands, children before parents, servants before masters (Ephesians 5:22-6:9; Colossians 3:18-4:1). The rationale for the first two of these relationships[15] would seem to be that the divinely instituted relationship is best preserved when the divine order inherent in it is made plain by urging compliance on those under authority first, before addressing those in authority. The apostle may then command those in authority to exercise their authority with loving concern that does not run roughshod over those under authority, tempting them to challenge the divinely established relationship. Having established the divinely given character of the institution and the divinely given roles, the apostle now spells out the attitudes with which those in that institution should fulfill their respective roles.

The Attitudes of Love and Respect

On this backdrop Paul addresses husbands: "Husbands, love your wives . . ." (Ephesians 5:25; Colossians 3:19). The key word, *love*, appears six times in Ephesians 5:25-33. It denotes the husband's duty to his wife. Interestingly enough his role, headship, was stated in the section addressed to his wife (verse 23), not in the section addressed to him. Paul does not say to husbands, "Be head over your wife!" Instead he commands them, twice, to love their wives (verses 25 and 28): "Husbands, love your wives," and, "husbands ought to love their wives as their own bodies." The command is explicated by reference to the analogy of Christ's love for the church (verses 25ff.) and by the way one loves one's own body (verse 28): by nourishing and cherishing it (verse 29). In the comparison made with Christ's love for the church, Paul emphasizes the self-giving character of that love (verse 25) and its concern to benefit the other so that life together will be wonderful (verses 26, 27).

Loving as Christ Loved

Paul's direct command to husbands is to "love your wives, just as Christ loved the church and gave himself up for her . . ." (verse 25). This is clearly how the apostle demands that the husband exercise his leadership in everything as the head over his wife. He is to love her "just as" (*kathōs*) Christ loved the church. Just as the church, in submitting to Christ, was the model for the wife in submitting to her husband as her head (verses 23, 24), so now Christ, in His love for the Church, is the model for the husband in loving his wife. The character and description of that love are stated in the words "and gave himself up for her" (verse 25). In these few key words are contained the description of what the love of a husband for his wife should be.

First, the loving husband gives of himself. In his leadership role as head, he seeks to lead by giving of himself to his wife in ways analogous to how Christ gave Himself to His bride. Christ's giving of Himself was personal and sacrificial. This great principle of self-giving sets the tone and points toward the many ways in which this love can be manifested and realized.

Second, Christ's giving of Himself was for the benefit of His bride—He gave Himself up "for her." Just so, the husband's self-giving should be for his wife's benefit. In short, we may speak of this love as a giving of oneself for the benefit of the other.

Paul specifies the intended result of Christ's giving up of Himself for the church in verses 26 and 27: "to make her holy, cleansing her by the washing with water through the word, and to present her to himself as a radiant church, without stain or wrinkle or any other blemish, but holy and blameless." Here we see two forces at work. First, Paul writes of Christ's redeeming work for us. Paul always delights in explicating this, and so he seizes on this opportunity to develop these ideas. Yet the uniqueness of the redemptive work of Christ means that these aspects cannot be imitated precisely by the husband. Nonetheless, second, Paul uses the imagery of marriage to tell of Christ and the church: Christ serves her "to present her to himself as a radiant church" (verse 27). Is it not likely, therefore, that he intended to teach that the husband's love, like Christ's, was to be beneficial to the wife, just as Christ's love was to the church?[16] Just as Christ works to present His church to Himself as a glorious bride in a glorious marriage, should not the husband work to make his wife glorious and their marriage glorious?

The Implications of Being One Flesh

The apostle continues with his insistence on the husband's loving his wife by restating the charge in verse 28. This time he states it in terms of a husband's loving his wife as he loves his own body and thus as he loves himself. Thus he not only introduces a new dimension to that love but also intertwines it again with the imagery of Christ's love for the church, His beloved, His body.

The new element is that the husband "who loves his wife loves himself" (verse 28b). Many commentators have suggested that this reflects the command to love one's neighbor as oneself (Leviticus 19:18; compare the reflexive "himself" in Ephesians 5:33).[17] More importantly, Paul first states the command by speaking of husbands' loving "their own bodies" (verse 28a). This use of "bodies" instead of "themselves" may have come about by the influence of Genesis 2:24, quoted in verse 31, which speaks of the couple as "one flesh." The analogy of Christ and the church may also have influenced the choice of words, since it is *body* (*sōma*) rather than *flesh* that Paul has already used in Ephesians to denote the church (1:23; 2:16; 4:4, 12, 16, and, most importantly, in the beginning of this account in 5:23) and that he reiterates shortly (5:30). Thus the command to "love their wives as their own bodies" reflects the love of Christ for the church,

His body (verse 30). At the same time, the word *body* provides a link to the one-flesh concept of Genesis 2:24, a verse Paul quotes in verse 31.

Paul does all this while applying the general commandment of Leviticus 19:18, "love your neighbor as yourself," in a very direct way to the love the husband should have for his nearest and dearest neighbor, his wife. In so doing, Paul ties together the creation ordinance about marriage (Genesis 2:24), the great commandment about loving one's neighbor (Leviticus 19:18), and the sublime pattern of Christ's love for His bride, the church. No greater combination could be conceived of than the combination of God's sanctions in creation, commandment, and redemption.

Having joined these concepts together, the apostle shows how this love is to be expressed by reminding the husband that he "feeds and cares" for his own flesh (verse 29). With these two verbs, *ektrephei* and *thalpei*, Paul uses the emotionally evocative language of nurturing care to communicate what it means to love one's wife. The word *thalpō* literally means "to keep warm" and, figuratively, "to cherish" and "to comfort." Paul's only other use of this verb is in 1 Thessalonians 2:7, where, in powerful imagery, he speaks of his love for the Thessalonians: "we proved to be gentle among you, as a nursing mother tenderly cares (*thalpō*) for her own children" (NASB). He develops his thought in the next verse by saying: "Having thus a fond affection for you, we were well-pleased to impart[18] to you not only the gospel of God but also our own lives, because you had become very dear [beloved][19] to us" (1 Thessalonians 2:8, NASB). In Thessalonians we see again the same elements we find in Ephesians, although in a different but similar setting. The one "cherished" is the one to whom one gives not only the highest good, the gospel, but also one's very own life because that one is "beloved." Ephesians says that because a husband loves his wife, he will give his life for her good and will express his love by nourishing and cherishing her, the beloved. The terms *feed* and *care* communicate these truths with a delightful fragrance that must be worked out and applied in the numerous, variegated, nitty-gritty situations of life.

The Tenderness of Godly Headship

Paul also addresses the danger of husbands' being overbearing toward their wives, or "harsh with them" (Colossians 3:19). Paul alludes to that attitude in Ephesians in his remark that "no one ever hated his own body" (Ephesians 5:29), and in the Colossians account (where he does not develop the concept of love as he does in Ephesians) he explicitly demands as a corollary to the command, "Husbands, love your wives," the parallel command, "do not be harsh with them."

In so doing Paul emphasizes that the headship of the husband over his wife must not be negative, oppressive, or reactionary. Instead, it must be a headship of love in which the husband gives of himself for his wife's good, nourishing and cherishing the beloved one who, as his equal, voluntarily submits to his headship. Paul has thus given two great truths with respect to the husband: first, that he is the head of his wife, and second, that he must exercise his headship in love.

Submitting as the Church Submits

Similarly, Paul has given two great truths with respect to the wife's role and how she should carry it out. The introductory verses of this section, with which we have already dealt in part, insisted that her role is to submit (as an equal) to her husband as her head (verses 22-24). We have left aside for the time being Paul's instructions about how this should be done, except to note the helpful analogy of the church's submission to Christ. Now we need to return to this matter.

The key phrases in this portion of Paul's instructions to wives are "as to the Lord" (Ephesians 5:22), "as is fitting in the Lord" (Colossians 3:18), "in everything" (Ephesians 5:24, which we considered above under the role itself), and "the wife must respect her husband" (Ephesians 5:33).

Because the headship of the husband is established by God, the husband who fulfills that role does so as a servant of God, and the leadership given to him in this role expresses God's authority in the marriage. Hence Paul finds it appropriate to appeal to the wife to submit to her husband "as to the Lord" (Ephesians 5:22). "As" (*hōs*) indicates the manner of her submission. She should submit to her husband as she submits to the Lord. The comparative "as to the Lord" conjures up what should and does characterize the godly submission a Christian renders to the Lord Jesus. This one qualification says it all, even though Paul goes on to explicate it in the verses that follow. (In view of Paul's calling for submission "as to the Lord," we gain a better appreciation of Peter's commendation of Sarah's calling Abraham "lord" and, particularly, of the fact that, as evidence of her submission to her husband, Sarah "obeyed Abraham" [1 Peter 3:6.])

The phrase "in everything" (Ephesians 5:24)[20] denotes the comprehensiveness of her submission. In view of the previous use of the word *Lord* with specific reference to Christ (verse 20), "the Lord" in view in Ephesians 5:22 is undoubtedly Jesus Christ, a fact reinforced by Paul's writing next of Christ's Lordship over the church and the church's submission to His headship as the model for how the woman is to submit to her husband.

The words in Colossians 3:18, "Wives, submit to your husbands," are qualified by the words "as is fitting in the Lord" (the Greek for "in the Lord" is *en kuriō*[21]). Here again "as" (*hōs*) is used. Therefore to say that such submission "is fitting"[22] "as . . . in the Lord" means that it is appropriate to being under the Lordship of Christ[23] or, to paraphrase, of being a Christian.[24] The apostle thus asserts that such submission is proper for Christian wives because it is what our Lord expects. The best illustration of this is another passage commanding this submission, Titus 2:4, 5. There also wives are urged to "be subject to their husbands"[25] (verse 5). Paul insists that this exhortation is "in accord with sound doctrine" (Titus 2:1). Thus the submission of wives to their husbands is not some concession to contemporary mores but is that which abides by scriptural teachings of Christianity (including the doctrine that in Christ there is neither male nor female, which Paul taught in Galatians 3:28).

To return to Colossians 3:18, to "submit to your husbands" is "fitting" or appropriate to the standing wives have "in the Lord." To put it theologically, redemption in Christ undergirds and commends the wife's submission to her husband according to God's design at creation rather than, as some feminists claim, overturning a submission rooted only in the fall. Since Paul warns husbands against sinful abuse of their headship through harshness (Colossians 3:10), perhaps this admonition to wives to submit "as is fitting in the Lord" is not only an encouragement to them to render voluntary submission but also a warning lest they presume that their standing in the Lord justifies their acting as if there were no distinguishable roles for wives and husbands "in the Lord."[26]

Showing Respect for the Husband's Headship

The last exhortation to wives about how they should submit to their husbands is found in Ephesians 5:33: ". . . the wife must respect her husband." The key word here is the verb *respect* (so rendered by a number of modern English translations, e.g., RSV, NASB, NIV, NEB).[27] This rendering of the Greek *phobeō* is proper. Paul uses *respect* here in the sense of treating the husband's leadership with dutiful regard and deference. The Greek verb is used similarly in an analogous situation where one human is urged to render respect (or reverence) to another (Leviticus 19:3, LXX: "Let every one of you reverence his father and his mother"). There, as here in Ephesians, the respect called for is primarily to the role the person occupies and not to the particular merits of the person.

Probably Paul chose *phobeō* in his final charge to wives to correlate his exhortation to them with his exhortation to all Christians, "Submit to one another out of reverence (*phobō*) for Christ" (Ephesians 5:21). By using a concept he had previously used of the Lord Jesus Christ, he also correlates this concluding exhortation to wives with his initial one (verse 22), which said that they should be subject to their own husbands "as to the Lord."

The respect asked of a wife recognizes the God-given character of the headship of her husband and thus treats him with dutiful regard and deference. Just as husbands have been asked to display their headship through likeness to Christ's headship over His church, that is, through a love that cherishes and nourishes (verse 25, 28, 29), so now wives are asked to render their submission in a way that is most like that of the submission of the church to Christ, that is, a truly respectful submission because it is rendered voluntarily from the heart. A wife's respecting her husband and his headship therefore implies that her submission involves not only what she does but also her attitude in doing it. As with the husband, so with the wife, it is the heart's attitude of grateful acceptance of the role God assigns to each and the determination to fulfill the particular role with all the graciousness God gives that Paul is urging on both wives and husbands in this last verse of his instruction.

The Analogy of Christ and the Church

Before concluding this discussion, we need to call attention to one more remarkable aspect of this passage. After quoting Genesis 2:24, "For this reason a man will leave his father and mother and be united to his wife, and the two will become one flesh" (Ephesians 5:31), Paul gives an interpretation that shows God's purpose in marriage: "*This is a profound mystery*—but I am talking about Christ and the church" (verse 32).

Unbeknownst to the people of Moses' day (it was a "mystery"), marriage was *designed by God* from the beginning to be a picture or parable of the relationship between Christ and the church. Back when God was planning what marriage would be like, He planned it for this great purpose: it would give a beautiful earthly picture of the relationship that would someday come about between Christ and His church. This was not known to people for many generations, and that is why Paul can call it a "mystery." But now in the New Testament age Paul reveals this mystery, and it is amazing.

This means that when Paul wanted to tell the Ephesians about marriage, he did not just hunt around for a helpful analogy and suddenly think that "Christ and the church" might be a good teaching illustration. No, it was much more fundamental than that: Paul saw that *when God designed the original marriage He already had Christ and the church in mind.* This is one of God's great purposes in marriage: to picture the relationship between Christ and His redeemed people forever!

But if this is so, then the order Paul is speaking of here (submission and love) is not accidental or temporary or culturally determined: it is part of the *essence of marriage*, part of God's original plan for a perfect, sinless, harmonious marriage. This is a powerful argument for the fact that Christlike, loving headship and church-like, willing submission are rooted in creation and in God's eternal purposes, not just in the passing trends of culture.

Wives, Children, and Slaves?

It is argued sometimes that this list of duties and responsibilities simply reflects the cultural approach to these matters found in the New Testament period and that the apostle is simply asking for conformity to the practices of the day so that the gospel itself will not be hurt by Christians' violating contemporary mores. The argument is then pressed by saying that if we today do not maintain slavery on the basis of Ephesians 6:5-9, we should also not argue from this passage about the differentiating roles of wives and husbands, because we now know (better than the first-century Christians, and Paul) that they are on a par. That is, the existence of slavery and slaves' submission to their masters and the submission of wives to their husbands stand or fall together.[28]

Space does not permit a full response to this argument here,[29] but certain remarks are necessary. It is true that these three relationships (husbands and wives, parents and children, masters and slaves) are dealt with here as a kind of unit. They are treated one after another as different relationships within the larger household moving from the most central (husbands and wives) to the next most crucial (parents and children) to the extended relationship that might exist in some households (masters and slaves). But if the argument advanced above is true, then it cuts all the way across the board. Not only would the teaching about husbands and wives cease to be normative and fall away with slavery, but so would the teaching about parents and children, which is positioned between the other two relationships! The argument would have this effect by insisting that these three are on a complete par. But that aspect of the argument is flawed. It assumes that these relationships treated one after another in this section are thereby placed on the same level and are presumably handled by Paul with the same kind of considerations. Further reflection on these different relationships shows that this is not so.

Take, for example, parents and children. Paul appeals to the Fifth Commandment, "Honor your father and mother" (Exodus 20:12, cited in Ephesians 6:2) to substantiate his command, "Children, obey your parents in the Lord, for this is right" (Ephesians 6:1). Thus Paul reaches back to a permanent moral command from God (given in a time and place much earlier than and quite different from that of Ephesians) as the linchpin for his instruction to children. Thus the demise of slavery does not sweep this permanent moral command for children away, for the two relationships are *not* inseparably connected as to their essence, but only exist side-by-side because slavery fit into the larger household setting of that day.

The inherent differences are seen also by noticing that no permanent moral command or any other moral absolute with reference to slavery is used in Paul's instructions to slaves. He simply gives them instructions on how to carry out appropriate work duties and relationships with appropriate Christian attitudes as they fiind themselves in the then existing institution of slavery. This is analogous to the way Moses is represented by Jesus as having given instruction about what a man must do when he divorces his wife ("because of your hardness of heart") without thereby indicating (as some then and there implied to Jesus) that Moses approved of or encouraged divorce (see Matthew 19:7-8). Furthermore, Paul elsewhere indicates that a slave could properly become free (1 Corinthians 7:21) and therefore he does not treat slavery as a divinely ordained institution as he does that of parents and children—and as he does that of husbands and wives. For both the existence of the marriage relationship and the roles required of each one in it are in the Ephesians passage (and elsewhere) related by Paul to the creation account and God's decisive actions and instructions in that most basic and foundational event. Thus there is a great divide between husband and wives, and parents and children on one side of this list of household relationships, and masters and slaves on the other side.

So we see that the appeal to the fact that slavery is handled alongside the relationships of husbands and wives and parents and children and that therefore they must be regarded in the same way is an error which is popularly referred to "as comparing apples with oranges" and also as the error of "guilt by association." Each relationship must be evaluated in terms of the degree of absoluteness and permanence the apostle inteded for it. It certainly is evident that he was both treating marriage as a permanent and absolute institution ordained by God and teaching respectively a specific role for the wife and a specific role for the husband as a divinely prescribed duty for each.

Conclusion

The instruction about wives and husbands found in Ephesians and Colossians, expressed in the key terms "be subject" for wives and "head" for husbands, teaches distinctive roles for wives and husbands. That instruction may be summarized both as a divinely mandated leadership role for husbands in the marriage relationship and a divinely mandated submission to that leadership for wives. The fact that Paul appeals to the creation activity of God with reference to husbands and wives in Ephesians and that in 1 Corinthians 11 he grounds the headship of men in that creation activity of God shows that the apostle regards these roles and the pattern of the role relationship itself as divinely given. His instruction also demands that the respective roles be expressed and fulfilled according to the analogue of the relationship between Christ the head and the church his body. Thus the roles should reflect the actions and attitudes appropriate to that wonderful relationship between Christ and His church. Husbands must therefore exercise their headship with a "love" that "nourishes and cherishes" and that puts aside all "bitterness." Wives must voluntarily submit themselves to their husbands "as to the Lord" with "all respect" because this is in accord with their standing "in the Lord."

The apostle has expressed in Ephesians (5:21-33) and Colossians (3:18-19) the same pattern as that which is found elsewhere in the New Testament (1

Corinthians 11:1-3, 8-9; Titus 2:4-5; 1 Timothy 2:11-14; 1 Peter 3:1-7). And he has also demanded, as was done similarly by the Apostle Peter (1 Peter 3:1-7), that the respective roles be carried out with all the graciousness that the redeeming grace of Christ has brought to each and continues to accomplish in each in their respective roles as a wife and as a husband. In short, as analogues of Christ and His church, the husband is asked to exercise, with love, a headship over his wife and the wife is asked to submit, with respect, to her husband.

9

What Does It Mean Not to Teach or Have Authority Over Men?

1 Timothy 2:11-15

Douglas Moo

The New Testament makes it plain that Christian women, like men, have been given spiritual gifts (1 Corinthians 12:7-11). Women, like men, are to use these gifts to minister to the body of Christ (1 Peter 4:10); their ministries are indispensable to the life and growth of the church (1 Corinthians 12:12-26). There are many examples in the New Testament of just such ministries on the part of gifted Christian women (see Chapter 5 in this volume). To be true to the New Testament, then, the contemporary church needs to honor those varied ministries of women and to encourage women to pursue them.

But does the New Testament place any restrictions on the ministry of women? From the earliest days of the apostolic church, most orthodox Christians have thought so. One important reason they have thought so is the teaching of 1 Timothy 2:8-15:

> [8]I want men everywhere to lift up holy hands in prayer, without anger or disputing. [9]I also want women to dress modestly, with decency and propriety, not with braided hair or gold or pearls or expensive clothes, [10]but with good deeds, appropriate for women who profess to worship God. [11]A woman should learn in quietness and full submission. [12]I do not permit a woman to teach or to have authority over a man; she must be silent. [13]For Adam was formed first, then Eve. [14]And Adam was not the one deceived; it was the woman who was deceived and became a sinner. [15]But women will be kept safe through childbirth, if they continue in faith, love and holiness with propriety.

Has the church been right to think that this passage imposes certain permanent restrictions on the ministry of women? Certainly this is what the passage, as translated above, seems to say. Women are not to teach or to have authority over men. They are not to do so because of the order in which God created man and woman and because of how man and woman fell into sin. However, many in our day think this passage does not require the contemporary church to limit the ministry of women. Others think it may limit only certain women from certain ministries in certain circumstances.

Many people refuse to apply this passage to the church today because they question whether it has authority over us. For example, non-evangelical New Testament scholars generally believe that all three pastoral epistles (1 Timothy, 2 Timothy, and Titus) were written by an unknown person in Paul's name long after he was dead. While this unknown author admired Paul and wanted to use his authority, he also contradicted Paul. In such cases, if anyone is to be able to speak to the church today with authority, it is the "true Paul," not the "pseudo-Paul" of the pastoral epistles. And the "true Paul" taught that in Christ there is neither male nor female (Galatians 3:28).

We are not, however, concerned here with those who hold this view, or others like it.[1] For such a viewpoint can only be refuted at a basic critical and theological level. We would want to show why Paul should be considered the author of the pastoral epistles; how the teaching of these epistles, although different in tone and emphasis from other letters of Paul, is nevertheless compatible with their teaching; and, most basically, why Christians should accept whatever Scripture says as holding unquestioned authority for the church today.

Yet there are many sincere Christians who agree with everything we have just said but still do not think that 1 Timothy 2:8-15 puts any general restriction on the ministry of women in the contemporary church. Are they right? Has the position of the Christian church on this issue for twenty centuries been the product of cultural conditioning from which we finally are able to free ourselves?

We do not think so. We think 1 Timothy 2:8-15 imposes two restrictions on the ministry of women: they are not to teach Christian doctrine to men and they are not to exercise authority directly over men in the church. These restrictions are permanent, authoritative for the church in all times and places and circumstances as long as men and women are descended from Adam and Eve. In this essay, we will attempt to justify these conclusions. In doing so, we will be concerned particularly to show why the arguments for alternative interpretations are not convincing.

The Setting

Paul writes this first letter to his disciple and coworker Timothy to remind him "how people ought to conduct themselves in God's household, which is the church of the living God" (1 Timothy 3:15). Paul must send this reminder because the church at Ephesus, where Timothy has been left to continue the work of ministry, is beset by false teaching (see 1:3). Certain people from within the church have departed from the true teaching of the gospel, have become quarrelsome and argumentative, and are propagating doctrines that are erroneous. Many interpretations of 1 Timothy 2:11-15 rely heavily on the nature of this false teaching at Ephesus in explaining what Paul means in these verses. There is nothing wrong with this in principle; good exegesis always takes into consideration the larger context in which a text appears. However, Paul tells us remarkably little about the specifics of this false teaching, presumably because he knows that Timothy is well acquainted with the problem. This means that we cannot be at all sure about the precise nature of this false teaching and, particularly, about its impact on the women in the church—witness the many, often contradictory, scholarly reconstructions of this false teaching.[2] But this means that we must be very careful about allowing any specific reconstruction—tentative and uncertain as it must be—to play too large a role in our exegesis.

We will, then, take a cautious approach to this matter. In our exegesis, we will use only those aspects of the false teaching that may be clearly inferred from the pastoral epistles and related New Testament passages to shed light on the text. Some of the aspects specifically relevant to 1 Timothy 2:11-15 are:

1. The false teachers sowed dissension and were preoccupied with trivialities (1 Timothy 1:4-6; 6:4-5; cf. 2 Timothy 2:14, 16-17, 23-24; Titus 1:10; 3:9-11).

2. The false teachers stressed asceticism as a means of spirituality. They taught abstinence from certain foods, from marriage, and probably sex generally (1 Timothy 4:1-3). In keeping with these ascetic tendencies, they may also have stressed physical training as a means of spirituality (4:8).

3. The false teachers had persuaded many women to follow them in their doctrines (1 Timothy 5:15; 2 Timothy 3:6-7).

4. The false teachers were encouraging women to discard what we might call traditional female roles in favor of a more egalitarian approach to the role relationships of men and women. This is not stated explicitly as a plank in the false teachers' platform anywhere in the pastoral epistles. Nevertheless, it is an inference with a high degree of probability for the following reasons:

First, an encouragement to abstain from marriage, which we know was part of the false teachers' program, is likely to include a more general denigration of traditional female roles. Second, the counsel in 1 Timothy 5:14 to young widows "to marry, to have children, to manage their homes"—i.e., to occupy themselves in traditional female roles—is issued because some "have . . . turned away to follow Satan" (verse 15). Since Paul labels the false teaching as demonic (1 Timothy 4:1), it is likely that this turning away to follow Satan means following the false teachers and that they were teaching the opposite of what Paul commands in 5:14.

Third, the false teaching that is besetting the church at Ephesus sounds very similar to the general problem that seems to lurk behind 1 Corinthians. In both situations, the problem arose from within the church, involved the denial of a future, physical resurrection in favor of a present, "spiritual" resurrection (see 2 Timothy 2:18; 1 Corinthians 15, coupled with 4:8), and led to incorrect attitudes toward marriage and sex (1 Corinthians 7; 1 Timothy 4:3), toward food (1 Corinthians 8:1-13; 1 Timothy 4:3, although the specific issues are a bit different), and, most importantly, to a tendency on the part of the women to disregard their appropriate roles, especially vis-a-vis their husbands (see 1 Corinthians 11:2-18; 14:33b-36; 1 Timothy 2:9-15; 5:13-14; Titus 2:3-5).

While we cannot be sure about this, there is good reason to think that the problem in both situations was rooted in a false belief that Christians were already in the full form of God's kingdom and that they had accordingly been spiritually taken "out of" the world so that aspects of this creation, like sex, food, and male/female distinctions, were no longer relevant to them.[3] It may well be that these beliefs arose from an unbalanced emphasis on Paul's own teaching that Christians were "raised with Christ" (Ephesians 2:6; Colossians 2:12; 3:1) and that in Christ there is neither "male nor female" (Galatians 3:28). What Paul would be doing in both 1 Corinthians and the pastoral epistles is seeking to right the balance by reasserting the importance of the created order and the ongoing significance of those role distinctions between men and women that he saw rooted in creation. Whether this specific interpretation of the data of 1 Corinthians and the pastorals is correct or not, the similarity between the battery of problems in the two situations strongly suggests that in Ephesus, as in Corinth, a tendency to remove role distinctions between men and women was part of the false teaching.[4] Very likely, then, Paul's teaching about the roles of men and women in church ministry in 1 Timothy 2:11-15 is occasioned by the need to counter the false teachers on this point.

Appropriate Behavior for Christian Women—Verses 5-11

In order to understand 1 Timothy 2:11-15, we need to back up and begin with verse 8, where Paul requests that "men everywhere . . . lift up holy hands in prayer, without anger or disputing." The word *everywhere* would be translated better "in every place" (*en panti topō*). Paul is probably referring to the various "places" (house-churches) in which Christians at Ephesus met for worship. With the word *likewise* (*hōsautōs*, verse 9), Paul connects this verse with his admonitions regarding the deportment of Christian women. This may suggest that Paul wants the reader to carry over from verse 8 both the verb *want* (*boulomai*) and the verb *pray*; hence: "Likewise, [I want] women [to pray], in modest dress. . . ." But it is more likely that we should carry over only the verb *want*, making verse 9 an independent exhortation directed to women: "Likewise, I want women to dress modestly . . ." (see the NIV). This reading is to be preferred both because of syntax—since both *pray* (verse 8) and *adorn* (verse 9) are infinitives, it is natural to think they both depend on the verb *want*—and context—at the end of verse 8 Paul's focus has shifted to appropriate behavior ("without anger or disputing"), and he does not come back to the topic of prayer.

This caution about anger and quarreling during prayer is almost surely occasioned by the impact of the false teaching on the church, for one of the most obvious results of that false teaching was divisiveness and discord (see 1 Timothy 6:4-5). The exhortation of verses 9-10, in which Paul encourages Christian women to "dress modestly, with decency and propriety," with "good deeds" rather than with elaborate hair styles and ostentatious clothes, might also be directed against the impact of the false teaching in Ephesus. For ostentatious dress, in the ancient world, sometimes could signal a woman's loose morals and independence from her husband. These connections are clear in a passage from the intertestamental Jewish book,[5] *The Testaments of the Twelve Patriarchs*, Reuben 5: "Women are evil, my children, and by reason of their lacking authority or power over man, they scheme treacherously how they might entice him to themselves by means of their looks. . . . They contrive in their hearts against men, then by decking themselves out they lead men's minds astray. . . . Accordingly, my children, flee from sexual promiscuity, and order your wives and your daughters not to adorn their heads and their appearances so as to deceive men's sound minds."[6] The problem addressed in 1 Corinthians 11:2-16 is of the same general nature, in which the Christian women were adopting a style of dress (or hairstyle) that implicitly proclaimed their independence from their husbands. And, as we have seen, the situation at Ephesus is very similar to that at Corinth some years earlier.

Having reminded Timothy that Christian women are to adorn themselves with "good deeds," Paul now warns them about certain activities that do not fall into this category. In verse 11, he commands them to "learn in quietness and full submission." That Paul wants Christian women to learn is an important point, for such a practice was not generally encouraged by the Jews. But this does not mean that Paul's desire for women to learn is the main point being made here. For it is not the *fact* that they are to learn, but the *manner* in which they are to learn that concerns Paul: "in quietness" and "with full submission." The situation may be compared to my saying to my wife: "Please have the children watch TV quietly and without fighting." My wife or I might or might not already have given permission for the children to watch television, but in this sentence, the stress falls not on the command to watch it, but on the manner in which it is to be done.

How, then, were the women to learn? First, Paul says, "in quietness." The word Paul uses (*hēsuchia*) can mean "silence," in an absolute sense, or "quietness," in the sense of "peacableness" (a cognate word, *hēsuchion*, is used in 1 Timothy 2:2: ". . . that we may live peaceful and *quiet* lives . . .").[7] Although the point is much the same in either case, there is good reason to think that the word should be translated "silence" in this context, since its opposite is "teaching." Clearly, Paul is concerned that the women accept the teaching of the church "peaceably"—without criticism and without dispute. Certainly, as Aida Besancon Spencer argues, Paul is encouraging the women at Ephesus to be "wise learners."[8] But the encouragement does not come in a vacuum—almost certainly it is necessary because at least *some* women were *not* learning "in quietness." These women had probably picked up the disputatious habits of the false teachers, and Paul must therefore warn them to accept without criticism the teaching of the properly appointed church leaders. But there is probably more to the problem than this. There is good reason to think that the underlying issue in verse 11 is not just submission to the teaching of the church but the submission of women to their husbands and, perhaps, to the male leadership of the church. This is suggested by Paul's use of the word *submission* (*hypotagē*). Submission is the appropriate response of Christians to those who are in authority over them (e.g., to government [Titus 3:1] and, for those who were slaves, to masters [Titus 2:9; the intention of Ephesians 5:21 is debated—see Chapter 8 of this volume]). The word (or its related verb) is a consistent feature in passages dealing with the appropriate response of wives to husbands (see Ephesians 5:24; Colossians 3:18; Titus 2:5; 1 Peter 3:1, 5; perhaps 1 Corinthians 14:34). The facts that this verse is directed only to women and that verses 12-14 (and perhaps also 9-10) focus on the relationship of men to women incline us to think that the submission in view here is also this submission of women to male leadership. (Reasons for thinking that this submission in this context is not just to husbands but to male leaders in the church generally are given below.) In light of our suggestions about the nature of the false teaching at Ephesus, we may surmise that women at Ephesus were expressing their "liberation" from their husbands, or from other men in the church, by criticizing and speaking out against male leaders. (The basic issue may, then, be roughly the same as in 1 Corinthians 14:33b-36.) This tendency Paul encourages Timothy to counter by enforcing the principle of submission of the women to the appropriate male leadership.

Spencer further argues that the very fact that women were to learn implies that they should eventually teach, since many ancient texts emphasize that the purpose of learning is to prepare one to teach.[9] But two replies may be made to this reasoning. First, we can grant the point without damage to our interpretation of the text, since we think Paul is only prohibiting women from teaching *men*. For women to be prepared to teach other women (see Titus 2:3-4), they would naturally need to learn and learn well. But, second, can we really conclude that learning must lead to teaching? Certainly if we mean by *teaching* an officially recognized activity of expositing and applying a section of Scripture, this is not the case. Neither do the texts cited by Spencer prove this. All Jewish men were encouraged to study the law; did they all become rabbis? Similarly, all Christians are encouraged to study the Scriptures; but Paul expressly limits "teaching" to a restricted number who have the gift of teaching (cf. 1 Corinthians 12:28-30). Of course, if we define *teach* in a broader sense—the communication of Christian truth through private conversation, family devotions, etc.—we may conclude that all Christians do indeed "teach."

But this is not the kind of teaching Paul is talking about in this context. Neither does it seem to be what Spencer means, for her point is that this verse validates women as teachers even in positions of authority in the church. It is manifest, then, that the encouragement to women to learn gives no reason to think that they were also to be engaged in expositing and applying Biblical truth to men.

Prohibitions on the Ministry of Women—Verse 12

The phrase *full submission* is the hinge between the command in verse 11—"A woman should learn in quietness and full submission"—and the prohibitions in verse 12—"I do not permit a woman to teach or to have authority over a man." The word that connects these verses is a particle (*de*) that usually has a mild adversative ("but") force. But, as so often with this word, its mild adversative force arises from the transition from one point to another rather than from a contrast in content.[10] In this case, the transition is from one activity that women are to carry out in submission (learning) to two others that are prohibited in order to maintain their submission (teaching and having authority). We may, therefore, paraphrase the transition in this way: "Let the women learn . . . with full submission; *but* [*de*] 'full submission' means also that I do not permit a woman to teach or to exercise authority over a man."

Verse 12 is the focus of discussion in this passage, for it is here that Paul prohibits the women at Ephesus from engaging in certain ministries with reference to men. There are six distinguishable issues that must be decided at the exegetical level: (1) the significance of the verb *permit* (*epitrepō*), which is in the present tense; (2) the meaning of *teach* (*didaskein*); (3) whether the word *man* (*andros*) is the object of the verb *teach*; (4) the meaning of the verb translated in the NIV "to have authority" (*authentein*); (5) the syntactical and logical relationship between the two words *teach* and *have authority* (they are connected by *oude*, "neither"); and (6) whether the Greek words *gynē* and *anēr* mean, respectively, "woman" and "man" or "wife" and "husband."

A. The Word *Permit*

Paul's use of the word *permit*—instead of, for instance, an imperative—and his putting it in the present tense are often taken as indications that Paul views the injunction that follows as limited and temporary.[11] The fact is, however, that nothing definite can be concluded from this word. No doubt Paul viewed his own teaching as authoritative for the churches to whom he wrote. Paul's "advice" to Timothy is the word of an apostle, accredited by God, and included in the inspired Scriptures. As far as the present tense of the verb goes, this allows us to conclude only that Paul was *at the time of writing* insisting on these prohibitions. Whether he means these prohibitions to be in force *only* at the time of writing, because of a specific situation, or—as in Romans 12:1: "I urge [present tense] you, brothers, in view of God's mercy, to offer your bodies as living sacrifices . . ."—to be applied to any church at any time cannot be known from the verb *permit*, but must be decided by the context in which it occurs.[12] It certainly is *not* correct to say that the present tense in and of itself shows that the command is temporary; it does not.

B. The Meaning of *Teach*

In prohibiting women from teaching, what exactly is Paul prohibiting? And is he restricting them from all teaching or only from teaching *men*? The word *teach* and its cognate nouns *teaching* (*didaskalia*) and *teacher* (*didaskalos*) are used in the New Testament mainly to denote the careful transmission of the tradition concerning Jesus Christ and the authoritative proclamation of God's will to believers in light of that tradition (see especially 1 Timothy 4:11: "Command and *teach* these things;" 2 Timothy 2:2; Acts 2:42; Romans 12:7). While the word can be used more broadly to describe the general ministry of edification that takes place in various ways (e.g., through teaching, singing, praying, reading Scripture [Colossians 3:16]), the activity usually designated by *teach* is plainly restricted to certain individuals who have the gift of teaching (see 1 Corinthians 12:28-30; Ephesians 4:11). This makes it clear that not all Christians engaged in teaching.[13] In the pastoral epistles, teaching always has this restricted sense of authoritative doctrinal instruction. As Paul's own life draws to a close, and in response to the false teaching, Paul is deeply concerned to insure that sound, healthful teaching be maintained in the churches. One of Timothy's main tasks is to teach (1 Timothy 4:11-16; 2 Timothy 4:2) and to prepare others to carry on this vital ministry (2 Timothy 2:2). While perhaps not restricted to the elder-overseer, "teaching" in this sense was an important activity of these people (see 1 Timothy 3:2; 5:17; Titus 1:9).

At this point the question of application cannot be evaded. What functions in the modern church would be considered teaching in this sense? Some have suggested that we have no modern parallel to it since, as the argument goes, the New Testament canon replaces the first-century teacher as the locus of authority.[14] However, it does seem right to claim that we have teaching that is substantially the same as what Paul had in mind here as he advised the first-century church. The addition of an authoritative, written norm is unlikely to have significantly altered the nature of Christian teaching. Certainly the Jewish activity of teaching that probably serves as a model for the early Christian teaching was all along much dependent on the transmission and application of a body of truth, the Old Testament Scriptures, and the developing Jewish tradition.[15] Before the New Testament Scriptures, early Christian teachers also had authoritative Christian traditions on which to base their ministries, and the implication of passages such as 2 Timothy 2:2 is that teaching, in the sense depicted in the New Testament, would continue to be very important for the church. Moreover, the Scriptures should be regarded as replacing the apostles, who wrote Scripture, not the teachers who exposited and applied it. Certainly, any authority that the teacher has is derived, inherent in the Christian truth being proclaimed rather than in the person of the teacher. But the *activity* of teaching, precisely because it does come to God's people with the authority of God and His Word, is authoritative.

In light of these considerations, we argue that the teaching prohibited to women here includes what we would call preaching (note 2 Timothy 4:2: "Preach the word . . . with careful instruction" [teaching, *didachē*]), and the teaching of Bible and doctrine in the church, in colleges, and in seminaries. Other activities—leading Bible studies, for instance—may be included, depending on how they are done. Still others—evangelistic witnessing, counseling, teaching subjects other than Bible or doctrine—are not, in our opinion, teaching in the sense Paul intends here.

C. Is Every Kind of Teaching Prohibited, Or Only Teaching of Men?

Is Paul prohibiting women from all teaching? We do not think so. The word *man* (*andros*), which is plainly the object of the verb *have authority* (*authentein*), should be construed as the object of the verb *teach* also. This construction is grammatically unobjectionable,[16] and it alone suits the context, in which Paul bases the prohibitions of verse 12 on the created differences between men and women (verse 13). Indeed, as we have argued, this male/female differentiation pervades this passage and comes to direct expression in the word that immediately precedes verse 12, *submission*. Paul's position in the pastoral epistles is, then, consistent: he allows women to teach other women (Titus 2:3-4),[17] but prohibits them to teach men.

D. The Meaning of *Have Authority*

The verb translated in the NIV "have authority" (*authentein*) has generated a great deal of discussion. We will confine ourselves to three points that we think are most important. First, the frequent appeal to etymology—the roots that make up the word—in explaining this word is understandable, given the limited number of relevant occurrences, but must always remain a precarious basis for conclusions. Not only is the etymology of the word debated, but also the usage of words often departs, in unpredictable ways, from their etymological meaning (e.g., the word *butterfly*). Second, the occurrences of this word—the verb—that are closest in time and nature to 1 Timothy mean "have authority over" or "dominate" (in the neutral sense of "have dominion over," not in the negative sense "lord it over").[18] Third, the objection that, had Paul wanted to say "exercise authority," he would have used the word *exousiazō*[19] does not bear up under scrutiny. Paul's three other uses of that verb hardly put it in the category of his standard vocabulary, and the vocabulary of the pastoral epistles is well known to be distinct from Paul's vocabulary elsewhere. For these reasons, we think the translation "have authority over" is the best English rendering of this word.

Again, we must ask the question of application. What kind of modern church practice would Paul be prohibiting to women in saying they are not to have authority over a man? First, we must, of course, recognize that it is not a question of a woman (in the New Testament or in our day) exercising ultimate authority over a man; God and the Scriptures stand over any Christian in a way no minister or human authority ever could. But, within these spheres of authority, we may nevertheless speak legitimately of a governing or ruling function exercised *under* God by some Christians over others (see 1 Thessalonians 5:12; Hebrews 13:17). In the pastoral epistles, this governing activity is ascribed to the elders (see 1 Timothy 3:5; 5:17). Clearly, then, Paul's prohibition of women's having authority over a man would exclude a woman from becoming an elder in the way this office is described in the pastoral epistles. By extension, then, women would be debarred from occupying whatever position in a given local church would be equivalent to the pastoral epistles' governing elder (many churches, for instance, call these people deacons). This would be the case even if a woman's husband were to give her permission to occupy such a position, for Paul's concern is not with a woman's acting independently of her husband or usurping *his* authority but with the woman's exercising authority in the church over *any man*.

On the other hand, we do not think Paul's prohibition should restrict women from voting, with other men and women, in a congregational meeting, for, while the congregation as a whole can be said to be the final authority, this is not the same thing as the exercise of authority ascribed, e.g., to the elders. Nor do we think Paul would intend to prohibit women from most church administrative activities. But what about women teaching or having authority over men in other activities in society generally (for example, in government, business, or education)? While this broader issue is addressed in another essay in this volume (see pages 50-52, 88-89, and 388-393), it is appropriate to note here that Paul's concern in 1 Timothy 2:11-15 is specifically the role of men and women in activities *within the Christian community*, and we question whether the prohibitions in this text can rightly be applied outside that framework.

E. Are Teaching and Having Authority Two Activities or One?

Thus far we have spoken of Paul's prohibiting women from two specific activities: "teaching" men and "having authority over" men. It has been argued, however, that the two verbs should be taken together, in a grammatical relationship called hendiadys, such that only one activity is prohibited: teaching in an authoritative (*authentein*) way.[20] If the meaning of *authentein* is "exercise authority," this interpretation would not materially change the first prohibition identified above—for the teaching Paul has in mind here has, as we have argued, some authority in itself—but it would eliminate entirely the second prohibition (against having authority over a man). We do not, however, think this interpretation is likely. While the word in question, *oude* ("and not," "neither," "nor"), certainly usually joins "two *closely related* items,"[21] it does not usually join together words that restate the same thing or that are mutually interpreting, and sometimes it joins opposites (e.g., Gentile and Jew, slave and free; Galatians 3:28).[22] Although teaching in Paul's sense here is authoritative in and of itself, not all exercising of authority in the church is through teaching, and Paul treats the two tasks as distinct elsewhere in 1 Timothy when discussing the work of elders in the church (3:2, 4-5; 5:17). That teaching and having authority are "closely related" is, of course, true, as it is true that both ministries often are carried out by the same individuals, but here and elsewhere they are nonetheless distinct, and in 1 Timothy 2:12, Paul prohibits women from conducting either activity, whether jointly or in isolation, in relation to men.

F. Are Only Husbands and Wives in View?

The final item on our list of exegetically significant issues in verse 12 is the relationship intended by the words *gynē* and *aner*. The difficulty arises from the fact that these words are used to describe both the marital relationship (wife/husband) and the larger gender relationship (woman/man). If, as many think,[23] Paul is here using the words in the former sense, then what he is prohibiting is not the teaching or exercising of authority of women in general over men in general, but only of wives over their own husbands. However, the wording and the context both favor the broader reference. If Paul had wanted to confine his prohibition in verse 12 to wives in relationship to their husbands, we would have expected him to use a definite article or possessive pronoun with *man*: "I am not permitting a woman to teach or to exercise authority over *her* man." (Paul readily made a similar distinction elsewhere in writing of male/female relationships. Women, he said, are to submit to "their own [*idiois*] husbands" [Ephesians 5:22, NASB; cf. Colossians 3:18.) And the context (verses 8-9) clearly addresses men and women generally as members of the church, not (as in Ephesians 5:22-33; Colossians 3:18-19) as husbands and wives, as members of family units; it is not only husbands who are to lift holy hands in prayer, but all the men, and not only wives who are to dress modestly, but all the women (verses 9-10). Therefore, the prohibitions of verse 12 are applicable to all women in the church in their relationships with all men in the church.

The Basis of the Instruction: Creation and the Fall—Verses 13-14

In verse 12 Paul prohibits women in the church at Ephesus from teaching men and having authority over them. But we now face the crucial question: Does this prohibition apply to the Christian church today?

We cannot simply assume that it does. The New Testament contains many injunctions that are intended only for a specific situation, and when the situation changes, the injunction may change its form or lose its validity. For instance, most Christians agree that we are no longer required to "Greet one another with a holy kiss" (1 Corinthians 16:20); forms of greeting have changed, and in our day, to obey this injunction, we may, as J. B. Phillips puts it, "shake hands all round as a sign of Christian love."

On the other hand, it is not a matter simply of identifying a local or temporary circumstance to which a text is directed and concluding that the text is therefore limited in its application. Almost the entire New Testament is written to specific circumstances—correcting certain false teachings, answering specific questions, seeking to unify specific church factions, etc.—but this does not necessarily mean that what is written applies *only* to those circumstances. For instance, Paul develops his doctrine of justification by faith in Galatians in response to specific, Judaizing teachers for a specific group of first-century Christians. But the specific nature of these circumstances in no way limits the applicability of his teaching. We might say that the circumstances give rise to his teaching but do not limit it. This point is particularly important, because some studies of 1 Timothy 2:12 imply that if one can identify local or temporary circumstances against which the passage is written then one can conclude that the text has only limited application. This is manifestly not true. Therefore, the question to be asked of 1 Timothy 2:12 is, Can we identify circumstances that limit its application to certain times and places?

Many think so, and the suggestions about local circumstances that have been proposed are legion. Lacking space to deal with all of them, we will focus on the two that are both the most popular in recent literature and that we think have the best claim to be accepted: that Paul is addressing only women who have succumbed to the false teaching at Ephesus, and that he is requiring only conformity to existing cultural conceptions of the woman's role.

The first suggestion emphasizes that 1 Timothy is directed throughout to the false teaching at Ephesus and that 1 Timothy 2:9-15 must, therefore be interpreted against this background. While we think the claim that "the whole of 1 Timothy . . . is dominated by this singular concern [that is, the false teaching]"[24] is exaggerated, we may grant the point without being any further along on the issue at hand. In fact, it is likely that the false teaching does give rise to Paul's instruction in 2:9-15;[25] but the crucial question is, How does it affect his instructions? As we have suggested above, we think Paul is correcting the erroneous views of the place of women vis-a-vis men taught by the false teachers (although our conclusions do not depend on this) and that verse 12 restates Paul's customary position on this issue in response to the false teaching. In other words, it was Paul's position in every church that women should not teach or have authority over men. He must give explicit teaching on the subject here simply because it has surfaced as a problem in this church. Yet this would be his position in any church, whether or not some false teaching required him to write about it. We think this reading of the situation is well-grounded in the actual evidence of 1 Timothy and that any other reading must import ideas that are not plainly present.

But the advocates of the view we are now examining go further, insisting that verse 12 is directed only against women who had fallen prey to the false teaching. Paul's purpose, then, is not to debar all women at all times from teaching or "domineering over" men, but to prohibit women who have succumbed to false teaching from teaching and propagating these doctrines. In our day, we obey Paul's injunction by preventing women who are ill-trained and under the influence of false teaching from teaching such doctrine.[26]

What are the reasons for accepting this specific interpretation of the situation Paul addresses? The advocates of this view, which has become by far the most popular approach among those who do not think that 1 Timothy 2:12 has general application, point particularly to verse 14. Here, they argue, Paul cites Eve as typical of what the women at Ephesus were doing: teaching false doctrine and doing so without adequate preparation. Eve taught the man to eat of the tree, bringing the ruin of falling into transgression; the women at Ephesus must not repeat her mistake by propagating false teaching and bringing ruin to the church.

But this argument falls completely short of being convincing. Paul's reference to Eve in verse 14 is difficult, but there are two emphases in the verse that must be factored into any adequate interpretation: the focus on the relationship between man and woman ("*Adam* was not the one deceived; it was *the woman* . . .") and the focus on deception. This latter point suggests that Eve stands not as a "type" of Ephesian women who were *teaching* false doctrine, but as a type of Ephesian women who were *being deceived by* false doctrine—hence the need to warn them about learning "in quietness and full submission" (verse 11). Paul says nothing here about Eve's teaching of Adam, which, had this been his point, he could easily have done. Moreover, there is no evidence in the pastoral epistles that the women were teaching these false doctrines.[27] If the issue, then, is deception, it may be that Paul wants to imply that all women are, like Eve, more susceptible to being deceived than are men, and that this is why they should not be teaching men! While this interpretation is not impossible, we think it unlikely. For one thing, there is nothing in the Genesis accounts or in Scripture elsewhere to suggest that Eve's deception is representative of women in general. But second, and more important, this interpretation does not mesh with the context. Paul, as we have seen, is concerned to prohibit women from teaching *men*; the focus is on the role relationship of men and women. But a statement about the nature of women *per se* would move the discussion away from this central issue, and it would have a serious and strange implication. After all, does Paul care only that the women not teach *men* false doctrines? Does he not care that they not teach them to other women? More likely, then, verse 14, in conjunction with verse 13, is intended to remind the women at Ephesus that Eve was deceived by the serpent in the Garden (Genesis 3:13) precisely in taking the initiative over the man whom God had given to be with her and to care for her. In the same way, if the women at the church at Ephesus proclaim their independence from the men of the church, refusing to learn "in quietness and full submission" (verse 11), seeking roles that have been given to men in the church (verse 12), they will make the same mistake Eve made and bring similar disaster on themselves and the church.[28] This explanation of the function of verse 14 in the paragraph fits what we know to be the general insubordination of some of the women at Ephesus and explains Paul's emphasis in the verse better than any other alternative.

There is a more serious problem with the viewpoint according to which verse 12 may be applied only to women who are seeking to teach falsely: verse 13. It is telling that most of the advocates of this general approach pass over verse 13 very quickly, explaining it as simply an "introduction" to verse 14,[29] or ignoring it entirely. Yet this verse provides the first reason ("for" [*gar*][30]) for the prohibitions in verse 12. Paul emphasizes that man was created "first, then" Eve; the temporal sequence is strongly marked (*protos*, "first," and *eita*, "then"). What is the point of this statement? Both the logic of this passage and the parallel in 1 Corinthians 11:3-10 make this clear: for Paul, the man's priority in the order of creation is indicative of the headship that man is to have over woman. The woman's being created after man, as his helper, shows the position of submission that God intended as inherent in the woman's relation to the man, a submission that is violated if a woman teaches doctrine or exercises authority over a man. Some accuse Paul, or the "unknown author" of the pastorals, of using the Genesis accounts of creation unfairly for these purposes.[31] But Paul's interpretation can be shown to be a fair extrapolation from Genesis 2 (see Chapter 3 of this volume).[32] This is an extremely important indicator of how Paul understood the prohibitions in verse 12. For by rooting these prohibitions in the circumstances of creation rather than in the circumstances of the fall, Paul shows that he does not consider these restrictions to be the product of the curse and presumably, therefore, to be phased out by redemption.[33] And by citing creation rather than a local situation or cultural circumstance as his basis for the prohibitions, Paul makes it clear that, while these local or cultural issues may have provided the *context* of the issue, they do not provide the *reason* for his advice. His *reason* for the prohibitions of verse 12 is the created role relationship of man and woman, and we may justly conclude that these prohibitions are applicable as long as this reason remains true.

It is sometimes said in opposition to this line of reasoning that even an appeal to creation does not demand that the prohibition involved be permanent.[34] This may be granted, in the sense that New Testament authors will sometimes appeal to creation, or to the Old Testament generally, to establish a principle on which a specific form of behavior is demanded. In these cases, while the principle always remains in effect, the specific form of behavior will not. This seems to be the situation, for instance, in 1 Corinthians 11:2-16, where the appeal to creation grounds the headship of man, a theological principle, which is in turn applied to the specific issue of women's head coverings.[35] But the difference between this and 1 Timothy 2:12-13 is simply this: in 1 Timothy 2:12-18, the principle cannot be separated from the form of behavior. In other words, for a woman to teach a man or to have authority over a man is, by definition, to void the principle for which Paul quotes the creation account. Granted this and granted the complete absence of explicit temporal or cultural references in the whole paragraph, the prohibitions of verse 12 can be ignored only by dismissing the theological principle itself.

This last point also calls into question the other main attempt to confine the teaching of verse 12 to a local or limited situation. On this view, Paul wants the women to refrain from teaching or exercising authority over men because such activities would have been considered offensive to the great majority of people in Ephesus.[36] Now, the concern about Christians avoiding behavior that would bring the gospel into ill repute is mentioned in the pastoral epistles (see 1 Timothy 6:1; Titus 2:5), and, as we have seen, the false teachers were propagating an anti-traditional view of the role of women. But, in reacting against such false teaching in 2:9-18, we must ask a crucial question: does Paul restrict womens' activities *only* because such activities would be offensive in that culture? Certainly it is clear that Paul requires many forms of behavior in the pastoral epistles that are both in keeping with the culture of the day *and* are part of God's eternal will for His people. That the behavior required in 1 Timothy 2:11-12 falls into this category is clear from (1) the lack of any reference in this context to a concern for cultural accommodation, and (2) the appeal to the order of creation—a manifestly trans-cultural consideration—as the explicit basis for the behavior.

A further variant of this last interpretation holds that Paul does require submission of women to men as a permanent fixture of Christian life and that the Old Testament references in verses 12-14 ground this general demand only. The principle of submission would have been violated in the first century if women had taught men or exercised authority over them, but it would not be in our day because of our different conceptions of what constitutes submission.[37] However, not only is the requirement of submission a little further away (verse 11) than we might expect if verses 13-14 give the basis for it, but we must question whether changing conceptions of men's and women's roles affect the nature of the activities Paul prohibits here. However a society might view these matters, the person who teaches in the sense Paul has in mind here and, obviously, the person who exercises authority over someone else is by definition in a position of authority with respect to that other person. For any woman in any culture to engage in these activities with respect to men means that she is violating the Biblical principle of submission.

Women's Role in a Positive Light—Verse 15

Before concluding, we must say something about the notoriously difficult verse 15. While we do not think that the interpretation of this verse is decisive for the meaning of the verses that precede it, the verse does conclude the paragraph and may shed some light on the whole.

One view of verse 15 holds that Paul is promising that women will be kept physically safe during childbirth, and this interpretation appears to be reflected in the NIV rendering: "women will be kept safe through childbirth. . . ." However, this is an unusual meaning for *save* (*sōzō*), which elsewhere always refers to salvation, in the theological sense, in Paul, and does not fit well with the qualifications that follow: "if they continue in faith, love and holiness with propriety." A second interpretation links this verse closely with the material about Eve that immediately precedes. Just as the curse that came upon Eve is mentioned in verse 14, so verse 15 alludes to the salvation that Eve (and other women) experience "through *the* childbirth," that is, the birth of the "seed" promised to the woman in Genesis 3.[38] This interpretation does more justice to Paul's language and to the context, but we must question whether a reference to the birth of Christ is naturally denoted by the word *childbirth*, or *bearing of children* (*teknogonia*), even when it is preceded by the article. The verbal form of this word (infinitive) is used in 1 Timothy 5:14 (albeit without the article) to denote bearing or raising children generally, and this is the meaning we would expect it to have in 2:15 also.

Another interpretation of verse 15 that depends on the reference to Eve in verse 14 is that the "bearing of children" is the trial, or hindrance through (*dia*) which women will experience salvation.[39] However, we must question whether childbearing can be considered a hindrance to the salvation of women. We think it is preferable to view verse 15 as designating the circumstances[40] in which Christian women will experience (work out; cf. Philippians 2:12) their salvation—in maintaining as priorities those key roles that Paul, in keeping with Scripture elsewhere, highlights: being faithful, helpful wives, raising children to love and reverence God, managing the household (cf. 1 Timothy 5:14; Titus 2:3-5).[41] This is not to say, of course, that women cannot be saved unless they bear children. The women with whom Paul is concerned in this paragraph are all almost certainly married, so that he can mention one central role—bearing and raising children—as a way of designating appropriate female roles generally. Probably Paul makes this point because the false teachers were claiming that women could *really* experience what God had for them only if they abandoned the home and became actively involved in teaching and leadership roles in the church. If this interpretation is correct, then verse 15 fits perfectly with the emphasis we have seen in this text throughout. Against the attempt of the false teachers to get the women in Ephesus to adopt "libertarian," unbiblical attitudes and behavior, Paul reaffirms the Biblical model of the Christian woman adorned with good works rather than with outward, seductive trappings, learning quietly and submissively, refraining from taking positions of authority over men, giving attention to those roles to which God has especially called women.

Conclusion

We want to make a final, very important point about all attempts to limit the application of 1 Timothy 2:12. The interpreter of Scripture may validly question whether any given command or teaching is to be applied beyond the situation for which it was first given. But the criteria used to answer that question must be carefully formulated. It is surely not enough simply to suggest local or cultural factors that may restrict the application of a text, for with such a methodology any teaching in Scripture could be dismissed. In the case of 1 Timothy 2:12, none of the factors that we have considered above, nor any of the many others that have been proposed (women were not educated enough to teach; Jews would have been offended by it; etc.) is stated, or even hinted at, in the text. Is it not a dangerous procedure to import such factors without clear warrant in the text? To be sure, there are commands of Scripture that we do not consider applicable today without any explicit restriction in the context; 1 Corinthians 16:20 ("greet one another with a holy kiss"), cited earlier, is an example. And we obey Titus 2:9-10 today in principle rather than literally. But the difference between such texts and 1 Timothy 2:12 is twofold. The activities involved in 1 Timothy 2:12 are, by definition, transcultural in the sense that they are permanent ministries of the Christian church, and the prohibitions of 1 Timothy 2:12 are grounded in theology. When we add to these factors the fact that the New Testament teaching on these matters is consistent (see other essays in this volume), we are justified in requiring very good reasons *from the text itself* to limit the application of this text in any way. We find no such reasons. Therefore, we must conclude that the restrictions imposed by Paul in 1 Timothy 2:12 are valid for Christians in all places and all times.

10

Wives Like Sarah, and the Husbands Who Honor Them

1 Peter 3:1-7[1]

Wayne Grudem

> [1]Wives, in the same way be submissive to your husbands so that, if any of them do not believe the word, they may be won over without words by the behavior of their wives, [2] when they see the purity and reverence of your lives. [3]Your beauty should not come from outward adornment, such as braided hair and the wearing of gold jewelry and fine clothes. [4]Instead, it should be that of your inner self, the unfading beauty of a gentle and quiet spirit, which is of great worth in God's sight. [5]For this is the way the holy women of the past who put their hope in God used to make themselves beautiful. They were submissive to their own husbands, [6]like Sarah, who obeyed Abraham and called him her master. You are her daughters if you do what is right and do not give way to fear.
>
> [7]Husbands, in the same way be considerate as you live with your wives, and treat them with respect as the weaker partner and as heirs with you of the gracious gift of life, so that nothing will hinder your prayers. [1 Peter 3:1-7, NIV]

This is a magnificent text for understanding God's plan for an ideal marriage. In a few verses Peter describes the complementary responsibilities of husbands and wives and guards against common abuses.

I. Directions to Wives

A. What Submission Does Not Mean

Because there is much misunderstanding today about what the Bible means when it says that wives are to "be submissive" to their husbands, this text is very helpful for correcting wrong understandings and practices. While Peter tells wives to "be submissive" to their husbands, the text also gives several indications of what such submission does not mean.

1. Submission does not mean putting a husband in the place of Christ.

The whole context assumes that allegiance to Christ takes priority over all human allegiance. The larger section begins, "Submit yourselves for the Lord's sake to every authority instituted among men" (1 Peter 2:13), and affirms that the Christian life above all means that we should look to Christ and "follow in his steps" (2:21).

2. Submission does not mean giving up independent thought.
Peter speaks directly to wives, not to the husbands so that they can tell their wives what he says. Peter assumes that they will hear, ponder, understand, and respond to God's Word themselves. Moreover, Peter knows that some wives have chosen Christ even though their husbands have not, and this was good for them to do. They have thought the matter through and departed from their husbands' way of thinking on this issue of supreme importance in life.

3. Submission does not mean a wife should give up efforts to influence and guide her husband.
The Christian wife should try to influence her husband to become a Christian. Peter helps her to do this; he does not tell her not to.

4. Submission does not mean a wife should give in to every demand of her husband.
If he should say, "Stop being a Christian, be like me," she will have to humbly say, "I cannot. My conscience must answer to a higher authority." If he should tell her to steal, or lie, or do something else contrary to the clear moral teachings of Scripture, she must refuse, thereby following Peter's command to maintain good conduct among the Gentiles (1 Peter 2:12). Moreover, the word *hagnos*, "chaste" (RSV, NASB; the NIV has "purity") means "pure, free from moral defilement," and serves as another reminder that the submission Peter commands must never go so far as to include obedience to demands to do something that is morally wrong.

This is consistent with other parts of Scripture where God's people have disobeyed some human authority and have been approved by God for so doing. Consider, for example, the Hebrew midwives in Egypt (Exodus 1:17), Esther before King Xerxes (Esther 4:16), Shadrach, Meshach, and Abednego (Daniel 3:13-18), the prophet Daniel (Daniel 6:10-14), the apostles (Acts 4:18-20; 5:27-29), and Moses' parents (Hebrews 11:23). The principle to be drawn from all these passages is to obey *except when it would be sin to obey*, which is consistent with Peter's general statement that it is "for the Lord's sake" (2:13) that all our submission to lesser authority is to be given.

5. Submission is not based on lesser intelligence or competence.
In fact, where there is a Christian wife with a non-Christian husband, she is shown to have greater spiritual insight than he does—she has seen the truth of Christianity, and he has not.

6. Submission does not mean being fearful or timid.
Peter tells wives to "not give way to fear" (verse 6). Thus the reference to the wife as "the weaker partner" (verse 7) cannot be due to any inherent lack of inner strength or courage in the face of danger or threat.

7. Submission is not inconsistent with equality in Christ.
We must remember that submission in regard to authority is often consistent with equality in importance, dignity, and honor—Jesus was subject both to His parents and to God the Father, and Christians who are highly honored in God's sight

are still commanded to be subject to unbelieving government authorities and masters. Thus the command to wives to be subject to their husbands should never be taken to imply inferior personhood or spirituality, or lesser importance. Indeed, Peter affirms just the opposite: wives are "heirs with you of the gracious gift of life" (verse 7).

It is important to note the relationship between this passage and Galatians 3:28-29:

> There is neither Jew nor Greek, slave nor free, male nor female, for you are all one in Christ Jesus. If you belong to Christ, then you are Abraham's seed and heirs according to the promise.

This text is often played off against submission as if the "neither . . . male nor female" in Galatians 3:28 ruled out any commands for submission within marriage. But 1 Peter 3:1-7 shows that the apostolic pattern of thought in Scripture did not feel any tension between a call for wives to submit to their husbands (verse 1) and a clear declaration that husbands and wives are joint heirs of the grace of life (verse 7). This is Peter's way of saying, "There is neither male nor female . . . you are all one in Christ Jesus," and the context shows that it is not inconsistent with female submission and male headship in marriage. Submission in role and equality in dignity and importance stand side-by-side in apostolic thought. In fact, the parallel between Galatians 3:28-29 and 1 Peter 3:1-7 is even closer when we see the theme of being "Abraham's seed, heirs according to the promise" (Galatians 3:29) compared to the theme of being daughters of Sarah in 1 Peter 3:6.[2]

A wife's submission to her husband therefore is more like the submission of Christ to God the Father (1 Corinthians 15:28), the submission of one to another who is equal in importance and essence.

B. What Submission Does Mean

1. Submission is an inner quality of gentleness that affirms the leadership of the husband.

"Be submissive to your husbands" means that a wife will willingly submit to her husband's authority and leadership in the marriage. It means making a choice to affirm her husband as leader within the limits of obedience to Christ. It includes a demeanor that honors him as leader even when she dissents. Of course, it is an attitude that goes much deeper than mere obedience,[3] but the idea of willing obedience to a husband's authority is certainly part of this submission, as is clear from verses 5-6. There Peter illustrates being "submissive to their own husbands" with the example of Sarah, "who obeyed Abraham," thus showing that obeying (*hypakouō*) is the means by which Sarah was being submissive (*hupotassō*, the same word used in verse 1). Moreover, this submission is a respectful affirmation, for Peter recalls that Sarah obeyed Abraham "and called him master" (verse 6).

Further understanding of the nature of this submission is gained from Peter's description of the beauty that accompanies it, the beauty of "a gentle and quiet spirit, which is of great worth in God's sight" (verse 4). The adjective *gentle* (*praus*) only occurs three other times in the New Testament, twice referring to Christ (Matthew 11:29; 21:5; also 5:5), but its related noun, translated "gentleness" or "meekness," is more frequent (Galatians 5:23; 6:1; James 3:13; etc.). It means "not insistent on one's own rights," or "not pushy, not selfishly assertive," "not demanding one's own way." Such a gentle and quiet spirit will be beautiful before other human beings, even unbelieving husbands (verses 1-2), but even more important, it "is of great worth in God's sight." Why? No doubt because such a spirit is the result of quiet and continual trust in God to supply one's needs, and God delights in being trusted (cf. 1 Peter 1:5, 7-9, 21; 2:6-7, 23; 5:7).

In describing the things that accompany this submission, Peter focuses on the inward attitudes of the heart. When he says that a wife's source of beauty should be "the inner self" (verse 4), he is speaking of her inward nature, her true personality. It is not visible in itself, but it is made known quickly through words and actions that reveal inner attitudes. *Unfading* (Greek *aphthartos*) is an adjective that the New Testament uses consistently to speak of heavenly realities, things that are not subject to aging or decay, things that will not fade away with the passing of this present world.[4] Peter uses this adjective without a noun following it, so the noun he intends must be supplied by the reader from the context. Various suggestions have been made (RSV, "imperishable jewel;" NIV, "unfading beauty;" NASB, "imperishable quality"), but the sense is roughly the same in all of them: a gentle and quiet spirit is something that has beauty that will last for eternity, in contrast to the fleeting beauty of jewelry or clothing.

2. *Submission involves obedience like Sarah's.*

There have been several attempts to avoid the conclusion that Christian wives today are to imitate Sarah's obedience to Abraham, which Peter gives here as an example of the "holy women of the past who put their hope in God" (verse 5). One prominent approach is taken by Gilbert Bilezikian, who attempts to deny the force of Sarah's example of obedience in two ways: (1) He apparently takes Peter's statement as a joke, for he says, "The use of Sarah as an example of obedience shows that Peter was not devoid of a sense of humor. In Genesis, Abraham is shown as obeying Sarah as often as Sarah obeyed Abraham," and he points to Genesis 16:2, 6; 21:11-12.[5]

(2) Bilezikian also denies that Sarah is a model for Christian wives to follow, for "the point of Peter's reference to Sarah is that wives in the new covenant can learn from their spiritual ancestress . . . who lived in the 'dark side' of the old-covenant compromise, when she had to 'obey' her husband. . . . Sarah obeyed Abraham, but Christian wives . . . are never told to 'obey' their husbands neither here nor anywhere else in the Bible."[6]

These statements are very troubling. (1) To say that a straightforward Biblical statement is an example of humor is simply an easy way to avoid the force of a verse whose plain meaning contradicts one's position. But is this the kind of argument that reflects submission to Scripture? As for Abraham's "obeying" Sarah, Genesis 16:2 is a classic example of role reversal leading to *disobedience* to God, for in this verse Abraham gives in to Sarah's urging and has a son by Hagar. In Genesis 16:6, Abraham does not obey Sarah but is clearly the family authority who (again wrongfully) gives in to Sarah's recriminations and allows her to mistreat Hagar and Ishmael. Why does Bilezikian refer to these examples of sin as positive examples of a husband's obeying his wife? To use such a procedure is to contradict the force of these passages.

In Genesis 21:11-12, God tells Abraham, "Listen to whatever Sarah tells you," but this was specifically with regard to casting out Hagar and Ishmael. It was not because of any general principle that husbands should obey their wives, but because of God's specific purpose for Isaac, for the verse continues, ". . . *because it is through Isaac that your offspring will be reckoned*" (Genesis 21:12). Abraham did what Sarah asked here not because he was being an example of a husband obeying his wife but because at this specific point God told him to do what Sarah said. God here used Sarah to convey His will to Abraham, but no pattern of husbands obeying their wives is established here. (Note, for example, that a child can call his or her father to supper without any implication of authority over the father.) In fact, the exceptional intervention of God here suggests that Abraham would not ordinarily accede to such a request from his wife.

(2) Although Sarah was not always a model wife, Peter does not choose to exploit that fact. However, whereas Peter uses Sarah as a *positive example* for Christian wives to imitate, Bilezikian uses her as a *negative example* showing what Christian wives are *not* supposed to do. Peter tells wives to act like the "holy women of the past who put their hope in God" and "were submissive to their own husbands" (verse 5), but Bilezikian says this was on the "dark side" of the "old-covenant compromise" (p. 191). Peter tells wives to act like Sarah, who "obeyed Abraham" (verse 6), but Bilezikian says that this verse does not tell wives to obey their husbands.

Readers should note carefully the result of Bilezikian's analysis of 1 Peter 3:1-7, because at several points he ends up denying what the text *does say* and affirming an opposite concept that the text *does not say*. Peter says that wives should be submissive to their husbands, but Bilezikian says that the motivations for a Christian wife's behavior should "have nothing in common with submission defined as obedience to authority" (p. 190). Peter does not say that husbands should be submissive to their wives, but Bilezikian says that husbands should be submissive to their wives and undergo a "traumatic role reversal" whereby they bestow honor on their wives "much like a servant to his master" (p. 192). Peter says that Sarah obeyed Abraham, but Bilezikian emphasizes his own claim that Abraham obeyed Sarah. Peter says that wives should follow the example of Sarah who obeyed her husband, but Bilezikian says that wives are nowhere told to be obedient to their husbands. We may well wonder if this can any longer be called simply a difference in interpretation of Scripture, or if it isn't rather a refusal to submit to the authority of Scripture at all, hidden under the smoke screen of "alternative interpretations"—which turn out on closer inspection to have no legitimate basis in the actual data of the text.

3. Submission acknowledges an authority that is not totally mutual.

Although Peter is speaking specifically to wives in this section, many people today object to any kind of submission that is required of wives and not of husbands. In order to avoid the force of any command that would tell wives to be submissive to their husbands' authority, evangelical feminists frequently talk about "mutual submission" within marriage. The phrase itself is slippery, because it can mean different things. On the one hand, it can mean simply that husbands and wives are to be thoughtful and considerate toward one another and put each other's interests and preferences before their own. If people use the phrase to apply to such *mutual consideration and deference*, then they are speaking of an idea that is fully consistent with the teachings of the New Testament and that still allows for a unique leadership role for the husband and a unique responsibility for the wife to submit to his authority or leadership. "Mutual submission" would then mean that the husband is to be unselfish in his exercise of leadership in the family and the wife is to be unselfish in her submission to and support of that leadership. Although we might think that this is using the word *submission* in a rather unusual way, we would probably agree that this is a possible sense of "mutual submission." We would then say that there is "mutual submission" in *some* senses in marriage, but not in *all* senses, because the wife still has to submit to her husband's authority and leadership in a way that the husband does not have to—indeed, *should not*—submit to his wife's authority or leadership. He has a unique leadership role in the family that he should not abdicate.

But the standard claim of evangelical feminists today is that "mutual submission" in marriage means something far different. They apply this slippery phrase to all the texts that say wives should submit to their husbands and *deny that any submission to authority is in view*. This is how they avoid the force of Peter's command, "Wives . . . be submissive to your husbands" (verse 1), if they discuss it at all. They say that mutual submission in marriage means that wives are to submit to husbands *and husbands are to submit to wives in exactly the same way*.[7] According to this view, the husband has no unique authority or leadership responsibility in the marriage. Usually Ephesians 5:21, "*Submit to one another* out of reverence for Christ," is claimed to support this view.[8]

But in order to make this argument, evangelical feminists must take two steps in the interpretation of Scripture that are simply incorrect and that show their position to be contrary to Scripture. First, they fail to account for the fact that, while wives are told several times in the New Testament to submit to their husbands, the situation is never reversed: husbands are never told to submit to their wives. Why? In fact, it is very significant that the New Testament authors *never* explicitly tell husbands to submit to their wives. The command that a *husband should submit to his wife* would have been highly unusual in that male-dominated culture, and if the New Testament writers had thought Christian marriage required husbands to submit to their wives, they certainly would have had to say so very clearly in their writings—otherwise, no early Christians ever would have known that that was what they should do. It is surprising that evangelical feminists can find this requirement in the New Testament when it is nowhere explicitly stated (with the possible exception of Ephesians 5:21, to which we now turn).

As for Ephesians 5:21, the misunderstanding comes when the verse is read apart from its context, which shows what Paul intends. He goes on to explain that he means that wives are to be subject to the authority of their husbands (verses 22-24), children to parents (6:1-3), and servants to masters (6:4-8). In each case Paul tells those in authority how they are to act, in love and thoughtfulness and fairness (Ephesians 5:25-33; 6:4, 9), but he does not tell them to submit to their wives, children, or servants respectively.[9]

Second, evangelical feminists take another illegitimate step in Bible interpretation when they change the meaning of the word *hupotassō* ("submit to," "be subject to"), giving it a meaning that it nowhere requires, something like "be thoughtful and considerate; act in love" (toward another), *without any sense of obedience to an authority*.[10] This is not a legitimate meaning for the term, which always implies a relationship of submission to an authority.[11] It is used elsewhere in the New Testament of the submission of Jesus to the authority of His parents

(Luke 2:51); of demons being subject to the disciples (Luke 10:17—clearly the meaning "act in love, be considerate" cannot fit here); of citizens being subject to governing authorities (Romans 13:1, 5; Titus 3:1; 1 Peter 2:13); of the universe being subject to Christ (1 Corinthians 15:27; Ephesians 1:22); of unseen spiritual powers being subject to Christ (1 Peter 3:22); of Christ being subject to God the Father (1 Corinthians 15:28); of church members being subject to church leaders (1 Corinthians 16:15-16 [with *1 Clement* 42:4]; 1 Peter 5:5); of wives being subject to their husbands (Colossians 3:18; Titus 2:5; 1 Peter 3:5; cf. Ephesians 5:22-24); of the church being subject to Christ (Ephesians 5:24); of servants being subject to their masters (Titus 2:9; 1 Peter 2:18); and of Christians being subject to God (Hebrews 12:9; James 4:7).

Note that none of these relationships is ever reversed; that is, husbands are never told to be subject to wives, nor government to citizens, masters to servants, disciples to demons, etc. In fact, the term is used outside the New Testament to describe the submission and obedience of soldiers in an army to those of superior rank (Josephus, *Jewish War* 2:566, 578; 5:309; cf. the adverb in *1 Clement* 37:2; also Liddell & Scott's *Greek-English Lexicon*, rev. Jones, p. 1897, which defines *hupotassō* [passive] as "be obedient").

Now we must recognize that submission to different kinds of authority may take many different forms. Members' submission to church leaders is far different from soldiers' submission to a general in the army, and both are far different from the submission of children to parents or of employees to employers. Within a healthy Christian marriage, as we explain elsewhere in this book, there will be large elements of mutual consultation and seeking of wisdom, and most decisions will come by consensus between husband and wife. For a wife to be submissive to her husband will probably not often involve obeying actual commands or directives[12] (though it will sometimes include this), for a husband may rather give requests and seek advice and discussion about the course of action to be followed (cf. 2 Corinthians 8:8; Philemon 8-9). Nevertheless, a wife's attitude of submission to her husband's authority will be reflected in numerous words and actions each day that reflect deference to his leadership and acknowledgment of his final responsibility—after discussion, whenever possible—to make decisions affecting the whole family.

What does Peter mean by the word *likewise* (RSV) in verse 1 (*NASB*, *NIV*, "in the same way")? Some have objected to Peter's teaching here, saying that he is viewing wives in the same category as servants and saying that wives should act toward their husbands as servants act toward their masters. But this is to misunderstand Peter's words. The word *likewise* (*homoiōs*) usually means "in a similar way," but the degree of similarity intended can vary greatly (cf. Luke 10:32, 37; 16:25; 1 Corinthians 7:22; James 2:25). Here the word might mean (a) similar to the example of Christ (2:21-25), or (b) similar to the way in which servants are to be submissive (2:18). A third possibility is (c) that *homoiōs* simply means "also," introducing a new subject in the same general area of discussion (relationships to authority), without implying similarity of conduct (see Bauer-Arndt-Gingrich/Danker, *Greek-English Lexicon*, rev. Danker, p. 568, and 1 Peter 3:7; 5:5).

The second option is best here. *Likewise* modifies "be submissive," and the reader would naturally make the connection with 2:18, the last time Peter used the verb "be submissive" (*hupotassō*): "Slaves, submit yourselves . . . . similarly, wives be submissive" (2:18; 3:1). (The form of expression is exactly the same in the Greek text, with the unusual use of a participle to express a command in both cases.) The point of comparison with Christ would be imitation of His patient endurance of suffering, but that is not what Peter commands in this sentence. And *homoiōs* never seems to mean merely "also" when a suitable referent for actual similarity is near at hand (as there is here), for then the idea of comparison can hardly be kept from the reader's mind.

Nevertheless, Peter does not use the stronger term *kathōs*, "even as, in the same way as," nor does he say "in every way (*kata panta*, Hebrews 4:15) be similar to servants in your submission." The similarity intended is apparently in motive ("for the Lord's sake," 2:13), in extent of application (to good or harsh masters [2:18] or husbands[13] [3:1]), and in attitude (with proper respect, 2:18; 3:2), as well as in the main concept of submission to an authority (2:18; 3:1).[14]

C. The Old Testament Examples of Submission

Peter illustrates what he means by submission by referring to the lives of holy women who hoped in God. Although he specifically mentions Sarah in verse 6, the plural "women" refers to godly women generally in the Old Testament. The pattern of their lives was that those who were hoping in God (the present participle suggests continuing in hope over time) used to adorn themselves "in this way," or "so" (*houtōs*, "thus," referring to adorning with a gentle and quiet spirit). The word "adorn" (RSV; *kosmeō*) is the verb related to the noun "adorning" in verse 3, and its imperfect tense indicates continuing or repeated action over time in the past, "they were repeatedly or continually adorning themselves" in this way.

"They were submissive to their husbands" (verse 5) brings us back to the theme of verses 1-2 and indicates the relationship between such submission and the inward beauty of verses 3-4. Quiet confidence in God produces in a woman the imperishable beauty of a gentle and quiet spirit, but it also enables her to submit to her husband's authority without fear that it will ultimately be harmful to her well-being or her personhood.

Peter uses Sarah's submission to Abraham as an example of such submissiveness to a husband. Wives are to be submissive to their husbands (verse 5) as Sarah obeyed Abraham, calling him her master (or "lord"). Peter does not seem to be referring to any one specific incident here, for the main verb and both participles in verse 5 all indicate a continuing pattern of conduct during one's life (see above).[15]

The example of Sarah's obedience would be an appropriate encouragement to the wives to whom Peter was writing, for Sarah became the mother of all God's people in the old covenant (Isaiah 51:2; cf. Galatians 4:22-26), even though there had been many times in which following Abraham had meant trusting God in uncertain, unpleasant, and even dangerous situations (Genesis 12:1, 5, 10-15; 13:1; 20:2-6 [cf. verse 12]; 22:3). Yet Peter says believing women are now her children (or "daughters"), the true members of her spiritual family.[16] To be Sarah's daughter is to be a joint heir of the promises and the honor given to her and to Abraham.

The condition for being Sarah's "daughters" is "if you do what is right and do not give way to fear" (verse 6). Both verbs are again present participles indicating a pattern of life continued over time: "If you are doing what is right and not giving way to fear," then you are (more accurately, "you have become") Sarah's daughters. Peter's insistence on doing what is right is a reminder that no acts of disobedience in Sarah's life are to be imitated by Christian wives (cf. Genesis 16:2, 6; 18:15; perhaps 20:5); it is her submission to her husband and her trust in God that Peter commends. The condition "if you . . . do not give way to fear" is another way in which faith finds expression. A woman with a gentle and quiet spirit who continues hoping in God will not be terrified by circumstances or by an unbelieving or disobedient husband (cf. Genesis 20:6).

D. The Rewards of Submission

Peter holds out one reward that wives are ordinarily to expect from this submission to their husbands: the unbelieving husband may be won to Christ.[17] Those who "do not believe the word" are husbands who are unbelievers; the present tense verb (*apeithousin*) suggests a pattern of life characterized by unbelief or rejection not only of the gospel but also of God's standards in other areas of life. The word does not mean just that they "do not believe the word" (NIV); it has a much stronger sense of active disobedience to the standards of Scripture and even rebellion against them. Note the use of this same word (*apeitheō*) in Acts 14:2; 19:9; Romans 2:8; 10:21; 11:30, 31; 15:31; Hebrews 3:18; 1 Peter 3:20; 4:17.[18] Some of these unbelieving, disobedient husbands (not all) would have been harsh and unkind to their Christian wives, but Peter says that even such husbands can be won for God's kingdom (note the same word for "won" in 1 Corinthians 9:19-22 (five times); also Matthew 18:15, and in a commercial sense, Matthew 16:26; 25:20, 22; James 4:13.[19]

These unbelieving husbands can be won without a word—that is, not by continually preaching or talking about the gospel, but rather simply by the behavior of their[20] wives, their Christian pattern of life. The word *behavior* (*anastrophē*) is frequent in Peter's writings (eight of the thirteen New Testament occurrences are in 1 and 2 Peter). He uses it to refer to the evil pattern of life of unbelievers (1 Peter 1:18; 2 Peter 2:7) and the good pattern of life of believers that is intended to lead to the salvation of others who observe it. Peter does not exactly say that Christian wives should never talk about the gospel message to their unbelieving husbands (indeed, it is hard to imagine that the Christian wives among Peter's readers would never have explained to their husbands what it meant to become a Christian), but he does say that the means God will use to win their husbands generally will not be the wives' words but their behavior. This knowledge should increase prayer both for grace to live rightly and for God's silent working in the husband's heart.

Another reward is to be daughters of Sarah (verse 6). As explained above, this certainly means being a member of the people of God, an heir of all the blessings of salvation. But it probably also includes a suggestion of sharing in Sarah's special dignity and honor, imitating the pattern of submission and trust in God that Sarah exemplified, and similarly receiving God's special approval as a result.

Finally, the greatest reward will be the combined joy of honoring God and receiving His favor. Dorothy Patterson rightly says of this passage, "Submission primarily honors the Lord who established the relationship."[21] Yet in honoring the Lord a Christian wife will also know His special favor. Peter says that the gentle and quiet spirit that accompanies such submissive behavior "is of great worth in God's sight" (verse 4). God will look on this behavior, which springs from a heart of faith, and will delight in this daughter of Sarah and show her His favor.

E. The Universal Rightness of a Wife's Submission to Her Husband

When Peter says that unbelieving husbands may be "won over" for Christ "by the behavior of their wives" when they are submissive to their husbands, there is a significant implication for the question of whether such submission is appropriate for all cultures and all times. The attractiveness of a wife's submissive behavior even to an *unbelieving* husband suggests that God has inscribed on the hearts of all mankind the rightness and beauty of role distinctions in marriage (including male leadership or headship in the family and female acceptance of and responsiveness to that leadership). Someone might object that female submissiveness is attractive to the unbelieving husband only because he is selfishly interested in gaining power for himself or because it fits his culture's current (and presumably wrong) perception of appropriate male-female relationships, and in either case—this position would argue—such role distinctions are still wrong or still incongruent with God's *ideal* plan for marriage. A similar objection would be made by those who say that this command was only a missionary strategy for that culture, to make the gospel inoffensive to non-Christians, but that it is not universally binding today.[22] In fact, those who make this objection would often say it would be wrong today to require all Christian wives to be subject to their husbands—it would fall short of God's ideal for marriage.

However, this position is unpersuasive because Peter would not encourage a *morally objectionable* behavior pattern (whether in the culture or in the husband himself) to continue in order to bring someone to faith. It is pure behavior, not behavior that falls short of God's ideal, that attracts unbelievers to Christ (1 Peter 3:2). And this pure behavior (verse 2), Peter says, especially involves wives being subject to their own husbands. The unbelieving husband sees this behavior and deep within perceives the beauty of it. Within his heart there is a witness that this is right, this is how God intended men and women to relate as husband and wife. He concludes, therefore, that the gospel that his wife believes must be true as well.[23] Perhaps, indeed, he sees his wife's submission to him in contrast with his own refusal to submit to God, who is infinitely more worthy of his submission, and is convicted of his own sinfulness by it.

Two other approaches that evade the implication that wives should submit to the authority of their husbands today are represented by Ruth Tucker and Walter Liefeld, who suggest that Peter's directions here are culture-specific and therefore need not apply today. They note that some maintain that "although Sarah is said to have expressed her submission to Abraham by obeying him and calling him 'lord' (or 'master'), that certainly does not mean that submission is expressed in every culture by obedience and calling one's husband 'lord.' Few would insist on the second part of Sarah's submission."[24] They also note that another way some argue that these injunctions are not binding on Christians today is to realize that they belong to a form of instruction known as a "household code" that was common in the ancient world and was included by the New Testament authors as a reminder that Christians should act in ways that would not give offense to unbelievers, but that the New Testament does not imply that these "household codes" were to be followed by all Christians in all cultures.[25] Although both of these approaches are simply presented as *possible* interpretations on pp. 81, 83, Tucker and Liefeld seem to adopt them as their own in the discussion of exegetical issues in Appendix B (pp. 462, 463).

The problem with the first argument is that it fails to recognize that Peter is requiring a general pattern of behavior (submission that results in obedience) rather than a carbon copy imitation of every word Sarah said (such as calling Abraham "lord" or "master"). The point is that Sarah gave respectful obedience to Abraham even in the words she used to refer to him, and so should Christian wives today be respectful (whatever words may be used from culture to culture to signify that respect). To say instead that submission itself is the general pattern and *obedience to a husband's authority* is the specific form that may vary from culture to culture (as Tucker and Liefeld do on p. 463) is to neglect the fact that submission in the New Testament (expressed by the word *hupotassō*) is always submission to an authority, and, therefore, the idea of obedience to authority seems inherent in this type of submission. Moreover, they neglect that it is not Sarah's specific words but her general obedience itself that Peter refers to when he says that Old Testament women who hoped in God were submissive to their husbands, *as* Sarah *obeyed* Abraham (verses 5-6). Obedience is one form that submission took for all of those referred to, but the mention of Sarah's words is simply a reminder of a specific example in Sarah's life.

As for the "household codes," there were lists of expected behavior for husbands and wives, parents and children, and servants and masters in the ancient world, but close comparison of ancient lists with those in the New Testament shows very few exact parallels except that these various groups are named.[26] The "form" (if the New Testament authors were even conscious of using such a form) was extensively "Christianized," so that few similarities remain. And at any rate, what we have in Scripture now is the morally binding authority of God's own words. If we say that no unique authority or leadership for husbands in marriage was the ideal, but that Peter gave in to cultural expectations and failed to teach that ideal, this would seem to impugn Peter's courage and integrity, because it implies that Peter was willing (and Paul, too!) to command Christians to follow a sinful, sub-Christian pattern of behavior in their homes—a most unlikely course of action for those accustomed to running against the tide! Moreover, it implies that God would command Christians to follow a sinful pattern of marriage just to attract unbelievers to the gospel—something inconsistent with God's own pattern of telling His people to use morally righteous means to achieve righteous ends. We may conclude that both of these attempts to avoid the force of Peter's directions today fail to be persuasive.

Another way that people sometimes have tried to avoid the permanence of these commands is to look at the commands about hair and jewelry and say that those are no longer binding today. This view says that Peter is forbidding the wearing of gold or braiding of hair when he writes, "Your beauty should not come from outward adornment, such as braided hair and the wearing of gold jewelry and fine clothes" (verse 3). This view reasons: (a) these commands are for that culture only, and cannot apply today; (b) therefore the other command in this paragraph, that a wife should be subject to her husband, does not apply today either.

But this view is certainly incorrect, because it misunderstands Peter. In this section Peter emphasizes not external, visible things that perish but unseen spiritual realities that are eternal, just as he has done frequently in the letter to this point (see 1 Peter 1:1 ["strangers"], 4, 7-9, 18-19, 23-25; 2:2, 5, 9, 11). "Let not yours be the outward adorning" (RSV) gives the sense of the phrase quite well and prepares the reader for the contrast with "inward adorning" (RSV) in verse 4. "Adorning" refers to what one uses to make oneself beautiful to others. The point is that Christian wives should depend for their own attractiveness *not* on outward things like braiding their hair, decorations of gold, and wearing fine clothing, but on inward qualities of life, especially a gentle and quiet spirit (verse 4). Furthermore, although the RSV and NIV speak of "fine clothing," the Greek text does not include an adjective modifying *himatiōn*, "clothing," and the text literally says, "Let not your adorning be the outward adorning of braiding of hair and wearing of gold or putting on of clothing." It is incorrect, therefore, to say that this text prohibits women from braiding their hair or wearing gold jewelry, for by the same reasoning one would have to prohibit "putting on of clothing." Peter's point is not that any of these is forbidden, but that these should not be a woman's "adorning," her source of beauty.

In fact, we should rather note that Peter in this very text is *opposing* dominant ideas in that culture. When he rejects the use of hairstyle, jewelry, or clothing as a means of winning the unbelieving husband, Peter writes counterculturally.[27] He commends not just any behavior or dress that would be approved by the culture, but a gentle and quiet spirit, which *in God's sight is very precious* (verse 4). Peter goes right to the heart of the Christian faith—hope in God (verse 5) and the gentle and quiet spirit that stems from faith and "is of great worth in God's sight" (verse 4). Peter is functioning from the center of the Christian faith here; he is not merely adapting to culture.

F. The Beauty of Submission

In an age when submission to authority is frequently denigrated and thought to be degrading and dehumanizing, Peter's words remind us that submission to rightful authority is beautiful and right in God's world. It is "for the Lord's sake" (2:13) that Christians are to be subject to God-ordained authorities, whether in civil government (2:13-17), in employment (2:18-20), in the family (3:1-6), or in the church (5:5). Specifically within marriage, the beauty of a wife's submission to her husband is evident to *unbelievers*, who are attracted to Christ through it (verses 1-2). Peter also expects this beauty to be evident to *believing husbands* and to *other people generally*, for this is the beauty that he tells Christian women to make their "adorning"—their source of beauty (verse 4). This is the beauty that adorned women of the Old Testament "who put their hope in God" and "were submissive to their own husbands" (verse 5). This beauty also ought to be seen and felt by the *Christian wife herself*, for it is not accompanied by fear (verse 6), but by reverence, purity (verse 2), moral uprightness (verse 6), quietness of spirit (verse 4), and hope in God (verse 5). Finally, the beauty of this submission is evident to *God*, for the gentle and quiet spirit that accompanies this submission in God's sight is "of great worth" (verse 4).

II. Directions to Husbands

A. What Considerate Leadership Is Not

Peter tells husbands, "Live considerately with your wives" (verse 7, RSV; similarly, NIV), or, more literally, "Live with your wives in an understanding way" (NASB).

This is the husband's counterpart to his wife's submissive attitude, and Peter here warns husbands against some potential abuses of their leadership role within the marriage. Because this section is the counterpart to Peter's command to wives to be submissive to their husband's leadership, we can speak of "considerate leadership" as a summary of the husband's responsibility.

1. Considerate leadership does not mean harsh or domineering use of authority.
Peter tells husbands to "be considerate" to their wives and says they should "treat them with respect as the weaker partner" (verse 7).[28] Peter does not specify how he understands the woman to be the "weaker partner," but the context would make it appropriate for him to have in mind any kind of weakness that husbands would need to be cautioned not to take advantage of. This would certainly include physical strength (most men, if they tried, could overpower their wives physically). But the context also shows that women are weaker in terms of authority in the marriage (verses 1, 5, 6), and Peter therefore tells husbands that, instead of misusing their authority for selfish ends, they should use it to treat their wives with respect. Yet there may also be a third sense of weakness that would fit the context (because it is something husbands should not take advantage of), namely, a greater emotional sensitivity (perhaps hinted at in Peter's admonition to godly wives, "do not give way to fear," verse 6). While this is something that is also a great strength, it nonetheless means that wives are often more likely to be hurt deeply by conflict within a marriage or by inconsiderate behavior. Knowing this, Christian husbands should not be "harsh" (Colossians 3:19) or fill their marriage relationship with criticism and conflict, but should rather be positive and affirming, living together in an understanding way and bestowing honor on their wives.

The word translated *partner* in "the weaker partner" is *skeuos*, which often means "vessel, jar, container," but is also used in the New Testament to speak of human beings as "vessels" created by God and intended for His use (Acts 9:15; Romans 9:21; 2 Corinthians 4:7; 2 Timothy 2:21). There is no derogatory or misogynistic nuance here, since the fact that the woman is called the "weaker vessel" (that is, the weaker of the two) implies that the man is also viewed as a "vessel." The term recalls God's creation of all people, both men and women, and is a reminder both of human frailty and of obligation to God our Creator.

2. Considerate leadership does not imply equal sharing of leadership in the family.
Although Peter tells husbands to act in a thoughtful and understanding way toward their wives, he never tells husbands to submit to their wives or suggests that roles in marriage are interchangeable. Considerate leadership is *how* the husband exercises leadership in the family; it does not contradict his headship.

The phrase "in the same way" in verse 7 has the sense "also" or "continuing in the same area of discussion" (see note above on the word at 3:1; also, Bauer-Arndt-Gingrich-Danker, p. 568, and 1 Peter 5:7), for the idea of similarity in submission is excluded by the fact that here (unlike 2:18; 3:1) Peter does not command submission to any authority but rather the considerate use of that authority.

3. Considerate leadership does not imply lesser importance for a wife.
The fact that husbands are to treat their wives with "respect" does not mean that

the wife, who has less authority, is less important. Peter's telling husbands that their wives are joint heirs of the grace of life reminds them that, even though they have been given greater authority within marriage, their wives are still equal to them in spiritual privilege and eternal importance. Here as elsewhere the New Testament authors couple their treatment of differences in roles of husband and wife with an implicit or explicit affirmation of their equality in status and importance (cf. 1 Corinthians 11:3, 7, 12; Ephesians 5:22, 33; Colossians 3:18, 19).

4. Considerate leadership does not mean always giving in to a wife's wishes.
Just as wives are not to obey their husbands when commanded to disobey God, so husbands must never allow love for their wives to become an excuse for sin—a principle tragically ignored by Abraham himself when he followed Sarah's urging and decided to have a child by Sarah's maid Hagar (Genesis 16:2, 5). The principle was also ignored by Solomon (1 Kings 11:1-3, 8), Ahab (1 Kings 21:25), and perhaps even Adam (Genesis 3:6). The mere fact that one's wife—even a godly, believing wife—*wants* to do something morally wrong does not mean that a husband is free before God to endorse or participate in that wrong. To do so would be to abdicate the leadership God has given the husband and would be the opposite of the righteous leadership God requires him to exercise. In actual practice, it will often take much prayer and knowledge of Scripture for a husband to be able to tell the difference between a morally wrong choice being urged on him by his wife and a morally right choice that just differs from his personal preference or judgment of how things should be done. But there will be times in every marriage when a godly husband simply will have to make decisions that affect the whole family, that go against his wife's desires and preferences and that he nonetheless is convinced, before God, are right.

5. Considerate leadership is not optional for husbands.
Just as submission to one's husband is not optional for Christian wives, so the considerate leadership that Peter commands is not optional for Christian husbands. Husbands cannot rightly opt out of family leadership and become passive non-participants in decisions and activities. Neither can they rightly make the opposite mistake and exercise harsh, selfish, domineering authority in their families. They are rather to live considerately and bestow honor. Yet in doing this they cannot escape the responsibility to lead that is implicit in the command for their wives to submit to them.

B. What Considerate Leadership Is

"[B]e considerate as you live with your wives" is literally, "living together according to knowledge."[29] Peter does not specify what kind of knowledge he means by "according to knowledge," so some general phrase like "in an understanding way" (NASB) is a good translation. The RSV's "considerately" (similarly, NIV) is generally acceptable, but it probably gives too much emphasis to a considerate attitude while neglecting the focus on actual "knowledge" or information that is implied by Peter's word. The knowledge Peter intends here may include any knowledge that would be beneficial to the husband-wife relationship: of God's purposes and principles for marriage; of the wife's desires, goals, and frustrations; of her strengths and weaknesses in the physical, emotional and spiritual realms, etc. A husband who lives according to such knowledge will greatly enrich his marriage—yet such knowledge can only be gained through regular study of God's

Word and regular, unhurried times of private fellowship together as husband and wife.[30]

"[G]rant her honor" as "a weaker vessel" (NASB) affirms a theme found frequently in the New Testament. God is often pleased to honor those who are weaker or less honored in the eyes of the world (cf. Matthew 5:3-12; 1 Corinthians 1:26-30; 12:22-25; James 2:5; 4:6; 1 Peter 5:5).[31] In this case, such honor may include kind and affirming words both in private and in public, as well as the highest human priority in allocation of time and money. (The NIV's "treat them with respect" is too weak—one can treat another person with detached, formal respect and yet give no special honor.)

In the phrase, "Bestowing honor on the woman" (RSV), the word "woman" translates *tō gunaikeiō*, a rare word that is used only here in the New Testament. It means more literally "the feminine one," and suggests that Peter is looking to the characteristic nature of womanhood or femininity and seeing in it an appropriateness for receiving honor. It is appropriate that those who are "feminine," those who give characteristic expression to "womanhood," should receive special honor, for this is what God has directed.

C. The Reasons for Considerate Leadership

The first reason for such considerate leadership is that there are differences between husband and wife: the wife is the "weaker vessel" (NASB) or "weaker partner" (NIV) and thus more vulnerable to being hurt by a selfish, domineering husband.

The second reason for considerate leadership is the equality between husband and wife: "since you are joint heirs of the grace of life" (RSV).[32] One who has equal standing in God's kingdom is certainly worthy of equal honor and thoughtful, loving attention.

D. The Rewards of Considerate Leadership

At the end of this passage Peter indicates a reward for husbands who live considerately with their wives, but he does so by giving a warning of what will happen if they do not live this way: "so that nothing will hinder your prayers." The implication is that if they *do* live in a considerate way with their wives, their prayers will not be hindered but helped, and God will answer them (compare 1 Peter 3:12, where Peter says, ". . . the eyes of the Lord are on the righteous and his ears are attentive to their prayer").

Some think that "your prayers" in this verse refers only to times when the husband and wife pray together, but this view is unpersuasive because Peter is addressing this sentence to husbands only, not to both husbands and wives. "Your" must refer to the "you" to whom Peter is writing: the husbands. The reference therefore is to the husbands' prayers generally. This hindering of prayers is a form of God's fatherly discipline, which Hebrews 12:3-11 reminds us is for our good and is given to those whom God loves. So concerned is God that Christian husbands live in an understanding and loving way with their wives that He interrupts His relationship with them when they do not do so! No Christian husband should presume to think that any spiritual good will be accomplished by his life without an effective ministry of prayer. And no husband may expect an effective prayer life unless he lives with his wife "in an understanding way, bestowing honor" on her. To take the time to maintain a good marriage is God's will; it is serving God; it is a spiritual activity pleasing in His sight.

11

The Valuable Ministries of Women in the Context of Male Leadership:

A Survey of Old and New Testament Examples and Teaching

Thomas R. Schreiner

This chapter focuses on the valuable ministries of women in the Scriptures. This is a crucial topic for at least three reasons. First, men often have hurt women. They have treated them as lesser citizens of the kingdom, and some men have denigrated or overlooked their contribution in ministry. An examination of the Scriptures will show that women have played a vital role in ministry. One reason for the current feminist movement, although not the only one, is that some women are responding to men who have oppressed them and treated them poorly.

Second, contemporary women should be encouraged by the women in the Scriptures who have contributed to the spread of God's kingdom message. God does not use men alone to accomplish His purposes. Both sexes are created in God's image, and both men and women have been used mightily by God. No woman who has a desire to please God should feel that there is no place for her ministry in the church.

Third, some contemporary evangelical writers appeal to the ministries of women in the Scriptures to support the notion that there should be no limits on women's roles in ministry today. They maintain that women and men should have equal access to every ministry function and that any limits on women derive from culture and tradition, not from the Bible, which they believe supports the full inclusion of women in any ministry.

This third area is particularly important. We will examine it carefully in this chapter, for if the examples of ministry by women in the Bible indicate that there should be no limits on women in ministry, then the church should open the doors of every ministry to women. We should be open to the possibility that we have misread the Scriptures by imposing some restrictions on women in ministry. Perhaps our culture and tradition have drawn lines and distinctions that cannot be supported from the Bible. Thus, we should listen to and evaluate carefully the arguments of those who contend that the ministries of women portrayed in the Bible demonstrate that every ministry that is open to men is also open to women.

I. Ministry in a General Sense

This chapter will focus on the third issue since that is a matter of particular debate today. Nevertheless, we should remind ourselves that ministry is a very broad word, stemming from the Greek words *diakonia*, *diakonos*, and *diakoneō*, and these words often convey the idea of "service" and "ministry" in the broadest sense. For example, Martha was distracted because of her "service" or "ministry" (*diakonia*), and the "service" being described is preparation of a meal (Luke 10:40). In Luke 22:27, one "one who serves" is contrasted to "one who reclines" (NASB) during the meal. The "ministry" in view is simply serving tables. Luke 8:1-3 tells of a number of women who were ministering (*diakoneō*) to Jesus and the apostles. The specific ministry they engaged in was not preaching the gospel but providing financial resources so that Jesus could carry on His ministry. First Peter 4:10 says that all spiritual gifts are to be used to "minister" (*diakoneō*) to one another in the church. And Paul says, "There are different kinds of service (*diakonia*), but the same Lord" (1 Corinthians 12:5). So in this broad sense, anything any Christian does to help the work of the church is a ministry.

Other examples of the use of the words *ministry* and service in this general sense could be cited, but the point to be made is this: Not all ministries that are valuable are public or official ministries. Providing food and support for others is crucial, and this ministry should not be scorned, even if one does not get public recognition for it. Many unnamed men and women of God have quietly and humbly worked behind the scenes in this way, and they have found great joy and blessing in doing so. I am not suggesting that this is the only ministry role for women. Nevertheless, it is a crucial one that should not be overlooked. Those who denigrate such a role are downplaying the function of many men and women who have labored with love.

Women, then, have engaged in significant ministries, even if those ministries were unofficial. One thinks of Abigail in 1 Samuel 25. Abigail was not a prophetess and had no other official ministry that we know of. Nevertheless, her humble and gentle advice to David persuaded him not to kill Nabal. How many unrecorded events there must be of women persuading men, humbly and gently, to pursue a more righteous course! What a good model this story is for traditionalists who think being a leader means they must always know the truth and that their opinion is always right. David was certainly the leader in this account, but his humility is evident in that he listened to Abigail and was persuaded. For women, Abigail is a model of gentle and humble persuasion. There was no stridency or imperiousness about her manner. She was winsome, yet bold.

The "unofficial" ministries of women, therefore, are of great importance, and some men, by desiring leadership for its status and power as the Gentiles do (Mark 10:42ff.), have contributed to the idea that these ministries are insignificant. Such a secular concept of ministry has done great damage in Christ's church.

II. The Argument for Full Inclusion of Women in All Ministries

The rest of the chapter will focus on the "official" or publicly recognized ministries of women in the Bible. What ministries did they have, and what are the implications of these ministries for today? We will begin by considering the evidence and arguments of those who think there are no limits on women in ministry.[1] We will not evaluate these arguments until all the evidence for the full inclusion of women in ministry is presented. Otherwise, we may be guilty of not giving both sides of the debate a full and fair hearing.

A. Prophetesses

Those who see no restrictions on women in ministry argue that the prophets of both the Old Testament and the New Testament were authoritative messengers of God. Women clearly functioned as prophetesses in both the Old Testament and the New Testament. Miriam is explicitly called a prophetess in Exodus 15:20, and she led the women in singing for Yahweh's triumph over Egypt (Exodus 15:21). The prophetess Huldah was consulted by the messengers of Josiah in 2 Kings 22:14-20. Other women probably functioned as prophetesses in the Old Testament but are unmentioned (cf. Isaiah 8:3), and Ezekiel pronounces judgment against daughters who prophesy falsely (Ezekiel 13:17-24). Compare also Nehemiah's words against the prophetess Noadiah (Nehemiah 6:14). The problem here was not that these women prophesied, but that they did not prophesy according to the word of the Lord.

For our purposes, the most significant example of a prophetess is Deborah (Judges 4:4-5). Evangelical feminists consider Deborah particularly significant because she functioned as a judge over Israel, which would include judging men, and she exercised authority over the man Barak, who was a commander of the Israelite troops.

In the New Testament, too, women prophesy, and there may even be some indication that it was more common for them to do so. The prophetess Anna thanked God and spoke of Him when Jesus was brought to the temple (Luke 2:36-38). Peter cites Joel's prophecy that when the Spirit is poured out both "sons and daughters will prophesy. . . . Even on my servants, both men and women, I will pour out my Spirit in those days, and they will prophesy" (Acts 2:17-18; cf. Joel 2:28-32).

Philip's four daughters are one indication that this promise was fulfilled, for they all prophesied (Acts 21:9). Paul also encourages women to prophesy, with proper adornment (1 Corinthians 11:5). Those who argue for full inclusion of women in every ministry point out that if Paul thought such prayer and prophecy were wrong, he certainly would not bother to explain in such detail how they should be adorned while they were sinning!

It is concluded, then, from both the Old Testament and the New, that women functioned as prophets, and they used this gift for the edification of the people of God. In addition, prophecy, according to those who argue for no limits on women's ministries, is defined as an authoritative declaration of God's Word; thus, if women can prophesy, they can perform any ministry. They argue that prophecy is just as important and as authoritative as teaching. In fact, in 1 Corinthians 12:28, the gift of prophecy is ranked *above* teaching. Now, nearly everyone agrees that women can function as prophets, for the evidence here is clear, but if women can function as prophets, it would seem that they can also function as teachers today, because prophecy is just as authoritative as teaching.

B. Women Teachers and Spiritual Gifts

Moreover, those who contend for no restrictions on women in ministry argue that women function as teachers. When Priscilla and Aquila heard Apollos teach, they took him aside and explained the gospel more accurately to him (Acts 18:26). The inclusion of Priscilla indicates that she must have taught Apollos as well. In fact, Luke mentions her first, and some suggest this implies that she did more of the teaching. Such ministry by Priscilla does not seem to be a one-time affair. In Romans 16:3, Paul greets both Priscilla and Aquila. He labels them his fellow-workers in the gospel, which implies that they shared in the gospel ministry with him. Their involvement in ministry is also confirmed by 1 Corinthians 16:19, for there Paul says that a church is in their house.

The argument for women teachers is also set forth from spiritual gifts. Teaching is a spiritual gift (1 Corinthians 12:28-29; Ephesians 4:12; Romans 12:7), and yet there is no indication that women are excluded from this gift. All Christians are told to teach one another (Colossians 3:16) and to share with the community what they have learned (1 Corinthians 14:26). Surely this must include women. Indeed, Priscilla, as we have seen above, seems to use the gift in instructing Apollos. Paul also mentions women in the role of teaching in Titus 2:3.

Those who advocate no restrictions on women in ministry say that passages like 1 Timothy 2:11-15 and 1 Corinthians 14:33b-36 should not be used to impose limitations on women today. First Timothy 2:11-15, they say, was not written to forbid all teaching of men by women. Paul here is only forbidding false teaching by women, or (according to others) preventing women who were uneducated from teaching men. First Corinthians 14:33b-36 was probably written to resolve a problem in the congregation where women were disrupting the assembly by speaking in tongues or by interrupting the service with questions. Or perhaps the passage quotes a Corinthian slogan or question that Paul rejects. Some also think that verses 34-35 were not part of the original text of 1 Corinthians and that they were added by a later scribe. These two passages, therefore, are designed to correct abuses by women in teaching, it is argued, not to forbid any teaching of men whatsoever. The fact that women could prophesy, which, it is claimed, cannot be distinguished from authoritative teaching, and that Priscilla engages in teaching, shows that the prohibitions in these two passages are not absolute.

C. Women as Fellow-workers and Laborers

It has already been noted that in Romans 16:3 Paul calls Priscilla a "fellow worker" (*sunergos*). It is instructive to note others who are called Paul's fellow workers: Timothy (Romans 16:21; 1 Thessalonians 3:2; Philemon 1), Apollos (1 Corinthians 3:9), Urbanus (Romans 16:9), Titus (2 Corinthians 8:23), Epaphroditus (Philippians 2:25), Aristarchus (Colossians 4:10; Philemon 24), Mark (Colossians 4:10; Philemon 24), Jesus Justus (Colossians 4:10), Epaphras (Philemon 24), Demas (Philemon 24), and Luke (Philemon 24). Some of those listed here we know very little about, but we know that Timothy, Apollos, Titus, Epaphroditus, Mark, Epaphras, and Luke proclaimed the gospel. Does it not follow, then, say those who espouse full inclusion of women in every ministry, that

Priscilla as a fellow worker did the same? Moreover, Priscilla is not the only woman whom Paul calls a fellow-worker. In Philippians 4:2, he exhorts two women, Euodia and Syntyche, to agree in the Lord. In 4:3, he says that they struggled together with him in the gospel along with Clement and the rest of the fellow-workers. The implication is that Euodia and Syntyche were fellow-workers. They struggled together in the gospel by helping Paul spread the good news of salvation.

The point can even be made more specific. In 1 Corinthians 16:16, Paul exhorts the Corinthians to be subject to the house of Stephanas and to "every fellow worker (*panti sunergounti*) and laborer (*kopiōnti*)." We have already seen that three women are called fellow workers: Priscilla, Euodia, and Syntyche. Paul says that the Corinthians are to be subject to all fellow-workers and laborers. It would seem to follow, according to those who reject any limits on women today, that since Priscilla, Euodia, and Syntyche were fellow-workers, these women held leadership positions in the church and, therefore, men were subject to them.

It is also noted that Paul says to be subject to "every laborer" (*panti . . . kopiōnti*) as well as every fellow worker (1 Corinthians 16:16). Paul often describes his ministry using this same word for labor (1 Corinthians 4:12; 15:10; Galatians 4:11; Philippians 2:16; Colossians 1:29; 1 Timothy 4:10). Indeed, the work of other leaders is also described in terms of laboring. The Corinthians are to submit to the house of Stephanas, which labors for them (1 Corinthians 16:16). The Thessalonians are exhorted "to respect those who work hard [or *labor*] among you" (1 Thessalonians 5:12), and these are clearly the leaders, because Paul goes on to say that they are "over you in the Lord and admonish you." The elders who rule well should receive double honor, according to 1 Timothy 5:17, "especially those whose work is preaching and teaching." Clearly, then, Paul often uses the verb *labor* to denote authoritative ministry and instruction. But Paul also mentions women who have labored. In Romans 16:6, he instructs the Romans to greet Mary, who labored much for them. And in Romans 16:12, three women, Tryphaena, Tryphosa, and Persis, are said to have labored much in the Lord. Some conclude, therefore, that women were leaders in the congregations, for the word *labor* is clearly used in this sense in 1 Corinthians 16:16, 1 Thessalonians 5:12, and 1 Timothy 5:17.

D. Women Deacons

It is also argued that women functioned in official positions in the church because they held the office of deacon. Many scholars have argued that this is the most probable interpretation of 1 Timothy 3:11. In 1 Timothy 3:8-10 and 12, the qualifications are given for men who are to serve as deacons. In 3:11, Paul says: "Women must likewise be dignified, not malicious gossips, but temperate, faithful in all things" (NASB). The word for "women" here (*gunaikas*) could be translated "wives" (as in NIV), and that is the view of some commentators. The following reasons are given to support the idea that Paul is speaking of women deacons: (1) Paul introduces the women mentioned here in the same fashion he introduced the men in 1 Timothy 3:8, i.e., he uses the word *likewise*. In 3:1-7, Paul lays out the qualifications for elders, and in 3:8 Paul says likewise there are similar qualifications for deacons. The *likewise* in 3:11 suggests that the qualifications for men who are deacons also apply to women deacons.

(2) If Paul were speaking of wives of deacons, he could have made this very

clear by adding *of deacons* (*diakonōn* or *autōn*). By leaving the word *women* without any modifier, he implied that he was speaking of women in general, not just of the wives of deacons. (3) The qualifications Paul mentions in 3:12 are identical with or similar to those required of deacons, and this suggests that an office is in view.[2]

Further evidence that women functioned as deacons is found in the case of Phoebe. In Romans 16:1, Paul says that she was "a deaconess of the church at Cenchreae" (RSV). Actually, the word *deaconess* here is the same as the one used in 1 Timothy 3:8 and Philippians 1:1, where Paul writes of deacons. Thus, Paul is not calling Phoebe a "deaconess," but a "deacon," some have claimed. In addition, Phoebe is called a leader (*prostatis*) in Romans 16:2. The most commonly used translations (RSV, NASB, NIV) use the word *help* or *helper* here, but it has been claimed that this term is a technical one used for a legal protector or leader. If such an interpretation is correct, Paul here recommends Phoebe as a deacon and as a leader of many.

E. Women Elders

Evidence is also adduced that women could function as elders. The letter of 2 John is addressed to "the chosen lady," and it is claimed that this does not refer to the church as a whole because the chosen lady is distinguished from her children (2 John 1, 4). The "chosen lady" refers to a woman who had authority over her children. Such authority is similar to the office of elder. Moreover, some suggest that Paul speaks of women elders in Titus 2:3. Although this is obscured by translations that render *presbytidas* by "older women," it is clear that this word is a feminine rendering of the term *presbyteros* (*elder*) that Paul uses in Titus 1:5 to refer to church office.

F. Women Apostles

Most significantly, it is frequently claimed that women also functioned as apostles. In Romans 16:7, Paul writes, "Greet Andronicus and Junias, my relatives who have been in prison with me. They are outstanding among the apostles. . . . " Some commentators have thought that Junias was a man, and that the name here is a contracted form of the word *Junianus*. Nevertheless, this is said to be an unpersuasive argument, for there is no example in Greek literature of this name being contracted. Thus, some have said that the name should be translated "Junia" (feminine) rather than "Junias" (masculine), showing that a woman is almost certainly included among the apostles here. Others have contended that the Greek (*en tois apostolois*) means "outstanding in the eyes of the apostles," not "outstanding among the apostles." Of course, such a rendering would exclude Andronicus and Junia(s) from the apostolic circle. The text would simply say that the apostles held them in high esteem. But it is claimed that this is an unnatural way to understand the Greek, and the most probable rendering is "outstanding among the apostles." To sum up: there seems to be evidence here that a woman was an apostle, and this raises a serious question against those who want to deny women full participation in leadership positions in the church.

G. Conclusion

To sum up, the argument often given for full inclusion in ministry is cumulative. Women functioned as prophets, and such a ministry is just as authoritative as teaching. Women possess all the spiritual gifts, and this includes the gifts of teaching and leadership. Indeed, there is evidence in the New Testament that women held the offices of deacon, elder, and apostle. All of this evidence is in accord with Paul's designation of women as fellow-workers in the gospel. The passages that seem to limit women in ministry can be explained from the situation that Paul addresses and thus should not be used to impose restrictions on women. The burden of proof, then, is said to be on those who want to impose restrictions on women in ministry.

III. The Argument for Some Restrictions on Women in Ministry

The preceding section has rightly shown that women participated in various forms of ministry in both the Old Testament and the New Testament. The question is whether its argument establishes the case that no restrictions are to be placed on women in ministry. I think not. I propose to prove below that women participated in ministry in the Scriptures, but their ministry was a complementary and supportive ministry, a ministry that fostered and preserved male leadership in the church. Thus, the ministry of women in the church was notable and significant, but it never supplanted male leadership; instead, it functioned as a support to male leadership. This view does not rule out all ministry for women. Instead, it sees the ministry of women as complementary and supportive.

A. Prophetesses

One of the strongest arguments for full inclusion of women in authoritative positions of leadership stems from the prophetic role women played in the Scriptures. Deborah, as we have seen, stands out as an authoritative messenger of Yahweh. Nevertheless, the evidence from prophecy actually indicates a supportive and complementary role for women. It buttresses the point that role distinctions between men and women are maintained. An examination of the evidence will indicate how this is so.

That women prophesied to men is clear in the case of Deborah, other women cited above, and 1 Corinthians 11:2-16. The last passage cited, however, is absolutely crucial for rightly understanding a woman's relationship to man as she prophecies. What is Paul's concern in 1 Corinthians 11:2-16? It is that women who prophesy do so with proper adornment. Why is Paul concerned about how they are adorned? Because a woman's adornment says something about her relationship with men (11:3-10). Indeed, as I show in Chapter 5 of this volume, 11:3 is the key to the passage: "Now I want you to realize that the head of every man is Christ, and the head of the woman is man, and the head of Christ is God" (*NIV*). Thus, the reason Paul wants women to be adorned properly is that this adornment shows that a woman is submissive to male headship, even while prophesying. The way she is adorned indicates whether the man is the head, i.e., the authority.

The implications for our study are clear. Paul affirms that women can prophesy, but even in the process of prophesying they are to do so in a manner and with a demeanor that will not violate male headship. Paul does not place the same limits on men, and thus upholds and preserves the notion that male leadership is God's ordained pattern in the church. Note carefully that this does not mean that women will not prophesy in church. Paul affirms that women have prophetic gifts, and he wants them to exercise those gifts in church, but he does not want them to overturn male leadership.

The only passage that creates any difficulty for such a supportive and complementary view of prophecy is Judges 4, where Deborah commands Barak what to do and is a judge in Israel. But there are several reasons why this is in harmony with the notion of male headship explained in 1 Corinthians 11:2-16: (1) Deborah is a special case because she seems to be the only judge in Judges who has no military function. The other judges also lead Israel into victory in battle, but Deborah receives a word from the Lord that Barak is to do this (Judges 4:6-7). Deborah is not asserting leadership for herself; she gives priority to a man. (2) There is an implied rebuke of Barak because he is not willing to go to battle without Deborah (Judges 4:8). Because of his reluctance, the glory that day will go to a woman (Judges 4:9), but note that the woman is not Deborah but Jael (Judges 4:17ff.). In other words, Deborah did speak the word of God, but her attitude and demeanor were such that she was not asserting her leadership. Instead, she handed over the leadership, contrary to the pattern of all the other judges, to a man.

(3) Both Deborah and Huldah (2 Kings 22:14-20) exercised their gift of prophecy differently from the men who possessed the gift. Isaiah, Jeremiah, Ezekiel, and other male prophets exercised a public ministry where they proclaimed the word of the Lord. But note that Deborah did not prophecy in public.[3] Instead, her prophetic role seems to be limited to private and individual instruction. Judges 4:5 says, "And she used to sit under the palm tree of Deborah between Ramah and Bethel in the hill country of Ephraim; and the sons of Israel came up to her for judgment" (*NASB*). Note that Deborah did not go out and publicly proclaim the word of the Lord. Instead, individuals came to her in private for a word from the Lord. The difference between Deborah's prophetic ministry and that of male Old Testament prophets is clear. She did not exercise her ministry in a public forum as they did. Note that even when she speaks to Barak she calls him and speaks to him individually (Judges 4:6,14). And the song of praise in Judges 5:1 was sung by both Deborah and Barak together. A confirming argument for this view is found in the case of Huldah (2 Kings 22:14-20). She did not publicly proclaim God's word. Rather, she explained in private the word of the Lord when Josiah sent messengers to her. She exercised her prophetic ministry in a way that did not obstruct male headship. The prophetic ministry of Miriam is no exception to this, because she ministered only to women. "Then Miriam, the prophetess, Aaron's sister, took a tambourine in her hand, and *all the women followed her*, with tambourines and dancing. Miriam sang *to them* . . ." (Exodus 15:20, my italics).

(4) It is perhaps also significant that most of the other prominent judges in the book of Judges are explicitly said to have been raised up by the Lord:[4] Othniel (3:9), Ehud (3:15), Gideon (6:14), Jephthah (11:29), and Samson (13:25; 14:6). But in the case of Deborah, there is no explicit statement that the Lord raised her up: we simply read, "Now Deborah, a prophetess, the wife of Lappidoth, was judging Israel at that time" (Judges 4:4). I am not suggesting that the Lord did not raise her up, for He did bring evident blessing to Israel through her, but it may indicate that the nature of her role as a prophet and a judge was different from that of the other judges in that she did not exercise leadership over men as the other judges did. Such an observation harmonizes with the three points above.[5]

Also, prophecy differs from teaching. Prophecy is based on spontaneous revelation (1 Corinthians 14:29-33a), while teaching is an exposition of received revelation. A prophet, therefore, does not hold the same office as a teacher. Prophets speak forth God's revelation to the people, but the people go to the priests in the Old Testament to receive authoritative instruction based on tradition (Leviticus 10:11; Deuteronomy 21:5; Malachi 2:6-7). It is instructive to note in the Old Testament that some women were prophets, but never priests. It is the priests who had the more settled and established positions of leadership in Israel. This is not to deny that the Old Testament prophets spoke with great authority. Indeed, they criticized priests who abused their authority. The point is that prophecy is a different kind of gift from teaching, and when women functioned as prophets they did so with a demeanor and attitude that supported male leadership.

In addition, Wayne Grudem has argued that the gift of prophecy in the New Testament is not the same as the prophetic gift in the Old Testament.[6] Old Testament prophets spoke the word of the Lord, and what they said was absolutely authoritative—no part of it could be questioned or challenged. Every word was to be received as God's very word. But the words of New Testament prophets do not have this kind of absolute authority. Paul calls on the church to sort and sift the good from the bad in prophetic utterances: "Do not despise prophesying, but test everything; hold fast what is good" (1 Thessalonians 5:20-21, RSV; cf. 1 Corinthians 14:29-33a). When Paul says, "Two or three prophets should speak, and the others should weigh carefully what is said" (1 Corinthians 14:29), he uses a verb for "weigh carefully" (*diakrinō*) that means "to sort or sift some things from others." This implies that in New Testament prophecies, not every word would be understood to be the word of God. By contrast, in the Old Testament, a prophet who spoke *anything* untrue was to be put to death (Deuteronomy 13:1-5; 18:20-22). Instead, New Testament prophecies are handled not as authoritative words from God but as spontaneous impressions or insights that may or may not be, either in whole or in part, from God. Thus, the church must judge and evaluate prophecies in order to determine whether they, either in whole or in part, are sound.

Why is this distinction relevant to our discussion? It provides further evidence, particularly with regard to New Testament prophecy, that the gift of prophecy is not as authoritative as the gift of teaching.[7] Teaching involves a sustained and orderly exposition of divine revelation already given, while prophecy in the New Testament occurs when someone has a spontaneous revelation or impression, the whole or parts of which may or may not be from the Lord. The church does not accept such "revelations" uncritically, but weighs them carefully. Thus, the fact that women utter prophecies in church does not logically imply that they can exercise a teaching gift over men, for the two gifts are quite different.

To sum up, those women who had the authoritative gift of prophecy in the Old Testament did not exercise it in a public forum as male Old Testament prophets did. The reason for this is that such a public exercise of authority would contradict male headship. In the New Testament, women could prophecy in a public forum, but Grudem has shown that prophecy in the New Testament is not as authoritative as either prophecy in the Old Testament or teaching in the New Testament. And even if one were to reject Grudem's interpretation, 1 Corinthians 11:2-16 makes it clear that women who prophesied in the New Testament were to do so in such a way that they acknowledged and supported male headship.

Thus, the Biblical teaching on women prophets does not contradict male headship; instead, it supports male leadership in the church.

B. Teaching and Spiritual Gifts

We noted above, however, that Priscilla taught Apollos (Acts 18:26), and women have all the spiritual gifts, including teaching (Titus 2:3-4) and leadership. Several things can be said in response to this: (1) It is hard to tell from the Acts account to what extent Priscilla taught Apollos, since both Priscilla and Aquila are named. It is precarious to base much on this text, since it is an argument from silence to say that Priscilla was the primary teacher. (2) Even if Priscilla did all the teaching, this is not the same thing as teaching publicly in an authoritative position of leadership. Surely, Abigail "taught" David in the passage we looked at in 1 Samuel 25, but no one would say she had a position of leadership over men. More is often established from the example of Priscilla and Aquila than is warranted from the text.[8] (3) The word Paul uses for teaching in Titus 2:4 is not the usual one, but derives from *sōphronizō*, which means "to advise, encourage, or urge." In any case, this passage does not support women teaching men, because the verses say that the older women are to teach the younger women. If anything, this text supports the traditional view that sees a complementary but distinct role for women.

(4) The argument from spiritual gifts is not phrased carefully enough. Women surely have all the spiritual gifts, but does that mean that there are no restrictions regarding the exercising of those gifts? If our interpretation of passages like 1 Timothy 2:11-15 is correct, then women cannot publicly exercise their spiritual gift of teaching over men. This is not to deny that women have the gift of teaching or leadership. The point is that they are primarily to exercise those gifts among women. The idea that women are to exercise their gifts of leadership and teaching with other women harmonizes beautifully with Paul's instructions to older women in Titus 2:3ff. It is inappropriate hermeneutically to conclude from Paul's teaching on spiritual gifts that there is no limitation on women in ministry. One must consider all of Paul's teaching on the subject, and then what he says about spiritual gifts should be integrated with his instructions elsewhere.

C. Women as Fellow-workers and Laborers

Several texts were cited above that spoke of women being fellow-workers and laborers. Since these terms are often used of men who exercised leadership, and since in 1 Corinthians 16:16 the church is called to submit to such, it was inferred that women had leadership positions in the church. But this argument is only convincing if these words are technical terms for positions of leadership, and it is not clear that the terms are technical. That women played a significant role in gospel ministry is clear from the use of these terms, but it is unwarranted to derive from these terms alone the nature of their ministry. The terms *fellow-worker* and *laborer* are vague. There are many ways that women could have been fellow-workers and laborers without holding leadership positions over men. The clear teaching of Paul elsewhere (1 Corinthians 11:2-16; 14:33b-36; 1 Timothy 2:11-15) must be the guide for understanding the role of women rather than the appeal to terms that are too vague to support the idea of women sharing full leadership with men. Women could, for example, be prophets and probably deacons (see below) without violating male leadership, and yet surely such women would be fellow-workers and laborers.

It could still be objected that Paul says to be subject to every fellow-worker and fellow laborer (1 Corinthians 16:16). Paul says in verses 15-16, "Now, brethren, you know that the household of Stephanas were the first converts in Achaia, and they have devoted themselves to the service of the saints. I urge you to be subject to such men and to every fellow worker and laborer" (RSV). What is crucial to see is that the command to be subject (*hypotassō*) to every fellow-worker and laborer is found in a particular context, and thus it cannot be generalized to prove that women were church leaders. Verses 15-16 make it clear that the household of Stephanas and others who worked with them were the leaders in the Corinthian church.[9] There is no evidence in the context that any of these fellow workers and laborers in Corinth were women. In fact, the only leader mentioned, Stephanas, is clearly a man. Since the words *fellow-worker* and *laborer* are vague and can refer to men or women, there needs to be indisputable evidence that women are included here as leaders in the church, especially since such leadership is not stated elsewhere. Let me put the same argument another way: The words *fellow-worker* and *laborer* do not indicate that someone is a church leader, although that does not mean that these terms are never used of church leaders. All church leaders would be fellow-workers and laborers, but not all fellow-workers and laborers are necessarily church leaders.[10]

One other objection should be handled. Some may conclude that the reference to the "household of Stephanas" shows that women must be included. This argument, however, proves too much. Surely, no one would say that the children in Stephanas's house were church leaders, and yet they were part of his house. Those who want to prove that women held positions of authority over men must prove their case with arguments from indisputable examples rather than from the vague wording that Paul uses here.

D. and E. Women Deacons and Elders

Does not the inclusion of women as deacons, however, prove that they can hold an authoritative office? We have seen that many think that Phoebe is called a deacon in Romans 16:1. It should be noted, however, that the word *diakonos*, as we pointed out above, is often a general term, and thus one cannot be sure that Phoebe was a deacon.[11] And it is very unlikely that the word *prostatis* (Romans 16:2) is being used to say that Phoebe was a leader, as an examination of that verse shows. Paul commends Phoebe to the Romans and says "help her in whatever matter she may have need of you; for she herself has also been a helper [this is the word some think should be translated "leader"] of many, and of myself as well (NASB)." That Phoebe is being called a leader here is improbable for three reasons. (1) It is highly improbable that Paul would say that Phoebe held a position of authority over him. He says that about no one except Christ, not even the Jerusalem apostles (Galatians 1:6-7, 11), so confident is he of his high authority as an apostle (cf. 1 Corinthians 14:37-38; Galatians 1:8-9; 2 Thessalonians 3:14). (2) There seems to be a play on words between the word *prostatis* and the previous verb, *paristēmi*, in 16:2. Paul says to help (*paristēmi*) Phoebe because she has been a help (*prostatis*) to many, including to Paul himself. It fits the context better to understand Paul as saying "help Phoebe because she has been such a help to others and to me." (3) Although the related masculine noun *prostatēs* can mean "leader," the actual feminine noun (*prostatis*) does not take the meaning "leader" but is defined as "protectress, patroness, helper."[12]

With respect to women deacons, we need not come to a firm decision, for even if women were deacons this does not refute our thesis regarding male governance in the church.[13] Even if women were appointed as deacons, they were not appointed as elders (1 Timothy 3:1-7; Titus 1:5-9). Two qualities demanded of elders—being apt to teach (1 Timothy 3:2) and governing of the church (1 Timothy 3:5)—are not part of the responsibility of deacons (cf. also 1 Timothy 5:17; Titus 1:9; Acts 20:17, 28ff.). The deacon's task consisted mainly in practical service to the needs of the congregation. This is suggested by Acts 6:1-6, where the apostles devote themselves to prayer and the ministry of the Word (6:4), while the seven are selected to care for the practical concern of the daily distribution to widows.[14] Elders were given the responsibility to lead and teach the congregation. Thus, women being appointed to the supportive and complementary role of deacons supports the major thesis of this chapter, as does the exclusion of women from the office of elder. So far, what we have seen is consistent with the Old Testament pattern. Women in the Old Testament functioned occasionally as prophets but not as priests. In the New Testament, women functioned as prophets and probably deacons but not as elders.[15]

Some have argued for women elders, as we have seen above, from the "chosen lady" in 2 John and Paul's reference to women who teach in Titus 2:3ff. The "chosen lady" in 2 John is almost certainly not an individual woman but a reference to the church.[16] (1) John uses the second person plural in verses 6, 8, 10, and 12. The plural demonstrates that he is not writing to one person only; he is writing to an entire church. (2) Second John is much more general and less specific than 3 John. Third John was clearly written to an individual, Gaius, but the lack of specificity in 2 John suggests that a community is being addressed rather than an individual. (3) The description of the church as a "lady" accords well with the rest of Scripture. Paul and John both portray the church as Christ's bride (Ephesians 5:22-33; Revelation 19:7). The new Jerusalem is described as a bride (Revelation 21:2). In the Old Testament, Israel is often portrayed as a woman (Isaiah 54:1; Jeremiah 6:23; 31:21; Lamentations 4:3, 22). (4) The distinction between the "lady" and "her children" in 2 John does not suggest that she is distinct from her children. The "lady" is the church as a whole; the "children" are simply the individual members of the church.

Those who find a reference to women elders in Titus 2:3 are clearly mistaken. Paul uses the word *presbytidas* here, which means "older women." The usual word for "elders" who served in church office in the Bible is related but different: *presbyteros* (Acts 11:30; 14:23; 15:2, 4, 6, 22ff.; 16:4; 20:17; 21:18; 1 Timothy 5:17, 19; Titus 1:5; James 5:14; 1 Peter 5:1, 5). Now, someone might say that Paul uses this different word because in Titus 2:3 he is referring to women elders. The problem with this is that the usual word for "elders," *presbyteros*, could easily have been made feminine (*presbytera*) if Paul wanted to refer to women elders. Paul did not use a feminine form of the word *presbyteros* here; he used a distinct word that never refers to elders.

Titus 2:2 demonstrates clearly that Paul was not speaking of women elders in Titus 2:3. In verse 2, Paul addresses the "older men." Now it is clear that Paul is not referring to elders here who hold a church office of authority, for he does not use the word that indicates such an office, *presbyteros*. Instead, Paul uses a word that always refers to "older men," *presbytas* (cf. Luke 1:18; Philemon 9). Paul could have used the word for elders that conveys church office in Titus 2:2, but instead he used a distinct word that refers to older men. He uses the related word that refers to older women in Titus 2:3. Thus, there is no doubt that Paul is speaking of older women in Titus 2:3, not of women elders.

F. Women Apostles

Of course, if Junias was a woman apostle (Romans 16:7), then a tension is created between the apostleship of Junias (if Junias was a woman) and the other arguments adduced in this chapter, for apostles were certainly the most authoritative messengers of God in the New Testament. But it should be said from the outset that this passage is unclear. Now, some scholars contend that lack of clarity is also a problem in texts like 1 Corinthians 11:2-16 and 1 Timothy 2:11-15, but the passages are not analogous in one respect. The texts in First Corinthians and Timothy, although they have their difficulties, contain a sustained argument, and the basic thrust of the passages is clear. Here, however, we have a single verse, and the meaning of that verse is not altogether clear. The passage is unclear in three ways. (1) It cannot be definitely established that Junias was a woman. The name may be a contraction of a man's name, Junianus.[17] Of course, if this is true, then the text is irrelevant for the question before us. (2) Even though some scholars claim confidently that the verse means that Andronicus and Junias are outstanding apostles, it is also possible that the text is saying that they are "outstanding in the eyes of the apostles." (3) Even if we grant that Paul is speaking of a woman and he designates her as a distinguished apostle, what does he mean by the word *apostle* here? It is by no means clear that he is assigning Junias the same position that he assigns to himself, the twelve, and James (1 Corinthians 15:7; Galatians 1:19). The word *apostle* in Paul could be used in a non-technical way refer to "messengers" or "representatives" (2 Corinthians 8:23; Philippians 2:25). In any case, the verse is too ambiguous to be used to establish the notion that there were female apostles in the technical sense. (See also Chapter 2, Question 38 in this volume.)

In contrast, it is remarkable that Jesus did not select a single female apostle, and the other clearly apostolic figures in the New Testament are men: Paul, James, and Barnabas. Not one indisputable example of a female apostle can be given in the New Testament. G. Bilezikian says that Jesus chose twelve men to be His apostles because of the "cultural constraints" that would have made the ministry of women "unacceptable."[18] There are at least two problems with this view. (1) Nowhere else does Jesus give in to cultural pressures when a moral issue is at stake. To imply that He gave in for this reason impugns His courage and integrity. Jesus associated with tax-collectors and sinners, healed on the sabbath, commended Gentiles who had great faith, and rebuked the scribes and Pharisees. All of these actions brought considerable cultural pressure on Jesus, and yet He continued to do what He thought was right. Thus, it is unlikely that Jesus did not appoint a female apostle because of merely cultural reasons. (2) If, as Bilezikian asserts, Junias was an apostle, then Jesus' reluctance to appoint a woman apostle becomes even more blameworthy. For just a few years after Jesus' resurrection, the church (according to Bilezikian) is willing to appoint female apostles. Had the culture changed so dramatically in the few years since Jesus' ministry that now such appointments were feasible? Bilezikian's view suggests that the early church was even more courageous than Jesus, and this is surely incorrect!

It should also be said that some who argue for no restrictions on women in ministry argue from isolated and ambiguous verses, such as Romans 16:7 or Priscilla's teaching of Apollos in Acts 18:26. Others have appealed to the fact that there were churches in a woman's house, but that says nothing about who the leaders of the church were. The church met in Mary's house in Acts 12:12, but there is no reason to think Mary was the leader of the church in that situation. If a woman has a Bible study in her house today, that is no indication that she is the leader of that study. It is also irrelevant to appeal to the fact that Jesus spoke to the Samaritan woman, treated women with dignity, and appeared to them first after His resurrection. Of course, Jesus treated women with dignity and respect, and we should learn from His example. But such examples are not directly relevant in discussing women in leadership roles.

G. Conclusion

In conclusion, men sometimes have gone farther than Scripture and suppressed the valuable ministry contributions of women. There are innumerable ministries with which a woman can become involved in order to further God's kingdom on earth. The ministries women do become involved in, however, should be complementary and supportive of the male leadership in the church. Such a supportive ministry does not rule out every public ministry of women when men are present. Many borderline cases depend on the demeanor and attitude of women.[19] There are inevitably some gray areas in applying any basic principle of Scripture. Nevertheless, in my opinion, it is clear that Biblical writers consistently ascribe ultimate responsibility to men for the leadership of the church.

IV. Valuable Ministries of Women

This chapter should not end on a negative note, for even though there are some restrictions on women in ministry, we want to highlight the valuable ministries of women in the church today. One could get the impression from this chapter that the main burden of Scripture is to limit women in ministry. Actually, Scripture lays only a few restrictions upon women. Indeed, the possibilities for ministry for women are myriad. It is not the case that there is nothing for women to do and so they might as well while away their time watching television.

No woman could possibly say that if there are some restrictions on women in ministry, then there is nothing valuable for her to do. Surely there is more work to do than can possibly be accomplished by men alone. Billions of people need to hear the gospel (most of them women and children), many people in our culture are without Christ, or they are hurting in innumerable ways. There is so much to do to advance the gospel of Christ that no woman should fear that there is no place for her ministry.

One of the most significant ministries for women (and men too!) is prayer. Without prayer, God's kingdom work on earth will not advance. If in practice we put prayer low on the list of our priorities, then we are actually saying that it is not crucial. How we need a revival of prayer in the church today, and a seeking after God that is intense and full of faith! What a significant ministry women can have in prayer for the work of God on earth![20] Both women and men should ask

God to pour out His Spirit on us so that the message of the gospel will go forth in power.

Women have advanced the gospel in missions, are advancing it, and will continue to advance it. A wife can aid her husband in innumerable ways in setting up a mission station. And as a wife she can exert, by word and quiet example, a remarkable impact on a godless culture, especially since so many people in that culture will be women and children. And I think women can proclaim the gospel to men in those cultures, for 1 Timothy 2:11-15 prohibits only authoritative teaching to a group of Christians within the church, not evangelism to those outside the church. Such proclamation of the gospel is not limited to men. She should clearly explain, however (as many missionary women have done in history), that men should assume leadership roles in the governance and teaching ministry of the church as soon as it is established.

Titus 2:3-5 indicates that mature women have the responsibility of instructing younger women regarding a life of godliness. There are more women in evangelical churches today than men, and how the church needs godly women who will instruct younger women in the Christian life! Any woman who has a gift for teaching will find great fulfillment in instructing other women in this way. The church is in great need of women who are theologically and Biblically sound to instruct younger women in the matters of the faith.

There are also some ways in which women can instruct both men and women, in my opinion, if the function of authoritative teaching to men is not involved. Thus, it is appropriate for women who travel as speakers to address a mixed audience as articulate and thoughtful representatives of a feminine perspective on many experiences of life. One thinks here of the ministry of Elisabeth Elliot, whom God has used significantly. Moreover, women can exercise their creative gifts through writing, including the writing of curriculum, fiction, nonfiction, scholarly writing about Scripture, and editing. Several of today's most widely read Christian books have been written by women.

There are so many ministries today in which a woman can advance the cause of Christ and righteousness! I will list a few here so that one can get some idea of the wide scope available: engaging in personal witnessing and joining campus organizations committed to spreading the gospel, ministering to the sick and elderly, fighting against abortion, fighting against pornography, helping with literacy, writing to government leaders to support the cause of righteousness, helping the disabled, aiding the poor, ministering in prisons, counseling and praying with the troubled and confused, supporting missionaries and the church financially, visiting newcomers to the church, extending hospitality to the lonely, using artistic gifts by ministering in music, the visual arts, drama, and theater, helping in youth ministry, etc.

Probably one of the most significant ministry roles for women, although it is not their only role, is their role as wives and mothers. Paul says that mature women are to "train the younger women to love their husbands and children" (Titus 2:4). One thinks of the godly mothers in Scripture like Sarah, Hannah, Ruth, and Mary. What a significant role they played in the history of redemption as wives and mothers! Their influence on their husbands and children is still not fully known to us. Countless unknown wives and mothers have had a tremendous impact on their husbands and children, and the influence of these women will only be revealed on the day of redemption. What a tragedy it is that women's role as wives and mothers is often viewed as second best today! God has ordained that most women will find the greatest fulfillment in these very callings, and those who do should also realize that the example of their lives, lived faithfully with "the unfading beauty of a gentle and quiet spirit" (1 Peter 3:4), will have a lasting effect on many others around them.

Another area in which women can have a powerful ministry is with children in the church. Of course, not all women are intended to work with children. But churches are crying out today for women to work with children, and it is harder and harder to find women who are available. I think part of the reason is that our culture, even in the church, does not think such a ministry is very honorable or significant. Now, we need men to work with children as well, but, as other parts of this book show, women are particularly fitted by God to work with children. How we need women who love children to help mold our children in churches and schools by teaching and example!

Of course, other examples of significant ministry by women could be mentioned, but as we noted, the possibilities in a hurting and lost world are endless. God has fitted women for particular ministries for their own fulfillment and satisfaction and for His glory. Such ministry builds up the body of Christ so that the church can truly accomplish its work in the world.

12

Men and Women in the Image of God

John M. Frame

The idea that we are made in the image of God has given comfort and moral stimulus to many. But what does it mean? The basic idea is simple.[1] An "image" is a picture or statue. Israel was forbidden to worship images, but, perhaps surprisingly, Scripture teaches that there is a true image of God, ourselves.

An image *resembles* and *represents* the one it pictures.[2] Let us look at each of these functions in turn.

I. Resemblance

To say that we are God's image is to say that we are like God. To be sure, in many ways God is very different from us (Isaiah 46:5; 55:8ff.). But Scripture often compares God to human beings, even deducing from our physical make-up what God must be like (Psalm 94:9). How are we like God?

A. Human Nature As Such

First, *everything we are* is like God. We *are* the image of God (1 Corinthians 11:7). To say we are "in" God's image is to say that we are made "to be" the image of God.[3]

I would infer that everything we are reflects God in some way, though of course everything we are is also different from God! Our souls, bodies, reason, will, goodness are like God, but also unlike Him, for He is the Creator, paradigm and infinite exemplar of these qualities. Even sin images God in perverse sorts of ways. In sinning, Eve sought to be like God (Genesis 3:5), not by imitating His goodness, but by coveting His prerogatives. And all sin is moral decision, a faculty that we share uniquely with God and the angels.

So human nature itself is the image of God. But more must be said. The fact that we image God in the totality of our being does not discourage but rather encourages us to find more specific kinds of correspondence.[4] So we move ahead.

B. Moral Excellence

When Scripture mentions specific ways in which people resemble God or Jesus Christ, it usually focuses on moral qualities like righteousness (Ephesians 4:24), ethical perfection (Matthew 5:48), purity (1 John 3:2ff., 9), love (John 13:14, 35ff.; Titus 3:4; 1 John 3:10, 16-18; 4:7-20), forgiveness (Matthew 6:14ff.; Colossians 3:13), humility (Philippians 2:3-11), holiness (Ephesians 4:24; Leviticus 19:1), and knowledge (Colossians 3:10).[5] Following John Murray, I call these qualities of "moral excellence," thereby distinguishing them from the mere fact (see below, C) that we are capable of making moral decisions.[6] Moral qualities are important in Scripture, because Scripture is the story of how God restores His righteousness in the world.

God renews His people. And that renewal is a renewal in the image of Jesus Christ (1 Corinthians 15:49; 1 John 3:2ff.). Christian love is defined as the imitation of Jesus, especially His atonement (John 13:34ff.; 15:12; 2 Corinthians 3:18; Ephesians 5:2; Philippians 2:5-11; 3:21; 1 John 3:11-16; 4:10ff.). Christ is *the* image of God (2 Corinthians 4:4; Colossians 1:15; Hebrews 1:3, cf. John 1:18; 12:45; 14:9). Adam defaced the image of God in which he was made, but Jesus honored and glorified the God whom He supremely pictured and represented. Salvation transfers us from the old humanity dead in Adam to a new humanity alive in Christ (Romans 5:12-19; 1 Corinthians 15:22, 45-49). As Adam begat sons in his defaced image of God (Genesis 5:1ff.), so Christ's children bear His pure image.[7] Thus the Lord removes from us the distortions of the image due to sin and leads us toward a perfect likeness to God.

Illustration: In photocopying, you can make copies from another copy as long as the latter is perfect. If you try to copy from a defaced copy, you will get defaced images. The only recourse is to go back to the original or to a perfect copy. To be restored in God's image, God must turn us away from our fallen nature in Adam and re-create us in Jesus Christ, who is both the original (John 1:1) and a perfect copy (Hebrews 1:3).

The Old Testament writers never said explicitly that the image of God was defaced by sin and required divine renewal. That theme emerges clearly for the first time in the New Testament, for the New Testament writers saw in Jesus what the image of God was really supposed to be.[8]

C. Moral Agency

Some theologians have argued that since God's image involves righteousness and holiness, Adam must have lost the image altogether when he fell into sin.[9] The unredeemed sinner, surely, is bereft of ethical knowledge,[10] righteousness and holiness (Genesis 6:5; 8:21; Romans 3:10-18; 8:5-8).[11] Scripture, however, does speak of man after the fall as bearing the image of God (see Genesis 5:1ff.; 9:6; 1 Corinthians 11:7; James 3:9).[12] We should expect that from the foregoing; had we lost the image of God after the fall, we would have lost our very humanity.

If that is so, then evidently the image does not consist only in the qualities of moral excellence discussed in the last section, though, as we have seen, Scripture has important reasons for stressing them. In what other ways do we reflect God? Well, certainly our reasoning power, creativity, ability to use language, ability to sense moral distinctions and to make moral choices, and above all our religious capacity distinguish us from the animals (Genesis 1:27-30) and make us like God. But beyond these, remember the fundamental principle: everything we are images God.

Sin disrupts and defaces the image, but it does not destroy our humanity. It is edifying (and appropriate to this volume!) to compare the God-human relationship with the man-woman relationship. As Scripture emphasizes the likeness between God and man, it also emphasizes the likeness between man and woman (Genesis 2:23). Human beings are to help God (1:28);[13] woman is to help man (2:20; cf. my later discussion of 1 Corinthians 11:7). Both relationships are hurt by sin, but the fundamental likeness on which they are based remains.[14]

D. The Body

Our fundamental principle, that everything human images God, requires us to hold that the human body, also, images God. Some theologians have denied that the body bears God's image, first because God has no body, and second because the commandment against idolatry seems to assume that God has no physical image. But the prohibition of idolatry is not based on the lack of a divine image, but on God's jealousy (Exodus 20:5).[15]

As to the objection that God has no body: True enough, but there are ways in which a body can picture a spirit. Psalm 94:9 asks, "Does he who implanted the ear not hear? Does he who formed the eye not see?" God does not have literal ears or eyes, but our ears and eyes image His ability to hear and see.

The body is an important aspect of human nature. *We* (not just our bodies) are made of dust (Genesis 2:7; 3:19). Sin pertains to the body as much as to the spirit (Romans 6:6). Even a dead body is a person, considered from his physical side (Matthew 28:6; John 5:28; 11:11ff., 43; 1 Corinthians 15:6, 18; 1 Thessalonians 4:13ff.). It is we ourselves who "return" to the dust (Genesis 3:19). The incarnate Son of God is both body and spirit, and His physical presence on earth was essential to His saving work (1 John 1:1-3; 4:1-3). So was His physical resurrection, which serves as the pattern for our resurrection (Romans 8:11, 23; Philippians 3:21). The division between soul and body on a person's death is something unnatural, a result of the fall.[16]

E. Sexual Differentiation

As is appropriate to this volume on Biblical manhood and womanhood, I have of course been laying a foundation to investigate how our sexual differences relate to the image of God. Our fundamental principle is that everything we are images God. Therefore (especially since the body itself participates in the image), we would expect that our sexual and social diversity, also, would picture God in some way.

1. The first thing that must be said is that both men and women are made in God's image (see especially Genesis 1:27; 2:20, 23; 5:1ff.).

Hurley points out that *man* in 1:26 and 27 is a collective noun (*adam* = "mankind"). The plural membership of that collectivity is indicated by the phrase "male and female" in verse 27, and then to both male and female is given the task appropriate to those created in the image of God (verse 28).[17] Any limitation of the image of God based on sexuality would also contradict the thrust of Genesis 9:6 and James 3:9: such limitation would imply that only males are protected against murder and slander because only they are in God's image. Re-creation in God's image also applies without sexual distinction (Colossians 3:9-11; and compare Galatians 3:26 with verse 28).

2. Are men and women equally in the image of God?

Some have answered in the negative because of Paul's statement in 1 Corinthians

11:7, "A man ought not to cover his head, since he is the image and glory of God; but the woman is the glory of man."

I agree with C. K. Barrett[18] that "in this context Paul values the term *image* only as leading to the term *glory.*" The reference to "image" is incidental to Paul's purpose, and therefore not mentioned with respect to woman; but it notifies his readers of the Old Testament basis for saying that man is the *glory* of God, "glory" and "image" being roughly, but not entirely, synonymous.

"Glory" in this context is the honor that one person brings to another. Man, Paul says, was made to honor God. Of course, woman was also made to honor God; but in addition, she is also made for a second purpose: to honor man. God made her specifically to be a helper for Adam (Genesis 2:18, 20; cf. Proverbs 12:4; Ephesians 5:25-29).[19] Man honors or glorifies God by uncovering his head, for covering the head connoted subservience to another creature.[20] Such subservience to men is especially inappropriate for a male prophet, whose whole function is to speak for God, or for one leading in public prayer, whose whole function is to lead the people to God's own throne. Woman, however, even when prophesying or praying in public, must not only honor God, but also honor man. Indeed, she honors God when she honors the specific task of "helper" for which God made her. Unlike the man, then, she honors God best by displaying a symbol by which she honors her fellow-creature.

Does such subordination itself detract from her capacity to image God? That is an important question for us to ask at this point. But the answer must surely be negative: (a) Men too are always placed in relations of subordination to other people (Exodus 20:12; Romans 13:1; Hebrews 13:17),[21] but that does not prejudice their being the image of God.

(b) Jesus Himself became subordinate to His Father, even subordinate to human authority structures, in order to redeem us. Human authority, therefore, imaging Jesus, is to be a servant-authority (Matthew 20:20-28). A willingness to subordinate oneself to others for God's sake is, indeed, itself a component of the image, not a compromise thereof. Even submission to *unjust* authority shows a special likeness to Christ (1 Peter 2:12, 19-25; 3:14-18).[22]

(c) It is often by submitting to others that we best display the ethical components of the divine image. How better to demonstrate God's love, His patience, His gentleness, His self-control, than by submitting to others?

3. Is sexual difference itself the image of God?

Karl Barth's famous discussion says that it is.[23] Genesis 1:27 may be divided into three parts: (a) "So God created man in his own image," (b) "In the image of God he created him," (c) "Male and female he created them." Barth argues that (b) and (c) form a "synonymous parallelism," typical of Hebrew poetry. Therefore, says Barth, the writer believed that the difference between male and female *is* the image of God. Some problems, however, attach to this idea:

(a) If this is the proper reading of Genesis 1:27, it would seem odd that this concept of the image is not found, suggested, or even alluded to elsewhere in the Bible. Indeed, as we have seen, Scripture elsewhere describes the image in other ways that, to say the least, would be hard to integrate with Barth's definition, should we adopt it.

(b) Although there is a corporate aspect of the image (see F below), the image also pertains to individual human beings. That is evident in Genesis 5:3, where

Adam transmits his "image" (the image of God, according to verse 1) to his son Seth. That is also evident in Genesis 9:6; 1 Corinthians 11:7; James 3:9; Colossians 3:10, and elsewhere. But individual human beings are *either* male *or* female, not "male *and* female," as in Genesis 1:27c. Therefore, the bearer of the image need not be "male *and* female" as Barth suggests.

(c) Scripture never represents God as sexually differentiated or as entering into marriage with Himself, although to be sure there are trinitarian pluralities within the one divine nature. It would therefore be odd to claim that sexuality is the *essence* of the divine image, though I do believe that it (together with everything else we are) is a component thereof.

(d) Meredith G. Kline presents a devastating exegetical critique of Barth's position.[24] He argues that the reference to "male and female" in Genesis 1:27 cannot state the essence of the image of God, because (i) it is not found in the statement of the divine intention in verse 26; (ii) sections (a) and (b) of verse 27 form a complete synonymous parallelism without 27c; so 27c serves, not as an additional parallel, but as a further description of *how* man is created in God's image. The point is simply that the image of God extends to both men and women (same in 5:1ff.); (iii) In Kline's view, 27c and 5:2a also point ahead to the following contexts. The "male and female" in 27c describes a prerequisite for the subduing of the earth in 28ff. In 5:2a, it presents the scope of the divine blessing in 5:2b.

(e) Barth does not stop with saying that the image is human sexual differentiation. Perhaps realizing the implausibility of that notion, he says that the sexual difference is only the original concrete form of *social* relationships that are more properly the content of the divine image.[25] There is some truth in this idea (see F below), but: (i) Though social differentiation is an aspect of the image, it is not the essence or definition of the image (see below). (ii) This move increases the exegetical implausibility of Barth's proposal. If it is unlikely that the writer of Genesis identified the image with sexual difference, it is even less likely that he was using that sexual difference as a kind of stand-in for social differentiation in general. Nothing else in Scripture suggests such an idea.[26]

4. Is sexual differentiation an aspect of the image?

Yes, for everything we are images God. The point is not that God is male, female, or both. To say that our eyes image God, remember, is not to say that God has eyes; it is rather to say that our eyes picture something divine. Similarly, our sexuality pictures God's attributes and capacities:

(a) It mirrors God's creativity, by which He brings forth sons and daughters (John 1:12; Romans 8:14ff.; etc.).

(b) The love of a husband for his wife pictures God's love for His people (Ezekiel 16; Hosea 1-3; Ephesians 5:25-33).

(c) Scripture describes God both in male and in female terms, though the overwhelming preponderance of imagery is male. The reason, I think, is basically that Scripture wants us to think of God as *Lord* (Exodus 3:14; 6:3, 7; 33:19; 34:5ff.; Deuteronomy 6:4ff.; cf. Romans 10:9f; 1 Corinthians 12:3; Philippians 2:11), and lordship, in Scripture, always connotes authority.[27] Since in the Biblical view women are subject to male authority in the home and the church,[28] there is some awkwardness in speaking of God in female terms. Our need today, in my opinion, is for a far greater appreciation of the *Lordship* of God and of Christ.[29]

Therefore, in my view, the movement to use unisex or female language in referring to God is fundamentally wrongheaded from a Biblical perspective.

(d) Nevertheless, the very submission of the woman also images God. See E(2) above. God the Lord is not too proud to be our "helper." Christ the Lord is not unwilling to be a servant. Godly women stand as models, often as rebukes, to all who would be leaders (Matthew 20:20-28).[30]

F. Social Differentiation

As we saw earlier, Barth regards the "sexual image" as a kind of stand-in for a "social image." We image God, he thinks, in social relationships.[31] For reasons noted, I reject the *identification* of the image with such relationships. Individuals, not just corporate groups, are in the image of God. On the other hand, there is a social aspect of the image, for the image contains everything human. In the Old Testament, God speaks as a plurality (Genesis 1:26; 3:5, 22; 11:7; Isaiah 6:8), which may reflect His trinitarian nature or, perhaps more likely, a heavenly "society" or "council" that God shares with His angels (Psalm 89:7).[32] The New Testament reveals God Himself as a Trinity, a society of Father, Son and Spirit. The task associated with the image (Genesis 1:28) is one that no one can perform fully as an individual. Through Scripture, God calls to Himself as his children not only individuals, but also families, nations, churches. Like godly individuals, godly families image God (Ephesians 5:22-6:4, noting 5:1; 1 Peter 3:1-7, noting 2:21-25; 4:1, 13-16). Godly nations also display the Lord's righteousness, peace, and glory. Preeminently, however, the corporate image of Christ in the world today is His body, the church. Note Romans 12:4ff.; 1 Corinthians 12:12ff.; Ephesians 2:16; Colossians 1:18, which show the corporateness of the body figure in the New Testament.[33]

Does a group image God better than an individual? Well, groups do resemble God in ways that individuals cannot by themselves, e.g., in taking counsel together or in displaying love for one another. Even the unity of God is imaged by the corporate body: note how in John 17 the unity of believers pictures the oneness of God the Father and God the Son. However, individuals in Scripture often image God precisely as they stand against the group, the crowd. Individuals, as we have seen, do bear the image of God (Genesis 9:6; 1 Corinthians 11:7; Colossians 3:10; James 3:9). There is not much value, I think, in such comparisons. God is one and many and is properly imaged both by groups and by individuals.

II. Representation

We have been discussing the image as resemblance; now we look at the image as representation. The distinction between resemblance and representation corresponds to the differences between structure and function and between nature and task.

Like the image of King Nebuchadnezzar (Daniel 3:1-6), images in the ancient world often represented those whose images they bore. Loyalty to the image was a form of loyalty to the one whose image it bore. Similarly, Adam represents God in the world. He does God's work, but under God: the task of ruling and filling the earth (Genesis 1:28). God is Lord, and Adam is God's assistant or vassal lord.

Elsewhere I have defined God's Lordship in terms of control, authority, presence.[34] "Control" is His working out "everything in conformity with the purpose of his will" (Ephesians 1:11). "Authority" means that He is the supreme lawgiver of the universe, the One whom all people and things *ought* to obey. "Presence" is God's will to be "with" His creatures, in various ways. He takes Abraham's family to be His people. He dwells with them in the tabernacle and the temple. Indeed, He dwells throughout His whole creation, so that we can never escape His presence (Psalm 139:7).

As vassal lord, Adam is to extend God's *control* over the world ("subdue" in Genesis 1:28). He has the right to name the animals, an exercise of *authority* in ancient thinking (Genesis 2:19ff.; cf. 2:23; 3:20, where he also names his wife!). And he is to "fill" the earth with his *presence*.

This dominion mandate continues after the fall (Genesis 9:1-3). But human beings apart from God's grace are unable to accomplish God's original purpose to subdue and fill the earth *to God's glory*. Hence Jesus proclaimed the Great Commission (Matthew 28:19ff.), also a command about filling and subduing, but in this case by the saving gospel of Jesus Christ. As evangelists, we are in a special sense God's representatives on earth (Matthew 5:14; 2 Corinthians 5:20; Philippians 2:14ff.).

Hence Scripture emphasizes the doctrines of sonship, adoption, and inheritance (John 1:12; Romans 8:14ff.; Galatians 3:26ff.; Hebrews 2:10; 1 John 3:1ff.). In these respects, man and woman share equally—Scripture makes no sexual distinction in such things. Indeed, Galatians 3:26 ("You are all sons of God through faith in Christ Jesus") precedes by two verses the famous "There is neither . . . male [n]or female. . . ." And, as we have seen, "male and female" equally are given the original dominion mandate (Genesis 1:27ff.).

Men and women, then, both have authority. But they are also under authority. There is no inconsistency there. Jesus Himself is both Lord and servant. A man rules his family, but he is subordinate to his employer and to the civil magistrate. A woman may have legitimate authority over her children (Exodus 20:12), her household (presumably including both children and servants, 1 Timothy 5:14), other women (Titus 2:4), a business (Proverbs 31:10-31), and the earth as part of Christ's body (Genesis 1:28; 1 Corinthians 3:21), even (in some sense) over everyone in her ministry as a prophet of God (Judges 4:4; Acts 2:17; 21:9; 1 Corinthians 11:5, 10).[35] But these facts do not conflict with the rule that a wife must be subject to her husband in the home and to male elders in the church (cf. above, I.E.2).

Citing Matthew 8:9, Stephen B. Clark well observes that one's own authority often finds its *basis* in submission to another.[36] Even the authority of prophets, priests, and kings in Scripture is based on their submission to God's higher authority. Thus the head covering of the woman (1 Corinthians 11:3-16), a sign of submission, also enables her to pray and prophesy in public.

Summary and Conclusion

Women and men equally image God, even in their sexual differences, even in their differences with regard to authority and submission. The reason is that the image of God embraces everything that is human. Both men and women, therefore, resemble God and are called to represent Him throughout the creation, exercising control, authority, and presence in His name. This doctrine is not at all inconsistent with the subordination of women to men in the home and in the church. All human beings are under authority, both divine and human. Their submission to authority, as well as their authority itself, images God.

Note: Will We Be Male and Female in Heaven?

Scripture doesn't explicitly address this question, so we should not be dogmatic in trying to answer it. But some broad Biblical principles may lead us in one direction or another.

We might be inclined to answer "no" to this question because of Jesus' statement in Matthew 22:30 that resurrected saints will neither marry nor give in marriage. In the resurrection, earthly families will be overshadowed by the great family of God (cf. Luke 20:36).

I am, however, inclined toward an affirmative answer: (1) Those who appear after death in Scripture always appear similar to their earthly forms (1 Samuel 28:11-15; Matthew 17:1-13; 27:52ff.; Revelation 11:1-12). I would assume that the men continued to appear as bearded (if they wore beards on earth), speaking with masculine voices. This fact seems to yield some presumption, at least, that we retain our sexual characteristics after death.

(2) Even angels (whom Jesus says we will resemble in the resurrection) tend to appear in Scripture as men, rather than as women or as asexual beings (Genesis 18:2, 16, 22; Joshua 5:13; Hebrews 13:2).

(3) Jesus' resurrection body also resembled the form He bore on earth, even down to the wounds in His hands and side (John 20:25, 27), although His new existence is mysterious in many ways. At the resurrection appearances, I have no doubt that the disciples saw a male figure.

(4) Sexuality, as we have seen, is part of the image of God, part of what it now means to be human. It is possible that this resemblance might in the next life be replaced with other kinds of resemblance. ("Image of God," we will recall, covers much territory.) But if we lose our sexuality, why should we not also lose our arms, eyes, and brains?

(5) Our sex organs and secondary sexual characteristics have functions other than procreation. They also image different attributes of God and express the variety of human personality. Sex, after all, is not just reproductive capacity. Stereotypes aside, men and women do differ in personality and in the distribution of their spiritual gifts. The body of a godly woman often serves as an appropriate accompaniment to her personality, reinforcing our impression of her inner meekness and quiet strength. Similarly for men, *mutatis mutandis*. We would, I think, sense something odd if Mother Teresa's personality were found in the body of, say, Sylvester Stallone, or vice versa.

So here's a weak vote in favor of the affirmative: I rather *suspect* that we will still be male and female in the resurrection.

13

The Church as Family:
Why Male Leadership in the Family Requires Male Leadership in the Church

Vern Sheridan Poythress

The Bible teaches us to call God "our Father" (Matthew 6:9). We who are redeemed by Jesus Christ are children of God (Galatians 4:1-7). These two Biblical affirmations are among many in which the Bible employs an analogy between a human family and the church. By means of this family analogy God makes some of His most precious promises to us concerning His present love, our future inheritance, and our intimate fellowship with Him (for example, Romans 8:12-17; Hebrews 12:5-11; Revelation 21:7).

The practical implications of these "family teachings" are so deep and so many-sided that we can never fully fathom them. Let us here concentrate only on one strand of implications, those for our conduct toward one another within the Christian community. The Bible invites us to use these family teachings to draw some particular inferences about the respective roles of men and women within the church. In brief, the argument runs as follows: Just as husbands and fathers ought to exercise godly leadership in their human families, so wise, mature men ought to be appointed as fatherly leaders in the church (1 Timothy 3:1-7). A particularly important role also belongs to more mature women (1 Timothy 5:9-16; Titus 2:3-5). Like wise mothers of the church, they are to train their spiritual daughters by example and word. But just as in the case of marriage (Ephesians 5:22-33), the respective functions of men and women are not reversible in all respects. Men—and not women—are called on to exercise the decisive fatherly leadership as elders.

New Testament Teaching Comparing the People of God to a Family

Now let us look in detail at the steps in the argument. First, consider the variety of New Testament teachings comparing the people of God to a family.[1] The confession that God is our Father belongs to a most fundamental strand of New Testament teaching, beginning with Jesus' model prayer in the Sermon on the Mount (Matthew 6:9) and continuing through the many instances where God is called "God the Father." The Bible never simply means that God is the Creator of all human beings. Having God as Father implies having intimate family fellowship with Him (Romans 8:14-17) and reflecting His holy character (1 Peter 1:14-17). Christ the only Son of God has God as His Father in a unique sense. In addition to Him, only Christians, that is, those who have received the Spirit of Christ, are rightly able to cry, "Abba, Father" (Romans 8:15). Those outside of Christ have the devil as their father and want to carry out their father's desires (John 8:44; cf. 1 John 5:19).

Thus, Christians are called "sons of God" and "children of God," in pointed contrast to non-Christians, who are outside God's family (1 John 5:1-5). To be called a child of God has many implications. We have intimate fellowship with God the Father (Romans 8:15). Jesus Christ is our elder brother (Romans 8:29). We are legally adopted out of a situation of bondage (Galatians 4:1-7). We are no longer slaves (Galatians 4:7; Romans 8:15). We are to receive the full inheritance from God as co-heirs with Christ (Romans 8:17). We are conformed to the pattern of death and resurrection life established through Christ (Romans 8:11-13). We share in the common family Spirit, the Holy Spirit (Romans 8:14-15). We are remade in God's image (Romans 8:29). We are born from God (1 John 5:4; John 1:12-13). As obedient children, we are to imitate the good character of our Father (Ephesians 5:1; 1 Peter 1:14-17).

Because God is our Father in this intimate sense, and because Jesus Christ is our brother and our all-sufficient advocate to the Father, we do not need any other human intermediary to bring us into contact with God. In relation to God the Father, we are brothers to all other Christians. We are to be servants to one another, and no one of us is to lord it over the others (Mark 10:42-45). Hence Jesus specifically criticizes the use of honorific titles that might contradict our status as children and undermine our sense of intimacy with God:

> But you are not to be called "Rabbi," for you have only one Master and you are all brothers. And do not call anyone on earth "father," for you have one Father, and he is in heaven. Nor are you to be called "teacher," for you have one Teacher, the Christ. The greatest among you will be your servant. For whoever exalts himself will be humbled, and whoever humbles himself will be exalted. (Matthew 23:8-12)

Jesus' own emphasis on humility and service and the larger context of Matthew 23, where Jesus is criticizing the Pharisees, indicate that Jesus is not setting forth a legalistic rule about the mere verbal use of the words "father" and "teacher." Rather, He is criticizing an attitude of the heart. We must always recognize the fundamental character of Christian brotherhood. Our common status as brothers implies that we should submit to Christ and serve one another.

In fact, then, Jesus' teaching is complementary to other teachings in the New Testament epistles that do assign a special role to pastors and teachers (for example, Ephesians 4:11). The most fundamental relationship is the Father-son relationship between God and Christian believers. But God's fatherly care ought to be reflected in the care Christians exercise towards one another within the church. For example, Christ is our Teacher in a most exalted sense (Matthew 23:10; John 13:13-14). From the fullness of His wisdom and His teaching gifts, He has distributed gifts to the church and thereby makes some people into subordinate or assistant teachers (Ephesians 4:7, 11). Christ is our Shepherd in a unique sense (John 10:11-18). He also imparts gifts to human beings who then become under-shepherds (1 Peter 5:1-4). God the Father and Christ are the ultimate models we ought to imitate (1 Peter 1:14-15; Romans 8:29). But in a subordinate sense we are supposed to imitate the good examples set by more mature believers (1 Corinthians 11:1; Philippians 3:17; 1 Timothy 4:12; Titus 2:4, 7).

God's Household in 1 Timothy

The theme of family relationships is particularly prominent in Paul's First Letter to Timothy. Paul repeatedly invokes the analogy of a family in order to enable Timothy better to understand the appropriate order and responsibilities within the Christian church. Paul calls Timothy his "son," expressing both his affection and the discipling relationship between them (1 Timothy 1:2, 18). He advises Timothy to treat an older man "as if he were your father. Treat younger men as brothers, older women as mothers, and younger women as sisters" (1 Timothy 5:1-2). If a widow has children or grandchildren, they should look after her (1 Timothy 5:4). But if the immediate family is lacking, the larger Christian family should care for her (1 Timothy 5:5, 16).

The overseers or elders ought to be respectable family men:[2]

> Now the overseer must be above reproach, the husband of but one wife, temperate, self-controlled, respectable, hospitable, able to teach, not given to much wine, not violent but gentle, not quarrelsome, not a lover of money. He must manage his own family well and see that his children obey him with proper respect. (If anyone does not know how to manage his own family, how can he take care of God's church?) (1 Timothy 3:2-5)

The requirement concerning "managing his own family well" is particularly important, because the same wisdom and skills necessary for good family management apply also to the management of God's church.[3]

Finally, the Apostle Paul explicitly indicates the prominent role of the family theme in 1 Timothy 3:14-15:

> Although I hope to come to you soon, I am writing you these instructions so that, if I am delayed, you will know how people ought to conduct themselves in God's household, which is the church of the living God, the pillar and foundation of the truth.

In fact, these verses summarize the thrust of the whole letter. The phrase "these instructions" is most naturally understood as referring to the contents of the letter as a whole. Thus the letter as a whole has the purpose of indicating "how people ought to conduct themselves in God's household."

The reference to "God's household" could theoretically involve either of two ideas, namely, the idea of communion with God in the "house" or "temple" of God, or the idea of a household managed by God. In some contexts within the Bible, the idea of God dwelling among His people as in a temple is emphasized (1 Corinthians 3:10-17). But in the context of 1 Timothy, the idea of household order and arrangements is obviously the most prominent. The order of the church is analogous to the order of a human household. Members of the church are to treat one another as they would members of their own family (1 Timothy 5:1-2). They are to care for one another in need (1 Timothy 5:5, 16). The overseers are to be men skillful at managing the household of God, as demonstrated by their earlier skill with their own immediate families (1 Timothy 3:1-7).

The Use of the Household Idea as the Basis for Inferences

In 1 Timothy the fundamental household analogy is not merely confined to one or two incidental illustrations or colorful flourishes of rhetoric. Rather, it used as a basis for arguments and inferences concerning Christian responsibilities. The central role of the analogy is particularly clear in 1 Timothy 3:4-5, which concludes with the sobering question, "If anyone does not know how to manage his own family, how can he take care of God's church?" Paul in effect presents an argument: good family leadership *must* be one of the criteria for appointment to a position of overseer because the very same skills and competencies are required for overseeing "one's own house" and the Christian "house." Paul does not expect Timothy simply to take Paul's word for the fact that such-and-such a criterion is suitable for elders. He expects Timothy to *see* the wisdom—yes, the inevitability—of this criterion on the basis of the validity of the analogy. Indirectly, Timothy is presumably even being invited to use the same argument himself, if someone else should have doubts about the matter.

Similarly, in 1 Timothy 5:1-2 we can see the beginnings of an argument. "Do not rebuke an older man harshly, but exhort him as if he were your father. Treat younger men as brothers, older women as mothers, and younger women as sisters, with absolute purity." The key comparative word *as* might possibly be interpreted as introducing mere illustrations. But all the illustrations are of exactly the same type, in that they all use the analogy between church and family. In view of the general statement about conduct in "God's household" in 1 Timothy 3:14-15, the comparisons in 5:1-2 are to be seen as so many ways of fleshing out the implications of being a member of God's household. We can perceive the obligatory nature of the inferences. You *must* treat the older men like fathers, the younger men like brothers, etc., not only because in some very general sense you must love them, but because you are part of the very same spiritual household. Conduct toward any other member of the household must take into account not merely sweepingly general obligations to love but the concrete distinctions introduced by differences in status within the household: treating some like fathers, others like brothers, others like mothers, others like sisters. Hence, 1 Timothy 5:1-2 presupposes the structure of an argument. The church is like a family. Therefore you must treat fellow church members like fellow family members.

The household analogy appears, then, to be one constituent element in Paul's own approach to articulating the nature of Christian church order. In fact, it might easily be one means by which the Holy Spirit led Paul himself to grasp the teaching that he presents in the pastoral letters (1-2 Timothy and Titus). Of course, we do not know for certain. Paul received spectacular special revelations from the Lord (Acts 9:1-8; Galatians 1:16; 2 Corinthians 12:1-7). But he was also one who had "the mind of Christ" (1 Corinthians 2:16). Through the wisdom and insight that the Holy Spirit had given to Paul, he understood the basic principles of Christianity in tremendous depth. Under the gentle superintendence of the Spirit, he was able to give inspired teaching in his letters even on matters that his spectacular experiences had not directly addressed.[4] Moreover, the Apostle Paul wants all Christians to arrive at a deep, principial understanding of the Christian faith. The Corinthians are rebuked for being carnal, not having the mind of Christ as he does (1 Corinthians 3:1-4). In Romans 12:1-2, Paul urges upon all the necessity of growing in their grasp of the will of God, concluding, "Do not conform any longer to the pattern of this world, but be transformed by the renewing of your mind. Then you will be able to test and approve what God's will is—his good, pleasing and perfect will." Similarly he says, "And this is my prayer: that your love may abound more and more in knowledge and depth of insight, so that you may be able to discern what is best and may be pure and blameless until the day of Christ, filled with the fruit of righteousness that comes through Jesus Christ—to the glory and praise of God" (Philippians 1:10-11).

How, then, do we know what sort of order is appropriate for Christian communal life? We know, in part, because Paul tells us in his letters. But how did Paul himself know? And how does he expect us to apply his teachings in circumstances slightly different from the ones he addressed in his letters? Paul had such wisdom partly because he had deeply absorbed the fundamental teaching of Christ about God being our Father and about Christ's saving work on the cross. Christ's work reconciled us to God and gave us intimate family communion with God, the communion of sons (Galatians 4:1-7). We are members of God's family. That family structure of God's church has definite implications about the specific forms of love to be exercised within the family (1 Timothy 3:1-7), the specific kind of management needed in dealing with family needs (1 Timothy 3:8-13), and so on.

In fact, almost the whole of 1 Timothy may be seen as a catalog of types of behavior and organization needed in a harmonious family. True doctrine is necessary because the family needs to know its own rules (1 Timothy 1:3-11, 18-20). Doctrine is therefore foundational for all the more specific kinds of organization and mutual relations within the family. Mercy and forgiveness bind the family together (1 Timothy 1:12-17). Protection is necessary from destructive outside interference and for the benefit of the family's relations to the larger world (2:1-7). The men in the family must not generate strife among themselves but be united in petitions (2:8). The women must devote themselves to family service and not to frivolities (2:9-10) or to usurping authority over men (2:11-14). The family must have wise, competent overseers (3:1-7). It must have wise care for family needs (3:8-13). In every respect it must conform to divine order (3:14-16). Proper rules and examples from the leaders are most important (4:1-16). Family members must all treat one another with the respect and honor and sensitivity appropriate to their mutual status (5:1-6:2). Those in need must be cared for, preferably by those closest to them (5:3-10). Use of money must support family goals (6:6-10, 17-19).

In sum, the theme of God's household runs through 1 Timothy and is validly used as the basis for inferences about Christian behavior, not merely as an incidental illustration.

Male Leadership in the Church

The central use of the household analogy naturally points toward inferences regarding authoritative leadership in the church. The leadership within a family is vested in the husband and father (Ephesians 5:22-6:4).[5] The church as God's household also needs wise and competent leadership. That leadership is to be sought among men who have already shown their abilities in the context of their immediate families (1 Timothy 3:1-7). Women, by contrast, are not to be placed in authority in the church, because such a role would not harmonize with the general relations between men and women in marriage, as established at creation (1 Timothy 2:11-14).[6] Thus, the differences between men and women within the context of marriage and family carry over into differences in roles that men and women may assume within the church.

Such a set of inferences is natural, once we have noticed the decisive connection between the natural family and the church as our spiritual family. But do these inferences really hold up? Let us look at the distinct steps more closely.

First, do families have a God-ordained structure of leadership and authority? Do husbands have a unique responsibility for leadership within the family? Ephesians 5:22-6:4 and Colossians 3:18-21 indicate that they do.

Second, are there irreversible relations of leadership and submission within the church? Clearly there are. The very title "overseer" used in 1 Timothy 3:1 indicates a position involving exercise of leadership. These overseers are also described as "elders" in Titus 1:5, 1 Peter 5:1-4, Acts 20:28-31. They are worthy of honor, especially when they discharge their responsibilities of leadership well (1 Timothy 5:17). Hebrews 13:17 makes it very clear that they deserve our obedience: "Obey your leaders and submit to their authority. They keep watch over you as men who must give an account. Obey them so that their work will be a joy, not a burden, for that would be of no advantage to you."

In fact, principles of submission should operate more broadly in the relations between older people and younger. Humility should characterize everyone (1 Peter 5:5b-6). But the younger men are particularly called on to be submissive to the older men (1 Peter 5:5). Paul counsels Timothy to exhort an older man "as if he were your father" (1 Timothy 5:1). Clearly, different people are to be treated differently, in accordance with the kind of people they are.

> Do not rebuke an older man harshly, but exhort him as if he were your father. Treat younger men as brothers, older women as mothers, and younger women as sisters, with absolute purity. (1 Timothy 5:1-2)

In fundamental matters pertaining to our relation to the Lord, all of us enjoy the same privileges.[7] We have all been justified by faith (Romans 5:1). We have all become a kingdom of priests and share in a heavenly inheritance (1 Peter 2:9-10; Ephesians 1:3-14). We have all put on Christ and are children of Abraham (Galatians 3:27-29). We are all members of God's family or household. But these fundamental privileges enhance rather than eliminate the distinctiveness of our gifts (1 Corinthians 12:12-31). Our privileges should stimulate rather than destroy our concern to treat each person in the church with the sensitivity and respect due to that person by reason of his or her gifts, age, sex, leadership status, and personality.[8] Such is Paul's point in the text of 1 Timothy 5:1-2 given above. Timothy is not exhorted to treat each person in a manner mechanically identical with every other person, but to take into account the full range of personal factors that go into an intimate family relationship. Each person in God's household is not an abstract, faceless mask to be treated according to an invariant recipe, but a full person who is to be recognized as such—as a man or a woman, an older person or younger, an adult or a child.

Must the church's leaders or overseers be men? The Apostle Paul assumes that they are to be men rather than women when he describes them as "the husband of but one wife" (1 Timothy 3:2). But could not this expression be incidental? We must consider carefully whether Paul's rule here is intended to be absolute.

According to Paul, the fundamental principles regarding the structures of the human family are to be applied to the church as God's household (1 Timothy 3:15). Our personal relations to others in God's household should take into account what kind of persons they are, whether young or old, male or female (1 Timothy 5:1-2). In particular, the structure of family leadership is to be carried over into God's household: qualified men are to be appointed as overseers, that is, fathers of the church. A woman, however capable and gifted she may be, can never become a father of a family. As a woman, she is simply not so constituted. Likewise, a woman may never become a father in God's household. She may indeed become a "mother" in God's household, and exercise the roles indicated in 1 Timothy 5:2; 3:11; 5:9-10, 14; Titus 2:3-5; 2 Timothy 1:5. The life of the church never overthrows but rather enhances the life of the family, based on God's design from creation.

Such reasoning on Paul's part is the best context for understanding Paul's teaching in 1 Timothy 2:8-15. There Paul sets out distinctive responsibilities for men (2:8) and women (2:9-15). The necessity of such distinction is best understood as flowing from the fact that men and women are not interchangeable within God's household, just as they are not within human families. Under the topic of women's responsibilities, beginning in 2:9, Paul includes the statement that a woman is not "to teach or to have authority over a man" (2:12). According to our previous arguments, this conclusion is a natural outcome of the analogy between the church and the human family, in which the wife is not to have authority over her husband (Ephesians 5:22-24). Paul then appeals to the background of the order of creation (2:13), in which the pattern for a husband's authority is initially established.[9] He also appeals to the fall (2:14), in which male and female roles were not identical. Paul concludes with a reminder of one of the central and proper services of women, the bearing of children (2:15). This particular distinctive service by women reminds us more broadly of the larger responsibilities that women have in rearing children within a family.[10] Thus the whole passage organizes itself naturally once we understand the centrality of the idea of family and the fruitfulness of using human households as a basis for discerning people's responsibilities within God's household.

In sum, Paul bases his reasoning on general principles, going back ultimately to the Biblical account in Genesis 2 and 3. Paul has an understanding of God's plans and purposes in creating marriage and the family. Paul teaches that in the church, God's household, women are not to exercise authority over men, just as in a human family they are not to exercise authority over their husbands. Paul understands the position of overseer as involving the exercise of fatherly care over God's household. Hence women are excluded from being overseers on the basis of general Biblical principles concerning the family, not on the basis of some temporary circumstances.

The Inevitability of Inferences Concerning People's Distinctive Roles

The conclusions that we have reached concerning distinctive roles of men and women in the church will doubtless be resisted in certain quarters. Nevertheless, in my opinion, church life in line with such conclusions inevitably results from the robust practice of Christian obedience and love within the body of Christ. Only temporary circumstances and difficulties within the body of Christ and within the surrounding society make genuinely Biblical practices seem less inevitable or even counterintuitive. Let us see how the process works.

Robust Christianity begins with fervent faith in Christ. When in faith we behold Christ in His true beauty and love, we begin to respond with vigorous love for Him. Love for Christ is in turn expressed and reflected in love for fellow Christians (1 John 4:20-21).

In particular, Christian love transforms the family. Husbands and wives begin to practice the Word of God in Ephesians 5:22-33 and begin to imitate the love that Christ has for the church and the submission that the church ought to practice to Christ. Christian love at its best and most intense is not merely a general, vague sentiment of love or an undefined impulse to do good. It is love in union with Christ. Our love ought to be enlivened by the supreme example of Christ, empowered by the resurrection of Christ, embodied in the practice of following Christ. In the family, such love will never find itself able to dispense with the power generated by the Christological analogy of Ephesians 5:22-33 and the Old Testament discourses about God as husband to Israel (for example, Hosea 2; Ezekiel 16; Isaiah 54:5-6). According to Ephesians 5:22-23, husbands have responsibilities like those of Christ, while wives have responsibilities like those of the church. The responsibilities are not simply interchangeable, any more than the roles of Christ and the church are interchangeable. The Bible thus moves us away from any pure identity in the roles of husbands and wives. The husbands grow in imitation of the love of Christ and the wives grow in imitation of the submission of the church. The roles of husband and wife are not reversible. The Bible contradicts radical egalitarian philosophy, that is, a philosophy that says that men and women are in virtually all respects interchangeable and that their roles ought to have no relation to their sexual constitution.

Of course there is *some* degree of overlap in the ways in which we may describe the responsibilities of husbands and wives. Though Ephesians 5 does not put it this way, it is nevertheless true that husbands ought to minister to the needs of their wives just as Christ serves the needs of the church, and wives ought to love their husbands as the church loves Christ. But the duties and practices of husbands and wives are not purely identical and interchangeable, precisely because they are modeled even more deeply on the irreversible Biblical patterns given once for all in the accomplishment of redemption through Jesus Christ.

Thus Christian marital practice gradually moves beyond the pure egalitarianism of some people and the immature domineering of others. Different Christian marriages may still have many differences, corresponding to the different gifts and different personalities of the two partners. But, as Christ transforms a marriage, a responsibility of overall family leadership and "headship"[11] begins to be practiced by husbands in distinction from wives.

Christian love also binds together all the members of the universal church. Since God is our Father, we really are in a fundamental sense one family. The

Holy Spirit as the Spirit of the family gives us yearnings toward our fellow family members. In the long run, Christians cannot be satisfied with nothing more than a large, anonymous meeting once or twice a week. The ties of love demand more frequent and more intimate relations, perhaps alongside a Sunday morning meeting with a very large group.

As Christians meet with one another and know one another more intimately, their sense of being one family grows. They begin to treat one another in the way Paul counsels: the older men as fathers, the younger men as brothers, the older women as mothers, the younger women as sisters (1 Timothy 5:1-2). People are no longer faceless masks, but real people, bound together by family ties. The same logic operative in natural families begins then to play itself out in the church as God's household. In the intimacy of this spiritual family, people find that they are treating one another in a manner that respects differences of age, sex, and personality.

The presence of Christ and the Holy Spirit in God's household, as well as God's own Fatherhood, demands the observance of household order. Quarrels, heresies, and various kinds of immaturity must be looked after rather than simply ignored or viewed with indifference. The intimacy of the spiritual family itself calls for loving involvement when there are sins and difficulties, not merely withdrawal or soupy tolerance.

In such situations, the "fathers" of the church stand out. Mature, sober, sound, godly men with exemplary family lives are the natural leaders in this extended family. First, the whole church naturally treats them as fathers and perceives the leadership abilities they exercise in their own immediate families. Second, church leadership in a situation of family intimacy is like family leadership—a matter not primarily of laying down formal rules but of setting a good example that naturally engenders admiration and that people attempt to emulate. Paul himself functions as an example in subordination to Christ, who is the example *par excellence* (1 Corinthians 11:1). Timothy is exhorted to set a good example (1 Timothy 4:12). The general godliness of overseers, and not merely their doctrinal orthodoxy or speaking ability, is important to Paul for the same reason. Of course mature men and women should both function as examples in a general way (Titus 2:2, 3-5). But in the particular case of overseers, we are dealing with people who must be an example specifically in their *family leadership*, both leadership in God's household and leadership in their own household. That natural qualification points the church away from looking for women and towards looking for men as overseers.

Finally, note that in situations of face-to-face intimacy, the church is largely made up of whole families who as a family come to the church meetings. The church is quite likely to meet regularly in small groups in members' homes, and the home atmosphere extends to the whole meeting. In the church meetings themselves, the fathers continue to exercise authority over their families. In Titus 1:6, Paul indicates that the elders should be men "whose children believe," in which case the whole family would regularly come to meetings and the obedience or disobedience of children to their father would be manifest at the meeting itself (see Titus 1:6; 1 Timothy 3:4). In fact, at a church gathering the lines between family and church are not very clearly drawn, because the family comes to the meeting as a family and not merely as isolated individuals. Family worship at home and family worship with a larger group might seem very like one another, except that the larger group is the extended family—that is, God's household.

All these factors, then, add up to generate a firm impulse to see the mature fathers in the church as the natural people to become fathers in a more extended and official sense, namely, fathers of the church as an extended spiritual family. If church life is as robust and intimate as it should be—if it is normal *family* life—the church will find itself recognizing male overseers even if hypothetically it did not have the specific instructions from the Apostle Paul in 1 Timothy 3:1-7 and Titus 1:5-9.

The Temporary Character of Modern Doubts

Of course, large sections of the church today have doubts about these matters, and some go so far as openly to oppose Biblical principles. But the doubts and oppositions arise, as I see it, from temporary aberrations and weaknesses in the life of the church and the larger society, rather than from the force of truth.

First, the Western church is deeply infected by theological modernism or liberalism. When the Bible is no longer acknowledged to be the Word of God, it is no longer clear that there is a divine standard for the church to obey, and love for Christ (if present at all) grows cold.

Second, the pace of technological and social change within post-industrial societies has made us reserved about the answers of previous generations, and our questioning extends to every aspect of society and church life. In addition, various changes in women's education, the nature of housework, and the involvement of women in work outside the home have raised many new and difficult questions about the nature of men's and women's roles in both family and church.

Third, radical philosophical and political egalitarianism, coupled with sin and envy, has generated hatred of all differences and differentiations among human beings. Many today think that the rich, the powerful, the gifted, and the possessors of official authority must be brought down to the level of the mediocrity of the mass, whether or not they have obtained their situation and function through righteous means. Such egalitarianism, when extended to the family and the church, refuses to acknowledge any differences between men and women.

Fourth, many people have become sincerely concerned about past and present oppression of women and unnecessary strictures on the use of women's gifts. Such evils do exist and should be opposed, but they do not justify radical egalitarian conclusions.

Finally, many evangelical churches today are seen primarily as lecture halls or preaching stations. People identify the church with its building, in contrast to the Biblical emphasis that those united to Christ are the real church. Moreover, the building is viewed merely as a place for hearing a sermon or enjoying religious entertainment. Such a view impoverishes our communal life as Christians. Certainly monologue sermons are important, since they are one means of bringing God's Word to bear on the church. But God intends the church to be much more. If we think only of sermons, we have lost sight of the riches expressed in the fact that the church is the body of Christ (1 Corinthians 12:12-27). Each member of the church is to exercise gifts for the benefit of the rest. We are all supposed to exhort and encourage one another, based on the love of Christ (Colossians 3:12-17). We are to be tender to one another as beloved children of God

(Ephesians 4:32-5:1). Christian fellowship is not supposed to mean merely a superficial social time, but sharing based on our relation to God the Father and to Jesus Christ (1 John 1:3-4). We are to express intimacy and care for one another as we would towards members of our own family, since we are in fact all members of God's family or God's household.

But in too many evangelical churches, people have little experience of the Biblical practice of common family life. There may also be no regard for the necessity of church discipline. The church leaders are nothing more than gifted speakers or counselors (paid ministers), or else managers of church property and/or programs (whether these people are called trustees or elders or deacons). Such "leaders" are just people whose useful gifts have brought them into prominence. In such situations, it is understandable that some people may fail to see why appropriately qualified women may not exercise the key functions they associate with leadership. In fact, Christians will not fully understand the logic leading to male overseers until they come to grips with what the church should really be as God's household.

Household Management Contrasted with Simple Communication

The analogy between family and church also helps to make clear what distinguishes the office of overseer from other roles in the church. Consider the situation within a natural family. Within a family we may find a variety of skills, abilities, and gifts. A wise husband and father will encourage the full development and use of these abilities. His leadership, properly understood, is enhanced rather than threatened by the full flourishing of the family as a whole.

For example, in a healthy situation family conversation involves rich communion, including give and take among all the members of the family. Even the children participate actively. As they learn from God and from outside sources at school or play, they may sometimes communicate to their parents things the parents did not know. The wife, as a mature person, is in an even better position to cause her husband to learn and grow through things she communicates to him. Thus the leadership belonging to the husband does not contradict many-sided communication among all the family members.

Similarly, all the family members have, in some broad sense, responsibilities for management. Even the youngest child may help to "manage" setting the table or doing dishes or caring for the cat. Wives exercise authority over their children, but they also may have very extensive projects in which they exercise management not only over the physical domain of the household but also over transactions with the surrounding society (Proverbs 31:10-31; cf. 1 Timothy 5:14). Thus management in a broad sense is everyone's responsibility. The father nevertheless exercises an overall authority over the household as a whole.

Advocates of women overseers are quick to observe that Christian women have many of the gifts and skills necessary for good communication and good management. If they have such gifts, they should exercise them for the benefit of the body of Christ (1 Peter 4:10). These observations are basically correct, but they are in fact just as relevant and useful to Christian families as they are to the church as an extended family. In both cases, wise leaders should encourage the use of gifts. But in neither case does the existence of gifts overthrow the legitimacy of investing unique leadership in the father. Quite the opposite: the comparison with the family shows that gifts, in and of themselves, can never be a sound reason for displacing an order grounded in other factors from creation.

Since management is crucial to the argument, let us become more specific about various kinds of management. The picture in Proverbs 31:10-31 illustrates several significant types of management: management of clothing, food, money, fields, charitable gifts, purchases, and sales. All these types of management ought to be treated as instances of stewardship, since the whole world belongs to God. We are never absolute owners, but only stewards who have been temporarily entrusted with some of God's property. In addition, management of other people should always respect the fact that people are created in God's image. Authority over them necessarily has a character different from authority over the subhuman creation.

Men and women may vary considerably in their skills in these various areas. Skills related to wisdom and general Christian maturity help in all types of management, but some people are still more skillful in some areas than in others. Moreover, people may improve their skills as they develop maturity and experience.

Within a family, the diversity of skills naturally results in division of labor. The husband, the wife, and the children may all have some specific areas of responsibility delegated to them. If grandchildren or other relatives are living together, they are naturally included as well. In addition, consultation and imitation help family members learn from one another. Some areas of management may work out best if they are the responsibility of the whole family rather than delegated to one person.

Ephesians 5:22-6:4 and other passages about the family clearly leave open a great many possibilities for the exact form of managerial arrangements. In these matters, a wise leader attempts to work out arrangements that best use and enhance the gifts of each family member. But Ephesians 5:22-6:4 does nevertheless draw some clear boundary lines. Children should submit to their parents, and conversely the parents have responsibility for managing their children. Wives should submit to their husbands, and husbands have managerial responsibility with respect to their wives, as well as for the rest of the household. These managerial responsibilities are fixed by God. Responsibilities can be delegated to other family members in accordance with their maturity and skills. In particular, they may all engage in various types of management of the subhuman creation. But there is still a leader where the buck stops. The roles of men and women in marriage are at this point irreversible, not interchangeable.

In sum, a wise husband leads his household using the fullest consultation and conversation, and he delegates authority. In all these practices, he is simply imitating Christ's care for the church. Christ involves us in two-way conversation and delegates responsibilities to us. Christ is nevertheless the ultimate authority in all of life; husbands, subject to Christ's authority, have been assigned as heads of their households.

When Paul's instructions are abused and husbands use their authority as an excuse for selfish and domineering behavior, a reaction sets in. Many people in our day deplore the oppression of women and the foolishness involving in refusing to encourage them to test and use their gifts. If people do not have proper godly models before them, it is understandable that they should think a pattern of completely interchangeable responsibilities is the only reasonable alternative consistent with the freedom given us in Christ. Yet the actual goal of Scripture is richer.

The analogy between the natural family and God's household therefore suggests the same procedures for God's household. Responsibilities for management may, in a broad sense, be delegated and distributed throughout God's household. But the overseers, as fathers in the household, possess more ultimate authority. The overseers ought to be men, in analogy with the fact that the father and not the mother of a family possesses higher authority.

Advocates of women overseers also appeal to the good that has been accomplished in the past by Christian women—in particular, by women who have exercised leadership. In evaluating this appeal, several factors must be borne in mind. First, Proverbs 31:10-31 shows that some types of leadership and management by women harmonize with a husband's more ultimate leadership (Proverbs 31:23). Second, bold but humble communication of the truth by wives to their husbands need not undermine their husbands' authority, any more than Paul intended to undermine general state authority by his criticisms of the actions of particular state authorities (see Acts 16:37; 22:25; 23:3-5; 25:10-11). Third, family cases involving widows, divorcées, and absent fathers show that sometimes women must exercise authority in the absence of any better alternatives; but such situations are far from ideal. Fourth, family cases involving domineering wives show that by the grace of God some good can be accomplished even through people and actions contaminated by sin.

All of these cases illumine by analogy what may happen within the church as God's household. None of these cases negates the principial point that ideally fathers are to exercise overall authority in both family and church.

In particular, we must avoid confusing leadership with ability to understand the Bible and ability to communicate its teaching to others. Such abilities are valuable within the body of Christ. But when they are present in women they obviously do not imply any lessening of their responsibilities to submit to their husbands in the Lord. Husbands on their part should encourage the full use of their wives' abilities, and they themselves may benefit greatly; but the husbands do not thereby relinquish their own responsibilities. The same holds for the overseers in God's household.

Evil Effects Arising from Disrupting the Order of God's Household

Maintaining male leadership in the church is not a matter of indifference. Evil effects inevitably arise when we deviate from God's pattern. Such effects are largely the reverse side of the picture that we have been drawing. Because of the close relation between family and church, godly family life stimulates appreciation of God as our heavenly Father, and appreciation of God stimulates godly family life. Both are enhanced by the example of mature, fatherly leaders within the church. Conversely, disintegration of household order within the church adversely affects both our consciousness of being in God's family and the quality of love within Christian families.

To begin with, absence of godly, fatherly leadership within the church makes the affirmation of the Fatherhood of God closer to an abstraction. God's Fatherhood is, of course, illustrated preeminently in the great deeds of the history of redemption that embody His fatherly rule, care, and discipline. But we are richer in our understanding of God because most of us have enjoyed having a human father, and we are richer still if we can see the fatherly care and the rule of God embodied at a practical level in the older men of the church (Titus 2:2) and especially in the overseers.

Church order can deviate from the ideal either by lacking overseers, by having unqualified overseers, by appointing women overseers, or by redefining the office of overseer. Any of these moves tends to make more vague people's experience of the church as a family. The lack of genuine practical correspondence between the church and Biblically-based natural families suppresses people's ability to see the analogy. Hence they lose some of their grip on the importance of family-like intimacy and support within the church. Moreover, they cease to understand that God's Fatherhood is expressed in His rule over us and that His rule is exercised in part through mature, father-like overseers.

In particular, radical egalitarian philosophy, which says that we are to treat all people exactly the same, hinders Christians from having the kind of sensitivity toward the age, sex, and position of others that Paul enjoins (1 Timothy 5:1-2, 17). Relations become more impersonal, and the realities of membership in one family of God recede out of Christians' consciousness and their practice.

The practice of Christian family life is also adversely affected. Most people learn far better from example, and from teaching closely related to their leaders' examples, than they do from teaching in the abstract. So how do they properly assimilate teaching about family life? Ideally, they imitate the family lives of their church leaders. But this imitation is most effective if they can actually see something of the family life of their leaders. For example, in a smaller group meeting in a home, they see the way the leader conducts himself with respect to the other family members present for worship. Christian worship in smaller groups becomes something very like family worship, which ought to be the heartbeat of life for each particular family. This whole process becomes confused when the distinctions between men and women, fathers and mothers, are overlooked. Ordinary families then have no direct models to build on.

Ostensibly, the feminist movement aims at freeing women from oppression. But such freedom in the true sense can come only through the divine powers of liberation and love contained in Jesus Christ. True freedom is found in obedience to Christ; anything else only constitutes some form of slavery to sin.

The family more than any other single institution in modern society desperately needs freedom and renewal through the love of Christ. That freedom comes most effectively when we are able, under God, to harness the full, rich resources that He provides. We are to teach people above all to embody in their families the model of Christ set forth in Ephesians 5:22-23. And we are to teach them by examples that we set forth in the family-like life of the church, including the godly example of mature spiritual fathers, the overseers. Hence we hinder true liberation if we deviate from the pattern of male overseers. It would be ironic if a sincere desire for women's liberation should be corrupted in practice into its opposite, a hindrance to the liberating power of God that is at work in His household.

Conclusion

Some Christian people think Christian marriage ideally should express a radically egalitarian pattern: a husband and wife should in every respect be able to function interchangeably. If they were right, the analogy between family and church would suggest that men and women could in every respect have interchangeable roles within the church.

But they are not right. Ephesians 5:22-23 resists them, as do the other passages comparing the relation of God and His people to marriage.[12] In time, we may hope that the Holy Spirit will use the power of these Biblical passages to generate godly marriages and so prevail over abstract egalitarian sentiments. If, as I believe, these Biblical passages do provide a warrant for assigning specific leadership responsibility to husbands and fathers, we need also to recognize the same pattern within the church. Mature men and not women are to be appointed overseers. But blind obedience to a formal rule is not sufficient. We must work towards more richly embodying in our churches the realities of our common life. We are children of God, members of one divinely ruled family. Only a full-orbed expression of Christ's love in the Christian community will bring to realization the freedom, power, and beauty derived from the manifestation of the glory of God in His household (Ephesians 3:10).

14

The Meaning of Authority in the Local Church

Paige Patterson

On February 11, 1989, Rev. Barbara C. Harris was consecrated a bishop of the Episcopal Church in the Diocese of Massachusetts. Harris thus became the first female bishop in the history of Anglicanism. The three-hour ceremony featured avowals such as "God with His mighty hand has exalted her," and "the Word of God is once again being made flesh among us."[1] Some churches were reticent to make such sweeping claims, whereas others suspected the hand of the devil rather than the hand of God and staged requiem services to lament the demise of the church.

The case of Bishop Harris is representative of the impasse developing over the past decade in ecclesiastical circles that, only a few years earlier, would have been considered sanctuaries for male clergy. At least two traditions had long since endorsed the preaching of women. Aimee Semple McPherson (1890-1944) of the International Church of the Foursquare Gospel mesmerized live audiences and radio clientele from her five-thousand-seat Angelus Temple in Los Angeles.[2] Pentecostalism in most of its expressions has sanctioned the ministry of women. By the same token, various denominations comfortable with a modern perspective, which more traditional groups labeled "liberal" but which viewed themselves as "progressive," welcomed women into the clergy. This participation of women at the highest level of church ministry was thought to represent the natural outgrowth of the socially liberating principles of the gospel.

Among more conservative and traditional denominations, the entrance of women into the clergy was consistently resisted until the decade of the seventies. Conservative Presbyterians, Southern Baptists, and other free church groups were joined by Episcopalians, Roman Catholics, and other communions of the episcopal tradition in rejecting the inroads of a growing feminist perspective. The recent confrontation in the Shelby County Baptist Association of Memphis, Tennessee, in which the Prescott Memorial Church (a Southern Baptist congregation) was disfellowshiped by the SBC Association because it had called Rev. Nancy Hastings Sehested as pastor, simply demonstrates that the issue of the rights of women to serve in pastoral roles has now been contested in arenas scarcely deemed possible a few years ago. This in turn has raised the question concerning the nature and authority of ordination, especially in communions that practice a congregational form of church government.[3]

I. The Nature of Ordination

Lexical investigations provide limited assistance on the subject of ordination. In the KJV, "ordain" is the English translation of more than twenty Hebrew and Greek terms. Most of these words also are translated at times by numerous other English words. The translators of the NIV have simplified the matter by almost uniformly translating the various Greek terms with the word *appoint.* Titus is instructed by Paul to "appoint elders in every town" on the island of Crete (Titus 1:5). In Mark 3:14, it is said that Jesus "appointed twelve," whereas in 1 Timothy 2:7 Paul confesses that he was "appointed a herald and an apostle." Such translations may reflect a conviction on the part of the NIV translators that "ordination" as practiced in most communions today has little in common with New Testament practice. A. H. Strong noted precisely that when he wrote, "The word 'ordain' has come to have a technical signification not found in the New Testament. There it means simply to choose, appoint, set apart."[4]

Even an ardent proponent of episcopacy such as Rudolf Schnackenburg admits that the primitive church was not highly organized in terms of ecclesiastical structure. "Now it would certainly be erroneous to try to affirm and defend in opposition to this an ecclesiastical juridical organization for the Pauline churches based on a starting point of later conditions in view."[5] C. H. Spurgeon, who was never ordained, considered ordination as practiced in his day to be essentially a vestige of Romanism void of foundation in the New Testament.

Examination of the salient "ordination" texts appears to sustain the judgment of Strong, Spurgeon, and the NIV translators. Mark 3:14 records that Jesus "ordained (*poieō*) twelve" (KJV; henceforward all Scripture citations in this chapter are from KJV unless otherwise noted). In Acts 14:23, Luke mentions that Paul and Barnabas traveled to certain cities in Asia Minor and "ordained (*cheirotoneō*) them elders in every church." Paul refers possibly to his own ordination in 1 Timothy 2:7, asserting that he was "ordained (*tithēmi*) a preacher and an apostle. . . ." Finally, Paul calls for Titus to "ordain (*kathistēmi*) elders in every city. . . ." Of the four texts, three use common words, each of which has the sense of "appoint," "place," or "establish." Only Acts 14:23 uses a word (*cheirotoneō*) that can mean "to stretch forth the hand," or "elect" or "appoint."[6] *Cheirotoneō* is a rare term, appearing in the Septuagint once (Isaiah 58:9) and in the New Testament only two times (Acts 14:23; 2 Corinthians 8:19, where Titus is appointed by the churches to travel with Paul to Jerusalem). The closely related compound word *procheirotoneō*, "to appoint beforehand," is found in Acts 10:41.

A possible connection suggesting formal ordination can be imagined by linking Acts 14:23 (Paul and Barnabas "ordained them elders in every church") with 1 Timothy 4:14. Timothy is told not to neglect the gift that he had received through "prophecy, with the laying on of the hands of the presbytery." This may parallel the experience of Paul and Barnabas, recorded in Acts 13:1-3, when the Lord instructed that the two apostles be separated for a particular work, in response to which, the church "laid their hands on them" (verse 3). On the other hand, the Acts 10:41 reference employing *procheirotoneō* seems to imply nothing except the sovereign choice of God, by which the apostles are called "witnesses whom God has already chosen."[7] Moreover, 1 Timothy 5:22 suggests that elders as a rule received the laying on of hands: "Do not be hasty in the laying on of hands" (in the context of instructions about elders) (*NIV*).

Even if there is an emerging pattern in Acts 14:23, 1 Timothy 4:14, and 5:22, the induction rites of the early church were probably simple in comparison to present practice. No concrete evidence can be generated to suggest that the ecclesiastical officers of the primitive church were inaugurated in any particular fashion or ceremony. This is not to suggest that elders and deacons were just announced without formal installation. The same diverse vocabulary that suggests absence of specific ceremony probably implies some public act of recognition and consecration.

First Timothy 4:14, as well as its probable parallel passage in 2 Timothy 1:6 ("... fan into flame the gift of God, which is in you through the laying on of my hands."), seems to have little connection to such events as those recorded in Acts 8:17, 9:17, 19:6, in which the laying on of the hands is associated with the impartation of the Spirit. Ronald Y. K. Fung notes that the experience of Timothy is more closely paralleled by the experiences recorded in the setting apart of the seven (Acts 6:6) and of Paul and Barnabas (Acts 13:3). He concludes that Timothy's experience was tantamount to ordination but also notes that the conferring of a charisma is exceptional in this case.[8] C. K. Barrett also sees 1 Timothy 4:14 as "ordination":

> The Pastorals are not inconsistent with Paul's teachings, though they probably mark a later stage of development. It was under the guidance of prophecy (cp. 1:18) that Timothy was selected for ordination (cp. Acts 13:1 ff.); that is, it had been ascertained so far as was possible that it was God's will that Timothy should be ordained to the work of ministry, and in the bestowal of the endowment for this work God's will was the cause, the laying on of the hands of the elders as a body being an accompanying act—not a means, for "through" is a mistranslation (*meta* with the genitive must mean "with," not "through").[9]

F. J. A. Hort recognizes the unique character of this event in Timothy's life, concludes that a prophetic oracle had singled Timothy out as Paul's chosen colleague, and hints that this precise event would probably not be duplicated.[10] But Bultmann views the incident more as the establishment of a pattern of ordination of elders based on practices known to exist in Jewish synagogues of the first century. While Bultmann suggests that this act did constitute the passing on of the pastoral office, he also acknowledges that the one being ordained was identified by "prophet-voices from the congregation" and that, based on 1 Clement 44:3, the congregations had to give their approval.[11]

First Clement may not sustain Bultmann's thesis of the role of charismatic prophets in the early church, but the idea of congregational ratification of the appointment of elders seems clearly to be present.

> We are of the opinion, therefore, that those appointed by them, or afterwards by other eminent men with the consent of the whole Church, and who have blamelessly served the flock of Christ in a humble, peaceable, and disinterested spirit, and have for a long time possessed the good opinion of all, cannot be

> justly dismissed from the ministry. For our sin will not be small, if we eject from the episcopate those who have blamelessly and holily fulfilled its duties. (1 Clement XLIV.2-4)[12]

Venturing no judgment as to whether contemporary ordination procedures are good or evil, it is sufficient to stress that no clear pattern or procedure for ordination is discernible in the New Testament. Neither can it be established that the various words translated "ordain" in the KJV mean anything more than "appoint." Insofar as the New Testament is concerned, ordination is not a major issue, if it exists as such at all. Most churches and denominations have developed ordination beyond New Testament precedent in both its form and its significance.

However, this is not to say that the New Testament does not recognize ecclesiastical offices. Furthermore, these officials were probably given formal recognition and installation. Apostles, prophets, evangelists, pastors, bishops, elders, and deacons all are clearly recognized in Acts and the epistles. Whatever the case may be regarding apostles and prophets,[13] it seems clear that pastors, bishops, elders, and deacons were names used for continuing offices in the churches.[14] The question for evangelical Christians who feel bound by the testimony of Holy Scripture then becomes not, "Who can be ordained?" but, more simply, "Who is qualified to serve in ecclesiastical offices?" More specifically, in light of the present debate, are women free to be appointed to the office of elder? And, if not, do elders have authority to authorize a woman to teach men? In fact, just exactly how much authority did elders wield in the primitive church?

II. Authority of the Elders

The picture of early church government that emerges from the New Testament presents elders as church leaders with substantive, but not unlimited, authority. A brief analysis of the extent of that authority will be followed by an assessment of the limitations of authority. The initial passage that suggests authority for elders is 1 Timothy 5:17-22:

> The elders who direct the affairs of the church well are worthy of double honor, especially those whose work is preaching and teaching. For the Scripture says, "Do not muzzle the ox while it is treading out the grain," and "The worker deserves his wages." Do not entertain an accusation against an elder unless it is brought by two or three witnesses. Those who sin are to be rebuked publicly, so that the others may take warning.
>
> I charge you, in the sight of God and Christ Jesus and the elect angels, to keep these instructions without partiality, and to do nothing out of favoritism.
>
> Do not be hasty in the laying on of hands, and do not share in the sins of others. Keep yourself pure. (NIV)

Elders who rule well are worthy of double honor, especially if their labor is in the Word and in doctrine.[15] Elders are subject to rebuke only if two or three witnesses are available; but if found guilty of sin, they are also to receive public rebuke. "Direct the affairs of" in verse 17 is a translation of *proistēmi*, a term with a variety of possible meanings. Here, however, it almost certainly indicates the being set over or being the head of something. Liddell and Scott cite multiple uses of the word in this regard, especially in Herodotus and in Xenophon's *Anabasis*.[16] Reicke agrees with this sense of the word and stresses that in the New Testament the idea of "leading" or "caring for" is the more prominent one (cf. 1 Thessalonians 5:12; 1 Timothy 3:4-5).[17] The emphasis of the word is that of decisive leadership undergirded by generally recognized authority.

C. K. Barrett is unsure that these "elders" have yet evolved into official status, suspecting that the word is still being employed here to denote the elderly men of the church.[18] But Hendriksen is almost certainly correct when he notes that instructions about wages (verse 18) and laying hands on future elders (verse 22; cf. 4:14) make clear that we are dealing here with officials.[19] Elders, therefore, are leaders who perform at least three functions: laboring in and teaching the Word of God, ruling or providing decisive leadership to the church, and presiding over the setting apart of future elders.

In Hebrews 13:7 and 17, the author uses a stronger term for "leader," namely *hēgoumenos*:

> Remember your *leaders*, who spoke the word of God to you. Consider the outcome of their way of life and imitate their faith. [verse 7, NIV]
>
> Obey your *leaders* and submit to their authority. They keep watch over you as men who must give an account. Obey them so that their work will be a joy, not a burden, for that would be of no advantage to you. [verse 17, NIV]

Not only are those who have the rule over the recipients of this epistle to be remembered, followed, and obeyed, but also their lifestyle is to be contemplated. They are not only described as ruling, but also charged with "watching for the souls" of God's people and being accountable for that responsibility. F. F. Bruce sees the leaders in verse 7 as distinct from those mentioned in verse 17. The former are those who had originally brought the gospel to the Hebrews, whereas the latter are the current leaders.[20] Regardless of who the leaders in verse 7 are, near unanimity seems to prevail regarding the identity of the leaders in verse 17:

> Obey your leaders and submit to their authority. They keep watch over you as men who must give an account. (NIV)

Johannes Schneider was both representative and explicit when he wrote:

> The bearers of the congregational ministries bear a specially heavy responsibility. They are accountable to God for the souls entrusted to their care and vigilance. But they can perform their ministry properly only when their God-given authority is fully acknowledged. The church of Jesus, like every other community, depends on officers and orders. It is expected of the members of the congregation that they do not obstruct the work of the leading men loaded down with heavy responsibilities, but rather that they lighten their burdens. In the church of Jesus no ministry ought to be performed with sighing. It is unsound and unworthy of the Christian brotherhood when discord or even unpleasant quarrels arise between congregation and the office holders. The latter have a claim to obedience. That is the clear directive of the Letter [to the] Hebrews. This sentence has proven an absolute necessity in the history of the Christian churches. It has as much validity today as then.[21]

The Ephesian elders are designated "overseers" and charged by Paul with feeding the church of God (Acts 20:28). In 1 Peter 5:1-4, an almost identical mandate appears:

> To the elders among you, I appeal as a fellow elder, a witness of Christ's sufferings and one who also will share in the glory to be revealed. *Be shepherds of God's flock that is under your care, serving as overseers*—not because you must, but because you are willing, as God wants you to be; not greedy for money, but eager to serve; not lording it over those entrusted to you, but being examples to the flock. And when the Chief Shepherd appears, you will receive the crown of glory that will never fade away. (NIV)

Like Paul, Peter unites the function of oversight with shepherding or feeding the flock of God. Moreover, he cautions that this oversight should be by way of example rather than acting as lords (*katakurieuontes*) over God's heritage.

Finally, some attention must be devoted to the exceptionally difficult quotations from Jesus in Matthew 16:19, 18:18, John 20:23. In the NIV they read:

> I will give you the keys of the kingdom of heaven; whatever you bind on earth will be bound in heaven, and whatever you loose on earth will be loosed in heaven. (Matthew 16:19)

> I tell you the truth, whatever you bind on earth will be bound in heaven, and whatever you loose on earth will be loosed in heaven. (Matthew 18:18)

> If you forgive anyone his sins, they are forgiven; if you do not forgive them, they are not forgiven. (John 20:23)

The technical aspects of the exegesis of this passage lie beyond the scope of this inquiry.[22] As the passages relate to the subject of the authority of the church, it scarcely can be doubted that Jesus invested His followers with significant authority. Whether the binding and loosing herein enjoined be understood as a rabbinic phrase involving excommunication or, as by many evangelical exegetes, as use of the keys of understanding, followed by confident declaration of the effects dependent on the response of hearers, obvious exercise of derived authority is in view.

Even if Peter is singled out as the recipient of this authority in Matthew 16:19, that is surely broadened to include a larger group in both Matthew 18:18 and John 20:23. If the commission is extended to others besides the elders, then the "binding and loosing" and the "remitting and retaining" must also be the responsibility of the church as a whole. Worth noting is the fact that the final step in church discipline in Matthew 18:15-20 is not "tell it to the elders" but "tell it to the church." This is, of course, not to be indiscriminately practiced, but rather as Westcott says:

> At the same time the exercise of the power must be placed in the closest connexion with the faculty of spiritual discernment consequent upon the gift of the Holy Spirit. Compare 1 John ii.18ff.[23]

We may, therefore, conclude that Jesus gave authority to the church, even if that authority is limited to announcing a decision that had already been rendered in heaven. While that decision may be announced by the elders, it seems in reality to be the prerogative of the church as a body.

Summarizing the situation as it existed in the New Testament era, Ronald Y. K. Fung notes:

> The existence of some kind of specialized ministry, or more specifically of church officers, is attested for the primitive church in Jerusalem, for all the Pauline churches with the sole exception of Corinth, and for some of the churches in the General Epistles (1 Peter, James). If a different picture obtains in the Gospel and Epistles of John and Revelation, this suggests only that church organization was still fluid during the New Testament period, that 'there is no such thing as *the* New Testament Church order,' and that different lines of development are discernible; the existence of an organized and official ministry remains unaffected.
>
> Further, it is possible, and perhaps even likely, that varying nomenclature used of church leaders refers basically to the same group, so that while "functional" terms are sometimes employed to emphasize that aspect of the ministry, they point to the same "functionaries" who are elsewhere described with a more official title; here we think especially of those who are referred to as *proïstamenoi*, 1 Thessalonians 5:12, *poimenas*, Ephesians 4:11, and *hegoumenoi*, Hebrews 13:17, 24, all of whom may well be identical with those designated elsewhere as elders and overseers. In any event, there is ample evidence which more than suffices to show that the early Christian communities were not amorphous associations run on haphazard lines; on the contrary, most if not all of them had at least a rudimentary, and some had a more advanced, form of church organization—although, on the other hand, there are no grounds for thinking that the monepiscopate is to be found within the pages of the New Testament.[24]

Fung may overstate the case for "fluidity" in the ecclesiology of the New Testament. What is remarkable is that elders existed in all the New Testament churches for which we have evidence: "in *every* church" (Acts 14:23); "in *every* town" (Titus 1:5); "let him call for the elders of the church" (James 5:14—written to *many churches*); "The elders which are among you I exhort" (1 Peter 5:1—to many churches). The elders of the churches, however formally or informally, exercised a teaching and governing authority throughout the New Testament churches. Nevertheless, as we will see presently, they were not the final authority in the local church.

Limitations placed on the authority of elders begin with the authority of the Scriptures, and authority is further restricted by the concept of the priesthood of believers. At no point could elders in the churches supersede the authority of the apostles or the apostolic testimony preserved in Holy Scripture. For example, the Corinthian church demonstrated little concern for the purity of the body, tolerating a man who maintained an incestuous liaison with his father's wife. In 1 Corinthians 5:4-5, Paul urges immediate action involving at least the offender's expulsion from the fellowship.[25] Worth noting is that the prescribed action is apparently the responsibility of the entire gathered assembly.

> *When you are assembled in the name of our Lord Jesus and* I am with you in spirit, and the power of our Lord Jesus is present, hand this man over to Satan, so that the sinful nature may be destroyed and his spirit saved on the day of the Lord. (1 Corinthians 5:4b-5, NIV)

This constitutes significant evidence of congregational polity. Equally obvious, however, is the fact that Paul's apostolic authority (which is equal to the present-day authority of the apostolic writings, the New Testament Scriptures) prevails in the church, since the church is to proceed with this action based on Paul's having already adjudicated the matter (1 Corinthians 5:3).

Again, in 2 Corinthians 10-12, Paul devotes considerable attention to his own apostleship and authority. He pleads with those Corinthians who were his critics to alter their course so that he may not have to be bold with them when he personally arrives in Corinth (2 Corinthians 10:2). Again, in Galatians 1-2, Paul not only argues the heavenly origin of his apostleship but also demonstrates his equality with the other apostles through a rebuke of Peter when the latter erred (Galatians 2:11-12). Paul considers his apostolic teaching to be normative for the churches (1 Corinthians 14:37-38), and Peter puts it on a par with Scripture (2 Peter 3:16).

Abundant evidence pointing to the authority of the Scriptures over even the elders of the church is available. An example of this occurs in 2 Peter 1:19-21, in which the author informs his readers that they possessed a "more sure word of prophecy" that was not "loosed upon" the church as a result of some individual's private decision but was rather the product of "holy men of God" who were "moved by the Holy Ghost." If the objection is raised that this is surely a reference to the Old Testament, the point may be conceded. However, in 2 Peter 3:15-16, Peter makes reference to the epistles of Paul, which he describes as subject to twisting in the same manner suffered by "the other scriptures." Here surely is a clear evidence of the authority of epistles penned by the apostles.

The authority of the elders was also limited by the priesthood of believers. Although this popular concept is mentioned as such only five times in Scripture (1 Peter 2:5, 9; Revelation 1:6; 5:10; 20:6) and is provided any sort of real explanation only in the 1 Peter passages, the idea does seem to be thoroughly ingrained in the New Testament. Jews, unless they were of Levitical lineage, were excluded from the Holy Place and the Holy of Holies no matter how devout they were. Gentiles were prohibited from entering even the Court of Israel. At the death of Christ, however, the veil separating the two inner chambers of the temple was torn in two, suggesting new and wider access for His people. The author of Hebrews leads his readers to believe that as a result of the rending of the veil of Christ's body, they may all enter directly into the Holiest through the blood of Jesus (Hebrews 10:19-20). Thus, every believer becomes a priest.

The functions of the priesthood are "to offer up spiritual sacrifices, acceptable to God by Jesus Christ" and to "show forth the praises" of the One who had called believers out of darkness and into light (1 Peter 2:5, 9). Each believer possesses the Spirit of God (Romans 8:9, 14-15) and is endowed with certain spiritual gifts that are to be exercised in behalf of the whole body of believers (1 Corinthians 12:7-11). This authority of the Spirit, which manifests itself in the lives of the believers, operates with freedom in the assembly. This activity of the Spirit in the life of the congregation is not subject to the rule of pastors or elders.

As Cyril Eastwood points out, the priesthood of believers is the doctrine that establishes the whole congregation as the ministers of Christ. "The first necessity, then, is to reinstate the general active part of the whole congregation in worship so that the members are no longer merely passive onlookers."[26]

Robert Saucy concludes:

> The nature of the church yields that conclusion in that each member is endowed with the Spirit to express the living presence of Christ and to participate in His ministry with His authority. The practice of the church corresponds to that reality in that the New Testament, through various examples and instructions, places the final responsibility for doctrine and practice on the church collectively.[27]

The picture of the primitive church appears to be that of an informal assembly of believers in Jesus, each of whom functions as a minister to the others through the Spirit-directed use of *charismata*. These congregations, however, are bound not to exceed or violate the authority of Christ as revealed through the apostles and the witness of the apostles contained in Holy Scripture. The congregation itself clearly acts as something of an authority. Within that congregation, there are presbyters or pastors who exercise a restrained authority of general oversight and direction. In the earliest church, these presbyters may have come to office either by apostolic appointment or by congregational selection. The New Testament pattern is clearly one of ruling elders with substantive, but not unlimited, authority.[28]

Today, whatever form of church government a church may have, the officers who have the highest governing authority in the local church (whether they are called elders, pastors, deacons, the vestry, the church board, the governing council, or any other name) are the ones who most closely correspond to the office of elder at the time of the New Testament. They do in fact have governing authority (of varying degrees) in their churches. The question now is whether women should be eligible to participate in that governing group, whatever it may be called.

III. Authority and Female Teachers

No legitimate question exists with reference to either the adequacy or the acceptability of a woman serving in some teaching roles. Apollos profited not only from the instruction of Aquila but also from that of Priscilla (Acts 18:26). Women are expressly commissioned to teach younger women (Titus 2:4), and Timothy, as a child and presumably even as a young man, was taught by his maternal mentors—Lois and Eunice (2 Timothy 1:5; 3:14).[29] Neither should there remain any uncertainty about the opportunity extended to women to participate in public prayer or prophecy (1 Corinthians 11:2-16). Any suggestion of an ontological inferiority of women cannot survive the first declaration of Adam, "This is now bone of my bones and flesh of my flesh" (Genesis 2:23), or the statement, "In the image of God created he him, male and female created he them" (Genesis 1:27).

Yet Clark Pinnock observed:

> . . . I have come to believe that a case for feminism that appeals to the canon of Scripture as it stands can only hesitantly be made and that a communication of it to evangelicals will have difficulty shaking off the impression of hermeneutical ventriloquism. . . . If it is the Bible you want, feminism is in trouble; if it is feminism you want, the Bible stands in the way.[30]

Why would a theologian of Pinnock's stature and egalitarian sympathies arrive at such conclusions in light of the acknowledged truths stated above? The answer is that for many evangelicals the Bible is intractably hierarchical. It teaches definite role assignments, together with their corresponding mandates, opportunities, and limitations. Great scholarly efforts have been made to prove this, but—as with other crucial truths—it seems obvious to average readers.

Careful scholarly analysis of the concept of love, for example, benefits the church. Such arduous research and thought will inevitably enhance our understanding of the nature of God's love and the love required of believers. But even in the absence of such noble research, an obvious sense of the nature of love can hardly be missed by even a cursory reading of the Bible. The spiritual leadership role of men in both home and church is obvious to many average Bible readers in the same way.

Equally obvious is it that role assignments and submission to various authorities are demanded in Scripture with no essential estimate of worth or value implied for the one in authority or the one who is subordinate. For example, Christians, who are after all the salt of the earth and the light of the world, are instructed by Paul to submit to the authority of magistrates (Romans 13:1-5). This mandate is not designed to depreciate Christians, much less suggest that a humble believer is in any sense inferior to the civil authorities. Instead, it is a matter of the nature of an ordered society in which the magistrate is to be viewed in his role as minister (*diakonos*) of God. By the same token, children are not of less worth than parents; yet they are counseled to obey and to submit to their parents. Learning to relate in an appropriate manner to those whose role assignments make them "authorities" assists us in learning to relate properly to God. Accountability is generally healthy and order almost always is desirable in church and society.

The most helpful paradigm is that of Jesus. According to Philippians 2:6, Jesus "did not consider equality with God something to be grasped" (NIV). In John 14:9, the Lord informs Philip that if one has seen Jesus, he has seen the Father. Or again, in the Good Shepherd discourse of John 10, Jesus flatly declares, "I and my Father are one" (verse 30). Yet, in John 14:28, Jesus also announces, "my Father is greater than I," and elsewhere emphasizes the importance of the Son's obedience to the Father. Such passages must be judged either to be contradictory or to be clumsy redactional mistakes unless we accept the thesis that Jesus was drawing a sharp distinction between essence and office. Evangelicals have opted for the latter, understanding that Jesus is equal with His Father in essence but subordinate in His office. Such a paradigm properly applied should remove the stigma from role assignments in the domestic, civil, or ecclesiastical arenas.

Other writers in this symposium examine the specific questions relating to those role assignments and whatever limitations may be imposed on the service of women in the church. Like many other evangelicals, I am convinced that 1 Timothy 2:12-15 is normative for the church in every age. The three reasons provided by Paul (verses 13, 14) for his limitation on the ministerial activities of women are both historical-theological, not cultural or situational.[31] The remaining purpose of this chapter is to determine, in light of the three restrictions of 1 Timothy 2:12 (and other supporting passages), whether a woman is to teach men or have authority over men and whether it is possible for the church or the elders to authorize women to function in a teaching role with men.

A general answer to that question is possible based on data previously mentioned. To review, the pattern of authority in the primitive church is as follows: All authority in heaven and in earth the Father has vested in Jesus (Matthew 28:18). That authority has been passed along to the apostles and to the church (Luke 10:19), though with some limitations. The apostolic witness to Christ, as found in the New Testament, is conceived to be the voice of God through the apostles (1 Corinthians 14:37; 2 Peter 1:21; 3:16) and thus carries full authority for the church. Elders governing and leading at the will of the churches, therefore, have general authority to adjudicate matters that have not already been settled either by Jesus or in the Scriptures. They do not, under any circumstances, have the authority to reverse the Scriptures or make exceptions to the teachings of Scripture due to circumstance or culture.

More specifically, the churches appear to have the authority and perhaps even obligation to encourage women to participate in the worship of the community of the saints with certain restrictions. Women, for example, are to keep silent in the churches according to 1 Corinthians 14:34. That this cannot mean "total silence" or mere passive participation is clear from the permission granted to pray and prophesy in chapter 11,[32] and from the verse itself when it is added that women are to be in submission ". . . as also saith the law." James Hurley is probably correct in rejecting interpretation of the phrase ". . . as also saith the law," which attempts to find some specific law of the Old Testament as one to which Paul refers.

> Paul's appeal to "the law" need not have any particular text in view. It is enough that he reminds them that men were called to exercise authority and to render judgment in matters in the home and in the "church in the wilderness," in the religious life of Israel. From his appeal, however, we may deduce that he considered that the Old Testament pattern of male headship in religious matters should continue in the church alongside the new freedom of women to participate in the worship.[33]

The appeal to "the law" settles the issue for Paul. And the appeal to "the law" also suggests strongly that at least the mandate of submission in the passage removes the passage from a merely temporal or cultural delimitation. Hence, elders, churches, or even apostles are not free to give directives that are contrary to the intent of the law of God.

Calvin properly interpreted 1 Timothy 2:11-15 in a similar fashion.[34] He acknowledges exceptions to the general rule but argues that these exceptions pose no threat to the ordinary and constant system of government. As if anticipating the current debate, Calvin says,

> If any one bring forward, by way of objection, Deborah (judges iv. 4) and others of the same class, of whom we read that they were at one time appointed

> by the command of God to govern the people, the answer is easy. Extraordinary acts done by God do not overturn the ordinary rules of government, by which he intended that we should be bound.[35]

Paul's appeal to Scripture in 1 Timothy 2:13-14 makes clear the ultimate source of appeal: Scripture itself. Thus, for theological and historical reasons, the church or the elders cannot elevate women to a formal office of rule or instruction over men without violating the whole spirit of the law.[36] In no other area of life would we be willing to say that a church or its elders can give a woman (or anyone) permission to disobey the teachings of Scripture. It is difficult to understand why some have claimed that such permission is acceptable in the area of women teaching or having authority over men in the church.

IV. Conclusion

In this chapter, I have attempted to show that the life of the early church was not highly organized. Nevertheless, authorities did exist and were recognized by those early churches. While ordination as a formal ceremony, such as is commonly practiced today, probably did not exist, the setting aside of persons for special leadership tasks does seem to have been the prerogative of the churches. This was at least sometimes accompanied by the laying on of hands. These authorities or elders exercised considerable authority but had no authority to abrogate the clear teachings of Scripture. Hence, an elder or a church apparently does not have the authority to elevate a woman to a formal role of instruction or spiritual authority over men. There are gifts and roles by which women may impart to both men and women their wisdom and spiritual insight, but this is not through the channels of authoritative office and teaching in the church. Dorothy Patterson's thought is worth noting in conclusion:

> The church has never sought to suppress gifts God has given but rather strives to ensure full and proper use of those gifts in a divinely given framework based upon natural order of creation and appropriateness of function within a master plan. One cannot accept the Bible as authoritative while rejecting its authority concerning home and church order. One cannot negate truths concerning the structure of church and home, such as the image of the relationship between God and Israel and between Christ and the church, just to satisfy cultural whim or to accommodate higher plateaus of education and opportunity. One cannot lift outward manifestations, such as a man's prayer posture or a woman's head covering (1 Corinthians 11), and use them to ridicule or belittle the timeless directives given to protect and edify men and women within the Kingdom.
>
> Without doubt women did have a variety of positions of service, influence, and even leadership and teaching in the early church. The text of Scripture, however, bears witness that the functions they assumed were done with modesty and order (1 Corinthians 11:2-16; 14:40), and that they did not teach or exercise authority over men.[37]

III

Studies from Related Disciplines

15

Women in the History of the Church: Learned and Holy, but Not Pastors

William Weinrich

If it was once true that women were a neglected factor in church history, that imbalance is quickly being rectified. There is a spate of recent books on the history of women in the church that chronicle their institutions, their influence, and their contributions. As typical examples one may mention the three-volume collection of scholarly essays, *Women & Religion in America*, edited by Rosemary Ruether and Rosemary Keller, and the monograph *Holy Women in Twelfth-Century England*, by Sharon K. Elkins.[1] There is little doubt that such scholarship is making a significant contribution to our understanding of the church's past and, specifically, of the place and importance of women in it.

From within evangelical circles, the most important contribution to the history of women in the church is *Daughters of the Church*, by Ruth A. Tucker and Walter Liefeld.[2] This book offers historical vignettes about women who have in one way or another exercised active, public leadership roles in the centuries of the church's past. While striving to be objective, Tucker and Liefeld nevertheless exhibit a predilection for feminist interpretations of the evidence. Yet, that aside, they have amassed a considerable amount of material so that their book can nicely serve as a kind of women's "Who's Who in Church History."[3]

In a short article we cannot encompass the full breadth of women's contributions to the church's life and faith through the centuries. We do wish, however, briefly to indicate some of the ways women have contributed to the church as well as the unbroken teaching and practice of the church that the recognized teaching and sacramental ministry of the church is to be reserved for men.

I. "Daughters of the Church" in Word and Deed

A. Service of Prayer and Charity

It is, I suppose, impossible to escape the trap of describing the contributions of women, or of men, to the church primarily in terms of leadership and influence. After all, historical sources tend to focus on persons who did something or said something of extraordinary importance and therefore have been remembered and recorded. Yet we ought not be oblivious to one-sided activistic assumptions. The life of faith can be "active" in prayer, contemplation, and charity, and there have been myriad women, and men, who have excelled in these "silent works."

In fact, the early church had a distinct group of women called "widows" who were dedicated to prayer and intercession.[4] The *Apostolic Tradition* of Hippolytus (c. 210 A.D.) speaks of widows as "appointed for prayer" (chap. 11), and the *Didaskalia Apostolorum* (Syria, c. 230 A.D.) similarly speaks of the widows as having prayer as their primary duty: "for a widow should have no other care save to be praying for those who give and for the whole Church."[5] Other early Christian writers make clear that widows as a group held a place of considerable honor and dignity. Often they are listed along with the bishop, elders, and deacons (e.g., Origen, *Hom. in Luc.* 17), and Tertullian calls them an "order" and says that widows were assigned a place of honor within the assembled congregation (*On Modesty* 13.4).[6] Although prayer and intercession were the primary tasks of the widow, the *Didaskalia* indicates that by the third century the widows in some churches were engaged in charitable work. Such charity would consist in hospitality, working at wool to assist those in distress, and visiting and laying hands on the sick.[7] The *Apostolic Church Order* (Egypt, fourth century) evinces a similar two-fold division of prayer and service. Three widows are to be appointed: "Two of them are to dedicate themselves to prayer for all those in trial and to be ready for revelations. . . . The one is to be ready to serve, attending upon those women who are ill" (chap. 21).[8]

Especially in eastern Christianity (Syria, Chaldea, Persia), social mores that severely limited social access to women required the creation of a distinctly female diaconal ministry for the evangelization and care of women. The order of deaconess first takes concrete form in the *Didaskalia*.[9] The first duty of the deaconess was to assist the bishop in the baptism of women by anointing their bodies and ensuring that their nudity was not seen. Beyond this duty, the *Didaskalia* says that the deaconess had the responsibility of teaching and instructing the newly baptized women, apparently serving as a spiritual mother exhorting them to chastity. In addition, the deaconess was to visit Christian women in the homes of the heathen, to visit women who were ill, to bathe those women who were recovering from illness, and to minister to women in need.[10]

Subsequent ecclesiastical legislation in eastern Christianity reiterates these functions of the deaconess, but they add other responsibilities. The *Apostolic Constitutions* (Syria, fourth century) indicate that the deaconess supervised the seating and behavior of the female part of the worshiping community. She was a keeper of the doors to prevent men from mingling in the women's section of the church, and she served as intermediary between the male clergy and the women of the congregation (*Apost. Const.* 2.57ff.; 2.26; 3.15ff., 19).[11] The *Testament of Our Lord Jesus Christ* (Syria, fifth century), which gives to the widow what other legislation gives to the deaconess, does give the deaconess one duty, to bring communion to pregnant women unable to attend Easter mass (*Test.* II 20.7).

Such legislation reveals a feminine ministry of considerable significance and responsibility. Indeed, the importance of the deaconess is indicated by the fact that she was an ordained member of the clergy.[12] In other regions, where the separation of the sexes was not so strict, such a female diaconate was not required, but the title of deaconess was introduced as a degree of honor to enhance the dignity of a woman religious called upon to oversee a convent. Such a deaconess-abbess not only would administer the life of the convent and oversee its charitable activities, but also could perform certain liturgical services in the absence of a priest.[13]

Typical of this kind of deaconess was Olympias. Born into wealth in fourth-century Constantinople, she used her wealth to found a convent that included a hostel for priests as well as a number of hospitals. Her fame was enhanced by her friendship with John Chrysostom, with whom she corresponded while he was in exile.[14] According to Palladius, Olympias "catechized many women."[15] Perhaps another such deaconess-abbess was a certain Mary who is known only from her tombstone (found in Cappadocia): "according to the text of the apostle, raised children, practiced hospitality, washed the feet of the saints and distributed her bread to those in need."[16] In the East where convents frequently were located in isolated places and priests might not be present, a deaconess-abbess could perform certain liturgical services: distribute communion to the nuns, read the Gospels and the holy books in a worship assembly, etc.[17]

Although the West never had a developed female diaconate[18] and the deaconess disappeared also in the East by the twelfth century, the deaconess ideal of charity and teaching for the sick and poor experienced a significant renewal in the nineteenth century. Indeed, Kathleen Bliss would write that in terms of its subsequent influence, the revival of deaconess in Germany in the early nineteenth century was "the greatest event in the life of women in the Church since the Reformation."[19] In Germany the deaconess trained primarily as a nurse and only secondarily as a teacher. The model for this nurse-deaconess was the deaconess home at Kaiserwerth begun in the 1830s by a Lutheran pastor, Theodore Fliedner. Its focus was the care of the sick poor, the orphan, discharged women prisoners, and the mentally ill.[20] Other deaconess training schools on the Kaiserwerth model began all over Germany, such as that in Neuendettelsau in 1854, but the success of Fliedner's enterprise was measured in international terms. By the mid-nineteenth century, Kaiserwerth nurses and teachers were staffing hospitals and schools in America, Constantinople, Smyrna, Alexandria, Jerusalem, Bucharest, and Florence.[21]

A different type was the Anglican deaconess, whose training was mostly theological and pastoral. The inspiration for this female diaconate came from Elizabeth Ferard, who—with six other women—founded the London Deaconess Institution in 1862. Unlike the German deaconess, who worked largely independently of the church, the Anglican deaconess was responsible to the bishop of the diocese in which she worked. Well trained theologically, the Anglican deaconess worked in the parish or taught in school.[22]

In her 1952 report on the function and status of women in the member churches of the World Council of Churches, Kathleen Bliss listed in addition to the deaconess these types of women parish workers: (1) the trained lay parish worker whose duties might include Sunday school and youth work, Bible study, home visitation, hospital visiting, preparation for confirmation, and social case work; (2) parish helpers; (3) directors of religious education; (4) trained youth leaders; (5) church social workers; (6) Sunday school organizers.[23] Throughout the history of the church thousands of dedicated women have carried on the tradition of prayer, Christian charity, and care begun in the early church by the widow and deaconess. Happily, the stories of some of these women are being told. An example of this is a recent book by Barbara Misner, who chronicles the history and work of eight different groups of Catholic women religious in America between 1790 and 1850.[24] Among their "charitable exercises" she mentions especially the care of the sick, work during cholera epidemics, and care of orphans.

B. Service of Mind and Pen

Although the opportunity to exercise their literary and intellectual abilities could vary considerably given historical circumstances, Christian women nonetheless have bequeathed to the church a respectable literary and intellectual legacy. From the beginning, Christian women have been interested in the study of the Scripture and Christian theology. Already in the second century we hear of a young woman named Charito who was martyred with Justin Martyr, most probably because she was associated with Justin's school in Rome (*Martyrdom of Justin* 4). We know also that the lectures of Origen were well attended by women, the most famous being Mammaea, the mother of Emperor Alexander Severus, who had a military escort bring Origen to Antioch so she could test his understanding of the divine things (Eusebius, *Hist. eccl.* 6.21.3ff.). Yet, it was the great Roman matrons of the fourth century whose combination of the ascetic life and the study of the Scriptures and the Church Fathers became, through the influence of Jerome, the ideal image of women dedicated to the religious life. Two of these highborn ladies, Marcella and Paula, founded circles of ascetic women in their homes whose central purpose was the intensive study of the Bible. Jerome became their mentor and introduced them to the study of the Old Testament in Hebrew. Paula learned Hebrew so well that she could chant the Psalms without a trace of Latin accent. Marcella is called by Jerome his "task-mistress" because she incessantly demanded of him complete explanations of Hebrew words and phrases.[25] "With her probing mind Marcella wished to have all the obscurities, especially the linguistic ones, of the text cleared up; and although their meetings were frequent, she often insisted on his setting down his solutions on paper."[26] Paula and Jerome eventually established monastic communities for women and for men in Bethlehem.

Another Roman ascetic matron who conjoined learning and monastic life was Melania the Elder. She, along with Rufinus of Aquileia, formed monasteries in Jerusalem. Palladius speaks of Melania's deep learning:

> Being very learned and loving literature, she turned night into day perusing every writing of the ancient commentators, including the three million (lines) of Origen and the two hundred and fifty thousand of Gregory, Stephen, Pierius, Basil and other standard writers. Nor did she read them once only and casually, but she laboriously went through each book seven or eight times. (*Lausiac History* 55)

A similar circle of studious women gathered in Constantinople around Theodosia, the sister of Amphilocius of Iconium. Olympias, deaconess and friend of John Chrysostom, was educated in this circle.

In this context we should mention also Macrina, whose strength as a woman ascetic and a theological mind is glorified by her brother, Gregory of Nyssa, in his *Life of Macrina*. Gregory's *On the Soul and the Resurrection* is presented as a Socratic dialogue between Gregory and Macrina in which Macrina is depicted as the protagonist and teacher.

The tradition of learned monastic women continued into the medieval period. Lioba (eighth century), sister of St. Boniface, "had been trained from infancy in the rudiments of grammar and the study of the other liberal arts." "So great was her zeal for reading that she discontinued it only for prayer or for the refreshment of her body with food or sleep: the Scriptures were never out of her hands." "She read with attention all the books of the Old and New Testaments and learned by heart all the commandments of God. To these she added by way of completion the writings of the Church Fathers, the decrees of the Councils and the whole of ecclesiastical law."[27] Princes and bishops, we are told, "often discussed spiritual matters and ecclesiastical discipline with her" because of her knowledge of the Scripture and her prudent counsel.[28] The Venerable Bede (eighth century) reports that Abbess Hilda of Whitby required those under her direction "to make a thorough study of the Scriptures" and that she did this to such good effect "that many were found fitted for Holy Orders and the service of God's altar."[29] Indeed, five bishops trained at Whitby under Hilda's direction.

The love of reading the Scriptures and the Church Fathers led convents also to the copying of manuscripts. In c. 735, St. Boniface wrote to Abbess Eadburga requesting that she have a copy of the epistles of Peter made in letters of gold. "For many times by your useful gifts of books and vestments you have consoled and relieved me in my distress."[30] Among other things, these words of Boniface reveal how logistically important and supportive English convents were to the Anglo-Saxon missionaries on the Continent.

Although the volume of theological and spiritual literature composed by Christian women is less than that written by Christian men, throughout the history of the church there have been capable women who have been productive with the pen. We have mentioned already women like Marcella and Olympias, who engaged in correspondence with Jerome and John Chrysostom. Their letters, unfortunately, no longer exist. However, a not inconsiderable body of writing by Christian women is extant.

Perhaps the earliest writing we have from a Christian woman is the account of Vibia Perpetua of her sufferings and visions as a Christian martyr. Martyred under Septimius Severus (c. 202 A.D.), Perpetua's personal account was included by an unknown redactor in the *Martyrdom of Perpetua and Felicitas*, which became a model for later Acts of the martyrs, especially in North Africa.[31] One of the most fascinating documents of the early church is the travel diary of Egeria (late fourth century). Egeria, a noble woman from southern France, spent several years as a pilgrim in the East, traveling to Egypt, Palestine, Syria, and Asia Minor. Taking notes along the way, she later wrote them up as her *Travels*. It is clear from her narrative that Egeria was steeped in the classics of the church, and "her language often echoes that of the Bible or of formal prayer."[32] Her account contains some of the most helpful and informative detail we possess of early monasticism and liturgy.

A rather unique contribution to Christian literature is the Virgilian cento by Proba. Born a pagan in fourth-century Rome, Proba was educated in the classical writers of Latin literature, especially in Virgil, whom she especially loved. In the fourth century it was fashionable to write cento poetry. A cento is a poem produced by piecing together lines from the works of another poet, resulting in a new poem with a new theme. After becoming a Christian, Proba wrote a cento, borrowing from the works of Virgil, in which she intended to present the whole of the Biblical history.[33] About one-half of the 694 lines relates the beginning of the Old Testament (creation, fall, flood, the exodus), but then Proba moves to the gospel story of Jesus. Although Jerome harshly criticized it, and the Gelasian Decretal "On Books to be Received and not to be Received" (496 A.D.) placed it among the apocryphal writings, Proba's *Cento* became a popular school text in the Middle Ages.[34] Its frequent use is attested by the number of manuscripts containing it and the catalogues of monastic libraries.

Eudoxia is another Christian woman who produced a respectable literary output. The daughter of a pagan philosopher, Eudoxia was instructed "in every kind of learning" (Socrates, *Hist. eccl.* 7.21). She was later baptized a Christian and became the wife of Emperor Theodosius II (408-450). The greater part of her writing has been lost.[35] However, much of a cento drawn from the works of Homer is extant, as is the so-called *Martyrdom of St. Cyprian*. The *Martyrdom* tells of a certain Antiochian magician named Cyprian who fails in his effort to tempt a young Christian virgin and is rather himself led to become a Christian. The story ends with the martyr death of Cyprian and of the young maiden under the Emperor Diocletian.[36]

The tradition of literary Christian women continued into the Middle Ages. Abbess Hildegarde of Bingen (1098-1179) was an extremely influential visionary and prophetess whose correspondence included "four popes, two emperors, several kings and queens, dukes, counts, abbesses, the masters of the University of Paris, and prelates including Saint Bernard and Thomas à Becket."[37] Commanded by a heavenly voice to write down her visions, Hildegarde wrote two major works, *Know the Ways of the Lord* (*Scivias*) and *Book of Divine Works*. Both works belong to the medieval genre that "combined science, theology, and philosophy in a description of the universe, internal (the human body) and external (the earth and the heavens)."[38] Her works evince a familiarity with Augustine and Boethius as well as with contemporary scientific writers. Portions of her *Scivias* were read by Pope Eugenius III and St. Bernard and elicited from the pope a letter of praise and approval.[39] In addition to her two major works and her extensive correspondence, Hildegarde wrote lives of St. Disibod and St. Rupert, hymns, books on medicine and natural history, fifty allegorical homilies, and a morality play.

In Spain, the Catholic Reformation had a major female voice in St. Teresa of Avila (1515-1582). As a young woman she entered the Carmelite convent at Avila. There, later in life, she began to experience visions and ecstasies, and these in turn led her to propose a reform of the Carmelite order according to its original, more austere rule. Although there was powerful opposition to Teresa, support from Pope Paul IV and from King Philip II enabled her to establish many convents for her "discalced" (barefoot) Carmelite nuns. Of her most important writings, two are autobiographical. The *Life* describes her visions and discusses the centrality of prayer, and *Foundations* describe the establishment of her convents. Teresa wrote her most important mystical writings for her nuns. The *Way of Perfection* teaches the virtues of the religious (monastic) life and uses the Lord's Prayer as the vehicle for teaching prayer. The *Interior Castle* presents mature Teresian thought on the spiritual life. Growth in prayer enables a person to enter into deeper intimacy with God, who dwells in the soul or "interior castle" of the person. Some thirty-one poems and 458 letters of Teresa are extant.

Not all significant writing by women, however, issued from the religious orders. Marguerite Porete (c. 1300) was an important leader in the Beguine movement. The Beguines were pious laywomen who practiced poverty, chastity, and charity but belonged to no monastic order and took no vows. Their independence from church authority sometimes brought them into suspicion of heresy, and this was the fate of Marguerite as well. Nevertheless, her book, *The Mirror of Simple Souls*, enjoyed considerable popularity in France, Italy, and England.[40] Another such woman was Mme. Jeanne Guyon, who—with Fenelon—was a spiritual leader in the Quietist movement in late seventeenth-century France. Her literary production amounted to some forty books, including a multi-volume commentary on the Bible.

In the nineteenth century, hymn writing by women came into its own.[41] Anna Laetitia Barbauld (1743-1825) wrote *Hymns in Prose for Children*, which was popular for many years and was translated into French, Spanish, and Italian. "Praise to God, Immortal Praise" is one of her best-known hymns. Charlotte Elliot (1789-1871) wrote around 150 hymns, including "Just As I Am." Sarah Adams (1805-1848) wrote "Nearer, My God, to Thee." But in addition to her hymns Adams wrote also *Vivia Perpetua*, a dramatic poem about the conflict between paganism and Christianity, and *The Flock at the Fountain*, a catechism and hymnbook for children. Cecil Frances Alexander (1823-1895) wrote around four hundred hymns, mostly for children. Among her most beloved hymns are "There Is a Green Hill Far Away," "Once in Royal David's City," and "Jesus Calls Us O'er the Tumult." Frances R. Havergal (1836-1879), well trained in the classics and mistress of several foreign languages, composed over fifty hymns. These include "Take My Life and Let It Be," "I Am Trusting You, Lord Jesus," and "Now the Light Has Gone Away." From the twentieth century we may mention Dorothy F. Gurney (1858-1932), who wrote "O Perfect Love," and Julia C. Cory (1882-1963), who wrote "We Praise You, O God." And it is hard to imagine how anyone can top Fanny J. Crosby (1820-1915), author of over three thousand hymns, including the well-known "Pass Me Not, O Gentle Savior," "Rescue the Perishing," and "Sweet Hour of Prayer."

Two women have been significant as translators of hymns. The foremost translator of German hymnody has been Catherine Winkworth (1829-1878), whose renderings are the most widely used of any from the German language. Her translations are contained chiefly in her *Lyra Germanica: Hymns for the Sundays and Chief Festivals of the Church Year* and *Christian Singers of Germany*. Winkworth was sympathetic with any practical efforts for the benefit of women, and from that interest wrote the *Life of Pastor Fliedner*, about the chief architect of the German deaconess movement. Second only to Winkworth as a translator of German hymns is Jane Borthwick (1813-1897). Her *Hymns from the Land of Luther* contains "Be Still, My Soul" (itself composed by a woman, Catharina von Schlegel, b. 1697).

The literary contribution of women to the faith and life of the church has continued into our own century. Of great influence was Evelyn Underhill (1875-1941). Born into an agnostic home, she converted to Roman Catholicism through a religious experience that led her to investigate spiritual experience. Underhill became an internationally recognized authority in mystical theology, and her book *Mysticism* (1911) became a standard text in that discipline. In *Worship* (1936), Underhill studied the nature and forms of Christian worship. Eventually

Underhill was led into the Anglican communion by Baron Friedrich von Hügel, with whom she shared a long and fruitful spiritual relationship. Underhill herself served as a spiritual director for many, and she conducted many retreats in spirituality. Underhill's distinction is indicated by the fact that she was the first woman invited to give a series of theological lectures at Oxford University (1921). She became a Fellow of King's College, Cambridge, and received a Doctor of Divinity degree from Aberdeen.

Dorothy L. Sayers (1893-1957) is another example of an influential woman thinker and writer. The daughter of an Anglican minister, Sayers studied medieval literature at Oxford. While her initial success was as a writer of detective novels, her renown comes from her work as an expositor of orthodox Christian faith through translations, plays, and books. Her play *The Man Born to Be King* (written for BBC) was a dignified presentation of the life of Christ. Her background in medieval literature bore fruit in her translation of Dante's *Divine Comedy*, which is perhaps the most-used English translation of that classic. Sayers was a lay theologian of some merit. Her treatment of God and the creative process, *The Mind of the Maker* (1942), argues that the creative process is analogous to the government of the world by the Trinity wherein both the sovereignty of God and the freedom of man are preserved. Sayers was a prolific writer, whose works, both popular and scholarly, require their own book to catalogue.[42]

Women also have written popular and devotional literature. As a representative of this writing we mention Corrie ten Boom, whose popular books—*The Hiding Place*, *Tramp for the Lord*, *In My Father's House*—detail her courageous love to Jew and Christian during and after World War II.

C. Service of Spiritual Power and Administration

Christian women have exercised spiritual power in many ways. The early church praised the steadfastness of its female martyrs and saw in them examples of Christ's victory over Satan and death. Some of these female martyrs were clearly instrumental in eliciting faithfulness also from others. Blandina (d. 177 A.D.), apparently a slave girl, was hung on a post and seemed to hang in the form of a cross. Her earnest prayer "aroused great desire in those who were suffering," for with their eyes they saw in the person of Blandina "Him who was crucified for them" (Eusebius, *Hist. eccl.* 5.1.41). Similarly, Potamiaena (d.c. 210 A.D.), a pupil of Origen in Alexandria, is said to have influenced the soldier who led her to her death to become a Christian martyr himself, and "it is related that many others of those at Alexandria came over all at once to the word of Christ . . . because Potamiaena appeared to them in dreams and invited them" (Eusebius, *Hist. eccl.* 6.5.7). Writing around a century later, Eusebius says that Potamiaena "is to this day still loudly sung by her fellow-countrymen" (*Hist. eccl.* 6.5.1).[43]

Female prophetic figures have on occasion exercised considerable spiritual direction and influence in the church. In the second century there were a number of female prophetesses in the churches of Asia Minor. We hear of the daughters of Philip the evangelist, who were active at Hierapolis (Eusebius, *Hist. eccl.* 3.31.4; cf. Acts 21:8ff.), and of a certain Ammia who prophesied at Philadelphia (*Hist. eccl.* 5.17.2-5). The *Acts of Paul* mention Theonoe, a prophetess at Corinth.

Yet, it is especially in the Middle Ages that one finds powerful, prophetic women. We have already mentioned Hildegarde of Bingen, who wrote her visions down and whose advice and counsel were sought by popes and princes so that her influence was perhaps not excelled in the Middle Ages. Of similar influence was Catherine of Siena (1347-1380) who was instrumental in the return of Pope Gregory XI to Rome from the Papal "Babylonian Captivity" in Avignon. Indeed, Walter Nigg can write that "no man has yet dared to speak to a wearer of the tiara as radically and openly as she spoke to Pope Gregory XI in Avignon."[44] Another prophetess contemporary to Catherine was Bridget of Sweden (1302-1373). Her visions and revelations led her also to work for the reform of ecclesiastical abuse and for the return of the papacy to Rome.[45] Finally, we may mention Caterina Fieschi Adorno, known as Catherine of Genoa (1447-1510). Following an ecstatic conversion, she committed herself to personal austerity and to the care of the poor and diseased at the Genoese hospital. She was also a mystical writer of merit.

Especially in the religious orders the spiritual power of Christian women could be ordered, officially recognized, and institutionalized. Nowhere was this more strikingly the case than with the medieval abbesses, whose powers could approach those of a bishop. The double monasteries in the seventh- and eighth-century Merovingian and Anglo-Saxon kingdoms were normally governed by abbesses. These women were ordinarily from royal or noble lineage, and the monasteries that they administered were extensions of royal power and were means for maintaining the wealth of the family.[46] "They were masterful and formidable ladies and they did not forget that they belonged to a ruling caste."[47] As such, these noble abbesses ruled their monasteries, nuns and monks alike. They were builders of churches and monasteries and demonstrated administrative wisdom.[48] They attended royal councils and ecclesiastical synods. One may mention Abbess Hilda at the Council of Whitby (664 A.D.) and Abbess Aelffled at the Synod of Nidd (706 A.D.).[49]

Yet, it is doubtful whether one can speak meaningfully of the "egalitarianism of the double monasteries," as do Tucker and Liefeld.[50] Although nuns and monks shared common functions in the scriptoria, the schools, and perhaps the divine services, the early double monasteries were, as noted, extensions of a ruling family's power and as such governed by a member of the ruling family, the abbess, who "ruled the whole organization in the spirit of one accustomed to command."[51] Moreover, nuns and monks lived separately, and their work was divided, the nuns doing the less strenuous work and the monks the rougher work. Finally, the abbesses had no episcopal power and no power to excommunicate or to administer the sacraments (note the case of the abbess of Quedlinburg, below, p. 272).

The institution of the double monastery and female monasticism in general declined during the ninth and tenth centuries. However, in the eleventh and twelfth centuries there was a revival of the double monastery, nurtured by the piety of the *vita apostolica* (which emphasized poverty and personal holiness) and utopian enthusiasm. This renewal culminated in the founding of the Premonstratensian Order by Norbert of Xanten and of the Order of Fontevrault by Robert of Arbrissel. In these foundations, nuns lived with monks, with an abbess usually at the head. In the case of Fontevrault, this rule of the abbess may have reflected the view that men should be obedient to women as St. John was to the Virgin Mary.[52] Similar were the Gilbertines founded by Gilbert of Sempringham. The Gilbertines were founded on a millennial vision of the kingdom of God encompassing all, men and women.[53]

Although there were variations, the abbesses of such foundations could have considerable authority. They administered community property, awarded benefices and spiritual offices, held their own chapter meetings, gave the benediction to their own nuns, and received ofttimes an oath of obedience from all those in the community, both men and women. And this power was not only tolerated but defended by the church, even against offending clergy. For example, in 1222 Pope Honorius III upheld the authority of the abbess of Quedlinburg, who had suspended from office and benefice a number of canonesses and clergy because of disobedience and certain other offenses. The Pope wrote to the abbot of Michelstein that he was to force the offenders, by ecclesiastical censure if necessary, to obey and defer to proper authority.[54]

However, in these institutions where the equal status of women in the communal life of the monastery was unquestioned and even held high, ultimate spiritual jurisdiction was not accorded to the abbess. Even the Gilbertines had a male master general who was "the judge to whom all controversial or difficult decisions were referred" and who heard "any confessions that the prioresses had reserved for his special attention, especially first confessions and those considered grave."[55] Also, in the case involving Pope Honorius III it is clear that the abbess had no power to excommunicate. It is for that reason that the abbot of Michelstein was called in. He could censure with excommunication.[56] The abbess was not merely the equivalent of the abbot or bishop.

The tradition of spiritual influence by women in religious orders continued after the Reformation. We have mentioned already Teresa of Avila, who gained the support of Pope Paul IV and King Philip II for her reform of the Carmelite Order. Closer to our own time is Elizabeth Bayley Seton (d. 1821). Born into a distinguished colonial, Episcopalian family, Seton early evinced great concern for the sick and poor, earning the name of the Protestant Sister of Charity. When she converted to Roman Catholicism, she went to Baltimore and eventually to Emmitsburg, Maryland, where she founded the American Sisters of Charity. Under her leadership, orphanages were opened in Philadelphia and New York, and in 1818 Seton started the first free parochial school in America. For such schools she trained teachers and prepared textbooks. After her death, the Sisters of Charity opened the first Catholic hospital in the United States (St. Louis, 1828).

In the same tradition was Frances Xavier Cabrini (d. 1917), the first American citizen to be canonized (1946). Born and raised in Italy, she was sent to America to work among the thousands of Italian immigrants. In that work she founded orphanages, schools, and hospitals, not only in the United States but also in South America and Europe.

Nor was it always the activist and organizer who exerted spiritual influence. Not until after her death did Therese of Lisieux (d. 1897) become known through her autobiography. But then her simplicity and humility elicited such worldwide reaction that Rome hastened the process of canonization. Therese was sainted in 1925.

Within Protestantism too the influence of women of faith has been significant. Wibrandis Rosenblatt (d. 1564) was married successively to three major reformers (John Oecolampadius, Wolfgang Capito, Martin Bucer) and gave gracious, intelligent hospitality to their guests. Calvin was supported by two prominent noblewomen: Marguerite of Navarre (d. 1549), the sister of King Francis I, and Renee of Ferrara (d. 1575). Especially supportive of the Protestant cause in France was Jeanne d'Albret (d. 1572), the daughter of Marguerite and the mother of King Henry IV.[57]

However, given the Reformation emphasis on proclamation, not surprisingly Protestant women too were interested in preaching and outreach. A central figure in the evangelical revival of eighteenth-century England was Selina Hastings, Countess of Huntingdon (d. 1791). Through her status and wealth she was the benefactress of John Wesley, George Whitefield, and other itinerant Methodist preachers. She founded colleges for the training of evangelical, even dissident, preachers and built chapels for them to preach in. Selina was interested in Whitefield's mission to Georgia and organized the sending of preachers to the Indians there. In that she was "a forerunner of those Wesleyan women in the nineteenth century who would find their first public identity in the development of missionary societies and social reform organizations."[58]

Indeed, the influence and participation of women in mission work has been considerable. Tucker and Liefeld document some of the primary figures and contributions in this area.[59] Here we may refer to those numerous women who have supported missions through various mission societies such as the Baptist Missionary Union, the Woman's Foreign Missionary Society of the Methodist Church, and the Lutheran Women's Missionary League.

As individual examples of women in missions we may mention Clara Swain (d. 1910), who was the first female medical missionary to a non-Christian land (India), and Mary Slessor (d. 1915), who served for thirty-eight years as missionary in Calabar (modern Nigeria). There she built churches and schools, preached, taught, and even served as a magistrate on behalf of the government.

II. "It is Not Given to Women to Teach": The Central Tradition

By selected example we have illustrated the broad and respected contributions that Christian women have made to the church throughout its history. These contributions have been intellectual, diaconal, and evangelical, and have carried with them spiritual power and recognized authority. Many women have achieved sainthood, and some have received titles of highest honor. Within Eastern Orthodoxy a number of women—Mary Magdalene, Thekla, Helena, and Nina, missionary to the Georgians—are regarded as "equal to the apostles," and Catherine of Siena and Teresa of Avila were named "doctors of the church" by Pope Paul VI.

In fact, women have done almost everything men have, and have done it just as well. The significant exception to that generalization is that, until the very recent past, the "office" of teaching and of the sacramental ministry, with the jurisdictional powers this implies, has been reserved for men. Of course, there have been historical anomalies, and there have been sects and peripheral groups that accepted women preachers who may also have offered the eucharist.[60] Yet, in its broad central tradition and practice, the church—East and West and in a multiplicity of cultural and social settings—has consistently maintained that to men alone is it given to be pastors and sacramental ministers.

Tertullian (second century) may be taken as a representative voice of this viewpoint: "It is not permitted to a woman to speak in church. Neither may she teach, baptize, offer, nor claim for herself any function proper to a man, least of all the sacerdotal office" (*On the Veiling of Virgins* 9.1). Photius, ninth-century

Patriarch of Constantinople, echoes the same sentiment for Eastern Christendom: "A woman does not become a priestess" (*Nomocanon* 1.37). This general prohibition did not rest on some idea of a natural inferiority of women to men in intellect or spiritual stature. John Chrysostom writes that "in virtue women are often enough the instructors of men; while the latter wander about like jackdaws in dust and smoke, the former soar like eagles into higher spheres" (*Epistle to Ephesians*, Hom. 13.4). Commenting on Priscilla's teaching of Apollos in view of 1 Timothy 2:12, Chrysostom says that "Paul does not exclude a woman's superiority, even when it involves teaching," when the man is an unbeliever and in error (*Greet Priscilla and Aquila* 3).[61] We have already noted Christian women whose counsel, advice, and intellectual gifts were valued by men. To those may be added the three "ammas" or "mothers" (Theodora, Sarah, Synkletika) whose sayings are included in the Eastern church's *Geronikon* ("Sayings of the Desert Fathers").[62]

Nor does the evidence suggest that the church's exclusion of women from the preaching and teaching "office" was an unevangelical accommodation to social and cultural pressures. In fact, the social and cultural context of Christianity at times favored the church's admitting women to the teaching "office." In first- and second-century Asia Minor, for example, the social position of women was well developed. There were female physicians, and Ephesus had its female philosophers among the Stoics, Epicureans, and Pythagoreans, who were known to teach, perhaps publicly. Likewise, female leadership and priesthood were well known in the local religious cults (Cybele, Isis, Demeter, Artemis).[63]

The first clear patristic opposition to female teachers and ministers is in reaction to Gnostic groups that often regarded women as the special bearers of revelation.[64] In their denial of the creation, the Gnostics refused to take seriously any fleshly, creaturely differences, so that Tertullian complains that among them no distinctions are made between catechumens and believers, women and men, neophyte and experienced faithful, layman and priest. In his rejection of such Gnostic egalitarianism, Tertullian writes of their women: "how wanton they are! For they are bold enough to teach, to dispute, to enact exorcisms, to undertake cures, it may be even to baptize" (*Prescription Against Heretics* 41.5). It is evident that Tertullian believes the Gnostics are engaging in a practice contrary to the standing practice of the church. Otherwise his point that in creed and practice the Gnostics are contrary to the church would lose all force. It is equally evident that a distinction of functions between man and woman in the church relates in some way to actual distinctions in creation. Against the Gnostic, to maintain a distinction of male and female function was to confess a creation theology that respected the concrete, fleshly differences between man and woman.[65]

Montanism was also important in early patristic prohibitions of women teaching and baptizing in the church. Montanism was an outburst of Christian apocalypticism that taught that a new outpouring of the prophetic Spirit had begun the last days. With Montanus and two prophetesses, Prisca and Maximilla, as its leaders, Montanism held to a spiritual egalitarianism based on the common outpouring of the end-time, prophetic Spirit. Montanism appears then to have granted women a more extensive participation in the worship services. Yet, even Montanism seems generally to have respected functional distinctions in the church. The general prohibition by Tertullian, "it is not permitted to a woman to speak in Church" (*Veiling of Virgins* 9.1), was written within his Montanist period. The account of a Montanist woman who had visions "amidst the sacred rites of the Lord's day in the church" and who "after the people are dismissed at the conclusion of the sacred services" reports her visions to the church's leaders illustrates how Montanist prophecy and Tertullian's prohibition coexisted (Tertullian, *On the Soul* 9).

The basic question raised by Montanism was whether the church understood itself to be essentially apostolic or essentially prophetic. The apostle, witness to the resurrection and confined to the first generation of the church, represented the finality of the revelation of the Word that happened once in history. The prophet, who rises again and again, does not and cannot represent Christ as final truth. When the prophet asserts his independence and autonomy, the finality of the revelation in Christ is threatened. The prophetic must be subordinated to the apostolic. Not surprisingly, therefore, the Fathers appeal to Pauline (apostolic) statements against women speaking in church as well as to the practice of Christ and the completed canonical histories of the Old and New Testaments.

Commenting on 1 Corinthians 14:34-35, Origen (third century) criticizes the Montanist prophetesses. Apparently the Montanists justified their prophetesses by an appeal to the four prophet daughters of Philip and to Old Testament prophetesses. To this Origen replies: "If the daughters of Philip prophesied, at least they did not speak in the assemblies; for we do not find this fact in the Acts of the Apostles." Deborah, Miriam, and Huldah were prophetesses. Yet, "there is no evidence that Deborah delivered speeches to the people, as did Jeremias and Isaias." Miriam and Huldah also did not speak to the people. Similarly, in the Gospel the prophetess Anna "did not speak publicly." The apostolic statements in 1 Corinthians 14:34 and 1 Timothy 2:12 correspond to the Biblical history.[66]

Epiphanius provides similar argumentation against two fourth-century "feminine" movements. The "Quintillians," an aberrant Montanist group, appealed to Eve, who had eaten of the tree of knowledge, as prototype for a female clergy. Epiphanius explicitly says that they had women bishops and women presbyters and that they justified this on the basis of Galatians 3:28. To counter the appeal to Eve, Epiphanius quotes Genesis 3:16 and 1 Timothy 2:14 ("Adam was not deceived, but Eve was first to be deceived") along with 1 Timothy 2:12 and 1 Corinthians 11:8 (*Against the Heresies* 49.1-3). The Collyridians venerated Mary as a virtual goddess, and women in the group served as priests in offering up a sacrifice of bread rolls in her name. Epiphanius attacks the women's claim to exercise the sacerdotal ministry: "Never from the beginning of the world has a woman served God as priest." In litany fashion Epiphanius runs through the Old and New Testaments pointing out that God's priests were always men but never a woman. Mary herself, the mother of the all-ruling Son of God, was not entrusted to baptize, that being given to John (*Against the Heresies* 78-79). Similar appeals to the Biblical history and to the example of Christ are made by the *Didaskalia* (Connolly, 133, 142), the *Apostolic Constitutions* (3.6, 9), and the *Apostolic Church Order* (24-28).

Fourth-century Latin opposition to women teaching in the church was probably occasioned by a Montanist-like revival named "Priscillianism." The sect was popular with women, and to give them an official function it seems to have imported from the East the title of "deaconess," which until then was not known in the West. In their commentaries on Paul, "Ambrosiaster" and Pelagius both express the view that it is contrary to the order of nature and against apostolic injunction for women to speak in an assembly of men. Ambrosiaster is especially harsh in his attitude.[67] In view of Priscillianism church councils also condemned the public teaching by women and reiterated the apostolic prohibition against women speaking in the church. The Council of Saragossa (380 A.D.) warned Catholic women not to attend Priscillian meetings where women might give readings and teach. The Council of Nimes (396 A.D.), reacting to reports that certain ones were admitting women to the "Levitical ministry," rejects such a practice as an innovation "contrary to apostolic discipline" and not permitted by the ecclesiastical rule.[68]

There were occasional instances into the early Middle Ages when women did serve at the altar. Invariably this practice received stiff ecclesiastical censure. To bishops in southern Italy and Sicily, Pope Gelasius I "with vexation" speaks of reports of women who "serve at holy altars": "everything that is entrusted exclusively to the service of men is performed by the sex that has no right to do so" (*Letter* 11.26). In the early sixth century, two priests in Brittany allowed women to assist them in the celebration and distribution of the Lord's Supper. This elicited a letter from three Gallic bishops. The distribution of the blood of Christ to the people by women was "a novelty, and unheard-of superstition."[69] In the early ninth century, several bishops wrote to Louis the Pious that "contrary to divine law and canonical directive, women enter the sanctuary, handle the consecrated vessels without fear, pass clerical vestments to the priests, and . . . distribute the Body and Blood of the Lord to the people." They had tried to take measures to prevent such liberties. "It is most astonishing that this practice, which is forbidden in the Christian religion, could have crept in from somewhere; . . . undoubtedly it took hold through the carelessness and negligence of some bishops."[70] While the details of what was prohibited and allowed to women might vary, "there was complete constancy regarding the bans on ministering and especially . . . on 'female ministers of Communion.'"[71]

It is perhaps necessary to mention the fifth- and sixth-century Gallic councils, for they have been cited recently as proof that there was a gradual suppression of ordained female ministry in the early Middle Ages. The Council of Orange (441 A.D.) ruled: "Deaconesses are absolutely not to be ordained; and if there are still any of them, let them bow their head under the benediction which is given to the congregation." The subsequent councils of Epaon (517 A.D.) and Orleans (533 A.D.) finally prohibited the consecration of women to the diaconate. Suzanne Wemple claims these councils were "a battle against female ministers." Of the Council of Orange she writes: "We do know that, by 441, the Gallican church had ordained deaconesses who regarded themselves as equals to the male clergy. . . . The bishops assembled at Orange were apparently determined to abolish the feminine diaconate, to humiliate the women who had already been ordained, and to assert the exclusivity of male authority in the church."[72] Tucker and Liefeld give a similar judgment. Quoting the "commonly used" ordination prayer for the deaconess in the *Apostolic Constitutions* (8.20), they comment: "By the sixth century, such consecrations were becoming less and less common in the Western church. . . . church councils during the sixth century gradually lowered the status of these women until the position of deaconess was virtually nonexistent."[73]

The fact is that "such consecrations" were never common, indeed never existed in the West. Also, to my knowledge the "commonly used" prayer of the *Apostolic Constitutions* was used nowhere else than in the provenance of the

Constitutions themselves, that is, in eastern Syria. The mixing of eastern and western evidence by Tucker and Liefeld produces quite a false historical reconstruction. Detailed study of the deaconess has amply shown that "there is no evidence that such deaconesses like those in the *Apostolic Constitutions* with social and limited liturgical duties ever existed in the West.[74] Ambrosiaster and Pelagius reveal no knowledge of deaconesses in the West. The language of the councils itself indicates that the practices they opposed were unfamiliar and uncommon. The Council of Nimes acts on a report and does not even know the location where the abuse is taking place ("one knows not where"). The Council of Orange wonders "if there are still any" of the ordained deaconesses. They also speak of innovation and novelty. The claim of Wemple that between 395 and 441 the ordination of deaconesses had become "common practice in the churches of Gaul" is wholly overdone.[75] The title *deaconess* appears to have been an import from the East. The reality behind the title in the West was the widow who wished to be consecrated to the ascetic life.[76]

In sum, there never was recognized ordained female ministry in the West (or East) that involved teaching in the assembly and ministering at the altar.

The canonical regulations that govern church life and circumscribe what is permissible are consistent throughout the Middle Ages in prohibiting women from teaching in the assembly and performing priestly and episcopal functions. The *Statuta Ecclesiae antiqua* of Gennadius of Marseilles (c. 480 A.D.), which adapts eastern practice for western life, allows the nuns and widows to teach women who are to be baptized ("to teach clearly and with exactitude unlearned women from the country"), but it also repeats the general prohibitions: "a woman, however learned and holy, may not presume to teach men in the assembly" (*in conventu*); and, "a woman may not presume to baptize." Again and again this text is cited in bans on teaching. Likewise, the ban of Pope Innocent III (thirteenth century) on the preaching and hearing of confession by powerful abbesses is a commonplace in canon law: "No matter whether the most blessed Virgin Mary stands higher, and is also more illustrious, than all the apostles together, it was still not to her, but to them, that the Lord entrusted the keys to the Kingdom of heaven."[77] The *Corpus Iuris Canonici*, the present-day book of canon law in the Roman Catholic Church, is the final recipient of the long tradition that has its origin in Paul: "Only a baptized man validly receives sacred ordination" (canon 1024).

Sometimes it is asserted that the canonical prohibitions were motivated by misogyny and false evaluations of women's intellectual and moral capacities. Misogynous remarks and opinions of inferiority do exist. Yet, Manfred Hauke correctly notes that the language of Gennadius' *Statuta*—"however learned and holy"—and of Innocent III—whether Mary "stands higher than all the apostles"—indicates that ultimately and officially considerations of intellect and sanctity were not determinative. Determinative were the Biblical history, the example of Jesus, and the apostolic injunctions.[78]

Within Protestantism, the major Reformation and post-Reformation leaders assumed without question the practice of reserving the office of pastor and sacramental minister to men. Their strong "Scripture alone" principle led them, however, to rely almost exclusively on actual apostolic prohibition. Appeal to the Biblical history and to the example of Jesus is correspondingly less frequent.

Against Rome's use of 1 Corinthians 14:34 to argue the existence of a special priesthood not common to all Christians, Martin Luther (d. 1547) consistently maintained a priesthood of all believers (especially on the basis of 1 Peter 2:9). This common priesthood possesses the right and power to exercise all "priestly offices" (teach, preach, baptize, administer the Eucharist, bind and loose sin, pray for others, sacrifice, judge doctrine and spirits).[79] Yet, Luther habitually combines 1 Corinthians 14:34 with Genesis 3:16 to assert that women are excluded from the public exercise of the common priesthood. In view of the "ordinance and creation of God" that women are subject to their husbands, Paul forbade women "to preach in the congregation where men are present who are skilled in speaking, so that respect and discipline may be maintained."[80] However, if no man is present to preach, then "it would be necessary for the women to preach."[81] For Luther, the apostolic prohibition of 1 Corinthians 14:34 was determinative.

John Calvin (d. 1564) also understood Paul's prohibitions as excluding women from speaking in an "ordinary service or where there is a Church in a regularly constituted state." The office of teaching is "a superiority in the Church," and therefore it is inconsistent that a woman, who is under subjection, should preside over the entire body.[82] Commenting on 1 Corinthians 14:34, Calvin writes: "It is therefore an argument from things inconsistent—If the woman is under subjection, she is, consequently, prohibited from authority to teach in public."[83] In his commentary on 1 Timothy, Calvin writes similarly: Paul "excludes [women] from the office of teaching, which God has committed to men only."[84] Although Calvin recognizes that some women in the Old Testament were supernaturally called by the Spirit to govern the people, "extraordinary acts done by God do not overturn the ordinary rules of government, by which he intended that we should be bound."[85]

The only significant group that denied the continuing applicability of Paul's prohibitions was the Society of Friends (Quakers). Their strong emphasis on the interiority of the Spirit militated against any distinctions in church life. George Fox (d. 1671), founder of the Quakers, and especially Margaret Fell (d. 1702) argued that the authority of the indwelling Spirit gave women equal right and obligation to speak, even in public assemblies.

John Wesley (d. 1791) repeatedly attempted to distinguish Quaker views and practices from those of Methodism, in which women also at times spoke in public. Wesley's own view was conservative. The ordinary rule of discipline, based on 1 Corinthians 14:34, was that women should be in subjection "to the man whose proper office it is to lead and to instruct the congregation."[86] Nonetheless, Wesley claimed that "an extraordinary impulse of the Spirit" suspends the apostolic regulation and allows a woman to speak in public.[87] Yet, the Methodists are not like the Quakers, who "flatly deny the rule, although it stands clearly in the Bible." The Methodists, however, "allow the rule; only we believe it admits of some exceptions." Indeed, Wesley regarded Methodism itself to be "an extraordinary dispensation" of divine providence, so that he did not wonder "if several things occur therein which do not fall under the ordinary rules of discipline."[88]

Other Reformation and post-Reformation groups largely concurred with the views of Luther, Calvin, and Wesley. The Anabaptists, the Anglicans, the Puritans, and the Separatists all prohibited women from the public ministry of preaching and teaching. While groups that emphasized religious experience and interior calling did allow women to assume (more or less restricted) public preaching, not until the nineteenth century did women begin to make significant strides toward a ready acceptance of any public ministry. It has been only in the last half of the twentieth century that the major Protestant church bodies have begun to accept women as regular preachers and pastors.

III. Conclusion

We have emphasized the practice and argument of the patristic and medieval periods of the church's history. It was during these centuries that patterns of conduct and ecclesial behavior were developed and solidified. The evidence shows that the Pauline statements against women speaking in the church were consistently upheld. Contrary practices were regarded as innovative and opposed to the truth and were, by ecclesiastical discipline and censure, excluded from the church. The practice of the early and medieval church was followed without question by the churches of the Reformation, both Reformed and Lutheran, and by virtually all other communions until the most recent past. Although they are favorable to the full participation of women in all functions of the church, Tucker and Liefeld note that even women who did seek a position of prominence rarely evinced "feminist impulse" but rather were "very hesitant to challenge the 'rightful' leadership of men."[89] That observation as much as anything testifies to the pervasive and universal faithfulness of the church to the Biblical and apostolic word throughout its history. The utter paucity of instances adduced where women were given or took the function of public preaching and teaching confirms it.

16

The Biological Basis for Gender-Specific Behavior

Gregg Johnson

I recall one Saturday afternoon telling my wife that I would occupy the children in the front yard so she could get some things done in the house. We live on a relatively busy street. Our four children were all under six years old at the time. I became immersed in the task of teaching Nicholas to ride his two-wheeler and was unaware that two-year-old Neil was toddling out into the street. Lois, glancing out the window, saw his intentions and arrived in time to intercept him and to offer me some helpful parenting advice.

On another occasion, we took Nate for his one-year-old picture. My wife and I were behind the camera. Nate was positioned on a stool on a countertop. The photographer began thrusting a fuzzy puppet on a stick toward Nate to get him to smile. On one final thrust of the toy, Nate suddenly lunged forward to grab it and fell headlong over the countertop into my wife's hands. We both had been standing about ten feet from the counter. It occurred to me that Lois initiated her dash to the counter well before there was any indication to me that Nate would respond in this way.

Such observations by numerous amazed fathers have perhaps led to the idea of maternal instinct and women's intuition. One cannot draw conclusions from these examples, but they provide a framework from which to ask the historically debated nature-nurture questions. Are there differences in male and female behavior patterns? If there are measurable differences, to what degree are they culturally or biologically based? The current scene suggests that such differences are largely culturally imposed, that such gender norms restrict our full potential, and that we should actively eliminate all cultural elements that continue to foster traditional attitudes that the sexes might be differentially gifted. Let us explore the evidence.

In our search for a Biblically informed and rational perspective on sex roles and gender identity, I would argue for including a search of our current biological understandings of sexual dimorphism. I am convinced that God has both anticipated and ordained our search for wisdom through the study of nature (Romans 1:20; Psalm 104:24). David identifies two sources of truth in Psalm 19 as: (1) evidence from the created world, and (2) declarations from God's Word. God bids Adam to "have dominion over the earth," which embodies the concepts not only of having control over but also of knowing, protecting, and exercising stewardship over. Scripture warns of the dangers in the pursuit of human wisdom and tendencies to rely on our own understandings to the exclusion of the simple truths of His Word (Proverbs 3:5-6; 1 Corinthians 1:19-31; 8:1). Yet we will be held accountable for the knowledge we have received from both Scripture and nature. It is important, then, to seek a balanced and concerted wisdom from each of these sources of truth. I am also convinced that if we seek wisdom in prayerful submission to God's leading we will not find truths in nature that directly contradict the Word of God. Yet we must expect that revelations through our study of nature may give us new perspective and insight into our understanding of Scripture and its Author. As God is the author of neither temptation nor confusion (James 1:13; 1 Corinthians 14:33), I continue to press the search for truth and wisdom through science.

Although our primary evidence in this chapter will come from biological studies, it is valuable to note a landmark review of psychological literature on the subject of gender differences. Maccoby and Jacklin made a rather complete survey of the literature to determine whether there was consistent experimental support for any of the traditional gender stereotypes. They found that the majority of studies revealed that males scored higher in levels of aggressiveness, dominance, self-confidence, and activity level. Females scored higher on verbal ability, compliance, nurturance, and empathy scales.[1] Women tend to socialize more intimately with a few friends. Men are more apt to form larger groups.

My purpose in this chapter is to demonstrate that these differences are not only real but likely have their roots in our unique biology as males and females. Furthermore, these differences are present at birth (and even before) and are amplified according to individual hormonal and genetic dictates. We are differently gifted as male and female not only in anatomy and physiology but also in behavior. It is a marvelous God-given pattern that enhances pair bonding, dual parenting, and extensive division of labor, characteristic not only of humans but of many of the higher social animals.

A couple of cautions are warranted here. First, some of the evidence presented here comes from animal studies of the brain and behavioral correlates. We must be cautious when extrapolating such data to human beings. However, when data on many different animals reveals universal characteristics or recognizable trends, such data can be very instructive in understanding our own biology. Indeed, drug testing, surgical procedures, and many other medical advances are first perfected on animals and then the technology is transferred to humans. This is possible since higher animal systems function similarly to those of humans. We have taken a strange position in the past that while the other nine systems function very similarly in higher animals and humans, we can expect no such parallels in the nervous system. A second caution is that we are speaking of averages and patterns that cannot be completely universalized. It is always possible to discover individual uniquenesses and variations that deviate markedly from the norm. There are certainly females who are more aggressive than the average male or males who are more nurturant than the average female. The data simply reflect trends and average differences seen between the sexes taken as groups.

Although some studies have come to different conclusions than those represented in this chapter,[2] most of the support for those conclusions appears to be based on psychological survey and test data that are more suspect than those underlying this survey because they depend on more uncontrollable variables. The following data and evidence seem compelling and tip the balance in this controversial issue in favor of a divinely ordained and biologically rooted division of gifts between the sexes.

The data and evidence for this view are arranged under the following subheadings: (1) ethological observations on sex, (2) sex differences in non-nervous-system physiology, (3) sex differences in the peripheral nervous system, (4) sex differences in the hind brain and limbic system, (5) sex differences in the cerebrum, (6) sex differences evident at birth, and (7) sex differences in stress management.

I. Ethological Observations on Sex

Ethologists are students of animal and human behavior who draw generalizations regarding social behavior across animal and human groups. They point out that among most higher social mammals studied, males are more aggressive than females and take dominant leadership roles in social groups. Males are more territorial, competing and sparring with other males for control of resources, societies, and, in particular, control of access to reproductive females.[3]

Among most mammals, males tend to build hierarchical social order. They are more reactive and less cautious. They are involved in breaking up squabbles of lesser ranking males, females, and juveniles. They set directions and courses of action for the group as a whole.[4] Females are more involved in parenting as a result of the close dependence of infants on maternal milk supply. Females of most groups studied are not as driven by competitive, territorial or hierarchical urges. They tend to socialize more horizontally and equally with other females. They are cautious in mating, solicitous particularly of males that are the most dominant and control the most resources. Females are more concerned with parenting, nurturing, and maintaining pair bonds with mates through grooming or care-giving behaviors. They tend in their broader social contacts to be less confrontive and combative and more interested in building and maintaining social bonds. They are peacemakers and conformists to group expectations.[5]

Anthropologists find similar kinds of universal sex-specific behaviors among human cultures. Of two hundred fifty cultures studied, males dominate in almost all. Males are almost always the rule makers, hunters, builders, fashioners of weapons, workers in metal, wood, or stone. Women are primary care givers and most involved in child rearing. Their activities center on maintenance and care of home and family. They are more often involved in making pottery, baskets, clothes, blankets, etc. They gather food, preserve and prepare food, obtain and carry firewood and water. They collect and grind grain.[6] The fact that these universals transcend divergent animal groups and cultures suggest that there must be more than a cultural basis for these sex differences. The data point to biological predeterminants of gender-related behavior. Indeed, as we survey the biology of mammals and humans in particular, we find sex-related differences in all of the organ systems, including the brain and nervous system.

II. Sex Differences in Non-nervous System Physiology

The conventional view on sex role development presented in psychosocial literature through the 1960s to 1980s has been that, apart from obvious morphological and physiological differences essential for reproduction, men and women are essentially the same in their potentials and capacities. Any behavioral differences that can be measured have been viewed as reflections of culturally imposed norms.

The biological profiles of males and females, however, reveal myriad basic physiological differences, many of which shape behavior. The basal metabolic rate is about 6 percent higher in adolescent boys than girls and increases to about 10 percent higher after puberty. During metabolism, girls convert more energy into stored fat, while boys convert more energy to muscle and expendable circulating reserves. At age eighteen, girls have almost twice the body fat (about 33 percent) of boys. Boys at age eighteen have about 50 percent more muscle mass than girls, particularly in the upper body. Males, on the average, have denser, stronger bones, tendons, and ligaments, which allow for heavier work.[7] Differences in metabolism and muscular ability likely give males a push in this more energetic direction.

Males have more sweat glands and can dissipate heat faster than females. Women have a thicker layer of subcutaneous fat that acts as insulation and energy reserve. Consequently, they can withstand cold better and have better energy supply for activities requiring extraordinary endurance. Women have raised their performance in long-distance swimming, running, and other endurance sports until it is similar to that of males, which their physiology favors. But males retain a significant advantage in sports that require short bursts of strength, such as sprints.

Men, on the average, have larger windpipes and branching bronchi and 30 percent greater lung capacity taken as a percent of their respective body weights. Men also have relatively larger hearts and can pump a larger volume of blood. Males have 10 percent higher red blood cell counts, higher hemoglobin readings, and consequently higher oxygen-carrying capacity. They have higher circulating clotting factors including vitamin K, prothrombin, and platelets.[8] Their rapid clotting and higher basal metabolic rate leads to more rapid healing of wounds and bruises. Males have fewer sensory nerve endings in the skin and higher peripheral pain tolerance. This combination of traits may aid in encouraging males to be more active and to be risk takers.

Women, on the average, have more stored and circulating white blood cells. They have more granulocytes and B and T lymphocytes for fighting infection. They produce more antibodies faster and thus have a more rapid and effective response to infectious invaders. They will develop fewer infectious diseases and succumb to them for shorter periods of time.[9] Ethologists argue that for females caring for multiple offspring and interacting with other females and their offspring in social groups, where communicable diseases can spread rapidly, this is a particularly advantageous trait. Males who have been historically less involved in these activities but more involved in hunting, protection, building, war, etc., are more in need of a good wound-healing system.[10]

The male digestive system functions at a higher pace. They have larger teeth, more salivary glands, more active gastric glands of the stomach. They are therefore more subject to ulcers. Their metabolic machinery converts more food to circulating energy and building blocks and less to fat. Their circulating blood sugar, cholesterol, and amino acids are higher. They eat more meat and protein and assimilate food faster. This perhaps accommodates the larger muscle mass that must be maintained. This is particularly true of young men still developing muscle. Males, however, often continue the protein and fat-rich diets well after the body-building years and years of high activity. The high levels of cholesterol and triglycerides then collect in blood vessel plaque, causing hardening of arteries and constriction of vessels. As a result, males are more at risk of heart attacks, strokes, hypertension, and related ailments such as headaches, ringing ears, and dizziness.

Women, whose metabolism favors fat storage, have more trouble eating enough to maintain their needed vitamin and amino acid requirements without putting on fat as well. There seems to be some relationship between a certain minimum level of body fat and fertility in women. Women athletes, body builders, or those who are particularly thin have higher levels of infertility.[11] It may be that a certain level of fat sufficient to carry the developing fetus and provide milk after birth is necessary before pregnancy will occur. This would be a logical, God-given feminine provision to prevent pregnancies during periods of unstable food supply or even famine. Today's emphasis on being thin may contribute to the concurrent high level of female infertility.

While both sexes have androgens and estrogens, these sex hormones are found in quite different concentrations in the two sexes. Males begin producing gonadal testosterone at about the sixth or seventh week of gestation. This has an immediate effect on all of the organ systems, such that heart rate, respiratory rate, red blood cell counts, and brain structure are already sexually divergent at birth. The male testosterone level is two to three times that of the female until puberty, at which time it becomes, on the average, fifteen times higher than that of a female. Females produce about twice the estrogen of males prior to puberty and eight to ten times the estrogen after puberty. Female estrogen varies considerably depending on the time of the menstrual cycle.[12]

All of the sexually dimorphic physiological traits mentioned above seem to be rather directly correlated with the level and ratio of these two sex hormones. In castrated males or estrogen-treated males, the red blood cell count, cholesterol level, clotting factors, basal metabolic rate, and many other factors decrease sharply to levels more like females. Likewise, in males with Klinefelter's syndrome (who have an extra X chromosome) and those with gonadal dysgenesis, where testosterone levels are more intermediate between males and females, physiological traits are intermediate. Such males with lower testosterone share females' longer life expectancies and better verbal than math scores on aptitude tests.[13] These data argue strongly for a biological rather than any cultural explanation for these sex differences.

Sex differences present in all the organ systems across various mammalian species go far beyond the superficial anatomical characteristics necessary for reproduction. These differences are direct responses to the levels of circulating hormones, which differ significantly between the sexes. It is difficult to avoid the conclusion that these physiological differences predispose males and females to certain behavioral and aptitude leanings. The debate heats up considerably when we suggest that there are fundamental differences in the structure and function of the brain and nervous system that predispose the sexes to certain behaviors and capacities. Nevertheless, it would be very strange to find hormones affecting all other systems and not the nervous system.

III. Sex Differences in the Peripheral Nervous System

The ability to discriminate two simultaneous pin pricks placed at close proximity on the skin is called the two-point discrimination test. Using this type of test, researchers find that women, on the average, have a more acute sense of touch. Females have finer body hair, on the average, which is more easily moved and results in finer sense perception. Females, likewise, have more acute senses of hearing, smell, and taste.[14] It has been argued that females are generally more perceptive and aware of context. Perhaps their more responsive sensory system allows them to monitor their environment more completely and with more discrimination. Such a system would give women an advantage in child care and social interaction. They would be able to pick up subtle environmental cues, such as a baby's cry or cough, or telltale odors or sounds that might escape the less discriminating male system.

There have been reports that females have finer discrimination of color, particularly in the red end of the spectrum, can tolerate brighter lights, and see better in dim light, while men can read finer print and are better at night vision.[15] Again, advantages in color discrimination might aid females in detecting rashes or slight flushes in infants and children that might indicate fever or diseases. They might be better able to detect slight facial flushing of peers or spouse, which may indicate anger or other emotional upset. Studies suggest that females are better able to read the emotional content of faces such as anger, sadness, or fear.[16] These more acute senses may give females a general advantage in social interactions. If males have better ability to read fine print or in general discriminate detail on which they are focusing, it may have been an advantage while hunting, tracking, or in other historically male pursuits requiring good hand-eye coordination.

The preceding arguments are an attempt to identify the original purpose for such differing allocated capacities given our heritage as hunters or agrarian people. At the core of our survival is the ability to find food and reproduce, roles that were associated with men and women respectively in Genesis 3:16-19. Females have been concerned more heavily with infant care due to breast feeding, and males with provision of food. In support of this basic division of labor, God has given each sex special gifts to carry out its task. This is not to argue that these gifts should only find expression in child rearing in the case of women or providing and protecting in the case of men. Yet it is out of this God-given design that these gifts arose and flourished. While today's technology may have reduced the need for such rigid division of labor, the gender gifts and aptitudes remain.

IV. Differences in the Limbic System

The limbic system includes the hypothalamus and amygdala and several other nuclei of the midbrain and lower forebrain. It is the seat of drives and emotions. It controls and regulates many involuntary visceral responses such as digestive, respiratory, and circulatory activities. It controls our thermoregulation, including sweating and shivering. Drives like hunger, thirst, sex, fighting, and fleeing are modulated in the hypothalamus. When drives are satisfied, the hypothalamus stimulates the pleasure center. Drives are continually shifting and being prioritized by the limbic system. Behavioral response to these drives results when impulses build and present an appropriate target object.

The thresholds to set off responses in the limbic system differ between males and females. In males, testosterone stimulates the production of neurotransmitters in the hypothalamic area. This excess of neurotransmitters waiting in readiness in the synaptic areas tends to lower the threshold of response in males, such that less stimulation is required to set off behavioral responses to such things as food, sexual, or threat stimuli. Elevated estrogen in females has the opposite effect, inhibiting synaptic firings in the brain region and requiring more sensory and cognitive stimulation in order to elicit the same response.[17] This may explain male tendencies to be more reactive and quicker to act and to make decisions. It may also explain feminine patience and tolerance of more stimuli without reaction. These differences may explain the gender-specific reactions of males and females in sexual interactions. It may also explain why females are more patient with children.

Males of most species studied, including humans, appear to be more aggressive, dominant, assertive, and seekers of control. Some social science studies suggest that the degree of difference in aggressive tendency is slight and that the variation with the sexes is far greater than the difference in the means. They suggest also that much of the difference may reflect cultural expectations. Studies on animals, however, reveal a more complex picture of aggression. Moyer has done much research on the types of aggression manifest in various animals. He contends that there are actually seven different types of aggression that can be identified. Three of these are found primarily in males, one primarily in females, and three seem to be found equally distributed between males and females. Researchers have been able to identify and map specific regions of the brain that control these types of aggression, using electrical implants in cats.[18] The stimulation of predator aggression results in an individual's adopting a stalking stance with ears back, fur sleek, and head low. On the other hand stimulation of competitive aggressive response is characterized by ears up, fur standing on end, back arched, teeth bared, often accompanied by hissing and snarling. Competitive male aggression and territorial aggression are evoked in animals that are electrically stimulated in the preoptic area of the hypothalamus.

In some animals, this area turns out to be eight times larger in males than females.[19] There are also more neurons and dendritic connections in the male preoptic area than in the female.[20] This enlarged male center has been reported in rats, cats, dogs, monkeys, and humans.

Predatory aggression is stimulated by centers in the amygdala. Males tend to have a larger amygdala and have more neural connections between the amygdala and other centers of aggression in the hypothalamus.[21] Intermale aggression appears to be a uniquely male trait, while predatory and territorial aggression appear to be stronger responses in males as well. One cannot be sure that because these centers are present in other animals they are also in humans; however, it is known that men have significantly larger preoptic areas and amygdalae than women, and it may be reasonable to assume that the cause of differences in human aggression do have a biological basis.[22] It may be, then that males gravitate to competitive sports, thrive better in a competitive business world, enjoy argumentation, etc., more than females. Males enjoy hunting and fishing more often, tend to collect and amass various resources from vintage cars to baseball cards to money, and may have more inclination to hoard. Among most higher mammals and human societies, it is the male that leaves the group during postpubertal maturing, while females stay in the group remaining bonded to their mother. The wanderlust and adventure-seeking disposition associated with young males may also have a biological basis. Males may simply have a predisposition to such behaviors due to larger centers for them with more neural connections as well as their lower threshold of stimulation in general. Castration of male animals reduces this behavior substantially and reduces the size of these centers and the amount of free neurotransmitters found in the area. Replacement of testosterone by injection restores normal size of centers and intensity of behavior.[23]

There is, then, a strong correlation between the amount of testosterone and the intensity of these behaviors. Among men there is a strong correlation between testosterone level and sexual activity and aggressive behavior. Juvenile delinquents and criminals incarcerated for violent crimes have, on the average, twice the level of testosterone found in the normal male population. (Of course, this does not excuse such criminal behavior or imply that it is unavoidable.) XYY syndrome men (having an extra male Y chromosome) have elevated levels of testosterone.[24] They are taller than average and have more problems with acne, but they are relatively normal in intelligence and other temperament characteristics. They are, however, more aggressive and twenty times more likely to have problems with the law. Men are more likely to be aggressive, assertive, confrontive, and reactive, not so much because of cultural expectation as because of their biological predispositions. The human male drive for power, wealth, fame, and resources may thus be rooted in hormones and brain differences.

Maternal aggression, described as females responding to impending danger or harm to their offspring, is common to mammals. This response, which is particularly strong during lactation, may be facilitated by prolactin, the hormone causing milk production.[25] It may also facilitate maternal instinct and bonding. This may explain why mothers are often more protective and aggressive in intervening on a child's behalf than fathers. Female-infant bonding appears to be innate. The baby's cries trigger involuntary responses in the mother such as oxytocin secretion, nipple erection, and pupil dilation. There are no such responses in males, and male bonding is likely a learned response.[26] Maternal instinct may be related to this center, which enhances bonding and protection of young. Such bonding may be important in later social development and learning skills.[27] Mothers show more stress when infants are cared for at day care or by multiple care givers than fathers. A mother may be better equipped to form this important bond due to centers in her brain. When cradling a baby, mothers tend to use the left arm, positioning the baby's ear over the aorta and strongest heartbeat. Babies likely imprint on the mother's heartbeat during gestation and derive comfort from it. We are now engaged in a large-scale experiment with significant numbers of mothers enlisting day care for their infants. We have relatively little information on the importance of bonding and maternal contact to social and intellectual development, but some reports suggest that it is an important factor.

V. Sex Differences in Cerebral Organization

In 1962, Roger Sperry published work on split brain patients for which he later won a Nobel Prize. Central to his work was the study of epileptic patients whose corpus callosum had been severed. The corpus callosum is the bridge of nerve fibers connecting the two cerebral hemispheres. Images on a projection screen presented to the right visual field of the eyes are transmitted to the left hemisphere of the brain. Images presented to the left visual field are transmitted to the right hemisphere. Sperry found that words or images easily described in words are perceived better from the right visual field and left hemisphere. Shapes, patterns, and abstract forms are better recognized if presented to the left visual field and right hemisphere. Through a process of such tests, the functions of the left and right hemispheres were characterized. The left hemisphere controls the right side of the body, written and spoken language, numerical calculation, logic, and reasoning. The right hemisphere controls the left side of the body and processes artistic and musical stimuli, visual spatial patterning, insight, imagination, and emotional responses.[28]

It became popular in the 1960s and 1970s to think of males as more left-brain dominant and females as more right-brain dominant. This does not now appear to be a correct interpretation of this work. More recently it has been discovered that the lateral isolation of functions into one hemisphere or the other is more characteristic of males. Herbert Lansdell worked with a group of epileptics whose right or left hemisphere had been partially surgically removed. He found that men did poorly on verbal tasks if the right hemisphere was affected. Women suffered far less speech and verbal skill loss as a result of a damaged hemisphere. Women tend to be less lateralized, with verbal centers and visual spatial centers in both hemispheres and with much greater communication between the two hemispheres. Women, then, could identify words flashed to either the right or left visual field more often than men. Likewise, they could identify abstract shapes and images relatively well from either visual field.[29]

Jeannette McGlone found that a shot of anesthetic administered to the right carotid artery (which supplies the right brain) would deaden only the right hemisphere for about thirty seconds before the anesthetic was pumped throughout the body and back to both hemispheres. She found that during this brief time, while the right hemisphere was deadened, males actually performed better on verbal tasks than with both hemispheres intact. When the left hemisphere was deadened, however, males had severe loss of verbal skill. Women had only slight loss of verbal skill when either hemisphere was disengaged.[30]

Sandra Witelson used dichotic stimulation tests to measure brain lateralization. She allowed subjects to touch briefly, simultaneously with both hands, a series of two dissimilar objects out of sight. Men identified the objects felt with the left hand while females more often identified both.

Doreen Kimura also used dichotic listening tests to measure brain lateralization. Through headphones, series of two different number words, like *two* and *nine*, were spoken simultaneously to the two ears. Men were able to report mainly words presented to the right ear (left hemisphere), while women could report numbers from both ears.[31]

Strokes result from blood clots or clogged arteries in the brain. They affect only one hemisphere or the other, depending on the artery involved. Aphasia, the loss of speech due to a stroke involving the left hemisphere, occurs much more commonly in men. Women are much more able to retain verbal skills or retrain their uninvolved hemisphere to take over.

Another observation that suggests that males are more asymmetrical in their cerebral hemispheres is that among most mammals studied, males have a slightly thicker, larger right hemisphere than left.[32] This is more pronounced early in life, and there is some likelihood that the left hemisphere in males is developmentally retarded by testosterone. Perhaps this helps explain why boys are far more likely to suffer from dyslexia, as well as reading, speaking, and spelling deficiencies in early grades. They are more likely to stutter during early development as a result of a conflict between the right and left hemisphere for control of speech.[33] While the left hemisphere begins to catch up during later development in males, even in adulthood brain asymmetry is more likely among males than among females. In general, females have a larger brain relative to their body weight than males.[34]

It was found that the bridge of nerve fibers or processes between the two hemispheres known as the corpus callosum was significantly larger and contained more nerve fibers in females. This difference was found at all ages of females.[35] Embryonic nerve cells grown in cell culture produce more dendritic processes in the presence of estrogen than in the presence of testosterone.[36] They also make connection with more neighboring cells. This fact may explain why there are more nerve fibers or processes through the corpus callosum connecting the two hemispheres. The female central nervous system may have more interconnections and more networking of nerve fibers.

It appears from all of the above data that women are generally capable of receiving and meaningfully processing more sensory nerve input. Because their nerves interact with more neighboring nerves, they are able to integrate more sensory and stored memory information to derive more complete analysis and assessment of a particular circumstance. It has been suggested, as an example, that if a male and female were both interviewing a potential new employee, the male might become very focused and engrossed in his line of questioning and the accuracy or clarity of responses, while a female would not only process the conversation but also the mannerisms, facial expressions, facial color, dress, hygiene, and many other cues to personality and temperament. The woman would come away from the same one-hour interview with a much more in-depth and complete assessment of the candidate and his suitability for the job. This might in fact be what has for years been called women's intuition. It may be simply women's ability to process, evaluate, and respond to more immediate simultaneous stimuli. A biological argument for the purpose of this ability of females to capture more stimuli would be that in the role of childrearing there is great advantage in being able to receive and process multiple stimuli in order to monitor multiple children and other social contacts. This may also explain my wife's ability to spot Neil's intentions to walk into our busy street while she is busy with other tasks in the house, or to anticipate Nate's lunge off the counter. It may explain how she is able to talk on the phone, write me a note, and continue to mix the appropriate ingredients into her batch of cookies, all at the same time. This kind of simultaneous activity appears to be more difficult for men.

Males, with their more lateralized brains, tend to have thought-processing more regionally isolated and discreet, with fewer interconnecting nerve interactions and perhaps more straightforward, quick reactions to important stimuli. This would be a strategy more conducive to the hunter, tracker, and builder. It may also be conducive to categorical thinking. It could allow more uninterrupted processing of visual/spatial data in the right hemisphere and computational analysis in the left, which could lead to a slight math advantage in males. The more lateralized male brain would be expected to be more single-minded, focused, less distractable, and perhaps less socially aware. This, coupled with the hot-wired limbic system, may increase males' competitive, goal-setting, rule-making, hierarchical approach to social interaction.

Aptitude tests have for years revealed that, on the average, girls perform better than boys in verbal skills and boys perform better than girls in math and visual-spatial skills. Camillo Benbow and Julian Stanley found that of forty thousand junior high students tested, two hundred sixty of the top two hundred eighty scoring over seven hundred on the SAT-M were male.[37] She suggested that there may be a biological basis for this. The prevailing explanation for such data has been cultural discrimination in education against mathematically inclined girls. This may in part be true, yet there may also be biological reasons for masculine superiority in this area. Girls generally do better in math up through the grade-school years. Girls probably are developmentally ahead of boys through these years and particularly ahead of them in left-hemisphere tasks, which include computational math. Boys begin to surpass girls in math after the involvement of geometry and algebra and more abstract problem solving, which may invoke thinking with the right hemisphere. Furthermore, this male advantage does not become pronounced until after puberty. In tests of seventh-grade boys, post-pubertal boys (who would have a sharp increase in testosterone) outperform pre-pubertal boys, on the average. Test scores of prepubertal boys improve after puberty. Girls with abnormally high testosterone levels due to hyperactive adrenal glands score more like boys on aptitude tests.[38] XXY boys and other males with low levels of testosterone score more like girls.[39]

VI. Sex Differences at Birth

A common response to these apparent biological sex differences is that brain structure and functional differences arise as a result of different learning environments and strategies between girls and boys. There is evidence that nurture and learning affect brain development. Rats raised in stimulus-enriched environments developed larger cerebral cortexes than stimulus-impoverished rats.[40] Rats that are continually paired with submissive rats and learn to win their conflict interactions develop elevated testosterone levels and resultant physiologies.[41] Yet there is also evidence that these differences are present at birth. Female infants have been noted to orient and fix their focus more often on faces, are comforted by voices and touch, and vocalize more often than boys. They respond earlier to smells and sounds. Female infants, on the average, learn to talk sooner and, when learning to draw, tend to draw people subjects. Male infants orient more to objects, lights, and toys, and are comforted more by patterned mobiles and ticking clocks. They develop speech later, draw objects more than faces, and learn three-dimensional drawing faster. Among infant brains studied, males more often show hemispheric asymmetry with a smaller left hemisphere. The female corpus callosum is larger in infants and their preoptic area of the hypothalamus is smaller.

Another line of evidence that suggests that differential male and female mental attributes have some innate biological basis comes from the various sex-anomalous syndromes that occur naturally. Males with lower testosterone levels score lower on visual/spatial tests. XYY males have higher-than-average testosterone and score higher in visual/spatial skills and lower in verbal than average males. Females with Turner's syndrome (with only one X chromosome and extremely low testosterone and estrogen) actually score better on verbal tests than the average female, but much poorer on visual/spatial. These individuals appear in most characteristics like normal girls and are raised that way. Often only at or near puberty is their condition recognized, when they require estrogen administration in order to develop normal secondary sex characteristics. It has been noted that Turner's syndrome females are particularly drawn to traditionally female pursuits, such as care and teaching of children and occupations involving more intensive use of their verbal skills, such as typing, word processing, and taking dictation.[42]

Men whose mothers were treated with diethylstilbestrol (DES), a synthetic estrogen, during pregnancy are less aggressive, less athletically coordinated, and less given to traditionally masculine interests.[43] Women whose mothers were given androgens during pregnancy to avoid miscarriage tend to be more masculine in their behavior. They are tomboyish and energetic and score more like boys on aptitude tests. In general, then, gender behavior and aptitudes follow more closely the hormonal make-up of an individual (and the hormonal influences of his or her mother during gestation) than whether the individual is a male or female. And certainly hormones are a more reliable predictor of gender-related behavior characteristics than cultural persuasions.

VII. Sex Differences in Stress Management

Biologists in the 1960s and 1970s raised concerns that humankind did not have the well-established inherent population control mechanisms exhibited in most higher animals. Since predators, disease epidemics, and famines had been brought under control, it seemed that the only way to control our reproduction was through educated family planning. This was the genesis of the zero population growth (ZPG) movement. More recently, however, we have discovered that human beings react much like other animals in response to stresses in our environment. Animals face long-term stress primarily when food or other resources are in short supply, or when populations are too dense. After long-term stress, higher social animals often react with these types of responses: (1) heightened aggressive behavior, particularly among males, often resulting in fighting and death, (2) elevated abuse and even eating of young, (3) homosexual behavior, (4) miscarriage of and reabsorption of fetuses, and (5) discontinuance of ovulation and infertility.[44] By many measures, human beings in modern societies are living in stressful conditions. Many of the same behavioral anomalies we see in animals have begun to manifest themselves in the human population.

Both animal and human males and females respond differently to stress, and herein lies another important difference in gender behavior. In both males and females, stress initially elevates adrenalin output, which in turn affects the hypothalamus to increase heart rate, blood pressure, basal metabolic rate, and responsiveness of the senses. Under initial pressure both sexes are able to put in long days, stay alert, and remain energetic. After a period of prolonged chronic hyperadrenalin, females begin to produce more cortisol and estrogen. Cortisol reduces the brain neurotransmitter serotonin, which is needed to maintain normal sleeping and waking patterns. It reduces norepinephrine, which is needed for a normal sense of well-being, leading eventually to a sense of ambivalence and even depression. Estrogen in high amounts acts as a sedative to quiet the system.

It reduces heart rate, respiratory rate, and blood pressure. After a prolonged stressful time under the influence of estrogen, women may become depressed. In various studies, women are found to struggle with depression, phobias, hysterias, anorexia and other depression disorders four to ten times more commonly than men.[45]

Men respond initially to stress in the same way as females. A burst of adrenalin incites a male to meet stress head on and overpower whatever the obstacles. When stress becomes chronic, the masculine system begins to enhance the aggressive adrenalin response by gradually increasing the level of testosterone. This androgen compounds the affects of adrenalin by lowering the neurotransmitter thresholds of the hypothalamus such that the whole male system becomes hyper-reactive. Reaction time decreases, while aggressive and sexual behavior are more easily provoked. Heart rate, blood pressure, clotting factors, cholesterol, and platelets increase. Men are able to maintain their elevated energy level perhaps longer than women under stress. They pay the price, however, of having higher levels of heart attack, hypertension, strokes, and other cardio-vascular problems. Their resistance to infectious diseases is diminished also. This, along with their higher basal metabolic rates in general, results in a shorter male life span, on average.

Some biologists argue that in social settings of early civilizations, where women were likely to band together to care for children and common household chores, depression served a purpose. It was an important nonverbal communication signal to other women in the social group of a need or problem. It often resulted in a corporate response from the small social group. Today, with the fragmentation of the family and with more working women, there is little remnant of these small kinship-based social groups to respond to needs. Depression smolders unnoticed or without meaningful response until it becomes clinically debilitating.

The male system of stress response (i.e., to go into overdrive) functioned well for males of hunting/gathering societies, whose stresses often meant higher energy output, which burned up the excess cholesterol and blood sugars. Today's male stress, however, is often more mental than physical, and these physiological changes are actually a health risk. It is then particularly advantageous for males to get regular exercise in order to offset this phenomenon.

Men and women respond differently to stress, and they are stressed by different environmental factors. By virtue of their gifts in language, their more networked nervous system, their acuity of perception, and their patience, women are more comfortable with and gravitate to social interaction and communication. They have physiologies and temperament traits that prepare them uniquely for child care. Their maternal instincts and bonding facility are stronger. Breeches of relationships, especially within the family, are particularly stressful for females. Inability to have children or to provide basic needs for a child are also common sources of feminine stress. Women need a sense that their social sphere of significant others is intact. They find fulfillment in caring for others and meeting needs. According to Willard Harley, women are stressed and vulnerable to an extramarital affair when one of these five needs is not met in their marriages: (1) need for affection, (2) need for conversation, (3) need for honesty, (4) need for minimal financial well-being, and (5) need for family commitment.[46]

Men appear to be more stressed when frustrated in goal achievement or when they feel a lack of control of their surroundings. They are stressed when frustrated in sexual fulfillment or when they sense a lack of support or respect from their wife and family. Harley proposes five reasons why a man would violate his marriage and seek fulfillment in an affair: (1) lack of sexual fulfillment, (2) lack of recreational companionship, (3) lack of an attractive spouse, (4) lack of domestic support, and (5) lack of admiration.

Men and women have different gifts and perhaps different needs. Men need a sense of accomplishment and achievement in goals. Women need a sense that their important social ties are healthy. I believe the admonition in Ephesians 5:28-32 for husbands to love their wives and wives to respect their husbands reflects a deep, important need of each sex. Men, who by nature are more assertive, who arrange their social organization hierarchically, and who seek to elevate their level of control and respect, can find fulfillment and daily stress relief through the admiration of a wife who respects her husband. A wife needs to have a sense of complete and healthy relationships with all of her significant social members. She needs an outlet for her nurturant urges and a sense of fulfilled communion. At the center of her social relationships is her husband and her family. She is then most fulfilled by the love, reception, and recognition of her husband and family.

These gifts and needs are by no means expressed and fulfilled only within marriage. Aggressiveness, nurturance, empathy, and verbal and visual/spatial gifts are all essential to a healthy society. My intent is not to suggest that individual fulfillment is dependent on marriage. I think, however, that males and females have been differently gifted in God's plan because of their historic roles in feminine child rearing and masculine provision and protection for the family.

Conclusion

Are we as men and women different? The evidence presented here suggests that we have some fundamental physiological and neural differences that are present at birth and predispose us toward certain behaviors dependent on gender. We should not conclude automatically that because men and women may have different gifts, traditional roles are the only way they may be expressed. Yet it seems very significant that these different gifts correspond very well to the different roles given to men and women in Scripture (see other chapters in this book). These unique abilities, coupled with the traditional roles, have served mankind well and enabled us to fulfill the commission to multiply and fill the earth very efficiently. It may well be that along with the fundamental division of labor in marriage referred to in Genesis 2-3, God gave the necessary gifts to uniquely accomplish those tasks.

Our culture has changed, and the demands for traditional roles may have varied, yet our basic, God-given physiological differences have not. We excel at different gifts, and all the gifts are needed. Let us hope that, by recognizing the existence of gender differences, we can better understand each other and help to maximize each other's potentials. Likewise, by accepting our God-given gifts, we can resist cultural pressures to become what we are not, to seek to master gifts we don't possess.

17

Psychological Foundations for Rearing Masculine Boys and Feminine Girls

George Alan Rekers

A fierce battle is being waged today over male and female roles in American family life. For thousands of years of Western culture, the overwhelming majority of people accepted and lived according to some basic distinctions between the roles of mothers and fathers, wives and husbands. The only legitimate way for a child to be born and reared was in a heterosexual marriage, providing both a mother and a father to share jointly in the rights and responsibilities of family life. Unmarried motherhood was considered tragic for the child because of the absence of a supportive father, who should have a role in cooperatively insuring a protective family environment for the child. Boys were reared differently from girls. Boys were dressed differently from girls. Boys were encouraged to identify with their fathers and other men, and girls were encouraged to identify with their mothers and other women. A person's sex was considered to be an important distinction in human personality.

But now this idea that sex makes a legitimate role difference is being fought by vocal and active social reformers. One of the official goals of the National Organization for Women (NOW) is to work toward "an end to all distinctions based on sex."[1] This is a concise definition of the unisex mentality that is gaining popularity in our society today. When advocates of unisex childrearing publish their ideas, it becomes immediately clear that when they argue for "an end to *all* distinctions based on sex" (italics mine), they include distinctions between men and women as sexual partners. In other words, they say that a woman should be free to choose either a man or a woman for a sexual partner and that an openly practicing lesbian is as fit to be a mother as is a heterosexual, married woman.[2]

Should the family be based on a heterosexual marriage? Should the mother's role in the family be different, in some significant respects, from the father's role? Do the child's long-term sexual identity and normal sexual adjustment depend, in some way, on unique fathering from the father and unique mothering from the mother? The unisex advocates say no to all of these questions.

The Source of Unisex Notions

The unisex notions are not based on the findings of child development research. Instead, the feminist and unisex ideas are rooted in the relativism of humanistic thinking.[3] The idea of natural sex-role boundaries embedded in creation is anathema to the relativistic humanists.[4] The relativistic humanists do not hold up heterosexuality as a desired norm:

> . . . neither do we wish to prohibit, by law or social sanction, sexual behavior between consenting adults. The many varieties of sexual exploration should not in themselves be considered "evil." Short of harming others or compelling them to do likewise, individuals should be permitted to express their sexual proclivities and pursue their lifestyles as they desire.[5]

So the proponents of unisex childrearing do not believe that children should be taught that committing oneself to marital fidelity to a woman for a lifetime is a masculine thing for a man to do.[6] The unisexist would be just as happy if a man had sexual relations with another man.[7] After all, the word *unisex* means that a person's sex doesn't make any difference! This is not a conclusion reached on the basis of scientific research. It is simply the idea of a relativistic, humanistic world view, a myth widely propagated in the media in the latter quarter of the twentieth century.

A Different Standard

NOW has a membership of less than .1 percent of the United States population. Yet its unisex and feminist values are loudly proclaimed in the mass media.

In sharp contrast, national polls[8] report that 90 percent of all Americans "favor the Christian religion," and 87 percent report that Jesus Christ has influenced their lives. Ninety percent of Americans pray to God. Eighty percent insist that they believe Jesus is God or the Son of God. Forty-four percent of all Americans attend church frequently, and seventy percent are church members. (This is a marked increase from less than 10 percent during the Revolutionary War, and no more than 20 percent throughout the nineteenth century.)

Seventy-two percent of Americans believe that the Bible is the Word of God. More than 50 percent of all Americans claim to have had a born-again conversion experience to Christ, and at least 40 percent claim they are evangelical. Thirty-three percent confess Jesus Christ as their "only hope of heaven," and 25 percent insist that the Bible is inerrant.

If I quote from the *Humanist Manifesto* and the radical feminists who constitute a tiny fraction of the population in America, I would hardly be out of place to quote the Christian Scriptures on these same issues. It is nonsense to capitulate to the charge that quoting the Bible is imposing Judeo-Christian values on a secular, non-Christian culture when our American government, law, and society were founded on Christian values and the vast majority of Americans identifies with Christian values.

Sex: To Be or Not to Be?

Should there be "an end to all distinctions based on sex," as the unisex proponents would have it? Or should parents shape the sexual identities of their boys to masculinity and of their girls to femininity?

If we took a vote in America, I suppose the results would be like these:

Is sex a meaningful distinction for human identity and roles?
All those in favor? 90 percent.
(Those Americans who favor Christian values.)

All those opposed? .1 percent.
(Members of NOW).

All those abstaining? 9.9 percent.
(Some folks always fail to vote!)

The Real Question

For the vast majority of parents, then, the question is not whether the unisex mentality is correct. They already know sex is an important distinction, and they have another, more complicated question: "*How* can I shape a normal sexual identity in my child?"

Parents have two key influences in shaping their children's sexual identities. First, parents shape normal sexual identities in their sons and daughters by properly contributing the distinctive roles of father and mother to their family life. Second, parents shape normal sexual identities in their children by encouraging their sons to behave in masculine ways and their daughters to behave in feminine ways. Let's examine each of these two key influences.

The First Key: Properly Contributing Distinctive Roles

We have looked at the unisex myth that tries to undermine the distinction between fathers' and mothers' roles. While the evil excesses of the menacing macho myth and male chauvinism are to be recognized, they should not lead us to the opposite and equally unreasonable evils of radical feminism and the unisex mentality. We should *not* end all distinctions based on sex just because those distinctions have been abused by some men in the past and present.

Sexual Identity Problem: Family Backgrounds of Troubled Children

For the past nineteen years, I have devoted the major portion of my professional career to the intensive study of more than one hundred children and teenagers who were identified by their pediatricians, psychologists, psychiatrists, schools, or other social agencies as having problems with their sex-role adjustment. With more than half a million dollars of support from research grants, I have been carefully studying these troubled children, both boys and girls, who are three to eighteen years old.[9] In addition to conducting a careful study of these youngsters, I have also written articles and invited textbook chapters about the psychological treatment desperately needed by these children with gender identity disorders.[10]

Not surprisingly, I have discovered that the family backgrounds of these young people tend to be quite a bit more troubled than those of normal children. The question has been, however, "Exactly how are these families different?"

Let's look at the importance of the family background of children troubled by sex-role deviations. We'll direct our attention to young children in order to illustrate the importance of family factors in early childhood adjustment to one's sex role. For the moment, we'll focus on what we have learned about families of young boys with sex-role difficulties. What do their family backgrounds tend to be like?

Male Role Example

One of the most obvious first questions had to do with whether the father was physically present in or absent from the home. If the father was present, I tried to find out what kind of relationship the biological father or the substitute father had with the boy. On the other hand, if the father was absent, I was interested in studying the age of the boy at the time of his separation from his father and the reason for the separation.

Whether or not the father was at home at the time of my study, I was also interested in whether the father had a psychiatric history. To round out my concern regarding the male role examples that these boys might have, I also recorded the number of older brothers the boy potentially had.

Mother's Role

I also thought it would be important to find the differences between the role that the mothers took in these families and the role taken by the fathers. For this reason, I developed a Behavior Checklist for Childhood Gender Problems,[11] which asked a number of questions about the fathers, the mothers, and the everyday home environment.

Psychological Testing

I was interested in finding out how involved emotionally the troubled boy was with his mother, his father, and other family members. For this reason, I hired other psychologists to administer a Family Relations Test[12] to as many of these boys as possible.

For the first three dozen of these boys that I studied, I wanted to make the most careful psychological diagnosis possible, given the state of the art in clinical psychology. For this reason, I asked two other senior clinical psychologists to join me in evaluating these boys.[13] One of these clinical psychologists extensively interviewed the mother and the father of the boy, first together and then individually. He then interviewed the child extensively and administered numerous standard clinical psychological tests.

The other clinical psychologist developed a Child Behavior and Attitude Questionnaire[14] and a Child Game Participation Questionnaire[15] based on research on normal boys and girls ranging in age from early to late childhood. Using norms based on the answers from these questionnaires, he was able to evaluate the boys with sex-role problems and to provide a psychometric diagnosis for each child.

In addition to these studies made by the other two clinical psychologists, I also interviewed the parents and the child and observed the child in play in controlled clinic situations in which I was able to compare the child's play with the play of normal boys and girls,[16] as well as make specific recordings of any effeminate gestures or mannerisms[17] of the child. When I interviewed the parents, I asked questions about how work was divided at home, how decisions were made on important questions at home, the parents' approach to discipline, the patterns of support and affection expressed by each of the parents toward the boy, and the amount of contact of each parent with the boy.[18] This was in addition to standard questions about the child's own appreciation of his physical sexual status and awareness of his sexual identity.

Then all three of us, as psychologists, made a diagnosis of each boy, on a scale from one to five. A rating of one indicated the most extreme sex-role disturbance and a rating of five indicated normal sex-role adjustment.

Psychological Problems in Parents

One of the most striking results of our research had to do with the high incidence of psychological problems in the families of these disturbed boys.[19] Of those families for whom we could obtain the information, a full two-thirds had at least one parent who had been under the extensive care of a psychiatrist, psychologist, or other mental-health professional. For 80 percent of the boys with sex-role problems, the mothers had mental-health problems. For 45 percent of these disturbed boys, the fathers had mental-health difficulties. It may be that these percentages are somewhat inflated because the parents who have sought psychological help for themselves might be likely to seek such treatment for their own child. But the results are so extreme as to suggest that the parents, and especially the mothers, of boys with sex-role problems have histories of serious psychological difficulties themselves.

The Boys' Fathers: We found that, unlike the majority of children in America, 67 percent of these boys with sex-role problems were not living in a home with their biological father. In fact, the biological father was absent for nearly all of the boys who had been diagnosed as having the most profoundly disturbed sex-role adjustment. In contrast, the boys with a moderate to mild sex-role adjustment problem had fathers absent in 54 percent of the cases. Our statistical tests of these data demonstrated our scientific findings. The more profoundly disturbed the boy is in sex-role adjustment, the more likely he is to be separated from his biological father.

On the average, we found that the boys were three-and-one-half years old at the time the father left the home. Eighty percent of the boys were five years of age or younger when their separation from their father occurred.

In 82 percent of the cases, the parents were separated or divorced. Only one of the fathers was dead, and in two cases the mothers had never legally married.

Fathers or Father Substitutes: For boys whose fathers had left, it is always possible that the mother has remarried so that the boys have father substitutes who can serve as an example of a male role. We found that 37 percent of these boys with sex-role problems had no adult male role model present in the home. This means that more than a third of the boys had neither a biological father nor a father substitute living at home with them.

This is a much higher rate of male role absence in the home than we find in the general population. According to United States census figures[20] contemporary with our testing, only 11.9 percent of all white children in the United States lived with their mothers without the benefit of a father or a father substitute in the home.

Once again, we separated these boys with sex-role problems into two groups: the most severely disturbed boys and the less severely disturbed boys. Making this simple grouping, we found that 75 percent of the most severely disturbed boys had neither the biological father nor a father substitute living at home with them, whereas 21 percent of the less severely disturbed boys had neither the biological father nor a father substitute living with them. (Once again, our statistical tests demonstrated that this was a scientific finding, not likely due to chance occurrence.)

Psychologically Remote Fathers: Tragically, we found that when a father figure was present physically, he was often psychologically remote from the rest of the family. In other words, the father was living in the same house, but he was not very involved emotionally with the other family members. In fact, for the boys with sex-role problems who were fortunate enough to have a biological father or father substitute living in the home, fully 60 percent of those father figures were found to be psychologically distant and remote from the other family members. This means that only about one in four of these boys with a sex-role problem had what might be described as a normal, close relationship with a father or a father substitute.

Older Brothers: It is possible that boys without a father can learn about the male role from the example of their older brothers. When we scrutinized our findings on this question, fewer than half of the boys had an older brother, and the results suggested a trend where the most severely gender-disturbed boys were less likely to have an older brother as an example of a male role than were the less severely disturbed boys.

Missing Male Models: We discovered a consistent picture that emerged from all the facts that we collected about these boys' families. As compared with most boys in America, these boys with severe sex-role problems are much less likely to have a father figure living in the home with them, and even when the father figure is present he tends to be psychologically remote from the boy. The boys with the most severe sex-role problems are much less likely to have a good male role example living in their own home than are the other boys with sex-role problems.

Mothers in Power: In those families that did have a father present, what was the family interaction like? On this question, we have accumulated clinical experience rather than research data. This means that we can only make a tentative description of what these families are like.

Our clinical records show that in the families of disturbed boys, the mothers held the balance of power with regard to financial decisions in more than half of the families. The mothers also held the balance of power with regard to decisions concerning the children in three-fourths of these families.

Our clinical records also show that in the majority of cases, the boys with sex-role problems typically go to the mother rather than to the father for sympathy. They are more likely to object to being separated from their mother than their father, and they are more likely to cling to the mother than to the father. It also appears that the mothers rather than the fathers are somewhat more likely to be the ones to discipline the child when both parents are present.

Feelings for Fathers: Based on the use of the Family Relations Test, our clinical record shows that the older boys with sex-role difficulties are more likely than normal children to endorse statements such as, "I wish this person [the father] would go away," "this person is not very patient," and "this person can make one feel very angry."

In conclusion, we have discovered that boys with serious sex-role disturbances live in families in which a male role model is usually absent or inadequate. In many cases, the boy did not have a father, a father substitute, or an older brother to look up to as an example of acceptable male behavior. In cases where a father or father substitute did live in the same home, he was usually psychologically remote from the boy. This means that these boys with sex-role disturbances did not have, in most cases, a male role model to identify with. In fact, the most severely disturbed boys had no father figure at home.

It was the less severely disturbed boys whose fathers were psychologically remote from the family if they were present at all. This means these fathers were not involved in making important family decisions and did not have affectionate, helping relationships with their sons.

This evidence from these clinical cases suggests that the father's role in the family is critically important for the development of sex-role adjustment.[21]

How Fathers Make a Difference

So far we have been considering the results of clinical experience with children with sexual-identity problems. These findings are similar to those of studies about the childhood and adolescence of adult homosexuals and transsexuals.[22] But there is yet another set of evidence that needs to be described to every serious parent. This is the extensive research about the effects on children when a father is absent from the home and the studies on the characteristics of fathers that lead to normal sexual-identity development.

Fathers' and Mothers' Roles

Should parents choose the unisex style of child rearing, or are there reasons why mothers and fathers should take different roles?

Results of Child-development Research

According to research findings, the special role of the father in the family is critically important for many different aspects of child rearing. It is not sufficient to say merely that two parents, regardless of their sex, are better than one, because there is a unique advantage for the child in having both a female parent and a male parent. As a male, the father makes a unique contribution to the child rearing of either a son or a daughter. While it is desirable for the father to be actively involved in rearing a child for the social, emotional, and spiritual needs of the child, I will focus my attention here on the special contribution that the father makes to the sexual identity of his children.

One of the most important roles that the father has in the family is to promote the development of a normal heterosexual role and normal sexual identity in his children. The father is more actively involved in heterosexual role development of his sons and daughters than the mother is.[23] The father usually fulfills an active role in the family, as compared with the expressive role of the mother.[24] The father is, therefore, more involved than the mother in preparing the children for their roles in society, including masculine roles for his sons and feminine roles for his daughters.

Effects of the Father's Absence on Masculine Development of Boys

Unfortunately, fathers often are absent from home due to a variety of reasons like separation, divorce, death, or military service. A number of research studies have been conducted on the question of whether a fatherless home has a detrimental influence on the development of boys.

One study found that young boys whose fathers were absent from the home were more likely to exhibit more feminine ways of thinking, low masculinity, dependence, and either less aggression or exaggeratedly masculine behaviors than were boys whose fathers were present.[25] Other studies have also reported the negative effects on the sex-role development of boys that are associated with the father's absence. Boys who were separated from their fathers during their preschool years were more often called sissies than were boys who had not been separated from their fathers.[26]

In studies that compare boys with fathers to boys without fathers, the fatherless boys are more likely to be perceived as effeminate than are the boys with fathers.[27] When fatherless boys become adults, they have less successful heterosexual adjustment than do males who grew up in homes with a father.[28] Therefore, all these studies indicate that the absence of the father can have a detrimental effect on normal heterosexual role development in boys.

Another body of evidence has suggested that sex-role problems in boys with serious sexual identity problems are correlated with either the physical absence or the psychological distance of the father from the young boy.[29] These studies of sex-role disturbances in boys parallel the findings of the other studies I have just reviewed.

We may conclude, then, that the absence of a father tends to have a detrimental effect on the normal masculine role development of boys. We may also conclude that the father is very important in fostering a normal heterosexual role development in his boy. This is not to say that the father is absolutely essential in order to rear a normal boy (there are cases in which widows, for example, have successfully reared normal boys), but as a general finding, the normal sex-role development of a boy usually depends on the presence of the father or a father figure in early childhood.

When Does the Father's Absence Have Its Biggest Effect?

Overall, the younger the age of the boy when the father departs, the more harmful is the impact on the boy's heterosexual role development. One psychological research study[30] found no difference in the sex-role behaviors of boys whose fathers left the home after they were five years old as compared with boys whose fathers were present all during childhood. But this same study found strong effects of the father's absence if the father left during the boy's first four years of life. Therefore, the younger the boy is when the father leaves, the more profound the effects will be on the boy's sex-role development.

Different Symptoms at Different Ages: The boy's age at the time of separation from the father not only is related to how strong the effect is on the boy, but also may determine the *kind* of effect that the father's absence will have on him. If the father leaves the boy before the age of five, effeminate behavior is likely to develop, whereas if the father leaves between the ages of six and twelve, hypermasculine problem behavior may result. The older boy without a father may have trouble in mastering what is appropriate masculine behavior, and in the process he may overcompensate for the loss of the father by acting in extremely "masculine" ways. For example, the boy may become belligerent, uncontrollable, insensitive to the feelings of others, and aggressive to the point of interpersonal violence. None of these is a desirable masculine quality, though all can be recognized as abnormal attempts to achieve a secure masculine image.

As a footnote, it should be pointed out that the research on heterosexual development is more complex than I can describe here, in that different aspects of heterosexual role development have been studied, including sex-role preference, sex-role orientation, and sex-role adoption. Father absence has its strongest effect on sex-role orientation, which is defined as the conscious or unconscious sense of basic maleness or femaleness in the child.[31]

Can the Effects of the Father's Absence be Counteracted?: The presence of a father substitute has generally been found to counteract, somewhat, the effects of the father's absence on a child's development.[32] One research study found that black preschool boys were more feminine, more dependent, and less aggressive if their father was absent than other boys who had fathers present in their home. However, a group of boys who had father substitutes were found to be less dependent than the boys with no fathers and no father substitutes.[33] But a father substitute may not be quite as effective as one continuous father in some cases, as suggested by another psychological study that failed to find a compensating effect from the presence of a father substitute.[34]

Even if a father or father substitute is not present in the home, there is another factor that has been found to lessen the effect of the father's absence. Research studies have identified this other factor as a positive attitude toward the father by the mother of the boy, as well as her positive attitude toward men in general.[35] This shows that the potential negative effects of the father's absence on the masculine role development of boys is not a simple thing. We must take into account other factors, such as the possibility that other male role models may be present for the boy and that a mother may be able to compensate for the effects if she has positive attitudes toward men and treats her boy with respect for his masculinity.

Effects of the Father's Absence on Feminine Development of Girls

Relatively fewer research studies have dealt with the effects of the father's absence on the development of the daughter than on sons. But the few studies available suggest that the father's absence is less devastating to the sex-role development of girls than of boys. In fact, some studies[36] have not found any differences in the heterosexual role development of girls in father-absent as compared with father-present homes. But more recent studies have found some subtle, complex effects of the father's absence on the development of girls.[37]

As with boys, the negative consequences of a fatherless home can have different effects depending on the reason for the father's absence. In a research study of a group of adolescent females, the girls were found to be inhibited in their interactions with males in general if the father had died.[38] On the other hand, if the parents were divorced, the girls were overly responsive to males and displayed early and inappropriate sexual behaviors. Sophisticated research studies are therefore finding that the absence of the father can have a debilitating effect on the sex-role development of girls.

What Characteristics of a Father Contribute to Normal Heterosexual Role Development in Children?

Earlier research studies focused on the differences in children in homes with fathers compared with those in homes without fathers. More recent studies have concentrated on which of the father's characteristics make a difference in the heterosexual role development of his children.[39]

Warm, Affectionate Fathers

The degree of the father's active, involved affection toward his children is the most important factor related to normal heterosexual role development in his child. Research studies have shown that the father who is affectionate and involved with his child is most likely to foster masculinity in his son. Appropriate sex-role development has been correlated with father-son interactions that can be characterized as warm, nurturant, and affectionate.[40] The warm affection of the father was more important than the father's actual, literal encouragement of masculine behaviors, and it was also more important than the extent to which the father himself was masculine as opposed to feminine. Many different studies have shown that appropriately masculine boys come from families with fathers who are affectionate, nurturant, and actively involved in childrearing.[41] Boys are more likely to identify with their fathers if their fathers are rewarding and affectionate toward them than if they are not.[42]

At the same time, normal feminine role development in girls is also related to a warm, nurturant relationship with the mother. The father's influence on daughters is different from the father's influence on sons. The normal feminine girls tend to have highly masculine fathers who encourage feminine behaviors in their daughters.

Quality of Father-Son Relationship

Other characteristics of fathers have been considered important to the appropriate and heterosexual role development of children. The results of research studies testing these ideas have not provided many absolute conclusions. For example, research has not found heterosexual role development dependent on how similar a boy feels he is to his father or how similar a girl feels she is to her mother.[43] Some fathers are more available than others to spend time with their boys, but better masculine role development has not been found for the boys whose fathers are more available.[44] If the father is living in the home and is usually available, it has been concluded that the quality of the father-son relationship may be more important than the number of interactions they have.[45]

Father's Assertion of Leadership

The different amounts of power assumed by the father and the mother in a family can also influence the heterosexual role development of children.[46] Generally speaking, the child is likely to identify with the parent who is the leader in the household. Boys from homes in which the mother asserted herself as the leader exhibited more feminine sex-role preferences than did boys from homes in which the father was leader. However, the sex-role preferences of girls were not influenced by whether the mother or father asserted leadership.[47]

In another research study, children were asked whom they wanted to be like when they grew up.[48] In many homes where the mother was the leading parent, there were many boys who chose to be a female when they grew up. At the same time, in homes in which the mother asserted leadership, the girls were likely to want to be a male.

It was also found that in homes led by dominant mothers, both girls and boys were likely to say that they disliked the opposite sex (as determined by sociometric ratings). Also, these girls and boys were frequently disliked by the opposite sex. These effects are not always observed, as reported by another study that did not find power distribution of the family to be related to some measures of sex typing in children.[49]

Father's Leadership Plus Affection

Clearly then, the father's assertion of leadership has a better effect on the heterosexual role development of both the boys and the girls than does the mother's assertion of leadership. When the mother asserts dominance, studies show that the sex-role orientation of the boys tends to be feminine and that of the girls tends to be masculine. Earlier, I reviewed the evidence that showed that the father's affection and nurturance toward the sons is very important to their masculine development. Other studies have shown that the father who both asserts leadership *and* is nurturant is more likely than the father who is remote to have sons who are masculine in their heterosexual role development.[50] In addition, there is evidence that suggests that effects of the father's leadership are expressed in the homes in which the father is also nurturant.[51]

Some of the most important factors, then, for the child's heterosexual role development are the affection and leadership of the father in the home. Additional studies have found that the father's ability to set limits for his sons is related to greater masculinity in boys if the father is also a nurturant and affectionate person.[52]

Family Fragmentation

Unfortunately, the role of the father in the family may be quickly changing in today's American society. The nature of the father's role for children of the future and the consequences of changes in the family structure will have profound influences on the sexual identity and sex-role development of children. The recent increase in the number of fatherless homes may result in larger numbers of sexual identity problems in children.

At the same time, there has been another trend of women being employed outside the home. Research studies indicate that child-rearing tasks are being shifted to group child care centers and temporary baby-sitters. By and large, fathers are not stepping into the vacuum created by the mothers' absence from the home. In cases where the father does increase participation in child rearing, it has been suggested that the differences in the mother's and father's role in the family may become blurred as the father becomes involved in historically feminine roles.[53] This may result in greater difficulty for children to distinguish between proper male and female roles.

The Straight Truth

Discarding the unisex myth as extremist, simplistic, and destructive to family life, my review of child-development research confirms the first key to shaping normal sexual identity in children—namely, the parents' proper contribution of the distinctive *father* and *mother* roles to their family life.

The Second Key: Encouraging Masculinity in Boys and Femininity in Girls

Little boys need to learn how to behave like boys and little girls need to learn how to behave like girls, and both need to learn in younger childhood. As the little boy learns how to behave like a boy—for example, by taking the role of "daddy" when he plays—he not only masters what it means to be a male but also sees himself behaving like a male, which will solidify or reinforce his identity as a male. By the same token, the little girl who is encouraged to act in a feminine way will feel more and more feminine as she grows up.

Sex-role behavior and sexual identity have certain connections:

> The boy who is encouraged to act in a masculine way will develop a firm male identity.
>
> The boy who develops a firm male identity will behave in a more masculine way.
>
> Similarly, the girl who is encouraged to act in a feminine way will develop a firm female identity.
>
> The girl who develops a firm female identity will behave in a more feminine way.

This means that parents need to be attentive to the proper sex-role behaviors for males and females and carefully teach these behaviors to their children.

What Are Masculinity and Femininity?

True Masculinity

The popular Playboy platitudes of our generation falsely preach that the most masculine attribute is unrestrained intercourse.[54] This irresponsible attitude pretends that we can isolate biological masculinity from social or moral aspects of the male role. But genuine masculinity acknowledges the interconnecting biological, psychological, social, and spiritual responsibilities attending the male role in all full sexual expression.[55] Therefore, promiscuous sexual acts outside the protective confines of permanent marriage are really counterfeit masculinity. Playboy's image of masculinity and the "gay liberation" view of sexuality are both pseudo-masculinity because sexual behavior outside of marriage is not socially and morally responsible masculinity.[56]

The sexual identity of a boy or man rests on much more than his genital functions. There are social and moral as well as physical attributes that define a man as a man. The male role has been understood throughout history as embodying much more than the male reproductive act. As a whole person, the man's role involves social responsibilities of father and husband that accompany sexual intercourse. As a whole person, the man's spiritual responsibilities as moral leader and provider attend the procreative sexual act. Marital fidelity and a leadership responsibility for children are intrinsic to the true and complete masculine role.[57]

We cannot understand the essence of masculinity or the fullness of male sexual identity if we separate the different aspects of being a man. Instead, we need to consider the physical, psychological, social, and spiritual dimensions of the male role together. If we take all of these aspects into account, then we have answers for these questions:

Can a man be fully masculine without fathering a child? Yes.

Can a man be fully masculine without marrying a woman? Yes.

At the same time, this holistic perspective teaches us that a man who promiscuously pursues heterosexual intercourse outside of marriage is diminishing his masculinity. And a male who engages in homosexual acts is also abandoning true masculinity.

True Femininity

Similarly, a true female sexual identity involves the whole person in her biological, psychological, social, and spiritual life.

It is true femininity to experience sexual intimacy in the protective confines of marriage with one's husband; extramarital promiscuity of the Playboy-bunny image is pseudofemininity. It is true femininity to conceive and bear a child in marriage; it is unfeminine to expose oneself to pregnancy out of wedlock. It is true femininity and motherhood to protect the unborn child from outside harm from tobacco or alcohol use; it is unfeminine and contrary to true motherhood to deliberately abort a child.

Scripture clearly defines the feminine role in terms of its biological, social, and moral dimensions taken together:

> So I counsel younger widows to marry, to have children, to manage their homes and to give the enemy no opportunity for slander. (1 Timothy 5:14)

> Likewise, teach the older women to be reverent in the way they live, not to be slanderers or addicted to much wine, but to teach what is good. Then they can train the younger women to love their husbands and children, to be self-controlled and pure, to be busy at home, to be kind, and to be subject to their husbands, so that no one will malign the word of God. (Titus 2:3-5)

In our twentieth-century culture, permeated as it is by Madison Avenue advertising, we might easily fall prey to the idea that a female identity is bolstered by the latest cosmetic wonders and the finest in feminine attire. This is a culturally-conditioned definition of femininity not supported in Scripture.

> I also want women to dress modestly, with decency and propriety, not with braided hair or gold or pearls or expensive clothes, but with good deeds, appropriate for women who profess to worship God. (1 Timothy 2:9-10)

Of course, this is not to say that girls should be prohibited from using modest amounts of cosmetics. The point is that true femininity is an inner quality and not mere outward adornment. In fact, overemphasis on outward appearance can actually detract from true femininity.

Distinctions in Male and Female Identity

Now that the reader has thoughtfully considered many important aspects of shaping the sexual identity of a child, a summary table (see Table 1) can be offered with minimal risk that it will be viewed in a simplistic or superficial way. I hope that studying this table will help to put everything I have discussed in perspective.

Contrary to the unisex myth, there are distinctions between male and female roles. Some of these distinctions are absolute differences, based on biological and moral realities. Other distinctions between the masculine and the feminine are culturally based.

Biologically Defined Sex Roles
Notice that each box in the figure is numbered in the upper left-hand corner. Look now at box 1 and box 2.

Box 1 gives examples of feminine sex roles that are *absolutely* feminine because they are based on the unique biology and anatomy of the female. For example, little girls learn to imitate a mother's role, which includes fantasizing or

TABLE 1 **Examples of Sex Role Distinctions**

		Feminine Sex Role	Masculine Sex Role
Absolute Sex-role Disctinctionas	**Biologically Defined**	[1] Breast-feeding an infant Delivering a baby Being a mother	[2] Impregnating a female by sexual intercourse Being a father
Absolute Sex-role Disctinctionas	**Morally Defined** Based upon Sex Differences	[3] Modest clothing of upper torso Abstaining from actions during pregnancy that would endanger the life of the child (such as abstaining from alcohol or illicit drug intake and from deliberate abortion) Abstaining from sexual relations with females Being submissive to husband's leadership at home	[4] Financially supporting one's children Abstaining from sexual relations with males Abstaining from sexual relations outside the protective confines of marriage Providing moral and spiritual leadership in the home
Culturally-based Sex-role Distinctions	**Culturally Defined** Based upon Biological Sex Differences	[5] Using the women's room Wearing a dress Singing in a female choir Living in a sorority	[6] Grooming a beard Shaving the facial hair Playing professional sports on all-male teams Using the men's room Serving in combat Singing in a male quartet Living in a fraternity
Culturally-based Sex-role Distinctions	**Culturally Defined** Based upon Arbitrary But Legitimate (Benign) Assignment	[7] Wearing lipstick Wearing fingernail polish Wearing mascara Shaving underarms or legs Carrying a purse	[8] Wearing a suit and necktie Having a man's haircut Opening doors for women and girls Paying for a date with a woman
Culturally-based Sex-role Distinctions	**Culturally Defined** Based upon Arbitrary and Harmful Stereotypes Which Should Be Abolished	[9] Nurse Airline cabin attendant Lower pay for same job done by a man Secretary	[10] Doctor Airline pilot Male chauvinism Macho male stereotypes Sexual harassment of women Lewd jokes, locker-room language

play-acting about growing up, being married, getting pregnant, delivering a baby, and breast feeding the little one. Parents should encourage and approve their little girl's play-acting in this feminine role. It helps the girl develop a normal female identity.

Box 2 gives examples of masculine sex roles that are *absolutely* masculine because they are based on the unique biology and anatomy of the male.[58] It is important, for example, for the boy to learn that he will *not* grow up with the biological possibility of having sexual intercourse with a man, getting pregnant, delivering a baby, or breast feeding the infant. This is essential in order to shape a normal male identity in the boy. While the boy should be encouraged to be nurturant, sensitive, and caring for infants (in preparation for fulfilling the command to fathers in Ephesians 6:4; Colossians 3:21; and 1 Timothy 5:8, for example), it is important to teach the boy that he cannot grow up to marry a man or to be a woman himself.

Morally Defined Sex Roles

Box 3 gives some examples of feminine sex roles that are *absolutely* feminine because they are based on unique moral responsibilities of women, as set forth in Scripture. Modest clothing of the upper torso should be taught to girls, and not boys, to train them to fulfill the moral teaching of 1 Timothy 2:9-10, for example. When parents emphasize this reason for having the girl dress differently from the boy, it reinforces her separate and distinct female identity. Protecting and preserving the life of the unborn child is a feminine responsibility taught by Scripture[59] and should be taught to every girl by her parents. The shaping of the girl's sexual identity also involves teaching her that women cannot select other women as sexual partners. In childhood and the teen-age years, the girl's mother should teach her daughter, by word and example, how to fulfill the uniquely feminine role of submissiveness in the home and the church. Of course, this moral distinction for the female is not expressed in the same ways outside the church and home. The domestic responsibilities of the woman, as Biblically defined (for example, 1 Timothy 5:8-14; Titus 2:3-5) are also morally based aspects of the female role.

Box 4 provides examples of absolute masculine distinctives that are based on unique moral responsibilities of men as set forth in the Bible. Fathers, in particular, should teach these truths to their sons by word and example. The male role includes providing spiritual leadership in the home and church, as well as supporting his wife and children in family life. The moral standards for sexual conduct teach that true masculinity enters into sexual union only within the protective and loving confines of marriage. Premarital and extramarital sexual intimacies are decidedly unmasculine and undermine the development of a confident and secure male identity. Similarly, boys should be taught that sexual relations with other males are not only wrong but also a symptom as well as a cause of a confused sexual identity. A male who has sex with another male calls his own masculinity into serious doubt. True masculinity reserves sexual acts for marriage, where the full moral, social, and biological responsibilities of manhood can be fulfilled as intended by the Creator.

Culturally Defined Sex Roles

There are three different kinds of culturally-based sex-role distinctions. Because these distinctions are not *absolutes*, it is essential that parents notice the real differences between these.

Culturally Defined, with Biological Basis: These male and female roles have come about by an interaction of cultural and biological factors.[60] Society has taken note of certain differences in the anatomy of males and females and has then made some cultural assignments based on these differences.

Look at boxes 5 and 6 in the table. These are simply examples of many ways that males and females do different things in our society because of their sex. It is important that you teach these differences to your children so they will get along well in everyday life. People in our culture expect different things from males from what they expect of females. To fit into society, your child needs to learn these things. But another benefit of teaching these distinctions to children is that they help boys feel like boys and girls feel like girls. It would be damaging to children's sexual-identity development if we parents failed to point out these sex differences to children in everyday life.

Consider some of these examples. Girls are taught to use the women's room and boys to use the men's room. Men either shave their beards or grow them out and groom them. Girls wear dresses and training bras. Boys and girls are placed on separate athletic teams that take into account their different rates of physical maturation and strength.

Culturally Defined, with Arbitrary But Legitimate Assignment: Every culture has different sets of behaviors that are arbitrarily classified as masculine or feminine (see boxes 7 and 8). There is nothing wrong with this if these arbitrary categories do not interfere with the freedom of individuals of both sexes to develop their potential competencies. As long as the arbitrary social labels of "for men only" or "for women only" do not hinder freedom to use one's talents, then they are benign or harmless sex-role stereotypes.

For example, in our culture, women may wear lipstick, fingernail polish, and mascara, as well as shave their underarms and legs. These things, along with wearing dresses and sometimes wearing their hair differently, all serve to highlight the differences between males and females. In the same way, men and boys often have their hair cut in a recognizable male fashion and they sometimes wear clothing, such as a suit and necktie, that is distinctively worn more by men than by women.

There are also various social roles and rules of etiquette that distinguish males from females. For example, men and boys often hold doors open for women and girls and let them walk in first. Men, in North American society at least, tend to shake hands more than women do, and women tend to hug one another more than men do.

All these kinds of male and female differences are largely culturally based, with little or no connection to the biological differences between men and women.[61] So a parent might ask, "Should I teach these kinds of arbitrary cultural distinctions to my children?"

The answer should be yes for most examples of benign cultural sex-role stereotypes. There are two reasons for this. First, if your child will be living for years in this culture, he or she will get along better with peers and society in general if these sex-role distinctions are learned. Boys, for example, might suffer severe ridicule and social rejection if they regularly appeared with lipstick, mascara, and bright red fingernail polish on. A youth who asks a girl out for a dinner date might be socially embarrassed—and the girl unprepared—if the young man did not realize the social expectation that the male pays for the female's dinner if he invites her out. Social and psychological adjustment depend on teaching the young person these sex-role stereotypes.

The second reason for parents' teaching these arbitrary sex-role stereotypes to their children is that such stereotypes help boys develop male identities and girls develop female identities. In childhood and adolescence, the boy and girl do not have the opportunity to experience many of the *absolute* sex-role distinctions. For instance, the girl cannot base her female identity on daily breast feeding of infants, because she must await marriage in adulthood for that. But she can feel quite feminine and different from boys by carrying a purse or putting on nail polish on a day-to-day basis. Little boys can feel "just like daddy" when they wear a little suit and tie.

In fact, in daily rearing of preschool children, parents should look for these kinds of social distinctions and tell the little boy he "looks just like daddy" when his clothes resemble dad's. The little girl will benefit when she's given her play cosmetics "just like mommy's." These things help to reinforce the crucial identification process that solidifies male identity in boys and female identity in girls.

These distinctions are important in childrearing. That is why the unisex myth that calls for "an end to all distinctions based on sex" is so destructive for normal sexual identification. Our culture has developed these sex-role stereotypes because they are useful in childrearing and help reinforce adolescent and adult sexual identities.

Culturally Defined, with Arbitrary But Harmful Assignment: These sex-role stereotypes (see boxes 9 and 10) are arbitrary because, once again, there is no biological or moral basis for them. But unlike the category we just considered, these stereotypes are harmful and should be abolished in our society.

This category includes the harmful attitudes of male chauvinism and the so-called masculine image of the menacing macho myth described earlier.

This category further includes those arbitrary classifications of employment categories that hinder the individual's freedom to develop talents and abilities. If your little children want to play a game of "hospital," it would be morally wrong to insist that the girl always play the nurse, letting only a little boy play the doctor. These are the kind of arbitrary, harmful stereotypes that overrule the consideration of individual ability. Intelligence, not sex, should be a criterion for choosing a career as a physician, dentist, psychologist, or optometrist.

Destructive male stereotypes, such as telling lewd jokes, using crass locker-room language, and sexually harassing women are part of this category of harmful stereotypes.

Obviously, these are the types of sex-role stereotypes that concerned parents should not teach their children by either word or example. In fact, when they become aware of them in everyday life, children need to be taught that these harmful stereotypes are morally wrong.

The existence of this category of harmful sex-role stereotypes provides fuel for the unisex proponents. But while this one category of sex-role distinctions needs to be eliminated in our society, it does not logically follow that the other four helpful types of sex-role distinctions need to be obliterated as well. Herein lies the fallacy of the unisex myth.

The Image: Male and Female

It is interesting that the unisex mentality is based on the godless world view of relativistic humanism, which includes the radical feminist movement.[62] Those who call for "an end to all distinctions based on sex" are those who simultaneously endorse the "right" to abortion, homosexuality, and divorce. The unisex mentality, therefore, is an assault against sex. It denies the existence of unique mother and father roles. It denies the existence of human rights for unborn babies. It denies the existence of the norm of heterosexuality by affirming the life-denying practice of homosexual acts. It denies the existence of divine sanction for marital permanence by its approval of divorce. In this sense, the unisex mentality denies the existence of God Himself, because it opposes the Judeo-Christian Scriptures' teaching about sexuality and family responsibility.

The Bible asserts: "So God created man in his own image, in the image of God he created him; male and female he created them" (Genesis 1:27). This means that sexuality in men and women reflects the "image of God." When the unisex mentality denies the human "distinctions based on sex," it is denying the image of God in the human personality. But what else would we expect from the godless worldview of relativistic humanism? The unisex mentality denies the existence of God and His Word's authority, and in the same sweep, denies one mark of God in the human personality—the distinctions of male and female.

Fortunately, most parents sincerely want to shape normal sexual identities in their sons and daughters. They have two basic ways of accomplishing this: by assuming distinctive and proper roles of mothering and fathering their children, and by directly encouraging masculinity in their sons and femininity in their daughters.

> Train a child in the way he should go, and when he is old he will not turn from it. (Proverbs 22:6)

Note: Professional writer and editor Carol Steinbach compiled and organized an initial draft of this chapter from excerpts of chapters 2, 3, and 10 of Dr. Rekers's book *Shaping Your Child's Sexual Identity* (Grand Rapids, MI: Baker Book House, 1982). For a more complete discussion of this subject, including case studies and treatment strategies, see *Shaping Your Child's Sexual Identity*, and chapter 3, "Biblical Perspectives for Goal Setting" in Dr. Rekers's book, *Counseling Families* (Waco, TX: Word, 1988), pp. 66-87.

18

The Inevitability of Failure:

The Assumptions and Implementations of Modern Feminism

David J. Ayers

It was late in the day. Just as I was preparing to go home, a single woman who was a staff member at our college walked into my office. A part-time editor for a major Christian publishing house, she had a "technical" question regarding a book manuscript that had been assigned to her.

Apparently, the hapless minister's wife who had submitted this piece had asserted that innate differences between the sexes existed and should be respected if marital harmony were to be obtained. A feminist professor in our psychology department had assured this editor that "no evidence whatsoever" existed for this claim of biological differentiation. Sexual differences, universal as they are,[1] are all caused by culture and socialization and thus are malleable and subject to redefinition. So she claimed. Based on this, the editor had quietly removed the offensive section from the manuscript. Now, she'd had second thoughts and was seeking another opinion.

I presented to her what I thought was an impressive set of documentation to the contrary, including anthropological evidences for the universality of many sex role differences, diagrams of male/female brain differences, and photographs comparing male and female nerve cells. While alternative arguments existed, I pointed out, there was extensive and reputable evidence in favor of what the minister's wife had written. In fact, historically, it was the psychologist's view that was novel, and it was difficult to sustain logically and empirically as well. The editor might personally disagree with this viewpoint, but to dismiss it uninspected and even censor it as if it really were pseudo-scientific and poorly documented would be unfair and unwarranted.

The editor listened intently and asked appropriate questions. Then, she startled me with her decision[2]—the debated passages would remain deleted!

My career in evangelical academia had begun only months earlier. Since then, I have continued to be alarmed by a growth in the kinds of phenomena I witnessed in that encounter. All the elements of censorship, intolerance of opposing viewpoints, fallacious reasoning, and argument-by-assertion that I have seen in contemporary feminism are evident in the "new" feminist evangelicalism.[3] This seems to be growing in influence. Evangelicals are, just as the general public is, increasingly accepting feminist portrayals of reality and prescriptions for change, even where these contradict not only Scripture but also their own personal experiences and aspirations.

To ignore competing arguments in an area of such broad ramifications as male/female differentiation is more dangerous than the Soviet refusal to debate Marx. As in Communism, we have seen repeatedly that if wrong assumptions and the theories flowing from them are not challenged, they will be accepted and applied. But they will fail. Naturally, proponents attempt to hide or discount these failures and the human misery associated with them. Still, denial can't last forever, and reality will have its day. But at what cost?

As we shall see, feminist ideology has profound implications for the family, business, the economy, politics, the military, marriage, sexual preference and identity, childrearing, and education. The mechanisms by which society has prepared, placed, and sustained each generation are being called into question. The requested changes are not just "reform"; they are truly revolutionary and are presented by feminists as such. Such alterations are far-reaching. Common sense demands, then, that they be seriously debated. But the truth is, enormous *de facto* censorship is directed toward any work questioning the basic tenets and consequences of feminism, and a decidedly slanted picture of this movement is being presented in the media.

For example, a recent "evaluation" of feminism in *Time* was written by an admitted feminist.[4] Amazingly, the widely recognized feminist neglect of the needs of full-time mothers and housewives was presented as overstated, and the idea prevailed that feminism was really "for" all women. This contradicts the views of feminist writers themselves, who tend to support theories and agendas that would completely eliminate such traditions as full-time mothering and male support of women and children, viewing women who live in such conditions as deceived, oppressed, and retrograde.[5] As late as 1981, "moderate" NOW founder Betty Friedan referred to stay-at-home mothers and male breadwinners as "obsolete." Her friend, feminist leader Simone de Beauvoir, asserted in 1975:

> No woman should be authorized to stay at home and raise her children. . . . Women should not have that choice, precisely because if there is such a choice, too many women will make that one.[6]

Yet this author continued to present feminism as a true "women's" movement that desires only "freedom of choice." This is a misnomer recognized clearly by their so-called "reactionary" targets at home with the children! That is why the article in *Time* failed to explain the widespread support for anti-feminist figures like Phyllis Schlafly and Beverly LaHaye and organizations such as Right-to-Life among precisely these women.[7]

Short on criticism and long on praise, the *Time* author punctuated her article with "objective" statements like those describing the "ERA" and "lesbian rights" as "noble causes." Not one interview with an educated critic of feminism was included. Although widely available, no alternative interpretations of the "feminist triumphs," "male feminization," evidence of "gender discrimination," etc., were considered. The term "women's movement" was used synonymously with "feminism," a highly inaccurate designation sociologically.

For poll items purporting to show positive responses to feminism, none dealt specifically with "hard" items like lesbian marriage, "unisexism" as an ideal for children, or placing women in combat. Like most popular media, the article dealt more with a "soft" image than with the real goals of feminists. In fact, as Nicholas Davidson has pointed out, the feminists' "dream" ticket of Mondale and Ferrarro in 1984 gave voters a meaningful referendum on the specifics of feminism and failed miserably to register with women.[8] As with the ERA struggle, poll data like those used in the *Time* article are biased and fail to detect the true feelings and practices of American women relative to most of the specific tenets of feminism.[9]

Such bias is understandable. A large number of studies have documented the strong and unrepresentative leftism, including pro-feminism, of the "social-cultural specialists," a group that includes artists, people in media and communications of all types, social and behavioral scientists, and to a lesser degree human service professionals and educators (especially those in the upper echelons).[10]

The result is that, as Davidson has pointed out, "No aspect of modern life has been so inadequately debated as feminism. Every year, thousands of feminist books pour off the presses. . . . In contrast, books that present opposing viewpoints are rare, and the 'Lace Curtain' of networked feminists make sure that they seem even rarer."[11] Feminist pressure makes the publication of works that challenge their position arduous and costly. Publishers are often hard to find. Many agree to publish, only to alter their decision later under external or internal feminist pressure. Two authors who, using respected and widely available studies, confronted the myth of male predominance in domestic abuse were threatened by feminists with loss of research grant monies.[12]

There is a price to be paid by any social scientist who challenges feminism. But the stakes are high, and the truth must be stated. Feminism is based on presuppositions that are simply indefensible. The analyses and bromides of modern feminism flow directly from these false assumptions. As a result, the application of feminism, while producing some positive benefit, has been coercive and tremendously destructive to society at all levels. It is to these issues that I now turn.

The Assumptions of Feminism

I was conversing with a friend at a party recently, a conservative fellow whose wife is a full-time mother and home schooler. Neither he nor his wife has much use for feminism. Yet, when I explained my deep concern to him that Christian feminism would produce the same kinds of fruit as the secular variety, he expressed some incredulity: "But they wouldn't believe all the same things as secular feminism, would they?"

His reaction is fairly typical among evangelicals—feminism in the church will take relatively benign forms. But this is to hope against hope, as so many Christian feminists have proven in recent years. Ultimately, this is because they make the same basic assumptions as do secular feminists, and these assumptions have logical correlates.

The foundation of feminism was stated by the feminist psychologist on my college's faculty, whom I cited at the beginning of this chapter: general sexual "non-differentness," full cultural determinism of sex roles, and the undoubted changeability of sex roles. States Levin:

> Feminism in its contemporary form is an empirical doctrine leading to recommendations for social action. The doctrine has three main tenets:
>
> 1. Physical differences apart, men and women are the same. Infant boys and girls are born with virtually the same capacities and if raised identically would develop identically.
>
> 2. Men occupy positions of dominance because the myth that men are more aggressive has been perpetuated by the practice of raising boys to be mastery oriented and girls to be person oriented. If this stereotyping ceased, leadership would be equally divided between the sexes.
>
> 3. True human individuality and fulfillment will come only when people view themselves as human repositories of talents and traits, without regard to sex.[13]

Generally, this is a pure "nurture" argument, reflecting a school of thought that sees all human morality, thought, and behavior, ultimately, as products of culture and socialization. Referred to broadly here as the "cultural determinist" school, this implies an extreme relativism. All aspects of human life, outside of necessary physiological functions (breathing, eating, etc.) are seen as subject to variation.

Given the evidence, some feminists do admit to some innate biological difference, but they minimize its impact and relevance. Most, however, ignore it entirely or deny its existence. This is a fatal mistake, since *"if there are important biologically-based differences between the sexes, the rest of contemporary feminism falls apart . . . what is obviously unattainable cannot be the object of rational human effort. In this sense, if the factual assumption of feminism is wrong, the rest is irrational."*[14]

In fact, all the major positions of feminism can be traced back to the assumption that there is no significant difference between the sexes. To feminists, all (or almost all) such social dissimilarities result from male dominance and oppression, and "justice" requires the eradication of such "unnecessary" differences. This is the basic theme of the *Time* article described above. Its headline statement, "And baby, there's still a long way to go,"[15] indicates more than bald support for feminism. It implies a march that must go on until female and male average wages are equal (which, of course, requires female participation in full-time work to the same extent as men); until all educational outcomes are exactly the same; until an equal distribution of males and females exists in every occupation, at every level; until our children's "subjective gender identification" is unisexual or at least completely nonpredictable based on their biological sex. All "gaps" must be eliminated, whatever the cost, because no gap is "chosen" or "natural"—gaps are all products of male oppression, they all prevent true actualization of self.

But if men and women are truly different, the vision crumbles. *If a "unisexual" world is unnatural, only force can maintain it, only failure and misery can accompany it.*

Are the Feminist Presuppositions True?

The fundamental feminist assumption is increasingly being shown to be fallacious. In spite of tremendous pressure and even bias, professionals in the biological and social sciences are generating findings that support the traditional viewpoint that healthy individuals and societies express, rather than deny, the complementary differences between the sexes.

As these facts steadily reveal feminist error in theory and practice alike, soul searching occurs, and some adjustments are made. For example, a "neo-feminist" reevaluation and glorification of femininity is emerging, based on the extensive research that uncovers the distinctive psychology of female cognition, morality, and behavioral response.

Still, on the whole, writers in these areas steadfastly refuse to apply a biological anchor to their findings and continue to believe in the possibility of an egalitarian, unisexual world.[16] Like our feminist psychologist friend, most have stuck with the theories of cultural determinism, "nurture," and male oppression to explain sexual differences.

But their belief in cultural determinism is simply incapable of standing up to logical, systematic observation of reality. Universally, social outcomes reflect what one would expect, given the kind of neurological, hormonal, and other physical sex differences uncovered by biologists and physiologists.[17] Stephen Goldberg, an expositor of the universality of sex role differentiation, has used empirical studies on humans, mostly anthropological, to sustain and defend this position through about seventeen years of intense debate. He states: ". . . the sexual stereotypes now so derided turn out to be basically correct."[18]

The arguments over the universality of sex differences are crucial and represent more than mere academic quibbling. Only through such discussion can biological differences be established as having social relevance. If, across the dazzling variety of cultures, such similarities consistently emerge, it is a distortion of logic to assume that each society has found an essentially similar way through socialization alone.

Mechanisms for evolving such universal sex role differences have been discussed, but none stands up to logical evaluation.[19] Socialization alone, though essential to human development and carried out in very different ways, cannot produce the same basic patterns of relationships and divisions of labor between the sexes without some innate qualities shared across cultures and time. The cultural determinist school, says Levin, ". . . ignores the question of why every society has chosen to do things the same way. . . . Given the universality of sex-role differentiation, the feminists' 'taught' collapses into 'innate': it is evidently an innate feature of human beings that they will train their male and female offspring differently."[20] Thus, feminists are left to abandon the nurture argument altogether, which requires denying their vision or proving that the universality of sex role differences is wrong after all and can be gotten around. Attempts at both of these, however, have failed.

The primary examples of universal male/female differences lie in the areas of male dominance, superiority in status achievement, and patriarchy. These have been accompanied by sexual division of labor, in which men are generally "instrumental" and oriented toward mastery of the external world, while women are "expressive," relationship oriented and directed toward domestic concerns, particularly child rearing.

Anthropologist William Stephens states:

> . . . these are the apparent near-universals of husband-wife rules:
>
> 1. A standard division of labor by sex.

2. The "essential femininity" of some tasks, such as child care, and the "essential masculinity" of other tasks, such as fishing.

3. Power and privilege: the husband's status is either equal or higher than the wife's; matriarchies are rare."[21]

Even this statement, powerful as it is, is probably too qualified. True matriarchies are non-existent; within all societies, on the average, male status is higher. Still, his three rules are cultural universals. This point has been extensively made by Goldberg.[22] In fact, Stephens points out in his own work that if there are any societies that even come close to full sexual egalitarianism, ours comes "as close as any."[23]

Scores of societies are put forward by angry feminists as evidence of a reversal of one or another of the above rules. All fail a review of their respective ethnographies. In fact, the evidence for universal sex role differentiation is often found in the same documents that were used by feminists to demonstrate the contrary.

For example, many Communist societies, based on their egalitarian rhetoric, have been put forward as "sex-neutral." Most commonly heroized have been Cuba, China, and the U.S.S.R.. All have turned out to be more than stultifying, cruel, and economically retarded. They are also far more patriarchal than the average Western nation!

One interesting example of a futile attempt by cultural determinists to disprove universality was the Arapesh. Margaret Mead wrote, "We found that men, as well as women, were trained to be co-operative, non-aggressive, responsive to the needs of others. We found no idea that sex was a powerful driving force either for men or for women."[24] But, in the same ethnography, Arapesh males were shown to abduct women, follow an all-male leadership,[25] and "oppress" their women by according them a more central role in childrearing.[26] Despite much "press" to the contrary, while Arapesh males were more child-centered than most, they did not behave like Alan Alda![27]

Such findings, amazingly, have not deterred feminists from looking for evidence of cultural determinism as a basis for what they believe to be widely varying sexual roles. In order to disprove the inevitability of sexual differences, they have found an unusual arena in which to demonstrate new "possibilities" for female involvement—crime.

Universally, males predominate in criminal activity. In cultures across the world, women rarely exceed 20 percent of total arrests and are usually a much lower proportion than that. Like all universal sex differences, this fact contains the obvious implication that innate qualities of the sexes make an enormous difference in social outcomes. Thus, it has been of paramount importance to feminists that a gender-crime connection prove *not* to be inevitable. One solution has been to show that, to the extent that men and women participate in similar activities, they will have similar rates of crime. Since this has occurred to some extent in the U.S. over the last twenty to thirty years, feminists have predicted that Americans would witness just such a shift.

In fact, some feminists believe that this has occurred. For example, as part of an attempted refutation of Goldberg's "universality of patriarchy" thesis, Cynthia Epstein wrote in 1986:

> Increasing convergence of gender role behavior is also seen in studies of crime. Girls' crime rates show increasing similarity to that of boys. Girls and boys both commit violent crimes and exhibit increasingly similar criminal histories.[28]

Epstein emphasizes violent crime, and this is appropriate, since such activity would be most closely correlated with innate male aggression and dominance patterns, if these actually exist. The problem is, her assertions are patently false.

Even if there had been *some* increase in female participation in violent crime, relative to men, the female crime rate would still be a drop in the ocean compared to the male rate. Until there is a very strong and prolonged increase, any discussion of "convergence" is grossly premature.

Yet, as Wilson and Hernnstein demonstrated in a highly regarded work published a year *prior* to Epstein's statement, the female proportion of the most frequently measured violent crimes remained steady from 1960 to 1980; about 10 percent. From 1965 to 1977, a time in which many of these alleged changes in violent crime and sex roles were said to have occurred, the female arrest percentage for murder *dropped* by 3.5 percent! Any "convergence" is minuscule in the various violent crimes, as in other categories of crime traditionally dominated by males. And while the female percentage of property crimes had increased a great deal, approaching 31 percent in larceny and almost 35 percent in fraud for the period 1973-1979, these increases are far more attributable to family breakdown and the resultant stress of single-parent homes than to any increased similarity in sex roles.[29]

Ultimately, the authors rejected any notion of a female revolution in sex roles *or* crime:

> Just as the gender gap in crime has survived the changes of recent decades, so also have the major sex roles, and most probably for similar reasons. The underpinnings of the sexual division of labor in human society, from the family to commerce to industry to government, may not be rigidly fixed in the genes, but their roots go so deep into the biological substratum that beyond certain limits they are difficult to change. At least until now, the gender gap in serious criminal behavior has fallen outside the limits of change in the sexual division of labor.[30]

The failure to find exceptions to patriarchy and sexual division of labor, even in crime, has not stopped feminists from looking, but their attention has turned to a more creative task—*constructing* an alternative. After all, as feminist Alice Rossi has anguished, "Even if they are sorely handicapped by lack of testosterone, it is inescapably necessary for women at this stage in human evolution to move to equality in society."[31]

How this might be done (legally) in the area of crime is a tough question. But with regard to other forms of social change, the answer seems clearer, at least to feminists: environmental and cultural alterations thorough and consistent enough to overcome any (insignificant) biological predispositions and especially the large residue of "sexism." This means eradicating male ideology in favor of an egalitarian, feminist one; providing unisex childrearing and universal day care to enable all women to work at "meaningful" (i.e., paid) jobs; providing equal access to all occupations and status positions, including political ones, and strongly encouraging female participation in these; downgrading the centrality of marriage and family life in favor of community work and individualized expression; and heightened sexual freedom (at least for adults). Such an experiment is best attempted with a highly dedicated group of egalitarians first, in order to demonstrate its viability. Then, once superior results have been demonstrated, it can be transferred to the larger society.

The problem for the feminists is that such an experiment has already been tried—the Israeli Kibbutz. And, at least from the standpoint of feminist egalitarianism, it has failed.

As Davidson points out, the Kibbutzniks sincerely and carefully "sought to implement a unisexist conception of equality between the sexes. The actual conditions of life in the kibbutz closely parallel the changes feminists advocate to eliminate gender distinctions in America."[32]

American conceptions of the Kibbutz, influenced by feminist dissemination of early research findings that favored their utopian expectations (and hostility to later ones that did not), provide an idealized picture of the alterability of sex roles. Feminists and cultural determinists of all types were exulting in the Kibbutz as "proof" that marriage, family, and sex roles were not universal. In 1954, Spiro claimed "the family . . . does not exist in the Kibbutz." Yet, four years later, he admitted that there was some minimal family life there; his earlier work had used too narrow a definition.[33]

By 1979, Spiro had completely rejected his earlier view and had begun a critique of feminist ideology itself.[34] The reason, as Tiger and Shepher documented in 1975, is that by then the Kibbutz had "reverted" to "male domination" in the political and economic sphere, sex-biased occupational patterns in the labor market, and disproportionate female attention to home and family. Worse (from a feminist point of view), the females in the Kibbutz had led the way, demanding more time with their children, insisting on larger homes and time to work in them, and asking their husbands to stay out of the "female" jobs at home! Women began to turn down "status" occupational and political opportunities consistently in favor of time at home, even where these were insistently offered, and even where female candidates had better qualifications than the available males. Thus, male "political oppression" and "sexist divisions of labor" were being demanded by ideologically committed, egalitarian women!

In contrast to feminist assertions to the contrary, Tiger and Shepher point out, there was no evidence of overt or even subtle coercion by males. Instead, the men often exerted great pressure on the women to forego children and home in favor of work and politics. The drive for "familism" in the Kibbutz was initiated and sustained by female pressure.

This was a surprise. After all, the Kibbutz system had professional child care and provided adequate living space for couples, so there was no "need" for wives to be domestically oriented. Compared to earlier times, there was less "need" for larger numbers, or more personalized care, of children. Also contrary to feminist ideology, childbearing obligations did not automatically prevent female out-of-home involvements. Women were choosing to have larger families and homes and voluntarily relinquishing available day care in favor of personal contact with their children.[35] The problem was not insufficient dedication to feminism, pervasive sexism, or female fear of success, as feminists tried to assert. If so, such "cultural residues" certainly would have prevented other aspects of the Kibbutz vision from being carried out. The realm of sex roles and child care simply seemed peculiarly resistant to change.

Many mothers, pulled between work and children today, could explain what the feminist critic finds incomprehensible. Day care and career opportunities aside, domesticity is uniquely desirable to women. As one Kibbutz woman exclaimed to Tiger and Shepher about the authors' supposedly "incredible" findings: "Why is it all so surprising? What did you expect women to do?"[36]

The feminist response to reports of the "failure" of the Kibbutz was typical—blame the men or question the good sense of the women. For, as with Marxism, those who fail to believe feminist tenets are thought to be suffering from oppression, or to be "mystified" by "false ideology." The authors state that the typical feminist "explanation" of the actions of Kibbutz women

> assumes that men are the center of all things, and that women, lacking any autonomy, must forego thoughtful and independent choices. . . . [Yet] they are not only independent of men in the Kibbutz, but willing and able to act in important ways frowned on and unsuccessfully opposed by the men. . . . [P]eoples' actions are not necessarily the unhappy performances of the duped and confused, and may well reflect what people wholeheartedly want to do. . . . As for those who claim that women who are eager to bear and raise children are tyrannized and obsolete, they can see for themselves how contemporary women on the Kibbutz are.[37]

I am glad that the Kibbutz was attempted. It not only supports universality of patriarchy but also humanizes the data to reveal the choice, even joy, in fulfilling many traditional roles. The complementary interests and aspirations of men and women seem to be not only functional but downright pleasurable, especially in comparison to the barren unisexism of the feminist.

Still, the Kibbutzniks, like all of those who have expended time and effort in an ideological crusade against common sense, might have foregone the pain. They were attempting to do what has never worked, and what most human beings have not even found desirable. No less an anthropologist than Margaret Mead, the leading advocate of cultural determinism and (until her death) reigning queen of American anthropology, stated in 1973:

> It is true . . . that all claims so glibly made about societies ruled by women are nonsense. We have no reason to believe that they ever existed. . . . Men have always been the leaders in public affairs, and the final authorities at home.[38]

With regard to her earlier work on the Arapesh, Tchambuli, and Mundugumor, cited by feminists like Epstein as "proof" that arguments for universal patriarchy are wrong,[39] Mead states, "Nowhere do I suggest that I have found any material which disproves the existence of sex differences."[40] Writes Goldberg,

> Just as patriarchy, male dominance, and male attainment of high status roles and positions are universal, so is the association of nurturance and emotional socialization with the women universal . . . [and] in every society it is women who are responsible for the care and rearing of the young.[41]

It is doubtful that we should lament this fact. Kibbutz women found it in their hearts to demand and celebrate it. Not only is it conducive to individual happiness, but the division of labor that exists in the supposedly "oppressive" Western system and nuclear family seems to do an excellent job of redirecting potentially harmful passions toward the common good, spurring human productivity, and producing the kind of attachment to children and home that insures a viable "next generation."[42] This "oppressive" family also provides a basis for political and economic freedom.[43] While people do not want to be forced into sexual molds, it seems fair to say that, given a choice, most decide to carry out their lives in very stereotypical, but pleasant, ways.

Implementing Feminism: Utopia, Spirituality, and Coercion

The feminist project ignores both man's fallenness and his God-given qualities and limitations. Like Marxism, it works against human nature rather than with it. And, also like Marxism, by replacing Biblical realism with humanistic utopianism, it will bring failure in the long run and coercion in the short run. Further, as with all such systems, to continue as a viable movement, feminism will find it necessary to employ censorship and propaganda as well, both to disguise failure and coercion and to encourage acceptance of its ideas.

As Levin points out, the reality of sex differentiation will not stop the feminist from pursuit of the unisex goal, even as repeated failure requires sterner action. Because, in the process, "evidence will have to be ignored," alternative ideologies suppressed, and "persuasion will give way to coercion."[44] Allan Bloom, author of the well-known *The Closing of the American Mind*, points out that the feminist vision ultimately favors equality over freedom. Its goals are so "unlimited and unconstrained" that it "ends, as do many modern social movements that want abstract justice, in forgetting nature and using force to refashion human beings to secure that justice."[45]

As utopians and advocates of state intervention to eradicate what they see as "inequality" produced by "male oppression," feminists show a remarkable affinity to Marxism and socialism. This includes a tendency to view "private" realms, such as voluntary associations and families, with great suspicion. These are seen as places where, because they are beyond the reach of the state, "male oppression" can be used against women without restraint.[46]

These coercive tendencies, like the presuppositions and comprehensive vision of feminism, are shared by so-called Christian feminists as well. They have the same tendencies toward education and "reform," the same suspicion of full-time motherhood, the same support for abortion, the same sexual "tolerance," etc., as the secularists.[47] They differ only in their special focus on applying these within the Christian community.

Another aspect of modern feminism strongly related to their utopian optimism is their increasing attention to Eastern mysticism, pagan beliefs, and New Ageism to create a spiritual dimension for their movement. Belief in androgyny (possession by each individual of masculinity and femininity in equal parts) is seen, for example, as a helpful way of overcoming the old "patriarchal" monotheism that Judeo-Christian beliefs represent. Old heresies like gnosticism and the Kabbalah are "celebrated." These are seen as more fully expressing the "femininity" in the divine. The essential sexual nature is seen as bisexual. In the quest to overcome old "rationalities" that lead to domination and to "transcend gender," androgyny becomes a "guiding principle of the New Age."[48]

Such a celebration of the feminine as a new spiritual force is not simply part of the backwaters of feminism. It has found a respected place within the mainstream feminist social agenda[49] and is strongly evident as a growing movement within Christianity, including evangelicalism, as well.[50] The growth of a spiritual component to feminism is understandable, given the historic barrenness of secular thought systems. But it is not comforting. These provide a "faith" basis for the utopian vision and increasingly denigrate what they see as "male dominated" tendencies toward rationality and order in favor of personal experience and "relationship" as mechanisms for determining truth.[51] This places the tenets and results of feminism outside the realm of logical debate. The extremely relevant and consistent evidence for sex differentiation becomes irrelevant. For the New Age feminist, it is simply a nuisance to be magically transcended rather than a reality to be seriously grasped and grappled with.

Implementing Feminism: The "Fall-out" of Abortion

Feminists continually talk about the idea that their input into the world will counteract what they see as a persistent violence and dominant spirit inherent in masculinity. The "feminization of culture" is presented as a bromide to cure everything from child abuse to ulcers, nuclear proliferation, and war.[52]

This not only exaggerates enormously the extent to which males are the source of the world's problems but also is negated in the very actions of feminists themselves. For, as they themselves claim proudly, feminism has been a major force behind the legalization, proliferation, and even government financing of abortion. And abortion itself must be seen as the baldest form of coercion of all.

Less obvious is the extent to which abortion is associated with the feminist denial of biology and the universal "nurturant" female sex role. They view their reproductive capacities as their only meaningful differences with men and as the barrier to be overcome for full participation in the male world. Particularly when combined with the feminist emphasis on sexual "freedom," *abortion becomes a necessary component* of the mainstream feminist vision. Abortion technology makes possible the full "emancipation" of women from home and male authority.[53] Nurturance and relationship orientation, then, to the extent that they are acknowledged as a special contribution of women, can be turned toward the public arena rather than "wasted" on home and children alone. Feminist sociologist Kristin Luker, in a lucid and fair comparison of pro-life and pro-choice worldviews, recognized the clear role of the rejection of biology and sex role differentiation in promoting abortion:

> . . . whereas pro-life people believe that men and women are inherently different and therefore have different "natural" roles in life, pro-choice people believe that men and women are substantially equal, by which they mean substantially similar. As a result, they see women's reproductive and family roles not as a "natural" niche but as potential barriers to full equality. . . . [M]otherhood, so long as it is involuntary, is potentially always a low-status, unrewarding role to which women can be banished at any time. Thus . . . control

over reproduction is essential for women to be able to live up to their full human potential.[54]

This deadly legacy, instituted in the name of equality, is the saddest "contribution" of feminism. Intricately tied to the basic assumptions and visions of their thought system, it is, predictably, being advocated increasingly by Christian feminists as well.[55]

Economic Coercion

Abortion, then, is a necessary social requirement for female participation in the marketplace, according to feminist ideology. This is an area in which their tendencies toward socialist-style coercions and utopian fantasy and denial seem particularly obvious. Their actions are informed by a strong belief that the traditional family, along with the idea that mothers and families are the preferable caretakers of children, is obsolete. In a recent seminar held by *Ladies Home Journal*, participants roundly rejected the idea of a female return to home as "a retreat to unreality" and a "return to Disneyland."[56] In spite of the strongly contrary evidence presented by cross-cultural studies and the Kibbutz, feminists persistently maintain that, given the right support, even mothers of small children and infants will gladly leave the home to pursue career-oriented lives in the marketplace.

Besides entailing a persistent negativity toward the intelligence, character, and worth of full-time homemakers, these views severely under-represent the extent to which women, like the Kibbutzniks, willingly forego status and career aspirations in favor of child care. A recent study found that only 19 percent of American families followed the "careerist" pattern advocated by feminism (dual-career couple with children cared for by an unrelated person). Fully four out of ten families followed the traditional pattern of a full-time mother and provider father, and another 18 percent were families in which, while both partners worked, child care was always provided by one of the parents or a close relative. The rest were "single parent" homes.[57] Fully 65 percent of American homes with children under five provide day care primarily though the parents. Some use flexible scheduling, but 54 percent of those primarily use mothers at home.[58] Furthermore, a recent Harris poll indicated that full-time motherhood is an ideal for the vast majority of Americans. Fully 82 percent felt that the best child care is that provided by a mother at home.[59] Clearly, while times have changed, the brave new world of feminism is not an ideal for most Americans. Many, including a large percent of those misleadingly classified by the Department of Labor as "working" or "full-time working" mothers,[60] are turning down material rewards in favor of the next generation, just as the Kibbutz women did.

In spite of the fact that almost all of the alleged "discrimination" in pay and promotions can be traced back to these kinds of choices (along with the natural effects of recent arrival in the work place and decreased experience), feminists continue to promote government intervention in order to create "equalization," i.e., near-complete female participation, in the workplace.[61] The most popular and well-known path is universal day care, a social policy proposal that has been growing in political support. Providing universal day care is, to them, an issue of basic "justice" and of meeting "huge unmet demands."

Through direct and indirect pressure, feminists have attempted to exaggerate support for day care and to suppress research that might reveal the extent to which such care is questionable in its effects on children, as pointedly shown by former leading day care advocate Jay Belsky.[62] Yet, this is a suspicion shared by fully 68 percent of the respondents in a 1987 Gallup poll on the subject. In fact, where day care is required, 75 percent of Americans state a clear preference for child care by relatives and 12 percent for care by neighbors. Only 13 percent see formal, group day care as the preferable option.[63]

Their concerns are well-founded. Such centers have been strongly related to the transmission of diseases such as hepatitis, meningitis, cytomegalovirus, and other illnesses.[64] Increasing evidence of negative psychological effects such as disruptions in maternal bonding, aggression, impulsivity, selfishness, and later school discipline problems is emerging in the research literature. Marked anger and a sense of rejection are seen in many day care children. There is also a growing recognition that many "findings" of positive day care effects were found in idealized child care situations, such as university-based centers, rather than in the kind of care that could reasonably be afforded and expected by average parents.[65] The potential harm of a broad emphasis on day care goes beyond the possible negative impact on children, however, and it is more than a probable waste of tax dollars. Government-sponsored universal day care would increase the favored financial status treatment of wealthier, two-career and single-parent families relative to the struggling majority, creating an economic and tax climate that would cripple the wage-earning power of primary (usually male) providers and further punish stable traditional or semi-traditional families. Eventually, as in Sweden, mothers would be forced into the workplace by financial pressures, and many would find marriage and childrearing themselves to be increasingly unprofitable options.[66] One recalls Simone de Beauvoir's statement that feminism should act to prevent women from having a "choice" to stay at home. Universal day care is a vehicle toward that end. By increasing the already disproportionate tax burden on traditional families,[67] the classic socialist advocacy of taxation as a tool for engineering the new order would be evident.

Another feminist-supported program to decrease "gaps" in the labor force is affirmative action for women. However, the idea that women should be proportionately (50 percent) represented in all or most occupations is unrealistic. As long as many women are not aspiring to be in the labor force as full-time career people (with hourly demands that often exceed 40 hours per week), there are likely to be serious "shortfalls" of women in many job categories. Furthermore, due at least partly to inborn differences in physical strength, aggression, status aspirations, and capacities and interests in areas like math, theoretical logic, mechanics, combat, etc., even stiffer quota problems will be likely to continue in areas that are traditionally male and favor male tendencies. Women simply avoid many "masculine" jobs, and high turnover generally prevails among women who enter them.[68]

The obvious result, which has already occurred in the armed services, military academies, and police and fire departments, is drastically lower standards for women to fill quotas. This has several insidious effects. First, it is discouraging to those who have met the traditional, higher standards. Second, it unnecessarily stigmatizes those women who have earned their jobs fairly, since an assumption of favoritism tends to emerge in jobs and population groups subject to massive affirmative action. Third, where specific skill superiority is critical, as in combat, police, and fire work, decreasing standards can also lead to negative performance and even loss of life.[69] Finally, organizations that are unable to fill quotas are consistently faced with the threat of government intervention and even lawsuits, a kind of constant sword of Damocles hanging over them.

However, the most far-reaching and dangerous feminist proposal to date is "comparable worth." Faced with a female population that continues to behave like women in terms of occupational choice and the reality that many of their jobs do not carry high status or high pay (usually for multiple reasons having little to do with discrimination against women), a large number of feminist thinkers have recommended that the government establish standard wages and salaries between occupations to decrease what they see as labor market injustice. These might, for example, command hospitals to lower payments to physicians and increase them for nurses to achieve a better "gender balance."

In practice, if seriously implemented, comparable worth would create extensive socialism. Massive and continuing government intervention, tremendously expensive, would be required to review existing jobs and update wage scales for the new occupational categories proliferating in our changing economy. Establishing a "just" basis for wages would also be arbitrary, and in practice this would become subject to the political activity of pressure groups.

Disguised under a cloak of "fairness," comparable worth would establish an incredible expansion of state bureaucracy and seriously undermine the potency of market forces.[70] It is one of the clearest illustrations of the fact that, even among so-called moderate feminists like Friedan, there is a Marxist-like willingness to brush away choice in favor of an elusive "equality of results." Given the failure of such state control of economy that has produced much of the current upheavals throughout the U.S.S.R. and the Eastern Bloc, that such a policy would be advocated at this time is utterly incomprehensible.

In all the feminist proposals targeted on the marketplace, there is a single unrelenting logic: to free women from the "male oppression" of the private sphere and to create the society that was originally sought in the Kibbutz—one of complete male/female "sameness." In spite of the wide rejections of a "careerist" norm for women, writes Gilder,

> Most feminist proposals seem designed to establish the working mother as the social norm by making it impossible for most male providers to support the family alone. The feminist attack on the social security system for giving housewives a right to the husband's benefits after he dies; the subsidies for day care; the affirmative action quotas for women who pursue careers outside the home—all such measures seek to establish the careerist woman as the national standard and incapacitate the woman who tries to care for her own children.[71]

Education

The feminist egalitarian and anti-biological vision is also clearly seen in the educational policies feminists promote. The school system is, for them, the realm in which their visions for sexuality, family, and career can be transmitted to the next generation and in which the often conservative influences of home and church can be overcome:

> Unlike other educational reforms, feminist pedagogy does not aim primarily at changing the way in which knowledge is transmitted to children. Rather, it aims to change children's personalities and attitudes toward each other, in the hope of producing children not crippled by sexism, children open to nontraditional goals and the adaption of characteristics once arbitrarily linked to sex.[72]

Sex differences in SAT and other educational test performance have long reflected well-known biological differences between the sexes, such as the male tendency to be more adept at and interested in the manipulation and observation of objects and the female tendency to focus on people, or the male tendency to have stronger motor skills and a predisposition toward "spatial visualization" that provides them an edge "in painting and certain branches of music."[73] Overall, as noted in hundreds of studies and as shown to be universal in cross-cultural studies, "Man would thus appear, on average, to be more gifted at perceiving the physical world and woman that of social relations."[74]

It is difficult, logically, to blame sex discrimination for test score differences such as exist in the SAT. Educational Testing Service researchers have pointed out that, as noted above, "categories designated 'world of practical affairs' and 'science' are typically easier for males, whereas the categories designated 'aesthetics/philosophy' and 'human relationships' are easier for females."[75] Furthermore, in its demand that males curtail their naturally higher rate of physical activity in favor of long hours of sedentary study, and through its emphasis on verbal ability, submissiveness, and regularity in study and attendance, schools clearly favor women. Males have much higher rates of dropout, grade failure, and disciplinary problems, and female students have a higher average performance.[76]

Still, based on their anti-biological theory and egalitarian agenda, feminists are forced to deny the validity of those differences in SAT test results. They have recently begun demanding that many SAT items in areas like science, economics, and math, in which males outperform females, be dropped or replaced as "sexist" and "discriminatory" by "gender-neutral" ones.[77] Not only would such manipulation contribute (conveniently) to feminist censorship of science by erasing a major indicator of sex differences; it is also silly. Given our strong national need to improve performance in these very subjects in order to compete successfully in our increasingly demanding world economy, it is not at all wise to subject measurement, training, or recruiting in these areas to the whims of feminist "sexual politics."

Another goal for feminists has been the effort, often coercive, to eradicate "sex bias" in the classroom. This includes techniques like breaking up even voluntary single-sex groups, avoiding praising girls for neatness, and calling on girls *more* often than boys to compensate for the female passivity and male aggressiveness that lead boys to raise their hands more often.[78] This occasionally approaches the absurd and the bizarre. Faced with evidence that boys are scolded more often by teachers than girls and receive lower grades, feminist Betty Levy asserted that it was really the girls who were being subject to discrimination! Why? "[T]eacher criticism, a seemingly negative response, may actually lead boys toward greater independence, autonomy, and activity."[79]

The final object of all of this, of course, is to prepare students, ideologically and practically, for the feminist world of full egalitarianism at home and work. With this in mind, feminists have demanded and instituted "unisex" education.

This depicts a world in which females and males are equally involved in all activities, from childrearing to the executive suite. It is to be promoted in school texts and the classroom, even where such a depiction grossly distorts reality, as in ludicrous attempts to eliminate the disproportionate historical representation of men as leaders in science and politics. Feminist leader Alice Rossi has even demanded that field trips be eliminated or modified, because "going out into the community in this way, youngsters would observe men and women in their present occupational roles." The goal is to confront children with the world the feminists believe *ought* to exist. A Senatorial investigation revealed that a committee with the old federal Department of Health, Education and Welfare was, in the late 1970s, "reviewing children's books for 'sexism,' on the grounds that schoolbooks should represent reality 'not as it is or was, but as it will be.'"[80] Such tactics are reminiscent of the Soviet system of brainwashing and censorship.

The feminist agenda in the schools is dangerous. It bypasses the role of parents in inculcating values and worldview to children and often dishonors them and their home by presenting their way of living as backward and unjust. It subverts the goals of education by placing the pursuit of indoctrination higher on the ladder of priorities than the traditional emphases on the transmission of skills, awareness of reality, and pursuit of truth.

Furthermore, it may have other direct and deleterious impacts on children. For example, Levin has submitted the common-sense observation that children will not trust educators who deliberately distort reality and the truth, and this will be plain to most students. Also, for some students, confusion of gender identity may occur,[81] and this is destructive for healthy human development.[82] Finally, children often become quite disturbed at the continual presentation of "non-stereotypical" or "gender-reversed" materials, particularly as they become more aggressive or obvious, simply because these do often violate reality and their innate sense of self. This, even where manifest, does not necessarily deter the teachers, and viewing student reactions as demonstrating latent "sexism" is common. For example, feminist author Judith Bardwick has categorized as "anti-feminist backlash" the anger, resistance, and conflict shown by pupils to school programs that directly attempt (as she phrases it) to "reduce children's sexism" through pointed discussions of "male oppression" and challenges to traditional sex stereotypes. She does not question the value of such programs, but ruefully notes:

> Another source of resistance to feminist goals is the conservatism of children. They seem very resistant to changing ideas about what the sexes are supposed to do and be like. This is probably because their gender is the only thing about them that does not change as they grow up.[83]

These reactions are a natural response to deep challenges directed against the most important aspect of human identity, consistent with all that we know about children biologically and cross-culturally. They reflect tendencies evident from infancy and confirmed, primarily, by their third birthday.[84] In light of this, Bardwick's response that these reflect deeply ingrained "sexism" that can and will give way to the feminists' vision is odd but typical. It is this kind of faith that causes feminists to pursue their program in the schools long after the negative responses and protests of the children themselves would make the more squeamish among us desist.[85]

Family

In the *Time* article described earlier, the fact that 94 percent of participants saw feminism as providing more "independence" for women and 86 percent thought it promised more personal "control"[86] was unashamedly celebrated. After all, female autonomy is "what it was all about."

Affirmative action and comparable worth will assure a job and adequate financial compensation. Contraception, abortion, and day care will secure freedom from children. The educational system will ensure that the next generation will partake of these fruits more fully than we did, by urging them toward their "opportunities" and stripping away the old "sex stereotypes" that might hold them back. And should any get squeamish about this brave new world—well, in Swedish fashion, high tax rates, Social Security reductions for housewives, inadequate child deductions, and special tax incentives for "working parents" will use the stick of financial necessity to lovingly ease us back into the path of dual-career egalitarianism. A great gift is being given, we are told—independence and control, freedom from the millstones of domestic obligation.

Is this a dream, or a nightmare? Reality suggests that there is, perhaps, a dark side to all of this.

The feminist revolution has made an incredible contribution to the soaring divorce rate. This is to be predicted, given feminists' consistently pessimistic evaluations of marriage.[87] Feminists directly promote eased divorce restrictions, a fact usually ignored in the popular media.[88] Indirectly, the kind of practical, often financial independence fostered in the "new woman" has been consistently linked to a heightened risk of divorce.[89] This is aggravated further by the amazing fact that, after having encouraged easy divorce laws (partly to provide a vehicle of escape from "male oppression") and denigrating the institution of marriage, feminists continually stress the need for women to develop the skills and outlook necessary to be able to provide for families on their own. Why? They are likely to have to do so, it is preached, because of the high divorce rate![90]

Feminist Judith Bardwick has described and lamented the causes of divorce as follows:

> We can predict a higher divorce rate *when the criteria of success in marriage change from family*, integrity, security, and contentment *to happiness in which people are to grasp opportunity to feel vital; when compromise is judged to be a sign of inadequacy; when "doing your own thing" and "getting yours" are legitimized.* . . . [W]hen divorce is easy to obtain . . . *when the negative costs of commitment are emphasized* . . . *when selfishness is idealized* as autonomy . . . and *moral responsibility is to the self* rather than to the relationship, divorce increases. . . . Commitment involves not only mutual feeling but also interdependent obligation.[91]

Interestingly, she fails to realize how severely she indicts the very feminist system she promotes.

Compare secular feminist Bardwick's ideas with the social-contract marital vision presented by Christian feminists Scanzoni and Scanzoni:

> In an equal-partner marriage, both spouses are equally committed to their respective careers. . . . Furthermore, there is role interchangeability with respect to the breadwinner and domestic roles . . . a woman should have autonomy and should find her fulfillment in her own achievement endeavors rather than through second-hand enjoyment of her husbands' success. Under these egalitarian sex-role norms, a woman should be free to pursue her own interests without subordination to those of her husband and children.[92]

At every point, the "dream" of the Scanzonis correlates with the nightmare of Bardwick!

Certainly, divorce itself is bad in its effects. For example, evidence is emerging regarding the long-term psychological traumatization of children from divorced homes.[93] The loss of a complete set of sex-role models leads to confusion in sexual identity for both boys and girls.[94] The single-parent home has also long been associated with enhanced poverty and vulnerability to juvenile delinquency (which, for many, leads to adult criminal careers) among children.[95]

Yet even more important, perhaps, is the atomization of society that is encouraged by feminism, of which divorce is merely a symptom. Like all aspects of feminism, this too is rooted in feminists' rejection of the biological sex role differentiation. Sex-complementarity demands interdependence, and heterosexual interdependence at that. The completion of the two as "one," the essential glue of family and society, implies a mutual need of the other. But where maleness and femaleness are arbitrary and interchangeable, autonomy becomes possible and interdependence is rendered optional and fragile.

Yet we do not work that way. That masculine and feminine strengths and weaknesses are not so easily "reprogrammed" has been amply shown in the failure of unisex and androgynous childrearing strategies.

Androgyny has been presented by feminists as the new goal for healthy parents and children. "Liberated" parents have rejected the old psychiatric orthodoxy that psychological health implies the development of distinctive masculine and feminine traits in children. This is seen as another evidence of "sexist ideology."

Logically, the idea seems puzzling. Many of the traits identified are somewhat mutually exclusive—such as aggression and passivity. To possess both in equal measure would be bizarre, demonstrating confusion rather than psychological health.[96] Yet this caution has been brushed aside. And for some, such as New Age androgynist June Singer, like the outmoded dichotomy of good and evil, androgyny unlocked a spiritual dynamic that was to transcend these puzzling dualities.[97] Early research, conducted mostly among college students, proved promising in its results.

But when data began to be collected on actual parents and children, a different reality emerged. Baumrind, in a very thorough study, found that sex-typed parents and their "stereotypical" children were much more competent and mentally well adjusted than were the androgynous sets.[98] Role reversals did not fare well either. As Carlson states, "[Baumrind] reported clear correlations between feminine fathers and cognitive incompetence in girls, and between masculine mothers and social irresponsibility in boys."[99] In research testing the relationship between androgyny and "neuroticism, . . . assertiveness, and self-esteem," Ray and Lovejoy discovered that "[t]hose who were androgynous were generally low scorers on the three indices of mental health."[100]

The attempt by feminists to prevent "sexism" in children by (forcibly) exposing them to cross-sex tasks and experiences, based on the androgyny ideal, or the similar notion that sex roles are arbitrary and should be "selected," has also fallen on hard times. Showing that little girls acquire their sexual identity (feminine) naturally, but that boys are more fragile, Harvard researcher Dorothy Ullian "warned that cross-sex play and other 'sex role interventions' could psychologically cripple little boys."[101] Sara Bonnet Stein's extensive study on unisex child rearing revealed a tremendous resistance among children to being made to be "gender neutral."[102] For example, when given the same toys, children do different things with them; given blocks, the tendency is for boys to build roads, while girls build rooms and houses.

Culture and socialization do not provide complete answers to this. The children's reactions are too strong, detailed, and spontaneous, appear much too early, and are too reflective of patterns seen across a wide variety of cultures to suggest that they have acquired them through the unwitting and residual "sexism" of their egalitarian moms and dads. They are striving to protect that most permanent and precious seed within them—their sexual identity.[103] And when parents become coercive in their attempts at "enlightened" childrearing, points out Davidson, this seems to prove damaging to the child.[104]

We should be thankful for what Bardwick has, so sadly, called the "conservatism" and "sexism" of children. For if unisexism and androgyny were successful, we would be creating children complete in themselves. They would not need "oneness" with the other sex, and thus (given optional sexual outlets, which they have today) they would not need marriage either. As the sad record of illegitimate children, "single parent" homes, and the pathological violence and personal instability of unattached, single men have shown us,[105] we cannot afford to disconnect people from marriage this way, as the feminists, wittingly and unwittingly, have done. And we certainly can't afford to deprive them of their sexual natures.

The truth is, in a way, as the androgynists claim. The masculine and the feminine do need to be brought together in one body. God has provided us a means, and it produces children, homes, stability, and love. It is marriage.

Our sexual conditions are not crosses meant to be transcended, overcome, or escaped. In this fallen world, we have enough of those. Rather, they were given to us to be celebrated and embraced.

Conclusion

The feminist viewpoint is destructive because it is grounded in a set of false presuppositions regarding the created order. It leads to coercion, failure, and censorship. It contributes, directly and indirectly, to the growing uncertainty and confusion of the post-Christian world.

The feminists' occasional insights, like their criticism of male neglect of the home and masculine tendencies toward violence and oppression and their emphasis on the special contributions of feminine moral viewpoints,[106] are not grounded in a worldview founded on truth. Thus, these illuminations are negated by faulty analyses and misdirected applications. In fact, their disregard for the real needs of most women and children far surpasses that of the old male order that they seek to replace. Their willingness to impose their will through almost any means at their disposal involves an embrace of power that is a match for most of their "male oppressors."

Feminists need to rethink their concerns from a presuppositional foundation that is consistent with reality and reflects a Biblical understanding of male and female. A worldview that is consistent with the order of things will be full of wisdom. It will not constrict us or make us miserable but will lead to greater social harmony and stability and to personal creativity, happiness, and fulfillment.

19

Is It Legal for Religious Organizations to Make Distinctions on the Basis of Sex?

Donald A. Balasa

Congress shall make no law respecting an establishment of religion, or prohibiting the free exercise thereof. . . . (First Amendment, United States Constitution)

[A]lthough Congress permitted religious organizations to discriminate in favor of members of their faith, religious employers are not immune from liability for discrimination based on race, sex, [or] national origin. . . . (*EEOC v. Pacific Press Publishing Association*, 676 F.2d 1272 (1982) at 1276)

The freedom of individuals and groups to practice their religious beliefs unfettered by government interference is a fundamental right guaranteed by the Constitution of the United States. By enacting landmark legislation such as the Civil Rights Act of 1964, Congress "clearly targeted the elimination of all forms of discrimination as a 'highest priority.'"[1] Balancing the First Amendment right of free exercise of religion with the Congressional mandate to eradicate discrimination has proven a monumental task for the judicial system.

The purpose of this chapter is twofold. First, court decisions determining whether religious organizations are exempt constitutionally from prohibitions of sex discrimination in employment will be examined. An attempt will then be made to derive practical guidelines for religious organizations desiring to make employment distinctions on the basis of sex. Second, the question of whether educational accrediting bodies can lawfully deny a religious school accreditation if the school assigns different roles to men and women will be discussed.

I. Are Religious Organizations Constitutionally Exempt from Prohibitions of Sex Discrimination in Employment?

A. Legislative History

Title VII of the Civil Rights Act of 1964[2] is the backbone of federal antidiscrimination legislation:

> *Employer practices* It shall be an unlawful employment practice for an employer—
>
> (1) to fail or refuse to hire or to discharge any individual, or otherwise to discriminate against any individual with respect to his compensation, terms, conditions, or privileges of employment, because of such individual's race, color, religion, *sex* or national origin; or
>
> (2) to limit, segregate, or classify his employees or applicants for employment in any way which would deprive or tend to deprive any individual of employment opportunities or otherwise adversely affect his status as an employee, because of such individual's race, color, religion, *sex*, or national origin.

The original House of Representatives' version of the Civil Rights Act exempted all religious entities from the Act's coverage. The Senate rejected this approach and limited the exemption to religious corporations, associations, or societies with respect to the employment of individuals *of a particular religion* to perform work connected with the carrying on by such corporations, associations, or societies of their religious activities. The Senate version was accepted by the House and became Section 702 of the Act. The "Section 702 exemption" has been analyzed by the courts in many Title VII cases against religious organizations.

In 1972 another attempt was made to remove religious organizations from the coverage of Title VII. This effort was unsuccessful, but the Section 702 exemption was broadened to allow religious employers to discriminate on the basis of religion with respect to *all* activities, not just *religious* activities.[3] Congress, however, has never explicitly permitted religious organizations to discriminate on grounds *other than* religion (e.g., race, color, sex, or national origin).

B. Court Decisions

Although Congress has not exempted religious groups from Title VII's prohibition of nonreligious discrimination, the courts have done so on a limited basis. There are several federal appellate cases that have held that certain employment distinctions made by a religious organization on the basis of sex are protected by the Free Exercise Clause of the First Amendment and thus are beyond the pale of Title VII scrutiny. A review of the most pertinent decisions is instructive.

In *McClure v. Salvation Army*,[4] a female "officer" (tantamount to a minister in other denominations), charging that she received "less salary and fewer benefits than similarly situated male officers,"[5] initiated a Title VII action. Conceding that Congress did not intend to insulate religious employers from all sex discrimination charges, the Fifth Circuit Court of Appeals nonetheless ruled that application of Title VII to the relationship between a church and its ministers infringed on constitutionally guaranteed religious liberties, and the court denied Officer McClure's claim. The following language from the court's opinion created a "ministerial exception" to Title VII's prohibition of sex discrimination:

> The relationship between an organized church and its ministers is its lifeblood. The minister is the chief instrument by which the church seeks to fulfill its purpose. Matters touching this relationship must necessarily be recognized as of prime ecclesiastical concern. Just as the initial function of selecting a minister is a matter of church administration and government, so are the functions which accompany such a selection. It is unavoidably true that these include the determination of a minister's salary, his place of assignment, and the duty he is to perform in the furtherance of the religious mission of the church.[6]

The "ministerial exception" articulated in *McClure* found fuller expression in *Rayburn v. General Conference of Seventh-Day Adventists*.[7] Carole Rayburn, who held a Master of Divinity degree from the denomination's seminary, did not receive an appointment as an unordained[8] associate in pastoral care in a Seventh-Day Adventist church and sought relief under Title VII. The position entailed serving as pastoral advisor to the children's Sabbath school, leading Bible studies, counseling and pastoring the singles group, and preaching occasionally from the pulpit. Noting the spiritual importance of the roles assumed by an associate in pastoral care, the Fourth Circuit ruled that "introduction of government standards to the selection of spiritual leaders would significantly, and perniciously, rearrange the relationship between church and state."[9] Ms. Rayburn's Title VII action, therefore, ran afoul of the First Amendment and was dismissed.

A more difficult set of facts confronted the Fifth Circuit Court of Appeals in *EEOC v. Southwestern Baptist Theological Seminary*.[10] Southwestern, a Southern Baptist seminary, refused to file a report used by the Equal Employment Opportunity Commission to ascertain whether unlawful employment practices were being committed. The EEOC sought to compel Southwestern to submit the report; the Seminary contended that compliance with the EEOC request would be repugnant to its First Amendment rights.

Relying upon the decision in *McClure*, Southwestern argued that the Free Exercise Clause barred the application of Title VII to the employment activities of a seminary. The court agreed in part. It held:

> (1) that the seminary was a "wholly sectarian" (i.e., wholly denominational) institution;
> (2) that it was entitled to the status of "church" for First Amendment purposes; and
> (3) that the seminary's employment relationship with "ministerial" personnel should be afforded the same protection as the church/pastor relationship.[11]

The court then grappled with the thorny question of which employees would be considered "ministers" according to the *McClure* standard. Faculty were deemed to be intermediaries between the Southern Baptist Convention and future SBC pastors. As a result, Title VII did not apply to the employment relationship between the seminary and its faculty. Members of the administrative staff were classified as either "ministerial" or "non-ministerial," with only the former being entitled to *McClure*-type protection.[12] Finally, support staff were considered non-ministerial and could seek redress under the antidiscrimination provisions of Title VII.

The end result of the case was that the Equal Employment Opportunity Commission was not constitutionally forbidden from obtaining information from Southwestern Baptist Seminary about its non-ministerial employees. The seminary, however, could not be ordered to provide information to the EEOC about ministerial employees.

Yet another matter balancing free exercise and Title VII considerations made its way to the Fifth Circuit. In *EEOC v. Mississippi College*,[13] Mississippi College—a Southern Baptist-affiliated four-year liberal arts institution—was accused by a female part-time assistant psychology professor of violating Title VII. The college allegedly discriminated against her on the basis of sex by hiring a male to fill a full-time position in the psychology department. In its defense, Mississippi College asserted that the male professor was selected because his educational and research background was a better fit for the vacant position. Moreover, the college had a written policy of preferring to hire Baptists—a practice unquestionably protected by the Section 702 exemption—and the male professor was a Baptist, but the female complainant was not.

Since Mississippi College's hiring decision was arguably based on religious factors, the court dismissed the case and did not reach the sex discrimination question. The court nevertheless did seize the chance to distinguish the facts in *Mississippi College* from the *McClure* scenario and left the unmistakable impression that the female professor would have had a full hearing on the merits of her sex discrimination charge had she been a Baptist.

> The College is not a church. The College's faculty and staff do not function as ministers. The faculty members are not intermediaries between a church and its congregation. They neither attend to the religious needs of the faithful nor instruct students in the whole of religious doctrine. That faculty members are expected to serve as exemplars of practicing Christians does not serve to make the terms and conditions of their employment matters of church administration and thus purely of ecclesiastical concern. *The employment relationship between Mississippi College and its faculty and staff is one intended by Congress to be regulated by Title VII.*[14] [emphasis added]

Another passing comment by the court in *Mississippi College* sheds some light on whether religious institutions may—without fear of legal reprisals—make employment distinctions on the basis of sex. The court remarked, "The only practice brought to the attention of the district court (i.e., the trial court) that is clearly predicated upon religious beliefs that might not be protected by the exemption of Section 702 is the College's policy of hiring only men to teach courses in religion. (Footnote 12: . . . Dr. Nobles [the President of the College] explained that the practice of not hiring women to teach religion courses was based upon Bible scriptures indicating that pastors and deacons should be men.)"[15] If the EEOC did attack the hiring of only male faculty to teach theology, the school would have the opportunity "to litigate in a federal forum whether Section 702 exempts or the First Amendment protects that particular practice."[16]

The final two cases move even more sharply away from the holdings in *McClure* and *Rayburn* and should be given careful heed by religious entities.

EEOC v. Pacific Press Publishing Association[17] involved a conflict between a Seventh-Day Adventist publishing house and a married female employee working as an editorial secretary. Pacific Press paid married men a higher rental allowance than single men, who in turn received more than female employees. The plaintiff, Lorna Tobler, objected to this practice, as well as to the facts that she was not given the annual utility allowance received by married men and was not paid the automobile allowance that married men, single men, and single women were given. Tobler filed a Title VII complaint with the Equal Employment Opportunity Commission.

During most of her tenure with Pacific Press, Mrs. Tobler's duties included administrative and discretionary responsibilities as well as secretarial tasks. Drawing upon the reasoning of *McClure*, *Southwestern* and *Mississippi College*, the Ninth Circuit decided that Tobler's duties did not "go to the heart of the church's function" as do those of a minister or a seminary teacher.[18] The court likened Tobler's duties to those of non-ministerial staff at Southwestern Baptist Theological Seminary. In addition, the court considered Pacific Press to be less sectarian than a church or a seminary.[19] Consequently, Pacific Press was not insulated by the First Amendment from Title VII charges and was held liable for discrimination.

The court took note of the fact that the Seventh-Day Adventist denomination "does not believe in discriminating against women or minority groups, and that its policy is to pay wages without discrimination on the basis of race, religion, sex, age, or national origin."[20] Not surprisingly, the nondiscrimination policy of the Adventist denomination worked to the disadvantage of Pacific Press. The court reasoned that applying Title VII's prohibition of sex discrimination to Pacific Press could not possibly abridge its free exercise rights, since the policy of the denomination supported equal treatment of the sexes.[21]

EEOC v. Fremont Christian School,[22] a Ninth Circuit decision, is a most unsettling case and has decidedly negative precedential value for religious organizations.

Fremont Christian School, a private school owned and operated by the Fremont Assembly of God Church, provided instruction from preschool through the twelfth grade. Because of its adherence to the belief that only the husband can be the "head of the household,"[23] the school provided health insurance to married men and single persons, but not to married women. A married female employee brought action against Fremont Christian School on the basis of the Equal Pay Act[24] and Title VII of the 1964 Civil Rights Act.

Emphasizing that wages and other conditions of employment at Fremont Christian School were comparable for all employees regardless of sex and that married female employees were eligible for group life and disability insurance, the court found that requiring the school to provide health insurance benefits to married females would not infringe on the free exercise of its religious beliefs. Even though the district (trial) court assumed the school's policy to be based on religious belief,[25] the Title VII action was allowed to go forward despite the fact that a plausible religious rationale for different treatment of the sexes was offered by the school. The court almost invites the inference that, if there had been a more consistent pattern of higher pay and more benefits for heads of households, a stronger argument for First Amendment protection could have been made.[26]

C. Practical Principles

What overarching principles can be gleaned from these diverse cases? How can a religious organization avoid challenge to its employment policies without compromising its doctrinal convictions? Are there certain practices that tend to arouse the curiosity (and the hostility) of the Equal Employment Opportunity Commission?

There appear to be three factors that the courts take into account in determining whether employment distinctions made by a religious entity on the basis of sex are immunized by the First Amendment from attack under antidiscrimination statutes:

1. The nature of the religious institution.
2. The nature of the employee's position and duties.
3. The religious institution's rationale for treating males and females differently.

The Nature of the Religious Institution and the Nature of the Employee's Position and Duties

Confronted with the assignment of preventing the antidiscrimination protections of Title VII from colliding with the free exercise of religion, the courts in the aforementioned cases have resorted to two devices:

(1) Ranking religious organizations according to how "sectarian" they were, and
(2) Determining how central the role of the employee allegedly discriminated against was to the religious character of the organization.

Mindful of how scrupulously the Supreme Court has sought to avoid meddling in internal church disputes, the courts in *McClure* and *Rayburn* treated churches as the most sectarian of all religious entities and refused to tamper with a church's selection of a pastor. *Prima facie* evidence of sex discrimination did not dislodge the courts from a hands-off posture toward the thoroughly religious position of pastor.

The *Southwestern* court deemed the seminary to be a "wholly sectarian" institution and thus on a par with a church. Faculty and "ministerial" administrators were analogous to pastors and beyond the reach of Title VII. But the Fifth Circuit would not allow the seminary to escape its Title VII obligations *vis-à-vis* support staff and "non-ministerial" administrators.

A Christian college was assigned a lower rank on the "sectarian scale." An examination of the purpose and operation of Mississippi College resulted in the Fifth Circuit classifying the school as "pervasively sectarian" rather than "wholly sectarian." Faculty teaching nonreligious courses (such as experimental psychology) could not be discriminated against without legal consequences.

Religious publishing associations (Pacific Press) and religious elementary and secondary schools (Fremont Christian School) were assigned an even lower station on the sectarian continuum. A female editorial secretary at the publishing house and a female rank-and-file employee of the school could prosecute sex discrimination claims against their respective employers without constitutional impediment.

Two general principles can be formulated from this line of cases:

1. *The more sectarian a religious entity, the more likely it is to be shielded by the First Amendment from sex discrimination actions.*
2. *The more directly the employee's responsibilities are related to the religious purposes and practices of the employer, the less likely a Title VII action could withstand constitutional attack.*

These two principles distill the case law into its essential elements. They also provide religious institutions with a practical framework for assessing the legality of their employment policies. But how will these principles be applied in marginal situations? Does a church face less legal peril than Fremont Christian School if it gives salary and benefits preferences to male heads of households holding non-ministerial positions? Even though a seminary's dealings with its faculty are beyond the reach of Title VII, is a Christian college courting a lawsuit if it prohibits women from holding certain positions in its theology department? Where would a court place a parachurch organization on the "sectarian continuum," and what constitutional privileges would it be accorded?

These questions are not easily answered. Indeed, the United States Constitution created a judicial branch for the very purpose of resolving controversies of this nature, and a case-by-case determination of the proper balance between the First Amendment and Title VII is inevitable. The third factor weighed by the courts in establishing boundaries between freedom of religion and the right to equal employment opportunities, however, may be the most determinative.

The Religious Institution's Rationale for Treating Males and Females Differently

For those situations in which the employment practices of a religious organization are not clearly sheltered by the First Amendment, it is imperative that the organization demonstrate that the distinctions between males and females are predicated on *religious tenets*. If the sex distinctions are motivated by prejudice or are the vestiges of nonreligious traditions, they probably will not pass muster under Title VII and other antidiscrimination laws. If the distinctions are solidly grounded on fundamental doctrines of the faith and are clearly articulated in the organization's governing documents and policies, a disgruntled employee would be hard-pressed to overcome a free-exercise defense raised by the religious body.

Pacific Press Publishing Association could not show that the smaller benefit package Mrs. Tobler received was necessitated by Seventh-Day Adventist beliefs. In fact, the denomination stated that its policy was to *not* discriminate between men and women. Given these facts, a finding for an employee like Mrs. Tobler was virtually a foregone conclusion.

Fremont Christian School's defense to the Title VII allegations was better conceived. Its views of headship in the family were well supported by the doctrines of the church, and the school did justify its denial of health insurance to married women by pointing to religious tenets reflected in the school's written policies.

Nevertheless, its failure to *consistently carry out* its "head of the household" beliefs proved to be its undoing.

The practice of paying married male employees more than married female employees was abandoned by the school because it was thought to be illegal. Ironically, Fremont Christian School's good-faith effort to abide by the law backfired. The district court opined that the school's policy of providing comparable wages to male and female employees, as well as its practice of extending eligibility for disability and group life insurance to married females, constituted an "implicit nondiscrimination policy." Limiting health insurance to married men, therefore, was inconsistent with the school's otherwise egalitarian practices and was sufficient to convince the court that doctrinal convictions could not have been the basis for denying health insurance to married females.

Religious organizations can learn from the mistakes of Pacific Press and Fremont Christian School. Employment distinctions on the basis of sex must be predicated on *previously articulated religious principles*. Furthermore, these principles must be *documented* by the religious body and must be *applied universally and consistently*.

II. May Accrediting Bodies Deny Accreditation on the Basis of School Policy Regarding Distinct Roles for Men and Women?

Another pressing issue of concern to seminaries and religious colleges is whether private accrediting bodies can lawfully make the granting of accreditation contingent on the abolition of distinct roles for men and women. The case law on this specific point is sparse; some broad legal concepts and one pertinent decision will be treated cursorily.

A. Broad Legal Concepts

Antitrust is the area of law relevant for this analysis. The foundation of American antitrust jurisprudence is the Sherman Act,[27] which was adopted by Congress in 1890. Section 1 of the Act states, in part:

> Every contract, combination in the form of trust or otherwise, or conspiracy, in restraint of trade or commerce among the several States, or with foreign nations, is hereby declared to be illegal.

An immediate interpretive problem confronted the courts. Which contracts, combinations, or conspiracies constituted "restraints of trade" as envisioned by the drafters of the Sherman Act? In the strictest sense, any contract restrains trade! Since the outlawing of all contracts was obviously not the intent of Congress, the United States Supreme Court created a "rule of reason" in evaluating Sherman Act cases. In *United States v. American Tobacco Co.*,[28] the Court pointed out that it had construed the words "restraint of trade" as embracing "only . . . acts or contracts or agreements or combinations which operated to the prejudice of the public interests by unduly restricting competition or by unduly obstructing the due course of trade or which, either because of their inherent nature or effect, or . . . evident purpose . . . injuriously restrain trade."[29]

How do antitrust principles impact accrediting bodies? First, the courts have ruled that all private sector associations, including accrediting entities, are automatically "combinations" within the meaning of Section 1 of the Sherman Act.[30] The activities of accrediting groups, therefore, can be reviewed to determine whether they are unreasonable restraints of trade.

Second, any standards of an accrediting body that exclude applicants must be *rationally related* to the purposes such standards are designed to further.[31] If, for example, an accreditor were to require the board of directors of a school to have female members and the school was denied accreditation for failure to comply with this criterion, the school might have grounds for antitrust action against the accrediting agency.

B. Case Law Precedent

Marjorie Webster Junior College v. Middle States Association of Colleges and Secondary Schools[32] remains the leading case applying antitrust law to accreditation.

Marjorie Webster was a proprietary junior college for women in the District of Columbia. Middle States was a nonprofit corporation accrediting secondary schools and institutions of higher learning in its geographical region. Marjorie Webster's application for accreditation was denied because it was not a nonprofit organization. The college sued Middle States on antitrust grounds, claiming that the denial of accreditation because of its for-profit status was an unreasonable restraint of trade. Because Middle States was assertedly a quasi-governmental entity, Marjorie Webster also maintained that it was deprived of property without due process of law in contravention of the Fifth Amendment of the United States Constitution.

The District of Columbia Court of Appeals refined and enunciated two points of law germane to the question at hand:

1. The more important the credential (e.g., accreditation) for the successful operation of the applicant, the greater the extent of judicial scrutiny of the exclusionary standard.
2. All standards must be "reasonable, applied with an even hand, and not in conflict with the public policy of the jurisdiction."[33]

Turning to the facts, the court noted that denial of accreditation by Middle States was not crucial to the successful operation of Marjorie Webster. Middle States accreditation was voluntary, and the college had been granted the credentials mandated by the state and federal governments. Many proprietary schools, including Marjorie Webster, had thrived without Middle States accreditation. Furthermore, for-profit schools were free to organize their own accrediting organs and could promulgate standards more suitable for proprietary education. Because withholding this particular accreditation would not appreciably hinder the viability of the college, the substantive reasonableness of the standard was not adjudicated.

C. Application to Religious Schools

What recourse does a religious educational institution have if it is denied accreditation because of differentiated roles for men and women? Assuming that the particular accreditation at issue has direct economic impact and that the distinctions on the basis of sex are founded on religious dogmas (see I.C. above), a school has a good chance of winning an antitrust suit if it can prove at least one of the following three points:

(1) The criterion invoked to deny different roles for men and women is not reasonably related to the purposes of the accreditor.
(2) The criterion is not "applied with an even hand."
(3) The criterion is not consistent with public policy.

Of these three bases for antitrust action, the third holds the most promise. Fortified by the decisions exempting religious organizations from certain antidiscrimination statutes (see I.B. above), a seminary or religiously affiliated school could contend that—if a certain distinction on the basis of sex is not unlawful—*it would be contrary to the public policy to allow a private sector accrediting body to deny a valuable accreditation status because of the very same distinction.*

For example, the *Southwestern Baptist Theological Seminary* court allowed a Christian educational institution to restrict theology faculty appointments and "ministerial" administrative positions to males. As a result, a strong argument could be made that it would be unconscionable for a private accreditor to withhold accreditation from a Christian school because of the accreditor's uniformitarian view of the proper roles of men and women.

* * * * *

It is likely that legal challenges to distinctions on the basis of sex by religious organizations will become more common. This author's hope is that this chapter will help religious entities develop policies and procedures that will avoid legal entanglements.

IV

Applications and Implications

20

The Family and the Church: How Should Biblical Manhood and Womanhood Work Out in Practice?

George W. Knight III

Introduction

As we have seen throughout this book, the Bible is quite clear that men and women are equally God's image bearers (Genesis 1:27) and therefore equal before God and in relationship with one another, and also that they are fellow-heirs in the Christian life, equal in their spiritual standing before God (1 Peter 3:7; Galatians 3:28). The Bible is also clear that men and women, who are equal with respect to creation and redemption and therefore share many things in common, are called to different and equally important roles in marriage and the church. It is God Himself (as we shall see later) who has determined distinctive roles for men and women in order that thereby they may fulfill the creation mandate that He has given to mankind (cf. Genesis 1:28; 3:15-19). God has called men to serve as leaders in marriage and the church, and women to submit themselves willingly to that leadership, as they labor together in their distinctive roles (Ephesians 5:23-24; 1 Peter 3:1-6; 1 Timothy 2:12; 3:1-13). In defining how men and women are to relate to one another in fulfilling their respective roles, God has called men to exercise a headship that is loving, gentle, and considerate (e.g., Ephesians 5:25ff.; 1 Peter 3:7), and He has called women to submit to that headship in a willing, gentle, and respectful way (e.g., Ephesians 5:24, 33; 1 Peter 3:1-2).

The question we all must face is how to carry out our Biblical roles with Biblical attitudes in specific, everyday situations. But before we proceed to the positive outworkings of Biblical manhood and womanhood, we need to be more aware of the forces working against us that must be overcome and the antidotes God's grace provides.

The Effect of Sin

The fundamental antithetical force is the effect of sin on our relationships. This we see from Genesis 3:16, in which God speaks of sin's effect on the relationship of men and women: "Your desire will be for your husband, and he will rule over you" (NIV; unless otherwise noted, all citations from Scripture in this chapter are from NIV). In these words, God is indicating that as a result of sin, rather than exercising a caring headship and leadership, men will seek to "rule" in an autocratic, unloving way. And He is indicating with reference to women that rather than being submissive helpers, they will "desire" to have mastery over their husbands. (We are understanding the word *desire* here in the same sense as that of its next occurrence [Genesis 4:7], where sin has the "desire" to master Cain.)[1] By saying this, God was indicating that just as sin, as a result of the fall, will bring pain (Genesis 3:16) to the joy of childbirth (the fulfillment of God's mandate to be fruitful, Genesis 1:28) and sweat and difficulty to the joy of work (the fulfillment of God's mandate to subdue the earth and rule over it, Genesis 1:28), so also it will bring strife into the role relationship God had established between man and woman at creation (Genesis 2:18). Thus, God has forewarned that sin will make the role relationship of man and woman a place beset by struggle that only God's grace can help us overcome.

We have seen and still see the horrible fulfillment of this curse's effect in man's domination of woman in those places and cultures where the effects of the gospel have not been felt. In contrast, in cultures and nations where the gospel has had strong influence, the joint-heir status of men and women has emerged as a wonderful by-product. But now we see in those same cultures and nations where secularization is replacing the effects of the gospel that a by-product of equality remains, while at the same time the society is giving expression to the sinful side of the curse pronouncement—women desiring to remove themselves from any distinctive role in their relationship to men and to be as much leaders in the home and church as men are, while men become increasingly passive or abusive in relation to women. We can see these outworkings of God's prophetic pronouncement in Genesis 3:16 on the broad scale of history and society, but we must also be aware of the presence of those very tendencies in every human heart, including the hearts of Christian men and women. Since Christians, like others, are affected by the "spirit of the age," these sinful tendencies within men and women will be compounded by the feminist push of our age as well as by a chauvinistic and macho backlash.

The Correlation of Role and Attitude

Any discussion of the practical outworking of the Biblical principles of headship and submission must take into account these sinful tendencies that so easily subvert us and work against compliance with the Biblical norm. We need to notice again how carefully the apostles present their teaching on the role relationship of men and women so as to affirm two things simultaneously and thereby to give balance to their teaching. First, they reiterate the mandate of God about the role relationship based on creation and speak of the headship of men and the submission of women. Second, they demand attitudes and actions that will seek to overcome the sinful tendencies that work against the proper functioning of these roles. Because people in authority, as a result of sin, often seek to rule and dominate with selfish or cruel attitudes, men are instructed not to be embittered against their wives (Colossians 3:19) but to love them and give themselves to them (Colossians 3:19; Ephesians 5:25), to nourish and cherish them (Ephesians 5:29), and to honor them as fellow-heirs (1 Peter 3:7). Because people under authority, as a result of sin, often resent their role and seek to minimize or escape it, or to take the position of leadership, women are repeatedly urged to submit (1 Peter 3:1; Ephesians 5:24; Colossians 3:18; Titus 2:5) because it is God's will and should be done as to the Lord (Ephesians 5:27; Colossians 3:18) and with respect (Ephesians 5:33) and a gentle and quiet spirit (1 Peter 3:4).

The balanced interrelationship of these two truths must control any discussion of the day-to-day situation, since these are the operative principles that the Scriptures give to guide us in all such day-to-day outworkings of male/female role relationship in marriage and the church. Thus we must constantly reiterate the roles of headship and submission and also constantly call for attitudes and actions that enable these roles to be fulfilled, by God's grace, in a world where sin works from within and without against those roles and against those attitudes and actions.

I. The Family

A. God's Delineation of the Distinctive Roles of Husband and Wife in Genesis 3

We can further delineate what is entailed in the roles of husbands and wives in marriage and family by taking careful account of the focused description that God gives of each in Genesis 3 on the basis of the truths first outlined in Genesis 1 and 2 at the dawn of human civilization and in a setting that antedates any particular culture or society.[2]

In this chapter, He gives the effects of sin, not only as it brings death and separation from God to all humans but also in its effects on men and women in their respective maleness and femaleness. In doing so, God relates the effect of the curse respectively to that portion of His creation mandate (as already established in Genesis 1 and 2) that most particularly applies to the woman on the one hand and to the man on the other hand. God had said to them: "Be fruitful and multiply, and fill the earth, and subdue it; and rule over . . . every living thing that moves on the earth" (Genesis 1:28, *NASB*). Now He relates the curse to that aspect of the creation mandate that is the particular responsibility of the woman and of the man and in so doing indicates the particular role that He has determined each is to fulfill. Thus, for the woman He speaks of her pain in childbirth (i.e., while seeking to be fruitful) and the struggles (as we have noted above) that will surface in the husband/wife relationship (Genesis 3:16): "To the woman he said, 'I will greatly increase your pains in childbearing; with pain you will give birth to children. Your desire will be for your husband, and he will rule over you.'" In short, God speaks about what is unique to her as a woman, namely, being a mother and a wife. To the man He speaks of the difficulties he will have in his toil (i.e., while seeking to subdue the earth) to secure bread (Genesis 3:17-19): "Cursed is the ground because of you; through painful toil you will eat of it all the days of your life. It will produce thorns and thistles for you, and you will eat the plants of the field. By the sweat of your brow you will eat your food until you return to the ground, since from it you were taken; for dust you are and to dust you will return." Thus He delineates what is the main calling for man, namely, the responsibility of breadwinner and provider for his wife and family. It will be helpful for all our discussion to keep this perspective in view and realize that it is the perspective God has given and not some "Victorian" or "traditional" view that has grown up out of some society or culture and been adopted unwittingly as the Biblical norm.

Therefore it is important in marriage and the family for a man to realize his responsibility as the primary breadwinner and to assume that responsibility willingly and gladly. It is equally important for a woman to realize her responsibility as the primary one to care for the children and the home, as these verses indicate, and as Proverbs 31 (see below) also indicates. This will provide the security and necessary time and energy for the woman to bear children but also to be with the children in their formative years when they are very dependent on their mother and need her presence. It is in this spirit that the Apostle Paul encourages young widows "to get married, bear children, keep house" (1 Timothy 5:14, NASB). Christ's apostle exalts the home and women's duties in it and encourages women to be "busy at home" (Titus 2:5).

Sad to say, when these distinctive emphases are not maintained, children often fail to develop healthy sexual identities (see Chapter 17 in this volume), and marriages tend to break up because husband and wife are no longer dependent on each other but are increasingly independent, ready to go their own ways.[3]

B. What About the Wife and Mother Working Outside the Home?

Some Christians have interpreted Titus 2:5 ("workers at home," NASB)[4] to mean that any work outside the home is inappropriate for the wife and mother. But the fact that wives should care for their home does not necessarily imply that they should not work outside the home, any more than the statement that a "overseer" in the church should "manage his own household" (1 Timothy 3:4-5) means that he cannot work outside the home. In neither case does the text say that! The dynamic equivalent translation of Titus 2:5 by the NIV, "to be busy at home," catches the force of Paul's admonition, namely, that a wife should be a diligent homemaker. Moreover, Proverbs 31:10-31 depicts a wife and mother whose support for the family extends well beyond ordinary domestic chores (cf. e.g., verses 16 and 24: "She considers a field and buys it . . . she plants a vineyard. . . . She makes linen garments and sells them, and supplies belts to the tradesmen," NASB). Since Scripture interprets Scripture and its teaching is consistent and unified, we realize that the picture of Proverbs is not contradicted by the Apostle Paul.

Furthermore, we must realize that the *emphasis* on the home is the very point of the Proverbs passage. The woman in Proverbs works to care for her family and to fulfill her responsibility to her family (cf., e.g., verses 21 and 27). She does this not only for her children but also to support her husband's leadership role in the community (verse 23). She is seeking the good of her family. Furthermore, she seeks to aid the poor and needy by her labors (verse 20).

Here, then, are keys to the question of a wife and mother working outside the home: Is it really beneficial to her family, does it aid her husband in his calling, and does it, in correlation with these first two, bring good to others? Can she do it while still being faithful to her primary calling to be wife and mother and to care for her home? It must be noted that even though the woman in Proverbs has not sought to "find herself" or to make her own career, but rather to serve her family, in the end she receives praise from her family (verses 28, 29) and recognition for her labors (verse 31) because she has conducted the whole endeavor in obedience to the Lord she reverences (verse 30). The decision in this realm must not be unilateral on the part of the woman but made under the leadership of her husband as the head of the marriage and the family.

C. Decision-making by Husbands and Wives

This brings us to the question of responsibilities and processes for decision-making. The delicate balance that must be maintained is that of the husband's leadership in a situation in which two equal image bearers of God are involved. The husband must honor his wife (1 Peter 3:7, "grant her honor as a fellow-heir of the grace of life, so that your prayers may not be hindered," NASB) and respect her views, opinions, feelings, and contributions about the issue at hand, and he must do so in a way that takes into account both his and her strengths and weaknesses (1 Peter 3:8, "husbands . . . be considerate as you live with your wives, and treat them with respect as the weaker partner").[5] He must not give over the leadership to the woman as Adam did to Eve, for then to him also the rebuke given to Adam will apply ("Because you have listened to the voice of your wife," Genesis 3:17, NASB).[6] Neither should he act rashly and harshly as Nabal did, not seeking the sensible and wise advice that his wife could and would have given him (cf. 1 Samuel 25:2-26:38). After all, the wife is given to the husband to be his chief "helper" (Genesis 2:18). The husband and wife should seek to come to a mutually satisfactory decision after discussion and through prayer and seeking the principles of God's Word, and they should do so under the leadership and guidance of the husband, who should initiate this process. In a world of sin in which both husband and wife are beset by the limitations sin brings to our understanding and to the evaluative and decision-making process, there will be times when a consensus may not be reached. In this situation, it is the husband's responsibility to exercise his leadership role and make the decision. The wife needs to submit to that decision (unless the decision is clearly and intrinsically evil [cf. 1 Samuel 25:14; Acts 5:29]).

D. Decision-making as It Relates to Changing Jobs and Relocation to Another Community

In a highly mobile age, it is appropriate to consider job location change. Therefore, to illustrate the matter of decision-making, let us take the question of changing jobs and relocating the family. Let the question be compounded by assuming that the wife also has a good position. In this case, let us assume that the wife is not inclined to move because she likes the locale and she does not want to give up her own paying job. This is understandable.

The husband should give due weight to all of these concerns. The two should pray about the matter and seek to understand each other's perspective and the good of the family as a whole, including the long-range as well as the short-range perspective. This decision-making must consider the total welfare of the family and not simply the benefits of the job. At the same time, it must include obedience to the creation mandate, on the part of the husband particularly but also the wife, who has agreed to be his helper in this responsibility, to fulfill to the best of his (and their) ability his primary calling as the one to be involved in work to support the family. A decision not to take the job and not to move, in light of the needs of the rest of the family, would be quite appropriate as long as no veto or coercion on the part of his wife has in actuality usurped the leadership or caused the husband to forfeit or surrender it. However, should he become convinced before God that the move is in the best interests of his family and will allow him and his wife to best fulfill the creation mandate and best glorify God, he should sympathetically lead the family through this transition, seeking to explain why the move is right from his perspective.

In such a case, it seems to me that two factors besides his general responsibility as leader are key elements. First is the recognition that the man, more than the woman—whose focus and energy are to be directed inward toward the family (cf. again Genesis 3:16-17 and Proverbs 31:27)—is called on to fulfill his role by directing his time and energy outward from the family in the work area (cf. again God's evaluation of what is characteristic of man as a male, Genesis 3:17-19). Second, the woman is created to be the man's helper (Genesis 2:18; 1 Corinthians 11:8-9). From these perspectives, the husband's work must take precedence (when necessary) over the wife's, and she must be willing to help her husband fulfill his calling in this realm even if it means that she must give up her position. A clear perspective on this subject will eliminate or remove many conflicts that could arise in this area.

E. Caring for the Children

The care and management of the home and children is another area in which Christians need to implement Biblical principles carefully. The Scriptures present the direct management of the children and the household as the realm of responsibility of the wife and mother. First Timothy 5:14 says that wives are "to manage their homes" (NIV). The Greek word *oikodespoteō*, which is rendered "manage," is a very forceful term. Proverbs 31 indicates some of the many ways in which this management is carried out (cf., e.g., verses 26 and 27: "She opens her mouth in wisdom, and the teaching of kindness is on her tongue. She looks well to the ways of her household, and does not eat the bread of idleness," NASB). The husband must recognize this calling and grant her the necessary and appropriate freedom of operation under his leadership. At the same time, the wife must recognize that her management is to be conducted in submission to her husband's leadership, who is responsible for the overall management of the household (cf. Titus 2:5, "to be busy at home . . . and to be subject to their husbands"). The Apostle Paul says that the man is responsible to manage his own household well (1 Timothy 3:4-5).

Although the wife and mother will have the most contact with the children, especially when they are young, and therefore will have the most direct responsibility for supervising them, the husband and father is held responsible for instruction and oversight of the children (Ephesians 6:4; 1 Timothy 3:4). It is imperative that fathers and mothers carry out this joint task in such a way that the leadership of both over the children is maintained and the headship of the father over the family is manifest. Thus neither should allow the children to play one parent off against the other in seeking to contravene the other's commands or prohibitions. The parents should resolve those questions in private away from the children; in public they should uphold each other's decisions, especially the mother upholding the headship of the father. Fathers should exercise an appropriate leadership by being careful to avoid exasperating or provoking comments or commands (Ephesians 6:4; Colossians 3:21) that not only discourage or anger their children but also provide occasion for their wives to feel the necessity of intervening and make it more difficult for them to be subject to their husbands' leadership. Exasperating or provoking comments or commands include commands that are unjust and comments that are given in a callous or unfeeling way. All parental give-and-take before children should manifest mutual respect and communicate before the children that the husband genuinely loves and respects his wife and the wife, too, respects and desires to submit to the leadership of her husband and their father. Such an attitude can itself be the best setting for the children to learn their own necessary submission to both father and mother.

The division of duties in the home and household must take seriously the respective roles of the woman and the man and their equal importance before the Lord and in the home. The direct care and supervision of the children is the specific calling of the wife/mother (cf. again Genesis 3:16; 1 Timothy 5:14; Titus 2:5). It would be unnatural in the normal family setting for the husband/father to assume this task and to surrender the task of "breadwinning" to his wife.[7] This is not to say that he is not to be as concerned and as involved in the training of their children as she is, but rather that he does so in correlation with his responsibility as the primary provider.

F. The Allocation of Other Duties and Responsibilities

Other duties and responsibilities should be allocated in such a way that the feminine and masculine proclivities come to their natural expression and the strengths and weaknesses of each partner are recognized and their mutual dependence on each other for distinct roles are a help to both. Yet we must realize also that there are many things in the daily affairs of a household that the specific teachings and broader principles of Scripture do not categorize as either "masculine" or "feminine." Here we must allow freedom and variation and not attempt to go beyond what is written in the principles we affirm and teach.

II. The Church

There are two basic Biblical truths relating to men and women that must be affirmed and upheld in the life of the church. The first is their equality as bearers of God's image (Genesis 1:27) and as fellow Christians (Galatians 3:28;[8] 1 Peter 3:7). The second is the leadership role to which men are called by God in the church so that by apostolic injunction, based on God's creative action, women are not allowed "to teach or exercise authority over a man" (1 Timothy 2:12, NASB).

A. The Use of Women's Gifts

The first truth has as its corollary that women are to use their gifts in every way that Christians in general are to do, except for those areas explicitly prohibited by Scripture. This is seen in Paul's treatment of the gifts in 1 Corinthians 11-14, where women are excluded only from speaking in church (1 Corinthians 14:34-35)[9] where congregational "teaching" is involved (1 Corinthians 14:26; notice that the items listed in verse 26 correspond with the subjects dealt with in verses 27 and 35 [with only the first item, "a psalm," not dealt with in these verses] and in particular notice that "teaching" [NASB] in verse 26 is the one-word description for the "speaking" Paul will deal with when it comes to women in verses 34 and 35).[10] These women are recognized as properly participating in praying and prophesying, for example, but are only asked not to throw off the cultural sign of their submission when they do so (1 Corinthians 11:1-16).

Some very practical deductions and applications can be drawn from these principles. If all other members of the church participate in voting at congregational meetings, then of course women members equally share that right. If all other worshipers are participating in the worship by sharing and praying, then women also should participate equally. The church of Christ, its men and women, must be equally concerned to uphold both these aspects of inclusion and any necessary exclusion in fidelity to God's Word.

One must not draw the false conclusion that the Scriptures are opposed to women teaching or exercising any kind of leadership. Far from it. Women are encouraged by the Apostle Paul to teach other women and to make full use of their gifts in that realm (Titus 2:3-5). Just as Paul directs how tongue speakers and prophets may use their gifts in accordance with God's order, so he encourages women to teach other women (Titus 2:3-5).

Similarly, the New Testament commends the activities of women in various sorts of ministries except those that would violate the male leadership principle. In an earlier work I summarized this range of ministries in the following words:

> Several passages indicate that women are involved in diaconal tasks and appropriate teaching situations. A sampling of those activities may be seen in the following: older women are called upon to teach and train younger women concerning their responsibilities to their husbands and children (Titus 2:3-5); wives (*gunaikas*) are referred to in the midst of the description of male deacons (1 Timothy 3:11); Phoebe is designated "a servant [*diakonon*] of the church which is at Cenchrea" (Romans 16:1); Paul refers in 1 Corinthians to women praying or prophesying (11:5); and Priscilla and Aquila, that inseparable husband-and-wife team, in a discreet and private meeting expound to Apollos "the way of God more accurately" (Acts 18:26).[11]

This brief Biblical summary, as true as it is and as helpful as it is, reminds us by these examples of the wide range of ministries available to women in the kingdom of God. The *Danvers Statement*, Affirmation 9, in this wide-ranging perspective and broad sweep, has attempted to express that range. Its words serve as a fitting conclusion to this particular section:

> With half the world's population outside the reach of indigenous evangelism; with countless other lost people in those societies that have heard the gospel; with the stresses and miseries of sickness, malnutrition, homelessness, illiteracy, ignorance, aging, addiction, crime, incarceration, neuroses, and loneliness, no man or woman who feels a passion from God to make His grace known in word and deed need ever live without a fulfilling ministry for the glory of Christ and the good of this fallen world. (See Appendix Two.)

B. The Biblical Principle of Male Leadership in the Church

Alongside our insistence on women's legitimate participation in the life of the church, we need to remind ourselves again that the apostolic teaching insists on men being the primary leaders in the church (just as in marriage) and therefore excludes women from that role. The clearest statement is 1 Timothy 2:12: "I do not allow a woman to teach or exercise authority over a man" (*NASB*). The contextual setting of this statement makes it plain that the apostle is speaking about women publicly teaching men in the religious realm and exercising authority over men in the Christian community. It is the male/female role relationship based on creation that requires this prohibition (cf. 1 Timothy 2:13). And thus, since the church by definition includes both men and women, those situations where both are present are situations in which this prohibition is in effect.

1. Applied to Church Officers

When the Apostle Paul moves on from this statement of principle to a description of the qualifications for the officers in the church (overseers and deacons; 1 Timothy 3:1-13), as an outworking and application of this principle, he describes them in masculine terms (i.e., the husband of one wife; cf. both 1 Timothy 3:2 and 3:12).[12] Similarly, the church today, as it seeks to apply the apostolic principle faithfully, has insisted that the primary leadership of the church must be male. This has meant that both the minister who serves as a full-time teacher and pastor and the ruling officers chosen from within the congregation (often called "elders" in line with the Biblical nomenclature) have been males. But this would also apply to other church officers, who may not be called "elders" but who have governing authority for the whole church similar to that of elders in the New Testament. The equivalent office to New Testament elders is called by other names in differing systems of church government: "deacons" in many Baptist churches, "the vestry" in an episcopal system, and often just the "church board" or "church council" in many churches. That the office of elder should be filled by men is particularly appropriate, since their labors are designated in terms of teaching (1 Timothy 3:2 and Titus 1:9) and of managing and caring for the church (1 Timothy 3-5)—the very roles denied to women in 1 Timothy 2:12.

Most Christians and churches who have made the application to "elders" have done so also for "deacons," noting that they, too, are designated in masculine terms (1 Timothy 3:12; also Acts 6:3, where the Greek word used for "men" [*anēr*] is the word used to distinguish men from women rather than one used for men as mankind whether male or female [*anthrōpos*]). They have noted furthermore that the role of deacons is still one of leadership, even if leadership in the area of service. At the same time it should be noted that women (or wives) are referred to in this section on deacons (1 Timothy 3:11). This has led to two understandings. The first is that the text distinguishes them from the deacons (who are males), does not designate them as deacons, but mentions them because they serve with and alongside the deacons in diaconal service. It is my judgment that this view understands the passage correctly and furthermore that it is the wives of deacons who are in view. A reference to wives would explain what would otherwise appear to be a seemingly abrupt statement in the midst of the passage but which, on such an understanding, is but the first of several comments about the deacon's family.[13] Others understand this verse as indicating that the New Testament recognized female deacons or at least deaconesses, and they appeal to Phoebe in Romans 16:1-2 for corroboration. If this understanding is correct, then the modern church should act accordingly. However, I think (as do others) the prior understanding is more likely, since the reference to Phoebe as a "servant of the church" has been widely understood to be a use of the Greek term *diakonos* in a non-technical and non-official sense, as it often is used elsewhere in the New Testament.[14] Even though we must recognize that 1 Timothy 3:11 and Romans 16:1-2 must be considered in their interaction with one another, the hermeneutical principle is that the section dealing most fully and explicitly with the office and with *deacon* as a technical term must be resolved first, and then the historical statement may more appropriately be evaluated in that light. Whichever position is adopted as to whether women are to be "deaconesses," there is still consensus that women should be involved in "diaconal" or service ministries in the church, whether they are elected as "deaconesses" or not.

2. The Biblical Principle of Male Leadership in the Church Related to Teaching Activities

Here it should be noted that the prohibition that the Apostle Paul gives in 1 Timothy 2:12 (and 1 Corinthians 14:34-35[15]) is not stated in terms of a prohibition of an office in the church or restricted to that sphere (e.g., a woman may not be an elder/overseer), but is stated rather in functional language indicating what she may not do ("I do not permit a woman to teach or to have authority over a man; she must be silent," 1 Timothy 2:12).

For this reason, it seems clearly contrary to the apostle's teaching for some to argue that the male elders in the church may give a woman the right to give the exposition of the Word of God to the church and to say that since she does it under the authority of the male leadership, this activity would be acceptable. Paul rules out such an activity and underscores this by saying that, in the public teaching situation where men are present, a woman must remain "silent" with respect to this activity and not "speak" (cf. again 1 Timothy 2:12; 1 Corinthians 14:34-35). No decision of male leadership can justify approving the exact opposite of what the apostle commands. This unqualified prohibition extends to every situation in the life of the Christian community where there is actual, recognized *teaching* of the Scriptures and the Christian faith to a group that includes men, e.g., a Sunday school class, a small group meeting, a couples group, etc. The statement in the text focuses on the activity of teaching and, by implication, includes the authority inherent in that activity. Other activities in which a group might be involved, such as participating in a group discussion on the meaning of a passage of Scripture or sharing the impact of the passage on their lives, which are neither teaching nor the exercise of authority, should certainly include the full and free participation of the women of the group. The prohibition is focused and specific, and thus the implication is that all other activities are open to women.

Since this is a statement of principles on the part of the apostle, it would seem that this principle extends to teaching the Bible to men in colleges, training men in seminaries, and teaching the Bible and Biblical truth to men in parachurch organizations. In women's colleges, in schools training women to serve as directors of Christian education, and in women's parachurch groups, according to the Scriptures (cf. Titus 2:3-5), women have every right to teach.

The question arises as to how this prohibition of women teaching men applies where boys are in transition to manhood; i.e., what is the cut-off point? It seems that the church must answer this question in terms of the society's evaluation of the time when, in that particular society, the boy becomes a man. If the young man is still under the direction of his parents and the instruction of a woman, his mother, at home, then it would seem appropriate for him to be under the instruction of a woman in the church. If he is regarded as on his own or as having reached manhood, whether married or not, then he should not be taught by a woman. Teaching a mixed group of high school students would seem, in our society, to be one kind of "borderline" situation. In such cases, if all involved agree on the basic Biblical principles involved and then pray for wisdom in applying those principles (cf. James 1:5-8), appropriate solutions will generally be found. Where doubt still remains, since we should not want to disobey the apostolic injunction, often the best solution would seem to be not to place a woman in that doubtful situation but rather to look to male leadership.

What of the Apparent Blessing When Women Seem to Have Violated These Principles? It may be retorted that in all these situations women have served in the church and their service has produced blessings in spite of the Apostle Paul's prohibitions. This kind of end-justifies-the-means argument surfaces more often than we think among Christians who would object to such an argument in other situations.[16]

But here we must realize that God often gives blessing in spite of our mistakes. We gladly admit that God's grace is greater than all our sins, including the unwitting ones in this and many other areas. And we gladly rejoice, as did Paul, in any proclamation of the gospel and teaching of the Word of God (cf. Philippians 1:14-18). However, in this passage Paul does point out the errors in that activity and their effects (e.g., "envy and strife," verse 15; "selfish ambition," verse 17), and it is to be hoped that the effect of his doing so would be that such errors would be remedied. We would seek to have the same Pauline balance, i.e., to rejoice in God's grace overcoming disobedience because His Word was present and effective. But we should not argue that such an outcome justifies the practice.

3. The Biblical Principle of Male Leadership in the Church Related to Leadership Activities

Just as we have sought to apply the principle of women not teaching men in the Christian community above, so also here in a similar way we must address the question of exercising authority over men in the life of the Christian community. Any board or committee in the local church or at other levels in the life of the church that exercises authority over that body should consist, by definition, of men who are called on to give leadership. Most denominations who hold this principle specify that the membership of denominational boards will be made up of church officers only, i.e., men. Since parachurch organizations (such as mission boards or campus ministries) and Christian institutions (such as Christian colleges and seminaries) are also part of the church universal, the body of Christ, it would seem that such restrictions should apply to their governing boards as well. They are part of the church; why should they act as though they were not? However, if a committee in the local congregation is formed to have representative input from various groups in the church, e.g., the women's group, etc., to give a cross-sectional perspective that can be used by the officers but that does not itself exercise authority, then, of course, all segments should be included. This would also be the case for advisory councils of parachurch organizations. On the other hand, it must not be argued that men cannot possibly conduct the affairs of the church involving men and women without the presence and input of women as members of the governing bodies. We have already seen that Christ's church, according to Scriptural teaching, is to be led by a male leadership. Thus, since male leadership can serve in the body of Christ that encompasses men and women, boys and girls, then a leadership of men also can function in other areas of the Christian community. This will entail, of course, that male leaders must be sensitive to and eagerly listen to the concerns of the whole spectrum of people whom they lead, with a special regard for the opposite sex. But that is the kind of male leaders the Scriptures call for—servants who lead with love, gentleness, and understanding as well as with strength and commitment (1 Peter 3:7).

4. Official Church Policies

Should specifications regarding male leadership in the family and church be formally included in the governing documents of a church such as the church constitution or by-laws, or in denominational affirmations of faith or statements of policies? In previous generations, such statements were included sometimes, but not usually, because male leadership was almost universally assumed to be Biblical (see chapter 15 in this volume). But in today's situation, with so many differing viewpoints expressed even within Christian circles, it would seem appropriate to include some policy statements at some level, at least concerning the most fundamental aspects of male/female roles. This is because the principle of male leadership in the church is a basic Scriptural principle based on the most fundamental of truths, God's creation order.

It must not be argued that only teaching about the Person and work of Christ and about salvation are teachings that can be considered fundamentals of the faith. The following Scriptural accounts, with their statements of principles based on God's creation order, make it abundantly plain that our Lord and His apostle regarded the implications of God's creation order as fundamental truths to be taught and observed by the people of God. Jesus makes the point that His teaching about marriage and divorce is based on God's creation order (Matthew 19:4-9). Furthermore, Paul indicates that teaching that repudiates marriage and regards foods God created as inherently unclean is absolutely unacceptable and is so because it denies the fact that what God created is good, i.e., it attacks God's creation order (1 Timothy 4:1-5). Because the principle of male leadership is based on the most fundamental of truths, God's creation order, it should be clearly and explicitly stated by the church as part of its basic teaching, and adherence to this general principle, especially as it applies to the ruling and teaching officers of the church, is an appropriate requirement of all officers in the church.

III. Correlation of the Family and the Church

We have dealt with the family and the church and have sought to work out and apply the principle of male leadership in both realms. In closing we may correlate these realms again to give perspective to the Scriptural teaching in its application to our lives. Those who recognize the Scriptural teaching about male leadership in marriage, both men and women, know that the leadership role of the husband/father does not in any way detract from or decrease the equally important role of wife/mother. That insight is helpful when we appraise male leadership in the church. Male leadership in the church does not decrease or detract from the gifts and graces women bring to the life of the body of Christ. Just as the male leadership in the home does not and should not keep the woman from exercising all of her God-given abilities, so also male leadership in the church does not and should not keep women from exercising, outside of the exclusively male realm of leadership itself, all of their God-given abilities within the church.

We wisely recognize in the family that being the male head is not all there is to the family life. We also need to recognize that, in the church, leadership over the church as a whole is not all there is to what is important and pleasing to God. Just as we recognize, accept, and acknowledge that God has wisely given man and woman different roles in the family, so we need to recognize and accept that in the life of the church God has also given man and woman different roles in relation to the leadership of the church, and we should gladly confess with the Apostle Paul that "God has placed the members, each one of them, in the body, just as He desired" (1 Corinthians 12:18, NASB).

21

Principles to Use in Establishing Women in Ministry*

H. Wayne House

A Biblical injunction against women exercising spiritual authority over men can be viewed from either a negative or a positive perspective. The exercise of authoritative teaching over men is but one facet of the overall scope of Christian service. Since the Scriptures confine that ministry to men only, the woman of God may either limit her ministry by her hardened resentment toward the one prohibition or expand her horizons to take in the full spectrum of ministry opportunities that are available to her.

For the woman willing to serve Christ by serving His people and for leaders of Christian ministries who long to see godly women used in His service, a number of principles should prevail in any decision concerning the placement of a woman in ministry. These guidelines are not new, and they are not limited only to women. New Testament principles concerning the suitability of the servant for service are universal. Those offered below are neither exhaustive nor restricted only to women, but they are important.

Spiritual Qualifications

Perhaps it goes without saying, but placing a woman into ministry in order to "make a statement" about one's church, to meet some type of master plan or quota, or to equalize some supposed "power structure" in the church is a terrible mistake—as it is any time a male is given a position of leadership for any reason short of the spiritual qualifications outlined in Scripture. What standard do we use to determine spiritual qualifications, for men and women? A good place to start is 1 Timothy 3:1-13, since the criteria listed there are predicated on a search for spiritual maturity in leadership. Another appropriate passage is 2 Timothy 2:21-26, which outlines characteristics of relational aptitude and the kind of even-temperedness required for anyone who deals daily with other believers.

*Adopted from H. Wayne House, *The Role of Women in Ministry* (Nashville: Thomas Nelson, 1990), pp. 148-158. Used by permission

A. Pure Motives

If a man were to accuse a Christian woman, particularly a feminist, of "smiling her way" into organizational leadership in order to aid her ultimate feminist goals, the accusations of sexism and paranoia would be deafening. Yet feminist author Patricia Gundry observes within a context of obvious sanction:

> One woman told me, "I smiled my way onto several committees in my church so I could be part of the decision-making body." She said she knew that in order to be effective (i.e. for feminism) as a lone individual she had to *do* something rather than wait for it to happen. She is an attractive and outgoing person. She used her personality to gain access to opportunity to help make decisions. Now she helps other women onto those committees. She also influences many decisions in the direction that will aid her ultimate goal.[1]

Any hidden agenda—whether feminism, moral laxity, legalism, social activism, doctrinal adjustment, or liberalism—can quickly erode and destroy an entire leadership team. The Bible is clear that any leader, male or female, must have pure and transparent motives.

B. A Proven Track Record

Of course, not every woman who desires to serve in some type of ministry will have experience to go along with her desire. Yet time by itself can add a great deal of credibility to a person's potential by confirming spiritual commitment and proving true humility. First Timothy 3:6 stipulates that a leader should not be a "novice, lest being puffed up with pride he fall into the same condemnation as the devil" (*NKJV*).

Time also allows a believer's basic beliefs and doctrine to solidify and become evident in practice as well as profession. Aberrant theology, while it may make for lively discussions and interesting articles, has no place at the spiritual core of a church's ministry, whether to three-year-olds or to thirty-year-olds.

A proven track record also includes the Christian's reputation in the "real world." This may not be much comfort to the recent Bible college graduate who wants to jump immediately into ministry, but it will safeguard that person's ministry and the reputation of Christ in His church.

C. A Willingness to Serve

It is unfortunate that the Christian church has bought the bill of goods pandered by our culture—one that equates leadership with prestige, power, and respect. This was not Christ's view of spiritual leadership. His approach to service for the kingdom was one of other-centeredness rather than self-centeredness; of availability rather than unapproachability; of respect for others rather than a demand of respect from others; of being prepared to lead but willing to serve, rather than aspiring to leadership because of its supposed "high" position.

D. Right Priorities

This may well be the acid test of one's suitability for ministry in any context. What is important to the person who aspires to leadership? Is it the opportunity to obey God's Word while taking the good news of salvation in Christ to every man, woman, and child possible? Is it the privilege of helping fulfill the Great

Commission, whether by administering the Christian education program of a church, teaching a Bible study for two hundred women, or discipling three hungry young believers?

Preoccupations reveal priorities, whether or not we want our priorities revealed. Little can stand in the way of the woman who aspires to spiritual leadership if she is preoccupied first with obedience to the Scriptures and second with fulfillment of Christ's Great Commission.

The Many Opportunities for Women

Throughout Scripture, one message comes through loud and clear when we observe those whom God would use in His work. Whether they are male or female, He is interested in using those who are entirely submitted to His will as expressed in His Word. Opportunities abound for women who desire to serve the church. Our focus needs to center on the many ministries that are Biblically open to all Christians, not on the few restrictions mandated by Scripture.

During Israel's wilderness wanderings, Korah and a following in excess of 250 rebelled against Moses and Aaron because they felt it was unfair that these two should be designated leaders while others weren't. According to Numbers 16, in fact, they accused Moses and Aaron of considering themselves a cut above everyone else because of what God had commanded and permitted them to do: "[F]or all the congregation are holy," they argued, "every one of them, and the *LORD* is in their midst; so why do you exalt yourselves above the assembly of the Lord?" (verse 3, *NASB*).

Korah and his companions felt that because all believers are equal, their roles should be completely interchangeable, whether or not God had commanded otherwise. Equality, to Korah and his companions, meant complete interchangeability of roles. What they failed to realize, however, is that for reasons of His own, God had limited the role of the priesthood. Though everyone in the redeemed community—each one who had been redeemed from bondage in Egypt—was equal, God had chosen to assign different roles to different segments of that community.

Of course, God's directives did not prevent Korah from rebelling against that principle and bringing on himself and his followers the wrath of God. For our purposes, the punishment in this episode is not the point. The point is that God chose to assign distinctly different roles to co-equal members of the redeemed community.

In 1 Samuel 13:8-14, we find another episode in which someone assigned one role aspired to fill another role assigned to someone else. In this case, Saul had been chosen by God to be king over Israel. It was as high an office as existed in human terms, and in this case there could be no feelings of insecurity—or so one would think.

After a great military victory, however, Saul decided that his time and prestige were more important than the command of God. After waiting seven days for Samuel to show up and make offerings to the Lord, Saul presumed that God did not really care about the distinction of roles and took it upon himself to assume the role of priest. After all, the people were scattering and needed to be reinforced spiritually. The offerings were ready. The people were waiting. And

Saul *was* king, after all. Why shouldn't he take on just one more duty and perform the priestly function?

Why? Because God had assigned specific roles to specific people and groups of people, and He expected His commands to be honored. Once Saul had made his presumptuous move, Samuel showed up and said to him, "You have acted foolishly; you have not kept the commandment of the LORD your God, which He commanded you, for now the LORD would have established your kingdom over Israel forever. But now your kingdom shall not endure" (1 Samuel 13:14).

There are other examples in Scripture that indicate that equality as persons, which the Bible freely attributes to all in the community of faith, does not necessarily imply interchangeability of roles. Within the context of human history, God chose to work His kingdom program through one man, Abraham, and his offspring. Yet that does not exclude anyone—Jew or non-Jew—from participating in His kingdom by faith. Within the nation of Israel, God limited the priesthood to the tribe of Levi, but that did not make any tribe superior or inferior to any other. And even among the Levites, anyone with a physical handicap was excluded from the priesthood—which in no way meant that he was inferior to the able-bodied or that God considered him less than his brethren.

The Scriptures teach clearly that submission to the Lord is going to include some kind of submission on the human plane. The great error of many feminists is their assumption that submission equals inferiority and precludes equality.

The fact that we are all equal in Christ does not exempt us from being obedient to God's Word. Neither does His Word limit us in any way from experiencing complete fulfillment in our relationship with Him. Why not? Because our greatest fulfillment comes in living in submission to Him, expressed in submission to the limits He has established. This is equally true for male and female, Jew and Greek, slave and free.

And how does all this help us better understand the myriad ministry opportunities open to godly, qualified women? More than anything else, it sets us free to look at every opportunity for service first in light of obedience to God's Word, then in light of the unlimited potential of every ministry pursued in a spirit of obedience and submission to Him.

What, then, of the godly woman who aspires to teach? Does the Biblical injunction against her authoritative teaching over men mean she is forever doomed to an unfulfilled Christian life and relegated to second-class citizenship in the kingdom? No.

The gifted female teacher can—and should—take every opportunity to teach women, whether in small groups or large. She can train other women to do the same. I believe she has been divinely equipped to teach children far better than most men can. She can write. She can author Bible study materials. She can do personal evangelism and discipleship among women, as men should do among other men. And a wide variety of administrative functions of ministry are Biblically available to women.

Does the Biblical model preclude a woman from giving her testimony in a church meeting or offering the Scripture reading, or making announcements, or leading songs, or offering a public prayer? These questions can be answered with another question: Are any of these ministries an expression of authoritative, elder-like teaching over men? Probably not, and thus they should not be excluded from the ministry opportunities afforded qualified women of God.

The Holy Spirit has bestowed spiritual gifts on all members of the body of Christ. First Corinthians 12:4-11 indicates that various gifts have been distributed to believers; there is no reason to believe any gift is limited to men. In view of this, local churches must provide ways in which women along with men can exercise their spiritual gifts. Women may be leaders in visitation to the sick, counseling other women and men, and leading Christian education programs, missionary programs, and evangelistic efforts.

Older women have special responsibilities toward younger women. They have a duty to teach the young women in Christian communities to love their husbands and their children, to be submissive to their husbands, and to fulfill their duties at home (Titus 2:4-5). The revered woman of Proverbs 31 acted in similar godly fashion.

It is indeed unfortunate that an overemphasis on trained male leadership fulfilling every aspect of ministry in the local church has excluded such "women elders of women" from serving Christ in a unique and valuable way by providing exemplary leadership for younger women. We needn't go into detail here about the risks and inadequacies inherent in the presumption that any and every male pastor is better equipped to counsel women in his church than are mature, godly Christian women in the same congregation. Suffice it to say that the pastor who fails to draw on the Biblical resource of qualified older women in the congregation to fulfill the church's ministry to younger women is not only risking the effectiveness of his ministry but also operating in clear contradiction to the instruction of Titus 2:4-5.

This type of ministry needn't be a formalized extension of the duties of a pastoral staff. In a large city in central California, for example, a woman (appropriately named Faith) for years conducted an annual "feminar" for the area's Christian college women. The all-day seminar was actually an outgrowth of a parachurch ministry led by Faith and her husband, a ministry that was usually attended by a mixture of Christian young women from the community. Included in this godly, mature woman's teaching was a combination of material concerning Christian maturity as well as Biblical womanhood. It was a successful ministry that simply could not have been effected by a man.

One church in the southwestern U.S. in recent years has made a transition from male pastoral staff counseling of women to counseling of women by a trained female staff. Since making the change, the success of the church's pastoral counseling has risen dramatically, a change everyone involved attributes to this small but Biblical adjustment.

In one parachurch organization, leadership by male directors over a mixed staff has been modified whenever possible so that both a director and his wife are responsible for the staff, he for the male staff and she for the female. Not only has this helped avoid romantic attachments and sexual pressures on all sides, but also the effectiveness of training and accountability has increased.

These are just a few examples. With so many opportunities available for fulfilling clear Biblical injunctions concerning female leadership, we should have precious little time left to force the application of questionable interpretations of Scripture into an already stressed context.

Conclusion

In short, the question of where women may minister in the church of Jesus Christ is not a question of who is superior and who is inferior, who gets the "good work" and who gets the "leftovers," or who is "sexist" and who is "open-minded."

It is, for its very essence, for both men and women, a question of submission to the Word of God. The would-be leader who is not submissive to the Bible's warnings against self-glorification and pride is not worthy to be a leader. The would-be leader who is not submissive to the Bible's clear teaching against greed is not worthy to be a leader. The aspiring teacher who is not submissive to the Bible's self-validation as inspired and inerrant, and who does not "rightly divide the Word of truth," is not to be a teacher.

And, no matter what it means in comparison to a contemporary social agenda—whether feminism, materialism, pacifism, socialism, imperialism, capitalism, racism, or any other "ism"—the would-be leader who is not entirely submissive to the liberating constraints of God's perfect Word should never be a leader at all.

22

The High Calling of Wife and Mother in Biblical Perspective

Dorothy Patterson

On completion of our graduate work in theology at New Orleans Baptist Theological Seminary in 1970, my husband and I moved with our two children to Fayetteville, Arkansas. My husband assumed the pastorate of First Baptist Church of Fayetteville, and I continued my role as his helper—but with some major adjustments. First, the responsibility of caring for a premature crying machine added to the already arduous task of keeping up with a card-carrying member of the Terrible Twos' Society was a life-changing jolt to the efficient routine of working as a highly paid executive secretary by day and amusing a drop-in toddler at night. Second, my weekend responsibilities as a pastor's wife in New Orleans, which I had previously fulfilled as a mere addendum to my role as a "professional woman," were certainly not from the script that had been presented to me on our arrival in Fayetteville. There I was to play the part of a young wife, following the steps of an accomplished pastor's wife who had enjoyed star billing for many years and whose wardrobe did not include two babies! Third, the intellectually stimulating and mind-stretching dialogue of a theological community definitely overshadowed the dissonant and monosyllabic monologue of a frenzied mother whose only moment for reflection came within the confines of the bathroom—and that only if she managed to enter the room alone, which was a feat in itself!

Confusion and frustration were mine as I wondered if this, too, really would pass and, if indeed it passed, whether I also would be passed by forever as to any worthwhile contribution to society. During my seminary days I had maintained a rigorous schedule as a full-time student, studying both Hebrew and Greek, coupled with multiple part-time jobs and the responsibilities of a pastor's wife. After completing my master's degree, I entered motherhood and moved to a full-time job while my husband completed his doctoral work. Though I pursued motherhood as enthusiastically as I had every other adventure in my life—I even breastfed my son for thirteen months, while working full-time—I can see in looking back that my first and freshest energies, not to mention the most productive part of my day, were devoted to professional pursuits away from home. When we moved to Arkansas, a void in my life came to the forefront. My theological training seemed a waste for the task of motherhood before me. In the midst of this frustrating time, I turned to the Lord. I determined in my daily quiet time to read through the Bible systematically with a new purpose: to determine God's message for me personally as a woman, a wife, and a mother. This experience became the catalyst for my life and ministry. From it came a series of messages titled "The Bible Speaks on Being a Woman," which I have been sharing with women over the years. My life and goals and perspective were forever changed. In every single book of the Bible I found God's word for me. That word was not always comforting; in fact, sometimes it was like a sword to my heart; but always I knew that it was authoritative and, if authoritative, true, regardless of culture, circumstances, or perceived relevance. I came to realize that God did not expect me to determine how to adapt His Word to my situation. Instead, He expected me to adapt myself to the consistently and clearly presented principles found in His Word. God did not expect me to interpret His principles in light of my gifts and intellect, but He admonished me "to be conformed to the likeness of his Son" (Romans 8:29),[1] including gifts and intellect and creativity. God was not waiting for me to determine what directives were relevant for me as a twentieth-century American woman, but He was making clear throughout Scripture His demand for my absolute obedience, even willing submission in the Spirit of Christ Himself, who said, "I delight to do Thy will, O my God" (Psalm 40:8, NASB).

Consequently, my chosen role of wife and mother took on new significance; my extensive academic preparation and professional experience I viewed in a new light; my commitment to marriage and home gained an added dimension—a divine contractual relationship reaching beyond my husband and me to include the Creator God Himself, who said "Therefore what God has joined together, let man not separate" (Matthew 19:6).

Bearing a new liberated identity, many women have devoted themselves to ambitious busyness everywhere but in the home. They are enmeshed in overwhelming voluntarism to achieve accolades and recognition in the community, or they are surrogate wives and mothers dedicated to hatching professional pursuits that promise power and pocketbook. Instead of encouraging adolescents to cut the apron strings of mother and venture out into society, we are begging mothers not to cut the apron strings on their babies and catapult them prematurely into a menacing world! Mom and hot apple pie have been replaced by institutional day care centers and cold apple turnovers at McDonald's!

Women have been liberated right out of the genuine freedom they enjoyed for centuries to oversee the home, rear the children, and pursue personal creativity; they have been brainwashed to believe that the absence of a titled, payroll occupation enslaves a woman to failure, boredom, and imprisonment within the confines of home. Though feminism speaks of liberation, self-fulfillment, personal rights, and breaking down barriers, these phrases inevitably mean the opposite.[2] In fact, the opposite is true because a salaried job and titled position can inhibit a woman's natural nesting instinct and maternity by inverting her priorities so that failures almost inevitably come in the rearing of her own children and the building of an earthly shelter for those whom she loves most. The mundane accompanies every task, however high paying or prestigious the job, so that escape from boredom is not inevitable just because your workplace is not at home. And where is the time for personal creativity when you are in essence working two jobs—one at home and one away?

In our quest to be *all* we are meant to be, let us not forget what we are *meant* to be! The question has never been whether a woman wants the best for her husband and children and even for herself. Rather the real question is this: Is being someone's wife and another's mother really worth the investment of a life? Does it take preparation of skills, concentration of energies, and the commitment of both to keep a home? The secular presuppositions of the present age, as well as one's own assumptions and priorities, must continually be tested against the sure written Word of God, which warns us, ". . . but test the spirits to see whether they are from God, because many false prophets have gone out into the world" (1 John 4:1).

Is Homemaking a Challenging Career?

A career or professional pursuit requires training and preparation as well as commitment and dedication over the long haul; it demands consistent activity and progressive achievement; it is a combination of training and preparation, commitment and loyalty, energy and time, excellence and achievement. Finding an efficient, capable person who is professionally adequate in many and varied careers simultaneously is rare indeed. For example, would you want your family physician to be your postman and policeman as well? I doubt it. Why? Because you want him to specialize and sharpen his expertise in medicine. Yet, you are certainly aware that your doctor dictates letters and reports and that he may on occasion sit down with a troubled patient as counselor. Within most careers there is a diversity of opportunity but never to the neglect of the priority responsibility. If the doctor gives the most productive part of his day to reports or counseling sessions and if, accordingly, he neglects updating his professional skills and treats patients haphazardly, the doctor will soon have no need to make reports or do counseling because his patient load will dwindle. In other words, there is specialization in purpose and preparation but generalization in service and opportunity.

Homemaking is a career. The dictionary defines the homemaker as "one who manages a household, especially a wife and mother." There are reasons why I believe this career is important enough to demand a woman's diligent preparation, foremost commitment, full energies, and greatest creativity. A homemaker does her job without the enticement of a paycheck, but she cannot be duplicated for any amount of money, for "She is worth far more than rubies" (Proverbs 31:10). Dorothy Morrison wrote, "Homemaking is not employment for slothful, unimaginative, incapable women. It has as much challenge and opportunity, success and failure, growth and expansion, perks and incentives, as any corporate career."[3]

Homemaking—A Divine Assignment

Keeping the home is God's assignment to the wife—even down to changing the sheets, doing the laundry, and scrubbing the floors. In Titus 2:3-5, Paul admonishes the older women to teach the younger women, among other things, "to love their husbands and children, . . . to be busy at home" (*oikourgous*, Greek, literally "home-workers"). The home was once described as ". . . a place apart, a walled garden, in which certain virtues too easily crushed by modern life could be preserved," and the mother in this home was described as "The Angel in the

House."[4] A 1982 Gallup poll showed that more than eight out of ten respondents (82 percent) assigned top priority on an eleven-point scale to the importance of family life. Families, health, and self-respect all were rated as more important than the possession of material goods.[5]

Few women realize what great service they are doing for mankind and for the kingdom of Christ when they provide a shelter for the family and good mothering—the foundation on which all else is built. A mother builds something far more magnificent than any cathedral—the dwelling place for an immortal soul (both her child's fleshly tabernacle and his earthly abode). No professional pursuit so uniquely combines the most menial tasks with the most meaningful opportunities.

The Book of Proverbs is for me the most practical book in the Bible. No other book is more saturated with home and family and the relationships therein. No other book has any more to say to women specifically.

Proverbs 31 contains a full-length portrait of a godly heroine finished in minute detail. The passage is significant not only for what it includes but also for what it omits. There is no mention of rights or pursuit of self-serving interests; neither is the husband assigned to domestic pursuits. In fact, his occupation with other tasks is clearly stated, "Her husband has full confidence in her. . . . Her husband is respected at the city gate, where he takes his seat among the elders of the land" (Proverbs 31:11, 23). This beautiful and perfect ode of praise to womanhood is written as an acrostic with the first word of each verse beginning with one of the twenty-two successive letters of the Hebrew alphabet.

This description of God's "Bionic/Wonder Woman" is often labeled an "Alphabetic Ode," "The Golden ABC's of the Perfect Wife," "The Portrait of the Wife of Many Parts," "A Paradigm for Brides-to-Be." Perhaps its literary form is designed to make the passage easier to commit to memory, or its acrostic style may be a literary device used to emphasize that these characteristics describe God's ideal woman—committed homemaker, chaste helpmeet, upright and God-fearing woman of strength. Though no woman can match skills and creativity perfectly with this model, all can identify their respective talents within the composite, and all can strive for the spiritual excellence of this woman of strength. This passage is recited in many Jewish homes on the eve of Sabbath, not only setting the high challenge for wife and mother but also expressing gratitude for her awesome service to the household.[6]

At least half of Proverbs 31:10-31 is occupied with personal and domestic energy. The New Testament, too, is clear in its emphasis on a woman's needed and necessary energy and efficiency in managing her household (Titus 2:5; 1 Timothy 2:10; 5:14). When Jesus reprimanded Martha, He did not condemn the vital housework she was doing; neither did He decry the gracious hospitality extended to Himself (Jesus did not say *only* one thing is needful but pointed to the one thing Martha had omitted). He did admonish her not to be encumbered or burdened by her work to the exclusion of spiritual sustenance, which Mary had so faithfully sought (Luke 10:38-42). One is never to neglect spiritual preparation—not even for the joy of serving others.

The best way to make homemaking a joyous task is to offer it as unto the Lord; the only way to avoid the drudgery in such mundane tasks is to bathe the tasks with prayer and catch a vision of the divine challenge in making and nurturing a home. Brother Lawrence, a member of the barefoot Carmelite monks in Paris in the 1600s, set a worthy example: "Lord of all pots and pans and things . . . Make me a saint by getting meals and washing up the plates! . . . The time of business does not with me differ from the time of prayer, and in the noise and clatter of my kitchen . . . I possess God in as great tranquillity as if I were upon my knees at the blessed sacrament."

Many people are surprised to discover how much time it actually takes to run a household and care for a family. Having a career was far easier for me than being a homemaker! None of my former positions required my being on the job twenty-four hours every day. None of my varied professional pursuits demanded such a variety of skills and abilities as I have exercised in homemaking. Automatic, labor-saving devices save much physical work, but increased mobility and multiplied outside activities add to the overall time demands so that the preparation and care of the family shelter are important enough for God Himself to assign that responsibility. Of course, much of the world would agree that being a housekeeper is acceptable as long as you are not caring for your own home; treating men with attentive devotion would also be right as long as the man is the boss in the office and not your husband; caring for children would even be deemed heroic service for which presidential awards could be given as long as the children are someone else's and not your own. We must not be overcome by the surrogacy of this age, which offers even a substitute womb for those so encumbered by lofty pursuits that they cannot accept God-given roles and assignments.

Homemaking—A Source of Self-Esteem

Women join men in the search for accomplishments and positive evaluations. We all have an innate desire to have worth. God's ideal woman has such worth. In fact, her worth cannot be fixed or estimated—it is "far more than rubies" (Proverbs 31:10). The question is, of course, clear: Who has such worth? The Hebrew word *hayil*, translated "virtuous" but more literally "strength,"[7] is found also in Proverbs 12:4; 31:29, and Ruth 3:11. It is further translated as *activity, ability, valor, wealth, efficiency, endurance, capability, energy*. This "woman of strength" enjoys dignity and importance in the administrative affairs of her home. She is a valuable helpmeet for her husband. She is a complement to her husband and a necessary completing part of his being.

There is beautiful reciprocity in this mutual relationship between husband and wife, just as there is between Christ and the church. Christ is the head of the church and the church is delighted to serve Him (Ephesians 5:23; Philippians 3:7-8). Christ finds joy in the church, and the church finds in Christ an inheritance of untold value. This husband has confidence in his wife's ability as the manager of the household affairs. She is absolutely dependable. The gain that accrues to her husband from her thrift and industry assures that he "lacks nothing of value" (Proverbs 31:11). This "woman of strength" is a visionary investor. With her savings or inheritance, "She considers a field and buys it" (Proverbs 31:16). Unlike the unfaithful servant who hid the talent given to him by his master (Matthew 25:24-25), this prudent wife is continually adding to her husband's investments because "she plants a vineyard" (Proverbs 31:16).

The woman of strength is an elegant lady. Tapestry for bedding, carpeting, pillows was a sign of a carefully-decorated home interior. Silk cloth had not yet been invented, but she undoubtedly used the fine flax or linen cloth that was the best of the day, and purple garments, indicating wealth or high rank, which were rare indeed (Proverbs 31:22). God's woman does give time and effort to her appearance. These words were written about the wife of the great eighteenth-century preacher Jonathan Edwards,

> But Sarah's husband made it clear that he treasured her as more than a housekeeping drudge and the mother of extra farmhands. So she stayed attractive, and fifteen years later she was still able to entrance men much younger than she was.[8]

The "woman of strength" was a source of tremendous pride to her husband. Her complete management of the household freed her husband to concentrate on his labors. Her husband respected her for neatness of dress, appreciated the fact that his wife was held in high esteem, and was willing to " . . . let her works bring her praise at the city gate" (Proverbs 31:31), but there is no hint in the passage that she had any other purpose than to meet the needs of her family in the best possible way.

Is Homemaking a Worthy Service?

In the Scriptures, the concern of godly women was not discrimination in vocation but rather the barrenness of the womb. Women were not pining away, pleading with the Almighty to be priests or prophets. They were praying for the blessing of bearing children. In Israel, every Jewish mother hoped to become the mother of the Messiah, who had been promised to Eve, the first mother (Genesis 3:15).

Hannah was brokenhearted over her childlessness (1 Samuel 1:1-2:1). Feeling forsaken of God, her maternal instinct prompted agonizing prayer with the burning intent of giving the boy back to God as a living sacrifice. Hannah deemed this the highest service. This motivation was not borne out of slavery to procreative responsibility. In conversations with her husband and Eli the priest, she was treated as an equal. The decision of when to go to Shiloh was left entirely with Hannah, and she not only was given the privilege of announcing the name of the child but also apparently chose the name Samuel, saying, "Because I asked the LORD for him" (1 Samuel 1:20, 22). Hannah was her own woman, but for her this meant committing herself to the purposes of God.

Hannah went from brokenhearted barrenness to extraordinarily privileged maternity. Though Hannah's psalm of thanksgiving marked her as a poetess and prophetess with a spiritual lyric equal to any psalm and full of theological truth, and though her words became the basis for Mary's Magnificat (Luke 1:46-55), Hannah did not reckon her literary acclaim equal to the nurturing of her child. Her greatest reward was not the birth of a son, however, but the gift to God of that son, who perhaps beyond all men had power with and from God. Moments of unequaled joy are coupled with difficult and time-consuming work. Children are not things to be acquired, used according to time and schedule, showcased for personal satisfaction, and then put aside for personal ambition and convenience.

Rearing the next generation is a coveted task despite the unprecedented attacks on motherhood. Some women want to limit parenthood to the labor room, settling for a "maternity sabbatical" in which they birth a baby during a few weeks' leave before rushing back to their lofty pursuits. Mrs. Uyterlinde returned to her job as an executive secretary at an insurance company four months after the birth of her triplets, saying, "I could only do that with the help of two full-time housekeepers." She continued, "Working is easier than being at home, but I give them my total attention when I am at home. Luckily they don't all want it at the same time."[9]

Others opt to take parenthood a bit more seriously and thus choose the "mommy track" work plan so that their hours have some flexibility while the children are very young.[10] Still others depict motherhood as an awful condition, suffocating and degrading—psychic suicide. Their banner is "Motherhood—Just Say No!" God's warning through the prophet Ezekiel could not be more timely:

> And you took your sons and daughters whom you bore to me and sacrificed them as food to the idols. . . . Everyone who quotes proverbs will quote this proverb about you: "Like mother, like daughter." You are a true daughter of your mother, who despised her husband and her children; and you are a true sister of your sisters, who despised their husbands and their children. (Ezekiel 16:20, 44-45).

Motherhood is both a demanding and a rewarding profession. Unfortunately, the reward often comes much later in life, but a prime characteristic of the good mother is unselfishness; she can wait for the final realization of her rewards. No one—not teacher, preacher, or psychologist—has the same opportunity to mold minds, nurture bodies, and develop potential usefulness like a mother. It is both practical and consistent with the basic qualities that nature has given male and female that the woman who bears and nurses the baby should care for the young and for the dwelling in which the young live. Though a woman approaching the twenty-first century is different in many ways from her foremothers, she is in at least one way forever the same. Some would say that she is a servant of her biological fate, to which she has to adjust her other pursuits. Of course, this may be interpreted as mere slavery with the procreative and nurturing tasks as the shackles; but, on the other hand, this biological duty may also be accepted as a divinely assigned destiny with the awesome opportunity for a woman to link hand and heart with the Creator God in bearing and preparing the next generation as the binding cord.

Despite pressures and difficulties, the job can be overwhelmingly satisfying and amazingly productive, because the result of really competent mothering will be passed from generation to generation. Products in the marketplace may come and go, but generation after generation we produce our sons and daughters. A child needs his mother to be all there; to be focused on him, to recognize his problems and needs; to support, guide, see, listen to him, love and want him. A young woman wrote to "Dear Abby" describing her mother as "a professional woman who collected a husband, a daughter, and a dog to enrich her life." According to the daughter, the only one not damaged by this enrichment was the dog![11] Susanna Wesley, the incomparably brilliant and well-educated mother of sons who shook two continents for Christ, wrote, "I am content to fill a little space if God be glorified." She described her now famous childrearing commitment in these words:

> No one can, without renouncing the world, in the most literal sense, observe my method; and there are few, if any, that would entirely devote above twenty years of the prime of life in hopes to save the souls of their children, which they think may be saved without so much ado; for that was my principal intention, however unskillfully and unsuccessfully managed.[12]

The emergence of inexpensive, effective birth-control measures, not to mention widespread abortion, has cut the size of average families. Women are giving less and less of their time to childbearing and rearing; marriage is being delayed to allow career preparation and pursuit. Motherhood has become as mechanical and insignificant as any other household task and is just as quickly farmed out to others—even the carrying of the child in the womb, i.e., surrogate childbearing through in vitro fertilization.

Marriage has become such a partnership that the household tasks are carefully divided and assigned as nonchalantly as clients to be serviced. Both husband and wife choose careers according to the best earning power and opportunity for advancement of both, which usually means the family loses the best opportunity for both. Despite all this egalitarian emphasis, Mary Jo Bane of the Wellesley Women's Research Center expressed a prevailing sentiment: "Everybody is in favor of equal pay, but nobody is in favor of doing the dishes."[13]

Feminism is a "social movement" that demands it all. Actress Katharine Hepburn said in an interview, "I'm not sure any woman can successfully pursue a career and be a mother at the same time. The trouble with women today is that they want everything. But no one can have it all. I haven't been handicapped by children. Nor have I handicapped children by bringing them into the world and going ahead with my career."[14] Actress Joanne Woodward says, "My career has suffered because of the children, and my children have suffered because of my career. I've been torn and haven't been able to function fully in either arena. I don't know one person who does both successfully, and I know a lot of working mothers."[15] Golda Meir of Israel confessed that she suffered nagging doubts about the price her two children paid for her career, adding, "You can get used to anything if you have to, even to feeling perpetually guilty."[16]

Each of these women chose to work, not because she had to do so to provide necessities for her family or because her husband demanded it, but because of personal gain and fame or because of what she perceived to be a contribution more valuable to the nation or world than full-time motherhood. In each case, attention to the child was less important than the career.

Even the politicians are convinced that children are a valuable resource to be protected. A new report released by the National Governors' Association Task Force on Children states, "The economic and social well-being of the United States rests on our ability to assure that our children develop into healthy, well-educated, and productive citizens. . . . To invest in their future is to invest in ours."[17]

A study of primarily middle-class children was conducted by University of Texas at Dallas researchers Deborah Lowe Vandell and Mary Anne Corasaniti. This study indicated that full-time child care was associated with poorer study skills, lower grades, diminished self-esteem, and inadequate social interaction. Those who went into full-time care after the first year did not develop as well socially, emotionally, and intellectually as those in part-time care or those whose mothers stayed home with them. Surely another concern must be in the development of the child's values and worldview, which are determined very early in life. Will forty hours a week in a day care center be a more formidable factor in forming those values than a worn-out mother? Because Vandell is a full-time professor and mother of three- and eight-year-old children, she had expected different results from the study. She clearly stated that she did not accept her findings as a call for mothers to stay at home.[18]

Napoleon was asked what could be done to restore the prestige of France. He replied, "Give us better mothers!"[19] The art of mothering surely demands as much training as a skilled waitress or craft worker, and thus we should not expect to be an expert as we begin this vocation but rather that slowly we would learn the needs of each child and how to meet those needs. Often those who are reluctant to begin the job of full-time mothering are just as reluctant to give it up when the results are both seen and enjoyed. Timothy Dwight, former president of Yale, said, "All that I am and all that I shall be I owe to my mother."[20] Good lives don't just grow like Topsy; they are built by people who care.

Isn't it amazing that legislators are looking for ways to enable families to send their children to day care rather than looking for ways to enable mothers to stay at home with their children? Megan Rosenfeld comments, "For the first time it is possible to envision a generation that will have spent the bulk of their childhood in an institution."[21] Sad but true is the fact that institutions are now set up to provide a substitute for the mother, who was the moral backbone and spiritual nurturer as well as the physical caretaker—the woman who is now no longer there!

Tatyana Zaslavskaya, president of the Soviet Sociologist Association, is quoted in a TASS interview as expressing deep concern for the ill effects on children of "the high rate of employment among working-age women." She pleaded for mothers to make children their prime mission, calling on the Communist Party to discuss ways to reduce the employment rate among mothers. She added that the problem that is often glamorized in the United States as the "Superwoman" phenomenon (the woman who is faster than a speeding two-year-old, able to leap tall laundry piles in a single bound, and possessed of more power than three teenaged boys and still able to go out and save the world in the midst of all) has been known in the Soviet Union for years as "the problem of two jobs."[22] Even Mikhail Gorbachev addresses this issue:

> We have discovered that many of our problems—in children's and young people's behavior, in our morals, culture and in production—are partially caused by the weakening of family ties and slack attitude to family responsibilities. This is a paradoxical result of our sincere desire to make women equal with men in everything.

He adds that Russia is now looking for ways to make it possible for women to return "to their purely womanly mission."[23]

Some women even claim to have a higher focus on serving God—putting the gospel ahead of "familyism."[24] While no one and nothing must come between a woman and her personal relationship to Christ ("But seek first his kingdom and his righteousness, and all these things will be given to you as well," Matthew 6:33), neither does the Bible contain any admonition to place the work of the church ahead of home responsibilities. When a woman has chosen the high calling of being a wife, her submission to her husband is "as to the Lord" (Ephesians 5:22). When she chooses the high calling of motherhood, "Sons are a heritage from the LORD, children a reward from him" (Psalm 127:3); this, too, is itself an offering to the Lord.

In another era the beautiful and godly mother of John Chrysostom was widowed at a young age. She refused her many suitors and committed herself totally to the responsibility of rearing her gifted son, who became the Patristic church's greatest orator.[25] Mothers, too, win most by losing all ("Whoever finds his life will lose it, and whoever loses his life for my sake will find it," Matthew 10:39). By developing the Christlike quality of abandoning personal demands and rights and seeking to serve and minister to those whom God has provided for their own personal ministry, these unselfish heroines gain worth and wonder and splendor beyond imagination.

There is no greater need for the coming years than a revival of interest in the responsibilities of motherhood. We need mothers who are not only family-oriented but also family-obsessed. We have seen much about the virtue of determined childlessness and the right to make one's own place in the sun; yet it is hard to locate an aging mother who believes she made a mistake in pouring her life into her children, and it would certainly be more difficult to find a child to testify that his mother loved him and poured herself into his life to his detriment and demise. Surely countless mothers would join me in saying, "Try it—you'll like it!" The Lord Himself says, "Like arrows in the hands of a warrior are sons born in one's youth. Blessed is the man whose quiver is full of them" (Psalm 127:4-5).

Homemaking—An Opportunity for Service

The wife was created by God to be her husband's "helper" (*ezer kenegdō*, Hebrew, literally "a help like or corresponding to himself," Genesis 2:18). There is nothing demeaning about being a helper. It is a challenging and rewarding responsibility. God Himself assumed that role on many occasions (Psalm 40:17, "You are my help and my deliverer; O my God, do not delay"; Hebrews 13:6, "So we say with confidence, 'The Lord is my helper'"). This did not mean that the Lord was an inferior but spoke rather of His desire to meet the needs of those whom He loves with an everlasting and unconditional love. Through the ages some have held that women are inferior to men, but the attempt to attribute such an idea to Scripture is unthinkable.

We must give attention to what Luther called "the plain sense of Scripture" as concerns the husband-wife relationship. It is really not terribly complicated. What the New Testament writers wrote and how they meant their words to be understood in their own time is far more important than the secular meanings assigned these Biblical terms in this generation, especially when those meanings depart from the clear teaching of Scripture. The fact is that there is no suggestion in Scripture that women are inferior or incapable in any sense—neither in personhood, which is the same as man's, nor in function, which is different from man's.

Any attitude or action suggesting a woman's insignificance, inferiority, or lack of personhood originated in the fall. The stigma of inferiority is no more appropriate for the wife than it would be for Christ. One can be subject to a superior as Israel was subject to the Lord (Deuteronomy 6:1-5) and as believers are subject to Christ (Philippians 2:9-11), or as Abraham submitted to the priesthood of Melchizedek

(Hebrews 7:7). But subordination is also possible among equals: Christ is equal to God the Father and yet subject to Him (Philippians 2:6-8); believers are equal to one another and yet are admonished to "submit to one another out of reverence for Christ" (Ephesians 5:21). In fact, one can be called to subordinate himself to someone who is inferior, as Christ submitted to Pontius Pilate, making "no reply, not even to a single charge" (Matthew 27:11-14). The mere fact that wives are told to be subject to their husbands tells us nothing about their status. It is the comparison of the relationship between husband and wife to the relationship of God the Father with God the Son that settles the matter of status forever.[26]

Submission and *authority*, which to the feminists are the offensive elements in Biblical womanhood, are not terms that in themselves connote sinful or evil characteristics. Neither are the terms limited to describe role relationships between the sexes. Both terms are used to describe relationships within the family, including, but not exclusive to, the relationship between husband and wife. In fact, these terms even reach far beyond the family. In every facet of organized society (see Romans 13:1-5 for application to government and Hebrews 13:17 as concerns the church), there must be both authority and submission to authority; otherwise, there is anarchy. There simply is no justification for labeling these words and the concepts they embody as innately objectionable and oppressive. Finally, and more importantly, these terms point to our common ground with the Lord Himself, who gave to us the highest example of servanthood, obedience, and selflessness, as "he humbled himself and became obedient to death" (Philippians 2:5-8; see also John 5:30).

Ideally, the care of one's partner is inherent in marriage. Each makes an active and unique (not passive and same) contribution to the marriage, and each depends upon the other for that contribution. Both husband and wife achieve their respective individuality by assuming different roles, for which each is needed and on which neither intrudes. In choosing to allow one's husband to support the family, a wife can turn her ingenuity toward producing a lifestyle even better than an additional salary would buy.

Subordination has been distorted before in the history of the church. Arius assigned inferiority of being to Jesus the Son, refusing to accept the Scripture's statement that Father, Son, and Holy Spirit are equal in being and personhood (John 1:1; 5:23; 10:30; 14:6-7, 9, 11) and yet different in office and function, as the Son voluntarily becomes subject and even subordinate[27] to the Father (John 5:19-20; 6:38; 8:28-29, 54; 1 Corinthians 15:28; Philippians 2:5-11), and the Holy Spirit is sent by, and thus under the direction of, the Father to glorify the Son (John 14:26; 15:26; 16:13-14). Arian subordinationism was condemned as heretical—a denial of Trinitarianism—because it ignored, distorted, or misread certain Scriptures and because of Gnostic tendencies that simply dismissed or abandoned passages that the human mind could not explain.[28] Can "Arian" feminism, which denies that women can have equal personhood along with a subordinate role, i.e., a different role with equal worth, be any more circumspect? I certainly think not. The Council of Nicea in A.D. 325 not only condemned this heresy but also ascribed to both Son and Spirit an equality of being, while clearly declaring subordination of order and function.[29] Likewise, I have no problem in accepting within my womanhood the equality of creation and personhood, while recognizing that my divinely bestowed womanhood is uniquely suited to the divinely assigned task.

Too many women rush headlong into a career outside the home, determined to waste no time or effort on housework or baby-sitting but rather seeking to achieve position and means by directing all talents and energies toward non-home professional pursuits. It is true that many "perfect jobs" may come and go during the childrearing years, but only one will absolutely never come along again—the job of rearing your own children and allowing them the increasingly rare opportunity to grow up at home.

Golda Meir, by her own testimony, devoted her adult life to the birth and rearing of Israel at the cost of her marriage. She separated from her reticent husband in pursuit of public life. To quote Mrs. Meir, "what I was made it impossible for him to have the sort of wife he wanted and needed. . . . I had to decide which came first: my duty to my husband, my home and my child or the kind of life I myself really wanted. Not for the first time—and certainly not for the last—I realized that in a conflict between my duty and my innermost desires, it was my duty that had the prior claim."[30]

How sad it is for a woman to try to build her life on the notion that she is going to pursue whatever momentarily happens to gratify her needs socially, emotionally, physically, or professionally. Though the duty of wifehood and motherhood may lay claim, the desires of personal ambition and success in public service can take hold, of which the Lord warned,

> but each one is tempted when, by his own evil desire [*epithumia*, Greek], he is dragged away and enticed. Then, after desire has conceived, it gives birth to sin [*hamartia*, Greek, literally "missing the mark"]; and sin, when it is full grown, gives birth to death. (James 1:14-15)

When a wife goes to work outside the home, often her husband and children go through culture shock. Suddenly the husband has added to his vocational work increased family assignments. He is frustrated over the increase in his own assignments and guilty over his wife's increased fatigue and extended hours to keep up at home. God did give the husband the responsibility of providing for the family (Genesis 2:15). To sabotage his meeting that responsibility is often a debilitating blow to the man personally and to the marriage. A woman's career can easily serve as a surrogate husband, as during employment hours she is ruled by her employer's preferences. Because the wife loses much of her flexibility with the receipt of a paycheck, a husband must bend and adapt his schedule for emergencies with the children, visits to the home by repairmen, etc. This leaves two employers without totally committed employees and children without a primary caretaker utterly devoted to their personal needs and nurturing. Note the prophet's warning, "Youths oppress my people, women rule over them. O my people, your guides lead you astray; they turn you from the path" (Isaiah 3:12).

Many women still see the paycheck as an inadequate trade for the sights and sounds and tastes of home. Though some see their paychecks as representing independence and achievement, to be bound to paychecks requires in exchange the time formerly allotted to work for the family in private, personal ways. This is not to say that there are never times when a woman should seek employment outside her home. Nevertheless, are we coming to a day when a woman's employment outside the home is the rule rather than the exception, leaving no one to give primary attention to the home and to producing the next generation.

The most outstanding ministering couple in the New Testament is the dynamic duo Aquila and Priscilla, who traveled the apostolic world together, sharing the gospel of Christ and expounding the Word more fully (Acts 18:2-3, 18, 26). Priscilla must have been a diligent and discerning student of the Word of God, or she could never have impressed the learned Apollos. On the other hand, she must have been a gracious hostess to have endeared her home and hospitality to Paul. Obviously, she was encouraged to take an active part in ministry by her husband. When a godly wife is all she ought to be, she completes, complements, and extends her husband. Their joint ministry reaches beyond what either of them could do alone (Psalm 34:3; Ecclesiastes 4:9-12).

When Paige Patterson invited me to link my life to his, irrevocably and inseparably, he asked me to join him in study and preparation. How grateful I have been for the formal studies of seminary, but how much more grateful I am for the hours Paige has spent as my teacher and mentor. Paige has encouraged me in multifarious ministry, but never has he given me the impression that these ministries were to be more important than keeping our home and rearing our children.

Conclusion

Despite the clear positive principles and the precise warnings of consequences for those who ignore or distort God's plan for the home and family, we find ourselves living in the very "upside-down" world the prophet Isaiah described:

> You turn things upside down, as if the potter were thought to be like the clay! Shall what is formed say to him who formed it, "He did not make me"? Can the pot say of the potter, "He knows nothing"? (Isaiah 29:16).

The efforts of contemporary society to eradicate the differences between the sexes have spawned an increase in strident lesbianism and open homosexuality, a quantum upward leap in divorces, an increase in rapes and sexual crimes of all sorts—and families smaller in size than ever before. We are part of a generation of women who have prostituted the creative purposes of God by prophesying "out of their own imagination" (Ezekiel 13:17), who have erected for themselves "male idols" to supplant the Creator's design (Ezekiel 16:17), and who have cast aside the greatest blessing of the Creator, i.e., the fruit of the womb (Ezekiel 16:20, 44-45). We have allowed Scripture itself to be distorted so that we are conforming ourselves to this age and letting the world squeeze us "into its own mold" (Romans 12:2, *Phillips*). The church today sounds like the world twenty-five years ago; it has lost its great power to stand against culture. Scripture has been shanghaied to suit the purposes of the age and to conform to the current cultural scene. The virtues and vices of Christianity have been inverted so that self-gratifying personal rights, selfishness, and self-interests are exalted, whereas self-effacing submission, humility, and service to others are degraded. While I am not implying that every career woman is selfish, I am saying that the social atmosphere that causes women to crave professional pursuits over the family is perverted by unbiblical assumptions and an ungodly spirit of assertion and self-gratification.

Evangelical or Biblical feminism is in large measure a product of the secular women's liberation movement of the late sixties and seventies. Few of these evangelical feminists have much in common with the radical wing of feminism.

Nevertheless, the movement of self-assertion in the home, church, and community cannot but extend into the spiritual realm with a determination to act independently of God and go one's own way (Proverbs 14:12; Isaiah 53:6). Human rights and reason have been exalted over responsibility and divine revelation. The reality in Scripture has been subordinated to the reason of man (and woman); the absolutes of the Creator have been replaced with the whims of the creation. Rejecting Scripture as authoritative, many male and female feminists put the focus of authority in human hands, usually through some hermeneutical casuistry. Whatever texts do not seem to affirm women are labeled as not authoritative, while texts judged as affirming are authoritative.

There is great resistance in the world of feminism to letting Scripture speak for itself. Instead of coming reverently to the Biblical text to see what it says and then declaring themselves to be feminists, many seem to have found something in secular feminism and in its claims for improving the lot of womanhood that seemed good and true to them. Thus, the feminists took a "leap of faith" to attach themselves to this movement, determining to legitimize their position Biblically and theologically and to change two millennia of church history and tradition to reflect this new church doctrine that more nearly fits the reality of their active professional lives—another tragic example of the world's setting the agenda for the church rather than vice versa.

Homemaking, if pursued with energy, imagination, and skills, has as much challenge and opportunity, success and failure, growth and expansion, perks and incentives as any corporation, plus something no other position offers—working for people you love most and want to please the most!

In the words of Scripture, I have found a worthy challenge:

> Teach them [God's words] to your children, talking about them when you sit at home and when you walk along the road, when you lie down and when you get up. . . so that your days and the days of your children may be many in the land that the LORD swore to give your forefathers, as many as the days that the heavens are above the earth. (Deuteronomy 11:19, 21)

Homemaking—being a full-time wife and mother—is not a destructive drought of usefulness but an overflowing oasis of opportunity; it is not a dreary cell to contain one's talents and skills but a brilliant catalyst to channel creativity and energies into meaningful work; it is not a rope for binding one's productivity in the marketplace, but reins for guiding one's posterity in the home; it is not oppressive restraint of intellectual prowess for the community, but a release of wise instruction to your own household; it is not the bitter assignment of inferiority to your person, but the bright assurance of the ingenuity of God's plan for complementarity of the sexes, especially as worked out in God's plan for marriage; it is neither limitation of gifts available nor stinginess in distributing the benefits of those gifts, but rather the multiplication of a mother's legacy to the generations to come and the generous bestowal of all God meant a mother to give to those He entrusted to her care.

23

Where's Dad?

A Call for Fathers with the Spirit of Elijah[1]

Weldon Hardenbrook

Lucille Ball was the first lady of American comedy. Some time before her death she did a remarkable television interview with Merv Griffin, who asked her a very pointed and serious question. "Lucille, you've lived a long time on this earth and you are a wise person. What's happened to our country? What's wrong with our children? Why are our families falling apart? What's missing?"

Lucy's startling yet matter-of-fact reply came quickly. "Papa's missing," she said. "Things are falling apart because Papa's gone. If Papa were here, he would fix it."

Lucille Ball was far better known for her comic performances than for her social insights. But she was right. For so many of the family problems that beset American culture have, at their root, dysfunctional fathers.

At the very beginning of the creation of our world, God proclaimed that it is not good for man to be alone, and through Adam He instituted the family as the center of human community. Throughout the historical transitions of a variety of cultures, the family existed as a natural society that provided the soul of each nation and that was to be nourished and protected through fatherhood.

But what is fatherhood? Certainly there is more to true paternity than merely breeding offspring. Author Clayton Barbeau does a good job of defining the essence of fatherhood when he writes, "The notion of responsibility is at the crux of true fatherhood. The conscious sense of responsibility for the physical and spiritual well-being of others is the mark of a true father."[2]

I humbly but firmly submit that the soul of our nation is in crisis in large part because American men have—from ignorance and for various and sometimes even subconscious reasons—abandoned their God-given role of fatherhood. They have discarded the notion of being responsible for the physical and spiritual well-being of those around them.

A series of historical events, beginning at the Industrial Revolution, traversing the search for American independence and the Second Great Awakening, and culminating in Victorianism, has had the net result of disestablishing American men from a true role of fatherhood and moral leadership in our land. The American male, at one time the ever-present guide of the close-knit colonial family, left his family for the factory and the materialistic lure that the Industrial

Revolution brought. The most numerous and most active members of the church, the men—who commonly debated theology in the colonial marketplace—were, in time, to be found arguing business practices in the tavern. The fathers who labored hard to instill the value of cooperation in their offspring, in time gave their children the example of unlimited individual competition. Men who once taught their children respect and obedience toward godly authority came to act as though independence were a national virtue. Men who once had an active hand in the education of their sons relegated this responsibility to a public school system dominated by female teachers and feminine learning patterns. Once the leaders of social progress, American men came to look on social reform and mercy movements as women's work and, in time, became themselves the objects of that social reform, in the case of movements such as the Women's Christian Temperance Union.

Over the course of 150 years, from the mid-eighteenth century to the end of the nineteenth century, American men walked out on their God-given responsibility for moral and spiritual leadership in the homes, schools, and Sunday schools of the nation. As sociologist Lawrence Fuchs notes, "The groundwork for the 20th-century fatherless home was set. By the end of the 19th century for the first time it was socially and morally acceptable for men not to be involved with their families."[3]

This disappearance of the American father has led writer Marion J. Levy in *Modernization: Latecomers and Survivors* to note that "for the first time in the history of humankind the overwhelming majority of little boys and little girls continued under the direct domination and supervision of ladies until they reached maturity. This has never happened before in history. Crusades, wars, migrations, pestilence—nothing for a people as a whole ever before took so large a percentage of young adult and older adult males out of the family context for so much of the waking time of the children. Most of us have not even noticed this change, nor do we have any idea of its radicality."[4]

Lucille Ball was right. Papa is gone. Consider these sobering statistics: One of every four American children has no father in the home to welcome him or her at the time of birth. Only 41 percent of today's children will grow up in a two-parent family. Almost a million children are left with one parent because of divorce each year. Nine out of ten of these are with their mothers. "Today's children are the first generation in this country's history who think divorce and separation are a normal part of family life," says Andrew Chrerlin of Johns Hopkins University.[5] From 1950 to 1980, the annual rate of illegitimate births increased by a staggering 450 percent. The 715,200 children born without fathers in 1982 represented 19.4 percent of *all* births for that year. On average, American fathers give each of their children a mere three minutes of undivided attention each day.

My own twenty-three years of pastoral experience bear out these figures. By far the most commonly recurring complaint I hear from married women is about phantom fathers who do not connect with their wives and children. Here is a letter I received, from the wife of a Christian friend, that tragically expresses the feelings of countless women in America today:

> The kids are in bed. There's nothing on TV tonight. I ask my husband if he minds if I turn the tube off. He grunts. As I walk to the set my mind is racing. Maybe, just maybe tonight we'll talk. I mean have a conversation that consists

of more than my usual question with his mumbled one-word answer or, more accurately, no answer at all. Silence—I live in a world with continuous noise but, between him and myself, silence. Please—oh God, let him open up. I initiate (once again; for the thousandth time). My heart pounds—oh, how can I word it this time? What can I say that will open the door to just talk? I don't have to have a DEEP MEANINGFUL CONVERSATION. JUST SOMETHING!

As I open my mouth—he gets up and goes to the bedroom. The door closes behind him. The light showing under the door gives way to darkness. So does my hope. I sit alone on the couch. My heart begins to ache. I'm tired of being alone. Hey, I'm married. I have been for years. Why do I sit alone? The sadness undergoes a change slowly—then with increased fervor I get mad. I AM MAD. I am sick and tired of living with a sissy. A wimp—a coward. You know, he's afraid of me!

Hostile, you say. You better believe it. I'm sick and tired of living in a world of passive men.

My two sons like sports. They're pretty good. They could be a lot better if their Dad would take a little of his precious time and play catch with them. (I'm sorry, catch once a year at the church picnic doesn't quite make the boys into great ball players.) But Dad's too busy. He's at work. He's at the health club. He's riding his four-wheeler. He's working on the car. He's playing golf. He's tired. He's watching a video movie. So who plays catch with my boys? Me. My husband says, "You shouldn't be playing men's sports." So who's going to do it? He *says* he will. But he doesn't. Remember? *He's* too busy. Satisfying himself doing what he likes. . . . So my poor sons have to be second-rate in sports. They could have been good. Really good. Yeah—I'm mad.

My daughter is a teenager. She likes boys. *They* notice her. *They* pay attention to her. She responds. I know what's coming. I try to talk to her. But it's not me she wants. It's Dad. Yeah, Dad! If he'd just hug her, notice her, talk to her—just a little—she wouldn't need those boys so much. But no . . . so she turns elsewhere for attention and love. And there's nothing I can do.

A mom isn't enough. Kids need a father. And not just a body, a passive, silent presence.

And here's the killer. My husband's father did the same number on him. Didn't hug him. Didn't take him to anything, let alone watch his baseball games. And he HATES his father. Now my husband's doing the same thing. Will our sons grow up to be passive? Will they be cowards?

Edwin Cole rightly labels father absence as the "curse of our day."[6]

That absence has dramatic effects on our children, especially our sons. My wife has been an elementary school teacher for over twenty-seven years. Most of this time has been spent in special education in California schools. Who has filled her classroom year after year? Boys. Ninety-eight percent of her special education students have been emotionally damaged young boys whose shared characteristic is father-loss. Of course, biological and chemical factors are involved in boys' problems. However, in many cases father-loss has exaggerated them.

The lack of the father's presence greatly damages the son's self-esteem and confidence. The lack of a male role model at home is compounded by the lack of male role models at school. Eighty-five percent of elementary school teachers are women. And a system that insists that little boys learn as if they were little girls contributes to this sad litany of educational problems. Some experts say that boys are not mature enough to begin school until they are six-and-a-half years old while girls seem to be ready for the classroom at five years and nine months. I agree that many boys are not ready for school at the usual age of five. But this is not necessarily because they are immature. Could it not also be that teachers are not ready for normal five-year-old male behavior? *Momism* author Hans Sebald argues,

> All too often these boys' fundamental learning process is left exclusively to females—the mother, the Sunday school teacher, nursery and kindergarten personnel, and the elementary school teacher. Thus, boys are exposed to the continuous authority and teaching of agents whom they may not imitate, but whose guidance and information about what they should be they are expected to accept and practice.[7]

More than two out of three students who fail one or more grades are boys. Learning and behavioral disorders are three to ten times as common among boys as among girls of the same ages. Three out of four retarded readers are boys. Four out of five school discipline problems are caused by boys.

Boys learn differently and at a different pace than girls. But school systems fail to allow for such differences. In classrooms, natural expressions of masculine behavior are commonly viewed as improper. Too often the boys of America find themselves in a conflict between "being good" and being male. Associating "being bad" with being masculine, many boys start behaving in destructive ways. These are the lads who are growing up to be the so-called bad boys of America. Four out of five of the nearly two million juveniles arrested in America every year are boys.

What is causing young people, particularly boys, to commit so much of the serious crime in this country? There are many reasons, but a key common factor is the absence of the father. "Fatherless families . . . generate far more delinquency and personality disorders than do normal or motherless families," declares Daniel Amneus. "The ratio of delinquent children living with the mother only compared to those living with the father only is about three to one."[8]

Psychologists and sociologists have been surfacing with evidence that identifies a new kind of disordered personality among these child criminals: a desensitized, almost passionless youth who has no feelings, no compassion toward those whom he strikes out against, no remorse. Thus we see such shocking phenomena as violent sexual crimes perpetrated by children against other children.

In 1982, more than eighty thousand juveniles were residing in juvenile custody facilities, not in their homes.[9] The year before that, over 51 percent of people arrested for what the FBI considers to be serious crimes were under the age of twenty.[10] *New York Times* writer William Shannon discloses, "Since 1963, crimes by children have been rising at a faster rate than the juvenile population. . . . The rate of armed robbery, rape, and murder by juveniles has doubled in a decade."[11] The FBI estimates that in 1983 youths under the age of eighteen accounted for more than 218,000 burglaries, 81,000 drug abuse violations, 45,000 motor vehicle thefts, 43,000 aggravated assaults, and 10,000 arsons. In that same year over 5,600 women were raped by youths aged seventeen and under, and over 1,400 people were murdered by the children of America.[12]

Who were these young perpetrators? You guessed it. They were overwhelmingly boys. In 1983, for example, there were approximately 1,722,531 people under the age of eighteen arrested in this country. More than 78 percent were boys.[13] What is causing young people, particularly boys, to commit so much of the serious crime in this country? The key common factor is the absence of a father.

Even more startling is the situation in the black community. In 1988, 75 percent of all black infants were born to unwed mothers.[14] Already in 1983 four out of ten black families in America had no father present, a ratio 300 percent greater than that of white families. Through a history of slavery, segregation, exploitation, oppression, overwhelming prejudice, emasculation, and well-intentioned but degrading government assistance programs, black families have lost their leaders—the fathers.

The effect on the sons is tragic. Richard Stengel wrote in *Time* about

> a frighteningly familiar but largely unspoken national scourge: the epidemic of violence by young blacks against other young blacks. The leading cause of death among black males, ages 15 to 24, in the U.S. is not heart disease, not cancer, not any natural cause. It is murder by other blacks. More than 1 out of every 3 blacks who die in that age group is the victim of a homicide. Across America, particularly among the underclass in the nation's urban ghettos, brother is killing brother in a kind of racial fratricide. More than 40% of all the nation's murder victims are black, and 94% of those who commit these murders are black. The 6,000 or so Americans who lost their lives because of black-on-black violence in 1981 alone rivals the number of black serviceman killed during the twelve years of the Vietnam conflict.[15]

The fatherless black youth, in his flight from the feminizing forces of a matriarchal culture, has pursued the only option he sees available to him to gain masculinity. In his mind, being physically tough is masculine. The main issue here is not poverty. "Poverty is not necessarily associated with crime because there are many poor and law-abiding people."[16] If poverty were the main reason for crime, almost everyone in the Third World would be a criminal. It seems that no one, for some hopeless or fatalistic reason, wants to touch on the raw nerve that needs to be healed—absent fathers, in both the white and black communities.

The plague of missing fathers is creating an American male who is confused about his identity and under a great deal of psychological stress, and who ends up lashing out in frustration. Our land is increasingly filled with angry, frustrated, isolated young men who no longer know who they are. In desperation, they are tearing everything to pieces. American husbands abused six million wives in 1988, four thousand of whom died as a result. And because of self-hatred, American men are destroying themselves also. They are the overwhelming majority of victims of substance abuse and murder. Of the 27,000 Americans who commit suicide each year, 75 percent are men.

Absent and disinterested fathers also take a toll on their daughters. Fathers play a crucial role in the development of girls' image of their femininity. Dad's positive feedback is essential. Ponder the following letter in *Seventeen* magazine from one girl whose father is not making contact:

> Have you ever heard of a father who won't talk to his daughter? My father doesn't seem to know I'm alive. In my whole life he has never said he loves me or given me a goodnight kiss unless I asked him to.
>
> I think the reason he ignores me is because I'm so boring. I look at my friends and think, "If I were funny like Jill or a superbrain like Sandy or even outrageous and punk like Tasha, he would put down his paper and be fascinated."
>
> I play the recorder, and for the past three years I've been a soloist in the fall concert at school. Mom comes to the concerts, but Dad never does. This year, I'm a senior, so it's his last chance. I'd give anything to look out into the audience and see him there. But who am I kidding? It will never happen.[17]

The lack of attention from her dad led this girl to the conclusion that she was dull, unintelligent, and all-around boring, hardly what you would call positive self-esteem. Girls like this are forced to seek male attention from other places. Usually they find a poor substitute in the American dating scene where, all too often, they end up victimized by a young man who takes advantage of their need for male approval. Each year three-quarters of a million teenaged girls become pregnant in America. Half of them will deal with their unwanted pregnancy by taking the life of their unborn child. Most of these girls are subconsciously trying to compensate for affection that should have come from Dad.

I sadly submit, America's children are lost.

It reminds me of the prophesy of Hosea, when the kingdom of Israel was in the darkest hour of her entire history. The land was polluted by greed, oppression, robbery, falsehood, adultery, and murder. The fathers of the nation had failed in their responsibility. Hosea summed up the tragic situation this way: "My people are destroyed for lack of knowledge. Because you have rejected knowledge, I also will reject you from being my priest. Since you have forgotten the law of your God, I also will forget your children" (Hosea 4:6, *NASB*).

American society has divorced itself from heaven because American fathers have ceased to pattern their fatherhood after the Fatherhood of God. There is no hope for the children of America unless their fathers return from the exile of self-serving behavior and offer their souls to the mercy of the Father who created them. The fathers of America must come to know God as Father and to see His Fatherhood as the pattern for their own.

This is what happened to the Apostle Paul at his conversion. This is how he could call Timothy his son. This is how he became the spiritual father we acknowledge him to be. This is how he can confidently say to his spiritual children, "Be imitators of me, as I also am of Christ" (1 Corinthians 11:1, *NASB*). He could say this only because he bowed his "knees to the Father of our Lord Jesus Christ, from whom all fatherhood (Greek *patria*) in heaven and earth is named" (Ephesians 3:14-15, author's translation). In doing this, St. Paul related all fatherhood to God's Fatherhood.

It is only when we, the men of today, like Paul, reconnect earthly fatherhood with the heavenly model that we will find out what is supposed to be true about ourselves, how we are supposed to function, how we can heal the hurts of

America's forgotten children. If American men are going to return to responsible fatherhood, we must look at what the Father does. Even Jesus said, "Truly, truly I say to you, the Son can do nothing of Himself, unless it is something he sees the Father doing; for whatever the Father does, these things the Son also does in like manner" (John 5:19, *NASB*).

When we look at the Father, we do not see a passive, uninterested father who refuses to be involved. Not at all! We see One who loves, One whose affection publicly bursts from heaven upon His Son, declaring, "You are My beloved Son, in whom I am well pleased" (Mark 1:11, *NKJV*).

When we look at the Father we do not see someone who is uninvolved with His creation. Not at all! We see One who initiates love toward His creation. "God so loved the world that he gave . . ." (John 3:16). "Behold what manner of love the Father has bestowed on us, that we should be called children of God!" (1 John 3:1, *NKJV*). "We love Him because He first loved us" (1 John 4:19, *NKJV*).

When we look at the Father we do not see someone who runs and hides and abandons His family. Not at all! We see One who commits Himself, who "bears all things" (1 Corinthians 13:7), who is so committed that He remains faithful even when we are faithless, for to do otherwise would be a denial of who He is (1 Timothy 2:13).

When we look at the Father we do not see someone content to have His family in discord, ripped apart by social chaos and anarchy. Not at all! We see One who unifies, One whose love is called "the bond of perfection" (Colossians 3:14, *NKJV*). We see a Father from whose headship peace and order flow.

When we look at the Father we do not see someone who is self-centered and unwilling to forsake personal pleasure for the good of others. Not at all! We see a Father who sacrifices. He was willing to sacrifice His only-begotten Son for the well-being of the human family.

When we look at the Father we do not see someone with a halfhearted, lukewarm, unfeeling attitude toward His family. Not at all! We see One who is zealous! We see an intense and passionate concern that declares, "I am zealous for Zion with great zeal" and "with great fervor I am zealous for her" (Zechariah 8:2, *NKJV*).

When we look at the Father we do not see someone whom His Son could not image. Not at all! We see One who models, and a Son who could declare, "He who has seen me has seen the Father" (John 14:9, *NKJV*). Christ is the image of the Father.

Because our view of God will determine our view of man, the essence of all fatherhood and family life can be found within the Holy Trinity. All the critical questions of our day regarding roles, functions, and equality can be solved by a better understanding of the relationship between the Father, the Son, and the Holy Spirit.

In the last few decades we have seen a Jesus movement and a Holy Spirit movement. Both of these movements contributed greatly to spiritual awareness. Yet neither of these movements has healed the American home. If anything, things are worse, even among Christians. Today America desperately needs a Father movement, where men can again get connected to the Heavenly Model. After all, it is the Father who is the very source and fountainhead of the Holy Trinity. We must see God as three persons in one divine nature, Father, Son, and Holy Spirit.

The same prophet Hosea who spoke of God forgetting our children if we reject knowledge of Him later declared, "Come, let us return to the LORD. For He has torn us, but He will heal us. He has wounded us, but He will bandage us. He will revive us after two days; He will raise us up on the third day, that we may live before Him. So let us know; let us press on to know the LORD" (Hosea 6:1-3, *NASB*). Our hope is in knowing God. If we are going to win the battle for the family in America, we must become people who are determined to know God the Father and commit ourselves to boldly call our nation back to Him and the model of fatherhood that He is for us.

We do not need a little squeak. We need the roar of a lion. We need the mighty spirit of Elijah to sing out in our churches and in our schools and in our nation. Why do we need the spirit of Elijah? Because he is the prophet who turns fathers back to their children. In the last two verses of the Old Testament the prophet Malachi says:

> Behold, I am going to send you Elijah the prophet before the coming of the great and terrible day of the LORD. And he will restore the hearts of the fathers to their children, and the hearts of the children to their fathers, lest I come and smite the land with a curse. (Malachi 4:5-6, *NASB*)

If the hearts of fathers are to turn to their children, and the hearts of children to their fathers, we need the spirit of Elijah at the highest level of government. For too long president after president has failed to exhort American men to responsible fatherhood. For too long passivity toward the American family has characterized the White House. For too long we have had Father's Day come and go without the father of our nation issuing a forceful call to the men of this country to engage in the battle for the survival of the basic building block of society, the family. For too long we have allowed bandages to be put on social cancers because no one at the highest level of government will dare to tell American men that we are going to continue to lose our children and see our marriages disintegrate until we get off our backsides and put the same sacrificial energy into our families that we put into our professions and personal amusements.

Mr. President, if you want a kinder and gentler America, we need you to use all the power and prestige of your God-given office to exhort the men of our land to turn their hearts to their families. Lyndon Johnson was right when he said, "History and instinct tell us that a society that does not encourage responsible fatherhood will pay for its failure in future generations."[18]

Mr. President, you have been a good father to your family. We need you, as the father of our nation, to use your Father's Day proclamation as a national platform to exhort American men to responsible fatherhood. We need you to push for legislation that will encourage men to abandon their preoccupations with personal pleasure and act in the best interests of their wives and children. We need the spirit of Elijah in the Oval Office to turn the hearts of American men back to their families.

But that is not the only place where we need the spirit of Elijah. The spirit of Elijah also needs to be felt in the classrooms of America. For too long the identities of our young boys have suffered from the absence of male teachers. For too long the government has sat on its own indisputable statistical evidence that proves this to be true. For too long the educational bureaucracy has closed its mind to the crucial need for teaching about masculinity. For too long educational bureaucrats have failed to incorporate masculine learning models into their curricula. For too long boys have been forced to choose between "being good" and being male, because of a system that does not allow for normal masculine development.

We need the spirit of Elijah to turn the hearts of fathers to their children and meet them in the classrooms of America. In private and public schools alike, the cry needs to be sounded for men to reenter the educational sphere. Only then will boys receive their instruction and guidance from models they can also imitate.

One last area where we desperately need the spirit of Elijah is in the church. For too long the boys of America have been viewing the church as a sanctuary for women and Sunday school as a place for sissies. For too long the most predictable fact about young males in the church is that the majority of them will leave by the time they are young adults. For too long the feminized clergy of our land have been known as nice guys rather than courageous leaders.

Fellow-clergy and lay leaders, we need the spirit of Elijah to be manifest among us most of all. If we are to remove the curse of father-loss from our land, the church more than any institution on this earth must face the responsibility of turning the hearts of fathers back to their families. Men must know that fatherhood is established in heaven and that only in the church can we experience the fullness of fatherhood. Men must again become the primary religious educators of their children. Men must enter the Sunday schools. Christian men must imitate God the Father and, like Him, become father to the fatherless. Big brothers are great, but the fatherless need more than big brothers.

I am not merely talking about biological fathers at this point. *All* men are called to be spiritual fathers, even single males and childless husbands. Men who are not biological fathers are still called on to devote time, effort, and energy to the guidance and care of the young people around them, comforting and counseling and instructing those who have no dads.

There is a desperate need for the single men and childless husbands of our nation to imitate God, the Father of us all, who is described as a "father to the fatherless" (Psalm 68:5).

At this point a Christian may ask, "Aren't you linking masculinity and fatherhood much too closely? Isn't Jesus Christ our highest standard for what it means to be manly? Yet He Himself is not a father."

Jesus Christ *is* a father. As Adam was the father of a fallen race, so Jesus Christ is the father of the new race. In fact, Isaiah's accurate prophecy concerning the Incarnate shows that one of the titles to be given to the Son of God would be "Everlasting Father" (Isaiah 9:6).

As to the Trinity, we keep the Father and the Son distinct. Jesus is not a father in relation to the Trinity, but He is in relation to His church. The first Adam was the father of the human race while Christ, the Second Adam, is the father of the new race that is born in Him. Thus, the Son of God the Father has Himself the attributes of fatherhood. Jesus' words are true when He says, "He who has seen Me has seen the Father" (John 14:9, *NASB*). In revealing the Father, He, as father of the faithful, is the perfect expression of fatherhood. He is the progenitor of the new humanity! Jesus Christ is both father *and husband* to the family of the faithful (Ephesians 5:22-33; Hebrews 2:13).

All men, married or single, can follow Christ in fatherhood, being spiritual fathers of those they bid to follow Him. If single men and childless husbands of this country see that God's call to fatherhood extends to them as well as to biological fathers, perhaps some of the millions of children who have no father present will have a chance of making it.

Real men do not just make babies. Real men take responsibility for the physical and spiritual care of children they beget and for those begotten and deserted by others. Responsibility lies at the heart of fatherhood as it was intended to be.

Let me end with a story. I was with a friend some time ago, driving home from Los Angeles. It was midday, and we were coming down a steep grade. In front of us was a new pickup truck with a family. The mother was driving, and the father was beside her in the cab. In the open bed of the truck were four small children. They had a picnic basket, fishing poles. The children were obviously excited to be going on vacation.

Suddenly, one of the back wheels snapped off. The truck veered sharply to the right and shot off a sixty-foot cliff. My friend and I were the only ones there. We stopped our car and started down the hillside. We ran to the children, doing what we could do. All of them were unconscious.

The mother was seriously injured. It looked as though she had broken her legs and pelvis. But she started crawling on her belly to each child. We couldn't prevent her.

The father could not restrain her either, although he tried. He was in the best shape of anyone, but he stayed in the truck, and called out to his wife to stop.

The scene is forever engraved in my mind. It says something to me about the fathers of our country. The children of America are lying wounded, strewn throughout our cities. In too many cases, their fathers are leaving them to their mothers' care. The children need the father to get out of the truck and join the mothers who care for them.

The fathers of America need to have such an extraordinary passion for God and be so consumed with the vision of responsible fatherhood that we will allow no obstacle to stand in the way of the healing of the American family.

This is our greatest challenge at the end of the twentieth century: turning the hearts of fathers to their children so that, as the prophet promises, the hearts of the children will turn back toward them.

24

Women in Society:
The Challenge and the Call[1]

Dee Jepsen

I was working as an unsalaried assistant in my husband's senate office when, one day in 1982, I was surprised to receive a call from the White House. President Reagan wanted to know if I would accept an appointment as special liaison to women's organizations.

I was startled by his invitation. I had never entertained ambitions of this sort. I was also acutely aware that women's issues were among the most hotly debated issues of the day. In the political arena, women and their concerns were on the front burner. Newspapers were full of the latest disputes and trends in the women's movement. There were charges and countercharges, and fists were shaken under the nose of anyone who disagreed with the basic tenets of the movement.

Knowing this, it was without much joyful anticipation that I said yes. But I believed that God had a plan, and I did not dare pass by an open door, especially one that others had been pushing to get open, without giving the matter a great deal of thought and prayer.

My position in the White House turned out to be just the political hot seat I had expected. If anything, the pressure was even worse than I had anticipated. The depth of emotion on both sides of the issues made rational discussion difficult.

As I worked with a wide variety of women, I began to notice something. It was clear that many of the women I talked to had been seriously mistreated. Some of them had faced great injustice in their lives. It was hardly surprising that they felt angry and bitter. Certainly, it was important to seek justice for them. Yet I noticed that these women had a problem whose roots went far deeper than discrimination. Even if they were given justice, they would still be left with the problem of their own anger and resentment, with their dissatisfaction with life.

At the same time, I witnessed the red-hot rhetoric flowing between women who were trying to defend the home and family and the more militant feminists. It seemed impossible to resolve the conflicts between different groups of women. That kind of conflict seemed to me to be yet another problem, not a solution.

The same was true of the divisions between men and women. Something was wrong with a society in which men and women were constantly accusing one another and being put on the defensive. Clearly, an essential element was being kept out of the public debate about women. I felt that we were missing the very core of the issue. But what was it? How could I articulate it?

Finally, I decided that the solution lay somewhere beyond the equal rights debate. After I left the White House at the end of 1983, I addressed this issue in my book *Women: Beyond Equal Rights*. Since then, I have spent a good deal of time traveling, speaking, and writing in order to communicate with Christian men and women what I believe to be of tremendous importance to God and to His people.

Let me begin by stating something fairly obvious: women constitute over half the population of this country. Even so, their contributions are often undervalued. The fact is that society needs the influence of women. Women are the ones who primarily pass on our culture and our values. We shape and mold the youth of the nation. We have profound influence. In fact, our influence is so great that we might have trouble with pride if we realized just how strong it really is.

To be co-creators with the God of the universe, to be able to conceive and bear new life, is a tremendous blessing. But the role of mother and homemaker has fallen into great disrepute and neglect. I can recall a time in Washington, D.C., when I participated in a discussion before a national committee of a large denominational church. In the course of the discussion I mentioned the word "family," and drew audible groans in the audience. I wanted to weep, not because those present disagreed with me—that wasn't the point—but because it grieved me that the family, which is God's idea and which is the basic unit of government within a nation, could be viewed with disdain even in the church. Sadly, some in the church have been influenced by the so-called sophisticated, intelligent, and modern view that says the family is passé.

But God is not impressed with our sophistication. The story of creation in Genesis tells us that when God called forth creation, He said, "Let us make man in our image. . . . So God created man in his own image, in the image of God he created him; male and female he created *them*" (Genesis 1:26-27, emphasis added). First He shaped Adam from the dust of the earth. Then, recognizing that is was not good for man to be alone, He drew Eve out of Adam. I believe that only in the fullness of Christian manhood and the fullness of Christian womanhood is the completed image of God reflected to the world around us. But both sexes seem to have amnesia about who they were meant to be.

Women need to learn one of Christianity's best-kept secrets—that Jesus values women. We need to realize how important we really are, not because of our own merits but because of the qualities God has given us to use on His behalf. We need to realize that we have a high call. He is the liberator, the One who frees us from our own sin as well as from our circumstances and the distortions of our culture. God is asking us to play our part in His plan. Something vital will be lost if women fail to respond to God's call.

Some women think the Bible makes us second-class citizens. But this is not true. First of all, consider that God chose Mary to give birth to His Son. The Son of God came into the world as any other human being would enter it—through the womb of a woman, and an unlikely woman at that. Mary was young, poor, and unmarried. She came from the insignificant village of Nazareth, and everyone thought that nothing good could come from Nazareth.

But Mary possessed something that pleased God, a humility and determination to do His will no matter the cost to herself. To the angel she responded, "May it be to me as you have said" (Luke 1:38). This is the kind of humility and dedication to the will of God that we all need.

We need to remember not only that God sent His Son into the world born of a woman, but also that Jesus performed His first miracle at the request of a woman, his mother.

Consider also the story of the Samaritan woman at the well. Jesus told her the greatest secret in the history of the world. This woman too was an unlikely choice. The Jews hated the Samaritans; rabbis did not talk to women in public; and this woman had a terrible reputation in her hometown. Yet Jesus told her that He was the Messiah, the long-awaited One. He began by telling her the sins she had committed, but He also spoke of the rivers of living water that He would give her. And the Samaritan woman did what we women are so good at. *She believed Him.* And she acted on her belief. She went into town and told everyone what Jesus had said to her. As a result, many of the people came to believe in Jesus.

The story of Martha and Mary is often told to emphasize the importance of having one's priorities in order. But there is another point to note. In the society of Jesus' day, women were not taught by rabbis. Jesus cut across cultural barriers to elevate women to a position of equality. He told Martha that Mary had chosen the better part, to be with Him and to learn from Him.

Women ministered with and to Jesus Christ during His ministry on earth. The women stuck with Him. Whom did He stop and comfort on the road to Golgotha? The women. "Daughters of Jerusalem, do not weep for me," He said. They loved Him and He knew it. We women are good at being loyal. Whom did Jesus see when He looked down from the cross but the faithful women? Most of the men had run away in disappointment or fear.

Who was the first at the tomb? The women. To whom did Jesus first appear when He rose from the grave? Who was the first evangelist? It was a woman. She went and told the others the good news that Jesus was alive. So let us not conclude that the Bible presents women as second-class citizens of the kingdom. Instead, let us acknowledge that women were and are important, in fact, essential, to the plan of God.

In the story of creation, after the fall, God said there would be enmity between the serpent and the woman. Through a woman, Mary, came the Savior of the world and Satan's defeat. Satan hates women, and through the centuries, either blatantly or subtly, he has put us down. Most of us have wondered if we were really as good as men.

When I was at the White House, I worked with many women who had highly successful and challenging careers and yet concealed low self-esteem underneath the facade of their success. Many women simply did not know that they had value. As someone said, "They're vogue on the outside and vague on the inside."

I am convinced that the enemy has tried to destroy womanhood. Today he is breaking up marriages, denigrating the home, and trying to do us in, because he hates us. But I also believe that God will use those very circumstances to move against his enemy and ours. In the latter half of the twentieth century, women have taken their place at center stage. Whether or not we like it, the spotlight is on us. I am convinced that God is now raising up godly women to reflect this character to the world around us.

When God created woman, He created her with sensitivities that most men possess to a lesser degree. We need these sensitivities because we were created to be the life-bearers, the nurturers. That's part of what it means to be a woman.

It's important that women are allowed to bring these womanly qualities into every area of life. The whole fabric of our society needs to be touched by the qualities women possess. But Satan has diverted us. As women began to ask why they were relegated to positions of lesser importance in the world's eyes, he stepped in to tell them that the men were doing all the important work. Consequently, child-raising and homemaking began to be viewed as lesser occupations. The enemy has convinced many women to go so far to the other side that they have modeled themselves on the very men they have criticized. In the process, they have denied their own womanhood. Once that happens, logic says that you no longer have one problem but two problems.

Consider abortion. Women were created to be life-bearers. Now the world is trying to tell us that it is actually noble for a woman to discard the fruit of her womb. She is simply exercising her "right to choose." But what of the child's right to be born, to be nurtured and loved by its mother? What happens to women who opt for abortions even though a mother's basic instinct is to protect her young? Such an action certainly does violence to a woman's soul.

The world has been telling us tremendous lies, and we have believed them. Our gullibility has caused us great stress and confusion. Some women are frustrated because they think they can and should be the best homemaker, the best mother and wife, and the very best in their profession—all at the same time. Many women feel pressured to become superwomen because of the message that society sends them. But there are no superwomen, only frustrated individuals attempting to live as though they have no personal limitations. Some of us have more energy than others, but we all have a limited supply. Part of growing up involves realizing that one has limits, that there are trade-offs in life.

For women especially, seasons of life are tremendously important. What is good for a woman at twenty-five may not be good for her at forty-five. I would not have been speaking, writing, and traveling, as I am today, twenty years ago when I had a family to raise. But now a season in my life has arrived when I can do all these things with the assurance that God is asking me to do them. But society says get it all—now. "Go for the gusto." But who wants the gusto if it means wearing yourself out in the pursuit of an unrealistic ideal?

One day I was privileged to sit at the table next to Mother Teresa of Calcutta. I had long admired her and her work with the destitute and dying in Calcutta and throughout the world. The Capitol Hill luncheon in her honor was held in the ornately decorated Senate caucus room in the Russell Building. As she entered, she seemed dwarfed by the enormity of the room. She was even tinier than I had expected. As she walked into the room, clad in a simple blue and white habit, I saw some of the strongest leaders in the world rise to their feet and applaud her with tears in their eyes. They were honored simply to be in her presence.

Here was a woman who obviously had tremendous power. She possessed more power than those who walked the marble halls of Congress. She had more power than I had seen in this city of power. "How has she done this?" I asked myself. She owned nothing, never shook her fist in anger for her rights, and never asked for anything for herself. Instead, she had reached down into the gutter and raised up and loved those the world calls unlovable. And she had done it simply because the poor were created by the God she loves and serves.

All of us that day were humbled in her presence because we knew how full of ourselves we were. God in His wisdom had once again used the simple to confound the wise. He had elevated this little woman to a place of international recognition and honor.

That experience with Mother Teresa impressed me so greatly that I began to wonder if she was so different from what we *all* should be. I thought of all the people who were rightly seeking justice but who did not know the Author of justice. Once again, I was struck with the realization that the needs of the women I had encountered would never be fully satisfied merely by acquiring equal rights.

Today, men as well as women are confused about who they are. Try imagining for a moment what is hiding behind some of those big, strong, noncommunicative walls that men walk around inside. Dr. James Dobson has said that he thinks feminism developed in this country, especially in some of its more militant forms, because men were not fulfilling the role they were called to in the home. Neither were they appreciating women for the important role they were playing.

Dr. Paul Tournier points out that our society has been shaped since the Renaissance by scientific rationalism, by an approach that focuses so totally on material things and on human achievement that we have forgotten the importance of relationships, of human emotion, and of the needs of people.

I frequently remind people to whom I speak that today all of us are one day closer to death than we were yesterday. When faced with our own death, what will be important? The title before our name? Our influence or power? Our great achievements? None of these things will make the slightest difference. What will matter will be the nature of our relationship with the God who made us and of our relationships with others—with friends, family, even our enemies. That is what will count. And that is what we women are best at—relationships that embody the kind of love the world needs so badly.

We live in a society of constant change and disposability. Not too long ago, the whole world watched the space shuttle *Challenger* explode just shortly after lift-off. The finest human technology had failed completely, and in an instant, seven lives, finely honed and trained to precision for the flight, were simply extinguished. All the plans and hopes of these men and women, their friends and families, were eternally disrupted. Over and over, we watched as the tragic spectacle replayed itself on our television screens. As the nation mourned, I wondered how long we would continue to focus exclusively on the things that are temporal to the neglect of those that are eternal.

Our society urgently needs the influence and action of Christian women. If the women of this country do not stand up in protest against the killing of a million and a half of their young a year, if they do not rise up against pornography, which demeans women and exploits children, who will? It has been said that if the women of a nation lose their virtue, the nation will lose everything. But how often is virtue talked about in public debate today? Anyone who appeared on "The Phil Donahue Show" and talked about virtue would be a laughingstock. But that is a risk we must take. Too many of us have been intimidated for too long. We have kept silent even when we knew we should speak out.

We live in a society that tries very hard to separate the sacred and the secular. When my husband, Roger, was in the Senate, I realized that any mention of spiritual values in the public sector was taboo. But a nation without underlying spiritual values cannot long endure. As Christians, we are supposed to be influencing the world rather than being influenced by it.

I am convinced that as Christian women learn who they are, they will begin to respond to God with deeper intercessory prayer. We are called, as are our brothers, to move the hands of God through prayer. We are called to listen to Him and to proclaim His Word. What God whispers in your ear, shout from the housetops!

I believe women will be used as instruments of healing, as peacemakers. We are the fixers of the world, able to bring people together, to help mend relationships.

I believe God is going to raise up women, first in our homes, then in our communities, and then in the nation. I am convinced that we can change the nation by responding to God's call. But how can you be the salt if you never get out of the shaker, the light if you are covered with a bushel basket, and the leaven if you never get into the loaf? It is time to let God have His way fully with us, to surrender absolutely to His plan for our lives.

Part of this surrender involves seeking God's plan for unity among His children. In John 17, Jesus prayed that we would all be one even as He and the Father are one. But how can the Father answer His prayer if we are unwilling to love one another as fellow Christians? By unity I do not mean uniformity. The body of Christ is made up of many parts, but the world cannot recognize His body if it is divided.

Recently I was asked to lead one of the prayers at the National Day of Prayer. As I walked up to the stage, I did not know what I was going to say. Then I looked down at the pamphlet in my hand, and on it was written 2 Chronicles 7:14: ". . . if my people, who are called by my name, will humble themselves and pray and seek my face and turn from their wicked ways, then will I hear from heaven and will forgive their sin and will heal their land." How often I had heard it. But it hit me for the first time that *we* are the instruments God wants to use to bring healing to the land. How can He use us if the body of Christ is so fragmented? How can He use us if men and women are constantly arguing? How can we be His instruments if our homes are falling apart and our lives are in chaos? The kingdom will only shine forth in us as we apply the principles of the kingdom to our lives. And then we will be able to bring the life of the kingdom to those around us.

The time has come for both women and men to grow up to maturity and to the fullness of Christ. We need to find out who we are in Christ. And when we go out and speak the truth—and that is what we need to do—we must speak it in love. It would be a hollow victory indeed to win in a righteous cause and yet to discredit Christ by our own self-righteousness. It is so easy to label those who disagree with us as evil men and women, but we cannot know the intent of their hearts. God knows and judges our hearts, and He commanded us to love others, even our enemies, and told us not to judge.

I believe that women really are key players in God's plan for the present age. We are not the only players, but our role is an important, even a crucial one. I am both glad and excited to be a woman living in these days. And I pray that Christian women will begin to understand who they are and how God wants to use them. It is my prayer that Christian men will begin to look at women through new eyes, through the eyes of the God who made them and fashioned them for His purposes.

25

The Essence of Femininity:
A Personal Perspective

Elisabeth Elliot

Feminists are dedicated to the proposition that the difference between men and women is a matter of mere biology. The rest of us recognize a far deeper reality, one that meets us on an altogether different plane from mere anatomical distinctions. It is unfathomable and indefinable, yet men and women have tried ceaselessly to fathom and define it. It is unavoidable and undeniable, yet in the past couple of decades earnest and high-sounding efforts have been made in the name of decency, equality, and fairness, at least to avoid it and, whenever possible, to deny it. I refer, of course, to femininity—a reality of God's design and God's making, His gift to me and to every woman—and, in a very different way, His gift to men as well. If we really understood what femininity is all about, perhaps the question of roles would take care of itself.

What I have to say is not validated by my having a graduate degree or a position on the faculty or administration of an institution of higher learning. It comes not from any set of personal tastes and preferences. It is not a deduction from my own genetic leanings or temperament. Instead, it is what I see as the arrangement of the universe and the full harmony and tone of Scripture. This arrangement is a glorious hierarchical order of graduated splendor, beginning with the Trinity, descending through seraphim, cherubim, archangels, angels, men, and all lesser creatures, a mighty universal dance, choreographed for the perfection and fulfillment of each participant.

For years I have watched with growing dismay, even anguish, what has been happening in our society, in our educational system, in our churches, in our homes, and on the deepest level of personality, as a result of a movement called feminism, a movement that gives a great deal of consideration to something called personhood but very little to womanhood, and hardly a nod to femininity. Words like *manhood* and *masculinity* have been expunged from our vocabulary, and we have been told in no uncertain terms that we ought to forget about such things, which amount to nothing more than biology, and concentrate on what it means to be "persons."

Throughout the millennia of human history, up until the past two decades or so, people took for granted that the differences between men and women were so obvious as to need no comment. They accepted the way things were. But our easy assumptions have been assailed and confused, we have lost our bearings in a fog of rhetoric about something called equality, so that I find myself in the uncomfortable position of having to belabor to educated people what was once perfectly obvious to the simplest peasant.

And here I must make a confession. Almost everything that constitutes an *issue* in modern American life I view from the vantage point of "peasants" in a Stone-Age culture where I once lived. I'm always asking myself, "What would those people make of all this? Where would I begin to try to explain it to them?" This exotic perspective does, in a way, throw a clearer light on the basics that helps me assess the issues.

For a number of years I lived with jungle Indians of South America who expressed their masculinity and femininity in a variety of ways, never pretended that the differences were negligible, and had no word for *role*. The femininity of woman was a deep-rooted consciousness of what she was made for. It was expressed in everything she did differently from men, from her hairstyle and clothes (if she wore any) to the way she sat and the work she did. Any child knew that women wove hammocks and made pots and caught fish with their hands, cleared underbrush, planted crops, and carried by far the heaviest loads, while men chopped down trees and hunted, caught fish with nets and spears, and carried no loads at all if there was a woman around. Nobody had any complaints. These responsibilities were not up for grabs, not interchangeable, not equal. Nobody thought of power or prestige or competition. Nobody talked about roles. This was the way things were.

Once, in the bungling way of foreigners, I "brought down the house," as it were, by picking up a man's eight-foot spear and pretending to be about to hurl it. They died laughing. If they had not taken it as a joke, I would have been in serious trouble. Women had nothing to do with spears. Their power did not lie in being equal with men but in being women. Men were men and women were glad of it. They understood that this was how things were arranged originally, and they liked it that way.

That perspective, among other things, convinced me that this civilized business of "roles" is nearly always, to put it bluntly, a power struggle. Coming back to this country and listening to a good many solemn dialogues on the roles of women in this or that or the other thing, I noticed that "this or that or the other thing" was never anything to do with fishing or farming or writing a book or giving birth to a baby, but always something that touched in some way on questions of authority or power or competition or money rather than on the vastly prior issue of the *meaning* of sexuality. In politics, in big business, in higher education, feminism is frequently discussed. But femininity? Never. Perhaps it should not surprise us that secular higher education has long since discarded the image of femininity as utterly irrelevant to anything that really matters, but it is calamitous when Christian higher education follows suit. This is what is happening. Shortly before he died, Francis Schaeffer said, "Tell me what the world is saying today, and I'll tell you what the church will be saying seven years from now."

It is my observation—and, I may add, my experience—that Christian higher education, trotting happily along in the train of feminist crusaders, is willing and eager to treat the subject of *feminism*, but gags on the word *femininity*. Maybe it regards the subject as trivial or unworthy of academic inquiry. Maybe the real reason is that its basic premise is feminism. Therefore it simply cannot cope with femininity.

Secular philosophy comes at us daily with terrible force, and we need Paul's admonition to the Roman Christians, "Don't let the world around you squeeze you into its own mold, but let God re-make you so that your whole attitude of mind is changed" (Romans 12:2, *Phillips*). Feminist philosophy, which sounds reasonable enough on the surface, is a subtle and pervasive poison, infecting the minds of Christians and non-Christians alike. I was amazed to find in *The Intercollegiate Review* (Fall 1987), a secular journal, a sharp critique entitled "The Barbarism of Feminist Scholarship," in which the author, Carol Iononne, laid bare its political motivation, suppression of data in the service of feminist politics, special pleading, and built-in contradictions.

The author cited the suit brought by the Equal Employment Opportunity Commission against Sears, Roebuck and Company, the largest employer of women in the country, charging discrimination against women because of the higher number of men promoted to commission sales. After eleven years of compiling evidence for their case, the EEOC found not one witness to testify that she had personally been the victim of discrimination. For the first time in the history of this kind of suit, Sears chose to fight back, countering that not enough women could be found willing to take the commission jobs, and that therefore factors other than discrimination must be the explanation. Trying to find an expert in women's history, they were turned down by one woman who declared that she would never testify against the EEOC and one man who refused out of fear of losing his feminist credentials. Only one woman, Rosalind Rosenberg of Barnard College, agreed to testify.

Rosenberg argued on the basis of the historical record: women and men have different interests, goals, and aspirations. Women are not quite so interested as men are, for example, in tires, furnaces, and aluminum siding. Rosenberg was vilified not because of the *content* of her testimony, but because she testified at all. This was an "immoral act," and she was called a traitor.

That any sensible person would find it necessary to argue in court that men and women have different interests only shows how far we have slid into absurdities. To speak even of scientifically verified differences in the structure of male and female brains, or endocrinological differences that affect the social behavior of men and women, is to risk charges of sexism, chauvinism, stupidity, or, as in Dr. Rosenberg's case, immorality.

The feminist theology of Christians (I cannot call it "Christian feminist theology") is a Procrustean bed on which doctrine and the plain facts of human nature and history, not to mention the Bible itself, are arbitrarily stretched or chopped off to fit. Why, I ask, does feminist theology start with the answers? One who spoke on "A Biblical Approach to Feminism" defined her task (a formidable one, I should say!) as the attempt to interpret the Bible in a fashion favorable to the cause of equality (Virginia Ramey Mollenkott at the Evangelical Women's Caucus, Washington, D.C., November 1975). The "interpretation" called for amounts to a thorough revision of the doctrines of creation, man, Trinity, and the inspiration of Scripture, and a reconstruction of religious history, with the intent of purging each of these of what is called a patriarchal conspiracy against women. Why must feminists substitute for the glorious hierarchical vision of blessedness a ramshackle and incoherent ideal that flattens all human beings to a single level—a faceless, colorless, sexless wasteland where rule and submission are regarded as a curse, where the roles of men and women are treated like machine parts that are interchangeable, replaceable, and adjustable, and where fulfillment is a matter of pure politics, things like equality and rights?

This is a world that the poets have never aspired to, the literature of the ages has somehow missed, a world that takes no account of mystery. The church claims to be the bearer of revelation. If her claim is true, as C. S. Lewis points out, we should expect to find in the church "an element that unbelievers will call irrational and believers will call supra-rational. There ought to be something in it opaque to our reason though not contrary to it. . . . If we abandon that, if we retain only what can be justified by standards of prudence and convenience at the bar of enlightened common sense, then we exchange revelation for that old wraith Natural Religion."[1]

Christian vision springs from mystery. Every major tenet of our creed is a mystery—*revealed*, not explained—affirmed and apprehended only by the faculty we call faith. Sexuality is a mystery representing the deepest mystery we know anything about: the relationship of Christ and His church. When we deal with masculinity and femininity we are dealing with the "live and awful shadows of realities utterly beyond our control and largely beyond our direct knowledge," as Lewis puts it.[2] We cannot at the same time swallow the feminist doctrine that femininity is a mere matter of cultural conditioning, of stereotypes perpetuated by tradition, or even the product of some nefarious plot hatched by males in some prehistoric committee meeting.

Please do not misunderstand me. We must and we do deplore the stereotypes that caricature the divine distinctions. We deplore the abuses perpetrated by men against women—and, let us not forget, by women against men, for all have sinned—but have we forgotten the archetypes?

Stereotype is a word generally used disparagingly to denote a fixed or conventional notion or pattern. An archetype is the original pattern or model, embodying the essence of things and reflecting in some way the internal structure of the world. I am not here to defend stereotypes of femininity, but to try to focus on the Original Pattern.

The first woman was made specifically for the first man, a helper, to meet, respond to, surrender to, and complement him. God made her *from* the man, out of his very bone, and then He brought her *to* the man. When Adam named Eve, he accepted responsibility to "husband" her—to provide for her, to cherish her, to protect her. These two people together represent the image of God—one of them in a special way the initiator, the other the responder. Neither the one nor the other was adequate alone to bear the divine image.

God put these two in a perfect place and—you know the rest of the story. They rejected their humanity and used their God-bestowed freedom to defy Him, decided they'd rather not be a mere man and woman, but gods, arrogating to themselves the knowledge of good and evil, a burden too heavy for human beings to bear. Eve, in her refusal to accept the will of God, refused her femininity. Adam, in his capitulation to her suggestion, abdicated his masculine responsibility for her. It was the first instance of what we would recognize now as "role reversal." This defiant disobedience ruined the original pattern and things have been in an awful mess ever since.

But God did not abandon His self-willed creatures. In His inexorable love He demonstrated exactly what He had had in mind by calling Himself a Bridegroom—the Initiator, Protector, Provider, Lover—and Israel His bride, His beloved. He rescued her, called her by name, wooed and won her, grieved when she went whoring after other gods. In the New Testament we find the mystery of marriage again expressing the inexpressible relationship between the Lord and His people, the husband standing for Christ in his headship, the wife standing for the church in her submission. This Spirit-inspired imagery is not to be shuffled about and rearranged according to our whims and preferences. Mystery must be handled not only with care but also with reverence and awe.

The gospel story begins with the Mystery of Charity. A young woman is visited by an angel, given a stunning piece of news about becoming the mother of the Son of God. Unlike Eve, whose response to God was calculating and self-serving, the virgin Mary's answer holds no hesitation about risks or losses or the interruption of her own plans. It is an utter and unconditional self-giving: "I am the Lord's servant. . . . May it be to me as you have said" (Luke 1:38). This is what I understand to be the essence of femininity. It means surrender.[3]

Think of a bride. She surrenders her independence, her name, her destiny, her will, herself to the bridegroom in marriage. This is a public ceremony, before God and witnesses. Then, in the marriage chamber, she surrenders her body, her priceless gift of virginity, all that has been hidden. As a mother she makes a new surrender—it is her life for the life of the child. This is most profoundly what women were made for, married or single (and the special vocation of the virgin is to surrender herself for service to her Lord and for the life of the world).

The gentle and quiet spirit of which Peter speaks, calling it "of great worth in God's sight" (1 Peter 3:4), is the true femininity, which found its epitome in Mary, the willingness to be only a vessel, hidden, unknown, except as Somebody's mother. This is the true mother-spirit, true maternity, so absent, it seems to me, in all the annals of feminism. "The holier a woman is," wrote Leon Bloy, "the more she is a woman."

Femininity *receives*. It says, "May it be to me as you have said." It takes what God gives—a special place, a special honor, a special function and glory, different from that of masculinity, meant to be a help. In other words, it is for us women to receive the given as Mary did, not to insist on the not-given, as Eve did.

Perhaps the exceptional women in history have been given a special gift—a *charism*—because they made themselves nothing. I think of Amy Carmichael, for example, another Mary, because she had no ambition for anything but the will of God. Therefore her obedience, her "May it be to me," has had an incalculably deep impact in the twentieth century. She was *given* power, as was her Master, because she made herself nothing.

I would be the last to deny that women are given gifts that they are meant to exercise. But we must not be greedy in insisting on having all of them, in usurping the place of men. We are women, and my plea is *Let me be a woman*, holy through and through, asking for nothing but what God wants to give me, receiving with both hands and with all my heart whatever that is. No arguments would ever be needed if we all shared the spirit of the "most blessed among women."

The world looks for happiness through self-assertion. The Christian knows that joy is found in self-abandonment. "If a man will let himself be lost for My sake," Jesus said, "he will find his true self." A Christian woman's true freedom lies on the other side of a very small gate—humble obedience—but that gate leads out into a largeness of life undreamed of by the liberators of the world, to a place where the God-given differentiation between the sexes is not obfuscated but celebrated, where our inequalities are seen as essential to the image of God, for it is in male *and* female, in male as male and female as female, not as two identical and interchangeable halves, that the image is manifested.

To gloss over these profundities is to deprive women of the central answer to the cry of their hearts, "Who am I?" No one but the Author of the Story can answer that cry.

V

Conclusion and Prospect

26

Charity, Clarity, and Hope:
The Controversy and the Cause of Christ

John Piper and Wayne Grudem

Two New Organizations: Council on Biblical Manhood and Womanhood Christians for Biblical Equality

The collection of essays in this book was undertaken as a project of the Council on Biblical Manhood and Womanhood. The Council was formed in 1987 by concerned evangelical pastors, professors, and lay people. Its rationale, goals, and affirmations are contained in the *Danvers Statement* (Appendix 2), which was finalized in Danvers, Massachusetts, in December 1987. It was first made public in November 1988 in Wheaton, Illinois, and then published as an advertisement in *Christianity Today*, January 13, 1989. One of the purposes of *Recovering Biblical Manhood and Womanhood* is to provide the *Danvers Statement* with Biblically faithful and culturally informed support and elucidation.

Emerging independently and simultaneously with the Council on Biblical Manhood and Womanhood has been an organization called Christians for Biblical Equality. It would be fair, we believe, to describe this group as theologically conservative, evangelical feminists. Its members are the primary persons we debate in this book. *Christianity Today* reported that, in 1987, women who had withdrawn from the Evangelical Women's Caucus (in disagreement with the apparent endorsement of lesbianism) formed the new organization. "The new group," wrote David Neff, "is a national chapter of Men, Women and God, International, an organization associated with John Stott's London Institute for Contemporary Christianity" (*Christianity Today*, October 16, 1987, p. 44).[1]

In July 1989 Christians for Biblical Equality unveiled their position paper entitled "Men, Women and Biblical Equality," a statement of twelve "Biblical Truths" and six points of "Application." A news release reported that "the declaration was drawn up by seven evangelical Biblical scholars—Gilbert Bilezikian of Wheaton College; Stanley R. Gundry of Zondervan Publishing; W. Ward Gasque, [then] of Regent College; Catherine Clark Kroeger of Hamilton College; Jo Anne Lyon of Asbury Seminary; Gretchen Gaebelein Hull, author of *Equal to Serve*; and Roger Nicole of Gordon-Conwell Seminary." The declaration was published as an advertisement in the April 9, 1990 issue of *Christianity Today*.

Pursuing Charity and Clarity Together

We are sure that neither the CBMW nor CBE flatters itself by thinking that it speaks for evangelicalism, let alone for the church as a whole. We do not know whether history will attach any significance to our statements. But both groups are persuaded that something immense is at stake. It is not merely a minor intramural squabble. It has important implications for marriage, singleness, and ministry, and thus for all of life and mission. Yet we sense a kinship far closer with the founders of CBE than with those who seem to put their feminist commitments above Scripture.[2]

The church of Christ will survive and triumph without either the CBMW or CBE. We have no Messianic infatuations. But we do have a burden—in large measure the same burden. When John Stott expressed his support for Men, Women and God (the parent organization of CBE), he used guarded language that we would be happy to affirm. He said, "I am very glad to express my support of Men, Women and God in its aim to understand and obey God's will for sexual roles today." That is our goal too: "to understand and obey God's will for sexual roles today." He went on to say, "The authentic evangelical way is neither the conservatism which reasserts traditional positions without reflection, nor the radicalism which sacrifices all tradition to the spirit of modernity."[3] Again we say a hearty Yes. The "reassertion of tradition *without reflection*" runs the grave risk of Jesus' indictment in Mark 7:9, "You have a fine way of rejecting the commandment of God, in order to keep your tradition!" (RSV; unless otherwise noted, all citations in this chapter are from RSV). We do not regard our book as a defense of tradition.

We hope this book represents a critical sifting of tradition, a rejection of all that is not Biblical, and a preserving of all that is. In profound ways we share a common passion with the members of CBE: a passion to be obedient to Biblical truth about manhood and womanhood; a passion to see men and women affirm the awesome reality of equal personhood in the image of God; a e passion to see marriages whole and lasting and freeing and happy for both husband and wife; the passion to resist the moral collapse of our culture in all manner of tolerated abuses and addictions and perversions; a passion to be a winsome countercultural outcropping of kingdom beauty and truth; a passion to equip all men and women for ministry according to their gifts, with none throwing life away in trivial pursuits; a passion to magnify Christ—crucified, risen and reigning—to a perishing society; and a passion to mobilize the whole church—men and women—to complete the great commission, penetrate all the unreached peoples of the world, and hasten the day of God.

But the heart-wrenching fact is that we have profoundly different interpretations of how God intends to fulfill this vision. We are thrilled that it is God Himself who will fulfill His plan for the church: "My counsel shall stand, and I will accomplish all my purpose" (Isaiah 46:10). We take heart that, in spite of all our blind spots and bungling and disobedience, God *will* triumph in the earth: "All the ends of the earth shall remember and turn to the Lord; and all the families of the nations shall worship before him. For dominion belongs to the Lord, and he rules over the nations" (Psalm 22:27-28). Yet one of the groanings of this fallen age is controversy, and most painful of all, controversy with brothers and sisters in Christ. We resonate with the Apostle Paul—our joy would be full if we could all be "of the same mind, having the same love, being in full accord and of one mind" (Philippians 2:2).

But for all his love of harmony and unity and peace, it is remarkable how many of Paul's letters were written to correct fellow Christians. One thinks immediately of 1 Corinthians. It begins with Paul's thanks (1:4) and ends with his love (16:24). But between those verses he labors to set the Corinthians straight in their thinking and behavior. For example, he addresses the danger of boasting in leaders (1:10-3:23), the limits of sexual freedom (5:1-8), the extent of true separation (5:9-13), the proper handling of lawsuits (6:1-8), the goodness of sexual relations in marriages (7:1-16), the nature of Christian freedom (8:1-13), the proper demeanor for men and women in worship (11:2-16), how to behave at the Lord's supper (11:17-34), the use of spiritual gifts (12-14), and the nature and the reality of the resurrection (15).

The assumption of the entire New Testament is that we should strive for peace by striving to come to agreement in the truth. Peace and unity in the body of Christ are exceedingly precious. Behold how good and pleasant it is when brothers and sisters dwell in *unity* (Psalm 133:1)! "Seek *peace* and pursue it" (1 Peter 3:11). "Let us then pursue what makes for *peace* and for mutual upbuilding" (Romans 14:19). "The wisdom from above is first pure, then *peaceable*" (James 3:17). But it is first *pure*. Peace is not a first thing. It is derivative. It comes from hearty agreement in truth.

For example, Paul tells us to set our minds on what is *true*, and honorable, and just; and the God of *peace* will be with us (Philippians 4:8-9). Peace is a wonderful byproduct of heartfelt commitments to what is true and right. Hebrews speaks of the "*peaceful* fruit of *righteousness*" (12:11). Paul tells Timothy to "aim at *righteousness* . . . and *peace*" (2 Timothy 2:22). The unity we strive for in the church is a unity in knowledge and truth. We grow up into the one body "joined and knit together" as we "attain to the *unity* of the faith and of the *knowledge of the Son of God*" (Ephesians 4:13, 16). "Grace and *peace*" are multiplied to us "in the *knowledge* of God and of Jesus our Lord" (2 Peter 1:2). And paradoxically, the weaponry with which we wage war for "the gospel of *peace*" begins with the belt of *truth* (Ephesians 6:14-15) and ends with the sword of the Spirit, the *Word of God* (6:17).

The reason for this is that truth frees us from the control of Satan, the great deceiver and destroyer of unity: "you will know the *truth*, and the truth will make you free" (John 8:32; cf. 2 Timothy 2:24-26). Truth serves love, the bond of perfection. Paul prays for the Philippians that their "love [may] abound more and more, with *knowledge and all discernment*" (Philippians 1:9). Truth sanctifies, and so yields the righteousness whose fruit is peace: "Sanctify them in the *truth*; thy word is *truth*" (John 17:17; cf. 2 Peter 1:3, 5, 12).

For the sake of unity and peace, therefore, Paul labors to set the churches straight on numerous issues—including quite a few that do not in themselves involve heresy. He does not exclude controversy from his pastoral writing. And he does not limit his engagement in controversy to first-order doctrines, where heresy threatens. He is like a parent to his churches. Parents do not correct and discipline their children only for felonies. They long for their children to grow up into all the kindness and courtesy of mature adulthood. And since the fabric of truth is seamless, Paul knows that letting minor strands go on unravelling can eventually rend the whole garment.

Thus Paul teaches that elders serve the church, on the one hand, by caring for the church without being pugnacious (1 Timothy 3:3, 5), and, on the other hand, by rebuking and correcting false teaching. "He must hold firm to the sure word as taught, so that he may be able to give instruction in sound doctrine and also to confute those who contradict it" (Titus 1:9; cf. 1:13; 2:15; 1 Timothy 5:20). This is one of the main reasons we have the Scriptures: they are "profitable for teaching, for *reproof*, for *correction*, and for training in righteousness" (2 Timothy 3:16).

The point is this: We do not love controversy; we love peace. We love our brothers and sisters who belong to Christians for Biblical Equality. We long for a common mind for the cause of Christ. But we are bound by our conscience and by the Word of God, for this very cause, to try to persuade the church that the vision of manhood and womanhood presented in this book is true and beautiful. It is a precious gift of God to the church and to the world.

Our aim is to carry on the debate with clarity and charity. By charity we have in mind mainly the good will that avoids caricature and seeks to state others' views in ways they would approve. We renounce the aim to "win" by concealing or distorting the points of disagreement. By clarity we mean the use of language that expresses as fully as possible what we affirm and what we deny.

We live in a day of politicized discourse that puts no premium on clear assertions that let people know exactly where one stands. The reason is that clarity will always result in more criticism than ambiguity will, and vagueness will win more votes in a hostile atmosphere than forthrightness will. But we want nothing to do with that attitude. Jesus refused to converse with religious leaders who crafted their answers so as to conceal what they thought (Mark 11:33). Our aim (if not our achievement) is always to be like Paul when he said, "We have renounced disgraceful, underhanded ways; we refuse to practice cunning or to tamper with God's word, but by the *open statement of the truth* we would commend ourselves to every man's conscience in the sight of God" (2 Corinthians 4:2).

The Declaration on "Men, Women and Biblical Equality" by *Christians for Biblical Equality*

We believe we share these aims for clarity and charity with the members of Christians for Biblical Equality. For this very reason we are perplexed that their declaration, "Men, Women and Biblical Equality," is written in such a way as to be unclear about the very issues that divide us. All of the seven authors of this declaration disagree with the thesis of this book: that men alone are called by God to bear the primary teaching authority in the church as elders or pastors. Yet the declaration does not clearly deny this. Moreover, most of the CBE authors disagree with our vision of marriage that calls the husband (precisely because he is husband) to bear the responsibility of primary leadership in the home. Yet this, likewise, is not explicitly denied; rather, the declaration makes general affirmations that, for the most part, we too could make. Thus the declaration does not make plain the important, distinguishing contours of their position.

The *Danvers Statement* (Appendix 2) is, we believe, more clear and distinct while not pressing for agreement on many specific applications. We do not regard this as a perfect or infallible document. Some things, no doubt, could be said better. Much less do we regard those of us who embrace the statement as perfect embodiments of its vision of mature manhood and womanhood. The statement was not written as a creed to test Christian orthodoxy. But we do believe it is true and is, therefore, one helpful test for right thinking on this part of Biblical teaching.

Our effort at clarity can be seen in our using enough precision and distinctness that, to our knowledge, the authors of the CBE statement "Men, Women and Biblical Equality" would *not* be able to ascribe to our affirmations 2, 3, 4, 5, 6, and 10 with the meaning each of these affirmations has in the context of this document. Therefore, the statement gives a clear option to the church and lets people know where we stand in distinction from others who disagree at crucial points. Our affirmations are worded to make plain what we deny as well as what we affirm about the crucial issues of headship in marriage and primary responsibility for leadership in the church.

We turn now to present the declaration of Christians for Biblical Equality along with our commentary.

A Commentary on "Men, Women and Biblical Equality,"[4] a Declaration of *Christians for Biblical Equality*

In what follows, we will present, point-by-point, the text of "Men, Women and Biblical Equality," followed by our own comments on that text.

> *The Bible teaches the full equality of men and women in Creation and in Redemption (Gen 1:26-28, 2:23, 5:1-2; 1 Cor 11:11-12; Gal 3:13, 28, 5:1).*

Comment: The difference in approach from the *Danvers Statement* is signalled at the outset. We made an effort to come to terms with the *nature* and *extent* of our equality as men and women and to be explicit about it: "equal before God *as persons* but *distinct in their manhood and womanhood.*" This is important because men and women are *not* equal in significant ways. Gregg Johnson, in Chapter 16, makes this plain from the physiological/neurological side. More importantly, in this day of increasing homosexual demands for marital rights, we need to say loudly and clearly that men are not equal with women personally or physically *as candidates for the spouses of men.* Men and women are *not* equal when they stand before *a man* as a possible marriage partner. (See Chapter 2, Question 41.) At that point, women have rights and privileges that men do not have, strictly on the basis of gender. We may speak, and should speak, of equal *worth*, even of the differences, but to speak of "full equality" in the context of this controversy with no clarifying explanation leaves the reader to wonder just how far the authors are willing to go. The nature and extent of our equality is at the heart of the controversy.

> *The Bible teaches that God has revealed Himself in the totality of Scripture, the authoritative Word of God (Matt 5:18; John 10:35; 2 Tim 3:16; 2 Peter 1:20-21). We believe that Scripture is to be interpreted wholistically [sic] and thematically. We also recognize the necessity of making a distinction between inspiration and interpretation: inspiration relates to the divine impulse and control whereby the whole canonical Scripture is the Word of God; interpretation relates to the human activity whereby we seek to apprehend revealed truth in*

harmony with the totality of Scripture and under the guidance of the Holy Spirit. To be truly biblical, Christians must continually examine their faith and practice under the searchlight of Scripture.

Comment: We rejoice in this strong affirmation of the divine inspiration of all the Bible. The aim to interpret the Bible "wholistically [sic] and thematically" and thus to apprehend revealed truth "in harmony with the totality of Scripture" is good. We would only alert the reader that the only way to find out what the totality of Scripture says is to interpret the smaller parts faithfully in their nearer context. This is called the hermeneutical circle: the parts determine the whole and the whole affects how we interpret the parts. Our concern is that any supposed "whole" or "theme" or "thrust" (like "the leveling of birth-based status differences"[5]) should not be used to nullify the contribution of any other part of Scripture (which may teach that gender is ordained by God to be significant in some role differences).[6]

Biblical Truths

Creation

1. *The Bible teaches that both man and woman were created in God's image, had a direct relationship with God, and shared jointly the responsibilities of bearing and rearing children and having dominion over the created order (Gen 1:26-28).*

Comment: We agree. We would only point out that just as God meant for the shared responsibility of bearing children to involve very different roles (in the process of fertilization, gestation, and nursing) so also He may mean for the shared responsibility of dominion to involve different roles. Acting "jointly" does not mean acting identically, and "sharing" responsibilities does not mean that each must bear the same ones. Yet CBE makes no affirmation of any distinctive responsibilities that men or women have in bearing or rearing children or having dominion over the earth, and their statement could be taken to mean that men and women have identical responsibilities.

2. *The Bible teaches that woman and man were created for full and equal partnership. The word "helper"* (ezer)*, used to designate woman in Genesis 2:18, refers to God in most instances of Old Testament usage (e.g. 1 Sam 7:12; Ps 121:1-2). Consequently the word conveys no implication whatsoever of female subordination or inferiority.*

The phrase "full and equal" has the same ambiguity referred to in the first paragraph of the declaration—some will take it to mean a partnership of identical roles, and some will take it to mean a partnership of different roles with equal value.

It is true that God is called our "helper," but the word itself says nothing about the kind of helper intended. The context must decide whether Eve is to "help" as a strong person who aids a weaker one, or as one who assists a loving leader. The context makes it very unlikely that "helper" should be read on the analogy of God's help, because in Genesis 2:19-20 Adam is caused to seek his "helper" first among the animals. But the animals will not do, because they are not "fit for him." So God makes woman "from man." Now there is a being who is "fit for him," sharing his human nature, equal to him in God-like personhood. She is infinitely different from an animal, and God highlights her value to man by showing how no animal can fill her role. Yet in passing through "helpful" animals to woman, God teaches us that the woman is a man's "helper" in the sense of a loyal and suitable assistant in the life of the garden. The problem with the CBE statement is the assumption that because a word has certain connotations in some places it must have them in every place.

With regard to the word *inferiority*, two comments: 1) the Bible never suggests that the differing roles of men and women imply differing worth; 2) women and men are inferior and superior to each other in various ways, but these are not made the sign of varying value as persons.

> 3. *The Bible teaches that the forming of woman from man demonstrates the fundamental unity and equality of human beings (Gen 2:21-23). In Genesis 2:18, 20 the word "suitable" (kenegdo) denotes equality and adequacy.*

Comment: We agree. But that is not all the Bible teaches about the meaning of taking woman from the side of man. It also teaches—and this is no contradiction of the other—that the man is the woman's "head" and that she should give evidence of her endorsement of his leadership (1 Corinthians 11:3, 7-10; see Chapter 5). If the CBE declaration aims to interpret the Scriptures holistically, why does the declaration omit this one place in the Bible outside Genesis where Genesis 2:21-22 is specifically used to teach on this issue?

> 4. *The Bible teaches that man and woman were co-participants in the Fall: Adam was no less culpable than Eve (Gen 3:6; Rom 5:12-21; 1 Cor 15:21-22).*

Comment: We agree. But this neglects and obscures the way the Bible talks about the role of man and woman in the fall. The Bible shows the woman and man reversing roles so that she becomes the leading spokesman as they enter into sin (Genesis 3:1, 17). The Bible speaks of the woman being deceived and not the man, though this does not lessen his guilt (1 Timothy 2:13). The Bible portrays the man as primarily accountable for the fall: the Lord came to him first and not to the woman to call them to account (Genesis 3:9); and the New Testament pictures Adam, not Eve, as the representative head of fallen humanity (Romans 5:17-19; 1 Corinthians 15:21-22). The specific thematic thrust of Scripture, which seems to give man peculiar responsibility, is ignored in the CBE statement.

> 5. *The Bible teaches that the rulership of Adam over Eve resulted from the Fall and was therefore not a part of the original created order. Genesis 3:16 is a prediction of the effects of the Fall rather than a prescription of God's ideal order.*

Comment: We agree with this point concerning Genesis 3:16. "He shall rule over you," is not a prescription of what should be, but a description of what happens through sin where redemption is not overcoming the effects of the fall. But the silence at this point regarding the reality of Adam's loving leadership *before* the fall gives the impression that fallen "rulership" and God-ordained headship are lumped together and ruled out. Again the Biblical thrust is ignored: Paul never appeals to the curse or the fall as an explanation for man's responsibility to lead; he always appeals to the acts of God before the fall (1 Corinthians 11:8-9; Ephesians 5:31-32; 1 Timothy 2:13). Why is this thrust and theme neglected when it bears exactly on the point at issue in this paragraph?

Redemption

> 6. *The Bible teaches that Jesus Christ came to redeem women as well as men. Through faith in Christ we all become children of God, one in Christ, and heirs to the blessings of salvation without reference to racial, social, or gender distinctives (John 1:12-13; Rom 8:14-17; 2 Cor 5:17; Gal 3:26-28).*

Comment: We agree. But we affirm more specifically that what Jesus redeems from corruption is the beautiful order of creation in which the distinct complementary roles for man and woman were ordained by God's creative acts.

Community

> 7. *The Bible teaches that at Pentecost the Holy Spirit came on the men and women alike. Without distinction, the Holy Spirit indwells women and men, and sovereignly distributes gifts without preference as to gender (Acts 2:1-21; 1 Cor 12:7, 11, 14:31).*

Comment: Men and women are indwelt and filled with the Holy Spirit and gifted to minister. But the texts do not say that the Holy Spirit takes no regard for gender. He is free to do so, if He wills. It would not limit His freedom in the least if, for example, He gave more women the gift of mercy (Romans 12:8). He apportions gifts to each "as he wills" (1 Corinthians 12:11; Hebrews 2:4). We need to make this plain because some may take this paragraph to mean that "pastor-teacher" (Ephesians 4:11) is a gift, and then say that the Holy Spirit is bound to be gender-blind in giving it. However, we agree that all the gifts (not offices) mentioned in the New Testament are given to men and women, though we do not know if the Spirit in His freedom sometimes takes gender into account when He gives them. (See Chapter 2, Question 34.)

> 8. *The Bible teaches that both women and men are called to develop their spiritual gifts and to use them as stewards of the grace of God (1 Peter 4:10-11). Both men and women are divinely gifted and empowered to minister to the whole Body of Christ, under His authority (Acts 1:14, 18:6, 21:9; Rom 16:1-7, 12-13, 15; Phil 4:2-3; Col 4:15; see also Mark 15:40-41, 16:1-7; Luke 8:1-3; John 20:17-18; compare also Old Testament examples: Judges 4:4-14, 5:7; 2 Chron 34:22-28; Prov 31:30-31; Micah 6:4).*

Comment: We agree, unless "empowered to minister to the *whole Body of Christ*" is a way of saying that a woman with the gift of teaching should exercise it toward the male half of the body of Christ the same way she does toward the female half. It is not easy to see what this paragraph might otherwise mean by ministering to the "whole Body of Christ." It would serve clarity better if CBE said plainly what is probably intended: God gifts women to teach men as well as to teach women in the body of Christ.

9. *The Bible teaches that, in the New Testament economy, women as well as men exercise the prophetic, priestly and royal functions (Acts 2:17-18, 21:9; 1 Cor 11:5; 1 Peter 2:9-10; Rev 1:6, 5:10). Therefore, the few isolated texts that appear to restrict the full redemptive freedom of women must not be interpreted simplistically and in contradiction to the rest of Scripture, but their interpretation must take into account their relation to the broader teaching of Scripture and their total context (1 Cor 11:2-16, 14:33-36; 1 Tim 2:9-15).*

Comment: Here the hermeneutical principle mentioned in the second paragraph of the declaration shows its power to silence Scripture. A broad and general statement about the priestly, royal, and prophetic function of women is used to determine what other texts "must not" mean.

Instead, what we recommend is that these so-called "isolated texts" be allowed to help *define* the nature of the prophetic, priestly, and royal role of men and women. But that possibility is obscured by caricaturing all alternatives to the CBE method. The problem here is that the language excludes the very possibility of our position by implying that any alternative to the CBE's method involves "simplistic" interpretation that "contradicts the rest of Scripture" and ignores the "total context" of passages to which we appeal. This is the fallacy of the excluded middle: one attempts to strengthen one's position by exposing the shortcomings of a weak alternative while giving the impression that there are no other alternatives but the weak one when in fact there are.[7]

But the alternative they reject is emphatically *not* the only alternative to their method. We offer interpretations of each of the texts in question that are *not* simplistic, do *not* ignore the Biblical context, and do *not* contradict the rest of Scripture. What is taken to be "the broader teaching of Scripture," namely, God's gender-indifference in assigning roles, proves on close examination to be a series of unwarranted inferences from many indecisive passages. This "broader teaching" then is used to govern the so-called isolated texts that were designed in the first place to help shape that "broader teaching" and guard us from the unwarranted inferences. This is not an approach to Scripture that secures the full authority of all that it has to say. (See note 57.)

Moreover it is unclear and misleading to speak of limiting a woman's "redemptive freedom" when the issue is whether she can "teach and have authority over men" (1 Timothy 2:12). "Limiting full redemptive freedom" is something none of us wants to do, because it sounds like we would be saying woman is not fully redeemed. That may be what the authors think we really are saying. But the problem is that many of their readers do not think that limiting the pastorate to men means women are less redeemed. So the authors have avoided the clear statement of what is at issue (women pastors or elders) and used a term that wins more support ("redemptive freedom"), but probably at the cost of true understanding.

10. *The Bible defines the function of leadership as the empowerment of others for service rather than as the exercise of power over them (Matt 20:25-28, 23:8; Mark 10: 42-45; John 13:13-17; Gal 5:13; 1 Peter 5:2-3).*

Comment: Again there is the fallacy of the excluded middle. What seems to be overlooked in the either/or of this paragraph is that leadership may exercise power not simply "over"—which may imply proud, self-aggrandizing domination—but "under" or "in front of" (that is, in the service of). What's missing is the fully Biblical notion of exercising servant-power to empower. This is what Jesus did as a leader (Luke 9:1); it is what Paul did as an apostle (1 Corinthians 4:19-21; 2 Corinthians 10:8; 13:10; Philemon 8-10); it is what church leaders "who govern well" are supposed to do for those they lead (cf. 1 Timothy 5:17 with 3:5); and it is what a husband is called to do for his wife as her head (Ephesians 5:25-26).

Family

11. *The Bible teaches that husbands and wives are heirs together of the grace of life and that they are bound together in a relationship of mutual submission and responsibility (1 Cor 7:3-5; Eph 5:21; 1 Peter 3:1-7; Gen 21:12). The husband's function as "head" (*kephalē*) is to be understood as self-giving love and service within this relationship of mutual submission (Eph 5:21-33; Col 3:19; 1 Peter 3:7).*

Comment: This statement lacks the clarity needed in the church at this time. It does not say whether the husband's "self-giving love and service" cancels out his role as a leader or simply describes the form his unique leadership should take. The result of this ambiguity is that people endorse this statement who have profoundly different views on one of the crucial issues at stake—the role relationship of husband and wife. How will it serve the cause of truth if CBE wins assent on this paragraph by omitting the assertion that really distinguishes their vision from ours? Omitted is the assertion, for example, that "mutual submission rules out hierarchical differences."[8] We gladly and urgently call husbands to "self-giving love and service." But we are persuaded that this does not cancel out the difference between *his* role and his wife's—it rather defines the kind of initiative and responsibility that most wives are glad for their husbands to take. (For more reflection on the phrase "mutual submission," see Chapter 2, questions 5 and 10.)

12. *The Bible teaches that both mothers and fathers are to exercise leadership in the nurture, training, discipline and teaching of their children (Exod 20:12; Lev 19:3; Deut 6:6-9, 21:18-21, 27:16; Prov 1:8, 6:20; Eph 6:1-4; Col 3:20; 2 Tim 1:5; see also Luke 2:51).*

Comment: We agree. But again the needed clarity is missing. Nothing is said about the point at issue: do fathers bear a distinct, primary responsibility in establishing a pattern of nurture and training and discipline in the home? We would say yes without denying anything of the partnership in parenting commended in this paragraph. Notice in Ephesians 6:1-4 how Paul moves from the shared honor of both parents to the special focus on fathers to take responsibility for their children's training: "Children, obey your parents. . . . *Fathers* . . . bring them up in the discipline and instruction of the Lord." (The same move from parents to fathers is found in Colossians 3:20-21).

Application

Community

1. *In the church, spiritual gifts of women and men are to be recognized, developed and used in serving and teaching ministries at all levels of involve-*

ment: as small group leaders, counselors, facilitators, administrators, ushers, communion servers, and board members, and in pastoral care, teaching, preaching, and worship.

In so doing, the church will honor God as the source of spiritual gifts. The church will also fulfill God's mandate of stewardship without the appalling loss to God's kingdom that results when half of the church's members are excluded from positions of responsibility.

Comment: Again there is the fallacy of the excluded middle. The last sentence implies that if women are not given access to "teaching ministries at all levels" including "preaching," then they are "excluded from positions of responsibility." This is not true. All of the hundreds of ministries women rightly undertake carry responsibility, many of them very great responsibility. The *Danvers Statement* (Affirmation Nine) makes it plain that we want every Christian, man and woman, to be responsibly and significantly engaged in ministry. But we do not so elevate the office of elder or pastor as to imply that the thousands of other believers—men and women—who serve Christ in a thousand other ways do not have positions of responsibility.

The other problem in this paragraph is again the ambiguity concerning the precise point at issue: namely, may women rightly fill the role of pastor or elder? The paragraph focuses on the generally permissible *function* of "preaching" and "teaching" but does not say explicitly that women may teach Scripture to men or hold the office of preaching pastor or teaching elder. Thus again, because of this lack of clarity, people may endorse this statement who have significantly different views on one of the crucial issues at stake—a woman's right to fill the role of preaching pastor or teaching elder. How is truth served in this crucial debate by formulating positions that win assent through ambiguity on the issues at the very heart of the debate?

2. *In the church, public recognition is to be given to both women and men who exercise ministries of service and leadership.*

In so doing, the church will model the unity and harmony that should characterize the community of believers. In a world fractured by discrimination and segregation, the church will dissociate itself from worldly or pagan devices designed to make women feel inferior for being female. It will help prevent their departure from the church or their rejection of the Christian faith.

Comment: No one can disagree with the aim to renounce "worldly and pagan devices designed to make women feel inferior." But we wish there had been some clarity about who or what is being indicted here. Is our interpretation of Scripture being called a pagan device? Are we the ones who by "design" aim to make women feel "inferior"? If so it would help readers make reasoned decisions about this matter if CBE said: "The view that endorses only men in the pastoral office is a pagan device and is designed to make women feel inferior." But again the language wins support without making clear what is being supported. We do not understand the rationale for such formulations in the present context of church controversy. It seems to us that we should all want to help our readers know as clearly as possible what is pagan and what is not, what is designed to make women feel inferior and what is not.

The desire to win the heart of contemporary women is tremendously important and praiseworthy. We share it. We too think the church should be a "city set on a hill that cannot be hid"—a beautifully attractive community of love and harmony and respect. But we caution that there will always be moral commitments in the church that are at first unattractive to the world. In one and the same context Jesus said two seemingly contradictory things: Men will "revile you and persecute you and utter all kinds of evil against you falsely on my account;" and, "Let your light so shine before men, that they may see your good works and give glory to your Father who is in heaven" (Matthew 5:11, 16). Which is it? Will they speak evil of us, or will they glorify God? The answer is: both—sometimes one and sometimes the other, and sometimes one followed by the other (1 Peter 2:12). The point is that we cannot shape all our life so as to win approval from the world. Some of it we can. But in other parts of it, rejection by the world may not be owing to our failure. We affirm with CBE that we must always struggle to discover the right missionary balance.

Family

3. *In the Christian home, husband and wife are to defer to each other in seeking to fulfill each other's preferences, desires and aspirations. Neither spouse is to seek to dominate the other, but each is to act as servant of the other, in humility considering the other as better than oneself. In case of decisional deadlock, they should seek resolution through biblical methods of conflict resolution rather than by one spouse imposing a decision upon the other.*

In so doing, husband and wife will help the Christian home stand against improper use of power and authority by spouses and will protect the home from wife and child abuse that sometimes tragically follows a hierarchical interpretation of the husband's "headship."

Comment: We agree that in a good marriage spouses will try to outdo one another in showing honor (Romans 12:10). Husbands and wives will often yield their own preferences to make each other happy. That is the way love is. "Through love be servants of one another" (Galatians 5:13). This is what husbands should use their leadership to cultivate. The responsibility of leadership that God calls a husband to bear is not conceived in terms of unilateral veto power. But the CBE statement does not make clear if they believe *any* unique leadership of the husband is good or if it is compatible with this kind of mutual kindness. This is another unfortunate ambiguity on a point that lies at the heart of the debate.

Again it seems to us that CBE is seeking to strengthen its case through the fallacy of the excluded middle. For example, CBE pictures, on the one hand, two humble spouses, each seeking to consider the other better than oneself; on the other hand, it pictures two spouses where one seeks "to dominate the other" and "impose a decision upon the other." In this way the CBE position is made to look like the only loving one, because the real middle position, the one we take, is excluded. We do not counsel any man to "dominate" his wife or to "impose" his decisions on her. We speak of a husband bearing the responsibility of servant-leadership and a wife gladly affirming that leadership. Moreover, we urge wives never to follow a husband's lead into sin. When we say that a husband should bear the responsibility to break a decisional deadlock, we do not mean that it will be without much interaction with his wife, or that he will always break it according to his own preference. Responsibility to lead is not synonymous with getting your way.

To say that wife and child abuse "sometimes follows a hierarchical interpretation of the husband's headship" is no doubt true. But it also sometimes follows an egalitarian interpretation of headship. Neither of us intends to give any encouragement for abuse. But the outcome of our teachings may differ from what we intend, and this cuts both ways. We would encourage those who minimize the husband's unique role as leader to consider the possibility that this may in fact be cultivating a milieu of gender confusion that in the long run brings about more abuse.

For example, sons who grow up in homes where the father gives no clear model of caring, strong, courteous leadership distinct from the role of the mother will find it much harder to develop their natural masculine identity in positive ways and will be likely candidates for the folly of macho distortions of manhood that ruin many homes. (See Chapter 17.) In the years to come, will it be enough to tell husbands and wives to love each other, without helping them discover what is unique about manhood and womanhood in the dynamic of marriage? If all the emphasis is on gender neutrality and undifferentiated roles, how will sons learn the answer to the question: What does it mean to grow up to be a man and not a woman? And how will daughters learn to answer the question: What does it mean to grow up to be a woman and not a man? If these questions are regarded as anything less than utterly crucial, we think the resulting frustrations and confusions, through the loss of clear sexual identity in the generations to come, will erupt with a tidal wave of hostilities and perversions that we can now scarcely imagine.

> 4. *In the Christian home, spouses are to learn to share the responsibilities of leadership on the basis of gifts, expertise, and availability, with due regard for the partner most affected by the decision under consideration.*
>
> *In so doing spouses will learn to respect their competencies and their complementarity. This will prevent one spouse from becoming the perennial loser, often forced to practice ingratiating or deceitful manipulation to protect self-esteem. By establishing their marriage on a partnership basis, the couple will protect it from joining the tide of dead or broken marriages resulting from marital inequities.*

Comment: It is astonishing to us that a Biblical vision for the inner workings of marriage can be proposed without reference to the deep and wonderful differences between male and female personhood. Another way to say it would be to ask: In a strictly competency-based pattern of leadership, where is the glorious parable of Christ and the church? What has become of the most beautiful marriage chapter in all the Bible, Ephesians 5:22-33? To us it seems not only naive but also sterile to portray the wonderful interweaving of manhood and womanhood in the fabric of marriage as the mere alignment of roles along lines of gender-neutral competencies, individual expertise, and schedule constraints. Something awesome is missing here. And its absence threatens the meaning of manhood and womanhood to such a degree that the church should be deeply concerned.

There is another way to protect spouses from being perennial losers. Let the husband learn to lead as Christ leads. And let the wife learn to affirm that Christlike leadership the way the church affirms Christ's. Is Christ or the church ever a loser in this relationship? Is Christ or the church ever forced to "practice ingratiating or deceitful manipulation to protect self-esteem"? Has a husband ever been guilty in marital breakup because he accepted the unique responsibility to lead like Christ? It is a great puzzle to us why the CBE declaration portrays its competency-based, gender-neutral, egalitarian option over against the corruptions and distortions of hierarchy while totally neglecting the beautiful portrait of marriage, visible today in many homes—namely, Christ and the church.

> 5. *In the Christian home, couples who share a lifestyle characterized by the freedom they find in Christ will do so without experiencing feelings of guilt or resorting to hypocrisy. They are freed to emerge from an unbiblical "traditionalism" and can rejoice in their mutual accountability in Christ.*
>
> *In so doing, they will openly express their obedience to Scripture, will model an example for other couples in quest of freedom in Christ, and will stand against patterns of domination and inequality sometimes imposed upon church and family.*

Comment: If Christ, in leading the church, does not "dominate" the church, and if God, in being the head of Christ (1 Corinthians 11:3), does not "dominate" Christ, and if elders "who lead well" (1 Timothy 5:17) need not "dominate" the flock, then domination is not the only alternative to the CBE gender-neutral conception of roles in marriage. There is a Biblical vision of warmth and respect and love that glories in the God-given, personal differences between manhood and womanhood. But in reading the CBE declaration one is left with the impression that the choice is between their view and "unbiblical 'traditionalism.'" We believe there is another choice. That is why we have written this book.

> We believe that biblical equality as reflected in this document is true to Scripture.
>
> We stand united in our conviction that the Bible, in its totality, is the liberating Word that provides the most effective way for women and men to exercise the gifts distributed by the Holy Spirit and thus to serve God.

Comment: See below for our summary assessment.

An Assessment of "Men, Women and Biblical Equality"

Apart from our disagreeing with the (apparent) CBE endorsement of women as preaching pastors and teaching elders and with their lack of endorsement of a man's responsibility to give primary leadership in his home, our summary concerns are these:

1. The CBE statement says nothing positive concerning the special responsibilities that a person should bear by virtue of being a man or a woman. The silence of CBE on such implications for sexual differences is typical of egalitarians. It is one of the reasons why so many young people today are confused about what it means to be a man or a woman. Readers are only told how their sexual differences *don't* count. They are not told in what sense they *do* count. We believe that

the resulting confusion and frustration over male and female identity will be increasingly responsible for the precise negative effects that CBE aims to avert.

2. We lament the absence of clarity on key points of disagreement. Only occasionally must we disagree with the actual *wording* of the declaration, even though its authors hold significantly different views from ours. This is because some affirmations are accepted by all evangelicals and others are so ambiguous as to allow clouded agreement by people with deep divergences. In other words, the CBE statement does not offer a clear contrary alternative to the *Danvers Statement*. The controversial positions that distinguish CBE from CBMW do not receive crisp, clear expression. This is doubly troubling from our point of view, because we regard ambiguity of this kind as the common prelude to liberalism. The loss of clarity and precision can easily create a fog in which it is much harder to discern what ideas are really coming and going.

3. We are troubled by the repeated fallacy of the excluded middle: the strengthening of one's position by exposing the shortcomings of an ugly alternative while giving the impression that there are no other alternatives when in truth there are. The CBE statement is a strangely oblique and ambiguous document. Chauvinistic abuses to our right are deplored. Controversial egalitarian convictions to our left are implicitly suggested in non-controversial language. But we do not recognize our own position as either the one suggested or the one rejected.

Almost all the denunciations in the CBE declaration refer to relational abuses that we reject, too. Thus CBE distances itself most often from a corruption of Biblical complementarity that we do not share, so that the reader is left wondering what CBE really thinks about a position like ours that rejects those same corruptions. Some examples:

- The "rulership" of man over woman is rightly rejected by CBE as part of the curse, but there is no explicit denial of our affirmation that the *loving headship* of husbands is rooted in creation before the curse.
- The "improper use of power and authority by spouses" is rightly rejected, but there is no explicit reckoning with the *proper* use of authority in a husband's loving leadership in the home, which is at the heart of CBMW's vision.
- CBE says the husband's headship is to be carried out "as self-giving love and service." Yes, but no explicit denial is made of our affirmation that this is the *form* of a husband's leadership, not an *alternative* to it.

4. The CBE hermeneutical procedure seems to us to pit Scripture against Scripture, with the result that crucial portions of God's Word are not allowed to have their proper say. For example, they speak of "the broader teaching of Scripture" and "the totality of Scripture" and the need to interpret "wholistically [sic] and thematically." Having defined this "totality" in terms of equality and the leveling of gender-based role distinctions, they say that the key texts that we appeal to as decisive "must not be interpreted" in a way that jeopardizes what they have determined to be the totality. This is very precarious and seems in fact to muzzle the most important passages on the issue at stake.

We do not claim to be above this very hermeneutical problem—determining the meaning of the parts by the whole, while at the same time defining the whole from the meaning of the parts. We all struggle here. And it is not just a problem in *Biblical* hermeneutics. Nevertheless we protest that CBE is heavy-handed in using the whole against the parts. And we appeal for the sake of 1 Timothy 2:12-14; 1 Corinthians 11:3-16; 14:34-36; Ephesians 5:22-33; Colossians 3:18-19;

1 Peter 3:1-7; Titus 2:5, etc. that they be given their say in shaping the "totality of Scripture" instead of being treated like outsiders with no exegetical vote—especially when these are the very texts that speak most explicitly and directly to the questions of distinct roles for men and women. This is all the more crucial today because the temptation to conform the "totality of Scripture" to contemporary egalitarian culture is just as strong today as the temptation to hold on to hierarchical tradition. This means that, contrary to the assumptions of many, the very texts of which we are being told what they "must not" mean are needed in all their special focus to protect the "totality of Scripture" from cultural distortion.

Again we want to confess explicitly that *we* have the same need in *our* effort of interpretation. We too are vulnerable to cultural, traditional, and personal influences that may distort our sense of what the totality of Scripture is saying. Yet we hope that in this book we have given evidence of being shaped and guided by all the Scripture, not just some of it.

Reasons for Hope

We not only want to pursue charity and cultivate clarity, but also to live in hope—hope that this controversy will move toward resolution in many fellowships and eventually in the church as a whole; hope that in the process we will become deeper and wiser and holier people; and hope that through it all our mission to a perishing world will not be hindered but advanced. What warrants are there for this hope? We see at least three. And, as with all signs of hope, these are also spurs to pray, because prophecies of this sort can be easily squandered. What will not be received by one generation God will save for the blessing of another.

1. There is hope because we stand together on the authority of God's Word, the Bible. As agonizing as the impasse may feel, there is reason to believe that while this common ground prevails, new light may yet break forth upon us. The Word is living and active; it will pierce through all our confusion. It is not passive, but "at work in you who believe" (1 Thessalonians 2:13). It will not suffer itself indefinitely to bear our misuses. It will set us straight, or it will drive us off, or it will show us how to live in peace and fulfill our mission to the world in spite of everything. "The testimony of the Lord is sure, *making wise the simple* . . . the commandment of the Lord is pure, *enlightening the eyes*" (Psalm 19:7-8). "You will know the truth, and *the truth will make you free*" (John 8:32). One can bemoan the puzzling impasse of multiple interpretations, or one can rejoice over the precious and auspicious privilege of standing together on one solid foundation. No doubt we feel both from time to time. May our footing remain firm and our common joy increase.

2. There is hope because of the ministry of the Holy Spirit. Not only do we believe in the Holy Spirit, but also each of us is indwelt by Him, for we confess heartily, on both sides of this issue, that Jesus Christ is Lord of all. And "no one can say 'Jesus is Lord' except by the Holy Spirit" (1 Corinthians 12:3). He is the Spirit of truth (John 16:13). He does not delight in disagreement among His people. He is urging and pressing us ever on toward "the unity of the Spirit" (Ephesians 4:3). Therefore we may dare to hear the words of the apostle as if spoken just for us: "Let those of us who are mature be thus minded; and if in anything you are otherwise minded, *God will reveal that also to you*" (Philippians 3:15). God is committed to correcting His people. He is not indifferent to dark-

ness. "If any of you lacks wisdom, let him ask God, who gives to all men generously and without reproaching" (James 1:5). "His anointing teaches you about everything" (1 John 2:27).

One of His indispensable contributions in the task of interpretation is teachability and humility. The "natural person" without the Spirit of God senses that the things of the Spirit are foolish. Therefore he cannot grasp them, because there is no welcoming attitude or spirit (1 Corinthians 2:13-16). Where the heart is averse, the mind will avert the truth. We have a thousand ways to justify with our brains the biases of the soul. More than we would like to think, our reason is the unwitting servant or our wishes. This condition is the special concern of the Holy Spirit. He works from within, sovereignly opening and humbling us to the truth of the Word. The "spiritual person assesses all things." Those who possess the Spirit eventually welcome the things of God. The template in the soul is cleansed of self and comes to feel the delight of meshing with its counterpiece in the Word of truth.

There is a specific application of this truth to the issue of manhood and womanhood. It is something we all suspect to be the case but are often fearful of articulating lest we sound presumptuous. But it is so vital in this matter that we should not avoid it. Do we not find ourselves again and again baffled that others cannot simply "feel" the rightness of what we are saying about the relationship of men and women? On the other hand, repeatedly people will say (on one side or the other): "That surely rings bells in my heart." Or: "That feels right to me." Or: "I really resonate with that." In fact, some have said to those of us speaking out in this controversy, "You're wasting your time arguing about this, because it's a matter of inner taste. Either you sense the vision as beautiful or you don't, and no amount of arguing is going to make something look attractive to the eyes of the heart if it doesn't see it in an instant."

There is something very profound being spoken here. Jonathan Edwards, the eighteenth-century preacher and theologian, developed it better than anyone we know. In describing how the saints are led by the Holy Spirit, he argues that, just as a good eye recognizes natural beauty, and a good ear knows harmony, and a good tongue tastes sweetness—all without a train of reasoning—so there is a spiritual sense in the regenerate soul that perceives immediately the fitness and beauty of a holy action or a relationship. Edwards puts it like this:

> Thus a holy person is led by the Spirit, as he is instructed and led by his holy taste and disposition of heart; whereby, in the lively exercise of grace, he easily distinguishes good and evil, and knows at once what is a suitable, amiable behavior towards God, and towards man . . . and judges what is right, as it were, spontaneously, without a particular deduction, by any other arguments than the beauty that is seen, and goodness that is tasted.[9]

This, Edwards explains, is why the simplest people are very often wiser and more holy than those who are very educated and scholarly. The ability to perceive what is morally good and beautiful is a function of a spiritual faculty, a discerning sense of fitness, a taste for what is lovely in the sight of God. Edwards sums up his discussion with the following sentence:

> There is a *divine taste*, given and maintained by the Spirit of God, in the hearts of the saints, whereby they are . . . led and guided in discerning and distinguishing the true spiritual and holy beauty of actions; and that more easily, readily, and accurately, as they have more or less of the Spirit of God dwelling in them. And thus *the sons of God are led by the Spirit of God in their behavior in the world.*[10]

What this implies is that discerning the beauty and goodness of any vision of manhood and womanhood involves more than just rational exegetical argumentation. Each of us has some capacity for immediate, moral perception of what Edwards calls the amiableness or suitableness of a pattern of behavior. He says that we will distinguish what is truly beautiful more "readily and accurately" as we have more or less of God's Spirit dwelling in us.

If Edwards is right—and we believe he is—there is reason to hope that we may come together under a vision of manhood and womanhood, notwithstanding all our exegetical disagreements. For the business of the sovereign Holy Spirit is to lead His people (Romans 8:14). And if He leads as Edwards says He does—by giving a divine taste for what is morally beautiful—then none of us dare say, "The day cannot dawn when we will not be drawn to the beauty of a different vision." Surely none is prepared to say that the influence of the Holy Spirit that we now have is all there is to have. Which of us needs more refinement in spiritual taste? God will make that plain in His time. More important than knowing that fact is the confession that each of us needs to be changed from one degree of glory to another. And if there were a great cry from us all, would God not answer—perhaps with a vision of manhood and womanhood none has yet seen or spoken?

3. Finally, there is reason to hope because the things that unite those of us on both sides of this issue are inexpressibly magnificent and infinitely valuable. This is why our mission to the world will not be blunted but will in fact prosper and triumph by the sovereign grace of God.

We serve the same omnipotent God, and there is none like Him. "I am God, and there is no other; I am God, and there is none like me, declaring the end from the beginning and from ancient times things not yet done, saying 'My counsel shall stand, and I shall accomplish all my purpose'" (Isaiah 46:10). The utter uniqueness of this omnipotent God that we serve together is not merely that He is sovereign and makes all His plans to stand. It is also the breathtaking truth that He works for us with His omnipotence! "From of old no one has heard or perceived by the ear, no eye has seen a God besides thee, who *works for those who wait for him*" (Isaiah 64:4).

Do we not share the faith that the earth is the Lord's and everything in it—that He made everything and everyone? Every human being is God's by right, whether they are in rebellion against Him or allegiance to Him. He is King over the nations.

Do we not share the faith that in these last days God has spoken to us by a Son, Jesus Christ, whom He appointed the heir of all things and through whom He made the world? Do we not believe together that Jesus reflects the glory of God and bears the very stamp of His nature, upholding the universe by the Word of His power? We believe that this great and glorious Son of God became flesh and dwelt among us. He was tempted but never sinned. He taught like no one else ever taught, and loved like no one else ever loved. He said He came to serve and to give His life a ransom for many. He suffered indescribable shame and pain, and died willingly. He identified the meaning of His own blood in advance: "This is my blood of the covenant, which is poured out for many for the forgiveness of sins" (Matthew 26:28).

Do we not share the faith that Jesus rose from the dead never to die again, that Satan was defeated, that death was conquered, and that Jesus now reigns at the right hand of the Majesty on high until He puts all His enemies under His feet?

Do we not share the faith that anyone and everyone who turns from sin and calls upon the name of the Lord will be saved? Every believer is delivered from the kingdom of darkness, the fear of death, and the dominion of sin. Every believer receives the gift of forgiveness, the indwelling of the Holy Spirit, the cleansing of conscience, and the hope of everlasting joy in the presence of God.

Do we not share the faith that God has a heart and a plan for all the nations? He has other sheep that are not of this fold. And the great assurance of our lives is that *these He must bring also*. His mission cannot fail, for He is God. What His Son has purchased He *will* possess. And He has purchased people from every tribe and tongue and nation. Therefore the gospel of the kingdom *will* be preached throughout the whole world, as a testimony to all nations, and then the end will come. The Son of Man will appear on the clouds with power and great glory. He will send out His angels with a loud trumpet call, and they will gather His elect from the four winds, from one end of heaven to the other. Every knee, in all the universe, will bow before Jesus Christ. He will establish His kingdom of righteousness and peace. All that is evil will be cast into outer darkness. And the glory of the Lord will fill the earth as the waters cover the sea.

These things and many more we cherish in common. There is no such thing as Christian fellowship if the shared revelling in these things is not fellowship. This is our united front of love and witness to the world. This is an unblunted point of unified penetration. Indeed, the mission is far advanced, and is moving today at an incredible pace.

In 1900 there were fewer than 10 million Protestants in sub-Saharan Africa. By the year 2000 there will be over 400 million—a growth rate 500 percent faster than the population growth. In 1900 there were only about 50,000 Protestants in Latin America. By the year 2000 there will be over 100 million—a growth rate 20,000 percent faster than the population growth. Just over one hundred years ago there were no Christian churches in Korea. Today there are 6,000 churches in the city of Seoul alone. More Muslims have become Christians in Indonesia, Bangladesh, Iran, and East Africa in the last ten years than in the last ten centuries. Christianity is the most extensive and universal religion in history. There are churches in every country in the world.

The task remaining is great. But we are gaining steadily. The goal is to reach every people group with the gospel and plant the church among them. Several thousand groups remain to be reached. But the number is shrinking steadily, and the number of Christians available to complete the job is growing. The great new reality in missions today is the emergence of non-Western missionaries and agencies. There are over 30,000 personnel and by the end of the century that number will be over 100,000 at the present rate of advance. Not only that, but also, lands once thought to be utterly inaccessible have opened, as it were, overnight under the sovereign hand of God. And as if that were not enough, God is reversing missions and bringing many of the unreached peoples to our own Western cities. In Toronto, Canada, live an estimated 67,000 Chinese Buddhists, 297,000 Indo-Pakistanis, 88,000 Portuguese, and 109,000 Japanese.

The point is this: there is great cause for hope today. Controversies notwithstanding—or perhaps through the very controversies themselves—Christ *will* build His church. All the families of the earth *will* be blessed. The nations may rage and the kingdoms totter, but God utters His voice and the earth melts. The victory will not come without suffering. Perhaps this is what will bind us together most sweetly in the end. May the Lord give us more light and more love as we hope in Him.

Appendices

APPENDIX 1

The Meaning of *Kephalē* ("Head"): A Response to Recent Studies

Wayne Grudem

In a 1989 issue of *Trinity Journal*, Richard S. Cervin published a critique[1] of my 1985 article, "Does *Kephalē* ('Head') Mean 'Source' or 'Authority Over' in Greek Literature? A Survey of 2,336 Examples."[2] My primary purpose in this appendix is to respond to Cervin's critique, but I shall also interact with a number of other studies of *kephalē* that have been published since my 1985 work (especially those of Berkeley and Alvera Mickelsen, Philip Payne, Gilbert Bilezikian, and Catherine Kroeger).

This discussion is of considerable interest today because of its relevance to women's and men's roles in marriage. What does the New Testament mean when it says that "the husband is the *head* of the wife as Christ is the *head* of the church?" (Ephesians 5:23), or that the "*head* of every man is Christ" and "the *head* of a woman is her husband" (1 Corinthians 11:3)? Christians throughout history usually have understood the word *head* in these verses to mean "authority over," but many authors have denied that in the last few years, claiming instead that *head* in these contexts means "source" or "origin," so that Christ is the *source* of every man, Christ is the *source* of the church, and—referring to Adam and Eve—the man is the *source* of the woman. Support for this view was claimed from some occurrences of the Greek word *kephalē*, "head," outside the New Testament, where it was said to take the meaning "source." Furthermore, some argued that the sense "authority over" was uncommon or unknown in Greek and would have been unintelligible to Paul's readers. (Dr. Cervin's recent article also denied the meaning "authority over" in these texts, but he proposed not "source" but "preeminence" as an alternative meaning.)

I. Brief Summary of My 1985 Article

My original article attempted to respond to these claims by making the following points:

1. The evidence to support the claim that *kephalē* can mean "source" is surprisingly weak, and, in fact, unpersuasive.
   a. All the articles and commentaries depend on only two examples of *kephalē* in ancient literature: Herodotus 4.91 and *Orphic Fragments* 21a, both of which come from more than four hundred years before the time of the New Testament, and both of which fail to be convincing examples: Herodotus 4.91 simply shows that *kephalē* can refer to the "end points" of a river—in this case, the sources of a river, but elsewhere, the mouth of a river—and since "end point" is a commonly recognized and

well-attested sense of *kephalē*, we do not have convincing evidence that "source" is the required sense here. The other text, *Orphic Fragments* 21a, calls Zeus the "head" of all things but in a context where it is impossible to tell whether it means "first one, beginning" (an acknowledged meaning for *kephalē*) or "source" (a meaning not otherwise attested).

b. A new search of 2,336 examples of *kephalē* from a wide range of ancient Greek literature produced no convincing examples where *kephalē* meant "source."

2. The evidence to support the claim that *kephalē* can mean "authority over" is substantial.
   a. All the major lexicons that specialize in the New Testament period give this meaning, whereas none give the meaning "source."
   b. The omission of the meaning "authority over" from the Liddell-Scott *Lexicon* is an oversight that should be corrected (but it should be noted that that lexicon does not specialize in the New Testament period).
   c. The search of 2,336 examples turned up forty-nine texts where *kephalē* had the meaning "person of superior authority or rank, or 'ruler,' 'ruling part'"; therefore, this was an acceptable and understandable sense for *kephalē* at the time of the New Testament.
   d. The meaning "authority over" best suits many New Testament contexts.

II. Response to Richard Cervin

At the outset it should be said that, even if I were to agree with all of Dr. Cervin's article (which is certainly not the case, as will be seen below), the outcome would be to finish this discussion much nearer to the position I first advocated than to the one I opposed. Specifically, Cervin concludes the following:

a. The meaning "source" is not "common" (as most egalitarians assert today). Rather, Cervin concludes that it is "quite rare" (p. 112), and he comes up with only one certain example where he thinks *kephalē* clearly means "source" (Herodotus 4.91, a fifth-century B.C. text on the sources of a river, which was analyzed extensively in my earlier article).

b. Cervin says that *head* does not mean either "authority" or "source" in Paul's epistles, but rather means "preeminent." Cervin writes:

> What then does Paul mean by his use of *head* in his letters? He does not mean "authority over," as the traditionalists assert, nor does he mean "source" as the egalitarians assert. I think he is merely employing a head-body metaphor, and that his point is *preeminence.* (p. 112)

Cervin goes on to explain how this would apply to the passages on husband and wife in the New Testament:

> How can the husband be *preeminent* over his wife? In the context of the male-dominant culture of which Paul was a part, such a usage would not be inappropriate. (p. 112)

So it seems to me that even if all of Cervin's criticisms of my article were valid, his article would still have to be seen as a rejection of the egalitarian claim that *kephalē* means "source" in the New Testament, and an affirmation of an understanding of the New Testament teaching on male headship that is congenial with (though not identical to) the one that I previously argued for. If his final explanation of the meaning "preeminent" with reference to "the *male-dominant* culture of which Paul was a part"[3] were correct, his article would have to be seen as a modification of my position, not a rejection of it.

However, my response to Dr. Cervin must go deeper than that, because I do not think that he has (1) used proper methodology, (2) correctly evaluated the evidence, (3) represented my own article with complete fairness, or (4) come to correct conclusions.

A. The Rejection of Data Closest to the New Testament Writings

1. Rejection of New Testament Examples

One of the most surprising aspects of Dr. Cervin's article is that he dismisses all the New Testament examples of *kephalē* without examining one of them. Yet he concludes his article by telling us what Paul did and did not mean by *kephalē* (p. 112).

With regard to the 12 New Testament passages in which I claimed that the context indicated that the meaning "authority over" was appropriate for *kephalē*, Cervin says,

> First of all, 12 of these passages (nos. 38-49) are from the NT, and are therefore illegitimate as evidence, since they are disputed texts. In citing these NT passages, Grudem commits the logical fallacy of assuming what he sets out to prove. The whole purpose of Grudem's study is to determine whether or not *kephalē* can denote "authority over" or "leader" in Paul's epistles. He cannot therefore cite Paul as supporting evidence. (p. 94)

But Cervin here fails to distinguish "assuming what one sets out to prove" from *arguing for a meaning from context*, which is what I did in my article in each case (pp. 56-58).[4] If Cervin disagrees with my arguments from the context of these New Testament examples, then it would be appropriate to give reasons why he disagrees. But it is hardly legitimate linguistic analysis to dismiss them out of hand.

This is especially significant when we realize that a number of the New Testament examples of *head* have nothing to do with husband-wife relationships in marriage but speak of Christ's universal rule. For example, "he has put all things under his feet and has made him the *head* over all things for the church" (Ephesians 1:22). Here *head* is clearly a metaphor, and it occurs in a context dealing with Christ's authority "over all things" and the fact that God the Father "has put all things under his feet." It is hard to avoid the sense of "authority over" or "ruler" in this case, since the fact of Christ's universal authority is so clearly mentioned in the very sentence in which the word occurs.[5]

Similarly, Colossians 2:10 says that Christ is "the *head* of all rule and authority"—clearly implying that Christ is the greater leader or authority over all other authorities in the universe.

Moreover, in a context in which Paul says that "the church is subject to Christ," he says that "Christ is the *head* of the church" (Ephesians 5:23-24). Once again the idea of Christ's authority over the church seems so relevant to Paul's statements in the immediate context that it is surprising that Cervin thinks such texts can be dismissed without any discussion at all.

Other New Testament texts could be mentioned, but at least it should be clear that it is highly unusual to conclude an article with a statement about what Paul could have meant by the word *kephalē* when one has not examined Paul's own uses of *kephalē* at any point in the article. I do not recall ever before reading an article that concluded with a pronouncement about what a certain author meant by the use of a word but did not examine *any* of the uses of the word by that author himself. Would Cervin do this for Plato or Aristotle? If the meaning of a certain term as used by Aristotle was "under dispute" because some author had recently challenged the traditional understanding of Aristotle's use of that word, I imagine Dr. Cervin would use the following procedure:

1. He would first look carefully at the uses of that term in Aristotle and try to decide from the context what meaning the word had in each case.
2. Next he would look at the uses of that word in literature *closest* to Aristotle in time (what linguists call "synchronic analysis" of a term).
3. Then he would look at uses further away in time, subject matter, and culture—writers who shared less of a common linguistic stock with Aristotle because of the possible

changes in language over time. ("Diachronic analysis" refers to such tracing of the different uses of a word over time.)

Such a procedure would be characteristic of sound linguistic analysis.

But this is just the opposite of what Cervin does, for he dismisses the New Testament texts without examining even one verse. Then by other means he dismisses examples from other literature closest to the New Testament.

2. Rejection of Septuagint Examples

The Septuagint (LXX) was the everyday Bible used most commonly by the New Testament authors and by Greek-speaking Christians throughout the New Testament world. Yet Cervin dismisses the value of its evidence because it is a translation: "As a translation, the LXX is valuable as a *secondary* source, not as a primary one" (pp. 95-96).[6] At the end of the article he says,

> Of the four clear examples, three are from the LXX and one is from the Shepherd of Hermas, and it is very likely that all four of these are imported, not native, metaphors. . . . Does *kephalē* denote "authority over" or "leader"? No. The only clear and unambiguous examples of such a meaning stem from the Septuagint and The Shepherd of Hermas, and the metaphor may well have been influenced from Hebrew in the Septuagint. The metaphor "leader" for *head* is alien to the Greek language until the Byzantine or Medieval period. (pp. 111-112)

But if the Septuagint was indeed the Bible used by the New Testament authors and Christians throughout the New Testament world (as it was), then the fact that it was a translation made two centuries earlier does not mean that its examples of the use of *kephalē* are irrelevant as evidence. To dismiss these as irrelevant would be similar to someone trying to find out what American evangelical Christians in 1990 meant by the use of a word and then saying that the use of that word in the NASB or NIV Bibles could not count as evidence because those Bibles were "translations" and therefore may not reflect native English uses of the word.

In fact, quite the opposite is the case. Though the Septuagint is not perfect as a translation, it was certainly adequate to be used throughout the Greek-speaking world for several hundred years. To some extent it reflected the use of Greek common at the time it was translated, and to some extent (as all widely accepted Bible translations do) it influenced the language of the people who used it. Because of both of these facts, the usage of a word in the Septuagint is *extremely important* for determining the meaning of a word in the New Testament. The standard Greek lexicon for the New Testament and other early Christian literature (by Bauer, Arndt, Gingrich, and Danker) quotes the Septuagint more frequently than any other corpus of literature outside the New Testament for that very reason. In fact, in his "Introduction" to this lexicon Walter Bauer says, "As for the influence of the LXX, every page of this lexicon shows that it outweighs all other influences on our literature."[7]

Sound linguistic analysis would recognize this and would pay closest attention to the literature *most closely related* to the corpus of literature in question. But Cervin fails to admit such evidence as relevant, and this must be counted as a major methodological flaw in his argument.

3. Rejection of the Apostolic Fathers

The other corpus of literature most closely related to the New Testament is commonly referred to as "the Apostolic Fathers" (the name originally was intended to signify authors who knew the apostles personally). These writings are also extremely valuable for understanding New Testament usage, because the proximity in time, culture, and subject matter means that these writers shared a linguistic stock that was almost exactly the same as that of the New Testament writers. Yet again with regard to a citation from the Shepherd of Hermas (*Similitudes* 7:3, where a husband is referred to as "the head of your household"), Cervin admits that the sense "leader" attaches to the word *head*, but he rejects this as valid evidence for the use of a word in the New Testament because he says that the author was unknown: "We do not know who wrote the Shepherd. . . . If the author were a foreigner, it is entirely possible that this metaphor could have been calqued from his own native language. If this were the case, then this would be another example of an imported, not a native metaphor" (p. 105).

But this is hardly a sufficient basis on which to reject the evidence of this quotation. The Shepherd of Hermas was so widely known in the early Christian world that for at least two centuries many thought that it should be included as part of the New Testament canon (in 325 Eusebius still classified it among the "disputed books"; see Eusebius, *Ecclesiastical History* 3.3.6).

4. Rejection of Examples from Plutarch

Plutarch (ca. 50-ca. 120 A.D.) was a secular Greek historian and philosopher. Because he lived so close to the time of the New Testament, his writings are another useful source for understanding the meanings of Greek words around the time of the New Testament. But Cervin rejects three examples of *kephalē* meaning "authority over" in Plutarch because he says they may have been a translation from Latin.

Regarding two examples in Plutarch, *Cicero* 14.4, where *head* is used as a metaphor for the Roman emperor, Cervin admits that they refer to a "leader," but objects that the examples are illegitimate primarily because[8] "Cataline was speaking *in Latin*, not Greek . . . and it is equally possible that Plutarch translated the Latin rather literally for the sake of the 'riddle.' If this were so, then this use of *head* for 'leader' is really a Latin metaphor, and not a Greek one. . . . These examples are therefore illegitimate" (p. 102).

Then regarding Plutarch, *Galba*, 4.3, he says, "Galba was a Roman, not a Greek, and that this passage, like the preceding, may have been influenced by Latin. Ziegler provides no known source material for this passage in Plutarch. This example is therefore dubious" (p. 103).

But in response we must remember that Plutarch wrote not in Latin but in Greek, and that Plutarch certainly thought himself to be writing Greek that was understandable to his readers. Whether or not the text was based on some Latin source material does not provide legitimate grounds for rejecting these examples.

5. Rejection of Patristic Evidence

Cervin then rejects any instances of *head* meaning "authority" from the period immediately after that of the Apostolic Fathers, the period of the Patristic writings. He admits that in Lampe's *Patristic Greek Lexicon* there are many citations referring to Christ as the "head of the church," and a few citations where *kephalē* refers to "religious superiors or bishops" (p. 107). These references would seem to be strong evidence that *kephalē* could mean "authority over" or "leader." But Cervin dismisses these examples with the following sentence: "It appears that the use of *head* in Patristic Greek is a technical term referring primarily to Christ, and occasionally to members of the ecclesiastical order" (p. 107).

But what kind of linguistic analysis is Cervin doing here? If the examples of *kephalē* meaning "authority over" are few, he calls them "rare." If the examples are many (as in the Patristic literature), he says it is a "technical term." One wonders what kind of evidence would satisfy him so that *kephalē* does mean "authority over"? He concludes, "Grudem's citation of Lampe is misleading" (p. 107), but by what kind of logic do examples that support a case become "misleading"? It is not clear to me how he can reason that instances of *kephalē* where it refers to Christ or to church officers in authority over the church do not show that *kephalē* can mean "leader" or "authority over."

6. Rejection of New Testament Lexicons

In addition to dismissing without examination, or explaining away, the instances of *kephalē* meaning "authority over" from the New Testament, the Septuagint, the Apostolic Fathers, Plutarch, and the Patristic writers, Cervin also dismisses evidence from all the lexicons that specialize in the New Testament period and impugns the competence of their authors. He asks,

> If "leader" is a *common* understanding of *kephalē*, as Grudem claims, then why is it apparently never so listed in any Greek lexicon outside the purview of the NT? I offer several possible reasons, not the least of which is *tradition* and a *male-dominant world view*.

As Cervin continues his explanation, he for some reason repeatedly refers to those who write lexicons specializing in the New Testament period as "theologians":

> The expertise of *theologians*[9] is the NT, not Classical, or even Hellenistic Greek, per se. While it may be true that some *theologians* have had a grounding in Classical Greek (especially those of the 19th century), they spend their time pondering the NT, *not* Plato, Herodotus, or Plutarch. . . . Another reason stems from Latin. . . . The Latin word for "head," *caput*, does have the metaphorical meaning of "leader." . . . Thus, for English speaking *theologians*, at least, English, Hebrew, and Latin all share "leader" as a common metaphor for *head*. Thus, the forces of tradition, a male-dominant culture, the identical metaphor in three languages, and a less-than-familiar understanding of the Greek language *as a whole*, could, in my mind, very easily lead *theologians* to assume that the metaphor of "leader" for *head* must be appropriate for Greek as well. (p. 87)

The result of this analysis is that Cervin rejects the judgment of the editors of those lexicons that specialize in the very period of the Greek language for which his article intends to give us a meaning for *kephalē*.

But several objections must be raised against Cervin's evaluation of the value of these lexicons:

(a) The assertion that the authors of New Testament lexicons do not read "Plato, Herodotus, or Plutarch" simply indicates a lack of familiarity with the Bauer-Arndt-Gingrich-Danker lexicon, whose pages are peppered with thousands of references to extra-Biblical authors, frequently including Plato, Herodotus, and Plutarch, as well as many, many others. The primary author of this lexicon, Professor Walter Bauer of Göttingen University, worked for more than thirty years at this task (see *BAGD*, pp. v-vi), during which time he "undertook a systematic search in Greek literature" for "parallels to the language of the New Testament" (*ibid.*). Moises Silva says,

> Bauer was fully sensitive to the need not to isolate the New Testament language from the contemporary speech and thus his work abounds with thousands of invaluable references to secular literature where parallel constructions occur—these references alone make Bauer's *Lexicon* a veritable treasure.[10]

While Cervin cites with approval many specialized lexicons for authors such as Xenophon, Plato, Sophocles, etc. (pp. 86-87), he makes the serious mistake of rejecting the value of Bauer's lexicon. By contrast, Moises Silva says of Bauer's lexicon, "It may be stated categorically that this is the best specialized dictionary available for any ancient literature."[11]

(b) One may wonder if Cervin would follow a similar procedure when attempting to determine the meaning of a Greek word in some other specialized corpus of literature. Would he reject the use of a specialized lexicon for Aristotle, for example, when attempting to determine the meaning of a word in Aristotle, simply because the authors of the lexicon spent more of their time looking at Aristotle's words? And would he call the authors of an Aristotle lexicon "philosophers" (rather than "linguists") because the subject matter about which Aristotle wrote was philosophy? Similarly, would he insist on calling the linguists who wrote a specialty lexicon for Herodotus "historians" (rather than "linguists") because Herodotus wrote about history? The editors of New Testament Greek lexicons (such as *BAGD*) should not be dismissed so easily.

(c) It is not immediately apparent why "tradition and a male-dominant world view" would have any effect on a scholar trying to determine what the New Testament means when it says that God made Christ "the *head* over all things for the church" (Ephesians 1:22), or says that Christ is the "*head* of all rule and authority" (Colossians 2:10). Rather than a male-dominant worldview, the only thing required for someone to see "authority over" in these passages would be an ability to recognize that the first-century authors had a "*Christ-dominant*" worldview and expressed that in their writings.

(d) The fact that *head* can mean "leader" in English, Hebrew, and Latin should not influence a competent team of editors to see that meaning in Greek unless the context required it in various places. The argument must simply be decided on the basis of the actual Greek texts in which such a meaning is claimed to be found—but Cervin does not provide us with any such analysis for the important New Testament texts.

7. Acceptance of Specialized Lexicons Distant from the New Testament Period

It is surprising that Cervin gives extensive weight to lexicons specializing in authors far distant from the New Testament period. Thus, he gives a long list of lexicons that he examined and in which he did not find the meaning "authority over, leader" for *kephalē*. What he does not tell the reader, and what certainly would not be evident to the non-technically trained reader of *Trinity Journal* who sees this long list of titles of Greek lexicons (many with Latin titles), is the *dates* of the authors for whom these specialty lexicons give definitions. But the authors covered by the lexicons (with dates) are as follows (following the order in Cervin's list, pp. 86-87):

Xenophon	4th century B.C.
Plato	5th/4th century B.C.
Thucydides	5th century B.C.
Sophocles	5th century B.C.
Aeschylus	5th century B.C.
Theocritus	3rd century B.C.
Homer	8th century B.C.
Herodotus	5th century B.C.
Polybius	2nd century B.C.
Plotinus	3rd century A.D.
Diodorus Siculus	1st century B.C.

What is proved by such a survey? The impression given the reader is that Cervin has found new evidence, but he has not. Rather, he has only shown my earlier study to be affirmed by these additional lexicons. I searched several of those authors exhaustively for the term *kephalē* in my earlier study, and (with the exception of one citation in Herodotus and one in Plato), I did not find the meaning "authority over" in any of those authors either. But most of them (with the exception of Polybius and Diodorus Siculus) are quite distant from the time of the New Testament—far more distant than the instances in the New Testament, the Septuagint, and the Apostolic Fathers, which Cervin dismisses.

But a further question arises. Why is a lexicon on Plato or Thucydides given more credence than a specialty lexicon in the New Testament period? In his selection of evidence from lexicons, as well as in his admission of examples of *kephalē* as relevant evidence, Cervin places evidence that is *most distant* chronologically on a much higher level than evidence that is chronologically *nearest* to the writings of Paul. He thus fails to carry out the careful synchronic analysis necessary to good lexical research.

8. Conclusion: A Flawed Methodology Producing an Erroneous Conclusion
What is the outcome of this procedure? Cervin by one means or another places all the examples where *kephalē* means "authority over" in special categories: the New Testament texts are "under dispute." The Septuagint is a "translation." Shepherd of Hermas may have been written by a "foreigner." The Patristic writings use *kephalē* as a "technical term." The citations from Plutarch "may have been influenced by Latin." And the New Testament lexicons were influenced by "tradition and a male-dominant world view" as well as "a less-than-familiar understanding of the Greek language *as a whole.*" Thus, by eliminating all the examples where *kephalē* means "authority over" in the New Testament period, Cervin is enabled to conclude that *kephalē* did not mean "authority over" "until the Byzantine or Medieval period" (p. 112). Yet we must keep in mind that he can do this only by the incorrect linguistic method of deciding that all the relevant texts from the second century B.C. to several centuries after the New Testament do not count as evidence. It seems fair to conclude that Cervin's article is fundamentally flawed at the outset in its methodology, a methodology that wrongly excludes the most relevant data for this investigation and thereby leads him to an erroneous conclusion. On this basis alone, we must reject Cervin's claim that *kephalē* did not mean "authority over" at the time of the New Testament.

We can now examine Cervin's analysis of specific texts in more detail.

B. The Claim that Kephalē May Mean "Source" in Some Texts

1. Herodotus 4.91.
Cervin does not claim that the meaning "source" is common for *kephalē*, but he thinks that it occurs at least once where it clearly takes that sense:

> Can *kephalē* denote "source"? The answer is *yes*, in Herodotus 4.91; *perhaps*, in the *Orphic Fragment* and elsewhere (in Artemidorus Daldianus, *T. Reuben* [no. 17], and in Philo [nos. 21-22]). Is the meaning "source" common? Hardly! It is quite rare. (p. 112)

But are Cervin's arguments convincing concerning the one clear example of the meaning "source," which he finds in Herodotus 4.91? Cervin says that "Grudem . . . has failed to comprehend Herodotus" (p. 89), and then he goes on to quote the Herodotus passage at length, showing that "in context, it is clear that Herodotus is discussing the 'source' (*pēgai*) of the Tearus River. . . . The context of this passage should make it abundantly clear that Herodotus is using *kephalai* as a synonym of *pēgai*, referring to the source of the Tearus" (p. 90).

But it is unclear from this how Cervin has said anything different from what I said in my first article when I said that "someone speaking of the 'heads' of a river is speaking of the many 'ends' of a river where tributaries begin to flow toward the main stream" (p. 44), and when I cited the Liddell-Scott reference to *kephalē* as "the source of a river," but pointed out that they only said that it had that meaning "in the plural." I agree completely that *kephalai* (plural) in this statement by Herodotus does refer to the sources of the Tearus River. But Cervin has said nothing in answer to my analysis of this statement, where I suggest that the quotation uses "head" in a commonly accepted sense, namely, "beginning point, furthest extremity, end point," and that the quotation does not show that *kephalē* could *mean* "source" in any general sense. In fact, the only "sources" that are called by the term *kephalē* are those that are also at the geographical or physical "end point" of something. This explains why the "mouth" of a river (the other *end point*) can equally well be called the *head* (*kephalē*) of a river. This fact would not make sense at all if *kephalē* meant "source" generally, but it does make sense if *kephalē* means "end point" generally. Cervin has failed to address this understanding of *kephalē* as an alternative explanation to the general sense "source."

Moreover, it should be noted that Liddell-Scott itself agrees with my analysis of the

Herodotus quotation. The overall structure of the *kephalē* article in Liddell-Scott is as follows (I have reproduced the outline structure exactly as it is in Liddell-Scott-Jones):

I.

1. Head of Man or Beast
   a. Down over the head
   b. On the head
   c. From head to foot
   d. Head foremost
2. As the noblest part, periphrastically for the whole person
3. Life
4. In imprecations, on my head be it!

II.

1. Of things, extremity
   a. In Botany
   b. In Anatomy
   c. Generally, top, brim of a vessel . . . *coping* of a wall . . . *capital* of a column
   d. In plural, *source* of a river, Herodotus 4.91 (but singular, *mouth*; generally, *source, origin, Orphic Fragments* 21a; starting point [examples: the head of time; the head of a month])
   e. *Extremity* of a plot of land

III. *Bust* of Homer

IV. Wig, head dress

V. Metaphorically

1. The *pièce de résistance*
2. Crown, completion
3. *Sum, total*
4. *Band* of men
5. Astronomy, "head of the world"

This outline indicates that the definition "source" (II.d.) was never intended by Liddell-Scott to be taken as a general definition applied to all sorts of "sources," but they were simply indicating that the general category "Of things, extremity" was illustrated by the fact that both the beginning point and end point (the source and the mouth) of a river could be referred to with the term *kephalē*.[12]

Neither Cervin nor Liddell-Scott give any citations where *kephalē* is applied to a person and clearly means "source."

2. Orphic Fragments 21a.

This text by an unknown author from the fifth century B.C. or earlier was analyzed at some length in my earlier article (see pp. 45-46). The text reads, "Zeus the head, Zeus the middle, Zeus from whom all things are perfected."

Cervin concludes that several different meanings are possible here and no clear decision can be made:

> Grudem's understanding of "beginning" for this fragment is quite valid. However, the understanding of "source" is also quite valid. . . . Zeus as the "head/beginning/source/ origin/ cause" are all plausible readings. This fragment contains a series of epithets of Zeus. Otherwise, there is really no context which can be appealed to in order to settle which meaning(s) were intended by the author. (p. 91)

At this point I concur with Cervin's analysis and simply note that the ambiguity of the text makes it illegitimate to use it as a clear example of *kephalē* meaning "source."

3. Other Possible Examples of the Meaning "Source"

Cervin briefly analyzes a few other texts that have been cited by Philip Payne[13] as examples of the meaning "source." These texts are Philo, *Preliminary Studies* 61; Philo, *On Rewards and Punishments*, 125; and six instances in Artemidorus Daldianus, *Onirocriticon* (Cervin, pp. 92-94). But Cervin does not see any of these as certain examples of the meaning "source," for he simply concludes that *kephalē* "*perhaps*" has this sense in some of those passages (he is doubtful about a number of the passages Payne cites).[14] I will discuss these passages more fully below in the section on Philip Payne's article.[15]

C. The Claim that "Kephalē" Does Not Mean "Authority Over"

After analyzing the forty-nine texts that I had categorized with the meaning "Person of superior authority or rank, or 'ruler,' 'ruling part'" (pp. 51-58), Cervin summarized his conclusions as follows:

> Of Grudem's 49 examples, the 12 of the New Testament are illegitimate as evidence on the grounds that one cannot logically assume what one intends to prove. This leaves 37 examples, only four of which are clear and unambiguous examples of *kephalē* meaning "leader" (examples 8, 10, 14, 30). Eleven examples are dubious, questionable or ambiguous (4, 5, 6, 7, 11, 12, 13, 23, 26, 36, 37); twelve examples are false (1, 3, 9, 15, 17, 18, 19, 20, 21, 22, 28, 29); seven other examples are illegitimate (24, 25, 27, 31, 32, 33, 34); two examples do not exist (2 and 16); and one example (35) cannot be decided. Of the four clear examples, three are from the LXX and one is from the Shepherd of Hermas, and it is very likely that all four of these are imported, not native, metaphors. (p. 111)

In what follows I shall look again at the texts involved and ask whether Cervin's evaluation of these texts is convincing.

1. Twelve New Testament Examples That Cervin Considers Illegitimate

First, he says that the twelve New Testament examples "are illegitimate as evidence on the grounds that one cannot logically assume what one intends to prove" (p. 111). But as I argued above, Cervin commits a major linguistic error when he fails to examine these uses in context, for they are the examples closest in use of language to the texts in question. To argue for the meaning "authority over" from the context of these texts (as I did in my previous article, on pp. 56-58) is not to "assume" what one intends to prove, but it is to *argue* for it by *giving reasons and evidence*. In the course of the discussion between Cervin and me, one wonders if the person who has "assumed what he intends to prove" might not rather be the one who dismissed twelve New Testament examples without examining them at all, rather than the one who examined each of them in context and gave reasons why the meaning "authority over" seemed appropriate.

Without repeating the earlier arguments from my first article, I will simply list those twelve examples here with their original enumeration. (Some of these texts are discussed later in this article, in response to the suggestions by other scholars that the meaning "source" might be appropriate in some cases.)

(38-42) 1 Corinthians 11:3: "But I want you to understand that the *head* of every man is Christ, the *head* of a woman is her husband, and the *head* of Christ is God. Any man who prays or prophesies with his head covered dishonors his *head*, but any woman who prays or prophesies with her head unveiled dishonors her *head*."

(43) Ephesians 1:22: "He has put all things under his feet and has made him the *head* over all things for the church."

(44) Ephesians 4:15(-16): "We are to grow up in every way into him who is the *head*, into Christ, from whom the whole body, joined and knit together by every joint with which it is supplied, when each part is working properly, makes bodily growth and upbuilds itself in love."

(45-46) Ephesians 5:22-24: "Wives, be subject to your husbands, as to the Lord. For the husband is the *head* of the wife as Christ is the *head* of the church, his body, and is himself its Savior. As the church is subject to Christ, so let wives also be subject in everything to their husbands."

(47) Colossians 1:18: "He is the *head* of the body, the church."

(48) Colossians 2:10: "And you have come to fullness of life in him, who is the *head* of all rule and authority."

(49) Colossians 2:18-19: "Let no one disqualify you, insisting on self-abasement and worship of angels, taking his stand on visions, puffed up without reason by his sensuous mind, and not holding fast to the *Head*, from whom the whole body, nourished and knit together through its joints and ligaments, grows with a growth that is from God."

Although the sense "authority over, leader" is clear in most of these texts, it is appropriate at this point to discuss Ephesians 4:15 and Colossians 2:19. Some writers (though not Cervin, since he does not examine New Testament verses) have said that the meaning "source" fits well in Ephesians 4:15 (since "bodily growth" is said to come from the "head") and in Colossians 2:19 (since the body is said to be "nourished" and "joined together" from the head, and thereby to receive growth from the head).

Certainly it is correct to note that the idea of nourishment and therefore growth coming from the head is present in these verses. The reason for such a description is not hard to discover: it is an evident fact of nature that we take in food through the mouth and therefore nourishment for the body comes "from" the head. So when Paul has already called Christ the "head" of the body, which is the church, it would be natural for him to say that we must hold fast to Him and that our nourishment and growth come from Him.

But do these verses show that *kephalē* could mean "source"? Not exactly, because in these cases the *function* of the head being the source of nourishment is simply more prominent. The metaphorical meaning "source" has not attached to the word *kephalē* sufficiently that this sense would be clear from the use of the word alone apart from the presence of this larger metaphor. That is, we could not substitute "source" in these verses and make any sense, for Colossians 2:19 would say, "Not holding fast to the *source*, from whom the whole body, nourished and knit together . . .," and Ephesians 4:15 would speak of "the *source* . . . from whom the whole body . . . makes bodily growth." But these are unintelligible statements. We need the actual meaning "head" in these verses or else the whole metaphor does not make sense. (This is not the case in several verses where "ruler" or "authority over" will substitute well and the sentence still make sense, as in Ephesians 1:22, "Has made him the *ruler* over all things for the church," or 1 Corinthians 11:3, "the *authority over* every man is Christ," or Colossians 2:10, "who is the *ruler* over all rule and authority.")

The fact that at times in using a head/body metaphor the New Testament calls attention to the idea of nourishment coming from the head to the body is clear in Ephesians 4:15 and Colossians 2:19. But it is not sufficient to show that the word *kephalē* itself *meant* "source." (This is similar to the vine and branches analogy that Jesus uses in John 15:1-8: if we "abide" in the vine, we bring forth much fruit. But that does not mean that the word *vine* means "source of life.")

Moreover, even in these contexts the nuance of "leader" or "authority" is never absent, for the person called "head" (here, Christ) is always the person in leadership over the others in view. In addition, we must recognize the close parallels in content and circumstances of writing in Ephesians and Colossians and realize that five of Paul's seven metaphorical uses of *kephalē* in Ephesians and Colossians have clear connotations of "authority" or "ruler" (Ephesians 1:22; 5:22-24 (twice); Colossians 1:18; 2:10, all cited above), and that these are in contexts quite near to Ephesians 4:15 and Colossians 2:19. When all of these considerations are combined, it seems very unlikely that these two references to Christ as "head" of the body would carry no connotations of authority or rulership over that body. In fact, it is probable that Christ's rule over the church is the primary reason why the "head" metaphor is applied to His relationship to the church at all, and this other connotation (that the head is the place from which food comes to nourish the body) was brought in by Paul as a secondary idea to it.

What shall we conclude about these examples? In the absence of specific objections from Cervin showing why the meaning "authority over" is inappropriate, it seems fair at this point in our discussion still to accept these as legitimate examples where such a sense is at least appropriate—and in several cases it seems to be required.

2. Four Examples That Cervin Considers Clear and Unambiguous

Cervin says there are four examples which are "clear and unambiguous examples of *kephalē* meaning 'leader'" (p. 111). These are the following examples:

(8) 2 Kings (2 Samuel) 22:44: David says to God, "You shall keep me as the *head* of the Gentiles: a people which I knew not served me."

(10) Psalm 18:43: David says to God, "You will make me *head* of the Gentiles: a people whom I knew not served me."

(14) Isaiah 7:9: "The *head* of Samaria is the son of Remaliah."

(30) Hermas *Similitudes* 7.3: The man is told that his family "cannot be punished in any other way than if you, the *head* of the house, be afflicted."

But if Cervin admits these four examples to be "clear and unambiguous" on p. 111, how can he conclude the following: "Does *kephalē* denote 'authority over' or 'leader'? No" (p. 112). This is an unusual kind of reasoning—to say that there are four "clear and unambiguous examples of *kephalē* meaning 'leader'" (p. 111), and then to say that *kephalē* does not denote "authority over" or "leader" at this period in the history of the Greek language (p. 112).

If we look for the basis on which Cervin has rejected the validity of the four "clear and unambiguous" examples, the only explanation given is his statement that "it is very likely that all four of these are imported, not native, metaphors" (p. 111). He also says that in these cases "the metaphor may very well have been influenced from Hebrew in the Septuagint" (p. 112).

But here he has shifted the focus of the investigation and the criteria for evaluating examples without notifying the reader. Whereas the article as a whole purports to be an investigation of whether *kephalē* could mean "authority over" in the New Testament, here he has shifted to asking whether the metaphor is a "native" one in Greek or has been "imported" into Greek under the influence of other languages. That is an interesting question, but it is linguistically an inappropriate criterion to use for determining the meanings of New Testament words. In fact, New Testament Greek *is* strongly influenced by the language of the Septuagint, and the Septuagint *is* certainly influenced to some degree by the Hebrew Old Testament. Moreover, the Greek language as a whole at the time of the New Testament had many words that had been influenced by other languages at that time (especially Latin), but words that were nonetheless ordinary, understandable Greek words in the vocabulary of everyday speakers. Cervin seems to be assuming that words can have no legitimate meanings that have come by the influence of other languages—certainly a false linguistic principle.

The question should rather be, "Was this an understandable meaning to ordinary readers at the time of the New Testament?" The clear New Testament examples cited above (which Cervin fails to examine) and the fact that these four other examples are from the literature *closest* to the New Testament in time and subject matter (see above) both give strong evidence that this was an understandable meaning for first-century readers. Cervin's introduction of the question of whether this is an "imported" metaphor (influenced by another language) or whether it is "native" (dating from the early history of the language) simply muddies the water here and skews his final conclusion.[16]

There is one further puzzling factor in Cervin's summary of his survey of instances of *kephalē*. Though in the summary he only mentions four "clear and unambiguous examples" of *kephalē* meaning "leader," this total does not include the examples from the article by Joseph Fitzmyer that Cervin discussed on pages 108-111. In that discussion Cervin admitted the meaning "leader" in some other contexts.

(1) In Jeremiah 31:7 (LXX 38:7) we read, "Rejoice and shout over the *head* of the nations." Cervin says about this statement, "Fitzmyer says that the 'notion of supremacy or authority is surely present' in this passage (p. 508). I do not necessarily disagree" (p. 108).

(2) Fitzmyer also gives an example from Josephus, *Jewish War*, 4.261, where Jerusalem is referred to as the "front and *head* of the whole nation." Cervin says, "The notion of 'leader' may be admitted here" (p. 111).

These citations apparently lead Cervin to admit that Paul could have used the word *head* in the sense of "leader" or "authority," for Cervin says,

> Fitzmyer argues that, from his examples (and those of Grudem), "a Hellenistic Jewish writer such as Paul of Tarsus could well have intended that *kephalē* in 1 Corinthians 11:3 be understood as 'head' in the sense of authority or supremacy over someone else" (p. 510). This may be so (p. 111-112).

But this statement seems to contradict directly his statement two paragraphs later where he says,

> Does *kephalē* denote "authority over" or "leader"? No. . . . The metaphor "leader" or *head* is alien to the Greek language until the Byzantine or medieval period. (p. 112)

Moreover, Cervin goes on to say, "What then does Paul mean by his use of *head* in his letters? He does not mean 'authority over,' as the traditionalists assert" (p. 112).

It is hard to understand how this analysis can be internally consistent. On the one hand Cervin admits that it "may be so" that Paul used the word *kephalē* in the sense of "authority or supremacy over someone else" (p. 112), and he cites several instances of literature close to Paul in which he admits the meaning "leader" or "authority over." On the other hand he says that *kephalē* does not take this meaning until the Byzantine period. Then he asserts (without examining any text in Paul) that Paul does not mean "authority over" when he uses the word *kephalē*. Such an argument gives at least the appearance of internal contradiction—and perhaps the reality.

3. Eleven Examples That Cervin Considers "Dubious, Questionable, or Ambiguous"

In this category Cervin puts eleven examples that he thinks are unpersuasive because of various factors that make them "dubious, questionable, or ambiguous" (p. 111). Here he lists the following passages:[17] (4) Judges 10:18; (5) Judges 11:8; (6) Judges 11:9; (7) Judges 11:11; (11) Isaiah 7:8a; (12) Isaiah 7:8b; (13) Isaiah 7:9a; (23) Plutarch 2.1.3; (26) Plutarch 4.3; (36) Libanius, *Oration* 20.3.15; (37) *Greek Anthology* 8.19.

Several of these examples Cervin dismisses because of the existence of a variant reading in the text. These are the following:

(4) Judges 10:18 (Alexandrinus): "And the people, the leaders of Gilead, said to one another 'Who is the man that will begin to fight against the Ammonites? He shall be *head* over all the inhabitants of Gilead.'"

(5) Judges 11:8 (Alexandrinus): "And the elders of Gilead said to Jephthah, 'That is why we have turned to you now, that you may go with us and fight with the Ammonites, and be our *head* over all the inhabitants of Gilead.'"

(6) Judges 11:9 (Alexandrinus): "Jephthah said to the elders of Gilead, 'If you bring me home again to fight with the Ammonites, and the Lord gives them over to me, I will be your *head*.'"

(12) Isaiah 7:8b (Sinaiticus omits): "The *head* of Damascus is Rezin" [Rezin is the king who rules over Damascus].

Now the question is, Are these examples valid evidence for the use of *kephalē* to mean "leader"? Cervin calls the examples "dubious, due to the presence of the variant readings" (p. 96). In response, the following points may be noted:

(1) These are not obscure variants, but three are from Alexandrinus, one of the three greatest ancient manuscripts of the Septuagint, and one is omitted only in Sinaiticus among the major manuscripts.

(2) The existence of a variant reading does make an example less weighty as evidence, but does not make the example entirely "dubious" as Cervin would have us believe, for the lexicons are full of examples of citations from texts where variant readings are found. The existence of these examples still indicates that *some* people in the ancient world (those who wrote and used these texts of the Septuagint, for example) thought that *kephalē* was a good word to mean "leader" metaphorically—and it was to show this fact that I cited these texts.

(3) If we were to rule out all texts with variant readings in discussions of the meaning of *kephalē* then we would have to exclude from discussion *Orphic Fragments* 21a ("Zeus the head . . ."), a text that those who claim the meaning "source" for *kephalē* cite with great frequency.[18]

(4) A better linguistic procedure than dismissing texts with variants (as Cervin would have us do) would simply be to do what I did in my original article: quote these texts as evidence and note the existence of a variant reading in each text. This would show what needs to be shown—that the examples are not as strong as if there were no variant, but that they are still valid examples and appropriate to use as additional evidence that some people in the ancient world thought that *kephalē* could be used metaphorically to mean "leader" or "authority."[19]

Next in this category of "dubious, questionable, or ambiguous" readings Cervin puts the following two items:

(11) Isaiah 7:8a: "For the *head* of Syria is Damascus."
(13) Isaiah 7:9a: "And the *head* of Ephraim is Samaria."

Cervin rejects these examples because they "refer to capital cities, not to people" (p. 97). This fact is certainly true, as I pointed out in my original article (p. 55). And because of that, we must recognize that these examples are not exactly parallel to the case where a *person* is called *kephalē* in the sense of "leader" or "ruler." Nonetheless, the idea of authority or rule is still prominent in such a reference to capital cities. Moreover, the connection between this "head" metaphor used of capital cities and its use to refer to persons is made quite explicit in a more full quotation of the context:

> For the *head* of Syria is Damascus, and the *head* of Damascus is Rezin. . . . And the *head* of Ephraim is Samaria, and the *head* of Samaria is the son of Remaliah. (Isaiah 7:8-9)

In both cases the mention of a capital city is followed by the mention of the king who rules in that city, thus making the connection between the "head" city and the "head" of the government twice in two succeeding sentences. Far from being dubious, these examples seem to be very strong and carry an unquestionable nuance of authority connected with the word *kephalē*.

Moreover, it is hard to understand what principle Cervin used to reject these examples where *kephalē* refers to a capital city and not to a person, but then to accept the meaning "source" for *kephalē* in Herodotus 4.91 (pp. 89-90). In that quotation *kephalai* refers to the "sources" of a river, items that are *entirely* non-personal and have no connection to any context where the metaphor is applied to a person as a "source" as well. If Cervin is to accept this Herodotus quotation (which he in fact claims as his *single certain example of the meaning "source"* [p. 112]), then consistent methodology would seem to require him to accept much more readily the examples from Isaiah 7:8-9 that speak of capital cities as "heads" in close proximity to the mention of the reigning kings in those cities as "heads."

The next text Cervin rejects in this category is:

(7) Judges 11:11: "So Jephthah went with the elders of Gilead, and all the people made him *head* and leader over them."

Cervin says that the presence of the phrase "as a leader" or "as a ruler" in the Septuagint following the word "head" is "sufficient to clarify the metaphor" (p. 96). I certainly agree that this statement does "clarify the metaphor" and show that the person designated "head" in this text was clearly the leader or ruler over the people. But then in the very next sentence Cervin simply asserts, "This example is also of questionable value" (p. 96). He gives no evidence or reason to support this statement, so there is really nothing to respond to except to say that this is a clear and unambiguous use of *kephalē* in the sense of "leader" or "authority over," and the mere assertion by Cervin that the example is of "questionable value" with no supporting argument to that effect does not make it of "questionable value."

The next example Cervin rejects as ambiguous is:

(23) Plutarch, *Pelopidas* 2.1.3: In an army, "The light-armed troops are like the hands, the cavalry like the feet, the line of men-at-arms itself like chest and breastplate, and the general is like the *head*."

Here Cervin says, "Plutarch is using the human body as a simile for the army. This is obvious in context, which Grudem again fails to provide[20]. . . . Plutarch does not call the general the 'head of the army'; he is merely employing a simile. This example is ambiguous at best, and may thus be dispensed with" (p. 101).

In response, Cervin is correct to point out that this is not a metaphorical use of "head" in which the general is called the "head of the army" but is indeed a simile in which Plutarch says, "The general is *like* the head." It is indeed a helpful distinction to point out these similes and put them in a separate category, for, while they may be helpful in clarifying the use of a related metaphor, they are not precisely parallel. But I would not agree that the example therefore may "be dispensed with," as Cervin says, for it is of some value in understanding the metaphor, but precision of analysis would be better served by putting it in a distinct category. I appreciate Mr. Cervin's suggestion at this point.

In the next quotation from Plutarch Cervin has a double criticism:

(26) Plutarch, *Galba* 4.3: "Vindex . . . wrote to Galba inviting him to assume the imperial power, and thus to serve what was a vigorous body in need of a *head*."

First Cervin says that "Plutarch is using the body as a simile. He is not calling Galba 'the head'" (p. 102). Yet the usage is a metaphor, not a simile, despite Cervin's assertion. (A simile explicitly compares things essentially unlike each other by using comparative words like *like* and *as*. A metaphor implicitly compares things essentially unlike each other without using comparative words.) Vindex does not say that Galba should "act like a head" to something that acts like a body, but should become "head" to a body that is seeking one. It is an extended metaphor, but it is nonetheless a metaphor in which the leader of a government is called the "head" of a body.

Cervin's other criticism is that "Galba was a Roman, not a Greek, and that this passage, like the preceding, may have been influenced by Latin. Ziegler provides no known source material for this passage in Plutarch. This example is therefore dubious" (p. 103).

But this objection is simply dismissing the example on the basis of speculation without supporting evidence. To say that a passage "may have been influenced by Latin" even though no one has found any Latin source material for it hardly constitutes a persuasive objection to its use and certainly does not provide adequate grounds for classifying it as "dubious."

Moreover, Plutarch is writing not in Latin but in Greek, and indeed in Greek that secular Greek-speaking people would find understandable. The example remains valid.

The last two examples Cervin puts in this category are the following:

(36) Libanius, *Oration* 20.3.15 (fourth century A.D.): People who derided government authorities are said to have "heaped on their own *heads* insults."

(37) *Greek Anthology* 8.19 (Epigram of Gregory of Nazianzus, fourth century A.D.): Gregory is called the "*head* of a wife and three children."

Cervin points out that both of these quotations are quite late, being written about "300 years after Paul" (p. 106). I agree with Cervin on this point and think that it is best not to use these late quotations as evidence for the New Testament meaning of *kephalē*. I included them in my original survey for the sake of completeness because these authors were part of the *Thesaurus Linguae Graecae* project's "Basic Text Package, Tape A," which I obtained for the original search. But it would have been better to exclude them from my examination, since they are so late.

In conclusion to this section, of the eleven examples Cervin says are "dubious, questionable, or ambiguous," eight remain legitimate examples of *kephalē* meaning "authority over" or "leader," one is a simile (the general of an army is like the head of a body) and gives supportive but not direct evidence, and two are too late to be used as valid evidence and must be rejected.

4. *Twelve Examples That Cervin Considers False*

Cervin considers twelve of my citations "false" examples of the use of *kephalē* to mean "authority over" or "ruler." In my original article these were examples 1, 3, 9, 15, 17, 18, 19, 20, 21, 22, 28, and 29. I will examine these in order in the following discussion.

(1) Herodotus 7.148: In a statement warning the Argives to protect those with full citizenship from attack and thus the remainder of the population will be protected: the Delphic Oracle says, "guarding your head from the blow; and the head shall shelter the body."

Cervin says, "*Head* here is literal—as long as one's head is safe, i.e., as long as one's brains are not splattered on the ground, one will continue to live. In hand-to-hand combat, each soldier protects *himself*, not his commanding officer!" (p. 95). Cervin therefore says this is a false example of *kephalē* meaning "leader."

However, Cervin's explanation is doubtful, for the Delphic Oracle is not speaking in the plural ("guarding your *heads* from blows") to all the individual soldiers in the Argive army, but is speaking to the tribe of the Argives as a whole, telling them to guard their "head" from the blow. Nor is Cervin correct in saying that protecting one's head prevents death, for in combat a spear thrust through the body will also be fatal. So Cervin's explanation is not persuasive. Much more likely is the explanation given by the editor in a footnote to the Loeb Classical Library edition of Herodotus: *head* means "those with full citizenship, the nucleus of the population; *sōma* being the remainder" (p. 456, note 2).

The statement of the Delphic Oracle is of course couched in metaphor, but the metaphor seems clear enough to count this as a legitimate example. Nonetheless, since the idea of rule or authority is not explicitly there in the context (though full citizens do have governing authority), it would seem better to classify this as a "possible" example of *kephalē* meaning "authority over" or "leader" rather than a certain one. Yet we can hardly count it a "false" example.

The next example is from Plato, *Timaeus* 44D. Here I will quote in full the original statement used in my first article:

(3) Although Plato does not use the word *kephalē* explicitly to refer to a human ruler or leader, he does say (in the text quoted earlier), that "the head . . . is the most divine part and the one that reigns over all the parts within us" (*Timaeus* 44D). This sentence does speak of the head as the ruling part of the body and therefore indicates that a metaphor that spoke of the leader or ruler of a group of people as its "head" would not have been unintelligible to Plato or his hearers.

Cervin says, "There is no political, social, or military metaphor here; rather, Plato views the head as the preeminent part of the human body, 'the most divine part,' which controls the body's movements. Understanding this metaphor of Plato's will be significant for several examples to come" (p. 95).

It is hard to see why Cervin has called this a "false" example. Since it is explicitly a statement about the head as the ruling part of the body (the Greek text says that it rules, *despoteō*, over all the parts within us), I classified it together in the general category, "person of superior authority or rank, or 'ruler,' 'ruling part'" (see category description on my p. 51). Several of my examples fit this last part of my original category, "ruling part." But I now realize that it would have been more precise to separate these examples into a distinct category in which the "ruling part" of the human body is both specifically said to rule the body and also called the "head," as in this example from Plato. (I specified this in my description of Plato's statement but did not count it in a separate category in my enumeration.)

Nonetheless, the example should not simply be dismissed as "false," for it does show clearly that a metaphor that spoke of a leader or ruler as a "head" would very likely have been understandable to native Greek speakers from a time several centuries before the Apostle Paul wrote.

Four other examples from my original survey should also be included here because they show that the Jewish writer Philo and the Roman historian Plutarch also recognized that the head was the ruling or governing center in the human body. These are as follows:

(18) Philo, *On Dreams* 2.207: "'Head' we interpret allegorically to mean the ruling (*hēgemona*) part of the soul."

(20) Philo, *Moses* 2.82: "The mind is head and ruler (*hēgemonikon*) of the sense-faculty in us."

(28-29) Plutarch, *Table Talk* 6.7 (692.E.1): "We affectionately call a person 'soul' or 'head' from his ruling parts." Here the metaphor of the head ruling the body is clear, as is the fact that the head controls the body in *Table Talk* 3.1 (647.C): "For pure wine, when it attacks the head and severs the body from the control of the mind, distresses a man."

My only objection to Cervin's comments on these passages (in addition to his general categorization of them as "false" examples) is at example 28, where Plutarch says, "We affectionately call a person 'soul' or '*head*' from his *ruling parts* (Greek *tōn kuriotatōn*)." Cervin translates this, "From his *principal* parts," but surely the word *kuriotatōn* (a superlative form of the adjective *kurios*) is much more likely to take the sense "having power or authority over" (Liddell-Scott, p. 1013) here than the sense "important, principal" (*ibid.*), since Plutarch speaks elsewhere of a "head" in a ruling function (see my examples 23, 24, 25, 26, 27, 29). Moreover, the translation "principal parts" does not fit the context as well because Plutarch also gives this as an explanation why people would call an individual "soul" (Greek *psychē*) as well as "head," and, though both "soul" and "head" could be thought to rule or govern the other parts of the body, the soul would not be thought of us as the most prominent or principal part of a human being. Finally, the immediate context shows that Plutarch is making a comparison with the part of the wine that gives its power: he explains that when the lees are filtered out of wine, "some substance that constitutes the edge and power (Greek *kratos*, 'strength') of the wine is removed and lost in the process of filtering. . . . The ancients even went so far as to call wine 'lees,' *just as* we affectionately call a person 'soul' or 'head' from his ruling parts." In each case, the metaphor is drawn not from the "principal" part of the thing named as much as from the dominating or strongest part of the thing named.

(9) 3 Kings (1 Kings) 8:1 (Alexandrinus): "Then Solomon assembled the elders of Israel and all the *heads* of the tribes."[21]

Cervin says that this statement "does not even have anything to do with 'leaders.' The word 'heads' is used of the tops of rods or staffs! This example must be rejected also" (p. 97).[22]

But Cervin's interpretation is hardly persuasive. It would make the sentence say, "Then King Solomon assembled all the elders of Israel with all the *tops* that had been raised up of the staffs of the fathers of the children of Israel." Did the Septuagint translators really think that Solomon had called together all the elders and all the tops of their staffs? Cervin fails to understand that "staff" here in the Septuagint (*rhabdos*) is being used in the sense of "staff of office" (see Psalm 44 [45]:7; 109 [110]:2; Liddell-Scott, p. 1562), and represents the "tribes" of Israel, similar to the way the Hebrew word here (*matteh*, "staff") can mean "tribe" (so Francis Brown, S. R. Driver, and Charles Briggs, eds., *A Hebrew and English Lexicon of the Old Testament* [Oxford: Clarendon Press, (1907) 1978], p. 641). The LXX here simply means that Moses assembled the elders "with the *heads* that had been raised up of the tribes of the fathers of the children of Israel." The heads of these tribes are of course the leaders of the tribes.

This text, therefore, is a legitimate one, and the "heads" of the tribes refers to the rulers or leaders of those tribes of Israel.

(15) Isaiah 9:13 (14): "And the Lord took away from Israel *head* and tail, great and small in one day, the elder and those who marvel at the people."

Cervin says, "Isaiah is using a 'head-tail' metaphor (hence the translation of *kephalē*), not an authority metaphor" (p. 98).

But Cervin here introduces a false dichotomy. We do not need to choose between a "head-tail" metaphor and an "authority metaphor," because a "head-tail" metaphor simply functions as a more full metaphor for "leader-follower." The head is a metaphor for the one who leads or rules, and the tail is a metaphor for the one who follows or obeys. In this text the leaders and rulers of the people are referred to as the "head," and the example is legitimate.

(17) Testament of Reuben 2:2: "The seven spirits of deceit are the 'heads' or 'leaders' of the works of innovation (or 'rebellion')."

Cervin says, "There is nothing in this text which is remotely political, social, or military, and so the translation of 'leader' which Grudem advocates is not justified. In fact, the notion 'source' is much more appropriate to the context, the seven spirits being the 'source' of rebellion. This example must be rejected" (p. 99).

However, Cervin fails to recognize that demonic spirits can certainly be thought of as leaders or rulers over works of "rebellion" (or "innovation," Greek *neōterismos*). The context is one of spiritual rulership or authority. This makes the translation "leader" (which I initially quoted from the translation of R. H. Charles[23]) a very good possibility. However, I agree that other senses such as "beginning" or even "source" would also fit in this context, and the context is not decisive enough to tell one way or another. Therefore this example should be reclassified as one in which the meaning "authority over" is possible but not required.

(19) Philo, *Moses* 2.30: "As the *head* is the ruling place in the living body, so Ptolemy [Ptolemy Philadelphos] became among kings."

Cervin does not think that "head" means "ruler" here because "Philo says that Philadelphos is the head of kings, not in the sense of ruling them, but as the *preeminent* king among the rest. Philadelphos is the *top* of the kings just as the head is the *top* of an animal's body. . . . This example is therefore to be rejected" (p. 100).

While Cervin's explanation at first seems plausible, it does not do justice to the actual words Philo uses. In fact Philo calls the head *to hēgemoneuon . . . tropon*, "the ruling place" in the body—a phrase that Cervin simply skips over and fails to translate in his own rendering of the passage (p. 100). But the adjectival participle *hēgemoneuon* here certainly has the sense of "leading" or "ruling," since the verb *hēgemoneuō* means "lead the way, rule, command" (Liddell-Scott, p. 762).

On the other hand, Cervin says that his suggestion that *head* here is used "as a metaphor of preeminence" is "fully in keeping with the use of *kephalē* as defined in [Liddell-Scott]" (p. 99). However, one searches in vain for such a definition in Liddell-Scott—it simply is not there (see the summary of meanings given in Liddell-Scott on p. 000 above). It would seem a better lexical procedure to stick with previously recognized and well-attested senses for *kephalē* if that is possible in the context in which we find the word than to postulate new meanings that might seem to be possible in a few instances but have not proved themselves convincing to any lexicographers in the hundreds of years in which the Greek language has been studied. Moreover, it seems that it would have been more appropriate for Cervin to notify readers that he was proposing a new meaning previously unrecognized in the lexicons than to say that this meaning "is fully in keeping with the use of *kephalē* as defined in [Liddell-Scott]" (p. 99) when it is simply not there.

(21-22) Philo, *On Rewards and Punishments* 125: "The virtuous one, whether single man or people, will be the head of the human race and all the others will be like the parts of the body which are animated by the powers in and above the head."

Cervin says, "It is fairly clear that 'head' here is the source of life. . . . Whether or not 'head' is taken to mean 'source' in this passage, Philo's simile of the animal and his statement that the head is 'the first and best part' makes it clear that 'preeminence' is Philo's point, not 'authority.' The 'virtuous one' will be preeminent among the human race. These examples must be rejected" (p. 101).

Here Cervin proposes two definitions: "source" and "preeminence," and it is not clear which one he is advocating. If it is "preeminence," then again it must be said that this meaning might possibly be an overlapping nuance that accompanies the "head" metaphor in this context, but it is probably not a necessary sense (it is not previously attested in any Greek lexicon), and it certainly is not the only nuance suggested in the metaphor here.

In fact, the context suggests much more than fame or preeminence—the rest of the human race is dependent in some way on this virtuous person or people. More explicit understanding of the meaning of "head" here is found when we recognize the larger context of Philo's discussion. The entire treatise *On Rewards and Punishments* is a discussion of the rewards God promised the people of Israel for obedience and the punishments He promised for disobedience. This particular section begins with an allusion to the fact that the mind of wisdom "was not dragged down tailwards but lifted up to the head" (124), an allusion to the promise in Deuteronomy 28:13 that if the people of Israel would be faithful to God, "the Lord your God will make you the head and not the tail" (compare Deuteronomy 28:44).[24] Then Philo says that "these last words contain an allegory and are figuratively expressed" (125). He then goes on to explain the allegory in the quotation that follows.

For our purposes it is significant that this passage in Deuteronomy 28 contains much about the people of Israel ruling over the nations and having the nations serve them if God exalts them to be the "head" and not the "tail" (see Deuteronomy 28:7, 10; and contrast with verses 43-44). There certainly is an idea of preeminence in this context, but it is preeminence that includes leadership and rule over the nations, and Cervin wrongly attempts to force a distinction between preeminence and leadership in this context.

But is the meaning "source" a better translation of *kephalē* in this context? Certainly the text does say that the rest of the human race will be like the limbs of a body that are animated by the powers "in and above the head." But the verb that I here translate "animated" (Greek *psychoō*) can simply mean "give understanding or wisdom" in Philo (see, for example, *On the Creation* 9; *On the Virtues* 14; *Who Is the Heir*, 185). This makes sense in the context: the virtuous man or people will be exalted by God to be the "head" and will thus be a leader who gives direction and wisdom to the rest of the human race—they will be quickened and directed by the powers and wisdom in this man or nation.

The idea of "source" does not fit the context nearly as well, both because no one would think that the *head* of an animal was the "source" of the entire animal, and because no one would think that a virtuous man exalted to leadership in the human race was the "source" of the human race! In both cases it is the leadership function that is in view when God makes one the "head" and not the "tail."

Given this larger context, it still seems most appropriate to conclude that Philo here uses the expression "head of the human race" to mean "leader of the human race," certainly not "source of the human race" (which would hardly make sense), and very likely not "preeminent one" (at least not preeminent one without leadership or authority in the human race). Cervin is incorrect to reject this example as "false."

What are we to conclude concerning the twelve examples Cervin classified as "false"? Five should be put in a separate category of examples where a person's "head" is said to rule over his or her body (examples 3, 18, 20, 28, 29). Two should be classified as "possible" but not clear or certain examples of *kephalē* meaning "leader" or "authority over" (examples 1, 17). The remaining five (9, 15, 19, 21, 22) remain legitimate examples of the meaning "leader."

5. Seven Examples That Cervin Considers Illegitimate

The first three examples are from Plutarch:

(24-25) Plutarch, *Cicero* 14.4: Catiline says to Cicero, criticizing the Senate as weak and the people as strong, "There are two bodies, one lean and wasted, but with a *head*, and the other headless but strong and large. What am I doing wrong if I myself become a *head* for this?" In saying this, Catiline was threatening to become the head of the people and thus to lead the people in revolt against Cicero. Therefore, "Cicero was all the more alarmed."

(27) Plutarch, *Agis* 2.5: A ruler who follows popular opinions is compared to a serpent whose tail "rebelled against the head" and insisted on leading the body in place of the head. The serpent consequently harmed itself. The implication is that a ruler should be like the "head" of a serpent and thereby lead the people.

Regarding the first two instances, Cervin admits that *kephalē* is "used by Cataline for a *leader* (himself)" (p. 101), but he then goes on to object that these two examples are illegitimate, first of all, because "Cataline's answer was in the form of a 'riddle,' as Plutarch points out" (p. 102). Then Cervin adds, "Secondly, and more importantly, Cataline was speaking *in Latin*, not Greek," and Cervin then provides a parallel passage from Cicero, concerning which he concludes, "It is entirely possible that Plutarch used this passage as source material for his *Life of Cicero*, and it is equally possible that Plutarch translated the Latin rather literally for the sake of the 'riddle.' If this were so, then this use of *head* for 'leader' is really a Latin metaphor, and not a Greek one. . . . These examples are therefore illegitimate" (p. 102).

First, whether the answer was a riddle or not, it is evident that Cicero understood it because he was immediately alarmed. We may assume that Plutarch also expected his readers to understand it.

The objection that this may have been translated from Latin does not make the example an illegitimate one for Greek. Cervin's objection here is similar to his objection to the use of Septuagint examples because the Septuagint was a translation from Hebrew. In both cases the translators were writing to be understood by those into whose language they were making the translation. Certainly it is true here that Plutarch's extensive historical writings are in Greek that would be understandable to Plutarch's readers, and whether or not the text was based on some Latin source material is not nearly as relevant as Cervin would have us think. These remain valid examples of *kephalē* meaning "ruler, authority over"—in this case referring to authority over the Roman Empire itself.

The third example, regarding the serpent whose tail led the head is certainly not a direct metaphor in which *kephalē* means "leader." It is closer to a simile in which Plutarch explains that a leader who is also a follower is like a serpent that follows its tail rather than its head. The example is of some importance to us because the leader is compared to the head of a serpent, but it is better classified as a simile (similar to example 23 [Plutarch, *Pelopidas* 2. 1. 3], above).

The remaining four examples that Cervin classifies as "illegitimate" are from Aquila's Greek translation of the Old Testament. Cervin objects that these are illegitimate "for the simple reason that Aquila's Greek translation of the OT was so slavishly literal that it was incomprehensible to native Greeks! . . . These examples from Aquila must therefore be rejected" (p. 105).

Although Cervin is right to caution us about the use of Aquila, he has greatly overstated the case. Though Aquila's translation was quite woodenly literal so that his grammatical constructions were at times foreign to Greek, his translation is not entirely without linguistic value for us. We must remember that "the Jews, however, held this translation in the highest esteem."[25] Moreover, Aquila himself was a Gentile who was a native Greek speaker long before he learned Hebrew.[26] Nor was he ignorant of the large vocabulary available in the Greek of his time:

> That the crudities of Aquila's style are not due to an insufficient vocabulary is clear from his ready use of words belonging to the classical or the literary type when they appear to him to correspond to the Hebrew more closely than the colloquialisms of the LXX.[27]

One wonders if Cervin's concern to dismiss these examples from Aquila has not led to some overstatement concerning Aquila's translation. An interesting example is seen in the comparison of two sentences. The first comes from the essay, "History of the Septuagint Text" in the preface to the Rahlfs edition, pp. xxxvi:

> Aquila's translation of the Bible must on occasions have proved altogether incomprehensible to non-Jews.

Cervin has apparently read this essay (for he quotes a sentence from a location two pages earlier in the essay), but his statement tells readers not that Aquila's translation "on occasions" was incomprehensible, but that the entire translation was incomprehensible. He says,

> Aquila's Greek translation of the OT was so slavishly literal that it was incomprehensible to native Greeks! (p. 105)

Certainly this is an overstatement, since the translation was used widely for centuries by Greek-speaking Jews.

It seems best to conclude that these examples from Aquila are of some value, though their weight as evidence is limited, both because of Aquila's translation style and because they come somewhat after the time of the New Testament (second century A.D.). It would not be appropriate to call them "illegitimate" examples, as Cervin does.

In conclusion, regarding the seven examples that Cervin calls "illegitimate," one (number 27) is better classified as a simile, and the remaining six should be seen as legitimate, though those from Aquila are less weighty than the others.

6. Two Examples That Cervin Claims Do Not Exist

Mr. Cervin has correctly pointed out that, in my original article, I incorrectly counted two examples where the word "head" was repeated in the English text but in fact the word *kephalē* was not found a second time in the Greek text itself. These two examples were the *second* instance of the word "head" in each of the following quotations:

(2) Herodotus 7. 148. 17: "guarding your *head* from the blow; and the *head* shall shelter the body."

In this example the synonym *karē* is used instead of *kephalē*.

(16) Isaiah 9:14-16: "so the Lord cut off from Israel *head* and tail . . . the elder and honored man is the *head*."

In this sentence the Greek word *kephalē* does not appear a second time.

In writing the original article, I examined all the occurrences in the original Greek text, then listed the English translation for each one, then made a final enumeration of the instances listed. But as I counted, in the two texts mentioned here I had failed to note that *kephalē* only represented one of the two occurrences of the word "head" in the English text. This was simply an unintentional oversight on my part. I am happy to correct this error in tabulation and note here that these two examples should be dropped from my tally.

7. One Example That Cervin Says "Cannot be Decided"
Here Cervin lists the following example:
(35) Theodotion, Judges 10:18: "He will be *head* over all the inhabitants of Gilead."
Cervin says of this, "Citing one verse by Theodotian tells us nothing. . . . The crucial question is how consistent is he in translating *ro'sh* into Greek. . . . Until more is known about Theodotion's translation(s) of *ro'sh*, judgment must be suspended on this example" (p. 105).

This is a puzzling statement. Cervin admits that Theodotion's translation was not as literal as Aquila's, and we know that it was written to be understood by Greek-speaking Jews in the second century A.D.. One wonders on what basis Cervin makes the statement, "Citing one verse by Theodotion tells us nothing." Since Theodotion, like most of the New Testament writers, was a Greek-speaking Jew, citing one verse by Theodotion (second century A.D.) probably tells us more about word usage by the New Testament authors (first century A.D.) than citing one passage in Herodotus (fifth century B.C.), to which Cervin gives so much weight. It is fair to conclude that this remains a legitimate example.

Where does this leave us with regard to the forty-nine examples of *kephalē* referred to in my original article? At this point we have the following tally:

Legitimate examples	36
Possible examples	2
Head as a simile for leader	2
Literal head said to rule over body	5
Illegitimate examples	4 (two very late, two do not exist)

But in addition to these examples, the following should be added from the study by Joseph Fitzmyer that Cervin discusses at the end of his article:[28]

Jeremiah 31:7 (LXX 38:7): "Rejoice and shout over the *head* of the nations."

Deuteronomy 28:12-13: "And you shall lend to many nations, but you shall not borrow. And the Lord will make you the *head*, and not the tail."

Deuteronomy 28:43-45: "The sojourner who is among you shall mount above you higher and higher; and you shall come down lower and lower. He shall lend to you, and you shall not lend to him; he shall be the head, and you shall be the tail. All these curses shall come upon you."

Josephus, *War*, 4.261: Jerusalem is the "head of the whole nation."

These four examples may be added to the thirty-six legitimate examples listed above, bringing that total to forty. In addition, as I explain below,[29] the articles by Payne and the Mickelsens have caused me to think Lamentations 1:5 should also be included here: [of Jerusalem] "Her foes have become the *head*, her enemies prosper." This would bring the total to forty-one.

Moreover, one passage from Philo quoted by Fitzmyer should be noted:
Philo, *The Special Laws* 184: "Nature conferred the sovereignty of the body on the head." This example should be added to the category "literal head ruling over the body," bringing that total to six. So the tally now should be:

Legitimate examples	41
Possible examples	2
Head as a simile for leader	2
Literal head said to rule over body	6
Illegitimate examples	4 (two very late, two do not exist)

D. The Meaning "Preeminent" as Proposed by Cervin

1. Cervin's Proposal

At the end of his article Cervin writes,

> What then does Paul mean by his use of *head* in his letters? He does not mean "authority over," as the traditionalists assert, nor does he mean "source" as the egalitarians assert. I think that he is merely employing a head-body metaphor and that his point is *preeminence*. This is fully in keeping with the normal and "common" usage of the word. Both Plutarch and Philo use *head* in this way and this usage is listed in Liddell-Scott-Jones (with other references). (p. 112)

The problem with this definition is that it is simply not found in Liddell-Scott as Cervin claims. His statement that it is listed there "with other references" is, as far as I can tell, simply false (see Liddell-Scott, p. 945, and the summary of meanings listed in that article that I gave above, p. 433). Moreover, so far as I know, the meaning "preeminent" is not found in any specialty lexicons for any period of the Greek language either (unlike *kephalē* with the meaning "leader, authority over," which is found in many if not all specialty lexicons for the New Testament and Patristic periods). Why then does Cervin suggest this meaning and claim that it is common and is found in Liddell-Scott?

One begins to wonder if there is not a commitment to find *any other* meaning than the meaning "authority over, leader," which gives us the sense—so unpopular in our modern culture—that the "husband is the authority over his wife, as Christ is the authority over the church" (Ephesians 5:23). Just as the Mickelsens in 1979 and 1981, in arguing against the meaning "authority over" for *kephalē* in the New Testament, proposed a new meaning ("source") that no lexicon in history had *ever* proposed in the category of definitions referring to persons, so now Cervin in this most recent article has rejected the meaning "leader, authority over," which is evident in so many texts, and has again proposed a meaning never before seen in any lexicon. Moreover, just as the Mickelsens earlier alleged (without evidence) that their new meaning, "source," was "common" in Greek literature,[30] so now Mr. Cervin has asserted that his new meaning is "fully in keeping with the use of *kephalē* as defined in [Liddell-Scott]" (p. 99). But this meaning is simply not there.

2. The Existence of Overtones in Metaphors

Is it necessary then for us to deny that there is any nuance of "preeminence" (or perhaps "prominence") in the uses of *kephalē*? Certainly not—for one who is in a position of authority often has some prominence as well. In fact, it is the nature of a metaphor to speak of one thing in terms of another with which it has some shared characteristics. Thus, if someone were to call her boss a "drill sergeant," she might be implying that he shares more than one characteristic of a drill sergeant—he might be thought to be not only very demanding but also highly disciplined, uncaring, and even given to barking commands in a loud voice. Part of the strength of a metaphor derives from the fact that there are often multiple nuances associated with it.

Therefore it would not be surprising if, when first-century people referred to someone as "the head," there would be nuances not only of authority but perhaps also of prominence or "preeminence" as well. But the notions of leadership, rule, and authority were so closely connected with the idea of prominence or preeminence in the ancient world that it would probably be impossible to separate them decisively at any point. Moreover, it must be recognized as significant that there are few if any examples where a person is called *kephalē* and the context shows preeminence *without* rule or authority. In the examples we have looked at, those who are called "head" are those with utmost authority in the situation in question—the general of an army, the king of Egypt, the Roman emperor, the father in a family, the bishop in a church (in the patristic examples given by Lampe), the heads of the tribes of Israel, the king of Israel, or (with cities) the capital city of a country.

Moreover, we have the examples of Christ as the head of the church and the head of all universal power and authority. Someone might wish to argue that the notion of "pre-eminence" is an "overtone" in many of these passages in addition to the primary suggestion of "authority" or "leader" or "ruler." That may well be so. But to argue that head means "pre-eminent one" *without any nuance of leadership or authority* seems clearly to fly in the face of an abundance of evidence from both the New Testament and numerous other ancient texts.

Moreover, is not this previously unknown meaning "preeminent" really contradictory to some very important New Testament teaching? The idea of "preeminence" suggests status and importance and honor, and if we were to say that the husband's headship means primarily that he is *preeminent* over his wife, we would almost have to conclude that the husband had greater status and importance and honor than the wife. Yet this is certainly not what the New Testament teaches about male/female relationships—men and women are "joint heirs" of the grace of life (1 Peter 3:7), and are "all one in Christ Jesus" (Galatians 3:28). In arguing for "preeminence," Mr. Cervin is ultimately arguing for a very distasteful male chauvinism that has no place in New Testament teaching or in the Christian church. Not only is this meaning (1) not required by the data and (2) previously unknown to the lexicons, it also (3) gives us a significant theological problem. If accepted, such a meaning would tend to push people toward rejection of Paul's writings on marriage as authoritative for today—a direction that Cervin himself seems to hint at in the last paragraph in his article:

> It might be objected that *preeminence* does not fit the context of 1 Corinthians 11. How can the husband be *preeminent* over his wife? In the context of the male-dominant culture of which Paul was a part, such a usage would not be inappropriate. . . . Just because *we* might have difficulty with a given metaphor does not mean that Paul would have had the same difficulty; it is after all *his* metaphor, not ours. (p. 112)

Personally I refuse to accept for myself any distancing of Paul's metaphor from my own personal convictions. Because these words are *Scripture* I want Paul's metaphor to become *my* metaphor as well, not one with which I have "difficulty," but one I can fully embrace and rejoice in. I can do that with the sense "leader, authority over," because (as I and others have extensively explained elsewhere) the idea of difference in authority is fully consistent with the idea of equality in honor and importance. But I cannot do that so easily with *preeminence*, because it inherently suggests greater status, honor, and importance for the one who is preeminent.

E. Some Inaccurate Representations of My Article

For the sake of completeness and factual accuracy, it is probably appropriate to mention here a few points at which Cervin seems (to me at least) to have represented my original article inaccurately.

First, regarding the use of Greek texts and translations, Cervin says,

> Grudem further states that the Loeb editions were used by him "where available; otherwise, standard texts *and translations were used*" (p. 65, emphasis mine). I find the last phrase of this sentence very disturbing. One *cannot* conduct a word-study of Greek (or *any* foreign language) by using translations! One *must* have the original text! (p. 88)

This statement contains an allegation that I sometimes used translations *without Greek texts*. This is simply a conclusion based on a misreading of my original sentence. I did not say that I used "standard texts or translations" but that I used "standard texts *and* translations." The original printout that I received from the TLG data base was entirely in Greek, and I did not in any case cite a translation without first consulting the Greek text itself.[31]

Second, Cervin says, regarding Liddell-Scott:

> Grudem has demonstrated that he does not really understand the significance of [Liddell-Scott]. Grudem wrongly claims that [Liddell-Scott] "emphasizes classical Greek" (*ibid.*). This is not so. [Liddell-Scott] is the *only* comprehensive Greek-English lexicon of *Ancient* Greek currently available. While [Liddell-Scott] was originally planned to cover only Classical Greek, it currently covers . . . a time span of roughly 1400 years, 800 B.C. to A.D. 600. (p. 86)

In fact, I said the same thing in the earlier part of the same sentence that Cervin quoted. I wrote:

> In fact, Liddell-Scott is the standard lexicon for all of Greek literature from about 700 B.C. to about A.D. 600 with emphasis on classical Greek authors in the seven centuries prior to the New Testament. (p. 47)

One may quibble about the relative emphasis placed on Greek writers prior to the New Testament, but my point was only to say that it is not nearly as detailed a lexicon in the New Testament and early Christian literature as some specialty lexicons like Bauer-Arndt-Gingrich-Danker. I was making this point only to critique the Mickelsens, who (in their 1979 article) quoted *only* Liddell-Scott for the meaning of a New Testament word and failed to inform their readers that their point could not have been supported by any specialty lexicon covering the time of the New Testament.

Finally, Cervin objects to my suggestion that the adjective *kephalaios* more commonly meant "leader" than the noun *kephalē* in the centuries before the New Testament. Cervin objects that "nouns and adjectives are not always used in the same ways" (p. 107). But I did not argue that they always are, only that there are examples that showed a similar meaning in *this* case. Then Cervin says, "Second, Paul did not use the adjective, he used the noun" (p. 107). But I did not claim otherwise. Cervin here simply misses my point, which was that there was a related term that was earlier used in the sense of "authority, leader" but that by the time of the New Testament the noun *kephalē* was quite clearly used in this sense as well.

Where does this leave us? I am grateful that Cervin's article has provided some helpful corrections to my earlier article, but the major point of his article, namely, that *kephalē* cannot mean "authority over, leader," and must rather mean "pre-eminent one," is disproved by his use of improper methodology and several internal inconsistencies in his argument, and it is contradicted by an abundance of evidence. It must therefore be rejected.

III. Response to Other Recent Studies

A. Articles Since 1985

I list here several articles written or published after my 1985 article, especially those that have contributed to the discussion within the evangelical world:

1. Berkeley and Alvera Mickelsen, "What Does *Kephalē* Mean in the New Testament?" in *Women, Authority and the Bible*, ed. Alvera Mickelsen (Downers Grove, IL: InterVarsity Press, 1986), pp. 97-110.
2. Ruth A. Tucker, "Response," in *Women, Authority and the Bible*, ed. Mickelsen, pp. 111-117.
3. Philip B. Payne, "Response," in *Women, Authority and the Bible*, ed. Mickelsen, pp. 118-132.

4. Walter L. Liefeld, "Women, Submission, and Ministry in 1 Corinthians," in *Women, Authority and the Bible*, ed. Mickelsen, pp. 134-154.
5. Gilbert Bilezikian, "A Critical Examination of Wayne Grudem's Treatment of *Kephalē* in Ancient Greek Texts," Appendix to *Beyond Sex Roles*, 2nd ed. (Grand Rapids, MI: Baker Book House, [1986] 1990), pp. 215-252.[32]
6. Catherine Clark Kroeger, "The Classical Concept of *Head* as 'Source,'" Appendix III in *Equal to Serve*, by Gretchen Gaebelein Hull (Old Tappan, NJ: Fleming H. Revell, 1987), pp. 267-283.
7. Gordon D. Fee, *The First Epistle to the Corinthians*, NICNT (Grand Rapids, MI: Eerdmans, 1987), pp. 501-505 [commentary on 1 Corinthians 11:3].
8. Joseph Fitzmyer, "Another Look at *Kephalē* in 1 Corinthians 11:3," *New Testament Studies* 35 (1989), pp. 503-511.
9. Peter Cotterell and Max Turner, *Linguistics and Biblical Interpretation* (Downers Grove, IL: InterVarsity Press, 1989), pp. 141-145.
10. Recent lexicons by Bauer (1988) and Louw-Nida (1988).

B. Analysis of Recent Articles

1. (1986) Berkeley and Alvera Mickelsen, "What Does Kephalē Mean in the New Testament?"[33]

In their 1979 and 1981 articles in *Christianity Today*, Berkeley and Alvera Mickelsen exerted wide influence in the evangelical world by arguing that "head" in the New Testament often meant "source" but never "authority over." I responded to those articles in my earlier study.[34] But in this 1986 article they give further development of what I will call "the Septuagint argument," an argument only briefly used in 1981.

a. "The Septuagint Argument": This is an argument that is also used by Philip Payne[35] (Article 3 above) and by Gordon Fee in his commentary on 1 Corinthians[36] (Article 7 above). It may be summarized this way:

> The Septuagint translators used *kephalē* to translate the Hebrew word *ro'sh* ("head") in a sense of "leader" or "ruler" in only eight out of the 180 cases[37] in which Hebrew *ro'sh* means "leader" or "authority over." In all the other cases they used other words, most commonly *archōn*, "ruler" (109 times). Therefore, since the Septuagint translators had about 180 opportunities to use *kephalē* meaning "leader," and they only did so eight times, it shows that the translators desired to avoid *kephalē* in the sense of "authority" or "leader over."

The Mickelsens, Philip Payne, and Gordon Fee all see this as a significant point. The Mickelsens say it shows that "the Septuagint translators recognized that *kephalē* did not carry the Hebrew meaning of leader, authority or superior rank."[38] Payne says, "When the Old Testament meaning of *ro'sh* was 'leader,' the Septuagint translators realized quite clearly that this would not be conveyed by *kephalē*, so they resorted to some other translation in 171 cases out of 180."[39] Fee says that the Septuagint translators "almost never" used *kephalē* to translate Hebrew *ro'sh* "when 'ruler' was intended, thus indicating that this metaphorical sense is an exceptional usage and not part of the ordinary range of meanings for the Greek word."[40] Several points of response may be made to this argument:

(1) That the Septuagint translators used another word much more commonly to translate *ro'sh* when it meant "leader" is not so significant when we realize that *archōn* was the common word that *literally* meant "leader," whereas *kephalē* only meant "leader" in a metaphorical sense. It is true that the Septuagint translators preferred *archōn* to mean "authority," as I noted in my earlier article (p. 47, n. 17). But I have never claimed, neither has anyone else claimed, that *kephalē* was the *most common* word for "ruler." In fact, the most common word for "ruler," the one that literally meant "ruler," was *archōn*. It is

not at all surprising that in contexts where the Hebrew word for "head" meant "ruler," it was frequently translated by *archōn*. All I have claimed is that *kephalē* could *also* mean "ruler" or "authority" in a metaphorical sense of "head." It is not the most common, but it is a clearly recognizable and clearly understood word in that sense. The fact that a word that *literally* meant "ruler, authority" (*archōn*) should be used much more often than a word that *metaphorically* meant "ruler, authority" (*kephalē*) should not be surprising—it is only surprising that people have made an argument of it at all.

(2) The Mickelsens and the others who have used this Septuagint argument fail to note that these eight examples are many compared to the Septuagintal examples of *kephalē* used to mean "source," of which there are zero. No one who has made this Septuagint argument has mentioned this fact. To use an athletic analogy, if the score at the end of a baseball game is eight to zero, one begins to wonder why anyone would declare the team with zero to be the winner because the team with eight did not score very many runs. Yet that is what the Mickelsens (and Payne, pp. 121-124, and Fee, pp. 502-503) conclude with respect to *kephalē* meaning "authority over"—they just say that the eight examples meaning "authority over" are very few, and fail to tell their readers that their preferred meaning ("source") has zero occurrences in the Septuagint.

(3) Those who make this argument also fail to mention that in Genesis 2:10, when the Hebrew term *ro'sh* means "source" or "beginning" (of rivers), the Septuagint translators used another term, *archē*, "source," "beginning," not *kephalē*, "head."[41]

(4) When those who make this argument from the Septuagint give the number of occurrences of *kephalē* meaning "authority" or "leader" in the LXX as eight, they give a misleadingly low number. The Mickelsens and Payne arrive at their low numbers by dismissing five texts[42] where there is a textual variant (apparently Judges 10:18; 11:8, 9; 1 Kings [LXX 3 Kings] 8:1, and one of the instances in Isaiah 7:8).[43] Yet these "variant readings" are in Codex Alexandrinus, one of the three great ancient manuscripts of the Septuagint.[44]

Moreover, there seems to be an inconsistency on the part of these authors when they dismiss these variant readings but fail to mention that the single text they most strongly appeal to for *kephalē* as "source" (*Orphic Fragments* 21a, "Zeus the *kephalē* . . .") also has *kephalē* only as a variant reading, with *archē* in other manuscripts. In short, there is no good reason not to count these additional five examples of *kephalē* meaning "authority" as well. This gives a total of thirteen in the LXX.

Furthermore, the Mickelsens dismiss three texts where God tells the people He will make them "the *head* and not the tail" with respect to the other nations, or, in punishment, will make *other* nations the "head" and them the "tail" (Deuteronomy 28:13, 44; Isaiah 9:14).[45] They say that "head" here is just used to complete the metaphor: it "would not make sense without the use of head in contrast to tail."[46] But Payne seems right to admit these three examples,[47] since they just extend the metaphor to include *tail* as "follower, one ruled over" as well as using *head* to mean "leader, ruler" (especially in the context of nations who rule other nations).[48] Allowing for a correction on one of the Septuagint instances I earlier counted, I have now adjusted my own count of instances in the Septuagint to sixteen instead of the earlier thirteen.[49]

Those sixteen instances of *kephalē* meaning "authority over" in the Septuagint are the following:

1. Deuteronomy 28:13: [in relationship to other nations] "And the Lord will make you the *head*, and not the tail; and you shall tend upward only, and not downward; if you obey the commandments of the Lord your God, which I command you this day." (Compare with the following passage, where rule and authority are in view.)
2. Deuteronomy 28:44: ["If you do not obey the voice of the Lord your God . . .," verse 15] "The sojourner who is among you shall mount above you higher and higher; and you shall come down lower and lower. He shall lend to you, and you shall not lend to

him; he shall be the *head*, and you shall be the tail. All these curses shall come upon you. . . ."

3. Judges 10:18 (A): "And the people, the leaders of Gilead, said to one another, 'Who is the man that will begin to fight against the Ammonites? He shall be *head* over all the inhabitants of Gilead.'"
4. Judges 11:8 (A): "And the elders of Gilead said to Jephthah, 'That is why we have turned to you now, that you may go with us and fight with the Ammonites, and be our *head* over all the inhabitants of Gilead.'"
5. Judges 11:9 (A): "Jephthah said to the elders of Gilead, 'If you bring me home again to fight with the Ammonites, and the Lord gives them over to me, I will be your *head*.'"
6. Judges 11:11: "So Jephthah went with the elders of Gilead, and all the people made him *head* and leader over them."
7. 2 Kings (2 Samuel) 22:44: David says to God, "You shall keep me as the *head* of the Gentiles: a people which I knew not served me."
8. 3 Kings (1 Kings) 8:1 (A): "Then Solomon assembled the elders of Israel with all the *heads* of the tribes."[50]
9. Psalm 17(18):43: David says to God, "You will make me *head* of the Gentiles: a people whom I knew not served me."
10. Lamentations 1:5: [of Jerusalem] "Her foes have become the *head*, her enemies prosper, because the Lord has made her suffer for the multitude of her transgressions; her children have gone away, captives before the foe."

11-12. Isaiah 7:8: "For the *head* of Syria is Damascus, and the *head* of Damascus is Rezin" (in both cases *head* means "ruler" here: Damascus is the city that rules over Syria, and Rezin is the king who rules over Damascus).

13-14. Isaiah 7:9: "And the *head* of Ephraim is Samaria, and the *head* of Samaria is the son of Remaliah."

15. Isaiah 9:14-16: (In the context of judgment) "So the Lord cut off from Israel *head* and tail . . . the elder and honored man is the head,[51] and the prophet who teaches lies is the tail; for those who lead this people lead them astray." Here the leaders of the people are called "head."
16. Jeremiah 31:7 (LXX 38:7): "Rejoice and exult over the *head* of the nations."[52]

(5) We should also note in this regard what it actually means to have sixteen (or even eight) instances of a term used in a certain sense in the Septuagint. It is really a rich abundance of examples. Many times in New Testament exegesis, if a scholar can find two or three clear parallel uses in the Septuagint, he or she is very satisfied. That means we can assume that first-century Jews could read and understand the particular term in that sense. Let me give a contemporary example. Imagine that I turn to a concordance of the RSV and see that there is only one occurrence of a certain English word, such as "aunt."[53] Do I conclude, "That means that twentieth-century readers don't know what *aunt* means, and we can be especially certain of this since *aunt* occurs only in an obscure portion of Scripture (Leviticus 18:14), a passage that people today seldom read"? Should I conclude that people speaking English today do not know the meaning of *aunt*?

Certainly this would not be legitimate. Rather, I would conclude that the translators of the RSV assumed that *aunt* was a good, understandable English word—so commonly understood that even a single use of it in the whole Bible would be understood without its having to appear time after time in various contexts comparison of which would make its sense clear. They put it in *expecting* readers to understand it. The fact that they used it meant that they thought it was a commonly understood term.

The same principle is true with the Septuagint. If I find even two or three clear instances of a word used in a certain sense, I can rightly conclude that readers in the first century A.D. could have understood the word in that sense. The translators wrote expecting that the readers would understand. But in the case of *kephalē* meaning "authority over, ruler," we have not two or three examples, but sixteen (or at least eight, even by the minimal count of the Mickelsens, or nine, according to Payne). That is really an abundance of evidence for *kephalē* meaning "leader" or "authority over."

In conclusion, to those who say, "Only eight examples in the Septuagint," I think it fair to respond, "A very significant eight examples, and more accurately sixteen, and compared to zero examples for 'source,' they look very convincing."

b. Other Meanings for kephalē Claimed by the Mickelsens: After rejecting the meaning "authority over, leader" for *kephalē*, primarily on the basis of its Septuagint usage and the absence of this meaning from Liddell-Scott,[54] the Mickelsens provide other meanings for the term *kephalē*.

In 1 Corinthians 11:3, they say *kephalē* means "source, base or derivation."[55] Now I recognize that one lexicon gives the meaning "source" for *kephalē*.[56] But when the Mickelsens affirm that "base" and "derivation" are possible translations of *kephalē* they are claiming senses that no lexicon has ever proposed, and they are doing it with no examples of *kephalē* meaning these things in any other literature either. Where do they get these meanings?

In Ephesians 5:23, where it says that the husband is the *head* of the wife, they say that *head* means "one who brings to completion" (p. 108). They explain, "the husband is to give himself up to enable (bring to completion) all that his wife is meant to be" (p. 110).

Then with respect to Colossians 1:18, where it says that "Christ is the head of the body, the church," the Mickelsens say that *head* means "exalted originator and completer" (p. 108). We should note that the Mickelsens call these "ordinary Greek meanings" (p. 105) for *kephalē*, and tell us that these are "Greek meanings that would have been familiar to the first readers" (p. 110). But a number of these "ordinary and familiar" Greek meanings have never been seen in any lexicon or claimed in any writing on the meaning of *kephalē* before the Mickelsens' work in 1986. The meaning "exalted originator and completer" is in no lexicon. The meaning "one who brings to completion" is in no lexicon. The meaning "base, derivation" is in no lexicon.

But if this is so, then what convincing examples from Greek literature do the Mickelsens give to show these to be "familiar" and "ordinary" meanings? They give none. Then what authorities do they quote to support these new meanings? They give none. In short, they have given no evidence to support their assertions that these are ordinary meanings. It would not seem wise to accept these meanings as legitimate senses for *kephalē*.

In fact, this attempt to give some alternate sense to *kephalē* in New Testament contexts where the meaning "authority over" seems so clearly evident from the contexts is one more example of a disturbing tendency among evangelical feminist scholars today, a tendency to search for "any meaning but authority" for the word *kephalē* in the New Testament. Even in Colossians 2:10 (where Christ is called "the *head* of all rule and authority") and Ephesians 1:20-24 (where God has exalted Christ "far above all rule and authority and power and dominion" and "has put all things under his feet and has made him the *head* over all things for the church"), the Mickelsens still are unable to admit the meaning "authority over," but say that *head* here means rather "top or crown (extremity)" (p. 106). When this can happen even in texts where authority is so clearly specified in context, one wonders if it is a prior doctrinal conviction rather than sound linguistic analysis that has led to their conclusions in these texts.

c. The Argument from Liddell-Scott: Although all the lexicons that specialize in the New Testament period list "ruler, leader, or authority over" as a meaning for *kephalē* at the time of the New Testament,[57] the Mickelsens and others have strongly emphasized that Liddell-Scott does not include this meaning. What is the significance of this? First, our earlier survey showed that the meaning "authority over" was not very common—indeed, is hardly found at all—*before* the Septuagint, about the second century B.C. Nonetheless, the evidence we have cited above showing around forty examples of this meaning indicates that the omission from Liddell-Scott must have been an oversight that we hope will be corrected in a subsequent edition. In fact, Joseph Fitzmyer recently wrote, "The next edition of the *Greek-English Lexicon* of Liddell-Scott-Jones will have to provide a sub-category within the metaphorical uses of *kephalē* in the sense of 'leader, ruler.'"[58]

Second, Liddell-Scott does list under the adjective *kephalaios* ("head like") the following meanings: "metaphorical, of persons, *the head* or *chief*" (pp. 944-945). Liddell-Scott then lists eight examples of this sense. Similarly, for *kephalourgos* (literally, "head of work"), it lists the meaning "*foreman of works*" (p. 945). Therefore, the meaning "authority over" for *kephalē* itself would probably have been understandable even if not commonly used in earlier periods well before the time of the New Testament.

This suggests a possible reason why the noun *kephalē* itself was not found in the earlier history of the language with the meaning "authority, ruler." Perhaps because the adjective *kephalaios* or this adjective used as a substantive could function with the meaning "chief, ruler" in an earlier period, there may have been no need for the noun *kephalē* to take a similar meaning. Yet later in the development of the language the noun *kephalē* also came to take this sense.

2. (1986) Ruth A. Tucker, "Response"

In this article Ruth Tucker finds examples of *kephalē* meaning "authority over" in Clement of Alexandria (ca. 155-220 A.D.), Tertullian (ca. 169-215 A.D.), Cyprian (ca. 200-55 A.D.), and other early writers. Tucker says:

> In conclusion, it is my impression that whatever the word *kephalē* meant to the apostle Paul as he wrote 1 Corinthians 11 and Ephesians 5, it was generally interpreted by the church fathers and by Calvin to mean authority, superior rank, or preeminence. These findings bring into question some of the Mickelsens' assumptions—particularly that the "superior rank" meaning of *kephalē* is not "one of the ordinary Greek meanings" but rather "a meaning associated with the English word *head*." More research needs to be done in this area, but it seems clear that the fathers used this so-called English meaning long before they could have in any way been influenced by the English language. (p. 117)

We can only note here that Tucker's survey of writings that followed the New Testament period gives some support to the idea that the meaning "authority over" was a recognized meaning at the time of the New Testament as well.

3. (1986) Philip B. Payne, "Response"

In this response to the Mickelsens' article, Philip Payne repeats "the Septuagint argument" concerning the infrequent use of *kephalē* to translate the Hebrew term *ro'sh* when it meant "leader, ruler." I have discussed that argument at length in the previous analysis of the Mickelsens' article.

Payne also adds some examples where he claims that *kephalē* means "source of life."

a. Philo: Payne's first example comes from Philo, *The Preliminary Studies* 61: "And Esau is the progenitor [*ho genarchēs*] of all the clan here described, the head as of a living animal [*kephalē de hōs zōou*]."

The sense of "head" here is difficult to determine. Payne suggests the meaning "source of life" for head, a specific kind of "source" that has never before been given in any lexicon. Yet it is possible that Philo thought of the physical head of an animal as in some sense energizing or giving life to the animal—this would then be a simile in which Esau (a representative of stubborn disobedience in this context) gives life to a whole list of other sins that Philo has been describing as a "family" in this allegory. However, the word translated above as "progenitor" (*genarchēs*) also can mean "ruler of created beings" (Liddell-Scott, p. 342). In that case the text would read: "And Esau is the ruler of all the clan here described, the head as of a living animal." Here the meaning would be that Esau is the ruler over the rest of the sinful clan, and *head* would mean "ruler, authority over." It seems impossible from the context to decide clearly for one meaning or the other in this text.

The next text cited by Payne is Philo, *On Rewards and Punishments* 125. This was discussed above in the response to Richard Cervin's article. In this quotation the sense "source of life" must also be seen as a possible meaning, but the sense "ruler, authority over" is also quite possible, and, as we argued above, in the context of commenting on God's promise to make the people the "head and not the tail" so that they would rule over other nations, the meaning "ruler, authority over" seems more likely.

b. Artemidorus: Next, Payne cites some texts from Artemidorus Daldiani (late second century A.D.) in his work *Oneirocritica* (or *The Interpretation of Dreams*). Payne gives the following citations:

> Another man dreamt that he was beheaded. In real life, the father of this man, too, died; for as the head [*kephalē*] is the source of life and light for the whole body, he was responsible for the dreamer's life and light. . . . The head [*kephalē*] indicates one's father. (*Oneirocritica* 1.2)
>
> The head [*kephalē*] resembles parents in that it is the cause [*aitia*] of one's living. (*Oneirocritica* 1.35)
>
> The head [*kephalē*] signifies the father of the dreamer. . . . Whenever, then a poor man who has a rich father dreams that his own head has been removed by a lion and that he dies as a result, it is probable that his father will die. . . . For the head [*kephalē*] represents the father; the removal of the head [*kephalē*], the death of the father. (*Oneirocritica* 3.66)

Do these examples show that *kephalē* could be used metaphorically to mean "source"? If we give a fuller context than Payne provided in his article, we can see that these do not provide an example of "head" meaning "source," for no person is in these texts *called* "head." But what the text does show is that Artemidorus pointed out various *functions* of the head in a human body and then said that these functions signified something in interpreting dreams (the whole text is an explanation of how to interpret dreams).

In the following context we see that Artemidorus gives *many* different interpretations to the dream of being beheaded, but in none of them would we say that this text adds new meanings to the word *head* itself:

> If a man dreams that he has been beheaded . . . it is inauspicious both for a man with parents and a man with children. For the head resembles parents in that it is the cause of one's living. It is like *children* because of the face and because of the resemblance. . . . Also, a man who owned a *house* has lost it. For the head is as it were the *house* of the senses. . . .
>
> To bankers, usurers, men who have to collect subscriptions, shipmasters, merchants, and all who collect money, it signifies loss of *capital* because the word for "capital" is derived from the word for "head." . . . To a slave who enjoys the confidence of his master, it signifies that he will lose that confidence. . . . But to other slaves, the dream signifies freedom. For the head is the *master of the body*, and when it is cut off, it signifies that the slave is separated from his master and will be free. . . .
>
> If someone who is at sea sees this dream, it signifies that the *sailyard* of the ship will be lost, unless it is one of the sailors who has seen it. For, in these cases, I have observed that it signifies death to their *superiors*. For the boatswain is the *superior* of the ordinary sailor; the officer in command of the bow is the boatswain's *superior*; the steersman is the *superior* of the officer who commands the bow; and the shipmaster is the *superior* of the steersman. . . .
>
> To have two or three heads is auspicious for an athlete. For he will be crowned in as many contests. (*Oneirocritica* 1. 35)[59]

This larger context shows us that in all of these examples the word *kephalē* simply *means* the *physical head* of a person's body. When Artemidorus speaks of losing one's head or having three heads in a dream, he is simply speaking of a physical head. When he says that the head *signifies* something in the dream, he is still speaking of the physical head and then giving a symbolic interpretation to it.

It would certainly be illegitimate to take this text and make a list of many new "meanings" that the word *kephalē* could take in ancient Greek. We could not take that text, for example, and say that *head* now also means (1) "house," because Artemidorus says that the head is the "house of the senses"; (2) "monetary capital," because Artemidorus says that the loss of the head "signifies loss of capital"; (3) "master of a slave," for Artemidorus says that "the head is the master of the body"; (4) "sailyard of a ship"; (5) "superior naval officer"; and (6) "athletic contest." All of these are simply symbolic interpretations that Artemidorus has given and do not constitute new metaphorical meanings for *kephalē*.[60]

However, one further observation must be made from this text. Because Artemidorus, in speaking about the physical head of a human body, says that "the head resembles parents in that it is the cause (Greek *aitia*) of one's living" (literally, of life, *tou zēn*), we must recognize that there was an awareness that the physical head was in some sense the cause (or one might say "source") of life. Perhaps this is just a common-sense observation of the fact that people who are beheaded do not continue to live! But it may also reflect a more complex understanding of the mental faculties located in the head—Artemidorus does say that the head is "the house of the senses." In this case it would be similar to the Philo quotations mentioned above where Philo apparently thought of the head as giving energy and direction to the body.

Whether the fact that (1) some in the ancient world thought of the *physical* head as somehow the "source" of energy and life for the body would have led to (2) a *metaphorical use* of *head* to actually *mean* "source," or not, we cannot say without some clear examples demonstrating such a use. It is very similar to the case of the quotations mentioned earlier from Plato, Philo, and Plutarch, in which the head was said to be the "ruler" of all the parts within us. Those quotations showed that a *metaphorical* use of *kephalē* to *mean* "ruler" would have been possible and probably understandable in the ancient world, but it did not mean that that metaphorical use *actually occurred*. In order to demonstrate that we needed to look at the thirty or forty texts where someone was actually called the "head" of something (such as the Roman empire, the church, the nation of Israel, etc.). In this case however, no metaphorical uses of *kephalē* in the sense of "source" have been found in the Artemidorus quotations.[61]

In conclusion, *kephalē* in all these Artemidorus texts simply means "physical head" of the human body.

c. Orphic Fragments 21a: As an additional example of *kephalē* meaning "source," Payne also cites *Orphic Fragments* 21a, "Zeus is the head, Zeus the middle, and from Zeus all things are completed." But Cervin's analysis of this text is quite valid: he says, "This entire fragment is ambiguous" (p. 90).[62]

d. 1 Corinthians 11:3: In 1 Corinthians 11:3 Paul writes, "I want you to understand that the *head* of every man is Christ, the *head* of a woman is the man, and the *head* of Christ is God." Payne objects to the sense "authority over" in this text because he thinks that it would imply a theological error:

> Under the interpretation that "head" means "authority" the present tense of *estin* requires that Christ now in the present time after his resurrection and ascension is under the authority of God. Such a view has been condemned throughout most of church history as subordinationist Christology. (pp. 126-127)

But Payne here has simply misunderstood the doctrine of the Trinity as it has been held throughout the church from at least the time of the Nicene Creed in 325 A.D. From that time the doctrine of the "eternal generation of the Son" has been taken to imply a *relationship* between the Father and the Son that *eternally* existed and that will always exist—a relationship that includes a subordination in role, but not in essence or being. Certainly Scripture speaks of that when it says, for example, that when Christ "had made purification for sins, he sat down at the right hand of the Majesty on high" (Hebrews 1:3). Jesus is at the right hand, but God the Father is still on the throne.

So Charles Hodge can write:

> The Nicene doctrine includes, (1) The principle of the subordination of the Son to the Father, and of the Spirit to the Father and the Son. But this subordination does not imply inferiority. . . . The subordination intended is only that which concerns the mode of subsistence and operation. . . .
>
> The creeds are nothing more than a well-ordered arrangement of the facts of Scripture which concern the doctrine of the Trinity. They assert the distinct personality of the Father, Son, and Spirit . . . and their consequent perfect equality; and the subordination of the Son to the Father, and of the Spirit to the Father and the Son, as to the mode of subsistence and operation. These are Scriptural facts, to which the creeds in question add nothing; *and it is in this sense they have been accepted by the Church universal.* (*Systematic Theology*, vol. 1, pp. 460-62)[62a]

Similarly, A. H. Strong writes:

> Father, Son, and Holy Spirit, while equal in essence and dignity, stand to each other in an order of personality, office, and operation. . . .
>
> The subordination of the *person* of the Son to the *person* of the Father, or in other words an order of personality, office, and operation which permits the Father to be officially first, the Son second, and the Spirit third, is perfectly consistent with equality. Priority is not necessarily superiority. . . .
>
> We frankly recognize an eternal subordination of Christ to the Father, but we maintain at the same time that this subordination is a subordination of order, office, and operation, not a subordination of essence.[62b]

Payne has simply misrepresented subordinationist Christology. Subordinationism has generally meant not the orthodox view that there is subordination in *role* in the Trinity, but the heretical view found, for example, in Arianism, in which a subordinate *essence* or *being* of the Son was advocated, so that Christ could not be said to be "of the same essence" (*homoousios*) as the Father. The orthodox doctrine has always been that there is *equality in essence and subordination in role* and that these two are consistent with each other. Certainly this is consistent with Paul's statement in 1 Corinthians 11:3 that "the head of Christ is God," thus indicating a distinction in role in which primary authority and leadership among the persons of the Trinity has always been and will always be the possession of God the Father.[63]

4. (1986) Walter L. Liefeld, "Women, Submission, and Ministry in 1 Corinthians"[64]
In this essay Dr. Liefeld comments on the dispute over the meaning of *kephalē*.

> The meaning "source," adduced by Bedale as a clue to some of Paul's passages, lacks clear evidence . . . in my judgment, however, it is no longer possible, given Grudem's research, to dismiss the idea of rulership from the discussion. (p. 139)

I would of course concur with Liefeld at this point. However, Liefeld then goes on to suggest a different sense for *kephalē*, "prominent part," or "prominent or honored member" (pp. 139-140).

This is similar to the suggestion by Cervin discussed above.[65] Once again it must be said that a number of texts might be found in which *kephalē* speaks of a kind of prominence derived from ruling authority or power that is possessed by (for example) the king of a nation or the head of a tribe, or from Christ's position as the head of the church. But it does not seem possible to demonstrate a sense of "honored part" or "prominent part" apart from a nuance of ruling authority as well.

Second, this suggestion has been mentioned previously in no lexicons (to my knowledge), and thus one wonders why it is necessary when the sense "leader, authority over" will fit as well or better.

Third, it is doubtful that the sense "prominent part" really fits the context of texts like 1 Corinthians 11:3. If Paul had meant to imply the idea of prominence in this text, then, instead of saying "the head of the woman is the man," he would have had to say, "the head of the *family* is the husband," and instead of saying "the head of every man is Christ," he would have had to say, "the head of *mankind* is Christ." Instead of saying, "the head of Christ is God," he would have had to say, "the head of *the Godhead* is the Father." But he did not say these things, in which he could have mentioned the prominent or most honored member of a larger group. Rather, he mentioned two individuals in each set of relationships, thus giving a sense that much more readily allows the meaning "authority over" than "prominent part."

5. Gilbert Bilezikian, "A Critical Examination of Wayne Grudem's Treatment of Kephalē in Ancient Greek Texts"[66]

Dr. Bilezikian has given some criticisms of my earlier article that I accept as valid and that are similar to those by Cervin in the article discussed above.[67] Among them are: (1) The need for a separate category, "ruling part," to distinguish five examples where the physical head of a person is said to rule over the human body (p. 220). I agreed with this suggestion in the discussion of Cervin's article. (2) The need to delete two examples from my list of forty-nine because I had miscounted them in my final enumeration.[68]

However, I must differ with Bilezikian's critique at several other points.

a. Lexicons: Bilezikian suggests that some lexicons list the meaning "source" and others list the meaning "ruler, authority over," and it is just a question of which lexicon one chooses to use. He says,

> This lack of lexical agreement on the meaning of *kephalē* is partly responsible for the frustration of scholars who have been attempting, in recent years, to understand the meaning of male/female relations in the Pauline epistles. Each one here is aware of the battle of the lexicons that has been waged by Bible scholars who have written on this issue during the last two decades. . . . They have been flinging their favorite lexicons back and forth at each other's heads. (pp. 218-219)

What Bilezikian fails to make clear is that, although one lexicon (Liddell-Scott) does list "source, origin" as a sense when *kephalē* is applied to the *end point* of something like a river or a span of time, nevertheless, *no lexicon has ever yet listed "source" as a metaphorical meaning for kephalē when applied to persons.* By contrast, *all the major lexicons for the New Testament period* list a meaning such as "authority over" or "ruler, leader" as a meaning for *kephalē* when applied to persons.[69] It is simply misleading to talk about a "battle of the lexicons."

b. Individual texts: In the examination of the individual texts where I found the sense "authority over," Bilezikian differs from Cervin in that he finds the meaning "source" in almost every text in which I saw the meaning "ruler" or "authority over." We do not need to examine every one of those quotations again, but a few instances will give the direction of Bilezikian's argument.

(1) *Herodotus* 7.148: The Delphic oracle warns the Argives to protect those with full cit-

izenship from attack and thus the remainder of the population will be protected, saying, "guarding your *head* from the blow and the *head* shall shelter the body."[70]

Here Bilezikian says, "The notion of an authority function is completely absent. . . . This text describes headship not as 'authority over' but as a source of protection . . . which item . . . should be classified as 'Source, origin'" (p. 221).

But here we can try substituting "leaders" and "source" to see which makes better sense:

My suggestion: "guarding your *leaders* from the blow; and the *leaders* shall shelter the body."

Bilezikian's suggestion: "guarding your *source* from the blow; and the *source* shall shelter the body."

The first alternative is preferable because the idea of guarding leaders is an understandable one for a population. To tell a population to guard its source would make no sense, for they would not know what was being referred to.

Bilezikian could respond that he was not arguing for the meaning "source" in this text, but the meaning "source *of protection*." But this illustrates a fundamental error in his argument: in order to make any of his explanations work, he must assume that *kephalē* means not just "source" but "source *of something*," and he then varies the "something" from text to text so that he actually gives *kephalē* many new senses (source of protection, source of vitality, source of well-being, etc.). But this is not sound analysis: *kephalē* does not take all these new specialized meanings, never before found in any lexicon, attested only in one text, and discovered only now for the first time by Bilezikian. In actuality, the fact that he must supply "source *of something*" and make the "something" different each time shows even more clearly that "source" alone is not a legitimate meaning for *kephalē*.

A few more examples will illustrate this point, and in each one when we try substituting the simple meaning "source" it will be evident how this meaning is unacceptable:

(23) Plutarch, *Pelopidas* 2. 1. 3: in an army, "the light-armed troops are like the hands, the cavalry like the feet, the line of men-at-arms itself like chest and breastplate, and the general is like the *head*."

Bilezikian says, "The general's function as the 'head' of the troops is explained as the general's being the source of their safety, the cause of their continued existence. . . . This instance of *kephalē* should be tabulated under 'Source, origin'" (pp. 226-227).

Bilezikian treats a number of examples in this same way: he looks around in the context until he can find something that the person called "head" is the "source" of, whether leadership or protection or financial support, etc. This is not hard to do because in the nature of things in this world, *everything* is the "source" of something else—the ground is the source of food, rivers are the source of water, trees are the source of leaves, cows are the source of milk, even rocks are a source of stability and support. Conversely, to take the example above, the soldiers are also a "source" of strength and support for the general. But that does not mean that "hand" or "foot" or "chest" can all mean "source."

Some other examples show the same procedure:

(26) Plutarch, *Galba*, 4. 3: "Vindex . . . wrote to Galba inviting him to assume the imperial power, and thus to serve what was a vigorous body in need of a *head*."

Although this was an invitation to Galba to become emperor of Rome, Bilezikian says, "They needed an emperor in Rome who would 'serve' them as the head 'serves a vigorous body.' . . . Headship is viewed in this text as a source of increased vitality. . . . This instance of *kephalē* is to be listed under 'source, origin'" (pp. 228-229).

In this quotation the "body" in question is the Gallic provinces. Once again we can substitute terms to see which is the most likely meaning:

My suggestion: To assume the imperial power, and thus to serve what was a vigorous province in need of a *leader*.

Bilezikian's suggestion: To assume the imperial power, and thus to serve what was a vigorous province in need of a *source*.

Once again, the meaning "leader" makes sense in the context, for it was leadership that this section of the empire needed. But the meaning "source" would have made no sense—who would have said that a province that already existed needed a "source"?

(30) Hermas, *Similitudes*, 7.3: The man is told that his family "cannot be punished in any way other way than if you, the *head* of the house be afflicted."

Bilezikian objects that the next sentence should be added to the quotation. It says, "For when you are afflicted, they also will necessarily be afflicted, but while you prosper, they cannot suffer any affliction!" He then says, "The full quote defines the role of the *head* in regard to the family as 'provider,' the source of its well-being. . . . This instance belongs in Grudem's category 3, 'Source, origin'" (pp. 230-231).

Once again we can substitute terms to see which is a more convincing translation:

My suggestion: The family "cannot be punished in any other way than if you, the *leader* of the house be afflicted."

Bilezikian's suggestion: The family "cannot be punished in any other way than if you, the *source* of the house be afflicted."

The idea of leader of a family would be quite understandable. But the idea that the father is the source of the family would make no sense with respect to the wife (or any possible servants) in the household, for the father was certainly not the source of them.

Bilezikian's error is simply this: whenever something *functions* as a "source," he says that the *name* of that thing can actually *mean* source. But on this account almost *any* word could mean "source." And in fact almost any word could mean anything else as well. Using this procedure, we could easily make *kephalē* mean just the *opposite* of "source"—we could make it mean, for example, "recipient": Since the general is the "recipient" of support from the army, we could say that *kephalē* means "recipient" in that text. Since the Roman emperor is the "recipient" of support and taxes from the provinces, we could say that *kephalē* means "recipient" here also, etc.

The fact that Bilezikian's procedure could lead to almost any noun meaning "source" and that it can also make a noun mean just the opposite of "source" should warn us against the error of such a procedure—it has no controls and no basis in sound linguistic analysis.

It is proper rather to ask exactly which characteristics of a physical head were recognized in the ancient world and were evident in contexts where people were metaphorically called "head." If those characteristics occur again and again in related contexts, then we can be reasonably certain that those characteristics were the ones intended by the metaphorical use of "head." In fact this is what we find. It is consistently people in leadership or authority who are referred to as "head." The examples cited above show that not only the general of an army, but also the Roman emperor, the head of a household, the heads of the tribes of Israel, David as king of Israel, and Christ as the head of the church are all referred to metaphorically by *kephalē*. What they share is a function of rule or authority. Moreover, several texts say explicitly that the head is the "ruling" part of the body.[71]

By contrast, where there are persons whose distinctive function is to be the source of something else, but where no leadership function attaches to them, the word *kephalē* is never used. Bilezikian recognizes this and finds it surprising:

> There exists no known instance of *kephalē* used figuratively in reference to women. This is especially surprising since the meaning of *kephalē* as source of life and servant provider would have been particularly suitable to describe roles assigned to women in antiquity. (p. 235)

He goes on to explain this absence of any examples by the fact that *kephalē* was not frequently used in a metaphorical sense and that women were not often referred to in Greek literature (pp. 235-236), but such an explanation is hardly sufficient. When there are over forty examples referring to persons in leadership as "head" of something, that shows that the metaphorical use of *kephalē* was not extremely rare. And to say that Greek literature does not talk much about women (especially in the role of mother and provider) is simply not true. What this statement of Bilezikian's actually indicates is that there are no clear examples to support his sought-after meaning, "source." But when no clear evidence turns up to support one's hypothesis, it would seem better to abandon the hypothesis than to stick with it and give unsubstantiated reasons why the expected data have not been forthcoming. At least we should realize that we are being asked to accept a meaning for *kephalē* for which no unambiguous supporting evidence has yet been provided.

Bilezikian's opposition to the idea of "authority" in any human relationships and in any texts that contain the word *kephalē* carries over into the New Testament as well. Even in the three texts where authority would quite readily be admitted by almost all commentators, Bilezikian does not acknowledge it:

(43) Ephesians 1:21, 22: Paul writes that God exalted Christ "far above all rule and authority and power and dominion, and above every name that is named . . . and he has put all things under his feet and has made him the *head* over all things for the church."

Here Bilezikian finds not authority but the idea of source. He writes, "In His headship, Christ is the source of life and increase to the church. In this passage there is no reference to headship as assumption of authority over the church" (p. 244). Yet the context of exaltation "above all rule and authority and power and dominion" certainly shows Christ's assumption of authority.[72]

(45-46) Ephesians 5:23: "For the husband is the *head* of the wife as Christ is the *head* of the church, his body, and is himself its Savior."

Here Bilezikian says, "As 'head' of the church, Christ is both the source of her life and her sustainer. . . . In this development on the meaning of headship, there is nothing in the text to suggest that *head* might have implications of rulership or authority" (p. 245). But once again the context indicates something quite different: The previous verse says, "Wives, be subject to your husbands, as to the Lord." And the following verse says, "As the church is *subject* to Christ, so let wives also be subject in everything to their husbands" (verses 22-24). Although Bilezikian speaks of the idea of "mutual submission," (p. 245), he fails to deal with the fact that the verb *hypotassō* always has to do with *submission to authority* in the New Testament and outside of it. Husbands are not told to be subject to their wives in this context, simply wives to husbands. And Christ is never said to be subject to the church, only the church to Christ. This idea of submission to the authority of Christ on the part of the church is impossible to remove from the context and makes it difficult to accept Bilezikian's claim that there is no suggestion of rulership or authority in the term *kephalē* in this context.

Bilezikian goes on to say that in Ephesians 5:23 "*head* designates the source of life ('Savior'), of servanthood ('gave himself up'), and of growth ('nourishes it')" (246), and says that "in their headship to their wives husbands fulfill servant roles similar to the servant ministries of Christ to the church" (245).

But Bilezikian's analysis here is simply an illustration of the fact that at this key text the contrived nature of the suggested meaning "source" for "head" most clearly shows itself: How can Paul have meant that the husband is the *source* of the wife as Christ is the *source* of the church? I am certainly not the "source" of my wife! Nor is any husband today, nor was any husband in the church at Ephsesus the "source" of his wife! The fact that this meaning will not fit is therefore evident in the fact that no evangelical feminist interpreter will propose the mere meaning "source" for this text, but each one will always shift the basis of discussion by importing some different, specialized sense, such as "source of *something* (such as encouragement, comfort, growth, etc.)". But the fact that the meaning "source" itself will not fit should serve as a warning that this suggested meaning is incorrect at its foundation.

On the other hand, we should realize the importance of this text: If the husband is indeed the head of the wife as Christ is the head of the church, and if "head" carries the sense "authority over" or "leader," then the feminist claim that there should be total equality and interchangeability of roles in marriage is simply inconsistent with the New Testament.

(48) Colossians 2:10: "And you have come to fullness of life in him, who is the *head* of all rule and authority."

Once again Bilezikian predictably gets the meaning "source" out of this passage: "Christ is 'the head of all power and authority' because he is the source of their existence" (pp. 246-247). But it is difficult to understand how Bilezikian can see "source" here without any connotation of authority. If (according to Bilezikian) Christ is the *source* of all other rule and authority in the universe, then is He not also a far greater authority and a far greater ruler than all of these others? Even if we were to take the meaning "source" for *kephalē* here (which is not necessary, for "ruler" or "authority over" fits much better), it would still be difficult to agree with Bilezikian's statement that "this text, like the others, is also devoid of any mention or connotation of rulership in reference to the headship of Christ" (p. 247).

In all of these individual texts, we must ask, is the meaning "authority, ruler" or the meaning "source" more persuasive? Bilezikian has not given us one example of a person called *kephalē* where he claims the meaning "source" but where the person was not someone in a position of authority. Would it not be unusual—if *kephalē* indeed means source and not authority—that people who are called "head" are all rulers and leaders? We do not find that wives and mothers are called "heads." We do not find that soldiers who are the source of strength and power for an army are called "heads." We do not find that citizens who are the source of strength for a nation are called "heads."

Rather, the king of Egypt is a "head," the general of an army is a "head," the Roman emperor is a "head," David the king of Israel is a "head," the leaders of the tribes of Israel are "heads," and, in the New Testament, the husband is the "head" of the wife and Christ is the "head" of the church and God the Father is the "head" of Christ. No one in a non-leadership position is called "head." Why? Perhaps because there was a sense in the ancient world that *kephalē*, when used of persons, meant someone in a position of rule or authority, just as the head was said by secular as well as Jewish writers to be the "ruling part" of the body.

c. 1 Corinthians 11:3: Bilezikian alleges, "Grudem adopts the view that this text describes a chain of command, moving from the top of a hierarchy of power to the bottom, whereby God the Father is the 'authority' over God the Son, Christ is the authority over every man, and man is the authority over the woman" (pp. 241-242).

This statement is simply false. I have never taught or written that there is a "chain of command" in 1 Corinthians 11:3. Neither (to my knowledge) have other responsible advocates of a complementarian position with regard to men and women. The idea of a "chain of command" suggests that the wife can only relate to God through her husband rather than directly. But this is certainly false. Paul in 1 Corinthians 11:3 simply sets up three distinct relationships: the headship of God the Father in the Trinity, the headship of Christ over every man, and the headship of a man over a woman. But certainly every woman is able to relate directly to God through Christ, not simply through her husband.

d. A Fundamental Opposition to the Idea of Authority: A fundamental commitment of Bilezikian's is evident in his unwillingness to see any authority in the New Testament view of marriage (or apparently in the relationship of Christ to the church):

> The New Testament contains no text where Christ's headship to the church connotes a relationship of authority. Likewise, the New Testament contains no text where a husband's headship to his wife connotes a relationship of authority. (pp. 248-249)

He then goes on to say that the existence of any authority structure in marriage would "paganize the marriage relationship." Regarding husband/wife relationships, he says:

> The imposition of an authority structure upon this exquisite balance of reciprocity would paganize the marriage relationship and make the Christ/church paradigm irrelevant to it. (p. 249)

As far as I can understand this sentence, it implies that any existence of authority within marriage is a "pagan" concept because it would "paganize the marriage relationship." Does Bilezikian mean, then, that the existence of any authority between parents and children is also a pagan concept? And if the existence of authority within marriage would "make the Christ/church paradigm irrelevant to it," he must mean that there is no authority relationship between Christ and the church either—for if Christ *did* have authority over the church, then certainly the paradigm of Christ and the church would not be "irrelevant" to an authority structure within marriage.

What seems to me to be both amazing and disappointing in this statement is the length to which Bilezikian will go in order to carry out his fundamental opposition to the idea of authority within human relationships. A commitment to oppose any idea of the husband's authority over the wife has apparently led him ultimately to say that authority within marriage is always a pagan idea and—it seems—to imply that Christ's authority over the church would be a pagan idea as well.

At this point we must object and insist that authority and submission to authority are not pagan concepts. They are truly divine concepts, rooted in the eternal nature of the Trinity for all eternity and represented in the eternal submission of the Son to the Father and of the Holy Spirit to the Father and the Son. To resist the very idea of authority structures that have been appointed by God (whether in marriage, in the family, in civil government, in church leadership, or in Christ's authority over the church) is ultimately to encourage us to disobey God's will. If effective, such an argument will only drive us away from conformity to the image of Christ. If we are to live lives pleasing to God, we must submit to the authority of our Lord Jesus Christ, whom God has placed "far above all rule and authority and power and dominion, and above every name that is named . . . and has put all things under his feet, and has made him head over all things for the church" (Ephesians 1:21-22).

6. Catherine Clark Kroeger, "The Classical Concept of Head as 'Source'"[73]

This article by Catherine Kroeger cites many passages from Greek literature in an attempt to demonstrate that *kephalē* meant "source" in the ancient world. Many have found this essay persuasive and thought it did what needed to be done; that is, they have read it and concluded that it finally produced *many* examples where *kephalē* clearly means "source" and found these examples in classical Greek literature as well. (Note that the title claims to be considering the "Classical concept" of head as source.)

In response, the first point that must be made is that the essay is wrongly and in fact misleadingly titled. The essay is not at all about "the Classical concept of head as source" but rather should be titled, "The Late Patristic Concept of Head as Source." In fact, four of the six authors Kroeger quotes in order to show that *kephalē* means "source" are taken from the entry in Lampe's *Patristic Greek Lexicon* (p. 749), and the actual quotations she gives in her article are also taken from that entry on *kephalē*.

Second, are these quotations persuasive? The actual new quotations given in Kroeger's article, in addition to the material from Philo, Artemidorus, and the *Orphic Fragments* (all of which have been examined above), include the following six authors (but Kroeger does not mention the date of any of them):

1. Athanasius (fifth century A.D.)
2. Cyril of Alexandria (died 444 A.D.)
3. Theodore of Mopsuestia (died 428 A.D.)

4. Basil (the Great) (329-379 A.D.)
5. Eusebius (died 339 A.D.)
6. Photius (died 891 A.D.)

Apart from these six late patristic writers, Kroeger cites *no new metaphorical uses of kephalē in her article.* (See below on her non-metaphorical examples from all periods of Greek literature.)

This means that in her article full of extensive citations of Greek texts, an article that therefore gives the appearance of extensive citations of "Classical" Greek literature (literature from long *before* the time of the New Testament), Kroeger has misleadingly claimed in her title to be giving such evidence. She has also concealed that fact from readers by failing to give any dates for the patristic writers she quotes.

Since all the additional metaphorical examples cited come from the fourth century A.D. and later, it does not seem that they are very helpful for determining New Testament usage, especially in light of Ruth Tucker's research showing that *earlier* Fathers took *kephalē* to mean "authority" and not "source."[74] Here it is appropriate to quote what Berkeley and Alvera Mickelsen say about such late material: "Our question is *not* what *kephalē* meant in A.D. 500 but rather what Paul meant when he used *kephalē* when writing his letters to the churches in the first century."[75]

Yet another highly misleading aspect of Dr. Kroeger's quotations is that she translates them in such a way that it appears that the authors are defining head to mean "source," whereas that is not at all a necessary translation. For example, she translates a quotation from Cyril of Alexandria as follows:

> Therefore of our race he become first *head, which is source*, and was of the earth and earthy. Since Christ was named the second Adam, he has been placed as *head, which is source*, of those who through him have been formed anew unto him unto immortality through sanctification in the spirit. Therefore he himself our *source, which is head*, has appeared as a human being. . . . *Because head means source*, He established the truth for those who are wavering in their mind that man is the head of woman, for she was taken out of him. (p. 268).

Kroeger then says, "In case you have lost count, *kephalē* is defined as 'source' (*archē*) no less than four times in this single paragraph" (p. 269). The texts would then all read, "head, which is ruler."

What Kroeger fails to tell the reader is that in every one of these sentences where she renders "head, which is source," we could also translate the word *archē* as "ruler" or "leader" or "beginning" (without any connotation of source). Kroeger fails to tell the reader that these texts are still somewhat ambiguous, because the word *archē* can mean either "beginning" or "ruler, authority."[76]

Moreover, several of the quotations Kroeger gives regarding authors who comment on 1 Corinthians 11:3 are from orthodox writers who were involved in the great Trinitarian controversy of the fourth and fifth centuries. None of them would have said that God the Father was the "source of being" of God the Son in any sense that would have meant that the Son was created. Yet we should note that in 1 Corinthians 11:3 Kroeger and many others who argue for the meaning "source" must have the meaning "source of being" in order for Christ to be the "head of every man" and the man to be the "head of the woman" in reference to Adam and Eve. But this sense of "source" will simply not fit any orthodox conception of 1 Corinthians 11:3, for then it would mean that the Son was created. How could these quotations then mean that God was the source of Christ in that sense? For no orthodox writer would have said anything that implied that the Father created the Son.

Furthermore, even if one were to grant that Kroeger has found some examples where *kephalē* takes the meaning "source," the point still remains that there is no instance of "source" *apart from authority*. For example, the Son is never said to be the "head" of the Father, nor is the wife ever said to be the "head" of the husband. The conclusion is that "head" again (and as in all the earlier cases) always applies to the one with greatest authority, and even if one sees a nuance of "source" in some of these texts, the nuance of authority inevitably goes with it.

Another line of argument in Dr. Kroeger's article is the listing of many examples in which the *physical head* of a person is seen as the "source" of various things such as hair, nasal secretions, earwax, and so forth (pp. 269-273). Kroeger asks, do these texts not show that *head* could mean "source" in Greek literature? (These texts come from various periods of Greek literature, including several near the time of the New Testament. In this respect they are unlike the late metaphorical examples that I mentioned above.)

No, they do not show that at all. These simply refer to the physical head of persons and describe *functions* that can be observed. These texts do not use *kephalē* metaphorically to mean source. We can see that if we try to substitute the word "source" in a statement like some of those mentioned in Kroeger's article: might someone say (for example), "I see luxuriant hair growing from your *source* today"? Or might someone say, "Your *source* is giving off abundant nasal secretions this morning"? Certainly those statements would be nonsense, and they show that "source" was not a suitable *meaning* or synonym for "head" in any of those statements.

An Important Unanswered Question

After all the research on this word by myself as well as by Cervin, Payne, Bilezikian, Kroeger, and others, there is still an unanswered question:

> Where is even one clear example of *kephalē* used of a *person* to mean "source" in all of Greek literature before or during the time of the New Testament? Is there even *one* example that is unambiguous?

If there is still not one clear example before or during the time of the New Testament, then how can many writers go on saying that this is a "common" meaning at the time of the New Testament? Or even a possible one? Perhaps such examples will be forthcoming, but until they are it would seem appropriate to use much more caution in the statements that are made about "source" being a common or recognized meaning for *kephalē*. We still see much reason to doubt that it was a recognized meaning at all.

7. (1987) Gordon D. Fee, The First Epistle to the Corinthians[77]

This treatment of 1 Corinthians 11:3, and particularly the meaning of *kephalē* in that text, quotes the 1954 article by S. Bedale, and then quotes the recent articles discussed above by the Mickelsens, Payne, and Kroeger. Fee calls Kroeger's paper on the "Classical concept of head as source" "a paper that appears to be decisive" (p. 502). In addition, from Payne's article Fee quotes the statement from *Orphic Fragments* 21a, the two quotations from Philo, and the quotations from Artemidorus.

Fee concludes that *kephalē* in the sense of "chief" or "person of highest rank" is "rare in Greek literature" (p. 502). He says, "Paul's understanding of the metaphor, therefore, and almost certainly the only one the Corinthians would have grasped, is 'head' as 'source,' especially 'source of life'" (p. 502). He gives as evidence the quotations just noted. Fee also takes issue with my study of *kephalē* for four reasons:

1. Of my 49 examples, he says 12 are from the NT, and these are examples that "[Grudem] prejudges exegetically" to mean authority over.
2. Of the other 37 examples, 18 are from the Septuagint, "which are exceptions that prove the rule."
3. He then says, "For most of the remaining 19 there is serious exegetical question as to whether the authors intended a metaphorical sense of 'authority over.'"

4. He says that I am "quite mistaken" in my use of Philo, because two passages in Philo show the meaning "source."[78]

In response to those four points:

1. I am not sure what Fee means when he says that I "prejudge exegetically" the New Testament passages. In my earlier article I discussed each passage. Fee by contrast offers no discussion in return. Is he implying that since my *discussion* concluded that *kephalē* means "authority over," it is invalid to count these examples? But when Fee provides no exegetical arguments of his own about any other passages than 1 Corinthians 11:3, one wonders if it is not he who has "prejudged" the meaning of these texts.
2. As I explained above, it seems inconsistent to say that 18 examples from the Septuagint are exceptions "that prove the rule" and then reject the sense "authority over," which is established by these 18 examples but accept the sense "source" where there are zero examples from the Septuagint.
3. Fee gives no evidence, no argument, no hint of what these "serious exegetical questions" are in the other citations. His statement is simply dismissal by assertion, with no argument or supporting evidence.
4. Regarding the two examples in Philo that speak of a person becoming the "head" of the human race and of the "head" of an animal, the meaning "source" is certainly not clearly established, as was indicated in the discussion above.[79]

Such analysis in a prominent commentary series is puzzling, to say the least. The survey above has shown that not only Fee, but also Kroeger, the Mickelsens, Payne, and Bilezikian all dismiss the meaning "authority over" as "rare," but say that the meaning "source" is "common." Perhaps we can be forgiven for realizing that all of these six writers have also been vocal proponents of an "evangelical feminist" position that seeks to deny any unique leadership role for men in marriage or the church and for wondering if their strong commitment to this viewpoint has affected their judgment on the meaning of *kephalē*.

It is of course possible that my own judgment on this issue is distorted as well, but as I review the data once again, it seems strange that they have taken the meaning "authority, ruler," which is attested over forty times in ancient literature, including about sixteen times in the Septuagint, and called it "rare." On the other hand, these authors have taken the meaning "source," for which there are only one possible example in the fifth century B.C. (*Orphic Fragments*, 21a), two possible (but ambiguous) examples in Philo, no examples in the Septuagint, and no clear examples applied to persons before or during the time of the New Testament, and called it a "common, recognizable, ordinary meaning." What kind of logic is this? Forty examples make a meaning "rare" but zero unambiguous examples makes the meaning "common"? The meaning "authority over," which is in all New Testament Greek lexicons, is unlikely and rare and "not part of the ordinary range of meanings for the Greek word," but the meaning "source," which is in no lexicon for the New Testament period and is reflected in none of the *early* Fathers, who took it to mean "authority," is called "almost certainly the only one the Corinthians would have grasped" (Fee, *First Corinthians*, p. 502). I confess that I find it hard to follow this line of reasoning. It seems to me that we have yet to see convincing evidence that *kephalē* ever did mean source at the time of the New Testament.

8. (1989) Joseph Fitzmyer, "Another Look at Kephalē in 1 Corinthians 11:3"[80]

In this study Fitzmyer, independently of my earlier study, finds a number of examples of *kephalē* meaning "authority or supremacy over someone else" in the Septuagint as well as in Jewish and Christian writings outside the New Testament. He concludes:

> The upshot of this discussion is that a Hellenistic Jewish writer such as Paul of Tarsus could well have intended that *kephalē* in 1 Corinthians 11:3 be understood as "head" in the sense of authority or supremacy over someone else. . . . The next edition of the *Greek-*

> *English Lexicon* of Liddell-Scott-Jones will have to provide a sub-category within the metaphorical uses of *kephalē* in the sense of "leader, ruler." (pp. 510-511)

I certainly concur with Fitzmyer at this point.

9. (1989) Peter Cotterell and Max Turner, Linguistics and Biblical Interpretation[81]
Here Cotterell and Turner express substantial agreement with my earlier study.[82] With regard to the suggestion of some that *kephalē* can mean "source," they note the absence of any examples of *kephalē* that cannot be explained by other established meanings and have to be explained by the meaning "source." They ask:

> And where have we evidence of this? Where do we find instances of such statements as "cows are the *kephalē* of milk"; "Egypt is the *kephalē* of papyrus", etc.? Only such a range of evidence could confirm that *kephalē* had the lexical sense "source" or "origin," generally understood rather than being specifically collocated with nouns referring to linear entities that have two ends. And we do not appear to have this kind of evidence. (p. 143)

They conclude, "We are not aware of any instance of 'head' unambiguously used with the sense 'source' before the third century A.D. . . . As far as we can tell, 'source' or 'origin' was *not* a conventional sense of the word *kephalē* in Paul's time" (pp. 144-145).

10. Recent Lexicons by Bauer (1988) and Louw-Nida (1988)
Since my previous article, two more New Testament lexicons have been published. The sixth edition of Walter Bauer's *Griechisch-deutsches Wörterbuch*, on pages 874-875, lists for *kephalē* no such meaning as "source" but does give the meaning "*Oberhaupt*" ("chief, leader") (p. 874-875). And the new *Greek English Lexicon of the New Testament Based on Semantic Domains*, edited by Johannes P. Louw and Eugene E. Nida, lists for *kephalē* the meaning "one who is of supreme or preeminent status, in view of authority to order or command—'one who is the head of, one who is superior to, one who is supreme over'" (vol. 1, p. 739), but they give no meaning such as "source, origin."

IV. Conclusion

The meaning "ruler, authority over" is still found quite clearly in forty-one ancient texts from both Biblical and extra-Biblical literature, and is possible in two or more other texts. In addition, there are six texts where *kephalē* refers to the literal head of a peron's body and is said to be the part that rules or governs the rest of the body, and there are two texts which are similes where a ruler or leader is said to be like a head. But four of the examples I previously adduced were shown to be illegitimate by subsequent studies, and those should no longer be counted as valid examples. In addition, all the lexicons that specialize in the New Testament period, including two very recent ones, list the meaning "ruler, authority over" for *kephalē*—it appears to be a well-established and valid meaning during the New Testament period.

On the other hand, the evidence for the meaning "source" is far weaker, and it is fair to say that the meaning has not yet been established. There are some texts which indicate that the physical head was thought of as the source of energy or life for the body, and therefore the possibility exists that the word *kephalē* might have come to be used as a metaphor for "source" or "source of life." There are two texts in Philo and one in the *Orphic Fragments* where such a meaning is possible, but it is not certain, and the meaning "leader, ruler" would fit these texts as well. There are still no *unambiguous* examples before or during the time of the New Testament in which *kephalē* has the metaphorical sense "source," and no lexicon specializing in the New Testament period lists such a meaning, nor does the Liddell and Scott lexicon list such a meaning as applied to persons or as applied to things that are not also the end point of something else. In fact, we may well ask those who advocate the meaning "source" an important question: Where is even one clear example of *kephalē* used of a *person* to mean "source" in all of Greek literature before or during the time of the New Testament? Is there even *one* example that is unambiguous?

Moreover, even if the meaning "source" or (as Cervin and Liefeld propose) "prominent part" were adopted for some examples of the word *kephalē*, we would still have no examples of "source" or "prominent part" *without the additional nuance of authority or rule*. Even in the texts where "source" or "prominent part" is alleged as the correct meaning, the person who is called "head" is always a person in leadership or authority. Therefore there is no linguistic basis for proposing that the New Testament texts which speak of Christ as the head of the church or the husband as the head of the wife can rightly be read apart from the attribution of authority to the one designated as "head."

APPENDIX 2

The Danvers Statement

The Council on Biblical Manhood and Womanhood

Rationale

We have been moved in our purpose by the following contemporary developments which we observe with deep concern:

1. The widespread uncertainty and confusion in our culture regarding the complementary differences between masculinity and femininity;
2. the tragic effects of this confusion in unraveling the fabric of marriage woven by God out of the beautiful and diverse strands of manhood and womanhood;
3. the increasing promotion given to feminist egalitarianism with accompanying distortions or neglect of the glad harmony portrayed in Scripture between the loving, humble leadership of redeemed husbands and the intelligent, willing support of that leadership by redeemed wives;
4. the widespread ambivalence regarding the values of motherhood, vocational homemaking, and the many ministries historically performed by women;
5. the growing claims of legitimacy for sexual relationships which have Biblically and historically been considered illicit or perverse, and the increase in pornographic portrayal of human sexuality;
6. the upsurge of physical and emotional abuse in the family;
7. the emergence of roles for men and women in church leadership that do not conform to Biblical teaching but backfire in the crippling of Biblically faithful witness;
8. the increasing prevalence and acceptance of hermeneutical oddities devised to reinterpret apparently plain meanings of Biblical texts;
9. the consequent threat to Biblical authority as the clarity of Scripture is jeopardized and the accessibility of its meaning to ordinary people is withdrawn into the restricted realm of technical ingenuity;
10. and behind all this the apparent accommodation of some within the church to the spirit of the age at the expense of winsome, radical Biblical authenticity which in the power of the Holy Spirit may reform rather than reflect our ailing culture.

Purposes

Recognizing our own abiding sinfulness and fallibility, and acknowledging the genuine evangelical standing of many who do not agree with all of our convictions, nevertheless, moved by the preceding observations and by the hope that the noble Biblical vision of sexual complementarity may yet win the mind and heart of Christ's church, we engage to pursue the following purposes:

1. To study and set forth the Biblical view of the relationship between men and women, especially in the home and in the church.
2. To promote the publication of scholarly and popular materials representing this view.
3. To encourage the confidence of lay people to study and understand for themselves the teaching of Scripture, especially on the issue of relationships between men and women.
4. To encourage the considered and sensitive application of this Biblical view in the appropriate spheres of life.
5. And thereby
   —to bring healing to persons and relationships injured by an inadequate grasp of God's will concerning manhood and womanhood,
   —to help both men and women realize their full ministry potential through a true understanding and practice of their God-given roles,
   —and to promote the spread of the gospel among all peoples by fostering a Biblical wholeness in relationships that will attract a fractured world.

Affirmations

Based on our understanding of Biblical teachings, we affirm the following:

1. Both Adam and Eve were created in God's image, equal before God as persons and distinct in their manhood and womanhood.
2. Distinctions in masculine and feminine roles are ordained by God as part of the created order, and should find an echo in every human heart.
3. Adam's headship in marriage was established by God before the Fall, and was not a result of sin.
4. The Fall introduced distortions into the relationships between men and women.
   —In the home, the husband's loving, humble headship tends to be replaced by domination or passivity; the wife's intelligent, willing submission tends to be replaced by usurpation or servility.
   —In the church, sin inclines men toward a worldly love of power or an abdication of spiritual responsibility, and inclines women to resist limitations on their roles or to neglect the use of their gifts in appropriate ministries.
5. The Old Testament, as well as the New Testament, manifests the equally high value and dignity which God attached to the roles of both men and women. Both Old and New Testaments also affirm the principle of male headship in the family and in the covenant community.
6. Redemption in Christ aims at removing the distortions introduced by the curse.
   —In the family, husbands should forsake harsh or selfish leadership and grow in love and care for their wives; wives should forsake resistance to their husbands' authority and grow in willing, joyful submission to their husbands' leadership.
   —In the church, redemption in Christ gives men and women an equal share in the blessings of salvation; nevertheless, some governing and teaching roles within the church are restricted to men.
7. In all of life Christ is the supreme authority and guide for men and women, so that no earthly submission—domestic, religious, or civil—ever implies a mandate to follow a human authority into sin.
8. In both men and women a heartfelt sense of call to ministry should never be used to set aside Biblical criteria for particular ministries. Rather, Biblical teaching should remain the authority for testing our subjective discernment of God's will.
9. With half the world's population outside the reach of indigenous evangelism; with countless other lost people in those societies that have heard the gospel; with the stresses and miseries of sickness, malnutrition, homelessness, illiteracy, ignorance, aging, addiction, crime, incarceration, neuroses, and loneliness, no man or woman

who feels a passion from God to make His grace known in word and deed need ever live without a fulfilling ministry for the glory of Christ and the good of this fallen world.

10. We are convinced that a denial or neglect of these principles will lead to increasingly destructive consequences in our families, our churches, and the culture at large.

The "Danvers Statement" was prepared by several evangelical leaders at a CBMW meeting in Danvers, Mass., in December, 1987. It was first published in final form by the CBMW in Wheaton, Ill., in November, 1988. We grant permission and encourage interested persons to use, reproduce, and distribute the Danvers Statement. Additional copies of this brochure are available for a donation of $9.00 for 50, and $15.00 for 100, postpaid, from CBMW, 2825 Lexington Road, Box 926, Louisville, KY 40280.

Council Members

Gary Almy, M.D.
Prof. of Psychiatry and Assoc. Dean
Chicago Medical School

Gleason Archer, Ph.D.
Professor of Old Testament
Trinity Evangelical Divinity School

Donald Balasa, J.D.
Attorney, Wildwood, Illinois

James Borland, Th.D.
Prof. of New Testament and Theology
Liberty University

Waldemar Degner, Ph.D.
Professor of Exegetical Theology
Concordia Seminary (Ft. Wayne, Ind.)

Lane T. Dennis, Ph.D.
President, Crossway Books

Thomas R. Edgar, Th.D.
Professor of New Testament, Capital Bible Seminary

John M. Frame, M.Phil.
Professor of Systematic Theology
Westminster Theological Seminary

W. Robert Godfrey, Ph.D.
Professor of Church History
Westminster Theological Serminary

Wayne A. Grudem, Ph.D.*
Assoc. Prof. of Systematic Theology
Trinity Evangelical Divinity School

H. Wayne House, Th.D., J.D.*
Vice-president and Professor of Theology
Western Baptist college

R. Kent Hughes, D.Min.*
Senior Pastor
College Church in Wheaton (Illinois)

James B. Hurley, Ph.D.
Professor of Counseling
Reformed Theological Seminary

Elliot Johnson
Professor of Bible Expostion
Dallas Theological Seminary

S. Lewis Johnson, Jr. Th.D.*
Minister, Believers Chapel, Dallas

Mary A. Kassian
Author, Women's Ministry Consultant
Calvary Baptist Church, Edmonton

Rhonda H. Kelley, Ph.D.
Associate Director, Innovative Evangelism
New Orleans, Louisiana

George W. Knight, III, Th.D.
Administrator, Dean and Professor of New Testament
Knox Theological Seminary

Beverly LaHaye
President
Concerned Women for America

Betty Jo Lewis
Homemaker
Atlanta, Georgia

Connie Marshner
Editor
Child & Family Protection Inst.

Richard Mayhew, Th.D.
Vice-Pres., Dean of Grad. Studies
The Master's Seminary

Douglas J. Moo, Ph.D.
Chairman, Dept. of New Testament
Trinity Evangelical Divinity School

Raymond C. Ortlund, Jr., Ph.D.
Asst. Prof. of Old Testament
Trinity Evangelical Divinity School

Dorothy Patterson, D.Min.
Homemaker
Dallas, Texas

John Piper, Dr. Theol.*
Senior Pastor
Bethlehem Baptist Church (Minneapolis)

Joyce Rogers
Homemaker
Memphis, Tennessee

Ken Sarles, Th.M.
Asst. Prof. of Systematic Theology
Dallas Theological Seminary

Siegfried Schatzmann, Ph.D.
Professor of New Testament
Oral Roberts University

Larry Walker, Ph.D.
Professor of Old Testament
Mid-America Seminary

William Weinrich, Ph.D.
Professor of Church History
Concordia Seminary (Ft. Wayne, Ind.)

*Currently serving on the Council's Executive Committee

Board of Reference

Hudson T. Armerding
Harold O. J. Brown
D. A. Carson
Edmund Clowney
Jerry Falwell
Carl F. H. Henry
Paul Karleen
D. James Kennedy
Gordon R. Lewis
Erwin Lutzer
John MacArthur, Jr.
Marty Minton
Thomas McComiskey
J. I. Packer
Paige and Dorothy Patterson
Pat Robertson
Adrian and Joyce Rogers
Bob Slosser
R. C. Sproul
James A. Stahr
Joseph M. Stowell, III
John F. Walvoord
Luder Whitlock
Peter Williamson

Notes

Endnotes to Preface (2006)

1. Bruce Ware, "Ethics in a New Millennium," *The Sourthern Baptist Journal of Theology* 4, no. 1 (Spring 2000): p. 92.
2. Dorothy Sayers, *Creed or Chaos?* (Manchester, NH: Sophia Institute Press, 1962): pp. 24-25.
3. James Boice et al. "Exposition." *Chicago Statement on Biblical Inerrancy* (Chicago: ICBI, 1978). Bible Research, ©2001-2006 by Michael D. Marlowe; www.Bible-researcher.com/Chicago.html (accessed May 9, 2006).

Endnotes to Foreword

1. Margaret Clarkson, *So You're Single* (Wheaton, IL: Harold Shaw, 1978), p. 10.
2. If you wonder why I quote more women singles than men in what follows, the answer is that there are probably six times as many ministering single women in the church and missions than single men. I base this on a survey taken in the late eighties of nineteen major mission agencies representing 20,333 missionaries. It showed that 16 percent (3,320) were unmarried. Of those, 15 percent were unmarried men. The unmarried women outnumbered the unmarried men in missions six to one. Howard Erickson, "Single Missionary Survey," *Fundamentalist Journal*, vol. 8, no. 1 (January 1989), p. 27. The women have certainly written more about their experience.
3. Trevor Douglas, "Wanted! More Single Men," *Evangelical Missions Quarterly*, vol. 24, no. 1 (January 1988), pp. 64-65.
4. John Piper, "Condom Ads Will Promote Promiscuity, Not Good Health," Minneapolis *Star-Tribune*, February 21, 1987.
5. This is an understated paraphrase from memory.
6. Luci Swindoll, *Wide My World Narrow My Bed* (Portland, OR: Multnomah Press, 1982).
7. Cheryl Forbes, "Let's Not Shackle the Single Life," *Christianity Today*, vol. 23, no. 10 (February 16, 1979), pp. 18-19.
8. Rhena Taylor, *Single and Whole* (Downers Grove, IL: InterVarsity Press, 1984), p. 71.
9. Douglas, "Wanted! More Single Men," pp. 65-66.
10. *Ibid.*, p. 66.
11. Ada Lum, *Single and Human* (Downers Grove, IL: InterVarsity Press, 1976), p. 34.
12. Ruth Tucker, *Guardians of the Great Commission: The Story of Women in Modern Missions* (Grand Rapids, MI: Zondervan, 1988), p. 84.
13. *Ibid.*, p. 40.
14. Elisabeth Elliot, "Virginity," *Elisabeth Elliot Newsletter*, March/April 1990 (Ann Arbor: Servant Publications), p. 1.
15. Douglas, "Wanted! More Single Men," p. 63.
16. Elva McAllaster, *Free to Be Single* (Chappaqua, NY: Christian Herald Books, 1979), p. 49.
17. *Ibid.*, pp. 50-51.
18. John White, *Eros Defiled* (Downers Grove, IL: InterVarsity Press, 1977), p. 22. Quoted in Clarkson, "Singleness: His Share for Me," *Christianity Today*, Vol. 23, no. 10, February 16, 1979. p. 15.
19. Lum, *Single and Human*, p. 22.
20. Douglas, "Wanted! More Single Men," p. 63.
21. Margaret Clarkson has no doubts in her own mind after six decades of singleness: "I may not blame my singleness on God. Singleness, like homosexuality, suffering, death, and all else that is less than perfect in this world, was not God's original plan for his creation. It was one of the many results of man's fall." Thus Jesus' singleness would not be sin but a participation in the calamities of the fallen world, like his mortality. "Singleness: His Share for Me," *Christianity Today*, vol. 23, no. 10, February 16, 1979, p. 15.
22. Dietrich Bonhoeffer, *Life Together*, trans. John W. Doberskin (New York: Harper and Row, 1945), p. 23.
23. Elliot, "Virginity," p. 3.

24. Edward F. and Gwen Weising, *Singleness: An Opportunity for Growth and Fulfillment* (Springfield, MO: Gospel Publishing House, 1982), pp. 5-6.
25. Clarkson, "Singleness: His Share for Me," pp. 14-15.
26. Ann Kiemel Anderson, *I Gave God Time* (Wheaton, IL: Tyndale House, 1982), p. 20.
27. Paul King Jewett, *Man as Male and Female* (Grand Rapids, MI: Eerdmans, 1975), p. 172.
28. Lum, *Single and Human*, pp. 44-45.
29. Forbes, "Let's Not Shackle the Single Life," p. 17.
30. Clarkson, *So You're Single*, p. 11.

Endnotes to Chapter One

1. Between November 1983 and May 1984 I carried on a debate concerning this issue with my friends and former colleagues Alvera and Berkeley Mickelsen in our denominational periodical, *The Standard* (of the Baptist General Conference). In these monthly articles I tried to lay the exegetical foundations for how men and women are called by God to relate to each other. The names of the articles are: "Male, Female and Morality" (November, 1983), pp. 26-28; "Satan's Design in Reversing Male Leadership Role" (December, 1983), pp. 33-35; "Jesus' Teaching on Men and Women: Dismantling the Fall, Not the Creation" (January, 1984), pp. 32-34; "A Metaphor of Christ and the Church" (February, 1984), pp. 27-29; "Creation, Culture and Corinthian Prophetesses" (March, 1984), pp. 30-32; "The Order of Creation" (April, 1984), pp. 35-38; "How Should a Woman Lead?" (May, 1984), pp. 34-36.
2. The cassette tapes of seven sermons on manhood and womanhood can be ordered by writing to Council on Biblical Manhood and Womanhood, P.O. Box 1173, Wheaton, IL 60189.
3. Paul K. Jewett, *Man as Male and Female* (Grand Rapids: William B. Eerdmans Pub. Co., 1975), p. 172.
4. *Man as Male and Female*, p. 173. The reference is to Emil Brunner, *Das Gebot und die Ordnungen* (Tuebingen: J.C.B. Mohr, 1933), p. 358.
5. *Man as Male and Female*, p. 178.
6. *Man as Male and Female*, p. 187f.
7. The teaching in 1 Peter 3:1-7 concerning the differentiation of roles is not based explicitly on the order of creation, but neither is it based on convention. Rather it is rooted in the example of "holy women who hoped in God" (v. 5). Sarah is cited as an example of submission, not because she complied with Abraham's wish that she pose as his sister (Genesis 20), which is the amazing example of submission we might have expected Peter to use, but rather because she said "my lord" when speaking offhandedly to herself about her husband. This seems to suggest that the root of Sarah's submission was a deep allegiance to Abraham's leadership that expressed itself without coercion or public pressure.
8. This is developed and defended exegetically by Ray Ortlund, Jr. in Chapter 3.
9. The limitation of this chapter is seen, for example, in that I will say very little about the capacity of a woman to bear children, and the special role that she has in nursing and nurturing them. Nor do I say anything about the man's crucial role in nurturing healthy, secure children. My focus is on the significance that manhood and womanhood have for the relational dynamics between men and women and the implications of these dynamics for the roles appropriate for each.
10. The fact that a Christian wife and church member, according to Acts 2:17, may "prophesy" implies, at least, that she may often have ideas and insights that a wise and humble husband and pastor will listen to and adopt. On women and prophecy see Wayne Grudem, *The Gift of Prophecy: In the New Testament and Today* (Westchester: Crossway Books, 1988), pp. 215-225.
11. This understanding of masculine responsibility will be developed, for example, from the way God comes to Adam first after the fall, implying his special responsibility in the failure even though Eve had sinned first. This accords with other pointers in the early chapters of Genesis before the fall that God meant for Adam to have a special responsibility for leadership (establishing a pattern of initiative) in relation to Eve. The sharing of initiatives

within that general pattern is implied in the image of Christ and the church as the model for marriage (Ephesians 5:21-33). Christ means for his bride to look to him for leadership, but not to the exclusion of her own thoughtful choices and initiatives in communication and in shared mission.

12. James Dobson, *Straight Talk to Men and Their Wives* (Waco: Word Books, 1980), pp. 64f.
13. Notice the move from "Children, obey your *parents*" in Ephesians 6:1 to "*Fathers* . . . bring them up in the nurture and discipline of the Lord" (v. 4). Both have responsibility to discipline, and children should hold both in high regard. But there is a special responsibility on fathers for the moral life and discipline of the home.
14. The Biblical teaching on nature's voice urging men and women not to exchange or confuse the cultural symbols of masculinity and femininity is very relevant here. When Paul says in 1 Corinthians 11:14, "Does not *nature teach* you that for a man to wear long hair is degrading to him?" he means that there is in man a *native sense* of repugnance against taking on cultural symbols of femininity. We would say, "Does not nature teach you that it is degrading to a man to wear a dress to church?" This voice of "nature" has great social benefits even in cultures untouched by special revelation from Scripture. But Romans 1:18-32 shows that a culture can become so corrupted that the native sense is ignored (vv. 26-27) and suppressed so that unnatural practices are even approved (v. 32). At such a point the call for Biblical repentance is not only a call to believe what the Bible teaches, but also to be transformed so deeply that the natural inclinations of mature manhood and womanhood are recovered, and society conforms once again not merely to what the Scriptures teach, but to "what nature teaches" among those who are now under the sway of Biblical truth and, more widely, under the rectifying social power of common grace. Alongside this teaching on the voice of nature should be put the teaching of 1 Corinthians 13:5 that love does not act in an "unseemly" way; it does not offend against good manners.
15. Another pointer from Scripture that this is the way God intends the relationship of husband and wife to be is the image of Christ as head of the church with man playing that role toward his wife according to Ephesians 5:23. The image of head implies that Christ is the *provider* as well as a leader. "Hold fast to the *Head, from whom the whole body, nourished* and knit together through its joints and ligaments, grows with a growth that is from God" (Colossians 2:19; cf. Ephesians 4:16).

This does not at all contradict the idea of leadership implied in "headship." On the contrary it strengthens it. The thought in Colossians 2:19 begins in verse 18 with a reference to people who are puffed up, "not holding fast to the Head, from whom the whole body, nourished and knit together through its joints and ligaments, grows with a growth that is from God." What is especially significant here for us is the implication that since Christ as head is *supplier*, the church must "hold fast" to him. The opposite of holding fast is being puffed up in mind and independent of Christ. So the implication is that headship is a role to be depended on and followed. There is to be an allegiance to the head as provider. This in essence implies a kind of leadership role for the head, as one to whom the body should ever look for what it needs. This is all the more evident when we note how Christ in fact does provide for his wife, the church. As the head he provides the body with truth (Ephesians 4:15, 21) and strength (Colossians 1:11) and wisdom (Colossians 2:3) and love (Ephesians 3:17-18; 4:16; Colossians 2:2). This means that the idea of provider implies loving leader because Christ leads with his truth and wisdom and he does this with love that lives out his teaching before us and for us.

There are numerous other Biblical evidences of the father's special responsibility to provide for his family. Consider, for example, 1 Timothy 3:5, "For if a someone (an elder) does not know how to manage (*proistenai*) his own household, how shall he take care of (*epimelesetai*) the church of God?" This idea of managing his own home well may have more than provision in mind (leadership for sure; see the use of *proistemi* in 1 Thessalonians 5:12), but I doubt that it has less. Elders/overseers are responsible to feed (1 Peter 5:2; Acts 20:28; Jeremiah 3:15) and protect (Acts 20:28-31) the flock.

Other evidences of the father's special responsibility to provide for his family portray the husband and father as the protector too. For example, Deuteronomy 10:18, "[God] executes justice for the fatherless and the widow, and loves the stranger giving him food and raiment." In other words, when the natural protector and provider is not there God steps in to take his place for the orphan and widow. Jeremiah 31:32 points in this same direction. God says concerning Israel, "My covenant which they broke, though I was their husband, says the Lord." How was he their husband? The context suggests that he was their husband in giving them protection at the sea and the provision in the wilderness.

16. The Biblical support for this is seen first in the texts like the ones cited above in note 15 (Deuteronomy 10:18 and Jeremiah 31:32). It is also implied in Ephesians 5:25, "Husbands, love your wives as Christ loved the church and gave himself up for her." Christ is here sacrificing himself to protect his wife, the church, from the ravages of sin and hell. Christ gives himself as the model for the husband in this regard because the husband is the *man*. This is not an arbitrary assignment. It is fitting because men were *created* for this. The "mystery" of marriage (Ephesians 5:32) is the truth that God designed male and female from the beginning to carry different responsibilities on the analogy of Christ and his church. The sense of responsibility to protect is there in man by virtue of this design of creation, not by virtue of the marriage covenant. Marriage makes the burden more personal and more intense, but it does not create it.

    Additional support for man's primary responsibility to protect women is found in the Old Testament pattern of men, rather than women, being given the duty to go to war. And nature itself seems to teach this duty of protection by endowing men, by and large, with greater brute strength.
17. Such customs, like all manners, are easily caricatured and satirized. But that is a mark of immaturity. Just as men and women know that some rough contact sports are not natural for women to play, so we know that there is a verbal rough-and-tumble among men, a kind of tough and rugged argumentation that is less appropriate when speaking to a woman than to a man.
18. J. I. Packer, "Understanding the Differences," in *Women, Authority and the Bible*, ed. by Alvera Mickelsen (Downers Grove: InterVarsity Press, 1986), p. 298-299.
19. One way of relating this definition to Scripture is to see it as an attempt to unfold some of what is implied in the old-fashioned phrase "help meet" in Genesis 2:18—"And the Lord God said, It is not good that the man should be alone; I will make him a help meet for him" (KJV). It may well be that the feminine inclination to help a man in his life and work signifies far more than I have been able to spell out in the phrases "affirm, receive, and nurture." But I have chosen to focus on what seems to me to be the heart of woman's feminine suitableness to man as a helper. The animals were helpful in some ways (Genesis 2:19). But the helpfulness of the woman is radically different. That unique human element is what I am interested in.
20. Ronda Chervin, *Feminine, Free and Faithful* (San Francisco: Ignatius Press, 1986), p. 15.
21. The Biblical warrant for this definition is 1 Peter 3:1-6, where a believing wife is married to an unbelieving husband. The text clearly teaches that she is to be submissive, but not in such a way that follows him in his unbelief. In fact, she is instructed how to get him to change, and be converted. The implication here is that her submission is not a de facto yielding to all that he says (since she has a higher allegiance to Jesus), but a *disposition* to yield and an *inclination* to follow. Her submission is a readiness to support his leadership wherever it does not lead to sin.
22. This paragraph is taken largely from my wider discussion of this issue in *Desiring God* (Portland: Multnomah Press, 1986), pp. 177-184.
23. For example, Gerald Sheppard, a professor of Old Testament at the University of Toronto, said in 1986, "I believe that the Gospel — as Evangelicals Concerned recognizes — should lead us at least to an affirmation of gay and lesbian partnerships ruled by a biblical ethic analogous to that offered for heterosexual relationships." "A Response to Anderson (II),"

TSF Bulletin, Vol. 9, No. 4, (March-April, 1986), p. 21. Similarly in July of 1986 the Evangelical Women's Caucus International under the influence of Virginia Mollenkott and Nancy Hardesty took a stand affirming the legitimacy of lesbianism to such an extent that members like Katherine Croeger and Gretchen Hull withdrew their membership. See "Gay Rights Resolution Divides Membership of Evangelical Women's Caucus," in: *Christianity Today* (October 3, 1986), pp. 40-44. Ralph Blair, the founder of Evangelicals Concerned, continues to debunk the claim that homosexuals can or should change their sexual orientation. He promotes monogamous homosexual relationships and claims Biblical support for it, arguing that the Bible is opposed to promiscuous homosexuality, not homosexuality itself. His views are cited by Tim Stafford, "Coming Out," *Christianity Today* (August 18, 1989), p. 19.

24. For a discussion of contemporary ministries that believe in the real possibilities of homosexuals to experience significant changes in the focus and power of their sexual preference see *Christianity Today*, August 18, 1989. See also George Rekers, *Shaping Your Child's Sexual Identity* (Grand Rapids: Baker Book House, 1982).
25. This is implied in the goodness and gladness of creation before the fall (Genesis 2) when man, created first, was called to the primary responsibility of leadership, and woman, created to be "a helper suitable for him," was called to use her gifts in helping carry that leadership through. This was all "very good" (Genesis 1:31) and therefore must have given man and woman great gladness. The same glad responsiveness to this order of things is implied in Ephesians 5:21-33 where man and wife are to model their relationship after that of Christ and the church. The church delights to accept strength and leadership from Christ. The delight that a woman takes in the strength and leadership of her husband is not merely owing to the marriage covenant. Just as man was created with a native sense of responsibility to lead and provide and protect in ways appropriate to his varying relationships, so woman was created as a suitable complement to honor this responsibility with gladness and satisfaction.
26. See page 46 for some examples of feminine strengths that enrich men.
27. Weldom M. Hardenbrook, *Missing from Action: Vanishing Manhood in America* (Nashville: Thomas Nelson Publishers, 1987), pp. 9-10.
28. Experience and psychology teach us that there are significant differences of many kinds between men and women. In each case one could establish a standard that would make one sex stronger and the other weaker. But Paul's teaching on the body of Christ warns us against demeaning those that have traits of weakness — male or female (1 Corinthians 12:21-26). The creation of male and female in the image of God (Genesis 1:27) forbids that we make our diversity a ground for variable worth as persons in God's eyes. And the Biblical declaration that all was "very good" when God created us with our differences means that a "weakness" by one narrow standard is a "strength" in its contribution to the total fabric of man as male and female in God's image.
29. When 1 Peter 3:7 refers to the wife as a "weaker feminine vessel," it is probably focussing on the most obvious fact, especially in that more rugged culture, that a woman has lesser brute strength. That is, she is more in need of protection and provision from the man than he is from her. He is to "recognize" this and honor her by supplying all she needs as a fellow-heir of grace. The verse does not contemplate the question I have raised, namely whether there are some other things about man that can also be described as weaker than woman.
30. I am assuming implicitly here what I said about submission on p. 47.
31. The elders are charged with the primary responsibility of leadership (Acts 20:28; 1 Timothy 5:17; 1 Peter 5:3) and Biblical instruction (Titus 1:9; 1 Timothy 3:2; 5:17) in the church. That's a summary of their job. So when Paul puts those two things together and says, "I do not permit a woman to teach or exercise authority," one very natural implication is, "I do not permit a woman to assume the office of elder in the church."

So the authority Paul has in mind in 1.Timothy 2:12 at least includes the authority of elders. We saw already from Jesus in Luke 22:26 what that is supposed to look like: "Let the greatest among you become as the youngest, and the leader as one who serves." Paul said in 2 Corinthians 10:8 and 13:10 that God gave him authority in the church not for tearing down or destroying, but for building up. And Peter said to the elders of the churches (1 Peter 5:3), "Do not domineer over the those in your charge, but be examples to the flock."

In other words elder-authority is servant-authority. Elder-leadership is servant-leadership. That's why teaching is at the heart of this calling. Biblical authority leads by persuasion — by teaching — not by coercion or political maneuvering. Elder-authority is always subordinate to Biblical truth. Therefore teaching is the primary instrument of leadership in the church. And authority refers to the divine calling of spiritual, gifted men to take primary responsibility as elders for Christlike, servant-leadership and teaching in the church. Their goal is not their own status or honor. Their goal is the equipping of the saints — women and men — to do the work of the ministry.

32. The Danvers Statement is the charter statement (Rationale, Purposes and Affirmations) of the Council on Biblical Manhood and Womanhood. Copies may be ordered from the Council at P. O. Box 317, Wheaton, IL 60189. It is presented in Appendix 2.

Endnotes to Chapter Two

1. This includes patterns stemming from negligence and abuses by both husband and wife. As the *Danvers Statement* (see Appendix 2) says, "In the home, the husband's loving, humble headship tends to be replaced by domination or passivity; the wife's intelligent, willing submission tends to be replaced by usurpation or servility." Our concern is to work from both sides for what Christ really intended His relationship to the church to look like.
2. One of the most pertinent Greek witnesses for the meaning of *head* in Paul's time describes an image of the head on the body as having a role of leadership. Philo of Alexandria said, "Just as nature conferred the sovereignty (*hēgemōnian*) of the body on the head when she granted it also possession of the citadel as the most suitable for its kingly rank, conducted it thither to take command and established it on high with the whole framework from neck to foot set below it, like the pedestal under the statue, so too she has given the lordship (*to kratos*) of the senses to the eyes" (*Special Laws*, III, 184.)
3. Mary Stewart Van Leeuwen, *Gender and Grace* (Downers Grove, IL: InterVarsity Press, 1990), p. 238.
4. The English work most cited on this question is the dissertation by J. E. Crouch, *The Origin and Intention of the Colossian Haustafel*, F.R.L.A.N.T. 109 (Göttingen: Vandenhoeck und Ruprecht, 1972). The examples of ostensible parallels translated into English can be read in this work.
5. The Greek word *prostatis* does not mean "leader" but "helper," "patroness." In the Bible it occurs only here.
6. Some contributors to this collection of essays do not endorse this view of New Testament prophecy. They would say that the New Testament gift of prophecy does not continue today because it was part of the unique revelatory moment in history and consisted of words having the infallible authority of God. They would say that women could prophesy in this sense but not teach because the authority attached so distinctly to the words and not to the person and the exposition as it does in teaching.
7. This understanding of prophecy in the New Testament is developed and defended in Wayne Grudem, *The Gift of Prophecy in the New Testament and Today* (Westchester, IL: Crossway Books, 1988); Roy Clements, *Word and Spirit: The Bible and the Gift of Prophecy* (Leicester: U.C.C.F. Booklets, 1986); Graham Houston, *Prophecy Today* (Leicester: InterVarsity Press, 1989); D. A. Carson, *Showing the Spirit* (Grand Rapids, MI: Baker, 1987). This view of New Testament prophecy is the one held by the editors of this book, but some other contributors hold a different view. See p. 530, n. 15.
8. See note 6.

9. See also Wayne Grudem, "Prophecy, Yes, but Teaching, No: Paul's Consistent Affirmation of Women's Participation without Governing Authority," *Journal of the Evangelical Theological Society*, 30:1, March 1987, pp. 11-23.
10. Ruth Tucker, *Guardians of the Great Commission: A History of Women in Modern Missions* (Grand Rapids: Zondervan, 1988).
11. *Ibid.*, p. 47.
12. *Ibid.*, p. 83
13. A. J. Gordon, "The Ministry of Women," *Gordon-Conwell Monograph* 61 (South Hamilton, MA: Gordon-Conwell Theological Seminary, n.d.), p. 10. Originally published in *Missionary Review of the World*, vol. 8, no. 12 (new series), December, 1894, pp. 910-921.
14. Dr. and Mrs. Howard Taylor, *Hudson Taylor and the China Inland Mission: The Growth of a Work of God* (London: The Religious Tract Society, 1940), pp. 397-398.
15. Tucker, p. 117.
16. John White, *When the Spirit Comes with Power* (Downers Grove, IL: InterVarsity Press, 1988), p. 128.
17. *Plutarch's Lives of Illustrious Men*, trans. John Dryden (New York: John Wurtele Lovell, n.d.), vol. 3, p. 359.
18. John Chrysostom, *Homilies on the Epistle of St. Paul the Apostle to the Romans*, xxxi.7, in *A Select Library of the Nicene and Post-Nicene Fathers of the Christian Church*, ed. Philip Schaff (Grand Rapids: Eerdmans, 1956), first series, vol. 11, p. 555.
19. However, we are perplexed about the fact that in the near context of the citation concerning Junias, Epiphanias also designates Prisca as a man mentioned in Romans 16:3, even though we know from the New Testament that she is a woman.
20. Gerald Sheppard, "A Response to Ray Anderson," *TSF Bulletin*, vol. 9, no. 4 (March-April 1986), p. 21.
21. Karen J. Torjesen, "Sexuality, Hierarchy and Evangelicalism," *TSF Bulletin*, vol. 10, no. 4 (March-April 1987), pp. 26-27.
22. "Gay Rights Resolution Divides Membership of Evangelical Women's Caucus," *Christianity Today*, October 3, 1986, pp. 40-43.
23. Paul Jewett, *Man as Male and Female* (Grand Rapids: Eerdmans), p. 178.
24. Paul Jewett, "An Overlooked Study: John Boswell on Homosexuality," *Reformed Journal*, vol. 33, issue 1 (January 1983), p. 17.
25. Robin Scroggs, *The New Testament and Homosexuality* (Philadelphia: Fortress Press, 1983), p. 129.
26. Paul Jewett, *Interpretation*, vol. 39, No. 2 (April 1985), p. 210.
27. Gerald P. Regier, "The Not So Disposable Family," *Pastoral Renewal*, vol. 13, no. 1 (July-August 1988), p. 20.
28. Nicholas Wolterstorff, "Hearing the Cry," in *Women, Authority and the Bible*, ed. Alvera Mickelsen (Downers Grove, IL: InterVarsity Press), 1986), p. 289.
29. Emil Brunner, *Das Gebot und die Ordnungen* (Tübingen: J. C. B. Mohr/Paul Siebeck, 1933), p. 358.
30. Otto Piper, *Christian Ethics* (London: Thomas Nelson and Sons Ltd., 1970), p. 299.
31. Elisabeth Elliot, "Virginity," *Elisabeth Elliot Newsletter*, March/April 1990 (Ann Arbor: Servant Publications), pp. 2-3.
32. These quotes are from the *Danvers Statement* of the Council on Biblical Manhood and Womanhood. It is printed in Appendix 2.
33. Gretchen Gaebelein Hull (Old Tappan, NJ: Fleming H. Revell, 1987), pp. 188-189.

Endnotes to Chapter Three

1. Ephesians 5:23, 25.
2. In this essay I will be interacting primarily with the evangelical feminist interpretation of Genesis 1-3 in Gilbert Bilezikian, *Beyond Sex Roles: A Guide for the Study of Female Roles in the Bible* (Grand Rapids: Baker Book House, 1985) and Aida Bensançon Spencer, *Beyond the Curse: Women Called to Ministry* (Nashville: Thomas Nelson, 1985).

3. I have put the *RSV*'s prose of verse 27 into its proper poetic form. Compare the *New International Version*.
4. Bilezikian, *Beyond Sex Roles*, p. 22.
5. Follow the reasoning in Calvin, *Institutes*, I, XV, 4. By contrast with original man, fallen man today is more like an image in a carnival house of mirrors—distorted, but not beyond repair.
6. See John Frame's interesting essay on this subject in Chapter 12 of this volume, pages 225-232.
7. The climactic power of verse 27 is underscored by the three-fold repetition of the verb "create," the great verb of verse 1. This feature of verse 27 implies that God's entire creative work reached its fulfillment in man.
8. Sexuality is *assumed* in verse 22: "Be fruitful and multiply. . . ."
9. Bilezikian, page 22. Italics his.
10. This usage should not be viewed as a mere accident of English translation, because God uses the one word *'adam*, "man," to refer to the first man Adam specifically (e.g., 3:17) and to the human race generally (e.g., 1:26-27; 5:1-2).
11. Bilezikian, p. 22. Italics his.
12. Spencer, *Beyond the Curse*, p. 39.
13. Spencer, page 21.
14. Note that the words *likeness* and *image* in 5:3 echo the wording of 1:26.
15. Spencer, p. 29.
16. By "Paradox" I do not mean a logical inconsistency or an absurdity. I mean a truth that bears an appearance of self-contradiction because it consists of two principles that *seem* to clash but, in reality, are mutually compatible. An illustration of a paradox would be the truth that one must lose one's life to find it (Matthew 10:39). Indeed, true Christian living is paradoxical to the core. Cf. 2 Corinthians 6:8b-10. This should be expected of a life lived for the God "whose service is perfect freedom" (*Book of Common Prayer*). Cf. *New Dictionary of Theology* (Downers Grove, IL: InterVarsity Press, 1988), s.v. "Paradox in Theology," by J. I. Packer.
17. The *RSV* of 2:20 reads, "but for the man there was not found a helper fit for him." But the Hebrew verb there is active, not passive. It should be construed to say, "but, as for the man, he did not find a helper fit for him." Adam now saw what God had known all along. For a well-reasoned argument advocating this interpretation, see U. Cassuto, *A Commentary on the Book of Genesis* (Jerusalem: Magnes Press, 1972), I:132ff.
18. Ephesians 5:28-29, RSV.
19. The reader will forgive me for using "Adam" and "Eve" from now on, for the sake of convenience, even though this usage does not appear until later in the Biblical text.
20. It has been argued that "a helper suitable for him" misinterprets the Hebrew. Instead, it is claimed, the true interpretation is "a power equal to him." Cf. R. David Freedman, "Woman, A Power Equal to Man," *Biblical Archaeology Review*, January-February 1983, pp. 56-58. Freedman reasons that, because the Hebrew word traditionally rendered "help(er)" *can* be construed in a few passages as "power," this latter sense *must* be accepted as a correction of the Hebrew lexicon. But he is assuming the very point which he must prove, because "help(er)" also functions meaningfully in every passage he cites. And even if he could demonstrate that the Hebrew may mean "power" in some contexts—although I very much doubt that it does—still, Freedman would have to prove further that "power" is the most meaningful interpretation of the word here in Genesis 2:18 and 20. That is most improbable. If an interpreter wishes his proposal to impress others as more than his own whimsical brainstorm, he must prove that his view is more than a merely possible construction of the sense; to be compelling, his interpretation must move toward its conclusion with inexorable, necessary logical force. Furthermore, a popularly-written, three-page article simply cannot treat a lexical question with sufficient depth to be convincing. For a more satisfactory approach to lexical argumentation see James Barr, "Semitic Philology and the Interpretation of the Old Testament," in *Tradition and Interpretation: Essays by Members of the Society for Old Testament Study* (Oxford, 1979), especially pp. 48ff.

21. By analogy, the dean of Trinity Evangelical Divinity School and I are equals before God. We both approach the throne of grace with the same boldness through the merit of Christ. Nevertheless, he is the dean of the Divinity School and I am an assistant professor. This fact requires that we love one another in different ways. He loves me by pursuing God's glory and my fulfillment through his leadership, and I love him by supporting his leadership and doing what I can to make him a successful dean.
22. Jack Crabtree, Philosophy 324, the University of Oregon, Spring 1989. I am indebted to Mr. Crabtree for allowing me to read his lecture notes, which contained a number of interesting insights.
23. Paul follows this same reasoning in 1 Corinthians 11:8-9 in arguing for sexual distinctions in dress and conduct.
24. That a "bone-and-flesh" relationship between people need not exclude hierarchical ranking is clearly evident in the logic of Judges 9:1-3 and 2 Samuel 5:1-3; 19:11-12.
25. George W. Ramsey, in "Is Name-Giving an Act of Domination in Genesis 2:23 and Elsewhere?" *Catholic Biblical Quarterly* 50 (1988): 24-35, argues that "it is very difficult to identify a [Biblical] passage where the narrator suggests that the name given is intended to shape the character of the recipient" (p. 34). From this he concludes that Adam's naming of Eve in Genesis 2 is an act of discernment, not domination. The argument is misplaced, as far as my interpretation is concerned, because: (1) I agree with Ramsey that naming does not "shape the character of the recipient" by a power-laden word; and (2) I agree with Ramsey that Adam's naming of Eve is not an assertion of domination. I do contend, however, that his naming of the woman makes sense as an act of his headship and that it does not make sense in any other way.
26. Strictly speaking, Adam *names* Eve in 3:20. By his act here in 2:23 Adam *identifies* who she is in relation to himself. But because this act was the climax of his naming of other creatures (vv. 19-20), it too may be referred to as naming.
27. Spencer, pp. 23ff.
28. *Ibid.*, p. 24. On page 26 she states, "The Hebrew text even literally signifies that the woman is 'in front of' the man or 'over' him!"
29. *Ibid.* English italics added.
30. The historical relationship between the preposition *neged* and the noun *nagîd* is unclear. What is obvious, but also semantically ambiguous, is the fact that the two words are etymologically related to one another.
31. *neged* in Psalm 119:168, then, suggests that the psalmist's whole life and soul are laid bare before the searching ministry of the law.
32. Spencer, p. 26. It would have been helpful if Spencer had stated clearly whether she believes the subordination in view is "inherent" to the woman's *person* or *position*. Presumably, however, Spencer would not acknowledge the validity of such a distinction. Feminism loses its logical power and moral attractiveness if one's personal worth and one's role are allowed to be registered independently of one another.
33. *Ibid.*, p. 27. Bilezikian argues along the same line in *Beyond Sex Roles*, only he goes further by misrepresenting our view. He states on page 28: "According to them [that is, "uninformed teachers of the Bible" in Bilezikian's preceding sentence], *helper* meant that man was boss and woman his domestic" (italics his). The male-boss/female-domestic relational model matches male domination, not male headship.
34. Patricia Gundry locates the heart of the evangelical feminist cause at this point: "There is but one central and watershed question in this conflicted issue: Are women fully human?" (A. Mickelsen, ed., *Women, Authority & the Bible* [Downers Grove, IL: InterVarsity Press, 1986], page 20).

    Gretchen Gaebelein Hull ups the ante with this challenge: ". . . I suggest we go further than Gundry did and ask the question: 'Are women fully redeemed?'" (*Ibid.*, p. 24).
35. Bilezikian, p. 36.
36. This should not be construed as a serious warning against marriage, as no doubt the reader detects. One gladly surrenders privacy to one's wife, and vice versa, in exchange for the satisfaction of marital intimacy and acceptance.

37. Cf. page 13, where Bilezikian explains that he is replying to James B. Hurley, *Man and Woman in Biblical Perspective* (Grand Rapids: Zondervan, 1981).
38. Please note that I am not interpreting the logic of the apostle in his making this connection, which logic I am not satisfied that I clearly understand. I merely observe the fact that Paul makes the connection, confident that his logic in doing so was compelling.
39. Eve's reply in verses 2-3 shows that she has been instructed in the command of 2:16-17, although she misquotes God. The inaccuracies in her quote are to be explained in terms of sin's operations in her mind, not in terms of "limited knowledge," as Bilezikian argues in *Beyond Sex Roles*, pp. 43-48. The latter interpretation trivializes Eve's moral dignity and misses the moral insight and power of the text. Moses' whole point is that we wickedly rebelled against the clear light of God's holy law. This alone can explain the ugly realities of life as we know it now.
40. The *RSV* does not include the words "with her," but their equivalent does lie in the Hebrew text.
41. The text literally reads, "But the LORD God called *to the man* and said *to him*, 'Where are you [second person *singular masculine* pronoun]?'"
42. Cf. 1 Timothy 2:14.
43. Derek Kidner, in his *Genesis: An Introduction and Commentary* (Downers Grove, IL: InterVarsity Press, 1972), p. 71, describes verses 14-19 as "oracles of destiny." This is an astute categorization of these three divine *dicta*. Cf. Genesis 27:28-29, 39-40; 49:1-27 as other "oracles of destiny."
44. At issue is not whether wives suffer *either* conflict with their husbands *or* domination by their husbands. Wives suffer both to one degree or another, being married to sinful men. At issue here is what God means by this particular utterance.
45. I am indebted here to the perceptive study by Susan T. Foh, "What Is the Woman's Desire?" *Westminster Theological Journal* 37 (1975): 376-383.
46. Paul uses the same moral reasoning in Romans 1:18-32, with his three-fold "God gave them up" (vv. 24, 26, and 28).
47. In this interpretation, the *waw* in *w*^{e}*hû'* is adversative and the *yqtl* form in *yimšol* is obligatory.
48. Here the *waw* in *w*^{e}*hû'* is coordinative and the *yqtl* verb form in *yimšol* is future.
49. This prescription for God-glorifying human fulfillment is precisely what we find in the gospel. Cf. Ephesians 5:22-33; 1 Peter 3:1-7.
50. God is not implying that husbands should disregard the counsel of their wives. Our natural limitations suggest that we husbands very much need our wives' perspectives, *as long as their opinions help us to keep moving in a God-glorifying direction*. And it is primarily our responsibility, as the heads of our households, to decide, in the light of Holy Scripture, what courses of action will most glorify God.
51. Spencer comments:

    It was the nature of Eve's command which was wrong, not the command in itself. (*Beyond the Curse*, p. 37)

    So, Spencer reasons, Eve could have assumed headship, urged obedience upon Adam, and that would not have clashed with the Creator's design. But if her leadership was in itself a matter of moral indifference, why does God mention it at all? God's logic is, "Because of X and Y, I curse the ground." Adam's submission to Eve is factor X and his eating of the forbidden fruit is factor Y.
52. My paraphrase and amplification of the import of verse 20.
53. Bilezikian, p. 56. On page 58 he writes:

    The ruler/subject relationship between Adam and Eve began after the fall. It was for Eve the application of the same death principle that made Adam slave to the soil. Because it resulted from the fall, the rule of Adam over Eve is viewed as satanic in origin, no less than death itself.

54. *Ibid.*, page 214. In "A Critique of Wayne Grudem's Treatment of *Kephalē* in Ancient Greek Texts," a paper read to the Evangelical Theological Society, Atlanta, 1986, Bilezikian states:

    The imposition of an authority structure upon this exquisite balance of [marital] reciprocity would *paganize* the marriage relationship and make the Christ/church paradigm irrelevant to it. (p. 33; emphasis added)

55. Cf. Ephesians 6:1-4; Colossians 3:20-21.
56. Cf. 1 Thessalonians 5:12-13; Hebrews 13:17.
57. Bilezikian, *Beyond Sex Roles*, p. 57.
58. Rosemary Radford Ruether, *Womanguides: Readings toward a Feminist Theology* (Boston: Beacon Press, 1985), page ix.
59. Cf. Romans 8:29-30; 2 Corinthians 3:18.

Endnotes to Chapter Four

1. For recent discussion of these issues see Richard N. Longenecker, "Authority, Hierarchy and Leadership Patterns in the Bible," in Alvera Mickelsen, ed., *Women, Authority and the Bible* (Downers Grove, IL: InterVarsity Press, 1986), p. 71.
2. Radical Christian feminists stand apart from evangelicals. When it suits them, they reject Biblical authority based on their subjective experiences which produce a women's theology of liberation. Elizabeth Fiorenza claims that her first principle of Bible interpretation is "(1) suspicion rather than acceptance of biblical authority," and in her opinion "without question, the Bible is a male book." Elizabeth Schussler Fiorenza, "The Will to Choose or to Reject: Continuing Our Critical Work," in Letty M. Russell, ed., *Feminist Interpretation of the Bible* (Philadelphia: Westminster Press, 1985), p. 130. She "locates revelation not in biblical texts but in the experience of women struggling for liberation from patriarchy. . . . " *Ibid.*, p. 136. Phyllis Trible holds that "A final unchangeable text is neither possible nor desirable," and believes Fiorenza has established that "only the nonsexist and nonandrocentric traditions of the Bible have revelatory power." Phyllis Trible, "Postscript: Jottings on the Journey," in Russell, *Ibid.*, pp. 148-149. "Human experience is both the starting point and the ending point of the circle of interpretation," and especially "women's experience is an interpretative key for feminist theology," according to Rosemary Radford Ruether, "Feminist Interpretation: A Method of Correlation," in Russell, *Ibid.*, p. 111.
3. Gretchen Gaebelein Hull, for example, calls herself a "biblical feminist" and lists the following who share her viewpoint: Gilbert Bilezikian, Richard and Joyce Boldrey, Patricia Gundry, Richard and Catherine Kroeger, Kari Malcolm, Aida Spencer, Elaine Storkey, Willard Swartley, and Don Williams. Hull, *Equal to Serve: Women and Men in the Church and Home* (Old Tappan, NJ: Fleming H. Revell, 1987), p. 60.
4. *Ibid.*, p. 55.
5. James B. Hurley, *Man and Woman in Biblical Perspective* (Grand Rapids: Zondervan, 1981), pp. 20-78, explains what women's lives were like in Old and New Testament times; Aida Besançon Spencer, *Beyond the Curse: Women Called to Ministry* (Nashville: Thomas Nelson, 1985), pp. 46-57, covers the position of women in rabbinic writings largely current at the time of Christ; and Mary J. Evans, *Women in the Bible: An Overview of All the Crucial Passages on Women's Roles* (Downers Grove, IL: InterVarsity Press, 1983), pp. 24-43, describes women in Old Testament society and in the Graeco-Roman world. Ben Witherington III, *Women in the Ministry of Jesus* (Cambridge, England: Cambridge University Press, 1984), p. 10, concludes, "It is fair to say that a low view of women was common, perhaps even predominant before, during and after Jesus' era."
6. Donald G. Bloesch, *Is the Bible Sexist?: Beyond Feminism and Patriarchalism* (Westchester, IL: Crossway Books, 1982), p. 25, has some helpful discussion highlighting these distinctions.
7. Evans, *Woman in the Bible*, p. 45.

8. Letha Scanzoni and Nancy Hardesty, *All We're Meant to Be: A Biblical Approach to Women's Liberation* (Waco, TX: Word Books, 1974), p. 56.
9. Evans, p. 45.
10. Hurley, *Man and Woman in Biblical Perspective*, p. 83.
11. Although opinions vary, the present writer regards John 7:53-8:11 as part of the genuine text of John's Gospel.
12. Bloesch, *Is the Bible Sexist?* p. 28.
13. Evans, p. 46.
14. Hurley, p. 109.
15. *Ibid.*, pp. 109-110.
16. Scanzoni and Hardesty, *All We're Meant to Be*, p. 58, suggest that Jesus' touch gave her a personal encounter, while "his public recognition brought social and psychological wholeness to this outcast."
17. Hurley, p. 86.
18. Philip Siddons, *Speaking Out for Women—A Biblical View* (Valley Forge: Judson, 1980), p. 55, calls this "the longest private conversation of Jesus with an individual as presented in any of the Gospels." If Siddons means the longest conversation time-wise, it would be impossible to prove. But as recorded, Jesus plainly spoke more words to Nicodemus than he did to the Samaritan woman (in both the Greek and English texts). Evans, p. 52, makes a rather large assumption when she claims that "the teaching of John 4 about the nature of the gospel and the nature of God *must* have come to the disciples through this woman" (italics my own). Jesus certainly talked to His disciples many times about God and His nature. He very naturally might have related his conversation with the woman to John the beloved and His other disciples. They frequently asked Him for further explanations (Matthew 13:36), which He gave. He even answered such requests from the crowds (John 6:41-47, 52-53, 60-65).
19. Witherington, *Women in the Ministry of Jesus*, p. 38.
20. Hull, *Equal to Serve*, p. 115. Mary was sitting with the other disciples in the position of a pupil, i.e., "at the feet of" (cf. Luke 8:35; Acts 22:3). Spencer, *Beyond the Curse*, p. 61, points out that Mary was not off to the side or in the back of the room but "was fact [sic] to face (*pros* is the preposition used in v. 39) with Jesus."
21. Hull, p. 116.
22. Hurley, p. 89.
23. *Ibid.*, pp. 57-58. Evans's excursus on Mary is on pp. 57-60. Hurley also has a good section dealing with Mary, *Man and Woman*, pp. 112-114. See in addition A. T. Robertson, *The Mother of Jesus: Her Problems and Her Glory* (New York: Doran, 1925), for a perceptive insight into Mary's thoughts that treats all relevant passages.
24. Although the *KJV*, *Knox*, *Phillips*, and *Moffatt* say the women ministered to "him," almost all other authorities have to "them." These include *ASV*, *RSV*, *NASB*, *NEB*, *TEV*, *Williams*, *Weymouth*, and the Catholic *NAB*, *Confraternity*, and *Jerusalem* versions. The UBS[3] text includes the reading "them" (*autois*) with a "B" level of certainty (their second highest of four categories). Although the evidence is divided, Hodges' and Farstad's *The Greek New Testament According to the Majority Text* (Nashville: Thomas Nelson, 1982), p. 211, also reads this way. Bruce M. Metzger, *A Textual Commentary on the Greek New Testament* (New York: United Bible Societies, 1971), p. 144, notes that the plural (them) has good support in the Alexandrian, Western, and Caesarean text-types, and that the singular (him), "appears to be a Christocentric correction, due perhaps to Marcion." If those women ministered to the twelve as well as to Jesus, it would increase their financial outlay considerably.
25. The word translated "ministered" or "served" in Luke 8:3, Matthew 27:56, and Mark 15:41 is from *diakoneo*, a verb meaning to serve in a general way. It is used of waiting on tables (Luke 22:27), and of service in general (2 Timothy 1:18; 1 Peter 4:10), even of the general ministry of deacons (1 Timothy 3:13). Although the ministering in Luke 8:3 is restricted to finances (as it is in Romans 15:25), each time it is used of these women the tense is the imperfect, indicating continued action over a period of time. Witherington, p. 114, suggests that these women did not "abandon their traditional roles in regard to

preparing food, serving, etc. Rather, serving Christ gave these roles new significance and importance, for now they could be used to serve the Master and the family of faith."

26. Hurley, p. 91. Spencer, p. 55, suggests that these women probably travelled in a group to appear more respectable.
27. Josephus, *Antiquities* iv. 8. 15. A note appended by the editor points out that "the Pentateuch says not a word about the exclusion of women as witnesses in courts of justice. It is very probable, however, that this was the practice of the Jews in the days of Josephus."
28. Evans, *Ibid.*, p. 50. Raymond E. Brown, "Roles of Women in the Fourth Gospel," *Theological Studies* 36 (1975), p. 692, applies the term "Quasi-apostolic role" only to the Samaritan woman and Mary Magdalene, each sent by Christ. Evans unadvisedly expands the use of the phrase to include the women at the tomb.
29. Hurley, p. 92. Still, Jesus rebuked the disciples for *not* believing the women's report (Mark 16:14; Luke 20:10). Evans, p. 55, asserts that the women showed "a greater perseverance, a greater loyalty and possibly a greater faith than even the twelve apostles." Thankfully, when the disciples had seen the Lord, they had the same glowing report to give Thomas (John 20:20, 25).
30. Siddons, *Speaking Out for Women*, p. 54. Evans, p. 57, acknowledges the all-male group of apostles, but hedges that "it is not clear what significance this was intended to have for the church."
31. The Samaritan woman gave a personal testimony (John 4:29, 39) that brought others to see Christ as Messiah.
32. Regarding the suggestion made by some that Romans 16:17 speaks not of a man (Junias), but of a woman, (Junia), who was an apostle, see the discussion in Chapter 11 in this volume, pp. 221-222; also Chapter 2, Question 38.
33. Spencer, p. 45, note 5.
34. Aida Bensançon Spencer, Review of Samuele Bacchiocchi, "Women in the Church: A Biblical Study of the Role of Women in the Church", *Trinity Journal* 8:1 (Spring, 1987), p. 100.
35. Evans, p. 50.
36. The word used for men here is *andrōn* from *anēr*, a word used only of a man, and in contrast to a woman. If just any human being had been meant, whether male or female, the word *anthropos* would have been used. See W. F. Arndt and F. W. Gingrich, *A Greek-English Lexicon of the New Testament*, 2nd ed. rev. F. W. Gingrich and Frederick W. Danker (Chicago: University of Chicago, 1979), pp. 66-67.

Endnotes to Chapter Five

1. Against Pauline authorship it has become quite common to regard this passage as an interpolation—a later insertion by a scribe—rather than an original Pauline passage. But this passage should be viewed as an interpolation only if there are convincing textual arguments, and this is hardly the case here. For bibliographical data on this question, see Gordon D. Fee, *The First Epistle to the Corinthians* (NICNT; Grand Rapids, MI: Eerdmans, 1987), p. 492, n. 3. Some scholars believe the first part of the passage (11:3-7b, Padgett; 11:2-9, Shoemaker) reflects the Corinthian position, and the last section of the passage (11:7c-16 and 11:10-16, respectively) is Paul's response to the Corinthians. In effect, then, Paul is an egalitarian and rejects the notion that women have to be veiled. See A. Padgett, "Paul on Women in the Church: The Contradictions of Coiffure in 1 Corinthians 11:2-16," *Journal for the Study of the New Testament* 20 (1984): 69-86; T. P. Shoemaker, "Unveiling of Equality: 1 Corinthians 11:2-16," *Biblical Theology Bulletin* 17 (1987): 60-63. The problem with this view of a Corinthian quotation in the first section is that the citation becomes incredibly long. Moreover there is no indication that Paul is citing the Corinthians in the first part of the text.
2. See especially James B. Hurley, "Did Paul Require Veils or the Silence of Women? A Consideration of 1 Cor. 11:2-16 and 1 Cor. 14:33b-36," *Westminster Theological Journal* 35 (1973): 193-200; cf. also James B. Hurley, *Man and Woman in Biblical Perspective* (Grand Rapids, MI: Zondervan, 1981), pp. 254-271; J. Murphy-O'Conner,

"Sex and Logic in 1 Corinthians 11:2-16," *Catholic Biblical Quarterly* 42 (1980): 488-489.

3. This reading is only found in a correction to the Alexandrinus text, not in the other early texts of the Septuagint.
4. The following arguments are largely taken from Fee (*1 Corinthians*, pp. 506-512). His footnotes on these pages are invaluable for a defense of his argument.
5. For some references to *katakalupto* in the LXX see: Exodus 26:34; Numbers 22:5; Leviticus 9:19; Esther 6:12 (variant reading); Habakkuk 2:14; Isaiah 11:9; Jeremiah 26:8; 28:42; Ezekiel 26:10, 19; 32:7; 38:9; Daniel 12:9; Sirach 24:3; Susannah 32 (T). In virtually every case the translation "cover" or "hide" is appropriate.
6. In the text, Plutarch refers to Scipio the Younger as *kata tēs kephalēs echōn to himation* ("having a toga covering his head") [*Mor.* 200ff). However, the addition of the word *himation* ("toga") makes this passage easier to comprehend.
7. The preposition *anti* in 11:15 need not refer to substitution. It can also indicate equivalence. The latter makes better sense in the context. See Walter Bauer, *A Greek-English Lexicon of the New Testament and Other Early Christian Literature* (henceforward *BAGD*), trans. William F. Arndt and F. Wilbur Gingrich, ed. F. Wilbur Gingrich and Frederick W. Danker, 2nd ed. (Chicago: University of Chicago Press, 1979), p. 73, 2.
8. So Fee, p. 529.
9. For a defense of the translation *source*, see Fee, pp. 502-505 and nn. 42-46 on these pages; Berkeley and Alvera Mickelsen, "What does *Kephalē* Mean in the New Testament?" in *Women, Authority and the Bible*, ed. Alvera Mickelsen (Downers Grove, IL: InterVarsity Press, 1986), pp. 97-110; C. C. Kroeger, "Appendix III: The Classical Concept of *Head* as 'Source,'" in *Equal to Serve: Women and Men in the Church and Home*, Gretchen Gaebelein Hull (Old Tappan, NJ: Fleming H. Revell, 1987) pp. 267-283.

   For the translation of *head* by *authority*, see Wayne Grudem, "Does *Kephalē* Mean 'Source' or 'Authority Over' in Greek Literature? A Survey of 2,336 Examples," 6 (1985): 38-59, and Appendix 1 in this volume.

   W. L. Liefeld seems to prefer the meaning "honor" for *kephalē* ("Women, Submission and Ministry in 1 Corinthians," in *Women, Authority and the Bible*, ed. Mickelsen, pp. 137-140), although he does not exclude the meaning "authority." He gives no example, though, of the word *head* meaning "honor." Liefeld makes the mistake here of confusing what is given to an authority—honor—with the position or status of an authority. In other words, just because the man as head deserves honor, it does not follow that the word *head* means "honor." All the lexical evidence suggests that the word *head* means authority, and therefore a woman should honor man as the authority.
10. Mickelsen and Mickelsen, "*Kephalē*," p. 104.
11. Kroeger, "*Head* as 'Source,'" pp. 282-283.
12. R. C. and C. C. Kroeger, "Subordinationism," in *Evangelical Dictionary of Theology*, ed. Walter A. Elwell (Grand Rapids, MI: Baker Book House, 1984), p. 1058.
13. *Ibid.*
14. G. Bilezikian, *Beyond Sex Roles: A Guide for the Study of Female Roles in the Bible* (Grand Rapids, MI: Baker Book House, 1985), p. 241.
15. R. C. and C. C. Kroeger, "Subordinationism," p. 1058.
16. John Calvin, *Institutes*, XII.6.128; see also XII.18.143-144 and XII.24.152.
17. Charles Hodge, *Systematic Theology* (Grand Rapids, MI: Baker Book House, 1975 rpt.), p. 462 (italics mine). Hodge argues (pp. 462-467) that we must distinguish between the Nicene Creed itself and the explanation of the Creed. He thinks the Creed is fully Biblical, although the explanation of that Creed by the Nicene fathers is more problematic.
18. Louis Berkhof, *Systematic Theology* (Grand Rapids, MI: Eerdmans, 1941), p. 88. The italics in the last part of the quotation are mine.
19. It may be that the Corinthian women had fallen prey to an overrealized eschatology, and they thought they were like the angels in heaven (Matthew 22:30), transcending sexual distinctions.
20. It is important to note that prophecy is not equivalent to either teaching or preaching. For an explanation of the distinction, see Wayne Grudem, "Prophecy—Yes, But Teaching—

No: Paul's Consistent Advocacy of Women's Participation Without Governing Authority," *The Journal of the Evangelical Theological Society* 30 (1987): 11-23.

21. Bilezikian, pp. 21-41, presents such an exposition of Genesis 1-2.
22. See M. D. Hooker, "Authority on Her Head: An Examination of I Cor. xi. 10," *New Testament Studies* 10 (1964): 410-416.
23. Objections two and three also apply to A. Padgett's view ("'Authority Over Her Head:' Toward A Feminist Reading of St. Paul," *Daughters of Sarah* 12 [1986]: 5-9) that Paul is giving the woman here the right or freedom to do whatever she wants with her head, i.e., she can wear her hair in whatever way she desires.
24. *BAGD*, p. 278, 5.
25. That the text was understood in such a way in the early church is indicated by the early variant reading *kalumma*, which means "veil." This reading is not original, but it probably arose because early readers understood *authority* to refer to wearing a veil.
26. See J. A. Fitzmyer, "A Feature of Qumran Angelology and the Angels of I Cor. xi. 10," *New Testament Studies* 4 (1957): 48-58. Incidentally, uncertainty on this point does not affect the significance of the passage for today since the main burden of the text is quite clear. For similar references to angels as observing the created order, see 1 Timothy 5:21 and 1 Peter 1:12.
27. See Bilezikian, pp. 143-144.
28. The word *phusis* in Paul often refers to what something is by virtue of creation. Thus, Paul can speak of Jews "by nature," i.e., Jews by birth (Galatians 2:15). Humans are "children of wrath *by nature*" because they are born in sin (Ephesians 2:3). Natural branches are those that are originally part of a tree, while branches *contrary to nature* are grafted in (Romans 11:21, 24). Romans 2:14 refers to Gentiles who do the law instinctively, i.e., by nature. Romans 2:27 refers to Gentiles who are uncircumcised *by nature*, i.e., physically. Galatians 4:8 speaks of those who are not gods by nature, i.e., they are not really gods at all. Of course, all of the uses of *phusis* do not have precisely the same meaning. For example, Romans 1:26-27 and 1 Corinthians 11:14 indicate how people *should* act due to the order intended by God from the beginning, while in Ephesians 2:3 the focus is on what man *is* by nature, not what he *should* be.
29. This does not mean that homosexuality could be culturally acceptable in some situations. Any homosexual relations are fundamentally contrary to nature according to Romans 1:26-27.
30. The failure to distinguish adequately between what speaks to the first-century situation and today's church leads some to the conclusion that women should wear coverings in church today. Cf. Bruce Waltke, "1 Corinthians 11:2-16: An Interpretation," *Bibliotheca Sacra* 135 (1978): 46-57; S. T. Foh, "A Male Leadership View: The Head of the Woman Is the Man," *Women in Ministry: Four Views*, ed. B. Clouse and R. G. Clouse (Downers Grove, IL: InterVarsity Press, 1989), pp. 86-87. R. D. Culver, in "Traditional View: Let the Women Keep Silence," in Clouse and Clouse, pp. 29-32, 48, seems to prefer the wearing of head coverings as well, although he allows some liberty on the question.
31. See Beth Spring, "Gay Rights Resolution Divides Membership of Evangelical Woman's Caucus," *Christianity Today* 30 (October 3, 1986): 40-42. For other indications of the acceptance of lesbianism in evangelical feminism, see K. E. Corley and K. J. Torjesen, "Sexuality, Hierarchy and Evangelicalism," *TSF Bulletin* 10 (March/April 1987): 23-25. Two issues of *Daughters of Sarah*, volume 14 reflect the same tendency: May/June and September/October 1988.

Endnotes to Chapter Six

1. This chapter is a considerable expansion and modest revision of D. A. Carson, *Showing the Spirit: A Theological Exposition of 1 Corinthians 12-14* (Grand Rapids, MI: Baker Book House, 1987), pp. 121-131, which is used by permission.
2. E.g., F. X. Cleary, "Women in the New Testament: St. Paul and the Early Pauline Tradition," *Biblical Theology Bulletin* 10 (1980): 78-82; D. J. Doughty, "Women and Liberation in the Churches of Paul and the Pauline Tradition," *Drew Gateway* 50 (1979): 1-21; W. O. Walker, "The 'Theology of Women's Place' and the 'Paulinist' Tradition,"

Semia 28 (1983): 101-112; G. W. Trompf, "On Attitudes Towards Women in Paul and Paulinist Literature: 1 Corinthians 11:3-26 and Its Context," *Catholic Biblical Quarterly* 42 (1980): 196-215; hesitantly, G. Zuntz, *The Text of the Epistles: A Disquisition upon the Corpus Paulinum* (London: British Academy, 1953), p. 17; not a few German scholars, most recently and notably Hans Conzelmann, *First Corinthians: A Critical and Historical Commentary on the Bible*, ed. George W. MacRae, tr. James W. Leitch (Philadelphia: Fortress, 1974). [Page numbers are omitted when referring to commentaries, unless the reference is to some passage other than the one under discussion, or I have entered into extensive debate with a particular commentator.] Strangely, Conzelmann, quite without textual warrant, lumps verses 33b-36 together as one gloss, even though the displacement in the Western tradition affects only verses 34-35.

3. Cf. Bruce M. Metzger, *A Textual Commentary on the Greek New Testament* (London: United Bible Societies, 1971), p. 565; and esp. E. Earle Ellis, "The Silenced Wives of Corinth (1 Cor. 14:34-35)," in *New Testament Textual Criticism: Its Significance for Exegesis*, Festschrift for Bruce M. Metzger, ed. J. Eldon Epp and Gordon D. Fee (Oxford: Clarendon, 1981), pp. 213-220—though I disagree with his interpretation of the passage, which is discussed below.
4. Gordon D. Fee, *The First Epistle to the Corinthians* (NICNT; Grand Rapids, MI: Eerdmans, 1987).
5. There is of course another pair of logical possibilities that Fee does not discuss, namely, that verses 34-35 are original, whether in one location or another, and that they were *accidentally* transposed to the opposite location. But these seem unlikely, and no one, to my knowledge, argues for them.
6. Fee, *First Corinthians*, p. 700.
7. *Ibid.*, p. 700, n. 9.
8. *Ibid.*, p. 701.
9. *Ibid.*, p. 702.
10. *Ibid.*, p. 702.
11. Cf. n. 1 of this chapter.
12. Fee, *First Corinthians*, p. 697, n. 48.
13. *Ibid.*, p. 707.
14. So Philipp Bachman, *Der erste Brief des Paulus an die Korinther*, 4th ed. (Leipzig: A. Deichertsche Verlagsbuchhandlung, 1936); Hermann Olshausen, *A Commentary on Paul's First and Second Epistles to the Corinthians* (Minneapolis: Klock and Klock, rpt. 1984 [1855]); John W. Robbins, *Scripture Twisting in the Seminaries. Part I: Feminism* (Jefferson, MD: The Trinity Foundation, 1985). Also to be noted is the argument of Noel Weeks, "On Silence and Head Covering," *Westminster Theological Journal* 35 (1972): 21-27, who holds that in 11:5 the "uncovering" is symbolic of the act of praying, and correspondingly that its dative form (*akatakaluptō*) has instrumental force: i.e., every woman praying or prophesying, *by means of the uncovering of the head*, dishonors her head. In this way the passage turns out to be an absolute prohibition, so far as public assembly is concerned. (It is worth pointing out in passing that Weeks, along with most commentators, assumes 11:2-16 deals with public meetings of the church—unlike the view we have just examined.) But this interpretation invokes a strained syntactical argument. If the "uncovering" is symbolic of praying and prophesying, then one cannot reasonably take such "uncovering" as an instrumental dative modifying praying or prophesying. Stripped of the symbolism, the verse would then read, in effect, "Every woman praying or prophesying, by means of praying or prophesying, dishonors her head." And as in the previous interpretation, Weeks's approach does not adequately reckon with the fulfilled Joel prophecy recorded in Acts 2, to the effect that both men and women will prophesy.
15. Robert L. Thomas, *Understanding Spiritual Gifts: The Christian's Special Gifts in the Light of 1 Corinthians 12-14* (Chicago: Moody Press, 1978), pp. 230-231.
16. E.g., John Loenig, *Charismata: God's Gifts for God's People* (Philadelphia: Westminster, 1978), p. 174; Jack W. MacGorman, *The Gifts of the Spirit: An Exposition of 1 Corinthians 12-14* (Nashville: Broadman Press, 1974), p. 113, who says Paul has already set a precedent for self-contradiction in 1 Corinthians 8:4-6 versus 10:21!

17. E. Kähler, *Die Frau in den paulinischer Briefen* (Zürich: Gotthelf-Verlag, 1960), p. 61; cf. also Karl Barth, *Church Dogmatics* 3/4, p. 172.
18. Elisabeth Schüssler Fiorenza, "Women In the Pre-Pauline and Pauline Churches," *Union Seminary Quarterly Review* 33 (1978): 153-166.
19. *Ibid.*, p. 161.
20. *Ibid.*, citing K. Niederwimmer, *Askese und Mysterium* (Göttingen: Vandenhoeck und Ruprecht, 1975), p. 115.
21. *Ibid.*, p. 161.
22. *Ibid.*
23. E.g., Richard and Joyce Boldrey, *Chauvinist or Feminist? Paul's View of Women* (Grand Rapids, MI: Baker Book House, 1976); J. Keir Howard, "Neither Male nor Female: An Examination of the Status of Women in the New Testament," *Evangelical Quarterly* 55 (1983): 31-42; Ralph P. Martin, *The Spirit and the Congregation: Studies in 1 Corinthians 12-15* (Grand Rapids, MI: Eerdmans, 1984), pp. 86ff.; William F. Orr and James Arthur Walther, *1 Corinthians*, vol. 32 of *The Anchor Bible* (Garden City: Doubleday, 1976).
24. Howard, "Neither Male Nor Female."
25. Cf. esp. Stephen B. Clark, *Man and Woman in Christ* (Ann Arbor, MI: Servant Books, 1980), pp. 185-186.
26. Martin, *Spirit and the Congregation*, p. 87.
27. *Ibid.*, p. 88.
28. E.g., Walter C. Kaiser, Jr., "Paul, Women, and the Church," *Worldwide Challenge* 3 (1976): 9-12 (which I have discussed in D. A. Carson, *Exegetical Fallacies* [Grand Rapids, MI: Baker Book House, 1984], pp. 38-40); Neil M. Flanagan, "Did Paul Put Down Women in 1 Cor. 14:34-36?" *Biblical Theology Bulletin* 11 (1981): 10-12; Gilbert Bilezikian, *Beyond Sex Roles: A Guide for the Study of Female Roles in the Bible*, 2nd ed. (Grand Rapids, MI: Baker Book House, 1989), pp. 144-153; G. Fitzer, "*Das Weib schweige in der Gemeinde*" (Munich: C. Kaiser, 1963); Jerome Murphy-O'Conner, "Interpolations in 1 Corinthians," *Catholic Biblical Quarterly* 48 (1986): 90-92.
29. Chris Ukachukwu Manus, "The Subordination of Women in the Church. 1 Corinthians 14:33b-36 Reconsidered," *Nouvelle Revue Théologique* 106 (1984): 23-58; D. W. Odell-Scott, "Let the Women Speak in Church: An Egalitarian Interpretation of 1 Cor 14:33b-36," *Biblical Thinking Bulletin* 13 (1983): 90-93.
30. It is simply astonishing to be told that the masculine plural *monous* "requires [!] some such paraphrase as 'you fellows only'" (so Charles H. Talbert, "Paul's Understanding of the Holy Spirit: The Evidence of 1 Corinthians 12-14," in *Perspectives on the New Testament*, Festschrift for Frank Stagg, ed. Charles H. Talbert [Macon, GA: Mercer University Press, 1985], p. 106.
31. For further application of these principles, cf. Carson, *Showing the Spirit*, pp. 53-55.
32. Fee, *First Corinthians*, p. 707.
33. *Ibid.*
34. Bilezikian, *Beyond Sex Roles*, pp. 286-288 n. 29 (1st ed., pp. 248-249).
35. Walter C. Kaiser, Jr., in *Christianity Today*, October 3, 1986, p. 124, citing Joseph Henry Thayer, *A Greek-English Lexicon of the New Testament*, 4th ed. (Edinburgh: T & T Clark, [1889] 1901), p. 275.
36. Bilezikian, p. 286.
37. *Ibid.*
38. *Ibid.*
39. Cf. also n. 30 in this chapter.
40. On which cf. Carson, *Showing the Spirit*, pp. 131-134.
41. Ellis, "Silenced Wives"; E. Earle Ellis, *Pauline Theology: Ministry and Society* (Grand Rapids, MI: Eerdmans, 1989), pp. 67-71. For yet another interpretation, cf. Robert J. Karris, "Women in the Pauline Assembly: To prophesy (1 Cor 11:5) but not to speak (14:34)?" in *Women Priests: A Catholic Commentary on the Vatican Declaration*, ed. Leonard and Arlene Swidler (New York: Paulist Press, 1977), pp. 205-208.
42. M. E. Thrall, *I and II Corinthians* (Cambridge, England: Cambridge University Press, 1965). She has been followed and expanded upon by James B. Hurley, *Man and Woman in Biblical Perspective* (Grand Rapids, MI: Zondervan, 1981), pp. 185-194; Grudem, *The*

Gift of Prophecy in 1 Corinthians (Washington: University Press of America, 1982), pp. 245-255; cf. W. J. Dumbrell, "The Role of Women—A Reconsideration of the Biblical Evidence," *Interchange* 21 (1977): 14-22.

43. Mary Evans, *Woman in the Bible* (Downers Grove, IL: InterVarsity Press, 1983), p. 95.
44. E.g., R. Banks, "Paul and Women's Liberation," *Interchange* 18 (1976): 100; and then he points out that this is not so much a command as a statement of the consequences of the first couple's sin.
45. Cf. Hurley, *Man and Woman in Biblical Perspective*, p. 192.
46. Cf. *Ibid.*, and Clark, *Man and Woman in Christ*; Douglas J. Moo, "1 Timothy 2:11-15: Meaning and Significance," *Trinity Journal* 1 (1980): 62-83; Douglas J. Moo, "The Interpretation of 1 Timothy 2:11-15: A Rejoinder," *Trinity Journal* 2 (1981): 198-222.
47. Verse 36 must not be understood to be addressed to women only: the masculine *monous* eliminates such a view. The entire Corinthian *church* is being held responsible for the deviations Paul disapproves, as is suggested already by the contrast between Corinthian *church* practice and that of other *churches* (verse 33b—assuming this clause is to be read with verses 34-36).
48. Cf. Grudem, *The Gift of Prophecy in 1 Corinthians*, pp. 250-251. The response of Fee, *First Corinthians*, p. 704, n. 23, is unconvincing.
49. Cf. Carson, *Showing the Spirit*, esp. pp. 91-100; Wayne Grudem, *The Gift of Prophecy in the New Testament and Today* (Westchester, IL: Crossway Books, 1988).
50. N. G. L. Hammond and H. H. Scullard, eds., *Oxford Classical Dictionary* (Oxford: Oxford University Press, 1970), p. 376.

Endnotes to Chapter Seven

1. Ronald & Beverly Allen, *Liberated Traditionalism: Men and Women in Balance* (Portland, OR: Multnomah Press, 1985), p. 134.
2. Mary Hayter, *The New Eve in Christ* (Grand Rapids, MI: Eerdmans, 1987), p. 134.
3. George W. Knight III, *The Role Relationship of Men and Women: New Testament Teaching* (Chicago: Moody Press, 1985), p. 7.
4. Paul King Jewett, *Man As Male and Female: A Study in Sexual Relationships from a Theological Point of View* (Grand Rapids, MI: Eerdmans, 1975), p. 142.
5. *Ibid.*, p. 145.
6. Robert Jewett, "The Sexual Liberation of the Apostle Paul," *Journal of the American Academy of Religion*, 47 (1979), Supplement, pp. 55-87.
7. Klyne R. Snodgrass, "Galatians 3:28: Conundrum or Solution?" in *Women, Authority and the Bible*, ed. Alvera Mickelsen (Downers Grove, IL: InterVarsity Press, 1986), p. 161.
8. James B. Hurley, *Man and Woman in Biblical Perspective* (Grand Rapids, MI: Zondervan, 1981), p. 195.
9. Ignatius, *To the Philadelphians*, iv, in *The Ante-Nicene Fathers: Translations of the Writings of the Fathers Down to A.D. 325*, ten volumes, ed. Alexander Roberts and James Donaldson, rev. A. Cleveland Coxe (Grand Rapids, MI: Eerdmans, 1973 rpt.), vol. 1, *The Apostolic Fathers—Justin Martyr—Irenaeus*, p. 81.
10. Justin Martyr, *Dialogue with Trypho*, cxvi, in *The Apostolic Fathers*, ed. Roberts and Donaldson, p. 257.
11. Clement of Alexandria, *Exhortation to the Heathen*, xi, in *The Ante-Nicene Fathers*, ed. Roberts and Donaldson, vol. 2, *Fathers of the Second Century*, p. 203.
12. Hippolytus, *The Refutation of All Heresies*, V.ii., in *The Ante-Nicene Fathers*, ed. Roberts and Donaldson, vol. 5, *Hippolytus, Cyprian, Caius, Novatian, Appendix*, p. 49.
13. Gregory of Nyssa, *On Virginity*, xx, in *A Select Library of Nicene and Post-Nicene Fathers of the Christian Church*, twenty-eight volumes in two series, ed. Philip Schaff and Henry Wace (Grand Rapids, MI: Eerdmans, 1975 rpt.), second series, vol. 5, *Gregory of Nyssa: Dogmatic Treatises, etc.*, pp. 343-371, p. 366.
14. John Chrysostom, *Commentary on the Epistle of St. Paul the Apostle to the Galatians*, iii, in *A Select Library of Nicene and Post-Nicene Fathers of the Christian Church*, ed. Schaff and Wace, first series, vol. 13, *St. Chrysostom: Homilies on Galatians, Ephesians, Philippians, Colossians, Thessalonians, Timothy, Titus, and Philemon*, p. 30.

15. Johannes Quasten and Walter J. Burghardt, eds., *St. Augustine on the Psalms*, in *Ancient Christian Writers*, vol. 1, *Psalms 1-29*, trans. and annotated by Dame Scholastica Hebgin and Dame Felicitas Corrigan (Westminster: The Newman Press, and London: Longmans, Green, 1960).
16. Martin Luther, *A Commentary on St. Paul's Epistle to the Galatians*, ed. Philip S. Watson (Westwood, CT: Fleming H. Revell, n.d.), pp. 341-344.
17. John Calvin, *Institutes of the Christian Religion*, IV.xx.1, ed. John T. McNeill, trans. and indexed by Ford Lewis Battles (Philadelphia: Westminster Press, 1960), vol. 2, p. 1486.
18. J. B. Lightfoot, *St. Paul's Epistle to the Galatians* (London and New York: Macmillan, 1896), p. 49.
19. *Ibid.*
20. A course in the exegesis of the Greek text of Galatians at Dallas Theological Seminary, 1945.
21. Ronald Y. K. Fung, *The Epistle to the Galatians* (Grand Rapids, MI: Eerdmans, 1988), p. 170.
22. I am separating the phrases, "through faith" and "in Christ Jesus," taking the latter as intended by Paul to be linked with the verb *are* and placed last in its clause for emphasis (cf. Romans 3:25; Fung, pp. 171-72). The change in meaning is slight.
23. John Calvin, *The Epistles of Paul the Apostle to the Galatians, Ephesians, Philippians and Colossians*, ed. David W. Torrance and Thomas F. Torrance, trans. T. H. L. Parker (Grand Rapids, MI: Eerdmans, 1965), p. 68.
24. *Ibid.*, pp. 68-69.
25. Herman N. Ridderbos, *The Epistle of Paul to the Churches of Galatia* (Grand Rapids, MI: Eerdmans, 1953), p. 147-148.
26. Fung, pp. 173-175. Fung agrees with Charles A. Anderson Scott (*Christianity According to St Paul* [Cambridge: Cambridge University Press, 1961], p. 114), who saw baptism as "the normal but not necessary" sign and seal of the faith that appropriates Christ.
27. Hans Dieter Betz, *Galatians* (Philadelphia: Fortress Press, 1979), pp. 186-189. To Betz, the rite is not a *ritus ex opere operato* but "the legal act of joining the Christian religion."
28. F. F. Bruce, *The Epistle to the Galatians: A Commentary on the Greek Text* (Grand Rapids, MI: Eerdmans, 1982), pp. 185-187.
29. James D. G. Dunn, *Baptism in the Holy Spirit* (Naperville, IL: Alec R. Allenson, 1970), pp. 109-113. The expression, *baptizesthai eis Christon*, meaning to be baptized into Christ, is to Dunn simply a metaphor taken from the rite.
30. Bruce, p. 185.
31. Calvin, *Commentary*, p. 68.
32. Cf. G. R. Beasley-Murray, *Baptism in the New Testament* (Grand Rapids, MI: Eerdmans, 1962), pp. 148-149; Bruce, p. 186. Moule thinks it "is difficult not to associate this metaphor with the actual movements of the baptized" (C. F. D. Moule, *Worship in the New Testament* [Richmond: John Knox Press, 1961], p. 52).
33. Betz, p. 190.
34. Bruce, p. 187; Snodgrass, pp. 169-170.
35. *Ibid.*
36. The apostle does not say, as one might expect, "there is neither male nor female" (*NASB*), but *there is no male and female*. The clause does not point to androgyny, as some early Gnostics thought. The equality of inheritance by male and female is Paul's point. The masculine form of the cardinal numeral points to a corporate unity (cf. Fung, p. 176; Ernst Burton, *The Epistle to the Galatians*, ICC [Edinburgh: T & T Clark, 1921], pp. 207-208).
37. Bruce, p. 189.
38. *Ibid.*
39. *Ibid.*, p. 190.
40. *Ibid.*
41. Paul King Jewett, *Man as Male and Female*, pp. 119, 143-147.
42. *Ibid.*, p. 113.
43. *Ibid.*, p. 142.
44. *Ibid.*, p. 144; cf. p. 147.
45. Cf. Bruce, pp. 128-134; Fung, pp. 110-111.

46. In a footnote, Jewett laments that scholars have not responded to Harnack's suggestion that the author of Hebrews was Priscilla. He speaks of their "erudite indifference and condescension" to the theory. He evidently does not know that, while the authorship of Hebrews remains a mystery, it surely was not Priscilla. The participle in Hebrews 11:32, rendered in the NASB by, "if I tell," and agreeing with the pronoun "me," is in the masculine gender. The author may have been Apollos, who learned significant things from Priscilla and Aquila (Acts 18:26), but he was not Priscilla (cf. p. 145).
47. *Ibid.*, p. 145.
48. *Ibid.*, p. 147.
49. Surely Professor Jewett does not wish to leave it for each group of professing Christians to decide for itself how sexual egalitarianism is to work. And, if there is no male or female in Christ, how will he oppose homosexuality?
50. Snodgrass, pp.174-175 (see n. 7).
51. *Ibid.*, p. 175. Hierarchy becomes "love, servanthood and mutual submission," a definition that Webster would not recognize.
52. *Ibid.*, pp. 180-181.
53. *Ibid.*, pp. 180.
54. *Ibid.*, pp. 180-181.
55. A careful perusal of David E. Aune's significant work, *Prophecy in Early Christianity and the Ancient Mediterranean World* (Grand Rapids, MI: Eerdmans, 1983) will enable one to distinguish prophecy from authoritative preaching.

    Cf. also Wayne A. Grudem, *The Gift of Prophecy in 1 Corinthians* (Lanham: University Press of America, Inc., 1982); David Hill, *New Testament Prophecy* (Atlanta: John Knox Press, 1979). See also Chapters 5 and 6 in this volume.
56. Snodgrass, p. 164.
57. *Ibid.*, p. 171.
58. Cf. George W. Knight III, *The Role Relationship of Men & Women* (Chicago: Moody Press, 1985), p. 32; "Male and Female Related He Them," *Christianity Today*, April 9, 1976, p. [711] 15.
59. Cf. Snodgrass, pp. 168, 179. The extent to which some feminists would go is indicated in Susie C. Stanley's response to Snodgrass. She, since Paul greeted "ten women colaborers in Romans 16," says that Priscilla, Phoebe, and Lydia are only "a sampling of the litany of women who labored with Paul as *protectors, teachers, deacons and apostles*" (italics mine)! Cf. p. 182.
60. *Ibid.*, p. 167.
61. Fung, p. 176.
62. Abraham Kuyper, *Principles of Sacred Theology*, trans. J. Hendrik De Vries (Grand Rapids, MI: Eerdmans, 1954), p. 577.

Endnotes to Chapter Eight

1. The summary statement of verse 21 is of course also a transition to his treatment of other groups found in the enlarged household, children and parents, 6:1-4, and slaves and masters, 6:5-9.
2. For the manuscript evidence, see the textual apparatus of *The Greek New Testament* of the United Bible Societies.
3. The other occurrences of *allēlōn* in Ephesians are 4:2, 25, 35.
4. Noted by F. F. Bruce, *The Epistles to the Colossians, to Philemon, and to the Ephesians* (NICNT, Grand Rapids, MI: Eerdmans, 1984), p. 382.
5. For example, James B. Hurley, *Man and Woman in Biblical Perspective* (Grand Rapids, MI: Zondervan, and Leicester, England: InterVarsity Press, 1981), pp. 140ff., with the qualification that it is "appropriate if it is addressed to the congregation at large and exemplified in these three relations in which one member must yield to another" (p. 141). The first part of this qualification ("addressed to the congregation at large") seems almost the same as the mutual submission position that is suggested above. The second part of this qualification, however, moves away from the idea of mutual submission by indicating

that the submission called for is in specific relationships, i.e., "exemplified in these three relations in which one member must yield to another."

6. Editor's note: Dr. Knight presents a clear argument for the view that verse 21 teaches mutual submission of all Christians to one another and that verses 22ff. teach specific kinds of submission. This interpretation is widely held and its implications are consistent with the overall argument of Dr. Knight's chapter and of this book. It is also consistent with the overall ethical teaching of Scripture that we should submit to one another in the way Dr. Knight defines submission, that is, to act in a loving, considerate, self-giving way toward one another.

   However, within the broad range of agreement in this book, there is room for another interpretation of Ephesians 5:21: that it does not teach mutual submission at all, but rather teaches that we should all be subject to those whom God has put in authority over us—such as husbands, parents, or employers. In this way, Ephesians 5:21 would be paraphrased, "being subject to one another (that is, *to some others*), in the fear of Christ."

   The primary argument for this alternative view is the word *hupotassō* itself. Although many people have claimed that the word can mean "be thoughtful and considerate; act in love" (toward another), it is doubtful if a first-century Greek speaker would have understood it that way, for the term always implies a relationship of submission to an authority. It is used elsewhere in the New Testament of the submission of Jesus to the authority of His parents (Luke 2:51); of demons being subject to the disciples (Luke 10-17—(clearly the meaning "act in love, be considerate" cannot fit here); of citizens being subject to government authorities (Romans 13:1, 5; Titus 3:1, 1 Peter 2:13); of the universe being subject to Christ (1 Corinthians 15:27; Ephesians 1:22); of unseen spiritual powers being subject to Christ (1 Peter 3:22); of Christ being subject to God the Father (1 Corinthians 15:28); of church members being subject to church leaders (1 Corinthians 16:15-16 [with 1 Clement 42:4]; 1 Peter 5:5); of wives being subject to their husbands (Colossians 3:18; Titus 2:5; 1 Peter 3:5; cf. Ephesians 5:22, 24); of the church being subject to Christ (Ephesians 5:24); of servants being subject to their masters (Titus 2:9; 1 Peter 2:18); and of Christians being subject to God (Hebrews 12:9; James 4:7). None of these relationships is ever reversed; that is, husbands are never told to be subject (*hupotassō*) to wives, the government to citizens, masters to servants, or the disciples to demons, etc. (In fact, the term is used outside the New Testament to describe the submission and obedience of soldiers in an army to those of superior rank; see Josephus, *War* 2,566, 578; 5.309; cf. the adverb in 1 Clement 37:2. Cf. also Henry George Liddell and Robert Scott, *A Greek-English Lexicon*, rev. Henry Stuart Jones and Roderick McKenzie, suppl. E. A. Barber, et al. [Oxford: Clarendon Press, 1968], p. 1897, which defined *hupotassō* [passive] to mean "be obedient.") The word is never "mutual" in its force; it is *always one-directional* in its reference to submission to an authority. This does not seem to be contradicted by the passages cited by Dr. Knight, because in none of those passages is the person in authority told to "submit" (*hupotassō*) to the person under that authority—rather, other words are used to encourage love, thoughtfulness, etc. So we may ask, why should we assign *hupotassō* a meaning in Ephesians 5:21 that it is nowhere else shown to have?

   Therefore it seems to be a misunderstanding of Ephesians 5:21 to say that it implies mutual submission. Even in Ephesians 5:22-24, wives are not to be subject to everyone or to all husbands, but to "their *own* husbands"—the "submission" Paul has in mind is not a general kind of thoughtfulness toward others, but a specific submission to a higher authority. But should not the verb *hupotassō* in verse 22 (whether implicit or explicit) take the same sense it does in verse 21?

   The reason the mutual submission interpretation is so common is that interpreters *assume* that the Greek pronoun *allēlous* ("one another") must be completely reciprocal (that it must mean "everyone to everyone"). Dr. Knight has cited some texts where *allēlous* does mean "everyone to everyone," but that is not the case in all of its uses, and it certainly does not have to take that meaning. There are many cases where it rather means "some to others;" for example, in Revelation 6:4, "so that men should slay *one another*" means "so that *some* would kill *others*" (not "so that every person would kill every other person," or "so that those people being killed would mutually kill those who were killing them," which would make no sense); in Galatians 6:2, "Bear *one another's* burdens" means not "everyone should exchange burdens with everyone else," but "*some* who are more able should help bear the burdens of *others* who are less able"; 1 Corinthians 11:33, "when you come together to eat, wait for *one another*" means "*some* who are ready early should wait for *others* who are late"; etc. (cf. Luke 2:15; 21:1; 24:32—there are many examples where the word is not exhaustively reciprocal). Similarly, in Ephesians 5:21, both the following context and the meaning of *hupotassō* require *allēlous* here to mean "some to others," so that the verse could be paraphrased, "those who are under authority should be subject to others among you who have authority over them."

Therefore, according to this (alternative) interpretation, it would seem best to say that it is not mutual submission but submission to appropriate authorities that Paul is commanding in Ephesians 5:21. (This view of Ephesians 5:21 would be consistent with how James Hurley views the structure of the passage, as noted in footnote 5 above.)

7. Cf., e.g., Gilbert Bilezikian, *Beyond Sex Roles* (Grand Rapids, MI: Baker Book House, 1985), pages 153ff. There is much to commend and agree with in Bilezikian's expression of his understanding of the New Testament teaching about mutual submission. What is terribly erroneous is that he plays this off against distinguishable roles so that, in effect, it serves for him to negate the distinguishable and different roles that Paul sets forth for the husband and the wife. Although one might not choose to use the word hierarchical, it seems evident that Bilezikian is attempting to use mutual submission to rule out role differences in the following quotes: "By definition, mutual submission rules out hierarchical differences" (p. 154), and, "We conclude that mutual subjection . . . renders hierarchical distinctions irrelevant within the Christian communities of church and family" (p. 156; cf. also his title *Beyond Sex Roles*).
8. Cf. J. E. Crough, *The Origin and Intention of the Colossian Haustafel* (FRLANT 109, Gottingen: Vanderhoeck und Ruprecht, 1972), p. 110, who indicates that this is a voluntary submission based on one's own recognition of God's order.
9. The respective passages in abbreviated form read as follows: "Wives, be subject to your own husbands"; "Wives, be subject (*hupotassesthe*) to your husbands"; "wives be submissive (*hupotassamena*) to your own husbands"; "the young women . . . subject (*hupotassamenas*) to their own husbands." When Paul deals with role relationships and leadership in the family of God, the church, he uses the related noun and expresses the same principle: "Let a woman quietly receive instruction with entire submissiveness (*hupotage*). But I do not allow a woman to teach or exercise authority over a man" (1 Timothy 2:11-12).
10. J. P. Sampley, *"And the Two Shall Become One Flesh": A Study of Traditions in Ephesians 5:21-23* (NTSM 16, Cambridge: University Press, 1971), p. 29.
11. Walter Bauer, *A Greek-English Lexicon of the New Testament and Other Early Christian Literature*, 2nd ed., trans. William F. Arndt and F. Wilbur Gingrich, rev. F. Wilbur Gingrich and Frederick W. Danker (Chicago: University of Chicago Press, 1979), p. 848, section 1bb.
12. Verse 24 begins with the word *but* (*alla*), which has caused some difficulty to commentators and has been omitted by various translations. F. F. Bruce's handling of the significance of this is so helpful that it merits quoting at length. His treatment incorporates statements of J. A. Robinson in *St. Paul's Epistle to the Ephesians* (London: James Clarke & Co., n.d.), pp. 124, 205, and they are indicated by quotation marks within the block quote that follows:

> J. A. Robinson points out that the conjunction need not have adversative force. It is used here rather "to fix the attention on the special point of immediate interest." The apostle, having made the general point that "it is the function of the head to plan for the safety of the body, to secure it from danger and to provide for its welfare," checks himself from a fuller exposition of this and resumes his main line of thought: "*but*—for this is the matter in hand—*as the church is subject to Christ, so* let *wives* be *to their husbands in everything*." This is the most satisfactory account of the connection between vv. 23 and 24, since v. 24 is largely resumptive of v. 22, adding a reference to the church's submission to Christ as the pattern for the wife's submission to her husband.

13. The principle that God expects His people to disobey when a human authority commands them to sin is affirmed in several passages of Scripture: see Exodus 1:17-21; Daniel 3:12-18; 6:10; Hebrews 11:23.
14. W. J. Larkin, Jr., *Culture and Biblical Hermeneutics* (Grand Rapids, MI: Baker Book House, 1988), p. 109.
15. Some people argue that because the submission involved in slavery has been done away with slavery itself, so also the submission of wives to husbands should be done away, since the two relationships are both treated in the same extended passage (Ephesians 5:21-6:9). Later in this chapter we will discuss the nature of the institution of slavery and how our understanding of it relates to and may or may not impinge on our understanding of the relationship of wives and husbands.
16. Cf. P. T. O'Brien's comment on what is entailed in the command to husbands to love their wives in Colossians 3:18. He says that the husband's love "involves his unceasing care and loving service for her entire well-being." (*Colossians, Philemon* [Word Bible Commentary, Waco, TX: Word, 1982], p. 223). His whole treatment of Colossians 3:18-19 (pp. 214-224) merits reading.
17. Bruce, *Colossians, Philemon, and Ephesians*, p. 391.
18. The Greek word is *metadounai* (from *metadidōmi*), which is akin to the Greek *paredoken* (from *paradidōmi*), used as the key word in Ephesians 5:25.
19. The Greek word *agapetoi*, "beloved," is a cognate noun to the Greek verb *agapaō* used throughout the Ephesians 5 passage in verses 25 (twice), 28 (three times), and verse 33.
20. For the phrase "in everything" see the discussion above.
21. The phrase is used forty-seven times by Paul. The occurrences in Colossians are 3:18, 20; 4:7, 17, with the closest use being the next occurrence, Colossians 3:20.
22. The Greek word is *anēken*, from *anekō*. For the question whether this "fittingness" refers rather to cultural non-offense, see the following section "Wives, Children, and Slaves?"
23. Cf., e.g., 1 Thessalonians 5:12, in which Paul reminds the Thessalonian Christians that their spiritual leaders "are over you in the Lord."
24. Cf., e.g., the expression of Romans 16:11, "Greet those . . . who are in the Lord."
25. This statement is almost identical to that in Colossians 3:18 using the same Greek verb, *hupotassō*, in the sense of "submit to."
26. Notice how Paul must resist that very misunderstanding in the early church (which is virtually identical to the argument among the feminists within the Christian church today) with his teaching in 1 Corinthians 11:1-16, which reminded them that the headship of the man (1 Corinthians 11:3) goes back to God's determinative action at creation (1 Corinthians 11:8-9).
27. Compare the word to wives in 1 Peter 3:2: "as they observe her chaste and respectful (Greek, *en phobō*) behavior."
28. Cf., e.g., Virginia R. Mollenkott, *Women, Men and the Bible* (Nashville: Abingdon, 1977), pp. 92ff., joining to slavery the government by kings. Cf. also Paul King Jewett, *Man as Male and Female* (Grand Rapids, MI: Eerdmans, 1975), pp. 137ff.; Letha Scanzoni and Nancy Hardesty, *All We're Meant To Be* (Waco, TX: Word, 1974), pp. 91, 107, 202-205.
29. See the author's *Role Relationship of Men and Women* (1985; reprinted Phillipsburg, NJ: Presbyterian & Reformed, 1989), pp. 9-15, for a fuller treatment of this question, including the matter of kings and civil government.

Endnotes to Chapter Nine

1. Some recent representative examples of this viewpoint are Mary Hayter, *The New Eve in Christ* (Grand Rapids, MI: Eerdmans, 1987), pp. 132-133, 142-143; Francis X. Cleary, "Women in the New Testament: St. Paul and the Early Pauline Churches," *Biblical Theological Bulletin* 10 (1980): 78-82. The extreme to which this can be taken is illustrated by William O. Walker, who thinks all the New Testament female subordination texts are post-Pauline, passages like 1 Corinthians 11:2-16 being insertions into the text of Paul's own letter. "The 'Theology of Woman's Place' and the 'Paulinist' Tradition," *Sēmeia* 28 (1988): 101-112.

2. See the surveys in Donald Guthrie, *The Pastoral Epistles* (Grand Rapids, MI: Eerdmans, 1957), pp. 32-38, and J. N. D. Kelly, *A Commentary on the Pastoral Epistles* (London: Black, 1963), pp. 10-18. Kelly notes that the picture of the false teaching is "incomplete and tantalizingly vague" (p. 11).
3. On the situation in 1 Corinthians, see especially Anthony C. Thiselton, "Realized Eschatology at Corinth," *New Testament Studies* 24 (1977): 510-528. P. H. Towner makes a clear and convincing case for the general similarity between the problems behind 1 Corinthians and the pastoral epistles: "Gnosis and Realized Eschatology in Ephesus (of the Pastoral Epistles) and the Corinthian Enthusiasm," *Journal for the Study of the New Testament* 31 (1987): 95-124. The paragraph above is heavily indebted to Towner's work.
4. See also David M. Scholer, "1 Timothy 2:9-15 and the Place of Women in the Church's Ministry," *Women, Authority and the Bible*, ed. Alvera Mickelsen (Downers Grove, IL: InterVarsity Press, 1985), p. 198.
5. While some think this book is a Christian production, we think it is a pre-Christian Jewish work with minor Christian interpolations. See the comments of H. C. Kee in *The Old Testament Pseudepigrapha*, two vols., ed. J. H. Charlesworth (Garden City, NY: Doubleday, 1983, 1985), 1:775-780 (the translation in the text is also from this volume).
6. For examples from ancient writers, see David Balch, *Let Wives be Submissive: The Domestic Code in 1 Peter* (Chico, CA: Scholars Press, 1981), pp. 101-102. On 1 Timothy 2:9-10, see Scholer, "1 Timothy 2:9-15," p. 201; Samuele Bacchiocchi, *Women in the Church: A Biblical Study on the Role of Women in the Church* (Biblical Perspectives 7; Berrien Springs, MI: Biblical Perspectives, 1987), p. 149.
7. The meaning of this word is thoroughly discussed in the interchange between Moo and Philip Payne; Moo, "1 Timothy 2:11-15," p. 64; Payne, "Libertarian Women at Ephesus: A Response to Douglas J. Moo's Article '1 Timothy 2:11-15: Meaning and Significance,'" *Trinity Journal* (1981): 169-170; Moo, "The Interpretation of 1 Timothy 2:11-15: A Rejoinder," *Trinity Journal* 2 (1981): 198-199; Payne, "The Interpretation of I Timothy 2:11-15: A Surrejoinder" (unpublished paper that is included in "What Does the Scripture Teach About the Ordination of Women?" produced by the Committee on Ministerial Standing of the Evangelical Free Church of America), pp. 99-100. (This series of articles will be referred to hereafter simply by the names of the authors, in the order above.)
8. Aida Besançon Spencer, *Beyond the Curse: Women called to Ministry* (Nashville: Thomas Nelson, 1985), pp. 75-79.
9. Spencer, *Beyond the Curse*, pp. 74-80.
10. Walter Bauer, *A Greek-English Lexicon of the New Testament and Other Early Christian Literature*, 2nd ed., trans. William F. Arndt and F. Wilbur Gingrich, rev. F. Wilbur Gingrich and Frederick W. Danker (Chicago: University of Chicago Press, 1979), p. 171, describes the word as follows: "one of the most commonly used Gk. particles, used to connect one clause with another when it is felt that there is some contrast between them, though the contrast is often scarcely discernible. Most common translations: *but*, when a contrast is clearly implied; *and*, when a simple connective is desired, without contrast: frequently it cannot be translated at all." The NIV rendering of the particle in 1 Timothy bears out this description: *de* is translated "but" eight times; "now," "rather," "as for," and "and" once each; and not at all sixteen times. The nature of this word, then, renders extremely precarious any exegetical decisions based on its exact meaning. Yet Spencer (p. 85) and Payne ("Surrejoinder," p. 97) claim that Paul's use of *de* here "indicates a consciousness of the contrast between the command to learn and the present prohibition of teaching." Nevertheless, even if we grant that *de* here is adversative—which, in light of what we said above, is hardly something we can be very sure of—this particular interpretation of that contrast has no basis in the text, as Mary J. Evans, who is sympathetic to the viewpoint of Spencer and Payne, recognizes. Evans, *Woman in the Bible* (Downers Grove, IL: InterVarsity Press, 1983), p. 103. Lacking such evidence, the simpler and more obvious mildly adversative transitional force suggested in this chapter should be adopted.
11. This argument is widespread. See, for instance, Don Williams, *The Apostle Paul and Women in the Church* (Van Nuys, CA: BIM, 1977), p. 112.

12. For further discussion of this point, see Moo, p. 65: Payne, pp. 170-173: Moo, pp. 199-200: Payne, pp. 100-101.
13. Against, for instance, Payne, "Surrejoinder," pp. 101-104.
14. See Walter Liefeld, "Women and the Nature of Ministry," *Journal of the Evangelical Theological Society* 30 (1987): 51.
15. See the discussion of K. H. Rengstorf, "*Didaskō*," *Theological Dictionary of the New Testament*, ten vols., ed. O. Kittel and O. Friedrich (Grand Rapids, MI: Eerdmans, 1964-1976), vol. 2, p. 157.
16. Despite Payne's objections ("Surrejoinder," pp. 107-108), Acts 8:21 is a valid illustration of the point at issue: that two words, connected by *oudé* ("nor"), can both depend on an object that follows the second only. The nature of the relationship of the two words and the fact that the object takes the case demanded by the second word only is immaterial. On the latter point, see Herbert Weir Smyth, *Greek Grammar* (Cambridge, MA: Harvard University Press, 1920), who notes specifically that in such cases the object will take the case demanded by the nearer verb (p. 1634). Payne objects further that the word order with *teach* separated from *man* by six words militates against construing them together. But not only is Greek word order notoriously flexible in such areas, but Paul has probably thrust *teach* forward in the sentence for the sake of an emphatic contrast with *learn* in verse 11: "Let the women learn, but, as for teaching. . . . "
17. The purpose clause in Titus 2:4, "in order that they might train young women to love their husbands . . .," shows that the "teaching" of verse 3 is restricted to teaching young women.
18. See particularly George W. Knight III, "*Authenteoeō* in Reference to Women in 1 Timothy 2:12," *New Testament Studies* 30 (1984): 143-157, and Leland Edward Wilshire, "The TLG Computer and Further Reference to *Authenteō* in 1 Timothy 2:12," *New Testament Studies* 34 (1988): 120-134. Despite the different methodological presuppositions—Knight includes only the verb, Wilshire all words from the *authen* root—and consequent broader scope of Wilshire's work, Wilshire comes to essentially the same conclusion as Knight: that the verb, during the New Testament period, was coming to mean "exercise authority/power/rights."

    Payne's attempt to dispute these findings (particularly in the case of the first-century B.C. papyrus BGU 1208) is unconvincing ("Surrejoinder," pp. 108-110). Particularly, he fails to come to grips with the fact that the verb is overwhelmingly used in Patristic Greek to mean "have authority," "exercise authority" (see G. W. Lampe, *Patristic Greek Lexicon* [Oxford: Oxford University Press, 1968], p. 262). And while Payne notes one occurrence of the verb in Chrysostom in the sense "domineer," he fails to note Chrysostom's other uses of the word, some of them with the neutral meaning of "have authority" (see Wilshire, "1 Timothy 2:12," pp. 131-132).
19. For this objection, see Liefeld, "Women and the Nature of Ministry," p. 52.
20. Payne, "Surrejoinder," pp. 104-107; see also his paper, read at the 1988 Evangelical Theological Society Meeting, "*Oude* in 1 Timothy 2:12."
21. Payne, "Surrejoinder," p. 104 (italics his).
22. We will not examine the texts here, but they are as follows: Romans 2:28; 4:15; 8:7, 10; 9:7, 16; 11:21; 1 Corinthians 2:6; 3:2; 4:3; 5:1; 6:5; 11:14, 16; 14:21; 15:13, 16, 50; 2 Corinthians 3:10; 7:12; Galatians 1:1, 12, 17; 2:3, 5; 3:28 (twice); 4:14; 6:13; Philippians 2:16; 1 Thessalonians 2:3; 5:5; 2 Thessalonians 3:8; 1 Timothy 2:12; 6:7, 16. As an example, we may cite a verse that Payne claims to parallel 1 Timothy 2:12–Romans 4:15: "where there is no law neither [*oude*] is there transgression." Payne is right when he says that we have here two separate items that form a single coherent idea, but the two things, "law" and "transgression," remain separate items and do not interpret one another in the way Payne argues for in 1 Timothy 2:12. That is, Paul does not mean "law of a transgression sort"; the two clearly do not modify one another.
23. Russell C. Prohl, *Woman in the Church* (Grand Rapids, MI: Eerdmans, 1957), pp. 31-32; Joyce Baldwin, *Women Likewise* (London: Falcon, 1973), pp. 21-22; N. J. Hommes, "Let Women Be Silent in the Church: A Message Concerning the Worship Service and the Decorum to be Observed by Women," *Calvin Theological Journal* 4 (1969): 13.
24. Gordon Fee, "Reflections on Church Order in the Pastoral Epistles, with Further Reflections on the Hermeneutics of Ad Hoc Documents," *Journal of the Evangelical*

Theological Society 28 (1985): 142-148. This statement, found also in Fee's commentary on the pastorals, is widely quoted.

25. This represents a change from my earlier view (see "Rejoinder," pp. 203-204).
26. This general approach is taken by a great many interpreters. See, for instance, Letha Scanzoni and Nancy Hardesty, *All We're Meant to Be: A Biblical Approach to Women's Liberation* (Waco, TX: Word, 1974), p. 37; Aida Besançon Spencer, "Eve at Ephesus [Should Women be ordained as pastors according to the First Letter to Timothy 2:11-15?]," *Journal of the Evangelical Theological Society* 17 (1974): 216-222, and *Beyond the Curse*, pp. 84-91; Payne, "Libertarian Women," pp. 185-197; Scholer, "1 Timothy 2:9-15," p. 211; Evans, *Women in the Bible*, pp. 104-106; Alan Padgett, "Wealthy Women at Ephesus, 1 Timothy 2:8-15 in Social Context," *Interpretation* 41 (1987): 25-27; Roger L. Omansen, "The Role of Women in the New Testament Church," *Review and Expositor* 83 (1986): 23-24; Gilbert Bilezikian, *Beyond Sex Roles* (Grand Rapids, MI: Baker, 1985), pp. 179-181.
27. See Towner, "Gnosis and Realized Eschatology," p. 110.
28. Verse 14 is frequently labelled "typological," on the analogy of Paul's other use of the deception of Eve in 2 Corinthians 11:3 (e.g., Padgett, "Wealthy Women at Ephesus," p. 25). While this is close to our view, we must point out that 2 Corinthians 11:3 has an explicit "just as . . ." construction that is lacking here.
29. See Spencer, *Beyond the Curse*, pp. 89-91; Evans, p. 104.
30. Although it has been argued that *gar* ("for") introduces simply an explanation, Paul much more often uses the word, particularly in contexts like this, with a causal meaning ("I am not permitting this . . . because . . ."). See Moo, "Rejoinder," pp. 202-204, arguing against Payne, "Libertarian Women," pp. 175-177. See also Payne's "Surrejoinder," pp. 110-111.
31. Paul King Jewett, *Man as Male and Female* (Grand Rapids, MI: Eerdmans, 1975), pp. 119-126; Karen W. Hoover, "Creative Tension in 1 Timothy 2:11-15," *Brethren Life and Thought* 22 (1977): 163-165; Catholic Biblical Association of America's Task Force on the Role of Women in Early Christianity, "Women and Priestly Ministry: The New Testament Evidence," *Catholic Biblical Quarterly* 41 (1979): 612.
32. Scholer's objection that Paul's use of Genesis is selective ("1 Timothy 2:9-15," pp. 208-211) is hardly to the point. The New Testament use of the Old Testament is always selective, since only specific points, not the interpretation of Old Testament passages per se, are at stake. The question is whether the Old Testament data selected really do relate to the issue involved.
33. The argument of some is that Paul viewed the prohibitions of verse 12 as temporary, culturally-related accommodations to the status of men and women under the curse of Genesis 3. But this line of argument founders on two counts: (1) Paul appeals here to the situation not after the fall, but before it (even Eve's deception is, technically, pre-fall [Bacchiocchi, *Women in the Church*, p. 180]), and (2) Paul, while anxious that Christians maintain a credible witness and not offend those without, would not, we think, in the new age that had dawned, treat people and require them to do things as if they were still under the curse. Nor is it clear that redemption nullifies the role relationship established at creation, as Ruth A. Tucker and Walter L. Liefeld suggest in *Daughters of the Church, Women and Ministry from New Testament Times to the Present* (Grand Rapids, MI: Zondervan, 1987), p. 451. Rather, redemption enables men and women to relate to one another as God originally intended (see Matthew 19:1-9).

    Furthermore, as Bertil Gärtner points out, Paul grounds the submission of women to men in the facts of redemption (Ephesians 5:22-24), not in the curse or even creation only ("*Didaskalos*: The Office, Man and Woman in the New Testament," *Concordia Journal* 8 [1982]: 59-60).
34. See, for instance, Scholer, "1 Timothy 2:9-15," pp. 208-211.
35. If, however, it were established that head-coverings for women are more directly involved in the appeal to creation, then exegetical faithfulness and hermeneutical consistency would demand not that we ignore the commands in both 1 Corinthians 11:2-16 and 1 Timothy 2:12, but that we obey both. We are all for consistency, but consistency may well be better attained by obeying more Biblical commandments than we now do rather than seeing

more of them as cultural accommodations (against, for instance, Fee, "Reflections on Church Order," pp. 150-151).

36. See Towner, "Gnosis and Realized Eschatology," p. 111; James G. Sigountos and Myron Shank, "Public Roles for Women in the Pauline Church: A Reappraisal of the Evidence," *Journal of the Evangelical Theological Society* 26 (1985): 289-298.
37. Grant R. Osborne, "Hermeneutics and Women in the Church," *Journal of the Evangelical Theological Society* 20 (1977): 348.
38. See, for instance, H. P. Liddon, *Explanatory Notes on St. Paul's First Epistle to Timothy* (London: Longmans, Green, 1897), p. 20; Williams, *Apostle Paul*, p. 113; Payne, "Libertarian Women," pp. 177-179.
39. Henry Alford, *The Greek Testament*, four vols. (London: Rivingstons, 1865-1876), vol. 3, p. 820.
40. The preposition *dia* ("through") would designate "attendant circumstances."
41. See, in more detail, my "Interpretation," pp. 70-72; Robert Falconer, "1 Timothy 2:14, 15: Interpretative Notes," *Journal of Biblical Literature* 88 (1941): 376-378; Scholer, "1 Timothy 2:9-15," pp. 195-202.

Endnotes to Chapter Ten

1. Several sections in this chapter are adapted from Wayne Grudem, *The First Epistle of Peter: An Introduction and Commentary* (Leicester, England: InterVarsity Press, and Grand Rapids, MI: Eerdmans, 1988), pp. 134-146, and are used by permission.
2. Note also in this regard Colossians 3:18, "Wives, submit to your husbands, as is fitting in the Lord." How can it be fitting "in the Lord" if there is "neither male nor female in Christ"? Only if we understand Galatians 3:28 to be talking about spiritual benefits and blessings of salvation, not about all created sexual differences and God-ordained differences in roles.
3. Dorothy Patterson says of this passage, "Submission actually is above and beyond obedience, which in itself could be the forcing and coercion to outward conformity." "Roles in Marriage: A Study in Submission: 1 Peter 3:1-7" in *The Theological Educator* (New Orleans, LA) 13:2 (Spring, 1983), p. 71. This entire article provides an exegetically-based perspective on submission as seen through the eyes of a wife who delights in her calling.
4. The New Testament uses *aphthartos* only of eternal heavenly realities, such as God Himself (Romans 1:23; 1 Timothy 1:17), God's Word (1 Peter 1:23), and our resurrection bodies (1 Corinthians 15:52; compare 9:25; 1 Peter 3:4).
5. Gilbert Bilezikian, *Beyond Sex Roles* (Grand Rapids, MI: Baker Book House, 1990[2]), p. 191. Patricia Gundry, *Woman Be Free!* (Grand Rapids, MI: Zondervan, 1977), also says of this passage, "The point is, Sarah and Abraham responded in the same way to each other. Abraham did what Sarah requested, and she did the same for him" (p. 83).
6. Bilezikian, *Beyond Sex Roles*, p. 191.
7. See, for example, Bilezikian, pp. 189. His section on 1 Peter 3:1-8 is titled, "Again, Mutual Submission—1 Peter 3:1-8."

   On page 190, Bilezikian sets up a dichotomy between what he calls "submission that is mere obedience" and "servant submission that walks the extra mile and turns the other cheek." He approves only the second kind and says of this "servant submission" that "the motivations for such submission have nothing in common with submission defined as obedience to authority" (p. 190). Such opposition to any idea of "obedience to authority" runs throughout Bilezikian's book and is a fundamental theme in his writings. (On p. 249 he says that the introduction of any authority into marriage "would paganize the marriage relationship and make the Christ/church paradigm irrelevant to it.")

   Bilezikian seems unable to understand that it is possible to have obedience to authority together with an attitude of love and concern for the one in authority. How does he think Jesus was subject to the authority of His parents, for example (Luke 2:51), or how should Christian children today be subject to their parents' authority, or how should we all be subject to God (James 4:7)? An attitude of love and willing submission characterizes all of these kinds of obedience to an authority. Further, Bilezikian seems unable to understand that someone in authority can act with love and consideration toward another who is under that authority (as God does with us, Christ does with the church, and Christian parents often do with their children).

Moreover, Bilezikian's argument on 1 Peter 3:1 is inconsistent with an earlier statement in his book. On p. 154 he says that the word for "submit" (*hupotassō*) means "to make oneself subordinate to the authority of a higher power. . . . [w]herever the word appears in the NT, except where its meaning is deliberately changed by a modifier such as in [Ephesians 5:21]." But here in 1 Peter 3:1 there is no such modifier (such as "to one another"), yet he still says that "mutual submission" is in view.

Finally, the fact that his definition of "mutual submission" without any obedience to authority is unworkable in the real world is seen in a self-contradiction on p. 155. He says, "The church thrives on mutual subjection." But then he says, "In a Spirit-led church, the elders submit to the congregation in being accountable for their watch-care, and the congregation submits to the elders in *accepting their guidance*." In a footnote to this sentence, he says, "The congregations submit to their leaders by *obeying* and accepting their guidance" (p. 289, emphasis mine). He wants to speak of "mutual submission" without obedience to authority, but he knows the church will not work without obedience to the authority of those in leadership. We must ask, if obedience to leaders is required in a Spirit-led church, then why not also in a Spirit-led marriage?

8. So Bilezikian, pp. 153-173.
9. The unsupported assumption in the feminist view of Ephesians 5:21 is that the word *allēlous*, "one another," *must always mean* "everyone to everyone." Of course, the word often takes that meaning, as in Ephesians 4:32, "Be kind and compassionate to one another," or John 15:12, "Love each other as I have loved you." In these cases the sense of the sentence shows that "everyone to everyone" is meant by "one another." But in other verses the word simply cannot take that meaning, and the sense "*some to others*" is required instead. For example, in Revelation 6:4, "men slay *each other*" means "*some* men slay *others*" (not "every man slays every other man," or "those people being slain 'mutually' slay those who are slaying them," which would make no sense); in Galatians 6:2, "Carry *each other's* burdens" means not "everyone should exchange burdens with everyone else," but "*some* who are more able should help bear the burdens of *others* who are less able"; 1 Corinthians 11:33, "when you come together to eat, wait for *each other*," means "*some* who are ready early should wait for *others* who are late"; etc. (cf. Luke 2:15; 12:1; 24:32; there are many examples where the word is not exhaustively reciprocal). Similarly, in Ephesians 5:21, both the following context and the meaning of *hupotassō* seem to require *allēlous* to mean "some to others," so that the verse could be paraphrased, "those who are under authority should be subject to others among you who have authority over them."

   Therefore, according to this interpretation, it would seem best to say that it is not "mutual submission" but submission to appropriate authorities that Paul is commanding in Ephesians 5:21.
10. Bilezikian, pp. 154-155, clearly opposes the existence of any obedience to authority in Ephesians 5:21-24.
11. Interestingly, Bilezikian admits that *hupotassō* in the New Testament "means to make oneself subordinate to the authority of a higher power . . . to yield to rulership" (p. 154). He says, "This is the natural meaning of 'submit' wherever the word appears in the New Testament, except where its meaning is deliberately changed by a modifier such as in verse 21 of [Ephesians 5]. The addition . . . of the reciprocal pronoun 'to each other' changes its meaning entirely. . . . By definition, mutual submission rules out hierarchical differences."

   Bilezikian sees the issue clearly: if "submit" (*hupotassō*) means to submit to a higher authority, then in that sense there can be no mutual submission. He also recognizes that this is the usual meaning for *hupotassō* in the New Testament. But his error is to assume that the meaning of the word must be changed when the expression "to one another" (*allēlous*) follows it. This is certainly not necessary, since *allēlous* can often mean "some to others," as explained in note 9. Then Ephesians 5:21 would be paraphrased, "Submit to one another (that is, *some to others*), out of reverence for Christ."

It is incorrect exegesis for Bilezikian to say that in Ephesians 5:21 a word *must* take a new meaning that has been nowhere else attested when a perfectly good sense for both words fits well in the context. Why should we assign *hupotassō* a meaning here that it is nowhere else shown to have? Even in Ephesians 5:22-24, wives are not to be subject to everyone or to all husbands, but to "their *own* husbands"—the submission Paul has in mind is not general thoughtfulness toward others but specific submission to a higher authority. But should not the verb *hupotassō* in verse 22 (whether implicit or explicit; it appears in some Greek manuscripts but not in others—in the latter, it clearly is understood as to be inferred by the reader) take the same sense it does in verse 21?

Therefore it seems to be a misunderstanding of Ephesians 5:21 to say that it implies mutual submission. And it is certainly incorrect to use Bilezikian's doubtful interpretation of Ephesians 5:21 to contradict the other four texts in the New Testament (Ephesians 5:22-24; Colossians 3:18; Titus 2:5; 1 Peter 3:1, 5-6) that speak clearly and explicitly of a wife's obligation to submit to her husband.

12. This is probably why the New Testament authors use the broader term *submit* when referring to wives in relation to husbands, rather than the specific term *obey* as they do with children and servants. The absence of the term *obey* (except in 1 Peter 3:6) with respect to wives does not mean that the idea is not there, only that the idea is included in a broader attitude of support for the husband's leadership.
13. However, nowhere does Scripture condone or support the abuse of wives by husbands, but explicitly forbids even harsh attitudes (Colossians 3:19; 1 Peter 3:7), and therefore certainly condemns any physical violence used by husbands against wives. Evangelical churches have a strong responsibility to prevent such abuse and to protect those threatened or harmed by it.
14. At this point Bilezikian apparently agrees, for he says about this word, "The servant attitude modeled by Christ and required of slaves is also the example for wives" (p. 189).
15. The aorist tense here for "obeyed" need not refer only to one incident, for the aorist indicative is used frequently in a constative sense simply to say that something "happened," with no implication of whether it happened at one point in time or over a very long period of time (cf. the aorist indicatives in Ephesians 5:25, "Christ loved the church"; Romans 5:14, "death reigned from the time of Adam to the time of Moses"; Revelation 20:4, they "reigned with Christ a thousand years"; also Blass-Debrunner-Funk, *Grammar*, sec. 332).

    E. G. Selwyn, *The First Epistle of St. Peter* (London: Macmillan, 1949), p. 185, and J. N. D. Kelly *A Commentary on the Epistles of Peter and Jude* (London: Black, 1969), p. 131, together with several other writers, say that Peter is referring to Genesis 18:12, the only place in the Old Testament where Sarah is reported as using the title *kurios*, "lord" (or "master," "sir"—it is a polite term of address when used of human beings in a position of leadership or authority, as is the Hebrew term *'adonî* behind it). It is possible that Peter is referring to this passage, but the difficulty is that no obedience to Abraham is mentioned in that immediate context. It is more likely that Peter deduces from this one example that Sarah ordinarily referred to Abraham as her "master" or "lord," and that this indicated her attitude of submission and respect for Abraham. This understanding would still mean that Peter is referring to Sarah's whole pattern of life, not only to one incident of obedience.
16. This is consistent with Peter's practice throughout the epistle of seeing the church, not those descended physically from Abraham and Sarah, as the new Israel, the true people of God (see, for example, 1:1 and 2:4-10).
17. Some commentators affirm that many or most of the wives to whom Peter was writing had unbelieving husbands. For example, Mary J. Evans, *Woman in the Bible* (Downers Grove, IL: InterVarsity Press, 1983), p. 118, suggests that "Peter's primary concern is for those whose husbands are not believers" (p. 118). Similarly, E. Margaret Howe says of 1 Peter 3:1, 6, "Here it is implied that the wives addressed are those whose husbands are not Christians" (*Women and Church Leadership* [Grand Rapids, MI: Zondervan, 1982], pp. 55-56). But the Greek text implies just the opposite: "So that *even if* some do not obey the word," and the phrase "even if" (*kai ei*) suggests that this would be an unexpected or

uncommon occurrence. It implies that Peter expected that most Christian wives among his readers had Christian husbands.

18. F. J. A. Hort, *The First Epistle of St. Peter 1:1-2:17* (London: Macmillan, 1898), says, "On the whole . . . the biblical use is best expressed by 'rebel' or 'be rebellious'" (p. 122). Although some have argued that this term can mean simply "disbelieve, be an unbeliever" (especially in John 3:36), such a sense is not required in any of the word's occurrences.

    Walter Bauer, *A Greek-English Lexicon of the New Testament and Other Early Christian Literature*, 2nd ed., trans. William F. Arndt and F. Wilbur Gingrich, rev. F. Wilbur Gingrich and Frederick W. Danker (Chicago: University of Chicago Press, 1979), accepts the sense "disbelieve" in John 3:36; Acts 14:2; 19:9; Romans 15:31, but adds that this meaning is "greatly disputed" and "is not found outside our literature" (p. 82). Moreover, it must be noted that to "disobey the gospel" in the New Testament can mean not just to "disbelieve" it but actually to "disobey" it: to refuse to respond to its command to repent and believe in Christ.
19. See note 13 on wife abuse.
20. The Greek text includes no word for "their" (Peter could have made it clear with *autōn*), leaving open the possibility that Peter intends to say that unbelieving husbands will be won not simply by seeing the submissive behavior of their own wives but by observing the pattern of Christian marriage exemplified by wives generally within the Christian community. But we cannot be certain of this, for Greek often omits possessive pronouns when the author thinks the meaning will be clear to the reader.
21. Patterson, "Roles in Marriage," p. 73.
22. Ruth A. Tucker and Walter Liefeld, *Daughters of the Church: Women in Ministry from New Testament Times to the Present* (Grand Rapids, MI: Zondervan, 1987), say, "This passage seems to present fewer problems, because the submissive attitude required of the woman has a clear purpose. The believing wife of an unconverted man is to fulfill the expectations of submission in order that she might win him to the Lord" (p. 462).

    But it is certainly incorrect to say that this is Peter's *only* purpose (if they are implying that), for Peter is addressing *all* the Christian wives in all the churches in four Roman provinces (see 1 Peter 1:1), not just the wives of unbelieving husbands. (See note 17 on the fact that Peter expected most of the wives to have believing husbands.) Moreover, the fact that such behavior would win the unbelieving husband does not imply that it was less than God's ideal, but quite the opposite. Finally, Peter's reference to Sarah (whose husband was hardly in need of saving) would ill suit a command to submission that was only a temporary expedient because it would help missionary work in that culture.
23. Someone might respond that a wife's submission was not exactly *sinful* but just morally neutral, something that might be adopted in one culture and not in another. But this is hardly persuasive, because it is not morally neutral behavior that wins the unbelieving husband, but morally "pure" (Greek *hagnos*) behavior—it is the *positive moral beauty* of Christian behavior that attracts the unbeliever. Moreover, if it were simply the fact that the believer was *unselfish* that would win the unbelieving spouse, it would not explain why Peter does not say the same to husbands as well. There seems to be something morally beautiful—not just neutral—in a wife's submission to her husband.
24. Page 82.
25. Pages 82, 83. This "household code" argument was extensively developed by David L. Balch, *Let Wives Be Submissive: The Domestic Code in 1 Peter* (Chico, CA: Scholars Press, 1981). Balch sees these New Testament teachings entirely in sociological terms, analyzing the possible motives for them as Christians attempted to avoid offending secular society. He does not consider the possibility that these New Testament standards are in fact divine commands with absolute divine authority attaching to them.
26. See further the discussion of this issue in chapter 2 of this volume, Question 17. Balch, *Let Wives Be Submissive*, especially pp. 96ff., lists several significant differences, even in form, with many pagan codes. He also adduces several parallel ideas (pp. 98-109), if not in actual household codes, at least in some ancient Platonic and neopythagorean literature, as well as in Jewish literature. Of course, this is what we would expect even from pagan Greek culture because of the influence of conscience and common grace. But direct borrowing of pagan Greek "household codes" simply did not occur.

27. Though a few ancient philosophers can be found with views similar to Peter's; see Balch, p. 101.
28. It should be noted that it is also possible to understand the two phrases "the woman" and "the weaker partner" as relating to the command "live together" rather than to "bestowing honor." This would give the sense, "live together with your wife according to knowledge, as with the weaker sex, the feminine one" (cf. NASB, TEV). It is not possible to decide between this reading and that of the RSV (and NIV, AV) on grammatical grounds alone; neither do the arguments from context seem to be conclusive on either side. But there is not much difference in the end since the commands to live together and to bestow honor are both part of one large command, and the husband's knowledge of the fact that Peter calls the wife "the feminine one" and "the weaker vessel" should in any case modify the whole complex of actions included in "living together in an understanding way" and "bestowing honor."
29. For the use of the participle as an imperative see 1 Peter 2:18; 3:1, 7; 4:8, 10; also David Daube, "Participle and Imperative in 1 Peter," in Selwyn, *First Epistle of St. Peter*, pp. 467-488.
30. One book that deserves mention here (simply because it contains so much practical wisdom on this subject) is James Dobson's *What Wives Wish Their Husbands Knew About Women* (Wheaton, IL: Tyndale, 1977).
31. Bilezikian states that the command for husbands to "bestow honor" on their wives indicated that Peter was commanding a "traumatic role reversal," since bestowing honor meant acting "much like a servant to his master" (p. 192). But this is simply false: when God bestows honor on His people, it does not indicate a "traumatic role reversal" whereby He becomes subject to our authority. Again Bilezikian refuses to admit that those in authority can act unselfishly and with love toward those under their authority, and this refusal skews his entire discussion.
32. The RSV's "since" expresses a possible relationship between this statement and the rest of the verse, but it could also be translated, "bestowing honor . . . as to those who are joint heirs . . ." (compare NASB). This would give slightly more emphasis to the way in which honor is bestowed instead of the reason for bestowing it, but the difference in meaning is not great.

Endnotes to Chapter Eleven

1. The argument for full inclusion of women in ministry presented here has been set forth by many authors, although there are differences among them. For a defense of full inclusion of women in every ministry similar to the position sketched here, see the following: A. J. Gordon, "The Ministry of Women," *Missionary Review of the World* 7 (1894): 910-921; A. H. Stouffer, "The Ordination of Women: Yes," *Christianity Today* 20 (February 1981): 256-259; S. S. Bartchy, "Power, Submission, and Sexual Identity Among the Early Christians," in *Essays on New Testament Christianity*, ed. C. R. Wetzel (Cincinnati: Standard Publishing, 1978), pp. 64-67 and 70-74; L. Scanzoni and N. Hardesty, *All We're Meant to Be*, rev. ed. (Nashville: Abingdon, 1986) pp. 78-81 and 85-90; Patricia Gundry, *Woman Be Free* (Grand Rapids, MI: Zondervan, 1977), pp. 89-104; E. Margaret Howe, *Women and Church Leadership* (Grand Rapids, MI: Zondervan, 1982) 30-36; Gilbert Bilezikian, *Beyond Sex Roles: A Guide for the Study of Female Roles in the Bible* (Grand Rapids, MI: Baker Book House, 1985), pp. 193-206; P. B. Payne, "Libertarian Women in Ephesus: A Response to Douglas J. Moo's Article, '1 Timothy 2:11-15: Meaning and Significance,'" *Trinity Journal* 2 (1981): 173-175, 183-185, and 190-197; J. Sigountos and M. Shank, "Public Roles for Women in the Pauline Church: A Reappraisal of the Evidence," *Journal of the Evangelical Theological Society* 26 (1983): 283-295; K. Snodgrass, "Paul and Women," *Covenant Quarterly* 34 (1976): 3-13; A. B. Spencer, *Beyond the Curse: Women Called to Ministry* (Nashville: Thomas Nelson, 1985), pp. 64-120.
2. Another argument in favor of woman deacons is that Paul says nothing about the wives of elders in 1 Timothy 3:1-7. Such an omission is hard to explain if he is speaking of the wives of deacons in 1 Timothy 3:11. One would expect that higher qualifications would

be demanded of wives of elders than of wives of deacons. But if Paul is referring to women who were deacons, then the omission of women among elders is because women could not be elders, although they could be deacons. Of course, those who argue for full inclusion of women do not use this particular argument because it would exclude women from being elders, even though they could be deacons.

3. That prophetesses in the Old Testament did not proclaim the word of the Lord publicly is also argued by Origen. He thinks the same pattern was followed in the New Testament, but 1 Corinthians 11:5 and 14:29-33a make this latter assertion questionable. For the original text of Origen's comments, see "Origen on 1 Corinthians," *Journal of Theological Studies* 10 (1908-09): 41-42, LXXIV.279-280. For an English translation, see R. Gryson, *The Ministry of Women in the Early Church* (Collegeville, MN: Liturgical Press, 1976), pp. 28-29.
4. Less prominent judges are only treated with a summary of one to three verses: Shamgar (3:31), Tola (10:1-2), Jair (10:3-5), Ibzan (12:8-10), Elon (12:11-12), and Abdon (12:13-15). The author devotes more attention to Abimelech (9:1-57), but he was clearly wicked and there is no indication that the Lord empowered or called him. All citations from Scripture in this paragraph are from the NASB.
5. Isaiah 3:12 should also be noted, where Isaiah asserts that women ruling over men is a sign of God's judgment: "O My people! Their oppressors are children, and women rule over them. O My people! Those who guide you lead you astray, and confuse the direction of your paths" (NASB). Note the theme of judgment in Isaiah 3:1-4. Surely Deborah's role as a judge was not the same as what Isaiah condemns here. Thus, we can conclude that Deborah's role as prophet and judge was not exercised in such a way that she ruled over men.
6. Such a distinction, of course, raises many questions. For a careful explanation of all the issues involved, see Wayne Grudem, "Prophecy—Yes, But Teaching—No: Paul's Consistent Advocacy of Women's Participation Without Governing Authority," *Journal of the Evangelical Theological Society* 30 (1987): 11-23. For a more extensive treatment of the same issue, see Grudem, *The Gift of Prophecy in the New Testament and Today* (Westchester, IL; Crossway, 1988).
7. Tertullian also made a distinction between prophecy and teaching, allowing prophetic utterances by women but not teaching. See *On the Veiling of Virgins*, 9,1; *Against Marcion*, 5, 8, 11.
8. The same point could be made regarding Colossians 3:16. That text refers not to public authoritative teaching by believers but to the mutual instruction and encouragement that occur when the community is gathered.
9. That the household of Stephanas held leadership in the Corinthian church is also suggested by 1 Clement 42:4 (95 A.D.), which reminds the Corinthians that the apostles appointed their "first fruits" (*aparchē*) as overseers and deacons, an apparent reference to the household of Stephanas, which is called the "first fruits (translated "first converts" by RSV) of Achaia" in 1 Corinthians 16:15.
10. Moreover, the word *fellow worker* in 1 Corinthians 16:16 is not from the noun form (*sunergos*), which occurs thirteen times elsewhere in the New Testament. Instead, Paul uses the participial form of the verb *sunergeō*. This verbal form is not necessarily a technical term for those who possess governing authority in the church, because in other contexts in the New Testament the verb is used in a general and non-technical way (cf. Romans 8:28; James 2:22). It is also most likely in the context that the fellow workers of Paul are described as "*my* fellow worker(s)" or "*our* fellow worker" (cf. Romans 16:3, 9, 21; 2 Corinthians 8:23; Philippians 4:3; 1 Thessalonians 3:2; Philemon 1, 24).
11. One of the problems with the otherwise fine study of E. E. Ellis ("Paul and His Co-Workers," *Prophecy and Hermeneutic in Early Christianity* [Grand Rapids, MI: Eerdmans, 1978], pp. 3-22) is that he interprets the terms *diakonos* and *adelphos* more technically than the evidence warrants. Both terms are often used in a very general way and often do not refer to specific ministry roles. Since *diakonos* is particularly relevant for our discussion, I list the texts where it occurs so that the evidence can be examined: Matthew 20:26; 22:13; 23:11; Mark 9:35; 10:43; John 2:5, 9; 12:26; Romans 13:4(2);

15:8; 16:1; 1 Corinthians 3:5; 2 Corinthians 3:6; 6:4; 11:15(2), 23; Galatians 2:17; Ephesians 3:7; 6:21; Philippians 1:1; Colossians 1:7, 23, 25; 4:7; 1 Timothy 3:8, 12; 4:6.

12. Walter Bauer, *A Greek-English Lexicon of the New Testament and Other Early Christian Literature*, 2nd ed., trans. William F. Arndt and F. Wilbur Gingrich, rev. F. Wilbur Gingrich and Frederick W. Danker (Chicago: University of Chicago Press, 1979; henceforward cited as BAGD), p. 718.

13. Although I incline to the opposite view for the reasons mentioned earlier in this chapter, there are several good arguments to the effect that women could not be deacons. We have noted previously that the use of the word *diakonos* (Romans 16:1) with reference to Phoebe does not establish that she was a deacon since the word is most often used of ministry in a general sense without any clear implication of church office. And a number of arguments can be adduced for the view that the women referred to in 1 Timothy 3:11 should be understood to be the wives of deacons rather than deacons:

    (1) The qualification "husband of but one wife" in 1 Timothy 3:12 would naturally exclude women.

    (2) Since the subject in verses 8-10 and 12-13 is male deacons, it would be unusual to switch the subject to female deacons in the middle of the discussion (verse 11) without giving explicit indication of that fact by some phrase such as "the women *who serve as deacons* likewise must be serious. . . . "

    (3) A requirement for the wives of deacons would be appropriate in this context, since Paul sees the status and conduct of a man's family as an essential qualification for church office (1 Timothy 3:2, 4-5, 12).

    (4) The word *likewise* (*hōsautōs*) in verse 11 does not necessarily prove that women were deacons, because Paul may be commanding the wives to have the same virtues as the male deacons without implying that they shared the same office. For example, in 1 Timothy 5:25 Paul uses the same word *likewise* to compare good deeds with the sins described in verse 24, but no one would claim from this comparison that sins and good deeds are the same thing. Similarly, the injunction to the older women in Titus 2:3, which is introduced with *likewise*, does not imply that the older women *are* the same as the older men of Titus 2:2.

    (5) Furthermore, the lack of a possessive genitive with *gunaikas* does not rule out the possibility that these women are wives of deacons, since elsewhere in the New Testament the possessive genitive is not used when it is clearly the case that the women or men being described are wives and husbands (cf. Colossians 3:18-19; Ephesians 5:22-25; 1 Corinthians 7:2-4, 11, 14, 33; Matthew 18:25; Mark 10:2).

    In conclusion, it cannot be established with certainty that women were deacons, although for the reasons stated earlier I am inclined to think they were.

14. Actually, the seven in Acts 6 are not called deacons, but they seem to carry out the function of deacons, and the verb related to the noun *deacon* is used in 6:2.

15. G. D. Fee, however, in *1 and 2 Timothy, Titus* (NIBC; Peabody, MA; Hendrickson, 1988), p. 22, argues that the term *elders* was used as "a covering term for both overseers and deacons." He says on p. 78, "It is altogether likely that *both* 'overseers' and 'deacons' come under the larger category *presbyteroi* ('elders')." If Fee is correct, then it would be wrong to distinguish between elders and deacons as I have done above, although one could still legitimately distinguish between overseers and deacons. But Fee's claim that both overseers and deacons belong to the larger category called "elders" is hard to sustain and should be rejected for the following reasons: (1) The New Testament nowhere identifies "elders" and "deacons" so that the latter would be construed as a subcategory of the former. (2) There is a clear and indisputable distinction between "overseers" (*episkopoi*) and "deacons" (Philippians 1:1; 1 Timothy 3:1-13). (3) But it is also clear that *overseers* and *elders* are two terms used to describe the same office. In Titus 1:5, Titus is charged to appoint "elders" in every city, and yet when Paul speaks of qualifications for this office he refers to an "overseer" in Titus 1:7. The singular *episkopos* ("overseer") in Titus 1:7 (and 1 Timothy 3:1-2) is generic and there is no indication that only one overseer is in view. Thus, these two terms describe the same office. Such an identification is confirmed by Acts 20:17-38. In verse 17 Paul summons the "elders" of the Ephesian church in order to address them. However, in verse 28 these same "elders" are called "overseers." So once

again we see that "elders" and "overseers" are two different terms for the same office. (4) Fee does not give any evidence to support his claim that *elders* is a covering term for both overseers and deacons, and the evidence we have adduced above points in the opposite direction. Thus, Fee's unsubstantiated assertion has no clear evidence to support it.

16. For a defense of this interpretation, see: R. E. Brown, *The Epistles of John* (Anchor Bible; Garden City: Doubleday, 1982), pp. 651-655; S. S. Smalley, *1, 2, 3 John* (Word Bible Commentary; Waco, TX: Word, 1984), p. 318; J. R. W. Stott, *The Epistles of John* (Tyndale New Testament Commentary; Grand Rapids, MI: Eerdmans, 1964), pp. 200-202.
17. A. T. Robertson, in *A Grammar of the Greek New Testament in the Light of Historical Research* (Nashville: Broadman, 1934), pp. 171-173, shows that such contraction of names was common in Greek and lists numerous examples in the Greek New Testament; cf. F. Blass and A. Debrunner, *A Grammar of the New Testament and Other Early Christian Literature*, trans. R. W. Funk (Chicago: The University of Chicago Press, 1961), henceforward cited as BDF], sec. 125). A. Spencer (*Beyond the Curse*, 101) responds that *Iounian* in Romans 16:7 could not be a shortened form of the common man's name *Junianus* because Latin names formed diminutives (or "nicknames") by lengthening, not shortening the name. But Spencer either misunderstands or inaccurately misrepresents the data here, for Paul is writing in Greek, not Latin, and Robertson (p. 171; similarly, BDF, sec. 125[2]) notes that "this custom of giving short pet-names . . . was used not merely with Greek names, but also with foreign names brought into the Greek." While Spencer cites James Hope Moulton and George Milligan, *The Vocabulary of the Greek New Testament* (Grand Rapids, MI: Eerdmans, [1930] 1976), p. 306, to show that "Junias" as a man's name has yet to be found in extra-Biblical sources, she fails to mention that in that same entry (p. 306) they say that *Iounian* in Romans 16:7 "is probably a contracted form of *Iunianus*, which is common in the inscriptions." In sum, no lexicon or grammar takes Spencer's view that *Iounias* in Romans 16:7 *could not be* a shortened form of the man's name Junianus, and all who comment on it (Robertson, BDF, BAGD, Thayer, and Moulton & Milligan) say not only that it *could* be but that it probably or possibly is a man's name. See further the discussion of this issue in Chapter 2 of this volume, Question 38.
18. Bilezikian, *Beyond Sex Roles*, p. 236.
19. This is not to deny, of course, that the demeanor and attitude of men are important as well. The point is that Scripture teaches that women should support male headship by their demeanor and attitude; men are also to be humble and servants, but their demeanor and attitude is not intended to support women in authority.
20. See E. Christenson with V. Blake, *What Happens When Women Pray* (Wheaton, IL: Victor Books, 1975).

Endnotes to Chapter Twelve

1. Neither in Genesis nor anywhere else in Scripture can we find an attempt to define the meaning of "image of God." Evidently the author of Genesis was using a concept familiar to his readers. Certainly the basic Hebrew terms for "image" and "likeness" were well known, as other contexts indicate.
2. Compare the distinction in Anthony C. Hoekema, *Created in God's Image* (Grand Rapids, MI: Eerdmans, 1986), pp. 65ff.
3. D. J. A. Clines, in "The Image of God in Man," *Tyndale Bulletin* 19 (1968): 53. The Hebrew preposition *beth*, often translated "in," is a "*beth* of essence."
4. Contrary to G. C. Berkouwer, *Man: The Image of God*, trans. Dirk W. Jellema (Grand Rapids, MI: Eerdmans, 1962), pp. 56ff.
5. Knowledge is a moral quality in Scripture. Sinners reject the true knowledge of God (Romans 1:21-25; 1 Corinthians 2:14). That knowledge is restored through the renewing work of the Spirit. Such knowledge is inseparable from obedience to God's commands, 1 John 2:3-6.
6. John Murray, *Collected Writings*, II (Edinburgh: Banner of Truth, 1977), p. 40.

7. All Christians bear the image of Christ from the beginning of their lives in Him (Ephesians 4:24). There is also a process of renewal by which God gradually and increasingly brings about more and more conformity to Jesus' image (2 Corinthians 3:18; Colossians 3:10). The fulfillment of this process, the perfection of the image, takes place at Jesus' return (1 Corinthians 15:49, in context).
8. Thanks to my colleague Robert B. Strimple, who makes this point in unpublished lecture notes.
9. This is the usual position of Lutheran theologians and that of G. C. Berkouwer. See Murray, *Collected Writings*, for a survey of views on this subject.
10. See note 5 on knowledge as an ethical quality. Unbelievers continue to know that God exists, who He is (Romans 1:18-21) and what He requires (Romans 1:32); but they utterly lack that knowledge (= friendship with God) that produces obedience (1 John 2:3-5). To have that they must be renewed by grace (Colossians 3:10).
11. What has been called "common grace" does produce even in unbelievers various degrees of external conformity to God's standards. However, unbelievers always fall short of that heart-righteousness by which alone God is pleased (Romans 8:8); thus God does not give them credit for having any righteousness or holiness. See Murray, "Common Grace," in *Collected Writings*, pp. 93-119.
12. Murray's exegetical observations on these passages are useful; *Collected Writings*, pp. 35-41.
13. In one sense, of course, God needs no help. But He has chosen to accomplish His great purposes (here and in Matthew 28:18-20) by means of human agents, thereby establishing a pattern that can be, and should be, imaged on the human level.
14. Thanks again to my colleague Robert B. Strimple (via his unpublished lecture notes) for this insight.
15. Berkouwer, *Man: The Image of God*, pp. 67ff.
16. In this paragraph I am summarizing Murray's argument (pp. 14-18). For other interesting suggestions about a physical aspect to the divine image, see Meredith G. Kline's *Images of the Spirit* (Grand Rapids, MI: Baker Book House, 1980).
17. James B. Hurley, *Man and Woman in Biblical Perspective* (Leicester, England: InterVarsity Press, 1981), p. 172.
18. *A Commentary on the First Epistle of Paul to the Corinthians* (New York: Harper and Row, 1968), p. 252.
19. I agree with those who say that "helper" does not in itself connote any subordination. God is Himself the helper of Israel (Psalm 30:10, etc.). It is, however, significant that Eve was made after Adam, for the specific purpose of helping him. That cannot be said of God's relationship to Israel (or of Adam's relationship to Eve). That fact, I believe, lies behind Paul's statements in 1 Corinthians 11:8-9 and in 1 Timothy 2:13. Note also that in 1 Corinthians 11:9 Paul does not base his argument on the word *helper* but on the fact that Eve was made for Adam.
20. Leon Morris, *The First Epistle of Paul to the Corinthians* (Grand Rapids, MI: Eerdmans, 1958), on 11:4. Also James B. Hurley, "Did Paul Require Veils or the Silence of Women?" *Westminster Theological Journal* 35:2 (Winter 1973): 205.
21. Even kings are usually answerable to someone, and even "absolute" monarchs get toppled if they do not succeed in pleasing other powerful members of society.
22. Noel Weeks wisely chides many in the feminist movement for confusing worth with ruling power. See his remarkable book, *The Sufficiency of Scripture* (Edinburgh: Banner of Truth, 1988), p. 137. The reader might also usefully peruse Royce Gruenler's *The Trinity in the Gospel of John* (Grand Rapids, MI: Baker Book House, 1986), in which he explores the relations of "mutual deference" within the Trinity. I don't agree with some of his points, but there is much stimulus here.
23. Karl Barth, *Church Dogmatics*, trans. J. W. Edwards et al. (Edinburgh: T. and T. Clark, 1958), III/1, pp. 184ff.
24. Kline, *Images of the Spirit*, pp. 30ff.
25. Barth, *Church Dogmatics*, p. 185.

26. I agree with Stephen B. Clark that "the notion is a modern preoccupation and is to be found neither in Christian tradition nor in the New Testament." See Clark, *Man and Woman in Christ* (Ann Arbor, MI: Servant Books, 1980), p. 14n.
27. Scripture also, of course, emphasizes God's masculinity over against the polytheism and degradation of pagan goddess-worship.
28. See other essays in this volume.
29. Hence the title of my series of theology books, *A Theology of Lordship*.
30. For this reason I disagree with Hurley's statement that according to 1 Corinthians 11:7 "The woman is not called to image God or Christ in the relation which she sustains to her husband" (*Man and Woman*, p. 173). The imaging is not precise, but, as we have seen, imaging never is. I think there are better ways to handle the problem of 1 Corinthians 11:7; see my earlier discussion.
31. A complete account of Barth's view cannot stop with his identification of the image with sexual, or even of social, relationships. Barth's ultimate view is, like all his theology, Christological: the image of God is the creation of man "in Christ" (see Barth, *Church Dogmatics*, III/1, 203ff.). He moves, then, from image as a reflection of the Trinity to image as our participation in Christ. As indicated earlier, I agree that there is a Christological aspect to the image: in salvation, God re-creates His people in Christ's image. Barth's view, however, regards all human beings as "in Christ" apart from their faith or unbelief. That position is in my view contrary to Scripture and certainly not to be found in Genesis 1:27 or other Biblical passages dealing with the image.
32. Kline sees the "image of God" as a reflection of that council on earth; *Images of the Spirit*, pp. 27ff.
33. The related figure of the temple is both corporate (1 Corinthians 3:16ff.; 2 Corinthians 6:16; Ephesians 2:21) and (I think) individual (1 Corinthians 6:19).
34. Frame, *The Doctrine of the Knowledge of God* (Phillipsburg, NJ: Presbyterian and Reformed, 1987), pp. 15-18.
35. There are different views as to the authority of New Testament prophecy. See Wayne Grudem, *The Gift of Prophecy in the New Testament and Today* (Westchester, IL: Crossway Books, 1988). I seek here only to establish that (a) there were women prophets in *both* testaments and (b) the authority of prophecy, whatever it may be in various historical circumstances, attaches equally to male and female prophets.
36. Clark, *Man and Woman in Christ*, p. 171.

Endnotes to Chapter Thirteen

1. In a more thorough analysis of New Testament teaching, it would be proper to attempt to delineate the distinctive contributions of the various New Testament authors. Paul emphasizes our legal adoption and our present and future participation in God's inheritance. John emphasizes that God has brought us to a new birth and transformed us into people characterized by faith and love. But these distinctive emphases are complementary contributions to a unified body of divine teaching with a single divine Author.
2. "Overseers" (*episkopoi*) and "elders" (*presbuteroi*) designate the same people, according to J. B. Lightfoot, *Saint Paul's Epistle to the Philippians* (London: Macmillan, 1913), pp. 95-99, and many other New Testament scholars.
3. In certain limited ways, both men and women must exercise skills in management. In 1 Timothy 5:14, women are instructed to "manage their homes." Proverbs 31:10-31 indicates in some detail the virtuous character and broad scope of a wife's management. But such management is not identical with the responsibility of fathers. Ephesians 5:22-6:4 makes it clear that while wives exercise authority over their children and over business affairs, husbands exercise authority over their wives as well as over these other areas. Thus the scope of authority is different in the case of husbands and wives. Such a distinction in scope is to be understood when we compare 1 Timothy 3:4-5 with 1 Timothy 5:14. In the subsequent argument, I aim to show that the same distinction extends to the church, since the church is the household of God.

4. The difficult statements in 1 Corinthians 7:12, 25, 40 are, I think, to be understood in this way.
5. See pp. 000-000 for further discussion of Ephesians and the leadership of husbands within their families.
6. See below on my understanding of 1 Timothy 2:11-14.
7. See further 000-000 on Galatians 3:28.
8. Thus Galatians 3:28 is in fundamental harmony with Paul's teaching elsewhere. Only by reading into Galatians 3:28 a social theory about the abstract interchangeability of individuals does one subsequently read out a principle at variance with Paul's teaching elsewhere. In fact, Paul's teaching fully affirms the richness of persons and the diverse complexity of social relations in creation.
9. See the discussion of Genesis 1-2 in Chapter 3 of this volume. Also relevant, though overstated at a few points, is the article by David J. A. Clines, "What Does Eve Do to Help? and Other Irredeemably Androcentric Orientations in Genesis 1-3," Society of Biblical Literature paper, December 7, 1987.
10. For an extended discussion of 1 Timothy 2:8-15 and for interaction with the competing interpretations of the passage, see Chapter 9 of this volume. Certainly the possibility of alternate interpretations must be considered. But my interpretation, arising naturally from the prominent family theme of 1 Timothy, has an innate advantage over interpretations that must introduce highly speculative reconstructions of special circumstances at Ephesus. When Paul's argument is understood against the background of the family analogy, it becomes clear that it would be apropos for any situation like Ephesus where people were having trouble understanding the distinctive responsibilities of men and women.
11. On the propriety of understanding headship in Ephesians 5:22-33 as involving exercise of authority, see Wayne A. Grudem, "Does *Kephalē* ("Head") Mean 'Source' or 'Authority Over' in Greek Literature? A Survey of 2,336 Examples," Appendix 1 in George W. Knight III, *The Role Relationship of Men and Women* (Chicago: Moody, 1985) pp. 49-80; also appearing in *Trinity Journal* 6 NS (1985): 38-59. Grudem is opposed by Berkley and Alvera Mickelsen "What Does *Kephalē* Mean in the New Testament?" in *Women, Authority and the Bible*, ed. Alvera Mickelsen (Downers Grove, IL: InterVarsity Press, 1986) pp. 97-110; Gilbert Bilezikian, "Hierarchist and Egalitarian Inculturations," *Journal of the Evangelical Theological Society* 30 (1987): 423-424; *idem*, "A Critique of Wayne Grudem's Treatment of *Kephalē* in Ancient Greek Texts" (ETS 0025; Theological Research Exchange Network, 1987); and Catherine Kroeger, "The Classical Concept of 'Head' as 'Source'" (see p. 486, n. 9, above). See the recent evaluation by H. Wayne House, "Should a Woman Prophesy or Preach before Men?" *Bibliotheca Sacra* 145 (1988): 146-148. For a thorough study of *kephalē*, see Appendix 1 in this volume.
12. Genesis 2 also resists them, as Chapter 3 of this volume demonstrates.

Endnotes to Chapter Fourteen

1. Stephen Goode, "Fretful Murmur in the Cathedral," *Insight on the News*, vol. 5, no. 17 (April 24, 1989), p. 46.
2. Earle E. Cairns, "Aimee Semple McPherson," *The New International Dictionary of the Christian Church*, ed. S. D. Douglas (Grand Rapids, MI: Zondervan, 1979), p. 620.
3. Reduced to the most simple level, the three forms of church government are episcopacy (with a system of bishops and local clergy who constitute a priesthood distinct from the laity), presbyterianism (with a system of elders who govern the local church and who also belong to a regional presbytery and a nationwide general assembly), and congregationalism (in which final governing authority rests with the local congregation as a whole). In both episcopacy and presbyterianism, the matter of ecclesiastical authority is more clearly defined and regulated because governing authority clearly rests with the priesthood (episcopalcy) or with the elders in general assembly (presbyterianism). The former invests much more extensive authority in upper-level clergy than does the latter.

    Evidence favoring one pattern of church government over another can be garnered both from early church history and from certain Biblical texts. This confusing malaise is doubtless what prompted Leon Morris to provide the following assessment:

A consideration of all this evidence, then, leaves us with the conclusion that it is impossible to read back any of our modern systems into the apostolic age. If we are determined to shut our eyes to all that conflicts with our own system, then we may find it there, but hardly otherwise. It is better to recognize that in the NT church there were elements that were capable of being developed into the episcopal, presbyterian, and congregational systems, and which, in point of fact, have so developed.

But, while there is no reason why any modern Christian should not hold fast to his particular church polity and rejoice in the values it secures to him, that does not give him license to unchurch others whose reading of the evidence is different. (Leon Morris, "Church Government," *Baker's Dictionary of Theology* [Grand Rapids, MI: Baker Book House, 1978], p. 127.)

Nonetheless, any highly developed system of episcopacy is clearly absent in the New Testament. No monarchial bishops are discernable in the New Testament. By the same token, such a doctrine as the priesthood of all believers surely favors systems that provide maximum participation and freedom for local assemblies and for individuals within these assemblies.

4. A. H. Strong, *Systematic Theology* (Philadelphia: Judson Press, 1907), p. 919.
5. Rudolf Schnackenburg, *The Church in the New Testament* (New York: Herder and Herder, 1965), p. 23. Hans Küng essentially agrees. He sees the early church developing with two different patterns but admits that neither pattern was highly developed. He sees only bishops and deacons as the first officers and doubts that ordination is present in Paul's letters at all. Hans Küng, *The Church* (New York: Sheed and Ward, 1967), pp. 388-480.
6. Walter Bauer, *A Greek-English Lexicon of the New Testament and Other Early Christian Literature*, 2nd ed., trans. William F. Arndt and F. Wilbur Gingrich, rev. F. Wilbur Gingrich and Frederick W. Danker (Chicago: University of Chicago Press, 1979; henceforward cited as BAGD), p. 881. According to Moulton and Milligan, *cheirotoneō* carries the usual meaning of "election by show of hands." "Nomination" is also sometimes intended. Only in Patristic literature is the word used for ordination of bishops or of deacons as it is, for example, in the Coptic ostracon. James Hope Moulton and George Milligan, *The Vocabulary of the Greek Testament* (Grand Rapids, MI: Eerdmans, 1974), p. 687.
7. *Procheirotoneō* Means "choose or appoint beforehand" (BAGD, p. 724)
8. Ronald Y. K. Fung, "Ministry in the New Testament," in *The Church in the Bible and the World*, ed. D. A. Carson (Grand Rapids, MI: Baker Book House, 1987), pp. 168-169.
9. C. K. Barrett, *The Pastoral Epistles* (London: Oxford, 1963), pp. 71-72.
10. F. J. A. Hort, *The Christian Ecclesia* (London: Macmillan, 1914), pp. 187-188.
11. Rudolf Bultmann, *Theology of the New Testament* (New York: Charles Scribner's Sons, 1955), pp. 107-108.
12. Alexander Roberts and James Donaldson, eds., *The Ante-Nicene Fathers*, ten vols. (Grand Rapids, MI: Eerdmans, 1975 rpt.), vol. 1, *The Apostolic Fathers with Justin Martyr and Irenæus*, ed. A. Cleveland Coxe, p. 17.
13. Beyond the scope of this paper is the interesting debate about what precisely constitutes the apostolate or the office of a prophet.
14. Also beyond the purview of this discussion is the assessment of the number of ecclesiastical officers. Some argue that there are only two, pastors and deacons. Others see three or even four, adding elders and perhaps bishops. Advocates of the two-office model point to passages such as 1 Peter 5:1-4, where the words *elder*, *pastor*, and *bishop* are used interchangeably. Only *elder* appears as a noun in the passage. But the verbs translated "taking oversight" and "feed" are clearly connected with the nouns *bishop* and *pastor* respectively. Also, in Philippians 1:1 and 1 Timothy 3 only two offices are listed. Other passages seem to suggest diversity of function among the elders with some being worthy of special honor (1 Timothy 5:17). The role of Timothy in Ephesus and Titus on Crete suggests to some that there is precedent for a regional bishop. Well-known defenses of the view that only two permanent officers were intended for the church may be found in the famous work of J. B. Lightfoot, *Saint Paul's Epistle to the Philippians* (Grand Rapids, MI:

Zondervan, 1953), pp. 95-99, and, for a distinctly free-church context, in H. E. Dana, *A Manual of Ecclesiology* (Kansas City: Central Seminary Press, 1944).

15. This, as Barth notes, is especially important because

> . . . the church must continually be occupied with the exposition and application of Scripture. Where the Bible becomes a dead book with a cross on the cover and gilt edging, the Church rule of Jesus Christ is slumbering. (Karl Barth, *Dogmatics in Outline* [New York: Harper and Row, 1959], p. 146.)

16. Henry George Liddell and Robert Scott, *A Greek-English Lexicon* (Oxford: The Clarendon Press, 1966), pp. 1482-1483; also BAGD, p. 707.
17. Bo Reicke, "*prohístēmi*," in *Theological Dictionary of the New Testament*, vol. vi, ed. Gerhard Friedrich (New York: Harper and Row, 1959), p. 146.
18. C. K. Barrett, *The Pastoral Epistles* (Oxford: The Clarendon Press, 1963), p. 78.
19. William Hendriksen, *New Testament Commentary: Exposition of the Pastoral Epistles* (Grand Rapids, MI: Baker Book House, 1957), pp. 179-180.
20. F. F. Bruce, *The Epistle to the Hebrews* (Grand Rapids, MI: Eerdmans, 1977), p. 407. In the Anchor Bible, George Wesley Buchanan is representative of those who believe that the expression "considering the end of their conversation" (KJV) is a reference to a departure from this life, possibly even martyrdom. See Buchanan's *To the Hebrews* (Garden City: Doubleday, 1981), p. 233. B. F. Westcott notes that the same position was taken with even greater specificity by Theodoret, who alluded to the martyrdom of Stephen, James the son of Zebedee, and James the Just as the subjects in view. See B. F. Westcott, *The Epistle to the Hebrews* (Grand Rapids, MI: Eerdmans, n.d.), p. 434.
21. Johannes Schneider, *The Letter to the Hebrews* (Grand Rapids, MI: Eerdmans, 1957), p. 132.
22. For one of the most objective and perceptive analyses of the passage in Matthew, see D. A. Carson, *Matthew*, vol. 8 of *The Expositor's Bible Commentary*, twelve vols., ed. Frank E. Gaebelein et al. (Grand Rapids, MI: Zondervan, 1984), pp. 367-374. Insights into the interpretation of John 20:23 may be derived from Leon Morris, *The Gospel According to John* (Grand Rapids, MI: Eerdmans, 1971), pp. 847-850; F. F. Bruce, *The Gospel of John* (Grand Rapids, MI: Eerdmans, 1983), pp. 391-392; Brooke Foss Westcott, *The Gospel According to St. John* (Grand Rapids, MI: Baker Book House, 1980), p. 352; and George R. Beasley-Murray, *John* (WBC; Waco, TX: Word Books, 1987), pp. 382-384.
23. Westcott, *Gospel According to St. John*, p. 352.
24. D. A. Carson, ed., *The Church in the Bible and the World* (Grand Rapids, MI: Baker Book House, 1987), pp. 174-175. For a different conclusion, see Robert L. Saucy, "Authority in the Church," in the Festschrift for John Walvoord edited by Donald K. Campbell. Not only does Saucy present a cogent and convincing argument for congregational government in the church, but he also insists, somewhat less convincingly, that terms such as *bishop*, *pastor*, *deacon*, etc. were purely functional descriptions void of "official" status. *Walvoord: A Tribute*, ed. Donald K. Campbell (Chicago: Moody Press, 1982), pp. 219-238.
25. For the view that removal from fellowship is all that the reference includes, see Leon Morris, *The First Epistle of Paul to the Corinthians* (Grand Rapids, MI: Eerdmans, 1980), p. 88, and Paige Patterson, *The Troubled Triumphant Church* (Nashville: Thomas Nelson, 1983), pp. 86-91. For the view that an apostolic judgment resulting in death was in Paul's mind, see Hans Conzelman, *A Commentary on the First Epistle to the Corinthians* (Philadelphia: Fortress Press, 1975), p. 97.
26. Cyril Eastwood, *The Priesthood of All Believers* (London: Epworth Press, 1960), p. 250.
27. Saucy, "Authority in the Church," p. 234.
28. The earliest non-canonical literature of the church tends to confirm this picture also. The First Epistle of Clement refers to the officers of the early church as deacons and bishops or presbyters. See Alexander Roberts and James Donaldson, eds., *Ante-Nicene Fathers*, Volume 1 (Grand Rapids, MI: Eerdmans, 1973), pp. 16, 17. The same is true of the Epistle of Polycarp, which orders that the presbyters ". . . be compassionate and merciful to all,

bringing back those that wander, visiting all the sick, and not neglecting the orphans or the poor . . ." (*ibid.*, p.34)

29. Calvin remarks, "Not that he takes from them the charge of instructing their family, but only excludes them from the office of teaching, which God has committed to men only." John Calvin, *Commentaries on the Epistles to Timothy, Titus and Philemon* (Grand Rapids, MI: Baker Book House, 1979), p. 67.
30. Clark H. Pinnock, "Biblical Authority and the Issues in Question," in *Women, Authority and the Bible*, ed. Alvera Mickelsen (Downers Grove, IL: InterVarsity Press, 1986), pp. 57-58.
31. As C. K. Barrett states the case, "The regulations governing the actions of women in public are dictated by practical consideration, but their relations to men rest on more fundamental grounds, which belong to the created order itself." *The Pastoral Epistles*, p. 56. See also Chapter 9 in this volume.
32. See chapter 6 in this volume.
33. James B. Hurley, *Man and Woman in Biblical Perspective* (Grand Rapids, MI: Zondervan: Academic Books, 1981), p. 192.
34. For a contrary opinion, see Paul K. Jewett, *The Ordination of Women* (Grand Rapids: Baker, 1980). For a mediating position see Walter L. Liefeld, "Women and the Nature of Ministry" in *Journal of the Evangelical Theological Society* (March 1987).
35. Calvin, *op. cit.*, p. 67.
36. For a thorough discussion of the theological reasons for this limitation, see H. Wayne House, "Should a Woman Prophesy or Preach Before Men?" *Bibliotheca Sacra* (April-June, 1988), pp. 141-161.
37. Dorothy Kelley Patterson, "Why I Believe Southern Baptist Churches Should not Ordain Women," *Baptist History and Heritage*, vol. xxiii, no. 3 (July 1988): 61-62.

Endnotes to Chapter Fifteen

1. Rosemary Radford Ruether and Rosemary Skinner Keller, eds., *Women & Religion in America*, three vols. (San Francisco: Harper & Row, 1982-1986); Sharon K. Elkins, *Holy Women of Twelfth-Century England* (Chapel Hill, NC: The University of North Carolina Press, 1988). The importance of women in the history of the church was never a totally neglected theme. Before it was fashionable to do so, Roland H. Bainton wrote his three-volume *Women of the Reformation* (Minneapolis: Augsburg, 1971-1977). See also Edith Deen, *Great Women of the Christian Faith* (New York: Harper & Brothers, 1959), and her bibliography, pp. 411-415.
2. Ruth A. Tucker and Walter Liefeld, *Daughters of the Church: Women and Ministry From New Testament Times to the Present* (Grand Rapids, MI: Zondervan, 1987).
3. More recently Ruth A. Tucker has produced a similar but more focused book on women in modern missions: *Guardians of the Great Commission: The Story of Women in Modern Missions* (Grand Rapids, MI: Zondervan, 1988).
4. See 1 Timothy 5:3-10. Ignatius of Antioch speaks of "virgins called widows" (*Smyrna* 13:1), a phrase that indicates that *widow* designated a specific group of women within the church. Polycarp of Smyrna calls the widow an "altar of God" (Philippians 4:3), probably because widows were recipients of Christian charity.
5. R. Hugh Connolly, *Didaskalia Apostolorum* (Oxford: The Clarendon Press, 1929), p. 132.
6. See also Tertullian, *Exhortation to Chastity* 13:4; *On Modesty* 13:7; *To His Wife* 1.7.4. This does not imply that widows were "ordained" or considered part of the clergy. Indeed, the *Apostolic Tradition* of Hippolytus expressly forbids the laying of hands on the widow. She is to be appointed "by the word alone" and is distinct from the clergy (*Apost. Trad.* 11).
7. Connolly, pp. 136, 138, 140.
8. The *Apostolic Constitutions* (Syria, fourth century), the *Canons of Hippolytus* (Egypt, fourth century), and the *Testament of our Lord Jesus Christ* (Syria, fifth century) continue to depict the widow as given to prayer and charity. The *Testament* gives the widow a place of considerable prominence and even appears to place her among the clergy. One should

note that the ministry of the widow was exclusively toward other women. For general discussion of the widow, see Mary McKenna, *Women of the Church: Role and Renewal* (New York: P. J. Kenedy & Sons, 1967), pp. 35-63; Bonnie Bowman Thurston, *The Widows: A Women's Ministry in the Early Church* (Minneapolis: Fortress Press, 1989); Roger Gryson, *The Ministry of Women in the Early Church* (Collegeville, MD: The Liturgical Press, 1976, 1980) *passim*.

9. That social conditions demanded an order of deaconess is evident from the *Didaskalia* itself: "for there are houses to which you (the bishop) cannot send a (male) deacon to the women, on account of the heathen, but you may send a deaconess" (Connolly, p. 146). The best study on the deaconess is Aimé Georges Martimort, *Deaconesses: An Historical Study* (San Francisco: Ignatius Press, 1986); see also Gryson, *Ministry of Women*.
10. Connolly, pp. 146-148.
11. See also the fifth- through seventh-century legislation from Chaldea and Persia adduced by Martimort, *Deaconesses*, pp. 52-58.
12. For discussion see Gryson, *Ministry of Women*, pp. 62-64; Kyriaki Fitzgerald, "The Characteristics and Nature of the Order of the Deaconess," *Women and the Priesthood*, ed. Thomas Hopko (Crestwood, NY: St. Vladimir's Seminary Press, 1983), pp. 84-89. *Apost. Const.* 8.20 gives an ordination prayer for the deaconess. It is necessary to make clear that ordination placed one into a *specific* service. It did not mean that one could perform any and all churchly acts. The deaconess performed by ordination the functions of deaconess. Her ordination did not authorize her to perform the tasks of elder or bishop. No office was simply interchangeable with another office.
13. For discussion of the deaconess-abbess, see Martimort, *Deaconesses*, pp. 134-143, 205-206; Gryson, *Ministry of Women*, p. 90.
14. See Martimort, *Deaconesses*, pp. 136-137.
15. Palladius, *Lausiac History*, 56.
16. Martimort, *Deaconesses*, pp. 125-126. Most likely "the text of the apostle" is 1 Timothy 5:10.
17. See especially Martimort, *Deaconesses*, pp. 138-143.
18. Martimort, *Deaconesses*, pp. 187-216.
19. Kathleen Bliss, *The Service and Status of Women in the Church* (London: SCM Press, 1952), pp. 80-81.
20. Perhaps the most famous of Kaiserwerth's nurses was Florence Nightingale, who went there after she could find no similar training in England.
21. For a brief account of the history and influence of the German type of deaconess, see Bliss, *Service and Status of Women*, pp. 80-89.
22. For the Anglican deaconess, see *ibid.*, pp. 89-91. Bliss noted a third type of deaconess as well, one common to Presbyterian, Baptist and Methodist churches. Their work ranged "from parish work to institutional work in orphanages, homes for the aged, and other church-supported institutions" (pp. 92-94).
23. *Ibid.*, pp. 94-103. This informative report, now almost forty years old, deserves an update, if it has not already received one.
24. Barbara Misner, *"Highly Respectable and Accomplished Ladies": Catholic Women Religious in America 1790-1850* (New York/London: Garland, 1988). The eight groups Misner discusses are the Carmelites, Visitation Sisters, Sisters of Charity-Emmitsburg, Sisters of Loretto, Sisters of Charity of Nazareth, Dominican Sisters of St. Catherine Kentucky, Oblate Sisters of Providence, and Sisters of Our Lady of Mercy.
25. Jerome, *Letters* 28; 29. These two letters answer Marcella's questions about "ephod" (1 Samuel 2:18) and "teraphim" (Judges 17:5).
26. J. N. D. Kelly, *Jerome: His Life, Writings, and Controversies* (New York: Harper & Row, 1975) p. 94. Jerome says that some, including priests, inquired of Marcella concerning "doubtful and obscure points" (*Letter* 127).
27. For these quotes, see the *Life of St. Lioba*, in *The Anglo-Saxon Missionaries in Germany*, ed. C. H. Talbot (London: Sheed and Ward, 1954, 1981), p. 215.
28. *Life of St. Lioba*, p. 223.

29. Bede, *History of the English Church and People*, 4.23. Whitby was a double monastery of both women and men. In Celtic and Anglo-Saxon monasticism, such monasteries were usually under the direction of an abbess.
30. Boniface's letter may be found in *Christianity and Paganism, 350-750: The Conversion of Western Europe*, ed. J. N. Hillgarth (Philadelphia: University of Pennsylvania Press, 1986), p. 175.
31. In the present form of the *Martyrdom of Perpetua*, chapters 3-10 constitute the prison diary of Perpetua. The *Martyrdom of Montanus and Lucius* and the *Martyrdom of Marian and James* (both c. 250 A.D.) are patterned after the *Martyrdom of Perpetua*.
32. John Wilkinson, ed., *Egeria's Travels* (London: SPCK, 1971), p. 5.
33. Virgilian cento poetry existed already at the time of Tertullian. In her *Cento*, Proba used especially Virgil's *Aeneid*, *Eclogues*, and *Georgics*.
34. For Jerome's criticism, see *Letter* 53.7, where he calls Christian cento literature "puerile" (also *Letter* 130). The most easily accessible English translation of Proba's *Cento* is in Patricia Wilson-Kastner, G. Ronald Kastner, et al., *A Lost Tradition: Women Writers of the Early Church* (Washington, D.C.: University Press of America, 1981), pp. 45-68. The *Cento* was not Proba's only writing. The beginning lines indicate that while still a pagan she had written of civil war, probably referring to the uprising of Magnus Magnentius against the Emperor Constantius (351-353 A.D.).
35. Socrates (*Hist. eccl.* 7.21) speaks of a "poem in heroic verse" that Eudoxia composed on the occasion of Theodosius' victory over the Persians (422 A.D.). Evagrius Scholasticus (*Hist. eccl.* 1.20) has preserved one verse of a poetic address to the people of Antioch. Photius, ninth-century Patriarch of Constantinople, mentions a poetic paraphrase of the first eight books of the Bible (*Bibliotheca* 183) and also a poetic paraphrase of the prophetic books of Daniel and Zechariah.
36. For an English translation of Eudoxia's *Martyrdom of Cyprian*, see Wilson-Kastner, et al., *Lost Tradition*, pp. 149-171.
37. Frances and Joseph Gies, *Women in the Middle Ages* (New York: Harper & Row, 1978), p. 84.
38. *Ibid*., p. 78.
39. *Ibid*., p. 81. Other nuns of the twelfth century who followed Hildegarde as intellectual mystics and writers were Herrad of Landesberg, Elizabeth of Schönau, Mechtild of Magdeburg, Mechtild of Hackeborn, and Gertrude the Great (*ibid*., pp. 85-86).
40. See Robert E. Lerner, *The Heresy of the Free Spirit in the Later Middle Ages* (Berkeley: University of California Press, 1972), pp. 68-78. For a theological description of *The Mirror of Simple Souls*, see Lerner, pp. 200-208.
41. Examples of pre-nineteenth-century female hymn writers are Emilie Juliane (1637-1706), to whom some six hundred hymns are attributed, and Henriette Luise von Hayn (1724-1782), who wrote over four hundred hymns, the most famous of which is perhaps "I Am Jesus' Little Lamb." For this topic, cf. Tucker and Liefield, *Daughters*, pp. 256-257.
42. See Colleen B. Gilbert, *A Bibliography of the Works of Dorothy L. Sayers* (Hamden, CN: Archon Books, 1978).
43. The story of Potamiaena is told also in Palladius, *Lausiac History* 3. Other female martyrs may be briefly mentioned: along with Blandina were martyred her mistress and a certain Biblis (Eusebius, *Hist. eccl.* 5.1.18, 25f); along with Potamiaena were martyred her mother, Marcella, and a certain Herais (Eusebius, *Hist. eccl.* 6.5.1). We have already mentioned Perpetua, who wrote of her visions. A certain Felicitas was martyred with her. Eusebius quotes a letter of Bishop Dionysius of Alexandria to Bishop Fabian of Antioch in which five women, martyred under Decius (c. 250 A.D.) are mentioned by name: Quinta, Appollonia, Mecuria, Dionysia, Ammonarion (*Hist. eccl.* 6.41). Finally, we mention Agape, Irene, and Chione, who were martyrs under Diocletian in Thessalonica (304 A.D.). The *Martyrdom* of these three women mentions another four women who were arrested but not killed (Agatha, Cassia, Philippa, Eutychia). The deaths of Agape, Irene, and Chione were adapted by the tenth-century nun, Hroswitha of Gandersheim, in her Latin play, *Dulcitius*.
44. Walter Nigg and H. N. Loose, *Katharina von Siena* (Freiberg: Herder, 1980), p. 8.

45. Bridget founded the Bridgettine Sisters (1370), who were dedicated to humility and simplicity. The original monastery in Vadstena, Sweden, established one of the first printing presses in Sweden.
46. See Jane Tibbets Schulenberg in *Women & Power in the Middle Ages*, ed. Mary Erler & Maryanne Kowaleski (Athens, GA, and London, England: The University of Georgia Press, 1988), pp. 105-109. Many of these noble women who exerted power as abbesses achieved sainthood (Schulenberg, pp. 105ff.).
47. R. W. Southern, *Western Society and the Church in the Middle Ages* (Baltimore: Penguin Books, 1970), pp. 309-310.
48. See Gregory of Tours, *History of the Franks* 2.17; Bede, *History of the English Church and People* 4.6, 19; also the discussion of Schulenberg, pp. 110-112.
49. The *Life of St. Wilfrid* 60 calls Aelffled "always the comforter and best counsellor of the whole province" and makes clear that Aelffled's speech was the determining factor at Nidd.
50. Tucker and Liefeld, *Daughters*, p. 137.
51. Southern, *Western Society*, p. 310.
52. See Jacqueline Smith, "Robert of Arbrissel: Procurator Mulierum," in *Medieval Women*, ed. Derek Baker (Oxford: Basil Blackwell, 1978), p. 180 n. 34. Smith points out that at Fontevrault the building that housed the virgins, widows, and matrons was dedicated to the Virgin Mary, while the men stayed in a building dedicated to St. John. For a general discussion of Prémontré, Fontevrault, and similar foundations for women, see Brenda Bolton, "Mulieres Sanctae," in *Women in Medieval Society*, ed. Susan Mosher Stuard (University Park, PA: University of Pennsylvania Press, 1976), pp. 141-158.
53. See Elkins, *Holy Women*, pp. 130-134. The utopian/millennial vision could go to heretical extremes. The Guglielmites believed that a certain Guglielma of Milan was the incarnation of the Holy Spirit and wished to establish a church with a female pope and female cardinals. Stephen E. Wessley, "The Guglielmites: Salvation Through Women," in *Medieval Women*, ed. Baker, pp. 289-303.
54. Ida Raming, *The Exclusion of Women From the Priesthood: Divine Law or Sex Discrimination?* (Metuchen, NJ: The Scarecrow Press, 1976), pp. 73-74.
55. Elkins, *Holy Women*, pp. 135-136.
56. Raming, *Exclusion*, p. 74.
57. For these women and others who played a role in the Reformation, see Bainton, *Women of the Reformation*. For Reneé of Ferrara, see F. Whitfield Barton, *Calvin and the Duchess* (Louisville, KY: Westminster/John Knox Press, 1989).
58. Martha Tomhave Blauvelt and Rosemary Skinner Keller, "Women and Revivalism: The Puritan and Wesleyan Traditions," in Ruether and Keller, *Women & Religion in America*, vol. 2, p. 325.
59. Tucker and Liefeld, *Daughters*, pp. 291-327.
60. For the anomalies, see Joan Morris, *The Lady Was a Bishop: The Hidden History of Women with Clerical Ordination and the Jurisdiction of Bishops* (New York: Macmillan, 1973), who vastly overrates the significance of her evidence; for the sects, see Friedrich Weichert, "Der Dienst der Frau ausserhalb der Grosskirche," *Eine Heilige Kirche* 21 (1939): 129-139; Gottfried Koch, *Frauenfrage und Ketzertum im Mittelalter* (Berlin: Akademie-Verlag, 1962).
61. Illustrations of this attitude can easily be multiplied. The *Acts of Peter* (second century) tell of Candida, who taught her pagan husband the gospel and converted him (chapter 1). In Syria, a widow could answer pagan inquirers in refuting polytheism and demonstrating the unity of God (*Didaskalia*, Connolly, 132; *Apostolic Constitutions* 3.5). Widows could not teach about the "mystical points" of Christ's incarnation and passion. For this the unbeliever should be sent to the elders.
62. The monk Isaias (c. 1200 A.D.) compiled a *Meterikon* ("Sayings of the Mothers") parallel to the *Paterikon* ("Sayings of the Fathers").
63. Manfred Hauke, *Women in the Priesthood? A Systemic Analysis in the Light of the Order of Creation and Redemption* (San Francisco: Ignatius Press, 1988), pp. 401-402.
64. The Simonians had Helen (Irenaeus, *Adv. Haer.* 1.23.2); the Naassenes had Marianne (Hippolytus, *Adv. Haer* 10:5); Mary Magdalene is revealer of secret knowledge in *Pistis*

Sophia, Gospel of Mary, and *The Dialogue of the Savior*. In the *Egyptian Gospel*, Salome is vehicle of secret tradition.

65. Tertullian, *Prescription Against the Heretics* 41.1: "I must not omit an account also of the heretics—how frivolous it is, how worldly, how merely human, without authority, without discipline, as suits their *creed*" (italics mine).
66. *Fragments on I Corinthians* 74. For the full Origen quotation, see Gryson, *Ministry of Women*, pp. 28-29.
67. See especially Ambrosiaster, *Comm. on I Corinthians*, 14:34-35, and Pelagius, *Comm. on I Corinthians*, 14:34-35. For Ambrosiaster and Pelagius, see Gryson, *Ministry of Women*, pp. 92-99; Martimort, *Deaconesses*, pp. 191-192; Hauke, *Women*, pp. 421-423.
68. For the Councils of Saragossa and Nimes, see Gryson, *Ministry of Women*, pp. 100-102.
69. See Gryson, *Ministry of Women*, p. 106; Martimort, *Deaconesses*, p. 195.
70. For the text, see Hauke, *Women*, pp. 423-424.
71. Hauke, *Women*, p. 424.
72. Suzanne Fonay Wemple, *Women in Frankish Society: Marriage and Cloister 500-900* (Philadelphia: University of Pennsylvania Press, 1981), pp. 138-140.
73. Tucker and Liefeld, *Daughters*, pp. 132-133.
74. Gryson, *Ministry of Women*, p. 102.
75. Wemple, *Women in Frankish Society*, p. 138.
76. Gryson, *Ministry of Women*, pp. 102-108; Martimort, *Deaconesses*, pp. 193-200.
77. Quoted in Hauke, *Women*, p. 447.
78. Hauke, *Women*, pp. 446-447.
79. *Luther's Works*, American Edition (St. Louis: Concordia Publishing House; Philadelphia: Fortress Press, 1955ff.), 40.21-34; 36.150, 152; 39.234-235.
80. *Luther's Works*, 36.152; 41.154-155; 30.55; 28.276-277.
81. *Luther's Works*, 36.152; 30.55. For discussion of Luther's position, see Wilhelm Brunotte, *Das geistliche Amt bei Luther* (Berlin: Lutherisches Verlagshaus, 1959), pp. 193-199.
82. John Calvin, *Commentary on the Epistles of Paul the Apostle to the Corinthians*, trans. John Pringle (Grand Rapids, MI: Eerdmans, 1948), vol. 1, pp. 467-468.
83. Calvin, *Corinthians*, vol. 1, p. 468.
84. John Calvin, *Commentary on the Epistles to Timothy, Titus, and Philemon*, trans. William Pringle (Grand Rapids, MI: Eerdmans, 1948), p. 67.
85. Calvin, *Timothy*, p. 67.
86. John Wesley, *Explanatory Notes upon the New Testament* (1754; Naperville, IL: Alec R. Allenson, rpt. 1966), p. 632 (on I Corinthians 14:34).
87. Wesley, *Explanatory Notes*, p. 632.
88. For Wesley's view and practice, see especially Earl Kent Brown, "Women of the Word: Selected Leadership Roles of Women in Mr. Wesley's Methodism," in *Women in New Worlds*, ed. Hilah F. Thomas and Rosemary Skinner Keller (Nashville: Abingdon, 1981), pp. 69-81. For the above, pp. 74-76.
89. Tucker and Liefeld, *Daughters*, p. 16.

Endnotes to Chapter Sixteen

1. E. E. Maccoby and C. N. Jacklin, *The Psychology of Sex Differences* (Stanford, CA: Stanford University Press, 1974), pp. 349-355.
2. James A. Doyle, *Sex and Gender: The Human Experience* (Dubuque, IA: William C. Brown, 1985); Laurel Richardson, *Dynamics of Sex and Gender: A Sociological Perspective* (New York: Harper and Row, 1988); Anne Fausto-Sterling, *Myths of Gender: Biological Theories About Men and Women* (New York: Basic Books, 1985); Ruth Bleier, *Science and Gender: A Critique of Biology and Its Theories on Women* (Elmsford, NY: Pergamon Press, 1984).
3. G. Siann, *Accounting for Aggression: Perspectives on Aggression and Violence* (Allen and Unwin, 1985), pp. 82-92.
4. I. S. Bernstein, "Analysis of a Key Role in a Capuchin (Cebus albifrons) Group," *Tulane Studies in Zoology* 13 (1966): 49-54.

5. M. Daly and M. Wilson, *Sex, Evolution, and Behavior* (Boston: Duxbury Press, 1978), pp. 55-79.
6. G. Murdock, "The Common Denominator of Cultures," in *The Science of Man in the World Crisis*, ed. R. Linton (New York: Columbia University Press, 1945), pp. 123-142.
7. A. Glucksman, *Sexual Dimorphism in Human and Mammalian Biology and Pathology* (Academic Press, 1981), pp. 66-75.
8. *Ibid.*, pp. 77-110.
9. *Ibid.*, pp. 77-85.
10. J. Durden-Smith and D. Desimone, *Sex and the Brain* (New York: Arbor House, 1983), pp. 71-73.
11. E. S. Gersh and I. Gersh, *Biology of Women* (Baltimore: University Park Press, 1981), pp 288-291.
12. J. Stein, ed., *Internal Medicine*, 2nd ed. (Boston: Little, Brown, 1987), pp. 2331-2338.
13. Glucksman, *Sexual Dimorphism*, pp. 66-86.
14. Durden-Smith and Desimone, *Sex and the Brain*, pp. 71-73.
15. Glucksman, p. 100.
16. M. McLaughlin and T. Shryer, "Men vs Women: The New Debate Over Sex Differences," *U.S. News and World Report*, August 8, 1988, pp. 50-58.
17. B. McEwen, "Neural Gonadal Steroid Action," *Science* 211 (1981): 1303-1311.
18. K. E. Moyer, *The Psychobiology of Aggression* (NY: Harper and Row, 1976), pp. 3-25.
19. R. W. Goy and B. S. McEwen, *Sexual Differentiation of the Brain* (Boston: M. I. T. Press, 1980), pp. 109-111.
20. A. P. Arnold, "Sexual Differences in the Brain," *American Scientist* 68 (1980): 165-173.
21. McEwen, "Neural Gonadal Steroid Action."
22. D. F. Swaab and E. Fliers, "A Sexually Dimorphic Nucleus in the Human Brain," *Science* 228 (1985): 1112-1114.
23. Arnold, "Sexual Differences in the Brain."
24. R. T. Rubin, J. M. Reinisch, and R. F. Haskett, "Postnatal Gonadal Steroid Effects on Human Behavior," *Science* 211 (1981): 1318-1324.
25. Moyer, *Psychobiology of Aggression*, pp. 3-25.
26. Goy and McEwen, *Sexual Differentiation of the Brain*, pp. 109-111.
27. K. Zinsmeister, "Brave New World: How Day-Care Harms Children," *Policy Review*, no. 44 (Spring 1988), pp. 40-48.
28. G. J. Tortora and N. P. Anagnostakos, *Principles of Anatomy and Physiology* (NY: Harper and Row, 1987), p. 323.
29. Durden-Smith and Desimone, pp. 62-74.
30. J. McGlone, "Sex Differences in Human Brain Asymmetry: A Critical Survey," *Behavioral and Brain Sciences* 3 (1980): 21-263.
31. Sandra Witelson and Doreen Kimura's work is summarized in Durden-Smith and Desimone, pp. 62-75.
32. McGlone, "Sex Differences in Human Brain Asymmetry."
33. Durden-Smith and Desimone, p. 162.
34. Gersh and Gersh, *Biology of Women*, pp. 153-154.
35. Christine de Lacosta-Utamsing, "Sexual Dimorphism in the Human Corpus Callosum," *Science* 216 (1983): 1431-1432.
36. C. Dominique Toren-Allerand, 1978, "Gonadal Hormones and Brain Development: Cellular Aspects of Sexual Differentiation, *American Zoologist* 18:553-565.
37. C. P. Benbow and J. C. Stanley, "Sex Differences in Math Ability: Fact or Artifact?" *Science* 210 (1980): 1262-1265; also, C. P. Benbow and J. C. Stanley, "Sex Differences in Mathematical Reasoning Ability: More Facts," *Science* 222 (1983): 1029-1033.
38. McLaughlin and Shryer, "Men vs Women," pp. 50-58.
39. Durden-Smith and Desimone, pp. 86-88.
40. M. R. Rosenzweig, E. L. Bennett, and M. C. Diamond, "Brain Changes in Response to Experience," *Scientific American* 226(2) (1972): 22-29.
41. K. J. Flannelly, R. J. Blanchard, and D. C. Blanchard, *Biological Perspectives on Aggression* (New York: Alan R. Liss 1984), pp. 207-260.
42. Durden-Smith and Desimone, pp. 86-88.

43. *Ibid.*, p. 127.
44. *Ibid.*, pp. 135-151.
45. E. O. Wilson, *Sociobiology* (Cambridge, MA: Harvard University Press, 1980), pp. 42-43.
46. Willard Harley, *His Needs, Her Needs* (Old Tappan, NJ: Fleming H. Revell, 1988).

Endnotes to Chapter Seventeen

1. Mary Smith, et al., *Revolution: Tomorrow Is NOW* (National Organization for Women, 1973), p. 9. This publication is described on page 1 as "a summary of NOW's existing resolutions and policies by issue."
2. *Ibid.*, pp. 20-21. See also page 27 of the *National Plan of Action* (Washington, DC: International Women's Year Commission, 1977), adopted at the National Women's Conference, November 18-21, 1977, in Houston, Texas. This publication states, "This National Plan of Action constitutes the official recommendations of the National Women's Conference, pursuant to Public Law 94-167." For recent thoughtful essays on homosexuality and contemporary society see G. J. M. Aardweg, *Homosexuality and Hope* (Ann Arbor, MI: Servant Publications, 1985) and W. Dannemeyer, *Shadow in the Land* (San Francisco: Ignatius Press, 1989).
3. See the extended discussion of the relationship between secular humanism and feminist thinking in Michael Braun and George Alan Rekers, *The Christian in an Age of Sexual Eclipse: A Defense Without Apology* (Wheaton, IL: Tyndale House, 1981), Chapter 2, "The Rhetoric of Revolt: The Sexual Propaganda of Humanism."
4. See *Humanist Manifestos One and Two* (Buffalo, NY: Prometheus Books, 1973). For example, *Humanist Manifesto Two* states, "We affirm that moral values derive their source from human experience. Ethics are autonomous and situational, needing no theological or ideological sanction. Ethics stem from human need and interest. . . . We strive for the good life, here and now" (p. 17); "We believe in maximal individual autonomy consonant with social responsibility. Although science can account for the causes of behavior, the possibilities of individual freedom of choice exist in human life and should be increased" (p. 18). See also David W. Ehrenfeld, *The Arrogance of Humanism* (New York: Oxford University Press, 1978).
5. *Humanist Manifesto Two*, p. 18.
6. A. Simon, "Promiscuity as Sex Difference," *Psychological Reports* 64: 802; D. M. Weisbrot, "The Politics of Sexuality in Adolescent Psychiatry," *International Journal of Adolescent Medicine and Health* 2: 27-37.
7. J. Money, *Venuses Penuses* (Buffalo, NY: Prometheus Books, 1986).
8. 1978 Harris Poll and 1983 Gallup Poll. J. C. Pollock, *et al.*, *The Connecticut Mutual Life Report on American Values in the '80s.' The Impact of Belief* (Hartford, CT: Connecticut Mutual Life Insurance Company, 1981). See also G. A. Rekers, *Counseling Families* (Waco, TX: Word, 1988).
9. My clinical research in this area has been funded by a graduate fellowship from the National Science Foundation at the University of California at Los Angeles, by a post-doctoral fellowship at Harvard University from the Foundations' Fund for Research in Psychiatry, and by United States Public Health Service research grants from the National Institute of Mental Health (grant numbers MH21803, MH28240, and MH29945), resulting in over sixty publications on gender identity disorder of childhood. The following publications are selected examples: G. A. Rekers, *Pathological Sex-role Development in Boys: Behavior Treatment and Assessment* (Ann Arbor, MI: University Microfilms), No. 72-33, 978; G. A. Rekers, "Sexual Problems: Behavior Modification," in B. B. Wolman, ed., *Handbook of Treatment of Mental Disorders in Childhood and Adolescence* (Englewood Cliffs, NJ: Prentice-Hall, 1978); G. A. Rekers, B. F. Crandall, A. C. Rosen, P. M. Bentler, "Genetic and Physical Studies of Male Children with Psychological Gender Disturbances," *Psychological Medicine* 9 (1979): 373-375; G. A. Rekers and S. L. Mead, "Early Intervention for Female Sexual Identity Disturbances," *Journal of Abnormal Child Psychology* 7 (1979); A. C. Rosen, G. A. Rekers, and S. L. Brigham, "Gender Stereotypy in Gender-dysphoric Young Boys," *Psychological Reports* 51 (1982): 371-374;

G. A. Rekers, "The Family and Gender Identity Disorders," *Journal of Family and Culture* 2 (1986): 8-37; G. A. Rekers, "Cross-sex Behavior Problems," in R. A. Hoekelman, S. Blatman, S. B. Friedman, N. M. Nelson, and H. M. Seidel, eds., *Primary Pediatric Care*, 2nd edition (St. Louis: C. V. Mosby, 1990).

10. George Alan Rekers, et al., "Child Gender Disturbances;" see also G. A. Rekers, "Assessment and Treatment of Childhood Gender Problems," in *Advances in Clinical Child Psychology*, ed. Benjamin B. Lahey and Alan E. Kazdin (New York: Plenum, 1977), volume 1, chapter 7. G. A. Rekers, "Therapies Dealing with the Child's Sexual Difficulties," in Jean-Marc Samson, ed., *Enfrance et Sexualite/Childhood and Sexuality* (Montreal and Paris: Les Editions Etudes Vivantes, Inc., 1990); G. A. Rekers, "Play Therapy with Cross-gender Identified Children," in C. E. Shaefer and K. J. O'Connor, eds., *Handbook of Play Therapy* (New York: John Wiley and Sons, 1983), pp. 369-385; G. A. Rekers, "Gender Identity Problems," in P. H. Borstein and A. E. Kazdin, eds., *Handbook of Clinical Behavior Therapy with Children* (Homewood, IL: Dorsey Press, 1985), pp. 658-699; G. A. Rekers, M. Kilgus, and A. C. Rosen, "Long-term Effects of Treatment for Childhood Gender Disturbances," *Journal of Psychology and Human Sexuality* 3(2) (1990).
11. G. A. Rekers, "Pathological Sex-role Development in Boys: Behavioral Treatment and Assessment" (Ph.D. diss., University of California, Los Angeles, 1972).
12. E. Bene and J. Anthony, "Bene-Anthony Family Relations Test: An Objective Technique for Exploring Emotional Attitudes in Children." Distributed by the National Foundation for Educational Research in England and Wales. Copyright 1957.
13. P. M. Bentler, G. A. Rekers, and A. C. Rosen, "Congruence of Childhood Sex-role Identity and Behavior Disturbances," *Child: Care, Health and Development* 5(4) (1979): 267-284. G. A. Rekers, "Psychosexual Assessment of Gender Identity Disorders," in R. J. Prinz, ed., *Advances in Behavioral Assessment of Children and Families, Volume 4* (Greenwich, CT: JAI Press, Inc., 1988), pp. 33-71; G. A. Rekers and S. M. Morey, "Personality Problems Associated with Childhood Gender Disturbance," *Italian Journal of Clinical Psychology* (1990).
14. J. E. Bates, P. M. Bentler, and S. Thompson, "Measurement of Deviant Gender Development in Boys," *Child Development* 44 (1973): 591-598.
15. J. E. Bates and P. M. Bentler, "Play Activities of Normal and Effeminate Boys," *Developmental Psychology* 9 (1973): 20-27.
16. G. A. Rekers and S. M. Morey, "The Relationship of Measures of Sex-typed Play with Clinician Ratings on Degree of Gender Disturbance," *Journal of Clinical Psychology* 46 (1990): 28-34.
17. G. A. Rekers and S. M. Morey, "Sex-typed Body Movements as a Function of Severity of Gender Disturbance in Boys," *Journal of Psychology and Human Sexuality* 2 (1989): 183-196.
18. G. A. Rekers and S. M. Morey, "Relationship of Maternal Report of Feminine Behavior and Extraversion to the Severity of Gender Disturbance," *Perceptual and Motor Skills* 69 (1989): 387-394.
19. G. A. Rekers, S. L. Mead, A. C. Rosen, and S. L. Brigham, "Family Correlates of Male Childhood Gender Disturbance," *The Journal of Genetic Psychology* 142 (1983): 31-42.
20. U.S. Bureau of the Census, *Statistical Abstracts of the United States: 1978* (Washington, DC: U.S. Department of Commerce, 1978).
21. S. L. Mead and G. A. Rekers, "The Role of the Father in Normal Psychosexual Development," *Psychological Reports* 45 (1979): 923-931; Rekers, et al., "Family Correlates." G. A. Rekers, "Parental Involvement with Agencies Serving Adolescents in Crisis: Adolescent Sexuality and Family Well-being," in hearings before the Subcommittee on Family and Human Services, Committee on Labor and Human Resources, United States Senate, on *Parental Involvement with Their Adolescents in Crisis* (Washington, DC: U.S. Government Printing Office, 1984).
22. L. B. Apperson and W. G. McAdoo, "Parental Factors in the Childhood of Homosexuals," *Journal of Abnormal Psychology* 73 (1968): 201-206; Alan P. Bell and Martin S. Weinberg, *Homosexualities: A Study of Diversity Among Men and Women* (New York: Simon and Schuster, 1978); A. P. Bell, M. S. Weinberg, and S. K.

Hammersmith, *Sexual Preference* (Bloomington, IN: Indiana University Press, 1981); E. Bene, "On the Genesis of Male Homosexuality: An Attempt at Clarifying the Role of the Parents," *British Journal of Psychiatry* 111 (1965): 803-813; Irving Bieber, *et al.*, *Homosexuality: A Psychoanalytic Study* (New York: Basic Books, 1926); R. E. Billingham and S. L. Hockenberry, "Gender Conformity, Masturbation Fantasy, Infatuation, and Sexual Orientation," *Journal of Sex Research* 23 (1987): 368-374; D. Boyer, "Male Prostitution and Homosexual Identity," *Journal of Homosexuality* 17 (1989): 151-184; D. G. Brown, "Homosexuality and Family Dynamics," *Bulletin of the Menninger Clinic* 27 (1963): 227-232; J. A. Cates, "Adolescent Male Prostitution by Choice," *Child and Adolescent Social Work Journal* 6 (1989): 151-156; R. B. Evans, "Childhood Parental Relationships of Homosexual Men," *Journal of Consulting and Clinical Psychology* 33 (1969): 129-135; R. Green, *The "Sissy Boy Syndrome" and the Development of Homosexuality* (New Haven, CT: Yale University Press, 1987); J. Harry, "Parental Physical Abuse and Sexual Orientation in Males," *Archives of Sexual Behavior* 18 (1989): 251-261; C. H. Jonas, "An Objective Approach to the Personality and Environment in Homosexuality," *Psychiatric Quarterly* 18 (1944): 626-641; G. A. Rekers, "The Formation of Homosexual Orientation," in P. F. Fagan, ed., *Hope for Homosexuality* (Washington, DC: Free Congress Foundation, 1988), pp. 1-27; G. A. Rekers, "AIDS: Behavioral Dimensions of Medical Care," *USC School of Medicine Report* 6 (1989): 7; Marcel T. Saghir and Eli Robins, *Male and Female Homosexuality: A Comprehensive Investigation* (Baltimore: Williams and Wilkins, 1973); S. F. Signer, "Homo-erotomania," *British Journal of Psychiatry* 154 (1989): 729; Charles M. Socarides, *The Overt Homosexual* (New York: Grune and Stratton, 1968); W. G. Stephan, "Parental Relationships and Early Social Experience of Activist Male Homosexuals and Male Heterosexuals," *Journal of Abnormal Psychology* 82 (1973): 506-513; E. D. Wilson, *Counseling and Homosexuality* (Waco, TX: Word, 1988); B. Zuger, "Homosexuality in Families of Boys with Early Effeminate Behavior," *Archives of Sexual Behavior* 18 (1989): 155-156.

23. B. I. Fagot, "Sex Differences in Toddlers' Behavior and Parental Reaction," *Developmental Psychology* 10 (1974): 554-558; J. Z. Rubin, F. J. Provenzano, and Z. Luria, "The Eye of the Beholder: Parents' Views on the Sex of Newborns," *American Journal of Orthopsychiatry* 44 (1974): 512-519.
24. David B. Lynn, *The Father: His Role in Child Development* (Monterey, CA: Brooks/Cole, 1974); G. A. Rekers, "Father Absence: The Effects on Children's Development," in hearings before the Subcommittee on Family and Human Services, Committee on Labor and Human Resources, United States Senate, on *Oversight on the Breakdown of the Traditional Family Unit* (Washington, DC: U.S. Government Printing Office, 1983).
25. L. Carlsmith, "Effect of Early Father-absence on Scholastic Aptitude," *Harvard Educational Review* 34 (1964): 3-21; Lois H. Stolz, et al., *Father Relations of War-Born Children: The Effect of Post-War Adjustment of Fathers on the Behavior and Personality of First Children Born While Fathers Were At War* (1954; reprint ed., Westport, CT: Greenwood, 1969).
26. Stolz, et al., *Father Relations of War-Born Children.*
27. G. R. Bach, "Father-fantasies and Father-typing in Father-separated Children," *Child Development* 17 (1946): 63-80; W. N. Stephens, "Judgment by Social Workers on Boys and Mothers in Fatherless Families," *Journal of Genetic Psychology* 99 (1961): 59-64.
28. R. F. Winch, "The Relation Between the Loss of a Parent and Progress in Courtship," *Journal of Social Psychology* 29 (1949): 51-56.
29. A. C. Rosen and J. Teague, "Case Studies in Development of Masculinity and Femininity in Male Children," *Psychological Reports* 34 (1974): 971-983.
30. E. M. Hetherington, "Effects of Paternal Absence on Sex-typed Behaviors in Negro and White Preadolescent Males," *Journal of Personality and Social Psychology* 4 (1966): 87-91.
31. H. B. Biller, "A Multiaspect Investigation of Masculine Development in Kindergarten Age Boys," *Genetic Psychology Monographs* 78 (1968): 89-138; C. T. Drake and D. McDugall, "Effects of the Absence of the Father and Other Male Models on the Development of Boys' Sex Roles," *Developmental Psychology* 13 (1977): 537-538.

32. G. A. Rekers, "Research on the Essential Characteristics of the Father's Role for Family Strength," in hearings before the Select Committee on Children, Youth and Families, United States House of Representatives on *The Diversity and Strength of American Families* (Washington, DC: U.S. Government Printing Office, 1986), pp. 55-69. G. P. Matthews, "Father-absence and the Development of Masculine Identification in Black Preschool Males," *Dissertation Abstracts International* 37, no. 3-A (1976): 1458; G. Sutton-Smith, B. G. Rosenberg, and F. Landy, "Father-absence Effects in Families of Different Sibling Compositions," *Child Development* 38 (1968): 1213-1221.
33. J. W. Santrock, "Paternal Absence, Sex Typing, and Identification," *Developmental Psychology* 2 (1970): 264-272.
34. Drake and McDugall, "Effects of the Absence of the Father."
35. H. B. Biller and R. M. Baum, "Father-absence, Perceived Maternal Behavior, and Masculinity of School Boys," *Developmental Psychology* 4 (1971): 178-181; Matthews, "Father Absence and the Development of Masculine Identification."
36. Santrock, "Paternal Absence"; Winch, "Loss of a Parent and Progress in Courtship."
37. G. A. Rekers and S. L. Mead, "Female Sex-role Deviance," *Journal of Clinical Child Psychology* 8 (1980): 199-203.
38. E. M. Hetherington, "Effects of Father-absence on Personality Development in Adolescent Daughters," *Developmental Psychology* 7 (1972): 313-326.
39. H. B. Biller, "The Father and Personality Development: Paternal Deprivation and Sex-role Development," in *The Role of the Father in Child Development*, ed. Michael E. Lamb (New York: Wiley, 1976), pp. 89-156; Lamb, ed., *The Role of the Father in Child Development*; Lynn, The Father: His Role in Child Development; D. B. Lynn, "Fathers and Sex-role Development," *Family Coordinator* 25 (1976): 403-409; G. A. Rekers, et al., "Family Correlates of Male Childhood Gender Disturbance," *The Journal of Genetic Psychology* 142 (1983): 31-42; S. L. Mead and G. A. Rekers, "The Role of the Father in Normal Psycho-sexual Development," *Psychological Reports* 45 (1979): 923-931; Rosen and Teague, "Case Studies in Development of Masculinity and Femininity."
40. P. H. Mussen and E. Rutherford, "Parent-child Relation and Parental Personality in Relation to Young Children's Sex-role Preferences," *Child Development* 34 (1963): 589-607.
41. E. M. Hetherington, "A Developmental Study of the Effects of Sex of the Dominant Parent on Sex-role Preference, Identification, and Imitation in Children," *Journal of Personality and Social Psychology* 2 (1965): 188-194; Lamb, *Role of the Father in Child Development*; P. H. Mussen and L. Distler, "Child Rearing Antecedents of Masculine Identification in Kindergarten Boys," *Child Development* 31 (1960): 89-100; D. E. Payne and P. H. Mussen, "Parent-child Relations and Father Identification Among Adolescent Boys," *Journal of Abnormal and Social Psychology* 52 (1956): 358-362.
42. Mussen and Distler, "Child Rearing Antecedents"; P. H. Mussen and L. Distler, "Masculinity, Identification, and Father-son Relationships," *Journal of Abnormal and Social Psychology* 59 (1959): 350-356.
43. S. Gray, "Perceived Similarity to Parents and Adjustment," *Child Development* 30 (1959): 91-107.
44. M. Reis and D. Gold, "Relation of Paternal Availability to Problem Solving and Sex-role Orientation in Young Boys," *Psychological Reports* 40 (1977): 823-829.
45. Biller, "The Father and Personality Development;" F. Earls, "The Fathers (not the mothers): Their Importance and Influence with Infants and Young Children," *Psychiatry* 39 (1976): 209-226.
46. Hetherington, "Developmental Study of the Effects of Sex."
47. *Ibid.*
48. L. W. Hoffman, "The Father's Role in the Family and the Child's Peer-group Adjustment," *Merrill-Palmer Quarterly* 7 (1961): 97-105.
49. J. M. Greenstein, "Father Characteristics and Sex Typing," *Journal of Personality and Social Psychology* 3 (1966): 271-277.
50. Lynn, *The Father: His Role in Child Development.*
51. E. M. Hetherington and J. L. Deur, "The Effects of Father Absence on Child Development," *Young Children* 26 (1971): 233-248.

52. Biller, "The Father and Personality Development;" Lamb, *The Role of the Father in Child Development.*
53. L. W. Hoffman, "Changes in Family Roles, Socialization, and Sex Differences," *American Psychologist* 32 (1977): 644-657; G. A. Rekers, "Adolescent Development in American Culture," *Contemporary Psychology* 31 (1986): 122-123; G. A. Rekers, *Counseling Families* (Waco, TX: Word, 1988); G. A. Rekers and A. P. Jurich, "Development of Problems of Puberty and Sex-roles in Adolescence," in C. E. Walker and M. C. Roberts, eds., *Handbook of Clinical Child Psychology* (New York: John Wiley and Sons, 1983), pp. 785-812.
54. C. S. Chilman, "Some Major Issues Regarding Adolescent Sexuality and Childbearing in the United States," *Journal of Social Work and Human Sexuality* 8 (1989): 3-25; C. S. Chilman, *Adolescent Sexuality in a Changing American Society* (New York: John Wiley and Sons, 1983); A. Parrot, "Acquaintance Rape Among Adolescents," *Journal of Social Work and Human Sexuality* 8 (1989): 47-61; A. C. Salter, *Treating Child Sex Offenders and Victims* (Newbury Park, CA: Sage Publications, 1988); D. A. Schetky, "Child Pornography and Prostitution," in D. H. Schetky and A. H. Green, eds., *Child Sexual Abuse* (New York: Brunner/Mazel, 1988); D. H. Schetky and A. H. Green, eds., *Child Sexual Abuse* (New York: Brunner/Mazel).
55. P. Allen-Meares, "Adolescent Sexuality and Premature Parenthood: Role of the Black Church in Prevention," *Journal of Social Work and Human Sexuality* 8 (1989): 133-142; J. McDowell and D. Day, *Why Wait?* (San Bernardino, CA: Here's Life, 1987); J. McDowell, *How to Help Your Child Say "No" to Sexual Pressure* (Waco, TX: Word, 1987).
56. A. W. Burgess and M. L. Clark, *Child Pornography and Sex Rings* (Lexington, MA: Lexington Books, 1984); E. Coleman, "The Development of Male Prostitution Activity Among Gay and Bisexual Adolescents," *Journal of Homosexuality* 17 (1989): 131-139; C. A. Gidycz and M. P. Koss, "The Impact of Adolescent Sexual Victimization," *Violence and Victims* 4 (1989): 139-149; D. B. Goldston, D. C. Turnquist, and J. F. Knutson, "Presenting Problems of Sexually Abused Girls Receiving Psychiatric Services," *Journal of Abnormal Psychology* 98 (1989): 314-317; M. Hancock and K. B. Mains, *Child Sexual Abuse* (Wheaton, IL: Harold Shaw Publishers, 1987); J. J. Haugaard and N. D. Repucci, *The Sexual Abuse of Children* (San Francisco: Jossey-Bass, 1988); G. E. Wyatt and G. J. Powell, *Lasting Effects of Child Sexual Abuse* (Newbury Park, CA: Sage Publications, 1989).
57. G. A. Rekers, *Counseling Families* (Waco, TX: Word, 1988); G. A. Rekers, "Developmental and Cultural Counters for Disorders in Adolescence," *Contemporary Psychology* 30 (1985): 813-814.
58. There are also gender-linked differences in abilities and in physical and psychological traits that are not discussed here in length (see Chapter 16 of this volume). The most obvious biological differences are that gestation, lactation, and menstruation occur in females only, and sperm production in the male only. Numerous research studies have also found that males, as a group, tend to score higher in measures of physical strength and fleetness (related to sex differences in muscles), certain mathematical skills, visual-spatial skills, and gross-muscle movements. On the other hand, females tend to score higher, as a group, in measures of certain verbal skills, resistance to certain illnesses and disease, tactile sensitivity, and fine-muscle movements involved in manual dexterity. In psychological traits, boys as a group are more aggressive, on average, than girls, and boys are more active in boisterous play than girls. On the other hand, girls score higher, as a group, on measures of nurturance, sociability, and empathy. The research studies demonstrating these sex differences are reviewed by several recent reports, including J. H. Block, *Sex-role Identity and Ego Development* (San Francisco: Jossey-Bass, 1984); J. Brooks-Gunn and A. C. Petersen, eds., *Girls at Puberty: Biological and Psychosocial Perspectives* (New York: Plenum Press, 1983); D. B. Carter, ed., *Current Conceptions of Sex Roles and Sex Typing: Theory and Research* (New York: Praeger, 1987); C. Hutt, "Biological Bases of Psychological Sex Differences," *American Journal of Diseases in Childhood* 132 (1978): 170-177; R. M. Lerner and T. T. Roch, eds., *Biological-Psychosocial Interactions in Early Adolescence* (Hillsdale, NJ: Lawrence Erlbaum Associates, 1986); L. B. Lueptow,

Adolescent Sex Roles and Social Change (New York: Columbia University Press, 1984); Eleanor E. Maccoby and Carol N. Jacklin, *The Psychology of Sex Differences* (Stanford, CA: Stanford University Press, 1974); Diane McGuinness and Karl H. Pribram, "The Origins of Sensory Bias in the Development of Gender Differences in Perception and Cognition," in *Cognitive Growth and Development—Essays in Honor of Herbert G. Birch*, ed. Morton Bortner (New York: Brunner/Mazel, 1978).

59. Compare the theological truths in Genesis 1:27-28; 3:16; Exodus 20:14; 21:22-25; Psalm 22:9-10; Philippians 2:3-4; Titus 2:3-5; and 1 Timothy 5:14. The feminine responsibility for protecting and preserving the life of the unborn child is discussed in more detail by Clifford E. Bajema, *Abortion and the Meaning of Personhood* (Grand Rapids, MI: Baker Book House, 1974); Braun and Rekers, *The Christian in an Age of Sexual Eclipse*; Harold O. J. Brown, *Death Before Birth* (New York: Thomas Nelson, 1977); Francis A. Schaeffer and C. Everett Koop, *Whatever Happened to the Human Race?* (Old Tappan, NJ: Revell, 1979). See also the article by Harold O. J. Brown, "Abortion and Child Abuse," *Christianity Today*, October 7, 1977, p. 34.
60. G. A. Rekers, J. A. Sanders, and C. C. Strauss, "Developmental Differentiation of Adolescent Body Gestures," *Journal of Genetic Psychology* 138 (1981): 123-131.
61. G. A. Rekers, J. A. Sanders, W. C. Rasbury, C. C. Strauss, and S. M. Morey, "Differentiation of Adolescent Activity Participation," *Journal of Genetic Psychology* 150 (1989): 323-335; Ray Raphael, *The Men from the Boys: Rites of Passage in Male America* (Lincoln, NB: University of Nebraska Press, 1988).
62. See Braun and Rekers, *The Christian in an Age of Sexual Eclipse*, chapter 2, "The Rhetoric of Revolt: The Sexual Propaganda of Humanism," and chapter 3, "Drawing the Battle Lines: The Radical Challenge of Sexual Extremists."

Endnotes to Chapter Eighteen

1. This professor admitted such universality of "stereotypical" sex differences in a private debate. She could not explain it through cultural means alone (no one has) but felt sure that such explanations did explain the phenomenon.
2. Perhaps changed later; I'm not sure.
3. I put quotes around "new" because feminist ideology bears a startling resemblance to the "old" Christian gnostic heresy. Cf. June Singer, *Androgyny: Toward a New Theory of Sexuality* (New York: Anchor, 1976), pp. 125-135, a feminist work. She celebrates this rebirth of gnosticism in the feminist resurrection of an androgyny ideal. See also Allan Carlson, "The Androgyny Hoax," *Persuasion at Work* (Rockford, IL: The Rockford Institute), vol. 9, no. 3 (March 1986), p. 4.
4. Claudia Wallis, "Onward Women," *Time*, vol. 134, no. 48 (December 1989), pp. 80-89.
5. This is clear in any reading of classic feminist works. A prime example of such views by a supposedly moderate feminist is Betty Friedan's *The Feminine Mystique* (New York: W. W. Norton, 1963). An excellent summary of major feminist works, through the most recent, is provided in Nicholas Davidson, *The Failure of Feminism* (Buffalo: Prometheus, 1988).
6. Davidson, *The Failure of Feminism*, p. 17.
7. *Ibid.* See also analyses of the ERA struggle in June Mansbridge, *Why We Lost the ERA* (Chicago: University of Chicago Press, 1986), and Kristin Luker, *Abortion and the Politics of Motherhood* (Berkeley: University of California Press, 1984). Both are written by feminists, yet both underscore the tremendous antipathy and sense of threat registered by traditional women toward feminism. The antifeminist vanguard has traditionally been led by women. See also Susan E. Marshall, "Ladies Against Women: Mobilization Dilemmas of Antifeminist Movements," *Social Problems*, vol. 32, no. 4 (April 1985), pp. 348-362.
8. Davidson, *The Failure of Feminism*, pp. 325-356.
9. Mansbridge, *Why We Lost the ERA*. Mansbridge points out that such polls purporting to show overwhelming women's support for the ERA failed to tap women's true complex of feelings on areas that the feminists claimed the ERA would alter, such as the primacy of heterosexual marriage, females in combat, child custody rules, etc.

10. Steven Brint, "New Class and Cumulative Trend Explanations of the Liberal Attitudes of Professionals," *American Journal of Sociology*, vol. 9, no. 1 (July 1984), pp. 30-71; Michael W. Macy, "New Class Dissent Among Social-Cultural Specialists: The Effects of Occupational Self-Direction and Location in the Public Sector," *Sociological Forum*, vol. 3, no. 3 (Spring 1988), pp. 325-356; S. Robert Lichter, Stanley Rothman, and Linda S. Lichter, *The Media Elite* (Bethesda, MD: Adler & Adler, 1986).
11. Nicholas Davidson, ed., *Gender Sanity* (Lanham, MD: University Press, 1989), p. v.
12. Davidson, ed., *Gender Sanity*, p. v. See also George Gilder, *Men and Marriage* (Gretna, LA: Pelican, 1986), p. viii, for a chilling account of the power of feminist editors in major publishing houses to prevent publication of anti-feminist works.
13. Michael Levin, "The Feminist Mystique," *Commentary*, vol. 70, no. 6 (December, 1980), p. 25.
14. *Ibid.*, emphasis added.
15. Wallis, "Onward Women," p. 80.
16. Cf. Davidson, *The Failure of Feminism*, pp. 215-231, on "The New Female Psychology."
17. The biological and psychological evidence has been adequately presented elsewhere in this volume. In addition to the excellent work and bibliography of Gregg Johnson (Chapter 16), I recommend the following: Melvin Konner, *The Tangled Wing* (New York: Holt, Rinehart and Winston, 1982), pp. 106-126; Stephen Goldberg, *The Inevitability of Patriarchy* (New York: William Morrow, 1974); Stephen Goldberg, "Reaffirming the Obvious" and "Utopian Yearning versus Scientific Curiosity," *Society*, vol. 23, no. 6 (September/October 1986), pp. 4-7, 29-39; James C. Neely, *Gender: The Myth of Equality* (New York: Simon and Schuster, 1981); Corinne Hunt, *Males and Females* (Baltimore: Penguin, 1973); Gilder, *Men and Marriage*; Davidson, *The Failure of Feminism*; Yves Christen, "Sex Differences in the Human Brain," in *Gender Sanity*, ed. N. Davidson, pp. 146-161; Michael Levin, *Feminism and Freedom* (New Brunswick, NJ: Transaction, 1987), especially pp. 70-97. All of these cite, in turn, many other worthwhile studies.
18. Goldberg, "Reaffirming the Obvious," p. 5.
19. A good summary and refutation of arguments that admit universality but attempt to deduce a "nurture" mechanism to explain it can be found in Stephen Goldberg, "The Universality of Patriarchy," in *Gender Sanity*, ed. N. Davidson, pp. 133-146. See also Levin, "The Feminist Mystique," pp. 25, 27-28.
20. Levin, "The Feminist Mystique," p. 27.
21. William N. Stephens, *The Family in Cross-Cultural Perspective* (Lanham, MD: University Press, 1963), p. 305.
22. Goldberg, *The Inevitability of Patriarchy*; Goldberg, "Reaffirming the Obvious" and "Utopian Yearning versus Scientific Curiosity"; Goldberg, "The Universality of Patriarchy"; see also Konner, *The Tangled Wing*, pp. 112-113; and Gilder, *Men and Marriage*, p. 21.
23. Goldberg, *The Inevitability of Patriarchy*, p. 42; Stephens, *The Family in Cross-Cultural Perspective*, p. 306.
24. Quoted in Davidson, *The Failure of Feminism*, p. 168.
25. *Ibid.*, p. 170.
26. Gilder, *Men and Marriage*, p. 42.
27. For another refutation of Mead's finding of a supposedly unisex tribe, the Tchambuli, see Goldberg, *The Inevitability of Patriarchy*, pp. 43-44, and Davidson, *The Failure of Feminism*, p. 170.
28. Cynthia Fuchs Epstein, "Inevitabilities of Prejudice," *Society*, vol. 23, no. 6 (September/October 1986), p. 8.
29. These data are synthesized from James Q. Wilson and Richard J. Hernnstein, *Crime and Human Nature* (New York: Simon and Schuster, 1985), pp. 104-125. Wilson is one of the top criminologists in the world today. Their arguments are extraordinarily well-documented, and while I cannot replicate the complexity of their analysis here, I do present a fair and accurate summary of their work on gender and crime.
30. *Ibid.*, pp. 124-125.
31. Levin, "The Feminist Mystique," p. 25.
32. Davidson, *The Failure of Feminism*, pp. 233-234.

33. Lionel Tiger and Joseph Shepher, *Women in the Kibbutz* (New York: Harcourt Brace Jovanovich, 1975), pp. 206-207.
34. Davidson, *The Failure of Feminism*, p. 366.
35. These issues are thoroughly discussed in Tiger and Shepher, *Women in the Kibbutz*, see especially pp. 242-281.
36. *Ibid.*, p. 260.
37. *Ibid.*, pp. 276-281.
38. Quoted in Goldberg, "Utopian Yearning versus Scientific Curiosity," p. 31.
39. Epstein, "Inevitabilities of Prejudice," p. 12. Deceptively, Epstein implies that Mead did not believe in the universality of patriarchy and sex differences. She stated that while Mead's work on complete sex role changeability had been "questioned," these criticisms are not of "sufficient merit." She does not point out that Mead sided with Goldberg and did *not* believe that her research demonstrated non-universality at all. For a similar erroneous treatment of Mead's work from an "evangelical" perspective, see Winston Johnson, "Gender, Society, and Church," in *Gender Matters: Women's Studies in the Christian Community*, ed. June Steffensen Hagen (Grand Rapids, MI: Zondervan/Academie, 1990), p. 228. Although Mead could be inconsistent (see Davidson, *The Failure of Feminism*, p. 361) her statements regarding gender differences are fairly representative of other leading anthropologists as well, such as George P. Murdock (e.g., *Atlas of World Cultures* [Pittsburgh, PA: University of Pittsburgh Press, 1981] and *Social Structure* [New York: Free Press, 1965]) and Stephens (*The Family in Cross-Cultural Perspective*).
40. Goldberg, *The Inevitability of Patriarchy*, p. 44.
41. *Ibid.*, p. 47.
42. A basic thesis of Gilder's *Men and Marriage*, amply supported by statistics on crime, illegitimacy, drug abuse, and decline of economic productivity in stable vs. broken homes, single vs. married males, etc.
43. A brilliant and well-documented defense of the "bourgeois" family along these lines is to be found in Brigitte Berger and Peter L. Berger, *The War Over the Family* (Garden City, NY: Anchor 1983).
44. Levin, "The Feminist Mystique," p. 25.
45. Allan Bloom, *The Closing of the American Mind* (New York: Simon and Schuster, 1987), p. 100.
46. Cf. Zillah R. Eisenstein, *Feminism and Sexual Equality* (New York: Monthly Review Press, 1984); Rosalind Brunt and Caroline Rowan, eds., *Feminism, Culture and Politics* (London: Lawrence and Wishart, 1982). On the feminist suspicion of "private spheres" (such as the family) particularly, see Diane Polan, "Toward a Theory of Law and Patriarchy," in *The Politics of Law: A Progressive Critique*, ed. David Kairys (New York: Pantheon, 1982), pp. 294-303, especially pp. 297-298.
47. See the discussion of a wide range of Christian feminists in Mary Pride, *The Way Home* (Westchester, IL: Crossway Books, 1985), pp. 3-23.
48. Singer, *Androgyny: Toward a New Theory of Sexuality*.
49. Cf. the very influential book by Elinor Lenz and Barbara Myerhoff, *The Feminization of America: How Women's Values are Changing Our Public and Private Lives* (Los Angeles: Tracher, 1985), pp. 138-156.
50. Pride, *The Way Home*, pp. 4-9.
51. Sara Evans, *Personal Politics* (New York: Vintage, 1979), pp. 166, 214-215.
52. Lenz and Myerhoff, *The Feminization of America*; see especially their chapter "Protecting Life!" Also extensively discussed in Davidson, *The Failure of Feminism*.
53. Edward Shorter, *A History of Women's Bodies* (New York: Basic, 1982).
54. Luker, *Abortion and the Politics of Motherhood*, p. 176.
55. Cf. Letha Scanzoni and Nancy Hardesty, *All We're Meant to Be* (Waco, TX: Word, 1974), p. 143; as quoted in Pride, *The Way Home*, p. 9. Another good example is a recent article by Virginia Mollenkott, "Reproductive Choice: Basic to Justice for Women," *Christian Scholar's Review*, vol. xvii, no. 3 (March 1988), pp. 286-293.
56. *Ladies Home Journal*, vol. cvi, no. 11 (November 1989), p. 58.

57. William R. Mattox, Jr., "Is the Traditional Family Dead?" *Family Policy*, September/October 1988, pp. 1-5.
58. *Family Policy*, "Who Will Care for the Children?" May/June 1988, p. 2.
59. *Family Policy*, "Day Care Attitudes," May/June 1989, p. 5. Nevertheless, there has been a sharp increase in the use of formal day care, and center-based care provides for 15 percent of the day care for children with full-time working mothers. William Dreskin and Wendy Dreskin, "Day Care and Children," in *Gender Sanity*, ed. N. Davidson, pp. 71.
60. Nicholas Davidson, "The Myths of Feminism," *National Review*, vol. xli, no. 9 (May 19, 1989), p. 44.
61. Some adjustments among moderate feminists have been made. Friedan is now advocating some government support for "mothers (or fathers)" to stay home with children. Note, however, that the assumptions are: a bias toward state action (socialist policy) such as direct cash payments for day care by stay-at-homes; an anti-biological view in which either male or female could provide for the mother role; and a strong expectation that most will choose a dual-career path requiring government-funded day care (otherwise, the policy would be clearly unaffordable). As quoted in *Family Policy*, May/June 1988, p. 7.
62. Jay Belsky, "Infant Day Care: A Cause for Concern?" (Washington, DC: Family Research Council, 1986; reprinted from *Zero to Three*, vol. 7, no. 1 [September 1986]), pp. 1-2.
63. *Family Policy* May/June 1989, p. 5.
64. Patricia A. Farnan, "Day Care Diseases," *Family Policy*, May/June 1989, p. 1-7.
65. Belsky, "Infant Day Care: A Cause for Concern?"; Otto Weininger, "The Daycare Dilemma: Some Reflections on the Current Scenario," unpublished manuscript presented at a meeting of the North American Social Science Network—1986; Dreskin and Dreskin, "Day Care and Children," pp. 71-81.
66. Gilder, *Men and Marriage*, pp. 151-153.
67. *Ibid.*, p. 153; William R. Mattox Jr., "The 'Parenting Penalty': How the Tax Code Discourages Parental Care," *Family Policy*, March/April 1989, pp. 1-7.
68. Gilder, *Men and Marriage*, pp. 147-148, 130-131, 144.
69. On the problems with women in combat, see Brian Mitchell, *Weak Link: The Feminization of the American Military* (Washington, DC: Regnery, 1989); Gilder, *Men and Marriage*, pp. 127-136; James Webb, "Women Can't Fight," in *Gender Sanity*, ed. N. Davidson, pp. 208-223; On the problem with female affirmation action, see E. J. Mishan, "Was the Women's Liberation Movement Really Necessary?" *Encounter*, vol. lxiv, no. 1 (January 1985), p. 14; Levin, "The Feminist Mystique," p. 28; and Levin, *Feminism and Freedom*, pp. 98-130. For a devastating and thoroughly documented critique of affirmative action generally, see Thomas Sowell, "Affirmative Action: A Worldwide Disaster," *Commentary*, vol. 70, no. 6 (December 1989), pp. 21-41.
70. Mishan, "Was the Women's Liberation Movement Really Necessary?" pp. 14-15; Gilder, *Men and Marriage*, pp. 149-151; Michael Levin, "Comparable Worth: The Feminist Road to Socialism," *Commentary*, vol. 74, no. 3 (September 1984), pp. 13-19; Levin, *Feminism and Freedom*, pp. 131-155 (chapter titled "Comparable Worth"); Davidson, *The Failure of Feminism*, pp. 137-142; Allan Carlson, "Toward 'The Working Family': The Hidden Agenda Behind the Comparable Worth Debate," *Persuasion at Work*, vol. 7, no. 7 (July 1984) (Rockford, IL: The Rockford Institute) (whole issue).
71. Gilder, *Men and Marriage*, p. 151.
72. Michael Levin, "The Impact of Feminism on Primary Education," in *Gender Sanity*, ed. N. Davidson, p. 82. See also Levin, *Feminism and Freedom*, pp. 157-207, for a broader discussion of the feminist program for education at all levels.
73. Levin, "The Feminist Mystique," pp. 26-27; see also Chapter 16 of this volume; Hunt, *Males and Females*, pp. 87-105; Goldberg, *The Inevitability of Patriarchy*, pp. 187-218; Christen, "Sex Differences in the Human Brain."
74. Christen, "Sex Differences in the Human Brain," p. 158.
75. *Chronicles*, vol. 13, no. 10 (October 1989), p. 7.
76. Christen, "Sex Differences in the Human Brain," p. 153; Gilder, *Men and Marriage*, p. 81; Levin, "The Impact of Feminism on Primary Education," p. 92.

77. *Chronicles*, vol. 13, no. 10 (October 1989). See also the excellent discussion by Joseph M. Horn, "Truth, Gender, and the SAT," *Academic Questions*, vol. 3, no. 1 (Winter 1990), pp. 35-39.
78. Levin, "The Impact of Feminism on Primary Education," pp. 89-92.
79. *Ibid.*, p. 89.
80. The above discussion and quotes are drawn from Levin, "The Feminist Mystique," p. 29; see also Levin, "The Impact of Feminism on Primary Education," especially pp. 82-89.
81. *Ibid.*, p. 95-96.
82. This will be discussed in more detail later in this chapter.
83. Judith M. Bardwick, *In Transition: How Feminism, Sexual Liberation, and the Search for Self-Fulfillment Have Altered Our Lives* (New York: Holt, Rinehart and Winston, 1979), p. 15.
84. Carlson, "The Androgyny Hoax," p. 8; Davidson, *The Failure of Feminism*, pp. 242-243.
85. Cf. ludicrous examples presented by Levin, "The Impact of Feminism on Primary Education," pp. 89-91.
86. Wallis, p. 85.
87. Cf. Midge Decter, *The New Chastity and Other Arguments Against Women's Liberation* (New York: Coward, McCann and Geoghegan, 1972); also Bardwick, *In Transition*, pp. 104-105.
88. Cf. our *Time* article, p. 85, compared to Davidson, *The Failure of Feminism*, pp. 314-315.
89. Scott J. South and Glenna Spitze, "Divorce Determinants," *American Sociological Review*, vol. 51, no. 4 (August 1986), pp. 583-590.
90. Cf. Davidson, *The Failure of Feminism*, p. 283.
91. Bardwick, *In Transition*, pp. 120-121, emphases added.
92. Quoted in Pride, *The Way Home*, pp. 18, 21.
93. Cf. Judith S. Wallerstein, *Second Chances: Men, Women, and Children a Decade After Divorce* (New York: Ticknor & Fields, 1989).
94. Neil Kalter, "Long-Term Effects of Divorce on Children: A Developmental Vulnerability Model," *American Journal of Orthopsychiatry*, vol. 57, no. 3 (October 1987), pp. 595-597. See also Wilson and Hernnstein, *Crime and Human Nature*, p. 252; though these find that the evidence for such confusion is not unequivocal, there is more of a tendency toward than away from it in the research literature. Also, see Chapter 17 of this volume.
95. Wallis, "Onward Women," pp. 85-86; Wilson and Hernnstein, *Crime and Human Nature*, pp. 124, 245-253, 476-481. The relationship between delinquency and broken homes is complex and equivocal but does seem to point more toward an exacerbation than against it.
96. Carlson, "The Androgyny Hoax," p. 6; Diana Baumrind, "Are Androgynous Individuals More Effective Parents?" *Child Development*, vol. 53, no. 1 (February 1982), p. 45.
97. Singer, *Androgyny: Toward a New Theory of Sexuality*.
98. Baumrind, "Are Androgynous Individuals More Effective Parents?"
99. *Ibid.*; Carlson, "The Androgyny Hoax," p. 7.
100. John J. Ray and F. H. Lovejoy, "The Great Androgyny Myth: Sex Roles and Mental Health at Large," *The Journal of Social Psychology*, vol. 124, no. 2 (December 1984), p. 237.
101. Carlson, "The Androgyny Hoax," p. 8.
102. Sarah Bonnet Stein, *Girls and Boys: The Limits of Nonsexist Childrearing* (New York: Charles Scribner's Sons, 1983), as summarized in Davidson, *The Failure of Feminism*, pp. 241-246.
103. *Ibid.*, pp. 243-234; Carlson, "The Androgyny Hoax," p. 8.
104. Davidson, *The Failure of Feminism*, pp. 245-246.
105. *Ibid.*, p. 187; Gilder, *Men and Marriage*, pp. 61-68.
106. Carol Gilligan, *In a Different Voice* (Cambridge: Harvard University Press, 1982).

Endnotes to Chapter Nineteen

1. *EEOC v. Pacific Press Publishing Association*, 676 F.2d 1272 (1982) at 1280. See also Senate Report No. 872, 88th Congress, 2d Session. pt. 1 at 11, 24 (1964).

2. Title VII, Section 702, 78 Stat. 255 (1964).
3. This expansion of the Section 702 exemption to all activities of the religious entity withstood constitutional challenge in *Corporation of Presiding Bishop v. Amos*, 107 S.Ct. 2862 (1987). The United States Supreme Court held that the 1972 amendment did not violate the Establishment Clause of the First Amendment.

   The current version of Section 702 reads thus:

   This subchapter shall not apply to an employer with respect to the employment of aliens outside any State, or to a religious corporation, association, educational institution, or society with respect to the employment of individuals of a particular religion to perform work connected with the carrying on by such corporation, association, educational institution, or society of its activities.

4. 460 F.2d 553 (1972).
5. *Ibid.* at 555.
6. *Ibid.* at 558, 559.
7. 772 F.2d 1164 (1985).
8. The Seventh-Day Adventist Church does not permit the ordination of women.
9. *Ibid.* at 1169. The court's sensitivity toward a church's right to control employment decisions is reflected in the following statement from its opinion:

   It is axiomatic that the guidance of the state cannot substitute for that of the Holy Spirit and that a courtroom is not the place to review the church's determination of "God's appointed." (At 1170)

10. 651 F.2d 277 (1981).
11. *Ibid.* at 281.
12. "The President and Executive Vice President of the Seminary, the chaplain, the deans of men and women, the academic deans, and those other personnel who equate to or supervise faculty should be considered ministers as well. On the other hand, those administrators whose functions relate exclusively to the Seminary's finance, maintenance, and other non-academic departments, though considered ministers by the Seminary, are not ministers as we used that label in *McClure*." Id. at 285.
13. 626 F.2d 477 (1980).
14. *Ibid.* at 485.
15. *Ibid.* at 487.
16. *Ibid.*
17. 676 F.2d 1272 (1982).
18. *Ibid.* at 1278.
19. *Ibid.* at 1282.
20. *Ibid.* at 1279.
21. *Ibid.*
22. 781 F.2d 1362 (1986).
23. "The tenets [of the Fremont Assembly of God Church] include the belief that the Bible is to be taken literally. Among the doctrinal beliefs held by the Church is the belief that, while the sexes are equal in dignity before God, they are differentiated in role. In light of this conviction, the Church believes, based on, *inter alia*, Ephesians 5:23, that in any marriage, the husband is the head of the household and is required to provide for that household." *Ibid.* at 1364.
24. 29 U.S.C.A., Section 206(d).
25. 609 F.Supp. 344 (D.C.Cal. 1984) at 349.
26. All of the cases dealt with in this section were decided by federal circuit courts of appeals, the courts immediately below the United States Supreme Court. These decisions carry great weight, and—although subject to limitation and refinement by the Supreme Court—are unlikely to be reversed outright.
27. 15 U.S.C.A. Section 1-7.
28. 221 U.S. 106 (1911).

29. *Ibid.* at 179.
30. *Eastern States Retail Lumber Dealers Association v. United States, 234 U.S. 600 (1914): American Tobacco Co. v. United States, 328 U.S. 781 (1946).*
31. Jerald A. Jacobs, *Association Law Handbook* (Rockville, MD: BNA, 1981), pp. 216-223.
32. *Marjorie Webster Jr. College v. Middle States Association of Colleges & Secondary Schools*, 432 F.2d 650 (D.C.Cir. 1970).
33. *Ibid.* at 655.

Endnotes to Chapter Twenty

1. See S. T. Foh, "What Is the Woman's Desire?" *WTU* 37 (1974): 376-385; also Chapter 3 in this volume (pp. 108-109).
2. See Chapter 3 for a full discussion of the distinctive roles of men and women in Genesis 1 and 2.
3. Cf. the observations of Allan Bloom, *The Closing of the American Mind* (New York: Simon & Schuster, 1987), pp. 97-132.
4. Probably the KJV rendering "keepers at home" lent itself to that misinterpretation.
5. See Chapter 1, p. 49, for a discussion of male and female weakness.
6. It is obvious from the text of Genesis that Eve encouraged wrongdoing when she gave Adam the fruit. It is equally obvious that she takes the leadership role in that activity and that Adam simply follows her leadership. She allows herself, though, to be drawn into the role of spokesman by the serpent. She does not turn to her husband, from whom she had received God's command (cf. Genesis 2:16-17, where God gives the command to the man before the woman is created, and Genesis 3:2-3, where the woman relays that command), to ask him about what God had said and meant by His command, but rather acted unilaterally in opposition to the command that her husband had given to her (Genesis 3:6). Furthermore, she leads her husband by taking the fruit and giving it to him to eat (Genesis 3:6). In both Genesis 3:6 and 3:17, the remarks about the woman are not superfluous asides, even though they easily could have been left out, as an examination of the text bears out, but they are there to indicate exactly what happened and who had assumed the responsibility of making the decision to eat. The fact that Adam was following Eve's leadership and not simply deceived by the serpent is borne out by Paul's inspired evaluative statement in 1 Timothy 2:14 that "Adam was not the one deceived; it was the woman who was deceived" (NASB). Thus it seems appropriate to say that God's first comment to Adam, "because you listened to your wife" (Genesis 3:17), is a rebuke to Adam for his failure to carry out his God-ordained leadership role, not simply a reminder to Adam that he had listened to bad advice from Eve.
7. First Corinthians 7:5 says a husband and wife may temporarily set aside their conjugal rights by mutual consent for a period of time in order to serve God. On this principle, a wife could properly be the primary breadwinner to assist her husband in securing his education so that he could assume, in a better-equipped way, that responsibility that is rightfully his. Of course, if the husband is prevented from assuming this responsibility by reason of health or being out of work, the wife will gladly do what he cannot do for the good of the marriage and their mutual welfare. But these should be considered exceptions to the norm and warranted either by necessity (the latter) or as a temporary situation making the norm possible (the former).
8. Since the first truth, especially the statement in Galatians 3:28, is often used to deny the second truth, it is necessary to understand not only the breadth of the implications of what Paul is asserting in Galatians 3:28 but also what is not being implied. Ronald Y. K. Fung wisely warns against an unwarranted appeal to this verse in the following statement drawn up after a careful exegesis of the verse in its context:

   It seems precarious to appeal to this verse in support of any view of the role of women in the Church, for two reasons: (a) Paul's statement is not concerned with the role relationships of men and women within the Body of Christ but rather with their common initiation into it through (faith and) baptism; (b) the male/female distinction, unlike the other two, has its roots in creation, so that the parallelism between the male/female pair and the other pairs may not be unduly pressed. (*The Epistle to the Galatians*, NICNT [Grand Rapids, MI: Eerdmans, 1988], p. 176, n. 44.)

See also chapter 6 in this volume.

9. Biblical students should not follow Gordon Fee, a very able exegete and textual critic and also an "evangelical feminist," in his argued conjecture that 1 Corinthians 14:34-35 is not authentically a part of 1 Corinthians and is therefore "certainly not binding for Christians." As he himself acknowledges, "these two verses are found in all known manuscripts" (*The First Epistle to the Corinthians*, NICNT [Grand Rapids, MI: Eerdmans, 1988], pp. 708 and 699, respectively). In spite of this uniform testimony to the authenticity of the text, Fee advances arguments relating to transcriptional and intrinsic probability that can be adequately answered (see Chapter 6 in this volume) and that have not convinced most textual critics, the most noteworthy recent example being the team of experts that edited the critical text for the United Bible Societies who gave these verses a "B" rating, i.e., the next-to-highest rating in terms of certainty and authenticity. Unfortunately, one reading the commentary will not be aware of many of these answers because Fee has not provided them for the reader or has denied the validity of some that he relates without, however, demonstrating that they lack validity.
10. See Chapter 6 in this volume, which understands 1 Corinthians 14:33b-36 in a different way from this, but one that is also consistent with the overall perspective of this chapter and this book as a whole.
11. George W. Knight III, *The Role Relationship of Men and Women* (1985; reprinted Phillipsburg, NJ: Presbyterian & Reformed, 1989), pp. 27ff. See also Chapter 11 in this volume, especially p. 218.
12. This masculine description, "husband of one wife," is not merely descriptive of the usual situation, as is the reference to his being married and having children, because it follows on the heels of the statement of principle in 1 Timothy 2:12 and therefore is normative, as are the other qualifications that do not in the nature of the case allow for a viable alternative. The New Testament commends singleness as a viable alternative (cf. Matthew 19:12 and 1 Corinthians 7:7ff.) and recognizes that Paul, who is single, is, like Peter, a "fellow elder" (1 Peter 5:1). Thus being married and having several children is not being stated as a requirement for an elder, but rather the requirement being stated is that of fidelity to his spouse if he is married and a godly oversight of his children if he has children. However, it is fair to say that the masculine aspect of the statement "husband of one wife" does indeed imply exclusively male elders, and particularly so (as we have noted) when it follows hard on the heels of 1 Timothy 2:12.
13. See author's forthcoming commentary on *The Pastoral Epistles* in the NIGTC series, which treats this question at some length. See also the discussion of this passage in Chapter 11 of this volume.
14. Compare, for example, the earlier, and only other, occurrences of the Greek word *diakonos* in Romans, i.e., Romans 13:4 (twice) and 15:8.
15. Those who understand 1 Corinthians 14:34-35 to be Paul's prohibition on women "judging" the prophets (cf., e.g., the very helpful book by J. B. Hurley, *Man and Woman in Biblical Perspective* [Grand Rapids, MI: Zondervan, and Leicester, England: InterVarsity Press, 1981], pp. 188-194), a view that I do not myself adopt, still concur that an activity or function is prohibited and that the text says that women should not seek to participate in that activity. Since the prohibition is related to women only, it may be said that Paul does not rule out men in general from participating in this activity. The entire section of 1 Corinthians 14 is dealing with the participation of members of the congregation in the congregational worship (see especially verse 26). The conclusion to be drawn, it seems to me, is that women are prohibited from even an occasional teaching of the church but that men, even though they are not officers, are not prohibited from this activity. This close consideration of the text evidences that Paul is concerned about prohibiting the activity of teaching and is not just concerned with a prohibition of a teaching office in the church, as is sometimes assumed—of course, the former also prohibits the latter.

16. For example, those who hold that only those who profess faith in Christ should be baptized will not be persuaded otherwise if those who practice infant baptism have spiritually successful ministries, and vice versa. God's general blessing on a person does not prove that a particular activity in his or her life is in accord with Biblical teaching.

Endnotes to Chapter Twenty-one

1. Patricia Gundry, *Neither Slave nor Free: Helping Women Answer the Call to Church Leadership* (San Francisco: Harper and Row, 1987), p. 120.

Endnotes to Chapter Twenty-two

1. All Scripture quoted will be from the *New International Version* unless otherwise specified.
2. Frank Zepezauer, "The Masks of Feminism," *The Human Life Review*, Fall 1988, p. 31.
3. "My Turn," *Newsweek*, October 17, 1988, p. 14.
4. Paul Fussell, "What Happened to Mother?" *The Wilson Quarterly*, vol. xii, no. 5 (Winter 1988), p. 154.
5. George Gallup, "Intangibles Rated Highest by Americans," *The Dallas Morning News*, January 28, 1982, p. 24D.
6. Hymen E. Goldin, *The Jewish Woman and Her Home* (New York: Hebrew Publishing Co., n.d.), pp. 130-131.
7. Francis Brown, S.R. Driver, and Charles Briggs, *A Hebrew and English Lexicon of the Old Testament* (Oxford: Clarendon Press, 1962), pp. 298-299.
8. Elizabeth Dodds, *Marriage to a Difficult Man* (Philadelphia: Westminster Press, 1976), p. 84.
9. *The Dallas Morning News*, September 22, 1981.
10. *The Dallas Morning News*, March 11, 1989.
11. Abigail Van Buren, "Dear Abby," *The Northwest Arkansas Times*, September 28, 1974.
12. Rebecca Lamar Harmon, *Susanna, Mother of the Wesleys* (London: Hodder & Stoughton, 1968), p. 57.
13. *San Francisco Examiner*, December 28, 1977.
14. "An Interview with Kate Hepburn," *Ladies Home Journal*, March, 1977, p. 54.
15. "Joanne and Paul," *Ladies Home Journal*, July, 1975, p. 62.
16. "Books," *Newsweek*, November 3, 1975, p. 88.
17. Kim A. Lawton, "Politicians Discover Children," *Christianity Today*, March 17, 1989, p. 34.
18. Sandra Evans, "Study Shows Negative Effects of Full-Time Child Care," *Washington Post*, April 23, 1988, p. A10.
19. Victor Wilson, "Book Garners Facts, Fancies about Mom," *Dallas Morning News*, May 13, 1984, p. 10F.
20. Dodds, *Marriage to a Difficult Man*, p. 209.
21. Megan Rosenfeld, *Washington Post* (November 9, 1986).
22. Associated Press, June 11, 1988.
23. Mikhail Gorbachev, "In His Words," *U.S. News and World Report*, November 9, 1987, pp. 70-79.
24. Kristin M. Foster, "Ministry and Motherhood: A Collision of Callings?" *Currents in Theology and Mission*, vol. 16, no. 2 (April 1989), p. 102.
25. W. R. Stephens, *Saint John Chrysostom* (London: John Murray, 1880), pp. 9-12.
26. "What Is Christian Marriage: a Debate between Larry and Nordis Christenson and Berkeley and Alvera Mickelsen," *Transformation*, vol. 5, no. 3 (July/September 1988), p. 3; see also Chapter 12 in this volume.
27. Defined as "one who stands in order or rank below another." *Webster's Third New International Dictionary* (Springfield: G & C Merriam, 1971), p. 2277.
28. "Subordinationism," *Oxford Dictionary of the Christian Church*, ed. F. L. Cross (London: Oxford University Press, 1958), p. 1301.

29. Augustus Hopkins Strong, *Systematic Theology* (Philadelphia: Judson Press, 1960), p. 342.
30. "Books," *Newsweek*, November 3, 1975, p. 88.

Endnotes to Chapter Twenty-three

1. Much of the material in this essay is taken from Weldon Hardenbrook's book *Missing from Action: Vanishing Manhood in America* (Nashville: Thomas Nelson, 1987). The editors recommend this book very highly and encourage all readers to pursue this matter of missing fathers further by reading Hardenbrook's book.
2. Clayton Barbeau, *The Head of the Family* (Chicago: Henry Regnery, 1961), p. xiii.
3. Lawrence Fuchs, *Family Matters* (New York: Random House, 1972), p. 109.
4. Quoted in Kevin Perrotta, "Why Bother About Modernization?" *Pastoral Renewal*, vol. 4, no. 11 (May 1980), p. 90c-d.
5. Quoted in Alvin P. Sanoff, "Our Neglected Kids," *U.S. News and World Report*, August 9, 1982, p. 58.
6. Edwin Louis Cole, *Maximized Manhood* (Springdale, PA: Whitaker House, 1984), p. 142.
7. Hans Sebald, *Momism* (Chicago: Nelson-Hall, 1976), pp. 111-112.
8. Daniel Amneus, *Back to Patriarchy* (New Rochelle, NY: Arlington House, 1979), pp. 26, 64.
9. U.S. Department of Commerce, Bureau of the Census, *Statistical Abstract of the United States 1985*, p. 182.
10. Donald MacGillis and ABC News, *Crime in America* (Radnor, PA: Chilton Book Co., 1983), p. 143.
11. Natalie Gittelson, *Dominus* (New York: Farrar, Straus and Giroux, 1978), p. 35.
12. *Statistical Abstract*, p. 182.
13. *Statistical Abstract*, p. 173.
14. "Demography Is Destiny," National Association of State Directors of Special Education, Inc., January 1989, p. 3.
15. Richard Stengel, "When Brother Kills Brother," *Time*, September 16, 1985, p. 32.
16. MacGillis and ABC, *Crime in America*, p. 40.
17. Abigail Wood, "The Trouble with Dad," *Seventeen*, October 1985, p. 38.
18. Presidential Proclamation #3736, June 15, 1966, as recorded in the Federal Register, May 17, 1966.

Endnotes to Chapter Twenty-four

1. Adapted from *Christian Allies in a Secular Age*, ed. Kevin Perrotta and John C. Blattner (Ann Arbor, MI: Servant Books, 1987), pp. 61-71.

Endnotes to Chapter Twenty-five

1. C. S. Lewis, "Priestesses in the Church?" in *God in the Dock: Essays on Theology and Ethics*, ed. Walter Hooper (Grand Rapids, MI: Eerdmans, 1970), p. 238.
2. *Ibid.*, p. 239.
3. I do not want to be understood as recommending a woman's surrender to evils such as coercion or violent conquest.

Endnotes to Chapter Twenty-six

1. A fuller description of the origin, statement of faith, and goals of CBE can be found in "New Organization Formed," *Priscilla Papers*, vol. 1, no. 4 (Fall 1987), pp. 1-3. For information one may write to CBE, 7433 Borman Ave. E., Inver Grove Heights, MN 55076.
2. Virginia Mollenkott wrote, in a letter to *Christian Century* (March 7, 1984, p. 252), "I am beginning to wonder whether indeed Christianity is patriarchal to its very core. If so, count me out. Some of us may be forced to leave Christianity in order to participate in

Jesus' discipleship of equals." Clark Pinnock said in response to this, "Apparently her commitment to feminism transcends her commitment even to Christian faith." "Biblical Authority and the Issues in Question," in *Women, Authority and the Bible*, ed. Alvera Mickelsen (Downers Grove, IL: InterVarsity Press, 1986), p. 51.

3. *Christianity Today*, October 16, 1987, p. 44.
4. The wording used here for the entire declaration is taken from the published advertisement in *Christianity Today*, April 9, 1990.
5. Mary Stewart Van Leeuwen, *Gender and Grace* (Downers Grove, IL: InterVarsity Press, 1990), p. 235. She expresses her confidence that the Bible's "main thrust is toward the leveling, not the maintenance, of birth-based status differences." This is an illustration of the Bible's "pilgrim principle," by which we are called to be aliens in our culture and bring God's countercultural vision to bear on the fallen world. But there is also a "missionary principle" that affirms "that, for the sake of advancing God's kingdom in a given time and place, temporary compromises can and often must be made with the societal status quo" (p. 236). This is what happened in Paul's restrictions on women. They were a temporary compromise with the status quo for the sake of the spread of the gospel. If we ask how we know what is a temporary compromise and what is abiding counsel, the answer is: the larger "theme" or "whole" or "main thrust" of Scripture tells us. This is very precarious. In the case of Biblical themes relating to manhood and womanhood, we think it results in canceling out crucial texts that are needed today precisely as pilgrim indictments of feminist alignment with egalitarian culture. (See Chapter 2, Question 15.)
6. This, it seems to us, is the Achilles heel of the hermeneutical approach adopted by Gretchen Gaebelein Hull in *Equal to Serve* (Old Tappan, NJ: Fleming H. Revell, 1987). See Chapter 2, question 50.
7. This was the most frustrating thing about reading Gretchen Gaebelein Hull's *Equal to Serve*. Literally nowhere did she interact with a vision of manhood and womanhood like ours—one that focuses on a man's primary responsibility to lead, not on the quest for power or control or dominance or supremacy. She consistently described "patriarchalism" and "traditionalism" as "preoccupied with [rigid, artificial] role playing" (pp. 34, 119, 128), propagating "male supremacy" (p. 84), ascribing less worth and dignity to women (p. 87), claiming that "one person must always be dominant" (pp. 104, 197), espousing "rigid vocational roles" and "rigid spheres of ministry" (p. 124), endorsing a "narrow female role" (p. 125), calling homemakers "non-working" mothers (p. 157), saying "child-related duties" belong only to the woman (p. 160), teaching a "chain of command" (p. 192), recommending that men "never submit" (p. 194), equating submitting with "knuckling under" (p. 195), seeking for men an "exalted position" (p. 198), equating headship with "power over" and having a "power-oriented" view of headship (pp. 205-206), returning "women to the nunnery" (p. 289) and excluding them from ministry (p. 222). Our point is not that there haven't been people who are guilty of all those things. Our point is that you cannot establish your case by implying yours is the only good alternative to the rejected view. This fallacy of the excluded middle runs throughout the CBE declaration, as we will see.
8. This is a quote from one of the authors of the CBE statement "Men, Women and Biblical Equality," Gilbert Bilezikian, *Beyond Sex Roles* (Grand Rapids, MI: Baker Book House, 1986), p. 154. Of course, if the only thing meant by "hierarchical differences" were abusive, domineering, arrogant, or insensitive patterns of power, we would agree that mutual submission rules them out. But that is not all that the CBE statement (or Bilezikian) means by it. They mean that mutual submission rules out patterns of relationship in which the man is called to be leader just because he is the man, no matter how loving and sensitive he is.

   But what Bilezikian says about marriage here does not seem to be true when he comes to talk about the church. He says, "The church thrives on mutual subjection. In a Spirit-led church, the elders submit to the congregation in being accountable for their watch-care, and the congregation submits to the elders *in accepting their guidance*" (p. 155, italics added). Again he says, "Leaders are specifically forbidden to 'exercise lordship' or 'rulership' over congregations. Instead they are to *provide guidance* by exemplifying authentic Christian life before them (1 Peter 5:1-4). In return, the congregations submit to their leaders by *obeying and accepting their guidance* (1 Thessalonians 5:12-13, Hebrews 13:17), while all members, elders included, approach each other in an attitude of humility (1 Peter 5:5)" (p. 251, italics added). What is clear in these quotes is that mutual submission is compatible with hierarchy—that is, with a differentiation in roles in which one group is called on to "provide guidance" (i.e., be leaders), and the other is called on to "obey and accept their guidance." If this is conceivable in the church as Bilezikian so well describes it, why is it inconceivable in marriage?

9. Jonathan Edwards, *Religious Affections*, in *Works*, vol. 1 (Edinburgh: Banner of Truth Trust, 1974), p. 286.
10. Edwards, *Religious Affections*, p. 286. If one should ask how this spiritual taste that discerns directly the beauty of an action relates to the rule and authority of God's Word, Edwards answers:

> The saints in thus judging of actions by a spiritual taste, have not a particular recourse to the express rules of God's word, with respect to every word and action that is before them: but yet their taste itself in general, is subject to the rule of God's word, and must be tried by that, and a right reasoning upon it. A man of a rectified palate judges of particular morsels by his taste; but yet his palate itself must be judged of, whether it be right or no, by certain rules and reasons. But a spiritual taste mightily helps the soul in its reasonings on the word of God, and in judging of the true meaning of its rules; as it removes the prejudices of a depraved appetite, naturally leads the thoughts in the right channel, casts a light on the word, and causes the true meaning most naturally to come to mind, through the harmony there is between the disposition, and relish of a sanctified soul, and the true meaning of the rules of God's word. Yea, this harmony tends to bring the texts themselves to mind on proper occasions; as the particular state of the stomach and palate, tends to bring such particular meats and drinks to mind, as are agreeable to that state. Thus *the children of God are led by the Spirit of God* in judging of actions themselves, and in their meditations upon the rules of God's holy word: and so God *teaches them his statutes, and causes them to understand the way of his precepts*; which the psalmist so often prays for. (p. 287)

Endnotes to Appendix One

1. Richard S. Cervin, "Does *Kephalē* Mean 'Source' or 'Authority' in Greek Literature? A Rebuttal," *Trinity Journal* 10 NS (1989), 85-112.
2. *Trinity Journal* 6 NS (1985), 38-59; reprinted from the appendix of George W. Knight III, *The Role Relationship of Men and Women*, rev. ed., (Chicago: Moody Press, 1985), 49-80.
3. Italics mine.
4. In this article I am citing the page references from my earlier *Trinity Journal* article rather than from the article as it appeared as an appendix to George Knight's book (see note 2).
5. Later in this article I discuss the claim of some recent interpreters that *kephalē* does not mean "authority over" in this and other passages dealing with Christ's rule. To my knowledge, no commentary and no lexicon in the history of the church has denied the meaning "ruler" or "authority over" in this passage until 1981, when Berkeley and Alvera Mickelsen suggested the meaning "top or crown" in their article, "The 'Head' of the Epistles" (*Christianity Today*, February 20, 1981, p. 22). But they give no argument for this interpretation except to assert it. And they admit that the context is discussing "Christ's authority over everything in creation" (*ibid.*).
6. Cervin also briefly mentions the argument that *kephalē* in the LXX only seldom translates Hebrew *ro'sh* when referring to leaders. Because this argument is developed more fully by the Mickelsens, I treat it below (pp. 450-453).
7. Walter Bauer, *A Greek-English Lexicon of the New Testament and Other Early Christian Literature*, 2nd ed., trans. William F. Arndt and F. Wilbur Gingrich, rev. F. Wilbur Gingrich and Frederick W. Danker (Chicago: University of Chicago Press, 1979; henceforth referred to as BAGD), p. xxi.

8. See below, p. 444, for more detailed discussion of Cervin's objection to this passage in Plutarch.
9. In this quotation, the emphasis on the word *theologians* is mine. Cervin seems determined to show that those who specialize in the interpretation of the New Testament do not have competence in understanding the meanings of terms. But why should the fact that one specializes in the study of New Testament literature automatically mean that one is incompetent in lexicography or linguistics or classical Greek? Especially in the case of Bauer's *Lexicon* this is certainly a false assumption. To continue to call such scholars "theologians" when their specialty is lexicography is both inaccurate and misleading to readers.
10. Moises Silva, *Biblical Words and Their Meaning: An Introduction to Lexical Semantics* (Grand Rapids: Zondervan, 1983), p. 172.
11. Silva, *Biblical Words*, p. 171.
12. Peter Cotterell and Max Turner, *Linguistics and Biblical Interpretation* (Downers Grove, IL: InterVarsity Press, 1989), comment on Herodotus 4.91:

    However, the singular word is also used of the *mouth* of the river . . . and the easiest explanation of both of these usages of *kephalē* is that they derive from the lexeme's established sense of "extreme end." . . . we do not need to posit that they represent *new senses*, "source" and "mouth" respectively, for which we have no corroborating evidence. . . . (p. 142)

13. Philip Payne, "Response," in *Women, Authority and the Bible*, ed. Alvera Mickelsen (Downers Grove, IL: InterVarsity Press, 1986), pp. 118-136.
14. He says that one example is not a metaphor at all but a simile and "has nothing to do with 'source' or 'authority.'" Regarding a number of other passages in Artemidorus he says, "Several of the passages cited by Payne do not warrant the interpretation of 'source,' however" (p. 92).
15. Some (though not Cervin) have also suggested (in personal correspondence to me, without attribution) that an example of *kephalē* meaning "source" may be found in *The Life of Adam and Eve* 19.3, which calls sinful desire (Greek *epithumia*) "the *head* of every sin." But once again this text is ambiguous: "Head" here could well mean just "beginning" or "starting point, first in a series." Moreover, the example is hardly reliable for NT evidence, since it is only found in two 13th A.D. century Italian manuscripts, designated A and B by R. H. Charles (*The Apocrypha and Pseudepigrapha of the Old Testament* [2 vols.; Oxford: Clarendon Press, 1913] 1:146; compare discussion of manuscripts on pp. 124-125). Charles himself does not think the reading *kephalē* to be correct here and follows manuscript C in its reading *rhiza kai archē*, therefore translating this different phrase "root and beginning" (p. 146). James H. Charlesworth (*The Old Testament Pseudepigrapha* [2 vols; Garden City, N.Y.: Doubleday, 1983-85] 2:279) translates "origin," but notes that *kephalē* here corresponds to Hebrew *ro'sh*, maning "head" or "first" (279, note e). (The Greek text is found in C. von Tischendorf, *Apocalypses Apocryphae* [Leipzig, 1866] 11).
16. We may of course ask the additional question, even if the metaphor of *kephalē* in the sense of "leader" was not a native Greek metaphor, would non-Jewish Greek speakers have understood it nonetheless? It seems quite likely that they would have understood it, because (1) the quotation from Plato, *Timaeus* 44d, noted below (example 3), shows that the idea of the head ruling over the body was commonly understood in Greek culture long before the time of the New Testament; (2) the quotations from Plutarch (my examples 23, 24, 25, 26, 27, noted below) are strong evidence of the use of *kephalē* meaning "leader" in a writer not influenced by the Hebrew Old Testament or the Septuagint; (3) the use of the adjective *kephalaios*, "head-like," in the phrase *ho kephalaios*, "the head-like one," to mean "leader" or "authority over" shows that a closely-related adjectival form of this word was used with that meaning in non-Biblical Greek (see Henry George Liddell and Robert Scott, *A Greek-English Lexicon*, rev. Henry Stuart Jones and Roderick McKenzie, supp. ed. E. A. Barber, et al. [Oxford: Clarendon Press, 1968; henceforth referred to as LSJ or Liddell-Scott], pp. 944-945: "metaphorically, of persons, *the head or chief*").

17. Once again the numbering of the passages follows that of my original article.
18. I realize that this point does not apply to Cervin's argument directly since he does not depend on *Orphic Fragments* 21a for his case, but I mention it here because of its relevance for the wider discussion.
19. One more question of a textual variant comes up when Cervin examines my example (9), 1 Kings (LXX 3 Kings) 8:1 (Alexandrinus): "Then Solomon assembled all the elders of Israel and all the *heads* of the tribes." Before commenting on the text itself, Cervin asserts, "The word *kephalē* does not even occur; rather it is found in a variation of Origen's" (p. 97). Cervin makes it sound as if I had quoted an example where the word does not occur in the Septuagint but rather was inserted by Origen (early third century A.D.). But in fact the word *kephalē* is found in the Alexandrinus text of the Septuagint (see H. B. Swete, *The Old Testament in Greek According to the Septuagint* [Cambridge: University Press, 1909], vol. 1, p. 691; cf. E. Hatch and H. A. Redpath, *A Concordance to the Septuagint*, 2 vols. [Oxford: Clarendon Press, 1897-1906; henceforth referred to as Hatch-Redpath], vol. 2, p. 761).
20. It is puzzling to be told several times in Cervin's article that I failed to provide the context for a quotation. In this example (which is not unlike a number of others), I originally quoted three lines, and Mr. Cervin quotes five and says I failed to provide the context. (The quotation from Plutarch above is a verbatim quotation from my original article, for example.) It seems quite clear from my original quotation that Plutarch is using a simile, and it does not seem to me that I omitted anything essential for the reader. Of course in these cases there are always questions of judgment about what must necessarily be included in an article without entirely losing its readability, but I do not think I was unfair to the reader or that I withheld essential information about the context in any of the cases in which Cervin suggests that I did so (as in this case).
21. For a discussion of the textual variant, see above, note 19.
22. Philip Payne, "Response," in *Women, Authority and the Bible*, ed. Mickelsen, p. 123, adopts the same interpretation as Cervin regarding this verse.
23. R. H. Charles, *Pseudepigrapha of the Old Testament* (Oxford: Clarendon Press, 1913), p. 297.
24. So also the editor in the Loeb Classical Library edition, p. 388, note c.
25. "History of the Septuagint Text," in Alfred Rahlfs, *Septuaginta* (Stuttgart: Württembergische Bibelanstalt, 1965), p. xxvi.
26. H. B. Swete, *An Introduction to the Old Testament in Greek* (Cambridge: University Press, 1900), p. 31.
27. *Ibid.*, pp. 39-40.
28. I did not include these examples in my earlier article because they seemed to me possibly to represent prominence instead of rule or authority. But reexamination of the contexts and the realization that exaltation to high position in the Old Testament seems inevitably to carry with it some idea of authority as well have convinced me that authority is in view in these examples also.
29. In subsequent personal correspondence to me (6/5/90), Dr. Cervin agrees that "pre-eminence" is not a meaning given in LSJ, and indicates that on reconsideration he now thinks the meaning "prominence" would be more appropriate, because this meaning "does not carry the overtone of superiority which is implicit in [the meaning pre-eminence]." Cervin indicates that, although this meaning "prominence" is not given in LSJ either, it seems to him a "valid aspect" of the Greek metaphorical use of *kephalē* because it is closely related to the idea of being the physical "top" or "end" of a person or object, and therefore the idea of prominence is "implicit in the metaphor." In response, the same objections given above seem to me also to apply to this new suggestion: though it may be an "overtone" of the metaphor, it is not a necessary meaning, it has never been suggested in any lexicon, and, in any case, when applied to persons it cannot be dissociated from the dominant sense of "authority, leader, ruler." Why must people search for any meaning but "authority over"?
30. Berkeley Mickelsen and Alvera Mickelsen, "Does Male Dominance Tarnish Our Translations?" *Christianity Today*, October 5, 1979, p. 23.

31. The existence of this unusual allegation in Dr. Cervin's article is particularly puzzling since I informed him in more detail about my procedure before he corrected the article for publication. In fact, this correspondence apparently led to a further footnote (p. 111, note 38), in which he says, "Grudem explains (p. e.) that he had based his count on English translations rather than on the Greek text." The impression given the reader is that my entire summary was "based on" counting English translations, whereas what I explained in the letter to Dr. Cervin was simply what I have said above regarding the two examples that do not exist (see above pp. 445-446), namely, that after I had listed all my examples for the article, my counting erroneously included two examples where the word "head" was repeated a second time in the English text. But the entire compilation of examples was certainly "based on" original Greek texts.
32. This was an address given at the Evangelical Theological Society meeting in Atlanta, October 20, 1986, to which I gave one of the scheduled responses. (My written critique below contains the major substance of my oral response given at that time.)
33. It should be noted that though the publication date of *Women, Authority and the Bible*, in which articles 1-4 appear, is 1986, the essays were written for a conference in 1984, before most of the authors had access to my 1985 article.
34. Pages 46-47, 52-53.
35. Philip B. Payne, "Response," in *Women, Authority and the Bible*, ed. Mickelsen, pp. 121-124.
36. Gordon D. Fee, *First Corinthians* (NICNT; Grand Rapids, MI: Eerdmans, 1987), pp. 502-503.
37. The Mickelsens use the number 8 out of 180; Payne (p. 123) uses 9, but the form of the argument is the same.
38. Berkeley and Alvera Mickelsen, "What Does *Kephalē* Mean in the New Testament?" in *Women, Authority and the Bible*, ed. Mickelsen, p. 104.
39. Payne, "Response," *ibid.*, p. 123. In footnote 35, p. 123, Payne explains that he only counts "nine exceptions" (verses where *kephalē* means "leader"): Judges 11:11; 2 Samuel 22:44; Psalm 18:43; Isaiah 7:8-9; Lamentations 1:5; Deuteronomy 28:13, 44; and Isaiah 9:14, because five others are in variant readings found in some but not all manuscripts (Judges 10:18; 11:8-9; 1 Kings (LXX 3 Kings) 8:1; 20:12), and he thinks that in yet three others (Deuteronomy 32:42; 1 Chronicles 12:19; Psalm 140:10) the word refers to the physical head and is not a metaphor for "leader" or "authority" (in these last three he is correct, and I did not cite those as examples of "leader").
40. Fee, *First Corinthians*, p. 503.
41. This is also the case when referring to a related idea, the "beginning point" of something, such as the "beginning" of a night watch (Judges 7:19; Lamentations 2:19), or the "beginning" of a period of time (Isaiah 40:21; 41:4, 26: 48:16; 1 Chronicles 16:7, etc.).

    This is interesting in light of the use of *kephalē* in *Orphic Fragments* 21a, where *kephalē* seems to mean "beginning" or "first in a series" (see below). If this meaning was commonly recognized at the time of the LXX, then *kephalē* could also have been used in these texts, but *archē* was preferred by the translators.

    We should also note that when the New Testament wants to say that Christ became "the *source* of eternal salvation" (Hebrews 5:9), it uses not *kephalē* but a perfectly good Greek word meaning "source," *aitios*, "source, cause." This does not of course prove that *kephalē* could not also mean source in a metaphorical sense, but it shows that in both the Old Testament (Genesis 2:10) and the New Testament (Hebrews 5:9), where there is a text that unambiguously speaks of "source" in the sense that the Mickelsens and others claim *kephalē* takes, the term used is not *kephalē* but something that means "source" without question.

    Philip Payne, "Response," p. 119, n. 21, quotes S. C. Woodhouse, *English-Greek Dictionary* (London: Routledge & Kegan Paul, 1932[2]) to show that *kephalē* does not mean "authority" or "chief." Although we think that may be an oversight in light of the examples we earlier adduced, Payne should perhaps also have mentioned that Woodhouse lists under "source of rivers, etc." *pēgē*, *krēnē*, and *krounos*, and under "origin" *archē*, *pēgē*, and *rhiza* ("root"), but not *kephalē* in either case. It does not seem fair to cite

Woodhouse to show lack of support on one side but fail to note that he gives no support to the other side either.

Moreover, Payne fails to tell the reader that Woodhouse's *Dictionary* is written to help students write compositions in Attic Greek and is specifically taken from the vocabulary of authors "from Aeschylus to Demosthenes" (pp. v, vi) (ca. 500 B.C.-322 B.C.). It does not cover the Koine Greek of the New Testament at all. Such a citation is troubling in a widely read popular book, for it conveys to the non-specialist reader an appearance of scholarly investigation while in actual fact there is little substantive relevance for it in the present discussion.

42. The Mickelsens actually dismiss six texts as having textual variants (p. 104), but they do not specify which those are. I am using the number five from the response by Philip Payne (pp. 122-123).
43. They do not specify exactly which texts they are not counting because of textual variants, but these five do have variants in the readings of Codex Alexandrinus, one of the major ancient manuscripts of the Septuagint.
44. The second instance in Isaiah 7:8 is found in several manuscripts and omitted only by Sinaiticus among major manuscripts.
45. Once again the enumeration is not exact between the Mickelsens and Payne. The Mickelsens say that four examples have the head-tail metaphor, but do not list them. Payne specifies these three texts in his response, and I have used his number here.
46. Mickelsen and Mickelsen, "What Does *Kephalē* Mean . . .?" p. 103.
47. Payne, "Response," p. 123, n. 35.
48. See note 38 with reference to my inclusion of Deuteronomy 28:13, 44; Jeremiah 31:7 (LXX 38:7).
49. In addition to the three verses listed in the previous footnote, the articles by Payne and the Mickelsens have persuaded me to look again at Lamentations 1:5 ("her foes have become the *head*; her enemies prosper"), and to count this as a legitimate instance of *kephalē* meaning "leader" or "authority over." These four examples, together with the deletion of the one I had erroneously counted (see above, p. 445, for discussion), bring my total to sixteen in the Septuagint rather than the thirteen I had previously listed.
50. Philip Payne (article 3, p. 123) disagrees with the sense "authority over" in this text because he says the translators replaced the idea of "leader" "with 'heads [meaning tops] of the staffs' they carried." I discussed this interpretation on pp. 441-442, above, in response to Richard Cervin.
51. In this second occurrence of *head* in this verse, the LXX has *archē* (here in the sense of leader, ruler), not *kephalē*.
52. Joseph Fitzmyer says of this passage, "The notion of supremacy or authority is surely present, and expressed by *kephalē*" ("Another Look," p. 508).
53. In fact, "aunt" only occurs once in the English Bible (*RSV*), at Leviticus 18:14. There are many other commonly understood English words that occur only once in the Bible, such as (using the *RSV*): *abstinence*, *acquaintance*, *afternoon*, *agent*, *anklet*, *anvil*, *armpit*, *aroma*, *arsenal*, *audience*. Other common words occur only twice:, *ambassador*, *ant*, *antelope*, *ape*, *awl*.
54. I discuss the absence of the meaning "leader, authority over" from Liddell-Scott in the next section of this article.
55. Page 107.
56. I discussed the legitimacy of using Liddell-Scott's definition of "source" above, pp. 432-433, 453-454.
57. My earlier article (pp. 47-48) cites definitions from BAGD, Thayer, Cremer, *New International Dictionary of New Testament Theology* (henceforth referred to as NIDNTT), and (for the Septuagint) *Theological Dictionary of the New Testament* (henceforth referred to as TDNT). See also note 69.
58. Joseph A. Fitzmyer, "Another look at *Kephalē* in 1 Corinthians 11:3," *NTS* 35 (1989), p. 511.

    Richard Cervin is hardly correct when he says "the contributors and editors of [Liddell-Scott] included a team of theologians, Milligan among them" (p. 86). In fact, the Preface to Liddell-Scott mentions no "team of theologians" but simply says that the results of the study of the meanings of words in the New Testament are "readily accessible" and mentions some lexicons that are "generally sufficient" (p. ix). H. Stuart Jones, the editor of the most recent edition of Liddell-Scott, mentions only that Professor Milligan sent him some advance proofs of his specialty lexicon of the papyri as they illustrate New Testament usage. Jones also mentions A. H. McNeil and A. Llewellyn Davies regarding their advice on the Septuagint and the Hexapla, but the preface mentions nothing else concerning any "team of theologians."

59. This translation is quoted from Artemidorus Daldianus, *The Interpretation of Dreams* (= *Oneirocritica*), translated by Robert J. While (Park Ridge, NJ: Nooyes, 1975), pp. 34-35; the Greek text is found in *Artemidori Daldiani Oneirocriticon Libre V*, ed. Robert A. Pack (Leipzig: Teubner, 1963), pp. 43-45.

60. Although Payne uses incorrect reasoning to derive the meaning "source" from these uses in Artemidorus, it is additionally disappointing to see that he quoted this very obscure text (accessible only at highly specialized libraries) to show instances where Artemidorus said that the head symbolized the "source" of something but did not inform the reader that in the very same section he quoted (*Oneirocritica* 1.35) Artemidorus also said that the head symbolized the "superior" of a sailor and the "master" of a slave, and that the head was the "master of the body"—all meanings that Payne denies.

    Moreover, in order to support his contention that "the ancient Greek world through the time of Paul commonly believed that the heart, not the head, was the center of emotions and spirit, the central governing place of the body" (pp. 119-120), Payne cites only one ancient author, Aristotle, and then cites the *Oxford Classical Dictionary* article on "Anatomy and Physiology" as saying about Aristotle that, "having found the brain to be devoid of sensation, he concluded that it could not be associated with it. The function of the brain was to keep the heart from overheating the blood" (Payne, p. 120. n. 26, citing *OCD*, 59). What Payne does not tell the reader is that the immediately preceding two sentences in the *OCD* article say that this view of Aristotle's was *contrary* to the commonly held view in the ancient world: "Among the noteworthy erros of Aristotle is his refusal to attach importance to the brain. Intelligence he placed in the heart. *This was contrary to the views of some of his medical contemporaries, contrary to the popular view, and contrary to the doctrine of the* Timaeus" (*OCD*, 59, italics mine).

    So in the use of both Artemidorus and the *OCD* Payne has given misleading and selective quotations, and has done so from technical works that will not be checked by even one in a thousand readers of such a widely-circulated and popularly written book.

61. Peter Cotterel and Max Turner, *Linguistics and Biblical Interpretation* (Downers Grove, IL: InterVarsity Press, 1989), p. 144, concur with this analysis:

    Least helpful of the types of evidence advanced, is the claim that amongst the ancients the head was often regarded as the source of a variety of substances and influences pertinent to life. The claim itself need not be doubted, but how is it *relevant*? Just because, say, Artemidorus . . . maintains that "the head is the source of light and life for the body" does not mean that the writer considered "source" to be a *sense* of the *word* "head." Our employers are the source of our income, books are the source of our knowledge, and the good, well-watered land the source of our food, but no one in their right mind would suggest that "source" is a *sense* of the *words* "employer," "books," or "land." Such would be a classic case of the confusion between the sense of a word and "adjunct" properties of the thing-in-the-world the word denotes.

62. See discussion above, p. 433.

62a. *Systematic Theology* (3 vols.; Grand Rapids: Eerdmans, 1970 [reprint]) 1:460-462 (italics mine).

62b. *Systematic Theology* (Valley Forge, Pa.: Judson, 1907), 342.

63. It is troubling therefore to find the evangelical feminists Richard and Catherine Kroeger writing the article "Subordinationism" in the *Evangelical Dictionary of Theology*, ed. Walter Elwell (Grand Rapids, MI: Baker Book House, 1984), and asserting in the first sentence that subordinationism is "a doctrine which assigns an inferiority of being, status, *or role* to the Son or the Holy Spirit within the Trinity. Condemned by numerous church

councils, this doctrine has continued in one form or another throughout the history of the church" (p. 1058, emphasis mine). When the Kroegers add the phrase "or role" to their definition they condemn all orthodox Christology from the Nicene Creed onward and thereby condemn a teaching that Charles Hodge says has been a teaching of "the Church universal."

A similar misunderstanding is found in Gretchen Gaebelein Hull, *Equal to Serve* (Old Tappan, NJ: Fleming H. Revell, 1987), who says, "If we define *head* as 'authority over,' then 1 Corinthians 11:3 can mean that there is a dominant to subordinate hierarchy within the Trinity, a position that does violence to the equality of the Persons of the Godhead. Early in its history, orthodox Christianity took a firm stand against any teaching that would make Christ a subordinate figure. To say that God is somehow authoritative over Christ erodes the Savior's full divinity and puts a Christian on dangerous theological ground" (pp. 193-194). And Katherine Kroeger says in her appendix to this same book, "The heretics would argue that although the Son is of the same substance as the Father, He is under subjection" (p. 283). But these statements by Hull and Kroeger are simply false. (A strong warning against this theological tendency of evangelical feminism is seen in Robert Letham's recent article, "The Man-Woman Debate: Theological Comment," *Westminster Theological Journal* 52:1 [Spring 1990], pp. 65-78.)

Such an attempt to shift the understanding of the doctrine of the Trinity as it has been held through the history of the church does not appear to be accidental, however, for the fact that God the Son can be eternally equal to God the Father in deity and in essence, but subordinate to the Father in authority, cuts at the heart of the feminist claim that a subordinate role *necessarily implies* lesser importance or lesser personhood. (Surprisingly, Millard Erickson, *Concise Dictionary of Christian Theology* [Grand Rapids, MI: Baker, 1986], p. 161, Similarly his *Christian Theology* [Grand Rapids, MI: Baker, 1983-85], 338, 668, expresses a position similar to the Kroegers here, seeing subordination in role as non-eternal, but rather a temporary activity of members of the Trinity for a period of ministry [similarly, his *Christian Theology*, pp. 338, 698].)

64. In Mickelsen and Mickelsen, *Women, Authority and the Bible*, pp. 134-154.
65. Pages 447-448.
66. Appendix in Gilbert Bilezikian, *Beyond Sex Roles*, 2nd ed. (Grand Rapids, MI: Baker Book House, 1990), pp. 215-252.
67. Although Dr. Bilezikian wrote these criticisms before Mr. Cervin's article, they apparently came up with the criticisms independently, because Mr. Cervin does not indicate that he has seen Dr. Bilezikian's article.
68. See above, pp. 445-446.
69. My earlier article (pp. 47-48) cites definitions from BAGD, Thayer, Cremer, NIDNTT, and (for the Septuagint) TDNT. Since then two more lexicons have been published: the sixth edition of Walter Bauer's *Griechisch-deutsches Wörterbuch*, ed. Kurt and Barbara Aland (Berlin: Walter DeGruyter, 1988), pp. 874-875, lists no such meaning as "source" but does give the meaning "Oberhaupt" ("chief, leader") (p. 875). And the new *Greek English Lexicon of the New Testament Based on Semantic Domains*, 2 vols., ed. Johannes P. Louw and Eugene E. Nida (New York: United Bible Societies, 1988), lists for *kephalē* the meaning, "one who is of supreme or preeminent status, in view of authority to order or command—'one who is the head of, one who is superior to, one who is supreme over'" (vol. 1, p. 739), but they give no meaning such as "source, origin." In light of such unanimity of testimony to one meaning and absence of testimony to another, it is difficult for me to understand how Dr. Bilezikian can speak of a "lack of lexical agreement on the meaning of *kephalē*" (p. 218).
70. See discussion above, p. 440.
71. See above the quotations from Plato, Philo, and Plutarch [quotations (3), (18), (19), (20), (28), and (29)], pp. 440-442.
72. Bilezikian's objection that the Greek phrase *hyper panta*, "over all things," cannot mean "authority over all things" because *hyper* means "above," not "over" (p. 244) carries little force: Whether Christ is head "*over* all things" or "*above* all things," He still has authority over all. Moreover, in the same sentence Paul says that God "has put *all things under his feet*" (Ephesians 1:22). Paul's use of *hyper* here to say that Christ is "over all

things" probably picks up on his use of the related preposition *hyperanō*, "far above," in verse 21, where Christ is said to be "*far above* all rule and authority and power and dominion." It is futile for Bilezikian to try to empty Ephesians 1:22 of the concept of Christ's universal authority.

73. Appendix 3 in Hull, *Equal to Serve*, pp. 267-283.
74. See above, p. 454.
75. Mickelsen and Mickelsen, *Women, Authority and the Bible*, p. 100.
76. See BAGD, p. 112; G. W. Lampe, *Patristic Greek Lexicon* (Oxford: Oxford University Press, 1968), pp. 235-236; Liddell-Scott, p. 252, for *archē* meaning "ruler, leader, authority." For the texts which Kroeger quotes from Chrysostom and Athanasius, the translations given in Philip Schaff, ed., *A Select Library of Nicene and Post-Nicene Fathers of the Christian Church* (28 vols. in two series [1886-1900]; reprint ed., Grand Rapids: Eerdmans, 1952ff.), are not "source" (as Kroeger translates) but "first principle" (Chrysotom, *Homily 26* on 1 Corinthians 11, *NPNF*, first series, 12:151, col. 2) and "beginning" (Athanasius, *De Synodis* 27:26, *NPNF*, second series, 4:465, col 2).
77. New International Commentary on the New Testament series (Grand Rapids, MI: Eerdmans, 1987), pp. 501-505 (commentary on 1 Corinthians 11:3).
78. These four objections are on pp. 502-503, n. 42
79. See above.
80. *NTS* 35 (1989), pp. 503-511. Fitzmyer is primarily responding to claims by R. Scroggs and J. Murphy-O'Connor that *kephalē* means "source" in 1 Corinthians 11:3.
81. (Downers Grove, IL: InterVarsity Press, 1989), pp. 141-145.
82. See above, p. 535, n. 12, for their comment on Herodotus 4.91.

Scripture Index

Matthew

Mark

Luke

John

Acts

2 Corinthians

Galatians

Ephesians

Philippians

Colossians

1 Thessalonians

1 Timothy

2 Timothy

Titus

Hebrews

Author Index

General Index

Greek/Hebrew Word Index

About the Authors

John Piper is Senior Pastor of Bethlehem Baptist Church in Minneapolis. He has authored a number of books, including *Desiring God* and *The Supremacy of God in Preaching*. He received his B.A. from Wheaton College, B.D. from Fuller Theological Seminary, and Dr. Theol. from the University of Munich.

Wayne Grudem is Associate Professor of Biblical and Systematic Theology at Trinity Evangelical Divinity School. He received his B.A. from Harvard, M.Div. from Westminster Theological Seminary, and Ph.D. in New Testament from the University of Cambridge, England. He has written three books, including *The Gift of Prophecy in the New Testament and Today and 1 Peter* in the Tyndale New Testament Commentary series. He and his wife, Margaret, have three children.

David J. Ayers is Assistant Professor of New Testament at Kings College. He is a graduate of Edinboro University, PA(B.A.), American University (M.A.), and is in the process of finishing his Ph.D. at New York University. He and his wife, Kathleen, have two daughters.

Donald A. Balasa is Executive Director and Legal Counsel for the American Association of Medical Assistants. He has a B.A. and J.D. from Northwestern University and an M.B.A. from University of Chicago. He and his wife, Kate, have one child.

James A. Borland is Professor of New Testament and Theology at Liberty Baptist Theological Seminary. He is a graduate of L. A. Baptist College (B.A.), L. A. Baptist Theological Seminary (M.Div.), Talbot Theological Seminary (Th.M.), and Grace Theological Seminary (Th.D.). He has written *Christ in the Old Testament*, *A General Introduction to the New Testament*, *Old Testament Life and Literature*, and *Lectures on Bible Prophecy*. He and his wife, Cheryl, have six children.

D. A. Carson is Professor of New Testament at Trinity Evangelical Divinity School. He received his Ph.D. from Cambridge University. He and his wife, Joy, have two children.

Elisabeth Elliot is a noted speaker and author whose books include *Shadow of the Almighty*, *Passion and Purity*, and *Let Me Be a Woman*. She is the mother of one and grandmother of seven.

John M. Frame is Professor of Apologetics and Systematic Theology at Westminster Theological Seminary and Associate Pastor of New Life Presbyterian Church (PCA). He is a graduate of Princeton University (B.A.), Westminster Theological Seminary (B.D.), and Yale University (M.A. and M.Phil.). He has written *Doctrine of the Knowledge of God*, *Medical Ethics*, and *Toward Reunion: A Critique of Denominationalism*. He and his wife, Mary Grace, have five children.

Weldon Hardenbrook has been pastor of St. Peter/St. Paul Orthodox Church for seventeen years. He is the editor of *Again* magazine and is the author of

Missing in Action. He is a former Campus Crusade for Christ staff member. He lives in Ben Lomond, California.

H. Wayne House is Vice-President for Academic Affairs and Professor of Theology at Western Baptist College. He has a B.A. from Hardin-Simmons University, an M.A. from Abilene Christian University, an M.Div. and Th. M. from Western Baptist Seminary, a Th.D. from Concordia Seminary, St. Louis, and a J.D. from O. W. Coburn School of Law. He is the author of *The Role of Women in the Ministry Today*, *Civilization in Crisis*, and *Dominion Theology, Blessing or Curse? A Biblical Look at Christian Reconstructionism*. He and his wife, Leta, have two children.

Dee Jepsen is Chairman of the Board at Regent University (formerly CBN University). She was formerly public liaison to President Reagan for women's organizations. She has authored three books, including *Women Beyond Equal Rights*. She is married to former Iowa senator Roger Jepsen. They have six children and eight grandchildren.

Gregg Johnson is Associate Professor of Biology at Bethel College, St. Paul. He has a B.S. from Bethel College and a Ph.D. from the University of North Dakota. He is the author of *Cyto-genetics*. He and his wife, Lois, have four children.

S. Lewis Johnson, Jr. is minister at Believers Chapel in Dallas, Texas. He is a graduate of the College of Charleston, SC (A.B.) and Dallas Theological Seminary (Th.M., Th.D.) and has done graduate study in Edinburgh, Scotland, University of Basil, Switzerland, and Southern Methodist Seminary in Dallas. He is the author of *The Old Testament in the New*.

George W. Knight, III is Administrator, Dean and Professor of New Testament at Knox Theological Seminary. He has earned a B.A. from Davison College, North Carolina, a B.D. and Th.M. from Westminster Theological Seminary, and a Th.D. from Free University in Amsterdam. He has written *Faithful Sayings in the Pastoral Letters*, *Prophecy in the New Testament*, and *The Role Relationship of Men and Women*. He and his wife, Virginia, have five children and four grandchildren.

Douglas Moo is Associate Professor of New Testament at Trinity Evangelical Divinity School. He is a graduate of the University of DePauw (B.A.), Trinity Evangelical Divinity School (M.D.), and the University of St. Andrews (Ph.D.). He wrote *The Old Testament in the Gospel Passion Narratives* and *A Commentary on James*. He and his wife, Jenny, have five children.

Raymond C. Ortlund, Jr. is Assistant Professor of Old Testament at Trinity Evangelical Divinity School. An ordained minister with the Presbyterian Church in America, he is a graduate of Wheaton College (B.A.), Dallas Theological Seminary (Th.M.), the University of California at Berkeley (M.A.), and the University of Aberdeen, Scotland (Ph.D.). He and his wife, Jani, have four children.

Dorothy Patterson is a homemaker and adjunct faculty member of the Criswell College. She has a B.A. from Hardin-Simmons University, a Th.M. from New Orleans Baptist Theological Seminary, and a D.Min. from Luther Rice Seminary. She is a contributor to the *NIV Women's Devotional Bible*, contributor of notes on James in the *NKJV Study Bible*, and assistant editor of the *Criswell Study Bible* and its revision *The Believer's Study Bible*. She and her husband, Paige (see below), have two children.

L. Paige Patterson is President of The Criswell College and Associate Pastor of First Baptist Church of Dallas. He is a graduate of Hardin-Simmons University (B.A.) and New Orleans Baptist Theological Seminary (Th.M. and Th.D.). He has written commentaries on Titus, 1 Corinthians, 1 Peter, and the Song of Solomon. He and his wife, Dorothy (see above), have two children.

Vern Sheridan Poythress is Professor of New Testament Interpretation at Westminster Theological Seminary. His degrees include a Ph.D. from Harvard University and a Th.D. from the University of Stellenbosch, South Africa. He is the author of *Philosophy, Science and the Sovereignty of God*, *Understanding Dispensationalists*, and *Science and Hermeneutics*. He and his wife, Diane, have two children.

George A. Rekers is Professor of Neuropsychiatry and Behavioral Science at the University of South Carolina School of Medicine. He also serves as an Adjunct Professor of Counseling at Tyndale Theological Seminary in The Netherlands. He has a B.A. from Westmont College and an M.A., C.Phil., and Ph.D. from the University of California, Los Angeles. He is the author of over eighty academic journal articles and seven books, including *Counseling Families*. He and his wife, Sharon, have five children.

Thomas R. Schreiner is Associate Professor of New Testament at Bethel Theological Seminary. He is a graduate of Western Oregon College (B.A.), Western Conservative Baptist Seminary (M.Div.), and Fuller Theological Seminary (Ph.D.). He has written *Interpreting the Pauline Epistles*. He and his wife, Diane, have three children.

William C. Weinrich is Professor of Early Church History and Patristic Studies at Concordia Theological Seminary, Fort Wayne, Indiana. He has a B.A. from Oklahoma University, an M.Div. from Concordia Seminary, St. Louis, and a D.Theol. from the University of Basel. He authored *Spirit and Martyrdom* and edited *The New Testament Age: Essays in Honor of Bo Reicke*. He and his wife, Barbara, have three children.